D0203241

WITHDRAWN

WITHDRAWN

Adversarial versus Inquisitorial Justice

Psychological Perspectives on Criminal Justice Systems

Perspectives in

Law & Psychology

Sponsored by the American Psychology-Law Society / Division 41 of the American Psychological Association

Series Editor: Ronald Roesch, *Simon Fraser University, Burnaby, British Columbia, Canada*

Editorial Board: Jane Goodman-Delahunty, Thomas Grisso, Stephen D. Hart, Marsha Liss, Edward P. Mulvey, James R. P. Ogloff, Norman G. Poythress, Jr., Don Read, Regina Schuller, and Patricia Zapf

Library of Congress Cataloging-in-Publication Data

Adversarial versus inquisitorial justice: psychological perspectives on criminal justice systems/edited by Peter J. van Koppen, Steven D. Penrod.
    p.   cm.—(Perspectives in law & psychology; v. 17)
    Includes bibliographical references and indexes.
    ISBN: 0-306-47362-3
    1. Criminal justice, Administration of—Psychological aspects. 2. Criminal investigation—Psychological aspects. 3. Judicial process—Psychological aspects. I. Koppen, P. J. van. II. Penrod, Steven. III. Series.

HV7419 .A384 2003
3644—dc21

2002034115

ISBN 0-306-47362-3

©2003 Kluwer Academic / Plenum Publishers, New York
233 Spring Street, New York, New York 10013

http://www.wkap.nl/

10 9 8 7 6 5 4 3 2 1

A C.I.P. record for this book is available from the Library of Congress

All rights reserved

No part of this book may be reproduced, stored in a retrieval system, or transmitted in any form or by any means, electronic, mechanical, photocopying, microfilming, recording, or otherwise, without written permission from the Publisher, with the exception of any material supplied specifically for the purpose of being entered and executed on a computer system, for exclusive use by the purchaser of the work

Printed in the United States of America

Adversarial versus Inquisitorial Justice

Psychological Perspectives on Criminal Justice Systems

CALVIN T. RYAN LIBRARY
U. OF NEBRASKA AT KEARNEY

Edited by

Peter J. van Koppen

Netherlands Institute for the Study of Crime and Law Enforcement
Leiden, the Netherlands

and

Department of Law, University of Antwerp
Antwerp, Belgium

and

Steven D. Penrod

John Jay College of Criminal Justice
New York, New York

KLUWER ACADEMIC / PLENUM PUBLISHERS
NEW YORK / BOSTON / DORDRECHT / LONDON / MOSCOW

Contents

1

Adversarial or Inquisitorial
Comparing Systems

PETER J. VAN KOPPEN AND
STEVEN D. PENROD

The most extensive reforms in criminal justice probably took place during the last decade in England and Wales. Following well known miscarriages of justice as the *Guildford Four* (Jessel, 1994) and *Birmingham Six* (Gilligan, 1990), the commission chaired by Runciman proposed a host of legislation (Royal Commission on Criminal Procedure, 1993). The objective of all these reforms "has been to create a criminal justice process which is administratively efficient and minimizes the 'risk' of an adversarial trial," Belloni and Hodgson (2000, p. 203) conclude. The Runciman Commission, according to its own contention, aimed at making mostly practical recommendations without a thorough theoretical basis, but admits that its recommendations "can fairly be interpreted as seeking to move the system to an inquisitorial direction" (Royal Commission on Criminal Procedure, 1993, p. 3). Would a turn to the inquisitorial system save the British?

Likewise, the inquisitorial systems on the European continent seem to incorporate more and more adversarial elements. This happens partly under the influence of the European Court of Human Rights in Strasbourg. This court, composed of justices from diverse legal backgrounds, seems to regularly introduce adversarial elements into the inquisitorial criminal justice systems on the continent (Harding, Swart, Jörg, & Fennell, 1995). Would such enhance the quality of these systems?

For more than a decade we two have, whenever we met, been arguing what system is better. Van Koppen, coming from the quite inquisitorial Dutch system, has taken the position that a carefully

1

designed inquisitorial system as the Dutch is in many ways better than any adversarial system. Penrod has always pointed to the superior elements in the system where he comes from: the United States. Being psychologists, the discussions always centered on more "psychological" comparisons of the systems.

The discussions became more interesting in recent years when we abstained from harassing each other and turned the argument on the following type of questions: How do we define 'better'? What are we actually comparing? And, most important: what would a decisive experiment or set of experiments look like, which might decide our dispute? This book is the result of our quest for the answers to these questions with, as you will notice, the help of many learned colleagues in our field. In the present chapter we will go into these questions and will try to define the problem under discussion.

COMPARING SYSTEMS

Comparing criminal justice systems is like shooting rabbits on a fair: you always shoot too high or too low, you always hit another rabbit than the one you were aiming at, and if you hit one in the belly, you are under the illusion that you shot the whole rabbit. Likewise, each inquisitorial system differs dramatically from each other, as great differences can be found between the criminal justice systems of every adversarial country. Each national system is also a moving target that keeps on changing all the time, both in practice and in law. And, all these systems differ in so many respects, that a system-wide comparison is foolhardy.

The most fundamental differences between systems of criminal law and procedure in European countries can be characterized on a rough dimension of *inquisitorial* and *adversarial systems* (cf. Damaška, 1986; Jörg, Field, & Brants, 1995). These systems have different roots (for an overview see Nijboer, 2000b, pp. 406 ff.), but also share common characteristics. In all systems there is, for instance, some form of standard of proof that differs only slightly from country to country; all systems have a presumption of innocence in one form or another; all systems have the right to counsel and, in varying degrees, a right of confrontation.

For our present discussion, however, the differences between the systems are of more importance. Under the adversarial model, legal proceedings are essentially contests between equivalent rivals (see also the chapter by Crombag in this volume). A contest is only a real contest if it is played in a fair way and the essential feature of fair play is the formal equality of the contestants. This feature constitutes, according to

Damaška, *essentialia* of the adversarial tradition. Under this model one is usually judged by one's peers (the jury) and the system emphasizes oral presentation of evidence. These features are "not indispensable to the adversary model. Yet ... the ideological assumptions underlying the model make ... these non-essential features a matter of natural choice." He therefore calls them *naturalia* of the adversary style (Damaška, 1973, p. 564). Because the adversarial system employs lay decision makers, heavy emphasis is placed on the development of rules of evidence designed to assure the flow of reliable evidence to jurors. There are concerns, for example—as reflected in general prohibitions against hearsay evidence—that lay jurors may have difficulty giving appropriate weight to evidence which, although relevant to the issues being tried, may be unreliable to some degree. In the adversarial system one major role of the trial judge is to serve as a gatekeeper for evidence—in this role the judge determines which evidence is admissible at trial and available for the jury to consider.

Under the inquisitorial model, on the other hand, a legal procedure is considered an inquest: "an official and thorough inquiry" directed at establishing the true facts. The "court-controlled pursuit of facts cannot be limited by the mutual consent of the participants. Once a case is brought before the court, the court takes its own responsibility for finding the truth" (Damaška, 1973, p. 564). Whenever technicalities of fair play threaten to get in the way of finding the truth, they are put aside. These are the *essentialia* of the inquisitorial tradition. Since, for instance, plea-bargaining "raises conflicts with the ... search of substantive truth" (Van Cleave, 1997), it must be considered irreconcilable with the *essentialia* of the inquisitorial procedure. Although oral presentation of evidence would be quite consistent with the inquisitorial model, it is a historical fact that inquisitorial systems have a preference for documentary presentation of evidence, which Damaška considers one of the *naturalia* of the inquisitorial model (see also Nijboer, 2000b). In contrast to adversarial systems reliance on rules of evidence, inquisitorial systems tend to be systems of "free proof" in which any relevant evidence may reach the judge and the judge is trusted to give weight to that evidence in a manner appropriate to the reliability of the evidence.

From these basic (formal) differences a host of practical differences between the systems in the manner in which courts handle cases are derived. The manner in which trials are handled has a consequence for the manner in which officers in other stages of the proceeding act (Nijboer, 1999). The emphasis on written documents in the Netherlands, for instance, makes the recording of witness and suspect statements in so-called *proces-verbalen* (sworn statements by police officers) of major importance during the police investigation. The emphasis on written documents causes Dutch courts to be reluctant to hear witnesses at trial. Thus, if during the trial the court considers it necessary to hear additional witnesses or further hear certain witnesses, the case is usually referred to a judge-commissioner to hear the witnesses and present the *proces-verbalen* of the interrogations to the court. But this, again, usually causes a postponement of the trial for another three months. Since it is quite common in more complex cases that additional witnesses need to be heard or additional investigations need to be conducted, these trials most often proceed in sessions many months apart, which can produce significant waiting times for the accused.

Relevant differences for the accused involve, for instance, the extent to which he or she plays an active role in different stages of the process, the immediacy of evidence presented against the accused, the role of plea bargaining, the amount and nature of information communicated to the accused at different stages in the process, the role of dossiers, processing times, treatment by criminal justice officials, role of judge and jury, and possibilities for appeal. It should be evident that such aspects may have considerable impact on experiences, perceptions, and attitudes of defendants who are involved in these criminal processes.

From a comparative perspective, some of these differences will have a positive effect on the experiences and attitudes of the accused and the flow of his or her case, while other aspects may work in the opposite direction. A systematic empirical comparison of these different criminal procedures from the point of view of the accused is, therefore, appropriate. Of course, the distinction between inquisitorial and adversarial systems is, however, not always clear-cut and frequently subject to debate. Most countries can in fact be characterized as more or less mixed or hybrid systems (Jörg et al., 1995).

None of the European criminal law systems can be considered a "pure" inquisitorial or a "pure" accusatorial system, but all are somewhere in between on this dimension. The Netherlands, however, can be considered the country that is probably the most inquisitorial in Western Europe, while the English/Welsh system, for instance, may be considered the most accusatorial. Both Sweden and Germany, for instance, belong to what is commonly called a Nordic continental law system that may be situated somewhere between the Netherlands and England and Wales on the dimension adversarial-inquisitorial (cf. Nijboer, 2000b; Toornvliet, 2000, Table 1 on p. 26).

Let us set the scene for the present volume. We primarily compare the United States criminal justice system to that of the Netherlands. Not only do we know these systems best but, at least at first glance, these two systems are somewhere at the extremes of the inquisitorial-adversarial continuum. Second, we compare the systems as they are now, knowing that especially the continental European systems may see dramatic changes in the next decade. Third, we take a psychological perspective, not a legal one. We are thus much more interested in how these systems work in practice, than in how they are supposed to work, as laid down in law and acts of Parliament.

DUTCH INQUISITION AND AMERICAN ADVERSARIES

To further set the scene, we give an overview of the most obvious differences between the Dutch and American system. We do so by following a suspect of an armed robbery in each country from the time he committed the crime to his punishment. In our description we take the point of view that a criminal justice system is some kind of organic body. It is quite fruitless to compare one point in one system to a comparable point in the other, without taking the rest into account. How can we, for instance, compare the decision-making behavior of jurors in the U.S.A. to the decisions of professional judges in the Netherlands without taking into account how prosecutors and attorneys may differ in both countries? Both attorneys and prosecutors may anticipate judge versus jury decisions differently, so they behave differently. The differences in their pretrial behavior may in turn result in a completely different selection of cases going to trial in the two systems and thus influence fact finder's behavior.

Indeed, many of the differences between the two systems seem to stem from the fact that the criminal legal system in the United States is based on the jury system while in the Netherlands decisions on guilt or innocence are always rendered by professional judges. The jury system is not essential to an accusatorial criminal legal system nor is decision-making by professional judges essential to the inquisitorial system. In fact, due primarily to widespread plea bargaining, only about 8% of the criminal cases in the United States are dealt by with a jury and a much smaller share of cases is decided in so-called "bench trials" in which the judge is the sole fact-finder (Hans & Vidmar, 1986, p. 43). Nonetheless, the jury model serves as the primary backdrop or frame of reference for the remaining trials. On the other hand, the Netherlands actually employed the jury for a short period during the unification with Belgium in the beginning of the 19th Century (Bossers, 1987). The Belgians reintroduced the jury system after the secession, but have fewer than a hundred cases a year tried by their so-called assissen court (Van Langenhove, 1989).

THE LIVES AND TIMES OF A DUTCH AND
AN AMERICAN SUSPECT

Both our Dutch suspect Jan Jansen and his American counterpart the defendant James Smith were arrested soon after their robbery, but there the differences already started. Following *Miranda* (*Miranda v. Arizona*, 1966), the American police officers inform James Smith at the time of his arrest of his right to remain silent, his right to legal counsel, and that anything he says can be used against him in court. The Dutch police did not do this while arresting Jan Jansen. Dutch policemen have to do something different: they begin every interrogation of the suspect by telling him that he has the right to remain silent (the so-called *caution*). Not that this difference may matter much, since most suspects do not understand the *Miranda* rules (Fulero & Everington, 1995; Stricker, 1985; Wall & Rude, 1985), and the police have a fine-tuned system to circumvent these rules (Leo, 1995, 1996b). Although there is no study on the effect or non-effect of the Dutch caution, it is a fair assumption that the effect of giving that caution is not any greater than reading *Miranda* in the USA, given all the possibilities for police officers to circumvent that caution (Leo, 1995, 1996a).

COUNSEL

Smith has the right to have counsel present during the police interrogations, but most suspects do not use that right (Leo, 1995, 1996a). Jansen does not have the right to counsel during police interrogations (Fijnaut, 1988; Lensing, 1988), but many police forces have the habit of routinely inviting the suspect's attorney to be present. Attorneys, however, seldom make use of the invitation, claiming that they have other duties. We suspect, however, that few of them like to spend much time in small rooms attending interrogations which are usually quite boring, except maybe in high profile cases.

In the Netherlands defendants who cannot afford an attorney can select an attorney themselves and he or she is paid for by the state. In the United States a defendant without money is provided with a government employed attorney. Since most criminal defendants cannot pay for their own attorney, this difference in arrangement may produce great quality differences in the defense of suspects. We are not sure, however, whether this makes much of a difference. Penrod's personal experience is that many public defenders are sharper and better prepared than privately retained counsel, although of course much money—as for instance in the O.J. Simpson case—can hire the best.

THE WRITTEN AND ORAL TRIALS

In both countries the police aim at obtaining a confession during inter-rogations (Van Koppen, 1998a; Leo, 1996a). If Smith confesses, he is asked to produce a handwritten statement. If Jansen confesses, he is not. Rather, the police write down his statement in a *proces-verbaal*, recounting in what can be called policemen's prose what the suspect told the interrogating offi-cers. Whether Jansen signs this proces-verbaal is quite unimportant. This is related to the hearsay structure of Dutch criminal procedure.

In 1926 the so-called 'principle of immediacy' was introduced in the then new Code of Criminal Procedure (*Wetboek van Strafvordering*; Sr.). Art 342 Sr. stipulates that a witness statement is a statement of "facts and circumstances that the witness has noticed or experienced personally." Witness statements should be given orally in front of the court at trial. The Supreme Court almost immediately after introduction of the new Code ruled that hearsay is acceptable, simply reasoning that a hearsay witness personally experienced what another person had said (HR 20 December 1926, *NJ* 1927, 87). This rather practical point of view had a dramatic influence on how Dutch criminal investigations are conducted by the police. Under the Supreme Court's ruling, the sworn statement of police officers containing a description of the suspect's statement is as good evidence as the suspect's statement itself. If the court uses such statements to prove its decision, formally, a document—the sworn statement by the interrogating police officers—instead of the suspect's statements is used as evidence. This is even done if the suspect later retracted the confession. This is also related to the great trust Dutch courts have in the work of the police. Recent discussions of police behavior (Crombag, Van Koppen, & Wagenaar, 1994; Van Traa, 1996; Wagenaar, Van Koppen, & Crombag, 1993), however, have caused courts to become more critical of police *proces-verbalen*.

It should be noted that suspect and witness statements are recorded in the words of the police officers conducting the interrogations. It is not uncommon for the *proces-verbalen* to contain all kinds of legal lingo intro-duced by the police in the statement or in other ways diverge from what the suspect or witness actually said. In a *proces-verbaal* a witness may, for instance, talk about a "four wheel vehicle," when he in fact said "car." Of course there may be less innocent examples of this. Recently, for instance, an admitted cocaine dealer told Van Koppen the following story. During all his interrogations, he used his right to remain silent. To each question by the interrogating officers he answered: "I use my right to remain silent." In one of the sessions, the police officers wanted to know who financed his cocaine trade and again he gave the same answer. In the *proces-verbaal*, however, this particular answer was recorded as follows: "I refuse to tell you who paid all my cocaine" (see for more examples Wagenaar et al., 1993). Statements by suspects and witnesses—with the exception of child witnesses—are usually not recorded on video or audio tape, so there is no way to check what a witness actually said.

The Dutch police are under "a duty to prepare an investigative record that is complete and formally correct, available to the defense as well as the prosecution, and able to withstand a searching examination" (Langbein & Weinreb, 1978, pp. 1553–1554). And that is what they do. They produce a dossier that in simple cases is about 2 cm thick, but in more complicated cases can grow to 2 meters thick or even more.

THE PROSECUTOR

In the Netherlands the police investigation is lead by the *Officier van Justitie* (OvJ), i.e. the public prosecutor. Usually this is only a formal position but in the more complicated cases the OvJ is actively involved in the guiding of the investigations. After the police submitted the case to the prosecution, more documents are added to the dossier. Also other participants play a role in shaping the dossier, as for instance the defense, the investigating judge, and the trial judges (Field, Alldridge, & Jörg, 1995, p. 235). If the defense considers it necessary—for instance because of discrepancies between its client's story and what is in the dossier—it may ask the prosecution to conduct additional investigation. This places the prosecutor in a position to engage in an impartial weighing of the all interests involved in the case (Van de Bunt, 1985, p. 398).

The Dutch prosecutor is a magistrate, who should independently come to a judgment on the merits of the case before it is submitted for trial. Thus, as in the United States, the prosecutor may dismiss a case (*seponeren; sepot*) for a host of reasons. The most important ones are dismissal for lack of evidence of any policy reason. The prosecutor can also offer the suspect *sepot* on the condition that he pays a fine. This can be done in every case, although it is usually limited to the less serious crimes. In most cases, however, the prosecutor only reads the dossier a few days before the trial is scheduled. If the prosecutors then consider the evidence too thin, they may actually ask for an acquittal at trial without loosing face.

In the Netherlands there is no system of plea-bargaining, for the simple reason that the defense does not have to issue a formal plea. To obtain a conviction, the prosecutor always has to bring the case to a full trial in which the court evaluates the evidence in cases where the suspect made a full confession. Of course, in the latter kind of case the discussion at trial centers more on the sentence than on the determination of guilt. In fact, most Dutch trials are minimal in length. Since all participants have read, or are supposed to have read, the file, even a murder trial may take less than a day and typically would consist mainly of the opening and closing statements of the prosecution and the defense.

In the United States plea-bargaining is a common manner to resolve criminal cases (Schulhofer & Nagel, 1997). This procedure poses a dilemma to the innocent defendant: the choice posed during bargaining is heavily influenced by the risk involved in a jury trial, rather than by the strength of the evidence against him. A now famous case in which plea-bargaining led to a miscarriage of justice is the Ingram case: his sentence was agreed upon just before his innocence became clear (Ofshe, 1989; Wright, 1993a,b). In the Netherlands plea-bargaining is (at least formally) not allowed and the evidence in each case is reviewed by the court, even after the defendant confessed. Formally, the court needs two pieces of evidence for a conviction, but after a defendant confessed, it may take the (written) report of the pathologist that the victim in fact died by a bullet as the second piece of evidence.

CUSTODY

The robberies of which Smith and Jansen are suspect are typically the more serious cases. In contrast to the United States, the Dutch system does not know bail. Suspects can be detained for six hours by the police. This can be extended for three days by the prosecution after which extensions have to be authorized by the court. For any extension there always has to be serious suspicion against the suspect and one of three additional requirements: (a) the risk of fleeing; (b) danger of committing other grave offense; or (c) the risk that the suspect may obstruct the investigations. An extension can also be based on the seriousness of the crime that shocked the community. The differences with the United States may be smaller than this suggests, since there "release on recognizance" exists, and "release on supervision" requires the defendant to report to someone periodically.

THE INVESTIGATING JUDGE

In many more serious crimes an investigating judge is involved. The prosecution may demand the start of a judicial inquiry (*Gerechtelijk Vooronderzoek*; GVO) by an investigating judge. He or she must do so if certain coercive measures (*dwangmiddelen*) are necessary, such as pretrial detention, phone tapping, or house searches. The role of the investigating judge in the Netherlands, however, is much more limited that the French *juge d'instruction*. The involvement of the investigating judge largely depends on the seriousness of the case. Usually it is no more that author-izing some coercive measures. Even if the judge is more involved—for instance hears witnesses—he or she never writes a report or draws con-clusions, but rather collects information to be placed in the dossier. The judge does not decide whether the evidence is enough to bring the case to trial, as his or her French colleague does.

In many ways, the role of the investigating judge is parallel to the role of magistrates and judges in the United States who are responsible for the issuance of search warrants, arrest warrants, and wiretap warrants—such warrants are issued by the judge or magistrate only on a showing or pres-entation of proof by the investigating police of probable cause that the defendant has committed a crime. In the case of search warrants, the war-rant must narrowly specify what the police are looking for and will, there-fore, be permitted to seize. Improperly issued warrants and improperly seized evidence can result in seized evidence being excluded at trial.

GOING TO TRIAL

In the Netherlands the prosecutor decides whether a case is brought to trial. This is done under the principle of opportunity: the prosecution can dismiss a case for many reasons. In addition to the ones mentioned above, Dutch prosecutors hold the attitude that non-criminal law solutions are usually preferable to a trial. The prosecutor may impose conditions on the suspect, as for instance taking therapy or not having contact with the victim.

In the United States, the prosecution of a case can travel several dif-ferent paths depending on the jurisdiction (that is, states have different procedures which may also differ from federal procedures). In almost all instances there are procedural hurdles the prosecution must cross before a case can be brought to trial. In some jurisdictions there may be a hearing before a judge—who makes a preliminary judgment about the merits of a case—before the case is 'bound over' for prosecution. In about half the states, the prosecutor must secure permission for prosecuting a case from a grand jury. The grand jury comprises a group of citizens who sit for varying periods of time and have responsibility for assuring that meritless cases do not proceed. In any event, a prosecutor may, once suitable evi-dence has developed, drop the charges against a defendant. There are also a number of plea bargaining arrangements in which a defendant can, for example, agree to some sort of supervision or program of treatment which, if successfully completed, will result in the dropping of charges. Another variant of this procedure is that charges will not be pressed against a defendant if the defendant stays out of further trouble (e.g., no further arrests) for a stated period of time. In many instances in the United States, plea bargains or arrangements which do not result in a prosecution or criminal conviction are a preferred method of handling cases in which a defendant is relatively young and does not have a prior criminal record.

AT TRIAL

In the Netherlands the trial is based on a very detailed and precisely written charge (*telastenlegging*) by the prosecution. If the defendant is charged with a number of crimes, the prosecution may charge him with a few of these and submit the dossiers of the other cases to the court *ad informandum*. The prosecution does not have to produce evidence on the *ad informandum* cases, but the court may take these in consideration for the sentence. In a USA trial, prior convictions and uncharged offenses are almost always not before the jury in the guilt phase of a trial—on the theory that this information could prejudice the jury against the defendant. However, prior convictions, and sometimes uncharged offenses, do play an important role in sentencing.

At trial, the most marked differences between the two systems become evident. In the United States, the model of a trial is that of a contest between two parties in from of a jury trial in which the judge serves primarily as an independent arbiter between the parties and is responsible for assuring that rules of evidence and procedure are followed during the trial. In the Netherlands misdemeanors and less serious crimes are decided by a *unus iudex*, while a three-judge court decides the more serious crimes. In the USA, the presence of a jury in some ways requires oral presentation of all the evidence anew at trial. Both parties call witnesses who are subject to cross-examination by the other party.

In the Netherlands decision-making is done by professional judges who decide most cases on the dossier without hearing witnesses at trial. They must arrive at the material truth. The legal criterion is that the court must be convinced that the suspect is guilty as charged based on legal evidence, i.e. evidence that is enumerated in the Code of Criminal Procedure. Since what is considered legal evidence is very broadly defined in the code, this means a system of free proof, with one exception: nobody can be convicted on one single piece of evidence—for instance a confession, a DNA match, or a witness statement; at least two pieces of evidence are necessary.

In contrast to the United States, the Dutch court is both gatekeeper of the quality of evidence and the decision-maker. As a consequence, Dutch judges routinely admit all evidence—it is in the dossier anyway—and just ignore evidence they consider too low of quality. Illegally obtained evidence usually does not lead to dismissal of the case, but can result in a reduced sentence for the defendant.

In the USA the quality of evidence is maintained by decisions of the judge on the admissibility of evidence. Thus, the difference between the two countries can best be characterized as follows: the United States is a country with admissibility rules; the Netherlands is a country with decision rules.

In the USA witnesses are called by the parties and are examined by the calling party and cross-examined by the opposing party. In the Netherlands, witnesses are called either by the prosecution or by the court. The defense has to ask the prosecution to call witnesses it deems necessary for the court to hear and must argue why the witnesses need to be heard at trial. The prosecution can refuse to hear all or certain witnesses, even with the argument that hearing a witness is "not in the interest of the defense." The defense can then ask the court to hear certain witnesses at the beginning of the trial, but this almost always leads to a postponement or continuation of the trial for three months (and a prolonged pretrial detention of the defendant).

In Dutch trials there is no formal cross-examination. Usually the judges in the court start asking questions of a witness and then give the prosecution and defense an opportunity to do so. As in the USA, the defendant has a right to speak at trial, but in contrast to American trials, the defendant is not sworn in as he does so.

VERDICT AND SENTENCING

In all cases in the Netherlands and most cases in the USA the court decides on the sentence if the defendant is found guilty. In the USA this is a second phase of the trial, in which additional witnesses may be called to testify on aspects that are relevant for the sentence. In the Netherlands there is a so-called one-phase trial in which all information relevant to both determination of guilt and the sentence is presented in the dossier at the beginning of the trial. This includes prior convictions of the defendant.

American judges have much less discretion in sentencing that Dutch judges have. American judges typically have to choose between a specific maximum for a crime and a specific minimum ("departures" from guidelines for sentencing are permitted though the judge typically has to explain the basis for the departure), and sometimes have even less options—for instance in the so-called three strikes laws (Ardaiz, 2000; Marvell & Moody, 2001). The Dutch courts can choose a sentence anywhere between a specific maximum and a general minimum for all crimes: one day in jail or a 7 euro fine. They can even find the defendant guilty without imposing a sentence.

The decision by a Dutch court is usually rendered two weeks after the trial formally ended and again is given is writing. Dutch courts at any level present their decisions as unanimous; dissenting opinions are not allowed because judges have to maintain the secrecy of the court chambers. Unlike the USA, the decisions are argued—that is, defended and justified in a written opinion. In the verdict, courts have to specify why they consider the defendant guilty and have to address the key arguments by both defense and prosecution on the evidence presented at trial. Also, the sentence has to be argued. It should be noted, however, that the argument on the evidence often is not more than an enumeration of the documents and parts thereof that support the court's decision. In most cases it is self-evident how the documents support the decision; sometimes is remains unclear why, for instance, the court believed one witness and not another who testified to the opposite state of affairs.

In the USA the jury, deciding on the guilt of the defendant, does not have to do anything other than make the finding that the defendant is guilty or not guilty, which (particularly in jurisdictions which do not permit interviews of jurors) will leave people completely in the dark on how the evidence was evaluated. Even in instances where jurors can be interviewed after trial, little they say—other than evidence of misconduct on the part of the jury—can be used as a basis for appealing the verdict. It is possible—though uncommon—for a trial judge to dismiss the charges against a defendant if, in the judgment of the trial judge, the evidence offered by the prosecution could not reasonably support a conviction of the defendant. It is even possible, but rarer yet, for a judge to do this after a jury conviction.

JUDGE OR JURY?

An interesting question—and the subject of intense dispute between the authors—is whether judges or juries render better or worse decisions. The question was addressed by Kalven and Zeisel (1966) in their hallmark comparison of American judges and juries. That study, however, is hardly relevant for a comparison of Dutch judges and American juries, since in the Netherlands trials of more serious crimes are handled by a three-judge bench, rather than by a single judge. The very size of panels may influence verdicts.

Apart from these effects, we know that decision-makers fall prey to all kinds of biases. These biases are much better documented for jurors than for professional judges who are vastly under-studied, so it would be unfair to point at the known biases for jurors as a basis for claiming superior decision-making by professional judges. Still, some of the biases may be absent in Dutch (or professional continental) judges and may make them better in handling criminal cases than jurors, at least to the extent they do not fall prey to any of the undesirable biases, cognitive limitations, and faulty inferences detected with American jurors (McEwan, 2000).

Because of their greater experience with deciding cases, judges may be better in some respects to jurors. There exists, for instance, poor juror sensitivity to variations in trial evidence in cases involving eyewitnesses (who, in some conditions, make identifications under conditions that are thought, by psychologists, to either promote or impair accurate identifications). Dutch judges may be better calibrated to these conditions, though American jurors are not (Cutler & Penrod, 1995). Jury research in Belgium by Van Langenhove (1989) shows that it is, with some exaggeration, virtually impossible to be juror if one has finished high school. Such selection effects may produce juries who on average are less informed than judges and thus their decisions may involve more errors.

On the other hand, another biasing effect may stem from the following. In a series of judgments, conviction rates on a weak case are lower when the weak case has been preceded by cases with strong evidence as opposed to weak evidence (Kerr, Harmon, & Graves, 1982). Since professional judges decide longer series of cases, they may be prone to this effect.

On other factors there may be no difference between professional judges and jurors. Jurors generally underutilize probabilistic evidence (Thompson, 1989), but there is no reason to expect professional judges to do better (Wagenaar et al., 1993). Also, pretrial publicity (Otto, Penrod, & Dexter, 1994; Studebaker & Penrod, 1997) seems to influence jury behavior and again there is no reason to expect judges to do better.

On some aspects juries may do better. For instance, defendants charged with multiple crimes are more likely to be convicted on any one of those crimes when all crimes are tried together rather than separately. A very strong argument can be made under US law that this should not happen (Tanford, 1985; Tanford & Penrod, 1982, 1983, 1984; Tanford, Penrod, & Collins, 1985). So, the extent to which multiple crimes are charged in one trial—quite common in the Netherlands—may influence decision-making.

APPEAL

With a few exceptions, all court decisions can be appealed in the Netherlands to the court of appeal (*Gerechtshof*). There, the case is tried *de novo*, meaning that in principle the case is tried anew. In the United States, although it is possible to secure de novo trials following judge-alone decisions on minor offenses in some jurisdictions, for the most part appeals are judged not de novo, but on the basis of appellate documents with reference to actions taken at trial. Appeals by the defendant are possible in all cases that go to trial, though the likelihood of success will largely depend on whether a serious error (e.g., evidence was inappropriately admitted or something prejudicial was said or done by the prosecutor) was made during the trial. Prosecutorial appeals are extremely limited and most likely to occur during trial over evidentiary issues.

WHICH SYSTEM IS BETTER?

Above we have tried to identify key differences in criminal procedure between the United States and the Netherlands. It should be evident that there is no way to answer the question "what system is 'better'" in any direct way. In part the difficulty arises from the problematic nature of the term "better." Let us just enumerate some possible definitions of "better."

Although some might be inclined to define "better" in terms of clearance rates for crimes or crime rates, we prefer a much more pronouncedly psychological perspective when defining "better" and from that perspective quality of decision-making within criminal justice systems and perceptions of the justice rendered by systems loom large. With respect to quality of decision-making, a most obvious criterion would be that the system that produces the least number of miscarriages of justice would be the better one, where a miscarriage of justice is defined as the conviction of somebody for a crime which is proved either to have been committed by somebody else or has not occurred at all.

Miscarriages of justice have been reported both in the United States, the Netherlands, but also in the United Kingdom, Germany, France, and elsewhere.[1] Of course, even though more miscarriages of justice have

---

[1] Dutch suspected miscarriages of justice have been described by Boumans and Kayser (1979), Bijnoord (1989), Blaauw (1996; 2000), Broekhuizen (1991) and Van Straten (1990). See for miscarriages of justice in the United States: J. C. Anderson (1999), Bedau and Radelet (1987), Borchard (1932; 1970), Crispin (1987), Dennis (1993), Dillon (1987), Dwyer, Neufeld, and Scheck (2000), Folsom (1994), Frank and Frank (1957), Frasca (1968), Gardner (1952), Gershman (1997), Gross (1987; 1996; 1998), Lassers (1973), Malcolm (1999), Platania, Moran, and Cutler (1994), Radelet, Bedau, and Putnam (1992), Radin (1964), Rattner (1988), Sharlitt (1989), Sotscheck (1990), Subcommittee on Civil and Constitutional Rights of the Committee on the Judiciary (1994), Uviller (1996), Westervelt (2001), Yant (1991) and Zimmermann (1964); in the United Kingdom: Belloni and Hodgson (2000), Bentley (1995), Blom-Cooper (1997), Blom-Cooper and Brickell (1998), Brandon and Davies (1973), Dickson (1993), Du Cann (1960), Engelmayer and Wagman (1985), Gilligan (1990), Greer (1994), Hale (1961), Hill, Young, and Sergeant (1985), Hill and Hunt (1995), Huff, Rattner, and Sagarin (1986), Huff and Rattner (1988), Huff, Rattner, and Sagarin (1996), Jessel (1994), Kee (1986), Mullin (1989), Nobles and Schiff (1995), Rolph (1978), Rose (1996), Royal Commission on Criminal Procedure (1993), Thornton (1993), Wadham (1993), Walker and

been detected in some countries, notably the United States, it is unclear to what extent detection depends on the number or rate of miscarriages of justice in each country and/or the methods used to detect miscarriages. As a practical matter, until recently miscarriages of justice have been most commonly detected by accident: somebody unexpectedly confesses to a crime for which somebody else has been convicted, the presumed dead victim suddenly reappears, or somebody cares enough about the misfortune of the convict and vigorously pursues the evidence in the case. A growing exception to this model of accidental discovery is the increasing use of DNA tests in cases tried before the widespread availability of DNA techniques. In the United States, at least, it seems that hardly a week goes by without a newly DNA-detected miscarriage of justice. As the use of post-conviction DNA testing increases, which, based on recent experience in the United States, it appears will happen, it is likely that a growing number of miscarriages will be detected and reported. Of course, once DNA testing is routinely applied in the narrow range of cases (e.g., sexual assault) where it is possible to collect DNA evidence, the source of those miscarriages will be exhausted.

Rather than relying on counts of miscarriages (which constitute a very small percentage of all convictions) a more fruitful way to assess the quality of system outcome might be to try to identify components of criminal justice systems which have a higher probability of generating miscarriages of justice. An example is the study by Wagenaar et al. (1993), showing that so-called dubious court decisions are often based on errors made in earlier stages of the proceedings.

A second major psychological variant on the notion of better concerns the perceptions of criminal justice participants that justice has been done. In their work on legal procedures, Thibaut and Walker (1975; 1978) have shown that variations in procedures can contribute considerably to the sense of justice felt by suspects, defendants, and the general public afterwards. It should be noted that most criminal cases, say 88% (Crombag et al., 1994), are clear-cut cases in terms of evidence. In these cases only the sentence is a decisional problem. Since defendants in these cases know there are going to be convicted anyway, procedural influences

Starmer (1993; 1999), Waller (1989), Woffinden (1987) and Young and Hill (1983); in Germany: Ebermayer (1965), Hirschberg (1960), Judex (1963), Kiwit (1965), Mostar (1956), Peters (1970; 1972), Preute and Preute (1979) and Vosskuhle (1993); in France: Beel (1993), Chemineau (1983), Floroit (1968) and Vidal-Naquet (1984); and in some other countries: Callaghan (1994), Carrington, Dever, Hogg, Bargen, and Lohrey (1991), Chamberlain (1990), Hatakka and Klami (1990), Hogg (1991), Karp and Rosner (1991), Luis Carlos (1973; 1975), Fijnaut (1983), Pizzorusso (1965), Stortino (1976), Sutermeister (1976), Tichane (1984), Tullock (1994), Walsh (1993), Wilson (1991) and Young (1989).

on perceptions of justice may be much more important than infinitesimal error rates. Research on procedural justice has shown that justice concerns of individuals likewise apply to police and prosecution behavior (Lind & Tyler, 1988; Tyler, 1990).

Although we are eager to consider and comparatively evaluate inquisitorial and adversarial systems, we are the first to acknowledge that we simply do not have an adequate empirical base upon which to make such judgments. Indeed, our primary objective in assembling this volume is to begin building that base and in doing so, we have placed particular emphasis on examining the quality of decision-making in the Dutch and American criminal justice systems.

SUBJECTS NOT COVERED

Of course a full comparison of systems should include all stages of criminal procedure, from police investigation to Supreme Court decision-making. That would involve many interrelated stages and many aspects of the criminal procedure in each country. Many of these aspects are not dealt with in the present volume. For example, most of police behavior is not covered (exceptions are the chapters by Slobogin and Vrij). The same holds for investigative techniques such as offender profiling (Canter & Alison, 2001; Godwin, 2000; Hazelwood & Burgess, 2001; Turvey, 1999). We also do not discuss many pre-trial procedures as reflected in plea-bargaining and the role judge commissioner.

To just mention some other subjects we do not cover in this volume, but of which both of us expect to find important differences: procedural justice considerations, advocates, battered women or other syndromes, effects of media on decision makers, expert versus lay cognitive psychology, and, of course, miscarriages of justice.

THIS VOLUME

Although we do not have space to cover everything, we do believe this volume presents an excellent overview of the primary features of the inquisitorial and adversarial criminal justice systems. In assembling this volume we have particularly emphasized contributors who bring a psychological perspective to the comparative process. Our contributors are drawn for the psychological legal communities and although we have sometimes been successful in our search for contributors who are familiar with both inquisitorial and adversarial systems, we recognize that it is the rare psychologist who is familiar with both legal systems and the rare legal scholar who is versed in psychological research or practice that is relevant to both systems. What we have tried to do in this volume is to find authors who bring a mix of psychology and comparative law to the volume. In some instances we have chapters from authors who can directly compare systems and in some instances we have paired chapters from authors who can examine a common set of issues by discussing their own systems. Our hope is that our selections will, in the whole, advance comparative psychological research on inquisitorial and adversarial systems.

In the second chapter, Hans Crombag describes why he considers a comparison of the two systems, though interesting, futile in the end. Please note that in Chapter 20 we continue that discussion anyway.

The two following chapters are devoted to pre-trial behavior. Christopher Slobogin compares American and European rules and practices of police investigations, while Aldert Vrij discusses the large differences in police interrogations of suspects.

One important difference between the American and Dutch systems is the manner in which suspects and defendants are evaluated and treated psychologically. First, John Monahan describes the American manner in which the risk of re-offending is assessed, after which Corine de Ruiter and Martin Hildebrand give an account of how that risk is evaluated in Dutch defendants and how they are treated after a conviction to an asylum.

The rest of the volume is devoted to the trial and trial behavior of the participants. Samuel Gross describes the peculiarities that are brought about by the fact that the USA still knows the death penalty. There is no sister chapter for the Netherlands, because there the death penalty has been abolished long ago. Harald Merckelbach writes on so-called recovered memory cases. As in the USA these are known in the Netherlands after recovered memory therapy practices have been imported from the USA.

As we described above, cross-examination as is practiced in the USA is unknown in the Netherlands. For whomever thinks that the Dutch then miss "the greatest legal engine ever invented for the discovery of truth," as Wigmore contended, should read the chapter on cross-examination by Roger Park.

In Chapter 10, Ingrid Cordon, Gail Goodman, and Stacey Anderson present current psychological knowledge on the manner in which children are heard in court in the United States. Again, there is no Dutch sister chapter to this, since in the Netherlands children are almost never interviewed at trial. We return to this subject in Chapter 20.

We go to Germany in the next chapter, because Siegfried Sporer and Brian Cutler give a comparison of identification evidence in practice between the United States and Germany. Their comparison, better than a comparison between the United States and the Netherlands, demonstrates what difference it makes if guidelines for identification evidence are well integrated in the legal system, as is the case in Germany.

The following five chapters are devoted to expert evidence. First, Petra van Kampen gives an overview of the state of the law in the Netherlands and the United States, which is necessary to appreciate where all the differences come from. Thereafter, both Michael Saks and Ton Broeders, each from his own perspective, compare the role of experts in the two systems. To give an appreciation that even on the European continent major differences exists, Claudia Knörnschild and Peter van Koppen, in the next chapter, compare psychological expertise in the Netherlands and Germany, especially in child sexual abuse cases. In the next chapter Peter van Koppen and Michael Saks analyze how, in different ways, the Dutch and the American systems are badly protected from unsound psychological expertise in the courtrooms and try to give guidelines how to prevent such evidence.

The next three chapters are devoted to comparisons of different systems of decision-making in criminal trials. Francis Pakes shows how judges from both adversarial and inquisitorial systems try to integrate their courtroom styles in the same court: the International Criminal Tribunal for the Former Yugoslavia. Shari Diamond makes the case for the jury in her chapter that follows, while Ruth Hoekstra and Marijke Malsch demonstrate the importance and fallacies of the so-called principle of open justice in the Netherlands.

The volume concludes with a chapter in which we draw together the observations made about the two systems in the preceding chapters and provide a summary overview of what we now call the "John Wayne and Judge Dee versions of justice."

2

Adversarial or Inquisitorial

Do We Have a Choice?

HANS F.M. CROMBAG

At first sight the difference between inquisitorial and adversarial legal systems appears to be a matter of form. Does this form hide substance or is it merely a matter of appearances? To answer this question one could make a list of objectives that one wants a legal procedure to serve, and next do a series of experiments to decide empirically which objectives are best served by which system. As a matter of fact, at one time this was done by John Thibaut, Laurens Walker and their co-workers (Thibaut & Walker, 1975). In a series of experiments they compared different procedures for settling legal disputes, ranging from inquisitorial to adversarial, and on the basis of these results they claimed that the adversarial procedure is superior to the inquisitorial when it comes to establish the facts of a case, and to combating external and internal bias. Moreover, when given a choice, experimental subjects invariably prefer adversarial procedures over inquisitorial ones, irrespective of what these experimental subjects were used to in their own countries.

The aspect of adversarial legal proceedings most alluring to litigants appears to be that under it, the parties have more control over the presentation of the facts of the case, ensuring both parties that the trier of fact becomes aware of all the facts they deem relevant. Under an inquisitorial regime it is the court that controls the presentation of evidence. There is, however, more to be said about the difference. In inquisitorial legal systems the facts of the case may, and often are, considered *de novo* on appeal, thus providing for a second opinion on their merits. This difference never found its way into the Thibaut and Walker experiments, which therefore only provided us with a bleak and even distorted representation of what actually goes on in inquisitorial legal proceedings, at least in complex cases that are almost always appealed.

Still, the results of the Thibaut and Walker experiments do have an alluring quality. Are we to conclude that adversarial legal proceedings are to be preferred, and that the continental European countries used to inquisitorial legal proceedings would do well to change over to the adversarial way of doing it? To a certain extent they actually appear to be faced with that choice. They are all party to the European Convention on Human Rights, which in its Article 6 contains a due process clause. Although the designers of that article originally have tried to phrase it in such a way as to be neutral with respect to inquisitorial-adversarial distinction, the decisions rendered by the Strasbourg Court since its phrasing suggest that the Court tends to interpret Article 6 in a rather adversarial manner (Crombag, 1992). And why not, one may well ask. If the adversarial manner is at least more appealing to litigants, why not change over to the adversarial manner altogether?

That is what the Italians decided to do in 1989 with their new Code of Criminal Procedure, although mostly for practical reasons (for details see Van Cleave, 1997). They wanted to do something about the ever-growing backlog in criminal cases. To this purpose they chose to introduce two trial avoidance techniques,[1] resembling the plea bargaining procedure by which the vast majority of criminal cases are dealt with in the United States. Both these new procedures, however, turned out to sit difficult with the Italian constitution, creating "tensions ... by the application of an accusatorial system, based on the control of the parties, to a system constitutionally defined by the domination of the judge at trial" (Van Cleave, 1997). This led to a long series of decisions by the Italian Court of Cassation that as yet failed to resolve these tensions. Why is that? The inquisitorial and adversarial procedures are *not* alternative ways to serve the same purpose. They represent basically different views of what the purpose of the law is, and even of what is the purpose of the state, so Mirjan Damaška tells us (Damaška, 1986).

Under the adversarial model legal proceedings are essentially contests between equivalent rivals. A contest is only a real contest if it is played in a fair way and the essential feature of fair play is the formal equality of the contestants. The parties play for irreconcilable stakes: one party can win only at the expense of the other. The legal position of one party may *prima facie* appear stronger than that of the other party, yet

---

[1] "Attagiamento" (bargaining as to punishment) and "Giudizio abbreviato" (bargaining as to procedure).

fairness requires that both have ample opportunity to present their respective positions with uninhibited and partisan zeal. Only if this is allowed, can the adjudicator "gauge the full force of the argument" (Fuller, 1968, p. 31) before rendering a decision. During the presentation of arguments the adjudicator is "an umpire who sees to it that the parties abide by the rules regulating their contest" (Damaška, 1973, p. 563) which are, like the rules of any contest, intended to guarantee fair play. However, what in a particular instance constitutes a breach of fair play is for the parties themselves to decide: the adjudicator "is to rule on the propriety of conduct only upon the objection of the side adversely affected" (Damaška, 1973, p. 465).

The features described this far constitute, according to Damaška, *essentialia* of the adversarial tradition. Under this model one is usually judged by one's peers (the jury) and the system emphasizes oral presentation of evidence. These features are, according to Damaška, "not indispensable to the adversary model. Yet … the ideological assumptions underlying the model make … these non-essential features a matter of natural choice." He therefore calls them *naturalia* of the adversary style (Damaška, 1973, p. 564).[2] Plea-bargaining may be added as one of the *naturalia*.

Under the inquisitorial model, on the other hand, a legal procedure is considered an inquest: "an official and thorough inquiry" directed at establishing the true facts. The "court-controlled pursuit of facts cannot be limited by the mutual consent of the participants." Once a case is brought before the court, the court takes its own responsibility for finding the truth (Damaška, 1973, p. 564). Whenever technicalities of fair play threaten to get in the way of finding the truth, they are put aside. These are the *essentialia* of the inquisitorial tradition. Since plea-bargaining "raises conflicts with the … search of substantive truth," (Van Cleave, 1997) it must be considered irreconcilable with the *essentialia* of the inquisitorial procedure. Although oral presentation of evidence would be quite consistent with the inquisitorial model, it is a historical fact that inquisitorial systems have a preference for documentary presentation of evidence, which Damaška considers one of the *naturalia* of the inquisitorial model.

Taking Damaška's analysis one step further, it seems to me that the two procedural models pursue different proximate goals. The ultimate goal of both systems is, of course, to serve justice. But "justice" is a theoretical concept in need of some practical way of achieving it. In the adversarial tradition it is assumed that justice is done if the parties are treated equally in presenting their (side of the) case. The tradition is not

---

[2] Still, in England jury trial was abandoned in civil cases, except in libel and a few other actions.

indifferent to the truth, but it adheres to a particular way of establishing the truth, a way best described by the well-known French dictum du *choc des opinions jaillit la vérité*. Fair play is the proximate goal of the adversarial model. Because fair-play is the proximate goal, the tradition occasionally appears willing to compromise its search for the truth in order to uphold the rules of fair-play.

In the inquisitorial model truth itself is the proximate goal of the system. The tradition is not indifferent to fair play, but on occasions may appear willing to sacrifice fair-play to the uninhibited pursuit of the truth. The parties themselves, blinded by their emotions, are considered incapable of pursuing the truth. A detached and wise adjudicator, using whichever method he or she deems fit, is much better placed to so.

Both traditions appear to have—and here I am quoting Damaška again—"a different commitment to the discovery of truth" (p. 583). One may try to get around this reproach by saying, as Van Cleave does, that there are "two types of truth: material truth and formal truth." To my mind, this is really just a play of words. However, even if we would agree that both procedures pursue the truth, albeit a different type of truth, it does not follow from this that plea-bargaining, which *de facto* is part of the accusatorial tradition, can be considered a device for pursuing any type of truth. On the contrary, plea-bargaining is a device for systematically sacrificing the truth to expediency. Honesty requires that we admit that both traditions have "contrasting ideas about the objective of the legal process. According to one, the process serves to resolve conflict; according to the other, it serves to enforce state policy" (Damaška, 1986, p. 88).

According to Damaška these different conceptions of what legal proceedings are about and the ways in which they are conducted correspond to different conceptions of the state itself and its objectives. On the one side there is the *reactive state*, whose *raison d'être* is to provide "a supporting framework within which its citizens (can) pursue their chosen goals." Such a state "contemplates no notion of separate interest apart from social and individual (private) interests....It does only two things: it protects order, and it provides a forum for the resolution of those disputes that cannot be settled by the citizens themselves" (p. 73). In such a state the law springs mostly from private agreements and contracts, because whenever possible it relies on the "social self-management" of its citizens.

On the other side of the spectrum there is the *activist state*, which "strives toward a comprehensive theory of the good life" of its own making. In such a society the law springs from the state and expresses its policies. "Projects and perspectives that arise spontaneously among citizens are suspect," because they may easily interfere with the state's conception of the good life (p. 80). Under these circumstances the legal process is a means to implement state policy and the procedure best suited to this purpose is the inquisitorial inquest.

The contrasting descriptions of these two systems are, of course, simplifications, if only because these models are really families of models, with lots of variations within each of these families. Still, if these vignettes do catch anything of the truth, they make clear that the question of the better model is unanswerable, because they do not serve the same (proximate) goals. They also make clear that the question of whether it would be wise to switch over from one system to the other is incredibly naive. One might as well ask whether it would be a good idea to rewrite a good part of history.

3

An Empirically Based Comparison of American and European Regulatory Approaches to Police Investigation

CHRISTOPHER SLOBOGIN

This chapter is a comparative and empirical look at two of the most significant methods of police investigation—searches for and seizures of tangible evidence and interrogation of suspects. It first compares American doctrine regulating these investigative tools with the analogous rules predominant in Europe. It then discusses research on the way the American system works that sheds light on the relative advantages and disadvantages of the two regulatory regimes.

Any effort of this sort is rife with pitfalls. A comparative analysis must not lose sight of the fact that a simple comparison of rules, without consideration of the cultural, systemic, and legal context, can be misleading. Similarly, social science research that reaches conclusions about how certain procedures work in the American context does not necessarily transfer to European settings. These caveats will be revisited throughout this chapter. They do not outweigh, however, the potential benefits that comparative empirical analysis brings in terms of improving our understanding of criminal justice and how best to regulate the police.

The following discussion is divided into two parts, the first on search and seizure, the second on interrogation. Each part begins by recounting the relevant doctrine from the United States and from Europe (more specifically, from three representative countries in Europe: England, France, and Germany). It then explains why, in theory, one approach might be considered superior to the other. Finally, each part examines empirical research on the American system that provides more insight into this issue and addresses the implications of that research for the American and European approaches. More often than not, the existing data call into question preconceptions about what "works." In particular, American reverence for search warrants, the exclusionary rule, and the *Miranda* warnings may be based on significant misimpressions about the effect of these aspects of American criminal procedure. Some suggestions that arise from this discussion are presented in the concluding section of the chapter.

SEARCH AND SEIZURE

UNITED STATES LAW

The Fourth Amendment to the United States Constitution prohibits "unreasonable searches and seizures" and also states "no Warrants shall issue, but upon probable cause, supported by Oath of affirmation, and particularly describing the place to be searched, and the person or things to be seized." Construing this language, the Supreme Court of the United States has established that, with some exceptions to be described below, every police action that constitutes a "search" for evidence of crime must be based on probable cause, which is usually defined as a level of certainty close to a more-likely-than-not standard (*Griffin v. Wisconsin*, 1987, p. 877, note 4; LaFave & Israel, 1984, § 3.3(b)). Arrests must also be based on probable cause (*Henry v. United States*, 1959). Furthermore, "subject only to a few specifically established and well-delineated exceptions," all searches must be authorized by a judicially-issued warrant that meets the probable cause and particularity criteria (*Katz v. United States*, 1967, p. 357).

At the same time, the Court has announced exceptions to the probable cause and warrant requirements that are neither "limited" nor always "well-delineated." The police only need reasonable suspicion—a level of certainty well below probable cause—to conduct a stop (as opposed to an arrest) or a frisk (a patdown for weapons), and of course no warrant is required in this situation (*Terry v. Ohio*, 1968). Police also do not need a warrant for searches of a validly arrested person or of the area within the "armspan" of that person (*Chimel v. California*, 1969); furthermore, if at the time of arrest police have reasonable suspicion to believe a confederate is on the premises in which the arrest occurs they may search areas in which he or she may be hiding (*Maryland v. Buie*, 1990). Nor is a warrant needed to conduct a search while in hot pursuit of a suspect (unless the suspect has committed a minor crime and is in his home) or for most searches of cars that have been stopped, although probable cause is still required in both of these situations (Whitebread & Slobogin, 2000, Chapters 6–8).

Neither a warrant *nor* probable cause is required for a whole host of administrative searches, such as health and safety inspections, drug testing of employees, and post-arrest inventory searches, although each must be justified by a rational regulatory scheme (Whitebread & Slobogin, 2000, Chapter 13). Finally, some types of police action (e.g., going through garbage, flying over backyards, most undercover activity) are not considered searches under the Fourth Amendment because they do not involve infringement on "reasonable expectations of privacy," and thus are not regulated *at all* as a constitutional matter (*California v. Ciraolo*, 1986; *California v. Greenwood*, 1988; *Hoffa v. United States*, 1966). Similarly, a voluntary consent to a search surrenders any expectation of privacy one normally might have in the place searched (*Schneckloth v. Bustamonte*, 1973).

If the search and seizure rules are violated, the typical remedy in the United States is exclusion of the evidence in the prosecution's case-in-chief, with the result that the case against the defendant must often be dismissed (*Mapp v. Ohio*, 1961). However, illegally seized evidence need not be excluded if it was obtained in good faith reliance on a warrant, is used solely to impeach a defendant who has taken the stand, or would have been discovered through legal means in any event (Whitebread & Slobogin, 2000, Chapter 2). Furthermore, a defendant does not have "standing" to exclude illegally seized evidence if the search did not violate his own privacy but rather merely intruded only upon a third party's (*Rakas v. Illinois*, 1978).

EUROPEAN LAW

Describing European law of search and seizure is more difficult, both because so many different countries are involved and because the law is often not as well developed in some particulars (although, as noted below, it is much more specific in other ways). As noted in the introduction, to make the task more manageable, this discussion will focus on the law of England, France, and Germany. Further, only an outline of that law, sufficient to enable gross comparisons with United States doctrine, will be provided. Thus, from among the many differences between the European and American search and seizure regimes, this chapter will focus on two in particular: the use of warrants and the exclusionary remedy. Warrants are not as important in European countries, either because they are not required as often, or because they are issued on something less than probable cause, or both. Similarly, European countries do not rely as heavily on exclusion as a means of sanctioning illegal searches and seizures, but rather resort to other remedial devices.

In England, under the Police and Criminal Evidence Act of 1984 (PACE), warrants must be based on the equivalent of probable cause and may only be issued if the police can show that they seek either evidence for an offense involving more than five years imprisonment, or drugs or stolen property (Bradley, 1993a, pp. 180–181). Warrants are required in the same circumstances in which they are required in the United States, with one significant exception. As noted above, when the police arrest someone in his home in the United States, the search incident to that arrest is limited to the arrestee's person, the area within the arrestee's armspan and, if police suspect a confederate is on the premises, areas in which confederates might be hiding; additionally, these searches must be contemporaneous with the arrest. In England, in contrast, police may conduct a *full* search of the arrestee's house without judicial authorization (although in some cases they may need to obtain a supervising inspector's authorization), so long as the search is for evidence related to the offense (PACE, sec. 18(4)(5); sec. 32(2)(b)). Furthermore, this warrantless search of the premises does not have to take place at the time of the arrest, but rather may be conducted some time afterward (perhaps up to a few hours later), and may even occur when the arrest takes place outside the home (Zander, 1995, pp. 51–79). According to one study, only about 12% of searches conducted in England are based on a warrant and about 55% of those that are not are searches incident to arrest (Bevan & Lidstone, 1985, pp. 45–46, 73).

Like England (and Germany), most rules governing search and seizure in France are found in statutes, most prominently the Code de Procédure Pénale (CPP). French police investigating a "recent" major felony (a "flagrant" offense) are never required to obtain a judicial order of the type envisioned under American law. Either they seek no authorization at all or an investigating judge delegates search authority to them through a "rogatory commission," which "need not meet any degree of suspicion, or specify the parties or places to be searched, or things to be seized" (Code de Procédure Pénale, 1988, arts. 151–155; Frase, 1999, p. 153). For non-flagrant offenses, either consent or permission from a judge or his delegate is needed to conduct a search, but "no actual warrant or other detailed order needs to be issued"; furthermore, the "delegate" can be a prosecutor or upper level police officer who then supervises the investigation (Bradley, 1993b, p. 119; Code de Procédure Pénale, 1988, art. 76; Frase, 1999, p. 154). However, French law does limit search authority to specialized "judicial police," and further requires that either the person whose premises are searched or other civilians be present during the search (CPP, arts. 16–21; arts. 95–97).

Under the German Code of Criminal Procedure (CCP), as in England, the premises of an arrestee may be searched without a warrant (Criminal Procedure Code Germany, 1973, § 102; Weigend, 1999, p. 194 note 27). Nor are warrants required in most other circumstances. The German Code permits foregoing a warrant not only in cases of "hot pursuit," but also when there is "danger in delay" (CCP, § 104). Although a three-decade old description of German law asserts that this latter concept is very narrowly defined (Mueller & Le Poole Griffiths, 1969, pp. 16–17), a more recent review concluded, based on research of the search process in Germany, that "the great majority of searches are conducted without any prior judicial authorization [because] police usually assume that there is 'danger in delay'" (Weigend, 1999, p. 194). Accordingly, perhaps 10% of house searches are conducted pursuant to a warrant (Weigend, 1999, pp. 194–195, note 32). If there is outside supervision of the search process, it is normally carried out by the prosecutor (Krey, 1999, pp. 597–98). Further, a "rather vague suspicion is a sufficient basis for search" (Weigend, 1999, pp. 193–94). However, similar to the system in France, the person who is the target of the investigation or an adult relative is entitled to be present during the search (CCP, § 106).

The second major difference between the European and American regimes of search and seizure regulation concerns the remedy if an illegality is perpetrated. In all three European countries, exclusion has become more common in recent years, but it is still a rarity (Bradley, 1993a). In England, exclusion is required only when, in the judge's discretion, admission of the evidence would make the proceedings unfair (PACE, sec. 78), which is generally interpreted to require exclusion only of unreliable evidence or evidence obtained through egregious police action (Feldman, 1999, p. 105). While this rule does lead to exclusion of illegally obtained confessions with some regularity, evidence from illegal searches is routinely admitted (Zander, 1995, p. 236). Likewise in France, there are a number of situations where an illegality may lead to a "nullity," but virtually none of them involve search and seizures (Frase, 1999, pp. 155–56; but see Pakter, 1985, p. 37, note 266). Germany's approach to exclusion is the most interesting. Put simply, German courts balance the degree of intrusion and bad faith on the part of the police against the seriousness of the offense and the importance of the evidence. If the intrusion is great enough (e.g., a seizure of a diary), exclusion may occur even if no illegality occurred. On the other hand, in serious cases exclusion of contraband or fruits or instrumentalities of crime is very unlikely (Bradley, 1993a, pp. 208–12).

All of these countries depend upon other means of ensuring that police obey the rules, in particular internal police discipline. In Germany, for instance, such discipline is taken very seriously by the police hierarchy (Langbein & Weinreb, 1978, p. 1559–61). However, it is unclear how often police are disciplined specifically for violations of search rules, as opposed to other types of transgressions (Weigend, 1999, p. 204).

EMPIRICAL ANALYSIS OF THE DIFFERENCES

American law is based on the premise that both warrants and the exclusionary rule are necessary to prevent police abuse of the search power. The usual reason advanced for the warrant preference was best described by Justice Jackson, who explained that the Fourth Amendment's protection "consists in requiring that … inferences [about criminal activity] be drawn by a neutral and detached magistrate instead of being judged by the officer engaged in the often competitive enterprise of ferreting out crime" (*Johnson v. United States*, 1948, p. 14). A number of rationales have been offered in support of the exclusionary rule (see Slobogin, 1999). But the only one that has stood the test of time is the belief that remedies other than exclusion have proven "worthless and futile" as means of ensuring that police obey the law (*Mapp v. Ohio*, 1961, p. 652). Although many exceptions to the rule now exist, the U.S. Supreme Court continues to exclude evidence obtained in violation of the Fourth Amendment on the ground that it is needed to deter police misconduct (see, e.g., *Bond v. United States*, 2000; *Florida v. J.L.*, 2000).

Thus, an American lawyer might criticize European search and seizure law for its relatively nonchalant attitude toward warrants and the failure to use exclusion as a mechanism for deterring police abuse. Of course, this criticism assumes, along with the Supreme Court, that warrants and the exclusionary rule *are* crucial mechanisms for controlling the police. Furthermore, it assumes that, even if warrants and exclusion are effective in this regard, the regulatory benefit outweighs any loss in crime control they may cause. A fair amount of research exploring these assumptions exists.

Warrants

The most authoritative information about the warrant process in the United States comes from a seven-jurisdiction study conducted by the

National Center for State Courts (NCSC). This study found that the "vast majority" of searches are conducted without a warrant (Van Duizend, Sutton, & Carter, 1985, p. 21), indicating that warrants do not play the significant role in regulating police behavior that Justice Jackson suggests. At the same time, warrants do figure prominently in searches of premises, universally considered the most private space (Van Duizend et al., 1985, p. 35). Unfortunately, we do not know the precise proportion of house searches that are conducted pursuant to a warrant in the United States. Given the law of search incident to arrest in England and Germany, however, it is very likely higher than the 10 to 12% figure given for such searches in those countries, and it is undoubtedly higher than the analogous figure in France.

Whether warrants provide any real protection of privacy is harder to tell. The NCSC study also revealed that, when police did seek a warrant, magistrates reviewed their applications in less than three minutes in 65% of the cases, devoted more than five minutes of deliberation to only 11% of the applications, and rejected an application in only 8% of the cases (Van Duizend et al., 1985, pp. 32–33). A separate study found that judges are even less likely to reject law enforcement requests for electronic surveillance warrants; of 20,107 applications submitted for such warrants at the federal level between 1968 and 1995, only 27 were denied, and none were denied between 1988 and 1995 (see Slobogin, 1998, p. 192). These findings suggest that magistrates usually rubberstamp the police application, and that the neutral, independent judgment of the type lauded by Justice Jackson rarely takes place. That conclusion is partially reinforced by the NCSC's finding that police often sought out particular magistrates believed to be friendly toward police views on investigation (Van Duizend et al., 1985, pp. 47–49).

Note, however, that another possible reason the rejection rate for warrant applications is so low is that most of them are meritorious. The NCSC study found that officers routinely request their supervisors or the prosecutor to check their application before submitting it to the magistrate, that magistrates more than occasionally ask the police to provide additional information before issuing the warrant, and that only 5% of the warrants that were issued were subsequently found invalid (Van Duizend et al., 1985, pp. 8–11, 24–25, 31). Perhaps in many cases a three-minute review is all that is necessary, because the warrant process encourages solid requests from police. Police knowledge that a judicial officer will check their investigative efforts and reasoning, even if only in a cursory fashion, may improve both.

There are also at least two theoretical reasons, both noted by Stuntz, for believing that the warrant process is useful in preventing illegal searches (Stuntz, 1991, pp. 910–18). First, the process may reduce judicial bias favoring the police, because a magistrate grants or denies a warrant application *before* he knows whether the police will find the evidence. In contrast, judicial review of a warrantless search occurs *after* the search, typically during a hearing to suppress evidence; because, inevitably, the magistrate in this hearing knows the police have found something, his probable cause determination could easily be tainted by hindsight reasoning, a phenomenon that has been found to infect other assessments of police behavior (Slobogin & Schumacher, 1993, pp. 765–68). The second way in which a warrant process may reduce illegality is by making police fabrication more difficult, again because the probable cause determination for a warrant must be made before the search takes place and thus before the officer knows what he will find. In contrast, fabrication is relatively simple during review of a warrantless search, when the officer can more easily "justify" his actions based on what has already happened.

Ultimately, however, we do not definitively know whether abolition or relaxation of the warrant requirement would lead to more frequent illegal searches. According to the NCSC study, approximately 12% of the warrant-based searches that were challenged were found to be invalid (Van Duizend et al., 1985, p. 42). That failure rate is only slightly lower than the suppression rate of 14.6% for *all* searches reported by Nardulli (1983, p. 597, Table 7). Furthermore, even if police are found in violation of the Fourth Amendment at a somewhat higher rate when they conduct warrantless searches, that differential could be due to a number of third variables, including a reviewing court's reluctance to second guess a fellow judicial officer's warrant decision.

Further, there is the possibility that a warrant requirement significantly detracts from effective law enforcement. According to the NCSC study, drafting and submitting a warrant application may take as long as half a day, although the advent of telephonic warrants, which permits oral applications, has reduced the warrant issuance period from an average of three or four hours to an average of one hour and a half in those jurisdictions where they are permitted (Van Duizend et al., 1985, pp. 85–87, 149). If the only searches discouraged by this process are those for which the police lack probable cause, then the warrant requirement is functioning as it should. But if the hassle of obtaining a warrant is discouraging police from conducting searches in cases where probable cause exists, then it is not. Furthermore, there is the possibility that the cumbersome nature of the process *encourages* illegal searches as police try to evade it through dubious consent searches or arrests staged in areas where warrants are not required (e.g., the car). As one officer quoted in the NCSC study stated, 98% of his searches were conducted after securing the target's "consent," sometimes obtained through (unfounded) threats to secure a warrant unless admission was granted (Van Duizend et al., 1985, p. 17).

Exclusionary Rule

The key issue in this context is the extent to which exclusion of illegally obtained evidence deters police violations of the Fourth Amendment. Several different types of research bear on this question. One strain of evidence consists of pre/post studies examining the effect of *Mapp v. Ohio* (1961)—the Supreme Court decision which applied the exclusionary rule to the 50 states—on various aspects of police conduct such as warrant applications and arrest statistics. Another group of studies consists of surveys of and interviews with the police and other actors in the legal system about the conduct of searches and their attitudes toward the exclusionary rule. A third type of study tests police knowledge of Fourth Amendment rules, on the theory that a sanction which deters should create an incentive to know the relevant law.

Unfortunately, the pre/post studies are seriously flawed methodologically. As Davies noted (1974, pp. 756–64), pre/post statistics on the number of search warrants issued, arrest and conviction rates, or the amount of recovered stolen property and seized contraband—although theoretically useful in evaluating *Mapp's* impact on search and seizure practices—are easily affected by a host of other factors (e.g., crime rates, police priorities, changes in Fourth Amendment rules). Poor record keeping before *Mapp* also afflicted the pre/post studies (see *United States v. Janis*, 1976, pp. 451–52). These difficulties have critically undermined this type of research on the exclusionary rule. For instance, Canon, although a supporter of the rule, had to conclude that his findings "do not come close to supporting a claim that the rule wholly or largely works" (Canon, 1977, p. 75). Similarly, Oaks, a researcher who argued against retaining the rule, admitted that his findings "obviously fall short of an empirical substantiation or refutation of the deterrent effect of the rule" (Oaks, 1970, p. 709). Such honesty by opponents in the debate over the rule is commendable, but its import is distressing for those trying to devise policy. As Davies concluded, "when all factors are considered, there is virtually no likelihood that the Court is going to receive any 'relevant statistics' which objectively measure the 'practical efficacy' of the exclusionary rule" (Davies, 1974, pp. 763–64).

Interviews of police and other actors in the system also produced ambiguous findings about the consequences of the rule. Surveys conducted shortly after *Mapp* was decided indicated agreement among attorneys and judges that exclusion had a much bigger impact on police behavior than the civil or criminal actions that comprised the main method of sanctioning illegal searches and seizures before that case was decided (see Katz, 1966, pp. 119, 132; Nagel, 1965, p. 302). That result, however, merely confirmed what the Court itself recognized in *Mapp*—that existing alternatives to the rule were "futile" as deterrents. Interviews with police suggest that the rule, while better than these other devices at influencing their search behavior, may not be significantly better. For instance, it is often reported that police say they resent the rule or that they learned valuable lessons when evidence they seized was suppressed, reports which are said to be indications that the rule affects their actions (see, e.g., Orfield, 1987, pp. 1066–67). Yet a survey of over 200 police from two southeastern cities found that 19% admitted to conducting searches of "questionable constitutionality" at least once a month, and 4% said that at least once a month they conducted searches they *knew* to be unconstitutional, meaning that several hundred constitutionally suspect searches occur each year in just these two departments (out of over 15,000 nationwide, Akers & Lanza Kaduce, 1986). Perhaps even more discouraging to proponents of the rule are the results of a survey of several hundred California police asking which remedy for illegal searches they preferred. Most officers picked the exclusionary rule, not only over damages (which would take money directly out of their pockets), but also over more training (Perrin, 1999, p. 733, Table 7). Apparently, the police would rather put up with the risk of exclusion than sit through a few more hours in the classroom.

One fairly robust finding of the pre/post research and the survey studies is that *Mapp* at least brought about a significant increase in such training programs, presumably because prosecutors and police departments, worried about losing cases, wanted their officers to know about Fourth Amendment law (see, e.g., Kamisar, 1990, pp. 557–59). The final category of research, examining the extent to which these programs have been effective, also offers frustrating results. One study involving over 450 officers, for instance, found that officers as a group did better than chance on only one out of six questions about search and seizure law (Heffernan & Lovely, 1991, p. 333). A second study testing police knowledge found that the "average officer did not know or understand proper search and seizure rules" and that "supervisors or senior officers only achieved slightly improved scores" (Hyman, 1979, p. 47). A third study involving 296 officers demonstrated a "widespread inability to apply the law of search and seizure or police interrogation" (Perrin, 1999, p. 727). These findings are supported by the observations of Wasby, who studied numerous police training programs in the 1970s, before many of the exceptions to the exclusionary rule had come into being. He came to the conclusion that "recruit training is sadly lacking in criminal procedure content" and that "[t]he spirit and tone of communication about the law, particularly when the law is favorable to defendants' rights, is often negative, with the need for compliance stressed only infrequently" (Wasby, 1978, pp. 464–466).

Why does the exclusionary rule have so little effect on individual officers or on training programs? After all, an illegal search could well mean dismissal of the case. Behavioral theory suggests one answer to this question. That theory posits that punishment, to be effective, must be frequent, consistent, immediate, and intense (Williams, 1973, pp. 154–155). The exclusionary rule, as applied in the United States, violates all of these precepts. First, exclusion only occurs when there is a prosecution, which is an infrequent event; the vast majority of police-citizen encounters never progress beyond the street level. Second, even when charges are brought, plea-bargaining often short-circuits them (perhaps as often as 95% of the time), which can mean that the validity of the search is never fully contested. When suppression hearings do take place, as discussed earlier, police lying and judicial hindsight bias often result in a finding for the prosecution in close cases. The many exceptions to the rule—good faith reliance on a warrant, impeachment, inevitable discovery, and lack of standing—also diminish the chance of exclusion. On those few occasions when suppression does occur, it may take place well after the illegal conduct and never be communicated to the officer. Finally, and perhaps most importantly, the exclusionary punishment is not directed at the officer or the department but at the prosecutor. Sociological research clearly establishes that the policeman is most interested in getting a "collar", with conviction a distant and often irrelevant consideration (see, e.g., Rubinstein, 1973, p. 45). That means that exclusion is a very indirect sanction on the average officer. For these and related reasons, the rule is not a very effective behavior-shaping mechanism (for elaboration of these arguments, see Slobogin, 1999, pp. 373–381).

Legitimacy–compliance theory, developed by Tyler (1990), may provide another explanation for the relatively weak impact of the exclusionary rule. Legitimacy-compliance theory posits that obedience to the law stems as much from respect for the law and those who promulgate it as from a fear of punishment for unlawful behavior. Because the rule "sanctions" the police by helping a clearly guilty person, and because it "punishes" virtually all police violations of the Fourth Amendment, even those that are inadvertent, suppression of evidence may not be perceived as legitimate, even by officers who are disposed to support the values underlying the Amendment. The previously reported resentment that police feel toward the rule, far from showing a willingness to comply with search and seizure doctrine, might instead indicate disrespect for this method of enforcing the Fourth Amendment and thus create passive-aggressive resistance toward it. Such resistance might be implemented through any number of mechanisms, including lying about probable cause or exigency, covering for other officers' transgressions, and simply avoiding prosecution when illegality is clear and cannot be hidden (see Slobogin, 1999, pp. 381–384).

None of this is meant to suggest that research and theory prove the exclusionary rule is inferior to other available means of controlling police misconduct. For instance, in the United States, civil, criminal, and administrative remedies for illegal searches and seizures are almost as impotent today as they were prior to *Mapp*. Even when police are sued or disciplinary actions are brought, proof that they acted in "good faith" generally prevents any action being taken. On those few occasions when a plaintiff is able to convince a jury to levy damages against a police officer, the officer is usually indemnified by the department, significantly undermining the effect of the verdict (see Meltzer, 1988, pp. 283–285; Patton, 1993, pp. 787–94). Thus, the exclusionary rule, despite its flaws, may be the most potent remedy currently available in the United States.

Perhaps for that reason, it also the most "expensive." Estimates of convictions lost because of the rule range from 0.5 to 7.1%, depending upon the jurisdiction and type of crime (see summary of data in *Leon v. United States*, 1984, p. 998, note 6). One commentator concluded that approximately 10,000 felons and 55,000 misdemeanants evade punishment each year because of successful Fourth Amendment suppression motions (Davies, 1983, pp. 669–670). Other more subtle "costs" of the rule include the exacerbation of adversarial tensions between police, suspects, and attorneys caused by the high stakes involved in assessing the legality of searches (Pizzi, 1999, pp. 40–42, 222–223), the distracting impact of suppression hearings on the quality of defense representation (Stuntz, 1997, pp. 31–45), and the damage to courts and government generally because of public outrage at the benefit criminals receive when cases against them are dismissed or damaged by exclusion (Kaplan, 1974, pp. 1035–36).

Existing alternatives to the rule are less costly on all these measures. In particular, they clearly sacrifice fewer convictions. Note, however, that this difference probably results primarily from their inadequacy. As many have pointed out (Kamisar, 1987, p. 47, note 211; Maclin, 1944, p. 56), an *effective* alternative to the rule (e.g., a meaningful damages remedy) would also result in "lost" convictions, because it would deter the police from conducting searches and finding the evidence in the first place.

IMPLICATIONS OF THE RESEARCH

Despite some good empirical efforts, we do not know how much extra protection a warrant provides, nor is there convincing evidence that exclusion deters police misconduct on a routine basis. However, the research does firmly suggest that warrants raise police officers' "standard of care" when they are deciding whether to conduct a search (Van Duizend et al., 1985, pp. 148–149), and that the exclusionary rule is superior to other means of deterring police conduct, at least in the United States. Can we then say that, because it is relatively more invested in warrants and exclusion, the United States does a "better" job at regulating searches and seizures than England, France and Germany? That conclusion does not necessarily follow. As the introduction to the chapter indicated, such comparative inquiries must take into account cultural, systemic, and legal differences.

First, various aspects of European culture may call for a very different cost-benefit analysis than policymakers and citizens in the United States might make. European societies tend to be more homogenous than the United States, which may reduce concerns about discriminatory treatment by law enforcement. Similarly, Europe's long tradition of centralized and often authoritarian regimes and its relatively compact living conditions may make its citizens more tolerant of strong police power and less concerned about privacy and autonomy. Finally, Europeans may tend to trust officialdom to a greater extent than Americans, meaning that they are more willing to believe, perhaps with good reason, that their police won't behave improperly (Damaška, 1973, p. 584). Thus, any relatively greater leniency toward law enforcement that does exist in Europe may reflect entrenched cultural differences rather than a lesser regard for "fundamental" values. Providing indirect support for this speculation is a study which revealed significant differences between American and Australian subjects in their evaluations of the intrusiveness of various police search techniques, with the Americans routinely gauging those techniques to be more intrusive than their non-American counterparts (Slobogin & Schumacher, 1993, p. 769).

Second, even if basic values concerning the relationship between the state and the individual were identical in the two societies, systemic differences between the United States and Europe might create a greater need for police regulation in the United States. For instance, the high crime rate and the prevalence of guns and drugs in the United States may place more pressure on American police to bend the rules, and thus require more restrictions on them. The adversarial nature of the American criminal justice system itself may make police in the United States more aggressive, and therefore more in need of regulation, than European police, who are immersed in a tradition of relatively neutral inquiry (Damaška, 1973).

Third, comparisons of individual legal rules can mislead because they ignore how other legal rules may compensate for or interact with the rules in question. This discussion has focused on warrants and exclusion, two areas in which European law is not as rigorous as United States law. Also noted, however, were ways in which European law might be more protective. For instance, the requirements that searches be conducted by certain types of police or under the supervision of the prosecutor, that they be limited to serious crimes, that they be monitored by third parties, and that they be sanctioned administratively if illegal—all components of one or more European systems—do not exist in the United States, at least on a national level. Some commentators have called into question the extent to which these aspects of the European system provide any meaningful limitation on the police (Frase, 1990, p. 586); for example, as in the United States, internal and monetary sanctions are rare in Europe, and third party monitoring only influences the execution of a search, not the decision to carry it out (and may even *increase* illicit intrusion into privacy). The point remains that comparisons of selected components of a system must be taken with the proverbial grain of salt.

INTERROGATION

UNITED STATES LAW

For many years, regulation of the interrogation process in the United States focused entirely on whether any statements obtained were "voluntary." If not, admission of the confession violated the suspect's "due process" rights under the Fifth and Fourteenth Amendments to the United States Constitution, both of which state in relevant part that the government may not deprive someone of life or liberty without due process of law. Voluntariness analysis requires looking at the "totality of the circumstances" surrounding the confession, which necessitates examination of the interaction of police conduct with the vulnerabilities of the suspect (*Fikes v. Alabama*, 1957). Under this test, for example, the U.S. Supreme Court declared "involuntary" both a confession obtained after a suspect was questioned continuously for 36 hours without rest or sleep (*Ashcroft v. Tennessee*, 1944), and a confession obtained from a suspect who was informed that welfare for her children would be cut off and her children taken away from her if she failed to "cooperate" (*Lynumn v. Illinois*, 1963). While originally the Court seemed concerned that such techniques would produce unreliable confessions, by 1961 it declared that such confessions were excluded "not because [they] are unlikely to be true but because the methods used to extract them offend an underlying principle in the enforcement of our criminal law; that ours is an accusatorial and not an inquisitorial system—a system in which the State must establish guilt by evidence independently and freely secured and may not by coercion prove its charge against an accused out of his own mouth" (*Rogers v. Richmond*, 1961, pp. 540–541).

Although the Court has never veered from this basic principle, it has since resorted to two other methods of regulating interrogation besides the due process clauses. First, in 1964, the Court held that, under the Sixth Amendment's guarantee of assistance of counsel in all criminal prosecutions, suspects who have been formally charged are entitled to counsel during interrogation (*Massiah v. United States*, 1964). More importantly, in *Miranda v. Arizona* (1966) it held that any suspects subjected to "custodial interrogation," even if *not* formally charged, are entitled to four "warnings": that the suspect has a right to remain silent; that anything he says may be used against him; that the suspect has a right to have counsel present during interrogation; and that if he cannot afford an attorney one will be appointed for him. If these warnings are not given, the Court held, any statements obtained must be excluded from evidence. Even if the warnings are given, statements that are "involuntary" in the due process sense must be excluded. Furthermore, the defendant who does talk has the right to cut off questioning at any time, and his refusal to answer questions may not be used against him in court. These holdings were based on the Fifth Amendment, the relevant portion of which states that "no person ... shall be compelled" to testify against himself.

Since *Miranda*, the Supreme Court has limited its holding significantly. First, police need not give the warnings when to do so would pose a threat to public safety because, for instance, a suspect's silence might prevent police from discovering a dangerous weapon (*New York v. Quarles*, 1984). Second, although questioning must cease if the suspect asserts the right to counsel, if the defendant who has invoked reinitiates conversation—a concept the Court has defined broadly (*Oregon v. Bradshaw*, 1983)—the police may continue questioning (*Edwards v. Arizona*, 1981). Moreover, if the suspect merely asserts his right to remain silent (as opposed to the right to counsel), police probably do not need to wait for the defendant to reinitiate conversation, so long as there is a decent interval between interrogations and they rewarn him (*Michigan v. Mosley*, 1975).

Third, the Court has sanctioned several forms of trickery after the warnings are given. For instance, on two occasions it has held valid a confession given by a suspect who apparently thought that so long as his statements were not reduced to writing they could not be used against him, a misimpression the police failed to correct (*Connecticut v. Barrett*, 1987; *North Carolina v. Butler*, 1979). In another case, the Court held valid a confession from a suspect who was misinformed about the subject matter of the investigation (*Colorado v. Spring*, 1987). The Court has also refused to exclude confessions obtained after police lied about finding fingerprints at the scene of the crime (*Oregon v. Mathiason*, 1977), after they falsely told the suspect that his colleague had already confessed to the crime (*Frazier v. Cupp*, 1969), and after they deceived the defendant's attorney about when interrogation would take place (*Moran v. Burbine*, 1986). Finally, a confession obtained by an undercover agent, even one posing as a cellmate, does not violate *Miranda* (*Illinois v. Perkins*, 1990). In all of these cases, the Supreme Court reasoned that the police action was insufficiently coercive to violate the Fifth Amendment prohibition against compelled testimony.

Finally, as with the Fourth Amendment exclusionary rule, the Court has narrowed the scope of exclusion after a *Miranda* violation. Although a statement obtained by an unwarned suspect must be excluded from the prosecution's case-in-chief, the Court has not required exclusion of evidence obtained as a result of such a violation (e.g., a witness identified in the statement, or another confession given under the impression the "cat was out of the bag"). Furthermore, even a statement obtained in violation of *Miranda* is admissible for impeachment purposes. On the other hand, confessions that are involuntary in the due process sense, as well as their fruits, continue to be excluded (see Whitebread & Slobogin, 2000, § 16.05).

EUROPEAN LAW

As with search and seizure doctrine, there are several differences between American rules governing police interrogation and the analogous European rules. The following discussion will note most of these differences, but will concentrate on the warnings requirement, the use of trickery and taping during interrogation, and the remedy for violation of the rules. As with the discussion of search and seizure law, the description is necessarily brief, sufficient only to provide grounds for comparison with American law.

English interrogation law is the most elaborate among the three countries. In England, a defendant must receive a "caution" about the right to remain silent as soon as there are "grounds to suspect" him of criminal activity (PACE, Annex C, para. 10.1). In contrast, *Miranda* is not triggered until the suspect is in "custody," meaning that English police may be required to give warnings at an earlier point than American police. However, beginning in 1994 with passage of the Criminal Justice and Public Order Act, the police must also inform the suspect that adverse inferences can be drawn from his silence (PACE, para. 10.4, Zander, 1995, pp. 303–311). Furthermore, although the suspect is entitled to counsel before and during interrogation, police need not tell him of that right until he is brought to the police station (Zander, 1995, p. 126, PACE, sec. 58), and this caution may be delayed if a superintendent or higher level officer decides that exercise of the right would lead to interference with evidence, harm to others, or escape of a suspect (ibid.). If the suspect does exercise the right to counsel, questioning must stop until one has been consulted, except in urgent circumstances of the type just described (PACE, Annex C, para. 6.6). Counsel may be present during the interrogation unless he begins answering questions for his client or in some other egregious way "prevents the proper putting of questions to his client" (PACE, paras. 6.9–6.11). Perhaps in part because of this latter provision, counsel in England often play a very passive role during interrogation, and seldom terminate it (Baldwin, 1992).

In addition to the cautions requirements, there are a number of other interrogation rules. All interviews in the police station must be tape-recorded, although interviews that take place elsewhere need not be (PACE, sec. 60). After the defendant is formally charged, all questioning must cease unless the police need information regarding other offenses (PACE, Annex C, para. 11.4). Various rules govern how often the suspect must be allowed breaks, food, and so on (PACE, paras. 8.6, 12.2). Finally, although trickery is not unknown in English interrogations (see Berger, 1990, pp. 23–24), English courts have declared that misrepresentation of the available evidence and others types of deceit are not permissible (Feldman, 1999, pp. 111–112) and research suggests that use of such techniques is rare (Baldwin, 1993, p. 331 and note 27).

Breach of these rules does not necessarily lead to exclusion of the confession, however. If the violation was inadvertent, a solicitor was present at the time, or the violation did not affect the suspect's decision to confess, then exclusion is unlikely (Feldman, 1999, pp. 113–114). On the other hand, complete failure to caution a suspect and wrongful refusal of access to legal advice are substantial breaches that will lead to exclusion. Intentional failure to abide by the recording requirements will usually lead to exclusion as well (Bradley, 1993a, pp. 188–191; Feldman, 1990).

Prior to June, 2000, French suspects were accorded very little protection during interrogation. Although they had a right to remain silent, they were not told of that right, and were not entitled to consult counsel during the first 20 hours of detention (Frase, 1999, p. 159). Today, they are informed of the right to silence and to consult counsel during detention (CCP, art. 63–1). Furthermore, records are kept of these various warnings, as well as of the length of interrogation (CPP, arts. 63–65). However, suspects are still not entitled to have counsel present during interrogation (CCP, art. 63–4). After charging, any interrogation that takes place will usually be conducted by a judge (who is permitted to tell the suspect that silence will be used against him), but further police interrogation is not barred. The defendant has a right to counsel during these post-charge sessions with the police, unless he waives it or the lawyer fails to appear (Frase, 1999, pp. 159–160). Exclusion for violations of these rules is rare, but has occurred when counsel was not provided after the 20-hour period, the 48-hour rule was violated, or the rights regarding detention were not recited (Frase, 1999, pp. 161–162).

In Germany, as in England, suspects must be told of the right to remain silent, as well as the subject matter of the investigation, whenever they are the focus of an investigation (CCP, § 136). They are also entitled to be told that they may consult a defense attorney prior to interrogation (ibid.). However, they have no right to counsel during interrogation and the state need not provide one for them if they are indigent. Furthermore, the German courts routinely admit evidence obtained during "informal" interviews that take place before the warnings are given, apparently on the ground that the interviewees are not being treated like suspects during these conversations (Weigend, 1999, pp. 200–201). Even if the suspect indicates a desire to remain silent, police may continue to question the suspect and can inform him of the disadvantages of remaining silent, although a request for counsel must end questioning unless there is reinitiation (Thaman, p. 602; Weigend, 1999, p. 201). Formal charging does not change any of these rules; police may continue to conduct interrogations. German courts do explicitly prohibit affirmative misrepresentations by the police, while permitting them to leave misimpressions uncorrected unless the misimpressions are about the law (Weigend, 1999, pp. 202–203). Questioning by undercover agents is also forbidden, at least when it takes place in jail (Frase & Weigend, 1997, pp. 333, 336–37, CCP, § 136a). Exclusion for violation of the rules is not automatic, but is likely to occur when the police fail to warn a person who should have been warned of his right to silence and the person appears not to have known of his right (Bradley, 1993a, p. 215; Weigend, 1999, p. 204).

In all three European countries, exclusion is required if the police use physical coercion to obtain the confession, although it is not clear that fruits of such a confession must be excluded. Additionally, in Germany exclusion is mandated when police use certain techniques, such as hypnosis, illegal promises, or undercover agents as inquisitors, regardless of whether the resulting confession is coerced (CCP, § 136a).

AN EMPIRICAL ANALYSIS OF THE DIFFERENCES

There are at least three independent reasons for telling a suspect he has a right to remain silent when police attempt to interrogate him. The primary rationale *Miranda* gave for this requirement was that knowledge of the right and the ability to exercise it in unfettered fashion is necessary to counteract the "compulsion inherent in custodial surroundings" (p. 458). The assurance that he may remain silent also lets the guilty defendant know that he is not confronted by what the Court has called, in other cases, the "cruel trilemma" of having to choose between self-accusation, fabrication, or some type of sanction for silence (see, e.g., *Murphy v. Waterfront Commission*, 1964, p. 54). Finally, the silence warning reminds the *police* that they may not resort to the inquisitorial practice of relying on the defendant for their information. The warning thus also protects the innocent, who otherwise might be subjected to prolonged interrogation by officers used to depending upon confessions as their main source of evidence. As Dean Wigmore stated, "if there is a right to an answer, there soon seems to be a right to the expected answer—that is, to a confession of guilt" (Wigmore, 1960, p. 309).

For the same sorts of reasons, the *Miranda* Court believed that suspects should be entitled to counsel during interrogation and to be told of that right. Without counsel present, suspects might become confused, on their own or with help from the police, about the scope of their right to silence. They may also need help in assessing the advisability of confessing. And, of course, counsel's presence should alleviate the coercive atmosphere of the stationhouse.

Miranda and its progeny implement these goals only imperfectly, however. The suspect is not told that he has a right to cut off questioning at any time. Furthermore, the suspect can waive the rights to silence and counsel relatively easily; indeed, as indicated above, even a waiver obtained through trickery may be valid, if it is not "coerced." Finally, the suspect is not told that statements made in response to illegal questioning can still be used for impeachment purposes, or that the fruits of such statements are admissible.

Despite the many loopholes in the *Miranda* regime, it appears to control certain facets of the interrogation process to a much greater extent than either English or German law, and clearly restricts police questioning more than French law does. In England and France, police may tell the suspect that silence may be used against him, a statement which is strictly forbidden in the United States on the ground that it would emasculate the right to silence. In France and Germany counsel is not entitled to be present during questioning. And in France and England, questioning may continue after a request for counsel, again something that American law prohibits unless the defendant reinitiates, on the theory that invocation of the right to counsel indicates that the defendant has decided he cannot face the police alone. Finally, incriminating statements obtained during interrogation are excluded much more frequently in the United States, where good faith failure to give the warnings is not excusable, and fruits of coerced interrogations are clearly excluded (see generally, Whitebread & Slobogin, 2000, Chapter 16).

On the other hand, England and Germany, and perhaps France as well, appear to put more limitations on the use of trickery or, as Vrij puts it in his chapter in this volume, on "American-style" questioning (Vrij, 2003). Whereas American courts focus on whether interrogation techniques are "coercive," and often find that trickery is not, European law appears to be less fixated on coercion per se and more on the propriety of police conduct. Furthermore, the taping requirement in England, designed to provide accurate information about the interrogation process, clearly goes beyond anything required under the United States Constitution. Finally, unlike English and French law, American constitutional law does not impose finite time limits on interrogation sessions or require any particular type of record-keeping.

These observations about the differences between the various countries raise several empirical issues. Because the focus of this chapter is a comparative analysis of how countries attempt to limit police abuse of the interrogation process, the following four issues are arguably the most important. First, does the warnings regime of *Miranda* and its progeny better alleviate coercion than either a no-warnings regime (pre-2000 France), or a quasi-warnings regime (England)? Second, what is the impact of "trickery" on suspects? Third, what is the impact of taping on suspect and police behavior? Finally, what is the "cost" of the *Miranda* regime, especially in terms of lost convictions?

All of these questions are very hard to answer empirically. The research does suggest, however, that the *Miranda* regime better protects against compelled statements than the other two approaches, at the same time it exacts a relatively small cost in crime control. On the other hand, the research suggests that trickery is an effective way of obtaining confessions and that taping may increase police ability to obtain incriminating statements. Most of this research comes from the United States, but research on the English interrogation process will also be noted occasionally.

Coercion with and without Miranda

There is no easy way of measuring "coercion" in the interrogation context because coercion is so hard to define and because, even if it is defined coherently, its subjective nature makes measurement challenging. Present research at best provides information that can act as a proxy for assessing coerciveness. Meares and Harcourt have identified three such proxies: knowledge of rights, number of interrogations conducted, and confession rates (Meares & Harcourt, in press). This proxy information suggests, but does not prove, that *Miranda* has diminished the coerciveness of police interrogation in the United States.

First, there is no doubt that more suspects and more police know about the right to remain silent and right to counsel now than before *Miranda* was decided. Suspects are routinely read their rights (Gruhl & Spohn, 1981; Leo, 1995), and over 80% of the population at large knows about them, a figure much higher than the analogous pre-*Miranda* figure (Walker, 1993, p. 51). If the three rationales for *Miranda* outlined above are correct, then knowledge about these rights, by itself, should reduce the coercive aspects of interrogation.

Second, some evidence suggests that police conduct proportionately fewer interrogations since *Miranda* was decided. At least one study attributes this trend to *Miranda* (Cassell & Hayman, 1996, pp. 854–858). If that conclusion is right, *Miranda* has reduced compulsion during interrogation by reducing the opportunity for it to occur.

Third, a considerable amount of pre/post research indicates that confession rates dropped due to *Miranda*, although debate has been vigorous over precisely how much. Cassell concluded, after looking at 12 studies and excluding three of them as unreliable, that the reduction in confessions resulting from *Miranda* averaged 16.1% (Cassell & Hayman, 1996, pp. 395 et. seq.). Schulhofer, examining the same studies and excluding five of them as unreliable, concluded that *Miranda* reduced the confession rate between 6.7 and 9.1%, and argued further that the reduction may have been between 4 and 5% if certain other adjustments were made (Schulhofer, 1996b, pp. 539–41). Even the lower figures show that *Miranda* has had some effect on the interrogation process.

One might wonder, however, why *Miranda* has not had a greater impact on the confession rate. After all, a rational guilty person who is told that he may remain silent and consult an attorney would presumably decide not to confess, at least until he had met with an attorney. In this volume, Vrij summarizes some of the reasons a suspect might nonetheless make incriminating statements, including a belief that confession will bring a better deal, the stress that accompanies detention, and a natural urge to talk (Vrij, 2003). All three of these phenomena may lead to a confession without any police prompting. On the other hand, police can also take advantage of all of these situations, which leads to the next topic.

Trickery and Confessions

As used here, trickery consists of either an outright fabrication or a failure to correct a misimpression that is not "coercive," as the U.S. Supreme Court has defined that term. For comparative purposes, understanding the impact of such techniques is most important, since it is allowed in the United States but limited to varying degrees in European countries. Examples of trickery, already noted, are false statements that a co-defendant has confessed or that certain evidence has been found at the scene of the crime, and continued questioning after it has become clear that the suspect believes oral statements will not be admissible. Showing false sympathy for the suspect, a technique widely recommended in American police manuals (see, e.g., Inbau, Reed, & Buckley, 1986, pp. 96–158), would also constitute trickery. On the other hand, telling the suspect that he does not have a right to remain silent or a right to counsel—in other words, lies about basic Fifth Amendment law—would not be permissible, because such statements recreate the coercive atmosphere the warnings are designed to diminish. Additionally, lies that are tantamount to threats—for instance, that the suspect's spouse will be detained or harmed if a confession is not forthcoming—are clearly coercive in the due process sense and should not be viewed as "American-style" questioning (cf. Vrij, 2003).

Observational research suggests that trickery so defined can be very effective at obtaining confessions. The most potent evidence in this regard comes from Leo, who found in his study of 182 interrogations that the only variables that were significantly related to the likelihood of a successful interrogation were the number of psychological tactics employed by detectives and the length of the interrogation (Leo, 1996, p. 275). In another article, he describes a number of specific trickery techniques which he has seen succeed. Foremost among these strategies are the creation of a relaxed, friendly atmosphere, de-emphasis of the warnings' importance, and persuading the suspect that it is in his legal interest to talk (Leo, 1995, pp. 660–65). Even more recently, in an article entitled "Adapting to *Miranda*," Leo and White described a number of other ways in which the police work around *Miranda*'s strictures (Leo & White, 1999).

This research suggests why *Miranda* has not caused confession rates to fall more precipitously. In the wake of that decision, the police may have abandoned their most coercive techniques, but devised more subtle ways of obtaining confessions. What we do not know is whether or how often such trickery induces innocent persons to confess. Although many false confessions have been documented (see, e.g., Kassin, 1997; Leo & Ofshe, 1998), most of them were obtained under conditions and in response to police techniques that were much more "coercive" than those this chapter is calling trickery.

The Effect of Taping

A National Institute of Justice survey provides the most detailed information on the American experience with taping interrogations

(Geller, 1993). That survey found that, although not constitutionally required to do so, at least one-sixth of American police and sheriff's departments audio- or videotape interrogations on a mandatory or discretionary basis. Despite initial reluctance, most police officers eventually found this innovation useful. They said it improved interrogation practices, facilitated the introduction of confessions into evidence, and made those confessions more convincing in court. From this account, one might conclude that taping *improves* confession and conviction rates, and in fact 59.8% of the departments surveyed stated that taping had increased the amount of incriminating information from suspects (Geller, 1993, pp. 54, 107–149). Reports on the English experience similarly indicate that, at worst, taping has not diminished the confession rate (Vrij, 1998a). At the same time, audio or videotaping would presumably reduce egregious police behavior (including trickery techniques that have been deemed illegal) while the tape is running.

Of course, the tape isn't always running. As noted above, in the United States taping is discretionary in many of the departments that use it. In England the taping requirement only applies to interviews in the stationhouse. Many interviews take place in the field, a practice that taping may actually encourage (McConville, 1992; Moston & Stephenson, 1994).

Costs of Miranda

As with the Fourth Amendment exclusionary rule, important to any assessment of the impact of *Miranda* is the effect it has on law enforcement's ability to solve crime. The data on confession rates, reported above, may furnish some indirect information on that score. But the conclusion that *Miranda* reduces confession rates does not dictate the conclusion that it also reduces conviction rates. Police unable to get a confession might nonetheless resort to other investigative techniques to obtain the evidence necessary for conviction. Indeed, that is one of the rationales underlying *Miranda*—that police must be swayed from their tendency to engage in inquisitorial practices.

Unfortunately, we do not have a clear empirical picture of *Miranda's* effect on conviction rates. Cassell and Schulhofer have debated this issue as well. Combining his estimate that *Miranda* caused a 16.1% drop in confessions with an estimate that confessions are needed to convict in 24% of the cases in which interrogations occur, Cassell concluded that *Miranda* caused a lost conviction in 3.8% of cases in which police resort to interrogation (Cassell, 1996, p. 484). Schulhofer, using his lower estimate of the reduction in confessions caused by *Miranda*, as well as a lower figure for the necessity of confessions (19%), concluded that, at most *Miranda* brought about a 1.1% drop in convictions (Schulhofer, 1996b, p. 545).

Cassell also attempted to calculate *Miranda's* effect on clearance rates, which report the number of crimes solved (through conviction or otherwise). He initially suggested that *Miranda* caused a drop in clearance rates from approximately 60% to approximately 45% (Cassell & Hayman, 1996), a conclusion which Schulhofer disputed on a number of grounds (Schulhofer, 1996a). Later, using more sophisticated regression analysis, Cassell and Fowles concluded that *Miranda* caused a 6.7% drop in the clearance rate for total violent crimes, and a 2.3% drop in the clearance rate for total property crimes (Cassell & Fowles, 1998, pp. 1086–1088). Using slightly different statistical methods on the same data, Donohue agreed that, around the year 1966 when *Miranda* was decided, there was a statistically significant drop in clearance rates with regard to larceny and total violent crimes, but concluded that there was no such drop for other property crimes or for the individual crimes that make up the category of total violent crimes (murder, robbery, rape, and assault). He also pointed to Cassell's failure to take into account the impact of unquantifiable variables that might account for the lower clearance rates, such as changes in police reporting of crime (Donohue, 1998). Still another author concluded that Cassell's analysis of clearance rates after *Miranda* is so faulty that no worthwhile conclusions can be drawn (Feeny, 2000).

Some have suggested other possible costs of *Miranda*. Perhaps, for instance, *Miranda* has distracted reviewing courts from the main goal of inhibiting coercive police techniques. Once the police show they gave the warnings, it is conjectured, further judicial inquiry into their actions tend to be cursory (Thomas, 2000, p. 4). Similarly, the police themselves may be less diligent about regulating their behavior in a *Miranda* regime, thinking that once they give the warnings they have discharged their legal obligation. These hypotheses about costs are still largely speculation, however. A more obvious, and prosaic, cost derives from the fact that *Miranda* requires the government to provide counsel to indigent defendants at a much earlier stage in the criminal process than is otherwise the case.

IMPLICATIONS OF THE RESEARCH

The research suggests that, compared to a regime in which no warnings are given, such as exists in France, the *Miranda* regime alleviates the coercive aspects of the interrogation process. That regime probably also marginally compromises police ability to solve crimes compared to a no-warnings system. But *Miranda* appears to have reduced inappropriate pressure to confess in a large number of cases without sacrificing an equivalent number of convictions.

A comparison of the warnings regime that exists in the United States to the quasi-warnings regime of England is harder to make, because the latter approach at least apprizes the suspect of the rights to silence and counsel, albeit in a fashion that significantly diminishes their worth. In theory, the quasi-warnings regime is closer to a no-warnings regime than a warnings regime. But statistics on confession rates suggest that the quasi-warnings approach may not be that different from *Miranda*, at least as the latter approach is implemented in the United States. Thomas, surveying a number of American studies, estimated the average post-*Miranda* confession rate to be 50 to 55% (Thomas, 1996, p. 958), while Leo found a 64% confession rate among his sample (Leo, 1996, pp. 300–391), and Cassell concluded the rate is much lower than 50% (Cassell, 1996, p. 434). To compare those rates with England's, it is instructive to look at pre-PACE data (when no cautions were required), data from 1986 to 1994 (when cautions were required and adverse inferences could not be drawn) and post-1994 data (the regime described above). Before cautions were required in England, confession rates were very high—between 65 and 75%—as one would expect (Van Kessel, 1986, pp. 127). After 1986, they fell significantly, with rates of from 40 to 55% reported (Baldwin, 1993, p. 335; Gudjonsson, 1992, p. 324). Post-1994, the one reported study indicated that the confession rate came back up, although not significantly, to 58% (Van Kessel, 1998, p. 829, note 129).

If the post-1994 confession rates in England are essentially the same as the post-*Miranda* confession rates in the United States, and assuming variables other than legal rules have no effect (an admittedly big assumption), either the quasi-warnings used in England are not as compulsive as earlier conjectured or the greater use of trickery in the United States makes up the difference. The reasons for rejecting the first explanation (i.e., the cautions in England essentially tell the suspect he should not exercise his right to remain silent) and for accepting the second explanation (i.e., trickery has been a successful interrogation technique) have already been advanced. If one accepts those reasons, a crucial normative question arises: Despite the likelihood that it would reduce the confession rate significantly, should trickery be prohibited (at the same time, perhaps, that taping is mandated to ensure that such a prohibition is followed)?

This is not the place to answer this question in full. I have recently advanced the argument that trickery which is not coercive may be permissible during custodial interrogation (although I would define coerciveness more broadly than the Court). Based on the work of moral philosopher Sissela Bok, I contended that if the police have probable cause that the suspect is guilty (which is normally the case if custodial interrogation is occurring), they may treat him as an "enemy," a situation in which Bok, normally hostile to deceit, would permit it (Slobogin, 1997). However, others have disagreed with this position, contending, *inter alia*, that it distorts Bok's premises and that it undermines the trust that is essential to good policework and to a well-functioning society (Mosteller, 1997; Paris, 1997). Inter-national differences might also affect this analysis. Perhaps Americans, whose "rampant individualism" (Bayley, 1986, p. 48) has helped create an adversarial process which more than occasionally leads to distortions of truth, are more comfortable with trickery than Europeans and thus more willing to endorse deceitful techniques.

Cultural and legal differences might also inform analysis of whether a quasi-warning regime is fundamentally unfair or unduly coercive. For historical reasons alluded to earlier, European legal culture may be comfortable with a greater level of police coercion. Further, given the adjudicatory procedures followed on the Continent, police coercion may be relatively irrelevant to the suspect. In both France and Germany, defendants are expected to testify at their trial and reveal information relevant to sentencing as well as guilt, since the same trier of fact decides both issues after a unitary trial. In addition, in both countries early cooperation brings lighter sentences (Van Kessel, 1998, pp. 833–835). This combination of pressures may be far more effective at motivating suspects to talk than anything the police do.

CONCLUSION

On paper, American search and seizure rules expressing a preference for warrants and requiring exclusion when illegality occurs provide greater protection of privacy than do European search and seizure rules. Likewise, in theory, the *Miranda* warnings regime protects autonomy to a greater extent than European interrogation rules. In practice, the American rules are not as potent as American courts and society seem to believe, in part because of legal loopholes, and in part because the police have been able to work around them. Consequently, the impact of American regulation of police investigation is not exceedingly different from the impact of the seemingly less restrictive regimes that exist in Europe. For the same reason, the American rules turn out to be less "costly" to law enforcement than some have made them out to be.

Borrowing from both American and European traditions, consider briefly various alternative regulatory systems that might better regulate the police without destroying their investigatory effectiveness. In the search and seizure context, warrants might be required whenever possible, on the ground that their ex ante nature eliminates judicial hindsight bias, foils police who want to lie, and improves the standard of care exercised by police who conduct searches. However, to alleviate the burden of consulting a magistrate, warrants could be issued (as they sometimes are in France and Germany) by prosecutors, who are more involved in the investigation process and more accessible. To reduce any tendency of these individuals to favor the police, evidence obtained as a result of an invalid warrant would be excluded, a sanction which has a much more direct effect on prosecutors than it does on either police or magistrates.

Alternatively, we might construct a system with substantive search and seizure rules similar to those in European countries, but with a meaningful damages sanction that required individual officers to pay for bad faith violations and the police department to pay for all other violations. Such a regime might deter officers much more effectively than the exclusionary rule, at the same time it would encourage them to seek warrants as insulation from liability. It would also create a stronger incentive for departments to develop serious training programs that would reduce ignorant mistakes by their officers. It might be supplemented by a German-style exclusionary rule, which suppresses evidence obtained through police action so egregious that it taints the judicial process.

In the interrogation context, we might combine a *Miranda* warnings requirement with a requirement that *all* interrogations be taped, an evidentiary ban on statements not on tape (about which the suspect must be told), and rules governing the length of interrogation and related matters. At the same time, police could be permitted to engage in trickery that is not coercive, a category that would become better defined as courts examine these techniques via audio or videotape. Alternatively, as some have suggested (Kauper, 1932), we could abolish custodial interrogation or render it irrelevant by providing that the only admissible incriminating statements are those obtained by a magistrate, who would conduct questioning as soon after arrest as possible, with defense counsel present. To facilitate information gathering, the magistrate would be allowed to advise the suspect that silence might increase suspicion, a process that is similar to the judicial questioning procedure that takes place in France (except that France also accepts statements made during police interrogation). Although this procedure undermines the right to remain silent, the fact that it occurs in open court and is conducted with counsel present makes it relatively uncoercive compared to the usual stationhouse encounter.

Finally, any proposals adopted should be codified in legislation. The disadvantages of relying on courts, which must wait for a case and controversy and may announce only those rules suggested by the facts of the case, have been well documented (Bradley, 1993b). The European codes of criminal procedure are far superior to the judicially created American rules in terms of comprehensiveness and clarity.

These concluding comments are offered merely as food for thought. One benefit of comparative analysis is that it renders proposals that seem radical from a domestic viewpoint less so because of foreign analogues. Much more comparative and empirical work needs to be done, however, before such proposals can be advanced with certainty.

4

"We Will Protect Your Wife and Child, but Only If You Confess"

Police Interrogations in England and the Netherlands

ALDERT VRIJ

The purpose of a police interrogation is to obtain further information about a crime that has been committed. The importance of the interview depends on the evidence available in the case. When there is substantial evidence, the interview would be used to clarify unsolved issues (e.g., the whereabouts of some of the stolen goods, the motives of the criminal, and so on). Cooperation of a suspect is often necessary to solve such issues but not crucial for a conviction. A recent example is the case of Dr. Shipman, Britain's "most prolific serial killer" (*The Independent*, 1 February 2000). He was a general practitioner and has been found guilty of murdering 15 women. He received 15 life sentences on 31 January 2000. Dr. Shipman denied all 15 charges and the 57-day trial uncovered no obvious motive of the killings. Dr. Shipman was convicted merely on the basis of evidence against him.

When there is no evidence, the interview should be used to obtain valid information in order to link the suspect or someone else to the crime. Cooperation of a suspect might then be crucial to solve the crime. It is therefore important for the police to get the suspect to talk.

To date, a number of (mainly American) manuals are available to advise police detectives how to get reluctant suspects to talk. Inbau, Reid, and Buckley's (1986) *Criminal Interrogation and Confessions* is probably the most popular among them. The book has been influential in England as well and has inspired Walkley (1987) to write his *Police Interrogation: Handbook for Investigators.* Inbau et al.'s book has been heavily criticized by various scholars (Gudjonsson, 1992; Kassin, 1997; Kassin & Fung, 1999; Leo, 1992; Ofshe & Leo, 1997b; Vrij, 1998a; Williamson, 1994), particularly because it advocates the use of trickery and deceit. Although using tricks and deceiving suspects is allowed in the United States, it is unlawful in many other countries, including England and the Netherlands (see Vrij, 1998a, for possible reasons why it is unlawful). This implies that the evidence obtained via trickery and deceit cannot be allowed as evidence in court in these countries.

Also, the use of trickery and deceit may, at times, cause innocent people to confess to crimes they did not commit. On the one hand, suspects might knowingly confess to crimes they did not commit to escape or avoid an aversive police interrogation or to gain a promised reward. Suspects also knowingly falsely confess sometimes without police pressure, for example, to protect somebody else (Crombag, Van Koppen, & Wagenaar, 1994; Wagenaar, Van Koppen, & Crombag, 1993). On the other hand, a police interrogation might induce a state that causes suspects to confuse truth and confabulation and to make them falsely believe that they actually have committed the crime (see Gudjonsson, 1992, 1999; Kassin, 1997; Kassin & Wrightsman, 1985; Leo & Ofshe, 1998; Ofshe & Leo, 1997b, for numerous documented real-life cases of false confessions and for social psychological explanations as to how police interrogations may elicit false confessions; Shuy, 1998).

What methods do the police use to obtain crucial information from a suspect if trickery and deceit are not allowed? This chapter reviews and compares literature published in England and the Netherlands concerning this issue (see Slobogin in this volume for a discussion of American interrogation techniques and for a comparison between European and American practices).

There is much more information available about interview techniques in England than about Dutch interview techniques. Unlike in the Netherlands, since 1986 all police interviews at police stations with suspects are audio taped in England, although this resulted in an increase in "off-the-record" (not audio taped and not registered) interviews (see below). A substantial number of English audiotapes have been made available to scholars for research purposes. The major part of the review therefore deals with police interviewing in England, particularly with reasons why suspects confess and which aspects of a police interview make it a good interview. I will also address the presence of legal advisers or other "third parties" during police interviews. Their presence should be a safeguard for suspects, but it will become clear that this is not always the case.

With the Dutch police keeping the interrogation room doors locked for observers, the review of Dutch police interviews is necessarily purely anecdotic. However, Dutch police literature contains guidelines about how to interview suspects. I will briefly discuss some of these guidelines, together with a recent English manual about police interviewing.

A striking finding is that researchers who listened to audio taped police interviews in England all came to the same conclusion: a main characteristic of English police interviewing is its general ineptitude (Baldwin, 1993, 1994; Cherryman, 2000; Gudjonsson, 1994a; McConville & Hodgson, 1993; Milne & Bull, 1999; Moston & Engelberg, 1993; Moston & Stephenson, 1993, 1994; Moston, Stephenson, & Williamson, 1993; Pearse & Gudjonsson, 1996b, 1997a, 1999; Pearse, Gudjonsson, Clare, & Rutter, 1998; Robertson, Pearson, & Gibb, 1996; Sear & Stephenson, 1997; Stephenson & Moston, 1994; Williamson, 1994). Researchers advocate that more guidelines for police detectives are needed about how to interview suspects. Guidance and police training on how to interview suspects is virtually non-existent in England (Gudjonsson, 1994a; Milne & Bull, 1999; Moston & Engelberg, 1993; Sear & Stephenson, 1997). For a long time it was believed that interviewing skills could not be taught, but only learnt through experience (Moston & Engelberg, 1993). Obviously, lack of training may contribute to the poor quality of police interviews noticed by so many researchers. I will conclude this article with some guidelines for police interviewing.

Theoretically, a suspect's willingness to confess in a police interview could be explained by social psychological theories concerning attitude change (Ajzen & Madden, 1986). I will commence discussing this framework in a police setting that could be used to evaluate the potential effectiveness of tactics used by the police to date (see also Ofshe & Leo, 1997a,b; Vrij, 1998b).

ATTITUDE CHANGE IN THE INTERROGATION ROOM

Attitudes are individuals' evaluations of particular persons, groups, objects, actions or ideas and are important in predicting somebody's behavior. Simply stated, somebody's attitude towards an attitude-object (for instance confessions) is based upon the perceived positive and negative aspects of that attitude-object. The more positive and the less negative aspects are perceived, the more positive the attitude will be; the more negative and the less positive aspects are perceived, the more negative the attitude will be. In sum, a suspect will be likely to confess if he believes that a confession will result in more benefits than costs. A suspect is unlikely to confess if he believes that a confession will results in more costs than benefits.

Perceived benefits of a confession could be factual or emotional. Examples of factual advantages are that a confession might result in a police caution rather than the case going to court (police cautions in England are only possible after guilty pleas) or in a lower sentence if the defendant is prosecuted and convicted. Two factors are particularly relevant: Perceived strength of evidence and seriousness of the offence. Suspects will only perceive factual benefits of a confession when they believe that the evidence against them is strong. In that case they might believe that they will be found guilty anyway, even if they do not confess. Confessing in that situation may lead to a milder sentence (police caution or low sentence). In cases where suspects believe that the evidence against them is weak, they might think that denying involvement in the crime will lead to discharge of prosecution or acquittal. In that case not confessing might have a more favorable factual outcome for the suspect than confessing.

The less serious the offence is, the more likely it is that a suspect will confess. If the offence is not serious, a suspect might believe that a confession will not lead to prosecution, but only to a police caution. The two factors interfere with each other. When the offence is very serious, suspects might be reluctant to confess even when they realize that the evidence against them is strong. In those situations, there is not much to gain for suspects with making a confession, as they will receive a severe punishment, even with a confession. One possible advantage of not confessing in such a situation is that it will save them the humiliation of having to discuss in detail the terrible crimes they have committed. Suspects are least likely to confess when they are suspected of a serious crime and when they perceive the evidence against them to be weak. In that case, a confession might lead to severe sentencing whereas the suspect might walk free if he or she remains silent.

It is possible that suspects confess even when there are no factual benefits for them to do so. In that case they probably do this for emotional reasons (feelings of guilt, remorse, or stress, Gudjonsson, 1992). Suspects might suffer from feelings of guilt or remorse and therefore confess in order to "get it off their chest". Alternatively, police interviews might cause a lot of stress and suspects might confess in order to escape further interrogation. This is more likely when the police put much emotional pressure on suspects. Obviously, the police then run the risk that the case will be dismissed in court because the interview was oppressive.

INTERVIEWING SUSPECTS IN ENGLAND

In January 1986 the Police and Criminal Evidence Act 1984 (PACE) and its Codes of Conduct came into force in England (and Wales). PACE included new legislation regarding the detention, treatment, and questioning of persons by police officers, and was introduced as a result of several serious miscarriages of justice. Among others, PACE (a) introduced the compulsory audio-taping of police interviews with suspects; (b) ensures that suspects are not subjected to undue police pressure, police tricks, or oppression; and (c) provides protection concerning the interviewing of "vulnerable suspects." Numerous audiotaped police interviews have been made available to researchers. Their analyses of these tapes are presented in Table 1.

Most studies mentioned in Table 1 served two different aims: They looked at reasons for suspects to confess or at the quality of the interview.

REASONS TO CONFESS

Table 1 reveals that most confession studies found confession rates between 50% and 60%. (see Slobogin in this volume for American confession rates). Apparently, the majority of suspects confess in police interviews. The studies also make clear that most interviews are short and that most suspects are co-operative during police interviews. For example, from a sample of 1,067 police interviews (fully reported in Moston & Stephenson, 1992), Moston et al. (1993) reported that only 5% of the suspects remained completely silent. The stereotypical belief that suspects tend to deny involvement in crimes or prefer to remain silent and that interviewing is a tough and long lasting process is simply untrue. It is not surprising that research findings contradict the stereotypical common beliefs. First, a refusal to talk might not be in the suspect's own interest. Baldwin (1994) pointed out that about a third of all cases end as police cautions. However, this option is only available to suspects who admit involvement in a crime. Second, being interrogated is often a very stressful experience, even for some experienced criminals (Gudjonsson, 1993; Sear & Stephenson, 1997). Cooperation will reduce the period of interviewing. Third, being detained in a police station is a stressful experience too (Gudjonsson, 1993). Once arrested, suspects are regularly detained in police cells for up to four hours, and in some instances for considerably longer periods (Evans, 1994). Suspects who are initially unwilling to talk are much more cooperative after a few hours in a police cell (Foppes, 2000, personal communication). Fourth, it is extremely difficult for people to

TABLE 1. OVERVIEW OF STUDIES ANALYZING ENGLISH POLICE INTERVIEWS WITH SUSPECTS

Authors	Aim of study	Number of interviews	Sample description	Length of interview	Confession/admission rates	Suspect cooperation	Dependent variables
Baldwin (1993)	Quality of interview	600	Random sample	30 minutes	75% within 55%	79% cooperative, 14% difficult to interview, 3% changed position in interview	"Experts": Give suspects opportunity to state their position, listen to suspect's responses, avoiding tactics, testing a suspect's account with fairness and integrity
Cherryman (2000)	Quality of interview	69	Random sample	33 minutes	Not reported	Not reported	29 characteristics. "Experts": communication detectives: no interruptions*, structure*, tactics*. Police supervisors: open-mindedness*, keep suspect on topic*, absence of long and complex questions*.
Evans (1993)	Reasons to confess	367	Juveniles	Not reported	59%	Not reported	Sex, age, police subdivision*, criminal history*, evidence*, offence type, seriousness*, legal advice
Evans (1993)	Reasons to confess	164	Juveniles	14 minutes	Not reported	77% readily confessed	Pointing out contradictions, confronting with evidence, "get it off your chest"
McConville and Hodgson (1993)	Reasons to confess	157	Random sample	54% less than 20 minutes, 2% longer than 2 hours	Not reported	Not reported	Accusation or abuse[a] pointing out evidence[a], consequences on self-esteem[a]
McConville and Hodgson (1993)	Reasons to confess	not reported suspects	Reluctant	Not reported	Not reported	Not reported	Downgrading[b], upgrading[b], rationalization[b], direct accusation[b], interpreting nonverbal behaviour[b]
Moston and Stephenson (1994)	Cooperation suspect's	641	Random sample	Not reported	51%	5% said nothing	
Moston, Stephenson, and Williamson (1992)	Reasons to confess	1067	Random sample	Not reported	42%	Not reported	Evidence*, seriousness*, legal advice*, age, criminal history, offence category, police station*
Pearse, Gudjonsson,	Reasons to confess	161	Random sample	22 minutes	58%, 3% confessed in	97% was polite, 83% was compliant,	Introduce evidence, emphasize seriousness of offense, challenge lies, age*, sex, ethnic origin,

Study				subsequent interview	
Clare, and Rutter (1998) (also reported in Pearse and Gudjonsson, 1996c, 1997)					solicitor present, appropriate adult present, experience of prison*, suspect's anxiety, suspect's suggestibility, suspect's mental state, use of drugs*, use of alcohol, mental state
Pearse and Gudjonsson (1999)	Reasons to confess	18	Reluctant suspects	1 hour 23 min	3 pleaded guilty	Intimidation, challenge inconsistencies, manipulation, introduce evidence, appeal, question style
Sear and Stephenson (1997)	Quality of interview	76	Random sample	Not reported	Not reported	Experts: dominance, agreeableness, conscientiousness, neuroticism, openness*.
Stephenson and Moston (1994)	Quality of interview	133	Reluctant suspects	Not reported	Not reported	Avoidance, downgrading, persistence, upgrading, rationalization

* Had a significant effect on the investigated issue.
[a] Used in interviews with at least 20 suspects.
[b] Used in interviews with at least 10 suspects.
Note: Williamson's (1993) assessments of police interviews are not incorporated in Table 1 because insufficient information is provided about the nature and content of these interviews.

keep information entirely private. For example, our ongoing research into secrets (Vrij, Nunkoosing, Oosterwegel, & Soukara, 2000) revealed that the vast majority of people confide a secret to somebody else, even when they believe that there are serious negative consequences in case these secrets come out.

Different studies reveal somewhat different outcomes to explain why suspects confess, but the following factors were significant predictors in more than one study: strength of evidence, perceived seriousness of the crime, the presence of a legal adviser, the police station where the interviews were conducted, and the criminal history of the suspect. As was predicted by the theoretical framework, the stronger the suspects perceive the evidence against them and the less serious the offence, the more inclined they are to confess. Moston et al. (1992) found that 67% of the suspects confessed when they evidence against them was strong, whereas only 10% confessed when the evidence was weak. Also Evans (1993) found that only 9% of (juvenile) suspects confessed when the evidence against them was weak. Also, suspects are less likely to confess when there is a legal adviser present during the interview. There are at least two explanations. It might be that legal advisers advise suspects not to confess. Alternatively, as conformity studies have revealed, people are less likely to comply in the presence of an ally (Allen & Levine, 1971; Asch, 1956). It may therefore be that the mere presence of a legal adviser strengthens the suspect's resistance to comply with the police detective.

Remarkably, two studies revealed that the police station where the interviews took place had an impact on confession rates. Evans (1993) suggested that interview styles may differ from station to station and may have an impact on the outcomes. Suspects with previous convictions were least likely to confess. Several explanations are possible. More experience with police interview tactics may make suspects better able to resist such tactics. Alternatively, people with previous convictions may also be more likely to be arrested and questioned for offences, which they have not committed. It may also be that for offenders with previous convictions the consequences to confess are more serious than for those without convictions, as previous convictions may contribute to harsher sentencing in case of a conviction.

Finally, the studies revealed that only a small minority of suspects changed position throughout the interview. The great majority of suspects (more than 95%) stick to their starting position (admission, denial, or somewhere in between), regardless on how the interviews were conducted. These findings inspired Moston et al. (1992, p. 38) to write: "Police officers would probably like to think that suspects make admissions because of skilled questioning techniques. The reality, however, is in all probability quite different." Although this conclusion probably makes good headlines, it is somewhat misleading. In many cases that were analyzed, the offences were minor, the evidence substantial and the suspects willing to talk. In such cases, interviewing is simple and straightforward and no enhanced question techniques are required. Such techniques, however, are required with reluctant suspects, especially if they are suspected of serious offences. There are numerous examples of reluctant suspects who are suspected of serious crimes and who do start talking as a result of interview tactics used by the police. The problem is that such tactics are often unprofessional, as will be outlined below.

QUALITY OF THE INTERVIEW

The new ethical framework of police interviewing in England (after the introduction of PACE) is based upon three principles (Sear & Williamson, 1999; Williamson, 1994): (a) to shift the police service from its traditional reliance in getting a suspect to confess to encourage its task as a search for the truth; (b) to encourage officers to approach an investigation with an open mind; and (c) to encourage officers to be fair. There are reasons to believe that these principles have not been achieved yet.

SEARCH FOR THE TRUTH

Both Moston et al. (1992) and McConville and Hodgson (1993) found that in the great majority of cases (in both studies 80%) the objective for the police was to secure a confession. There are several reasons why obtaining a confession seems attractive for police officers. First, often there is pressure on the police (from the general public, media, and political agenda) to solve crimes and to do this quickly. Clear-up rates are an important measure of police performance and obtaining a confession is one of the quickest routes to clearing up crime (Evans, 1994; Maguire, 1994; Milne & Bull, 1999). Second, confession evidence is often seen as a prosecutor's most potent weapon (Kassin, 1997). If a defendant's confession is admitted at trial, it may have considerable value and many other aspects on the trial will be viewed as less important (McCann, 1998; Otte, 1998; Stephenson & Moston, 1994). Indeed, few confessions are ever challenged in court; fewer still are challenged successfully (Baldwin, 1993). Third, police officers readily assume that a suspect is guilty (Evans, 1994; Moston & Stephenson, 1992; Stephenson & Moston, 1994). For example, Moston et al. (1992) found that in 73% of the cases the interviewers were "sure" of the suspect's guilt before they interviewed the suspect. Not surprisingly, the tendency to seek a confession increases when they are sure of the guilt of a suspect (Stephenson & Moston, 1994). Fourth, the English legal system might encourage police officers to obtain confessions. In England defendants can be, and sometimes are, convicted merely on the basis of their confessions, even when the confession is disputed at trial (Gudjonsson, 1999). In many other countries, such as the Netherlands and the USA, a confession has to be corroborated by some other evidence, although in practice the corroboration criteria allowed by judges are sometimes weak (Wagenaar et al., 1993).

OPEN-MINDEDNESS

Moston et al. (1992) observed two interview styles used by the police: (a) an accusational strategy (where suspects were confronted with the accusation against them at the very outset of the questioning) and (b) an information-gathering strategy ("open" questioning style intended to let suspects describe their actions in their own words, without an overt accusation being made). Although the latter corresponds with the desired open-mindedness of police officers, the first strategy was common as well. Moston et al. (1992) found that the choice of style did depend on the perceived strength of evidence and offence severity. An accusational strategy was used in case the officers perceived the evidence against the suspect to be strong, whereas the information-gathering style was used when the evidence was perceived as weak. The latter strategy was also commonly observed with serious offences, particularly sex-related offences. This finding was also obtained by Soukara (2000) in her ongoing research.

Lack of open-mindedness might also have to do with police officer's personality. Sear and Stephenson (1997) investigated personality measures amongst police detectives and found that many of them had "a cold, calculating and dominant approach to others" (p. 32). Obviously, such an interpersonal style goes well with accusational interview strategies.

Assuming a suspect's guilt makes it difficult for a police officer to be open-minded (see also Hargie & Tourish, 1999; Mortimer & Shepherd, 1999), as can be explained with the concepts of "confirmation bias" and "belief perseverance" (Brehm, Kassin, & Fein, 1999). The confirmation bias refers to people's tendency to seek, interpret and create information that verifies existing beliefs. People want to support their own "theories" and are therefore eager to verify their beliefs but less inclined to seek evidence that might disapprove them. In fact, people have the tendency to maintain beliefs even after they have been discredited (belief perseverance).

The reason is that once early impressions are formed it is difficult to "see straight" once presented with improved evidence. It is similar to looking to a slide that is completely out of focus and which gradually becomes less blurry. People have more difficulties recognizing the picture if they watch this gradual focusing procedure than if they simply view the final image.

According to Baldwin (1993, p. 329), a high quality interview contains the following characteristics: allowing suspects an unhurried and uninterrupted opportunity to state their position; listening to their responses; avoiding harrying, coercive, or authoritarian tactics; and testing a suspect's account with fairness and integrity. Cherryman (2000) asked four "experts" to listen to 69 audio taped police interviews and to rate them. They rated the presence of communication, empathy, open questions, and structure as the most important features of a skilled interview. In their analysis of audio taped police interviews, Sear and Stephenson (1997) found that openness as reflected in an officer's behavior was a major component of interviewing skill. These findings fit well in the new ethical framework of interviewing, outlined before. However, the question "what is a good interview" is difficult to answer, as it is a subjective judgment (disagreement about the relative importance of the objective criteria that might be employed). There is no guarantee that different people would reach the same assessments of the quality of any particular interview. Cherryman (2000) addressed this issue. She found that her four experts did agree amongst each other in their assessments of the quality of the interviews they were asked to listen to. However, none of these raters were police officers (neither were the raters in Baldwin's and Sear and Stephenson's studies). Cherryman therefore invited police officers (both police detectives and police supervisors) to assess the interviews, which were also rated by the experts. Perhaps the most interesting finding was the presence of a "confession-effect" amongst police officers. They evaluated interviews that contained a confession as more positively than interviews that did not contain a confession. Also Moston et al. (1992) reported that a confession is generally thought by police officers to be a sign of a "good interview." Cherryman (2000) did not find a confession-effect amongst police superiors and experts. A possible explanation for her confession findings is that officers who interview themselves are particularly inclined to perceive benefits of a confession (quick way of solving a crime; indicator of successful performance; unlikely to be challenged in court).

Baldwin (1993) criticized the communication skills of the interviewers. He found most attempts to build up a rapport highly artificial. Some interviewers tried an approach on the lines of "Tell me something about yourself"—an invitation that usually met with confusion and unease.

Moreover, most officers appeared nervous, ill at ease, and lacking in confidence throughout the interview. Several interview styles were questionable and unprofessional (e.g., misleading the suspect, interrupting the suspect, terminating the interview as quickly as possible after an admission, and losing control of an interview [i.e., overreacting to provocations of the suspects]). Similar findings were obtained by Moston et al. (1992). Interviewers appeared to be very nervous, often more nervous than the suspects. Police interviewing skills were, as Moston (1996, p. 92) recently described, "almost non-existent."

FAIR INTERVIEWING AND THE USE OF TACTICS

Pearse et al. (1998) observed that the police generally placed very little pressure on suspects. However, their sample included many straightforward cases in which the evidence was strong and the suspect willing to talk. In these interviews, pressure is not necessary. More insight into the use of police tactics would be obtained by looking at interviews with reluctant suspects, particularly when they are suspected of serious crimes. Evans (1993) found that persuasive tactics were most frequently used in these cases.

Several authors (Baldwin, 1993; Moston & Stephenson, 1992; Pearse & Gudjonsson, 1996b; Stephenson & Moston, 1994) noticed that police detectives had a somewhat limited repertoire of interview techniques and limited strategic flexibility. Baldwin (1993) pointed out that even when the suspects denied the allegation, the interviewer in almost 40% of the cases made no challenge. Stephenson and Moston (1994) came across several strategies but they noticed that each officer tried out only one strategy, and they tend to stick to it even when it clearly did not work.

McConville and Hodgson (1993) observed several persuasive techniques used in interviewing reluctant suspects, including downgrading (trying to get the suspect to talk about anything, for example lifestyle, relationships, if the suspect doesn't want to talk about the offence. Once a dialogue is established, the conversation can be transferred back to the offence in question), upgrading (providing information which tends to implicate the suspect) and direct accusation (suggesting that silence implies guilt). They concluded that sometimes these strategies were effective in persuading reluctant suspects to talk, but they also believed that sometimes these tactics soured the atmosphere and alienated suspects who might otherwise have been persuaded to co-operate. Moston and Engelberg (1993) and Stephenson and Moston (1994) observed police tactics in 133 cases where right of silence was exercised. Upgrading (explained above) was used most often, followed by persistence (merely repeating the same or similar question), which was found to be a highly unproductive and sometimes embarrassing strategy that revealed the officers at loss.

Perhaps the most detailed analysis of police methods in interviews with reluctant suspects was published by Pearse and Gudjonsson (1999). They examined the techniques used in 18 serious criminal cases. The police relied heavily on tactics to overcome resistance and secure a confession, such as intimidation (manipulating details, manipulation self esteem, maximize anxiety, threats and so on) and manipulation (minimize seriousness and responsibility). In three cases the interview style resulted in a guilty plea and conviction. Several times, however, the police resorted to tactics that were unprofessional, unethical, and illegal. As a result, in four cases the interviews were classified as inadmissible and two cases were withdrawn because the interview was found to be unreliable.

THE PRESENCE OF AN APPROPRIATE ADULT

PACE offered important provisions for interviewing "special groups" such as juveniles, persons who are hearing or sight impaired, those who are illiterate, and those who do not speak English sufficiently well to comprehend the interviewer. It also includes persons who are mentally disordered or who have learning disabilities (McKenzie, 1994; Sear & Williamson, 1999). A major reason for the introduction of provisions is that such interviewees may be especially prone to providing, in certain circumstances, information that is misleading or unreliable (Milne & Bull, 1999). The legal provision requires the presence of an "appropriate adult," a responsible adult called in by the police to offer special assistance to the detainee. The role of the appropriate adult is to advise the person being questioned and to observe whether or not the interview is being conducted fairly. It is also their role to facilitate communication with the person being interviewed (Pearse & Gudjonsson, 1996c; Sear & Williamson, 1999). The appropriate adult can be a relative of the detainee or a professional person such as a social worker. The suspect's solicitor cannot act as an appropriate adult (Gudjonsson, 1994b).

Robertson, Pearson, and Gibb (1996) visited seven police stations in London for continuous periods of 21 days at each station. A total of 902 detainees were interviewed and an appropriate adult was present at 131 (15%) of those interviews. However, 110 of those 131 interviews were with juveniles (under 17 years) and an appropriate adult was present at all these interviews. In only 13 out of 752 interviews with detainees over

18 years old an appropriate adult was present (2% of the cases). This rate is, according to Pearse and Gudjonsson (1996a), low compared with the rates of prevalence in the general population.

Gudjonsson and two fellow clinical psychologists attended two police stations over a substantial period and assessed 173 suspects who were about to be interviewed by the police (Gudjonsson, 1994b). The assessments lasted approximately one hour each and consisted of an interview where the detainees' mental state, background, and under-standing of their legal rights were assessed. In addition, psychological testing took place of intellectual and reading ability, anxiety proneness, and interrogative suggestibility. The researchers concluded that there were good clinical reasons for the presence of an appropriate adult in 25 cases (15%). The police called in an appropriate adult in only 7 cases (4%); all were from the group of 25 identified by the researchers.

Pearse (1995) and Pearse and Gudjonsson (1996c) explained the underrepresentation of appropriate adults by pointing out that it is diffi-cult for the police and even for trained clinicians, to identify who is "at risk," partly because at this moment no operational definition exists about what exactly constitutes "mental disorder" (Pearse & Gudjonsson, 1996c). Pearse (1995) described an experiment in which he asked police officers to read scenarios about background characteristics of detainees. He asked them to identify whether they considered the detainees to be "at risk." The results showed an "underestimation," relative to the researchers' judgments, by police officers of which detainees were at risk.

Problems also arise when an appropriate adult is actually present. Evans (1993, 1994) listened to 131 interviews in which an appropriate adult was present. In 98 interviews, they made no contribution whatso-ever. When parents were appropriate adults and did contribute they were as likely to be supportive as unsupportive to their children. In some cases, parents colluded with the police in trying to obtain a confession and fre-quently used the type of abusive or oppressive tactics that are examples of the worst police practices. Gudjonsson (1993) and Gudjonsson and Pearse (1996a) found that some relatives called in as an appropriate adult suffer from a mental disorder to a similar or greater extent than the suspect. They also noticed that parents are likely to have emotional attachment to their child, and that it is not unusual for parents to resort to intimidating, almost bullying, tactics towards the detainees once they are at the police station. They question whether relatives should be used as appropriate adults. Pearse and Gudjonsson (1996a) described the case of a 14-year-old who was suspected of kidnapping and robbery. His uncle was present as an appropriate adult. At the very beginning of the interview, the uncle launched a series of 15 challenging and sometimes hostile questions, before he was brought to a halt by the police officer. The uncle neverthe-less continued asking questions and making comments throughout the interview and accused the suspect of being a liar.

Inappropriate use of the appropriate adult is not without danger. The presence of an appropriate adult in an interview gives the interview legit-imacy and credibility. It might well be that the presence of an appropriate adult who remains totally passive throughout the interview makes an interview admissible which would have been inadmissible if that third party would have been absent (Robertson et al., 1996). The findings discussed above suggest that the public may be much more accepting of coercive techniques than do researchers, which is an issue worthy to investigate.

Aspects that hamper correct functioning of the appropriate adults system are that it is still unclear what the exact role of the appropriate adult is in a police interview and that there are instances where their role tends to be devalued. The latter situation was illustrated by one police officer's explanation of a social worker's expected role: "You are wallpa-per, pal" (Pearse & Gudjonsson, 1996a, p. 573). For this reason, training in the law of appropriate adults and the skills required in this role is recom-mendable (Evans, 1994; Robertson et al., 1996). For example, according to the law, an appropriate adult can act independently of the wishes of the detainees and seek legal advice on their behalf, but not many people seem to be aware of this (Robertson et al., 1996). Pearse and Gudjonsson (1997b) recently suggested utilizing trained and experienced legal advisers instead of appropriate adults. This can be established by giving solicitors additional training in the recognition and management of mentally disordered suspects.

THE PRESENCE OF A LEGAL ADVISER

The presence of an appropriate adult in interviews with adults sus-pects seems to be a bit of a rarity; the presence of legal advice is much more common. In Moston et al.'s (1992) study, 41% of suspects received legal advice either in person or via the telephone. Baldwin (1993) reported that up to 50% of suspects had a legal adviser actually present in interview, and in Pearse and Gudjonsson's (1997a) analysis of 161 police interviews a legal adviser was present in 56% of the cases. These percentages would even be higher if many suspects would not decline legal advice. They do this because they think legal advice would not assist their case, or that it would delay their release (Pearse & Gudjonsson, 1997a). However, Pearse and Gudjonsson (1997a) found that qualified solicitors accounted for only

24% of the 56% with "legal representatives" making up the remaining 32%. Baldwin (1994, p. 73) stated that "many firms of solicitors ... have adopted the practice of sending articled clerks and other junior and unqualified staff to advise suspects in police stations .... It is obvious that such personnel are not a match for an experienced police interrogator." Baldwin (1993) observed several cases where legal advisers sat in silence throughout the interview when one would have expected some intervention from them, and that much more could have been done by legal advisers to protect the interests of their clients and to check unfair police questioning. Also Pearse and Gudjonsson (1997a) noticed passivity amongst legal advisers. They intervened in only 15% of the cases and the interventions were mostly related to an administrative matter as opposed to challenging an improper tactic (although they also found that suspects more frequently remain silent in presence of a legal adviser). The passivity of legal advisers is worrying because, similar to the appropriate adult, the presence of a passive legal adviser during an improper interview can give the interview an unjustified legitimate and credible status.

SUMMARY

Analyses of English police interviews revealed that perceived strength of evidence and seriousness of the offence are the main factors to explain a witness's willingness to confess. Quality of the interviews is rather poor. Detectives are not open-minded and appear nervous. They do not seem to know what to do when interviewing reluctant suspects. They have a limited strategic flexibility in order to persuade reluctant suspects to confess, and are inclined to use "American style" oppressive techniques (officially banned in England) in order to get them to confess, sometimes with the case being dismissed as a result. Third parties that are present at the interview are often passive. Therefore, they are not always the safeguards as they are meant to be for the suspects.

INTERVIEWING SUSPECTS IN THE NETHERLANDS

Audiotapes, Videotapes, Solicitors, and Anecdotal Evidence

As mentioned before, Dutch police interviews are rarely audio taped or videotaped and these tapes are never made available to researchers. Neither have solicitors the right to be present during police interviews (although they are sometimes allowed to be present). Inspired by the situation in England, the Dutch Government was asked in the late eighties to consider audio taping police interviews and allowing solicitors to be present during these interviews (Lensing, 1998). The Government explicitly rejected the idea of introducing solicitors and ignored the plea for audio taping interviews (Lensing, 1998). However, defense solicitors increasingly claim in court that interviews are too oppressive or otherwise illegitimate (Lensing, 1998; Otte, 1998). In those cases, judges often decide to call the police detectives who conducted the interviews in court and ask them their opinion. Unsurprisingly, they mostly tell that the interviews were conducted fairly and legitimately (Lensing, 1998). The judge then could indicate who he believes was telling the truth (the suspect or the police officer) or, alternatively, could decide to further investigate the matter. The latter decision happens more and more (Lensing, 1998). I have little doubt that many people outside the Netherlands would think that this is a bizarre, outdated and time consuming procedure, with no guarantee that it could ever be established what really happened during the interviews. In fact, many Dutch people have similar thoughts and, again, numerous pleas have been made to audiotape or videotape police interviews (Fijnaut, 1998; Lensing, 1998; Nierop, 1998; Otte, 1998; Rassin, 1998; Vrij, 1997).

Fijnaut (1998), who is in favor of audio- and videotaping, recently summarized the Dutch discussion about the possible benefits and disadvantages of audio- and videotaping. Possible advantages are that (a) the court could easily obtain insight into what actually happened during the interview in case a suspect challenges the legitimacy of the interview; (b) the flow of the interview would no longer be disrupted by the police detectives making minutes on their typewriters; (c) videotaping would enable other police officers in a different room to view the interview "live" on a TV-screen and to instantly compare the suspect's statements with facts about the case which are known to the police; (d) at a latter stage, detectives could listen or view the interviews again to find out whether they initially did neglect some important information; and (e) information initially considered to be irrelevant might become relevant in the light of new evidence. The police could re-analyze the tapes with this new evidence in mind (Fijnaut, 1998). An additional advantage (not mentioned by Fijnaut) is that watching the videotapes could help with lie detection (see below).

According to Fijnaut (1998) possible disadvantages are that (i) a suspect might be less inclined to confess when they are audio- or videotaped (however, English studies comparing confession rates before and after the introduction of audio taping have shown that this is not the case, Vrij, 1998a); (ii) in case of videotaping, observers (judges, jurors) could become distracted by what they see and won't listen anymore to what the suspect actually says; (iii) videotaped interviews may be leaked to the media and broadcasted on television (in fact, this happened in the Netherlands, see below); (iv) in case of videotaping, the appearance of the suspect might have an impact on the impression judges and jurors form about the suspect's potential guilt.

The latter issue is an important problem. People have strong beliefs about how liars behave (Vrij & Semin, 1996). These beliefs are often inaccurate (Vrij, 2000). As a result, by watching videotapes, observers may well come to an inaccurate impression about a suspect's alleged guilt or innocence. Kassin (1997) mentioned additional problems with using videotaped interviews in the courtroom, such as the point-of-view bias (by focusing the camera on the suspect during the interview, this camera point of view can lead observers to underestimate the amount of pressure exerted by the "hidden detective") and the recap bias (observers are unlikely to see the whole interview, but only part of it, which is potentially very manipulative). Given the disadvantages of presenting videotapes in court and the advantages of videotaping for the police in conducting the interviews, a possible solution is to audio- and videotape the interviews and to allow only audiotapes in court (although this may have disadvantages for those with limited verbal ability). Obviously, the recap bias also applies to audiotapes, but audiotapes probably make a considerably less powerful impression on observers than videotapes. Finally, English scholars pointed out another disadvantage of audio- or videotaping police interviews. Interviews now seem to take place outside the police station as well, such as in the police car, where audio taping is not required (Evans, 1993, 1994; Gudjonsson, 1995; Moston & Stephenson, 1993, 1994). According to McConville (1992) in these "off-the-record" exchanges unallowed coercion (threats) and unallowed deals (promises) still occur.

Nowadays, some videotaping takes place in the Netherlands, particularly interviews with suspects who are suspected of serious offences. To date, solicitors still do not have the right to be present at police interviews, although Lensing (1998) and Otte (1998), two Dutch judges, made recent pleas.

As a result of the absence of taping interviews, little is known about what takes place in a Dutch interrogation room. Researchers depend on solicitors who sometimes ask them to give their expert view on the style of interviewing. Obviously, this only happens when the interviews are taped and when solicitors have concerns about these interviews. This sample of interviews is almost certainly not a representative sample of Dutch police interviewing. Both Blaauw (1998) and Van Koppen (1998) described recent examples of Dutch police interview conducted in the "American style."

In 1996, a solicitor asked me to give an opinion about a new interview method, the "Zaanse Verhoormethode," which was employed in the interrogation of a man (a hash-dealer) suspected of kidnapping and murdering. The suspect was extensively interviewed before, but remained silent throughout these interviews. He was therefore exposed to this new technique, which was claimed to be successful in dealing with reluctant suspects. At the beginning of the interview, the detectives (several were employed throughout the interviews which lasted nearly 30 hours in total) assured the suspect numerous times that they were always using an ethical interviewing style and were treating suspects fairly. Despite these assuring comments, the interview style was improper and unethical. For example, they suggested that his wife might be seeing somebody else and that his daughter would end up as a prostitute if he would not confess. Moreover several tricks were used, including downgrading: "We knew you did not intend to kill the person, you are just an honest hash-dealer, and there is nothing wrong with that" (dealing hash is illegal in the Netherlands); lying: "Your wife received several phone calls of people threatening to kill her and your daughter" (in fact, no threatening phone calls were made); bargaining: "I am sure you will get a lower sentence, if you confess" and "We will protect your wife and child, but only if you confess" (obviously, it is a police task to protect citizens in any case); and upgrading: "If you don't confess, your wife will end up in prison as well for complicity". Publicity about this "American style" of interviewing (copies of the videotapes were leaked to the press and shown on Dutch television) led to public outrage, expressed both in the media and in Parliament where questions were asked about the legitimacy of the method. Initially, the method was "successful," as the suspect confessed to both kidnapping and murdering and informed the police where the victim's body could be found. However, his confession was later dismissed in court, and the Dutch Government banned several elements of the interview technique. Perhaps most worrying, the police detectives who conducted this interview did not appear to think that anything was wrong with the technique at all; the team leader defended the method in court. This is not totally surprising given the fact that police officers tend to find several tactics more acceptable than non-police officers (Skolnick & Leo, 1992).

PUBLISHED GUIDELINES FOR INTERVIEWING SUSPECTS

Blaauw, now a retired Dutch police chief constable, published in 1971 his 99 guidelines for police interviewing (Blaauw, 1971). Similar to Baldwin and Williamson, who published their ideas more that 20 years later, he believes that a good police interviewer is flexible, has an analytic style of thinking, and is socially skilled. Already in 1971, Blaauw strongly opposed the use of trickery and deceit.

Nierop (1998), a researcher at the national criminal investigation institute (Centrale Recherche Informatiedienst; CRI), emphasized the importance of a detailed police investigation of the case before the interview takes place. She argues that sometimes—most likely in sexual offences, murder, and arson—case characteristics reveal important information about what type of person the offender might be. This information about his or her personality could be used to decide how to approach the suspect in the interview (see Nierop, 1998 for a detailed description of this method).

Van den Adel (1997), a former employee at the Dutch training institute for police investigations (Rechercheschool Zutphen) published the most detailed manual for police interviewing ever written in Dutch. In 1999, Brian Ord, a retired English detective superintendent and Gary Shaw, a detective inspector, published their detailed police manual in English (Ord & Shaw, 1999). Although the manuals were written by different authors working in different countries, they are remarkably similar. Both manuals emphasize the importance of detailed information gathering at the beginning of the police investigation. In both manuals it is argued that, before the interview starts, the detectives should have been to the scene of crime and therefore know how it looks; should know all the facts of the crime (evidence obtained at the scene of crime, statements of witnesses, any peculiarities); and should know the suspect (background characteristics, family circumstances, possible addictions, possible diseases, and so on).

Both manuals further describe how to use of open and closed questions in police interviews. They both advocate an information gathering strategy at the beginning of the interview as this increases the possibility of eliciting an account from the suspect. The use of open questions is generally preferable (see also Bull, 1999; Shuy, 1998). They usually elicit longer answers and therefore more information. They are an invitation to suspects to present their point of view and will increase the likelihood that suspects believe that the interviewer takes them seriously. Open questions encourage suspects to talk and therefore facilitate the desired format of a police interview: The suspect talks and the interviewer listens and asks for clarifications (Van den Adel, 1997). An interviewer who is prepared to listen is more likely to be liked by suspects, which, in turn, might make suspects more willing to talk. According to Ord and Shaw (1999) closed questions are also useful in interviews, particularly to obtain short, factual answers on specific points. However, these questions should be used sparingly at other times, and rarely in the early stages of the interview (Ord & Shaw, 1999).

Van den Adel (1997) describes several strategic tactics that could be used in a police interview, including the "blocking escape routes" method, which is a method to strengthen the evidence in a case. Evidence is sometimes thin and multi-interpretable. Presenting this evidence at an early stage during the interview may give the suspect the opportunity to "escape" by providing alternative explanations. The blocking escape routes methods intends to prevent this. For example, suppose that the suspect's car was noticed near the scene of crime just after the crime took place. This might be a link, but the link is not strong. By confronting the suspect with this piece of evidence at this stage, he might for example say that he used his car to go to a shop. The evidence is much stronger if the suspect, before the evidence is presented, has told the interviewer (after being asked about this) that he did not use the car that particular day, that he never lent his car to someone else, and that nobody has the keys to his car. After the escape routes have been blocked, the suspect could be confronted with his own statements and evidence: "You told me that you are the only one who uses that car, right? Well, a high-speed camera provided evidence that you drove with your car at high speed near the scene of crime just after the crime took place. Could you explain that?"

Summary

Due to the fact that not many police interviews are taped in the Netherlands, not much is known about what is going on in Dutch interrogation rooms. However, anecdotic evidence (discussed above) suggests that in order to get reluctant suspects to talk, American style police interviews take place especially in serious cases, despite the fact that the use of trickery and deceit is illegal in the Netherlands.

An Outline of a Police Interview

In conclusion I will briefly discuss aspects that I believe are essential for a good police interview. My aim is to accentuate some main aspects, not to give a complete guide to police interviewing. The outline is based upon the existing interview literature; most of it has already been discussed above.

In-Depth Analysis of the Case

The interviewer should know all the facts of the case before starting the interview. Obviously, interviewers will lose their authority over a suspect if the suspect realizes that the interviewer is badly informed about the case. Köhnken (1995) considered appropriate planning as a method to reduce cognitive load on the interviewer during the interview, and as a result of this, more cognitive capacity is available for information processing during the interview. In-depth analysis of the case might also facilitate lie detection during the interview (see below).

Preparation of the Interview

Prior to the interview, the interviewer should define the aims and objectives of the interview and decide how the suspect should be approached in order to obtain the desired information from the suspect. The latter depends on the personality of the suspect, as different suspects require different interview strategies (Nierop, 1998).

Identify Persons at Risk

Research has shown that some groups of people (the mentally disordered, the mentally impaired, juveniles) are at risk during police interviews as they are known to be suggestible, which may result them in giving unreliable information (Gudjonsson, 1994a,b). Introducing a third party, well trained in how to be an effective appropriate adult, is recommendable in order to protect vulnerable individuals against giving untrue statements during the interview.

Open-Mindedness and Rapport Building

The interviewer should be open minded and flexible. Being open minded is particularly difficult if the interviewer believes that the suspect is guilty, as this may lead to belief perseverance. Belief perseverance can be reduced by asking police officers to consider why an alternative theory, i.e., the suspect is not guilty, might be true (Brehm et al., 1999).

The interviewer should also try to obtain rapport with the suspect at the beginning of the interview. Rapport building is an important factor in the success of an interview, because it creates a more relaxing atmosphere in which people are more willing to talk (Köhnken, 1995), or, as Ord and Shaw (1999, p. 15) phrased it: "You catch more flies with sugar than you do with vinegar." In cases where an interviewer fails to establish rapport, it might be useful to change interviewers.

Don't provide too much information at the beginning of the interview. Police officers have the tendency to confront the suspect with the accusation and evidence against then at the very outset of the questioning (Stephenson & Moston, 1994). This might be acceptable when the evidence is very strong, but in other situations it is a poor strategy. As pointed out earlier, suspects might come up with alternative explanations for the evidence, thereby damaging the evidence in the case. It also makes it easier for the suspect to lie. One crucial aspect of lying is that liars should avoid saying something which contradicts the facts the interviewer knows, as such contradictions will reveal the lie. When interviewers inform suspects about their knowledge, lying suspects will know what the interviewers know, making the task not to contradict the facts known by the interviewers much easier.

Strengthen the Evidence

The use of evidence, contradictions, and blocking escape routes. As mentioned earlier, two main factors that induce suspects to confess are the seriousness of the offence and the perceived strength of evidence. The seriousness of the offence is often a fait accompli (the offence is serious or not) and cannot easily be manipulated by interviewers. Interviewers, however, could strengthen the evidence throughout the interview. When the suspect says something the interviewer knows to be untrue, the interviewer could confront the suspect with the available evidence and show the suspect that the interviewer knows that he is lying. This might put the suspect in an awkward position as he has to clarify why he was lying in the interview (see also Ord & Shaw, 1999). The interviewer also could point out contradictions in the suspect's statement and could ask for an explanation of these contradictions. Finally, by blocking escape routes (method described above) the interviewer could give thin evidence more weight.

Listen and Observe Carefully

Pointing out contradictions is only possible when the interviewer listens carefully to the story the suspect has to tell. Also, only by careful listening might the interviewer find out that the suspect's statement contradicts the available evidence. Detecting "lie signs" regularly occurs during police interviews (Baldwin, 1993; Evans, 1993; Inbau et al., 1986; Milne & Bull, 1999; Mortimer & Shepherd, 1999; Moston & Engelberg, 1993). However, the problem is that there are many misconceptions about the relationship between nonverbal behavior and deception and many invalid ways of detecting lies (Vrij, 2000). Lie detection through observation of behavior is clearly a very difficult task with many pitfalls, and many researchers suggest that the police should refrain from this task (Baldwin, 1993; Milne & Bull, 1999; Mortimer & Shepherd, 1999; Moston & Engelberg, 1993). However, I believe that it is possible if done properly.

One of the main problems with detecting lies via observing behavior is that there does not exist typical deceptive behavior. In other words, there is nothing like Pinocchio's nose (Vrij, 2000). Strategies such as "look at gaze aversion," "look whether the suspect puts his hand before his mouth," and so on are all certain to fail. A method which might be useful and which we have employed in a couple of cases is the baseline method (Vrij, 1998b; Vrij & Mann, 2001). In this technique, a suspect's behavior is scrutinized at different phases of the interview. Changes in behavior are detected and analyzed, and possible explanations for these changes are given. Vrij and Mann (2001) analyzed the videotaped police interview of a man suspected of murder. The man has been convicted for murder on the grounds of substantial evidence. Although he confessed at a later stage, he initially denied his involvement in the crime. In the first interview he was asked the question: "What did you do that particularly day?" The man gave a detailed account about his activities during the morning, afternoon and evening. We noticed a sudden change in behavior when he described his activities during the afternoon and evening. He spoke slower, added pauses to his speech, and made fewer movements. This behavior gave the impression of having to think hard. One explanation why it was more difficult for the man to talk about the afternoon and the evening was that he was lying in that part of the interview. Evidence supported this assumption.

Crucial in the use of the baseline technique is that the correct parts of the interview are compared. One should not compare apples with pears. Unfortunately, that happens often in police interviews (Moston & Engelberg, 1993). Small talk at the beginning of the interview is used to establish a baseline. The behavior displayed during the small talk is compared with the behavior shown in the actual interview. Moston and Engelberg (1993, p. 227) describes this way of using the baseline technique as "one of the most striking misuses of psychological research in police training." I agree. This is an entirely incorrect way of employing the technique as small talk and the actual police interview are totally different situations. Not surprisingly, research has shown that both guilty and innocent people tend to change their behavior the moment the actual interview starts (Vrij, 1995). In the case of the convicted murderer we were able make a good comparison. There are no reasons why different behaviors would emerge while describing the morning or the afternoon. Interestingly, the question on which we based our baseline method "What did you do that particular day?" could be asked in almost every police interview. Compared to innocent suspects, guilty suspects are more likely to face difficulties in keeping their behavior constant while describing their activities during different parts of the day. The changes in behavior which one might observe are usually small and therefore difficult to detect instantly. Videotaping the interview and analyzing the videotape is the best way to employ this technique.

Check the Confession

Police officers often consider the confession at the end of the investigation. They tend not to check whether the confession is true (Moston & Engelberg, 1993), perhaps because they believe that this is a task for the prosecution and not for the police (Milne & Bull, 1999). However, the police should always check whether a confession is true, as this will decrease the likelihood that someone will be convicted due to a false confession. The veracity of the confession could be established by checking the accuracy of the information elicited in the confession (Van Koppen, 1998; Ofshe & Leo, 1997b). There should be a fit between the suspect's narrative and the facts of the crime. Also, a suspect must provide information independent of that put before them by the interviewer (Moston & Engelberg, 1993). It may be that suspects provide incriminating answers not because of their first hand knowledge of the crime, but from their ability to listen to questions and draw inferences (Moston & Engelberg, 1993).

CONCLUSION

This contribution has shown that the police have difficulty in interviewing reluctant suspects. In order to get them to talk, the police are inclined to use tricks, deceit and other oppressive techniques which are unlawful in many countries. The positive aspect of the story is that reluctant suspects are in the minority, most suspects are willing to co-operate during police interviews, especially when they perceive the evidence against them to be strong.

I have also shown that most researchers criticize the police about their interviewing skills. However, they are remarkably passive themselves, and hardly offer guidelines to help the police (not surprisingly, many Dutch police detectives would like to have more guidance from experts, Nierop & Mooij, 2000). I would encourage researchers to give guidelines how interviews should be conducted, especially with reluctant suspects. The use of persuasive techniques will probably be necessary to get reluctant suspects to talk. Especially in serious cases it might be in the public interest to get suspects to talk. Guidance should therefore be given to the police about which persuasive techniques are effective and legitimate. The effectiveness of these techniques should be tested with experimental research paradigms.

5

Violence Risk Assessment in American Law

JOHN MONAHAN

Violence risk assessment is a critical and expanding part of the practice of clinical psychology and of psychiatry in the United States at the beginning of the 21st century. *Dangerousness to others* became one of the pivotal criteria for involuntary hospitalization of people with mental disorders in the 1960s. Tort liability was first imposed on clinicians who negligently failed to predict their patients' violence in the 1970s. Statutes authorizing involuntary treatment in the community for otherwise "dangerous" patients were enacted in many states in the 1980s. Risk assessments of violence were explicitly mandated during the 1990s in the Americans with Disabilities Act, which protects the employment rights of people with disabilities, unless those disabilities result in an employee becoming a "direct threat" of violence to co-workers or customers.

In this chapter, I address two topics relevant to the use of violence risk assessment in American law. First, I review the state of the *science* of violence risk assessment, concentrating on recent moves in the United States toward augmenting clinical prediction with statistical approaches to assessment. Second, I review the current state of American *law* on the admissibility of clinical and statistical risk assessments of violence as evidence in court proceedings.

STATE OF THE SCIENCE

THE VALIDITY OF CLINICAL RISK ASSESSMENTS

Five studies on the accuracy of clinicians at predicting violent behavior of others were available as of the late 1970s (Cocozza & Steadman, 1976; Kozol, Boucher, & Garofalo, 1972; Steadman, 1977; Steadman & Cocozza, 1974; Thornberry & Jacoby, 1979). The conclusion of one review of those studies was that

> Psychiatrists and psychologists are accurate in no more than one out of three predictions of violent behavior over a several-year period among institutionalized populations that had both committed violence in the past (and thus had high base rates for it) and who were diagnosed as mentally ill. (Monahan, 1981, pp. 47–49)

Only two studies of the validity of clinicians' predictions of violence in the community have been published in the past 20 years. Sepejak, Menzies, Webster, and Jensen (1983) studied court-ordered pre-trial risk assessments and found that 39% of the defendants rated by clinicians as having a "medium" or "high" likelihood of being violent to others were reported to have committed a violent act during a two-year follow-up, compared to 26% of the defendants predicted to have a "low" likelihood of violence (p. 181, note 12), a statistically significant difference, but not a large one in absolute terms.

More recently, Lidz, Mulvey, and Gardner (1993), in what is surely the most sophisticated study published on the clinical prediction of violence, took as their subjects male and female patients being examined in the acute psychiatric emergency room of a large civil hospital. Psychiatrists and nurses were asked to assess potential patient violence toward others over the next six-month period. Violence was measured by official records, by patient self-report, and by the report of a collateral informant in the community (e.g., a family member). Patients who elicited professional concern regarding future violence were found to be significantly more likely to be violent after release (53%) than were patients who had not elicited such concern (36%). The accuracy of clinicians' predictions of male violence substantially exceeded chance levels, both for patients with and without a prior history of violent behavior. In contrast, the accuracy of clinicians' predictions of female violence did not differ from chance. While the actual rate of violent incidents among discharged female patients (46%) was slightly higher than the rate among discharged male patients (42%), the clinicians had predicted that only 22 percent of the women would be violent, compared with predicting that 45 percent of the men would commit a violent act. The inaccuracy of clinicians at predicting violence among women appeared to be a function of the clinicians' serious underestimation of the base-rate of violence among mentally disordered women (perhaps due to an inappropriate extrapolation from the great gender differences in rates of violence among persons without mental disorder).

THE MOVE TOWARD ACTUARIAL RISK ASSESSMENT

The general superiority of statistical over clinical risk assessment in the behavioral sciences has been known for almost half a century (Grove, Zald, Lebow, Snitz, & Nelson, 2000; Meehl, 1954; Swets, Dawes, & Monahan, 2000). Despite this, and despite a long and successful history of actuarial risk assessment in bail and parole decision making in criminology (Champion, 1994), there have been only a few attempts in the past to develop actuarial tools for the specific task of assessing risk of violence to others among people with mental disorder (for reviews, see Blumenthal & Lavender, 2000; Borum, 1996; Douglas & Webster, 1999; Monahan & Steadman, 1994). In the 1990s, however, there has been move toward the development of actuarial tools for violence risk assessment. Three instruments are representative of this recent trend: the Violence Risk Appraisal Guide, the HCR-20, and the Iterative Classification Tree.

THE VIOLENCE RISK APPRAISAL GUIDE

The *Violence Risk Appraisal Guide* (VRAG, see Harris, Rice, & Quinsey, 1993; Quinsey, Harris, Rice, & Cormier, 1998; Rice & Harris, 1995) was developed from a sample of over 600 men from a maximum-security hospital in Canada. All had been charged with a serious criminal offense. Approximately 50 predictor variables were coded from institutional files. The criterion was any new criminal charge for a violent offense, or return to the institution for a similar act, over a time at risk in the community that averaged approximately seven years after discharge. A series of regression models identified 12 variables for inclusion in the VRAG, including the Hare Psychopathy Checklist-Revised, elementary school maladjustment, and age at the time of the offense (which had a negative weight). When the scores on this actuarial instrument were dichotomized into "high" and "low," the results were that 55% of the group scoring high committed a new violent offense, compared with 19% of the group scoring low.

THE HCR-20

Douglas and Webster (1999) reviewed ongoing research on a structured clinical guide that can be scored in an actuarial manner to assess violence risk, the HCR-20, which consists of 20 ratings addressing *H*istorical, *C*linical, or *R*isk management variables (Webster, Douglas, Eaves, & Hart, 1997). Douglas and Webster also reported data from a retrospective study with prisoners, finding that scores above the median on the HCR-20 increased the odds of past violence and antisocial behavior by an average of four times. In another study with civilly committed patients, Douglas, Ogloff, Nicholls, and Grant (1999) found that during a follow-up of approximately 2 years after discharge into the community, patients scoring above the HCR-20 median were 6 to 13 times more likely to be violent than patients scoring below the median.

THE ITERATIVE CLASSIFICATION TREE

The MacArthur Risk Assessment Study (Monahan et al., 2001) assessed a large sample of male and female acute civil patients at several facilities in the United States on a wide variety of variables believed to be related to the occurrence of violence and developed what its authors called an *Iterative Classification Tree*, or ICT. A classification tree approach to violence risk assessment is predicated upon an interactive and contingent model of violence, one that allows many different combinations of risk factors to classify a person as high or low risk. Whether a particular question is asked in any clinical assessment grounded in this approach depends on the answers given to each prior question. This contrasts with the usual approach to actuarial risk assessment in which a common set of questions is asked of everyone being assessed and every answer is weighted and summed to produce a score that can be used for purposes of categorization. The first test of the ICT method (Steadman et al., 2000) focused on how well the method performed in making violence risk assessments under ideal conditions (i.e., with few constraints on the time or resources necessary to gather risk factors). For example, the risk factor that most clearly differentiated high risk from low risk groups was the Hare Psychopathy Checklist: Screening Version (Hare PCL:SV, see Hart, Cox, & Hare, 1995). Given that the full Hare PCL-R requires several hours to administer—the Screening Version alone takes over 1 hour to administer—resource constraints in many non-forensic clinical settings will preclude its use. In a second test of this approach, Monahan et al. (2000) sought to increase the utility of this actuarial method for real-world clinical decision making by applying the method to a set of violence risk factors commonly available in clinical records or capable of being routinely assessed in clinical practice.

Finally, rather than pitting different risk assessment models against one another and choosing the one model that appears "best," Monahan et al. (2001) adopted an approach that integrates the predictions of many different risk assessment models, each of which may capture a different but important facet of the interactive relationship between the measured risk factors and violence. Using this multiple models approach, these researchers ultimately combined the results of five prediction models generated by the Iterative Classification Tree methodology. By combining the predictions of several risk assessment models, the multiple models approach minimizes the problem of data overfitting that can result when a single "best" prediction model is used. Monahan et al. (2001) were able to place all patients into one of 5 risk classes for which the prevalence of violence during the first 20 weeks following discharge into the community varied between 1% and 76%, with an area under the ROC curve of 88.

STATE OF THE LAW

CONSTITUTIONAL ISSUES

Concerns about whether violence risk assessments offered by psychologists and other mental health professionals were "good enough" to incorporate into mental health law and policy once drew a staple of commentary in the field (e.g., Ennis & Litwack, 1974). This is no longer the case. Courts across America and, in particular, the United States Supreme Court, answered with a resounding "No" the question, "Does a reliance upon clinical predictions of violence invalidate an otherwise valid law?" Consider just two of the many cases relevant to this point.

In 1978, Thomas Barefoot was convicted of the capital murder of a police officer. At a separate sentencing hearing, the same jury considered the two questions put to it under the Texas death penalty statute, namely (a) whether the conduct causing the death was "committed deliberately and with reasonable expectation that the death of the deceased or another would result," and (b) whether "there is a probability that the defendant would commit criminal acts of violence that would constitute a continuing threat to society." The jury's affirmative answer to both questions required the imposition of the death penalty. In *Barefoot v. Estelle* (1983) the Supreme Court considered the constitutionality of using clinical predictions of violence for the purpose of determining whom to execute. In an opinion upholding the Texas statute, Justice White wrote:

> It is urged that psychiatrists, individually and as a group, are incompetent to predict with an acceptable degree of reliability that a particular criminal will commit other crimes in the future and so represent a danger to the community … The suggestion that no psychiatrist's testimony may be presented with

respect to a defendant's future dangerousness is somewhat like asking us to disinvent the wheel. In the first place, it is contrary to our cases ... and if it is not impossible for even a lay person sensibly to arrive at that conclusion, it makes little sense, if any, to submit that psychiatrists, out of the entire universe of persons who might have an opinion on the issue, would know so little about the subject that they should not be permitted to testify. (pp. 896–897)

Little has changed since *Barefoot*. In *Kansas v. Hendricks* (1997), the Supreme Court upheld a civil means of lengthening the detention of certain criminal offenders scheduled for release from prison. The Kansas Sexually Violent Predator Act established procedures for the civil commitment to mental hospitals of persons who may not have a major mental disorder, but who have a "mental abnormality or personality disorder" (in Hendricks's case, pedophilia) which makes them "likely to engage in predatory acts of sexual violence." A "mental abnormality" was defined in the Act as a "congenital or acquired condition affecting the emotional or volitional capacity which predisposes the person to commit sexually violent offenses in a degree constituting such person a menace to the health and safety of others." In upholding Hendricks's civil commitment under the act, the Supreme Court emphasized two specific facts of the case: Hendricks's own admission of his uncontrollable urges and a risk assessment predicting high risk. The Court noted:

> Hendricks even conceded that, when he becomes "stressed out," he cannot "control the urge" to molest children. This admitted lack of volitional control, coupled with a prediction of future dangerousness, adequately distinguishes Hendricks from other dangerous persons who are perhaps more properly dealt with exclusively through criminal proceedings. (p. 360)

Not only courts, but also professional organizations in the United States have concluded that predictions of violence are here to stay. For example, the American Bar Association's *Criminal Justice Mental Health Standards* (1989) recommended that a person acquitted of a violent crime by reason of insanity be committed to a mental hospital if found to be currently mentally ill and to present "a substantial risk of serious bodily harm to others" (Standard 7–7.4). Likewise, the guidelines for involuntary civil commitment of the National Center for State Courts (1986) urged that

> particularly close attention be paid to predictions of future behavior, especially predictions of violence and assessments of dangerousness. Such predictions have been the bane of clinicians who admit limited competence to offer estimates of the future yet are mandated legally to do so. [However,] such predictions will continue to provide a basis for involuntary civil commitment, even amid controversy about the scientific and technological shortcomings and the ethical dilemmas that surround them. (p. 493)

EVIDENTIARY ISSUES

The legal issues concerning violence risk assessment are now evidentiary rather than Constitutional. The evidentiary test for the admissibility at trial of expert psychological testimony on violence risk assessment was given by the United States Supreme Court in *Daubert v. Merrill Dow Pharmaceuticals* (1993). Many American state courts—where the vast majority of psychological and psychiatric testimony is offered—have now adopted and attempted to operationalize the *Daubert* standard. For illustrative purposes, I will rely on one representative state case, *E.I. du Pont de Nemours & Co. v. Robinson* (1995) to frame the discussion. In *Robinson*, the Supreme Court of Texas specified six *Daubert*-derived factors "that a trial court may consider in making the threshold determination of admissibility" (p. 557). My evaluation of the points at issue will follow these six factors:

1. *The extent to which the theory has been tested.* As described above, at least seven empirical studies conducted since the 1970s have tested the proposition that psychologists and psychiatrists have greater-than-chance accuracy at predicting violent behavior to others in the open community. Many additional studies have tested the proposition that psychologists and psychiatrists have greater-than-chance accuracy at predicting violence to others within closed institutions (e.g., McNiel, Sandberg, & Binder, 1998).

2. *Reliance on the subjective interpretation of the expert.* The American Bar Association published a *National Benchbook on Psychiatric and Psychological Evidence and Testimony* (1998). The *Benchbook* is directed to state and federal judges and explicitly "designed to aid decision-making [...] regarding admissibility of evidence" (p. iii). While acknowledging that subjective clinical interpretations often play a role in predictions of violence, the *Benchbook* concludes:

> Despite recent commentary indicating that clinicians are better at addressing possible risk factors and probabilities than providing definitive predictions of dangerousness, courts have remained reluctant to totally exclude such [clinical] evidence, in part, perhaps, because courts are ultimately responsible for making these decisions and though the information may remain open to challenge, it is the best information available. The alternative is to deprive fact finders, judges and jurors of the guidance and understanding that psychiatrists and psychologists can provide. (p. 49)

3. *Subject to peer review and publication.* All seven empirical tests of the ability of psychologists and psychiatrists to clinically assess risk of violence in the community have been published. Five of the seven tests have been published in peer-reviewed scientific journals rather than in

books or student-edited law reviews, including the most methodologically sophisticated study (Lidz et al., 1993), which was published in the
Journal of the American Medical Association.

4. *Potential rate of error.*   No one questions that the state of the science is such that the prediction of violence is subject to a considerable
margin of error. But acknowledging this error rate, the American Bar
Association's *National Benchbook on Psychiatric and Psychological Evidence
and Testimony* (1998) nonetheless states:

> While the frustration with psychiatry and psychology from a legal standpoint
> centers on the certainty or lack thereof with which mental health experts speak
> to the ultimate issues in a case (for example, dangerousness ...), this frustration
> should not lead courts to reject all such input, but rather should encourage
> courts to recognize the proper role and limitations of expert evidence and
> testimony in the courtroom. (pp. 47–48)

5. *General acceptance in the relevant scientific community.*   The best-
known recent study of the validity of clinical predictions of violence, Lidz
et al. (1993) concluded: "What this study [shows] is that clinical judgment
has been undervalued in previous research. Not only did the clinicians
pick out a statistically more violent group, but the violence that the predicted group committed was more serious than the acts of the comparison
group."

Likewise, a critical analysis of existing risk assessment research
(Mossman, 1994) reached this measured judgment: "This article's reevalu-
ation of representative data from the past 2 decades suggests that clinicians are able to distinguish violent from nonviolent patients with a
modest, better-than-chance level of accuracy."

6. *Nonjudicial uses of the theory or technique.*   Violence risk assessment
not only permeates the legal system but is a significant component of general clinical practice in the mental health fields. As McNiel et al. (1998)
have recently stated, "Clinical assessment of violence potential and management of aggressive behavior are routine components of contemporary
practice in psychiatric emergency rooms and inpatient units" (p. 95).

CONCLUSION

The future of violence risk assessment is likely to see more precise
depictions of which specific risk factors are associated with violence in
which specific types of people. Violence risk assessment is likely to continue to move strongly in an actuarial direction, including the imminent
introduction of the first violence risk assessment software (Monahan et al.,
2001). American courts in the past generally have found violence risk

assessments to be admissible as evidence, and the likelihood is high that they will continue to do so under the *Daubert* standard. As the American Bar Association's *National Benchbook on Psychiatric and Psychological Evidence and Testimony* (1998) states:

> Even given the underlying uncertainties and discrepancies within the psychiatric and psychological communities, psychiatrists and psychologists—through their education and experiences—acquire special information and skills that are beyond that of the lay community to better understand and interpret human behavior (normal and abnormal). Thus, in many instances the knowledge of psychiatrists and psychologists can assist factfinders in understanding and interpreting human behavior within a legal context. (p. 47)

6

The Dual Nature of Forensic Psychiatric Practice

Risk Assessment and Management under the Dutch TBS-Order[1]

CORINE DE RUITER AND MARTIN HILDEBRAND

In this chapter the dual nature of forensic psychiatry as a medical profession on the one hand and a juridical specialism on the other will be the frame of reference from which several aspects of the treatment and risk management of mentally disordered offenders in the Netherlands will be discussed. First, we will focus on the legal provisions that apply in cases in which forensic assessment is conducted. Special attention is paid to the concept of diminished responsibility, which plays a central role in the penal system in the Netherlands. We then turn our focus to the treatment and risk management of mentally disordered offenders in one of the forensic psychiatric hospitals in the Netherlands, the Dr. Henri van der Hoeven Kliniek. Finally, the strengths and weaknesses of forensic psychiatric practice in the Netherlands are discussed.

[1] The opinions expressed in this chapter are those of the authors and do not necessarily represent those of other staff or officials of the Dr. Henri van der Hoeven Kliniek. The authors wish to thank J.R. Niemantsverdriet, Ph.D., for helpful comments on an earlier version of the chapter.

JURIDICAL FRAMEWORK

According to the Dutch Code of Criminal Procedure (*Wetboek van Strafvordering*, Sv., Article 352, Section 2) and the Dutch Code of Criminal Law (*Wetboek van Strafrecht*, Sr., Article 39), as a general rule, in cases where the criminal act is proven but the offender cannot be held responsible for his deed, because of a mental defect or disorder, the offender will not be considered punishable. Therefore, the non-punishable offender will not be sentenced but discharged.[2] The question whether the defendant has committed the offense precedes and is distinguished from the question whether he or she[3] is punishable, which depends (among other things) on whether the defendant is to be held responsible for the crime he committed (see Article 350 Sv.).[4]

Dutch criminal law recognizes two measures that can be applied to mentally disturbed offenders. First, the law offers the possibility for a defendant who is found not responsible for the crime, to be admitted to a psychiatric hospital, but only if he is a danger to himself or to others or to the general safety of persons or property (Article 37, Section 1 Sr.). Second, Article 37a of the Dutch Code of Criminal Law states that a defendant who, at the time of the alleged crime, suffered from a mental defect or disorder may receive what is called a "disposal to be involuntary admitted to a forensic psychiatric hospital on behalf of the state" (*maatregel van terbeschikkingstelling, TBS*). In the remainder of this chapter, we will refer to this penal measure as a "TBS-order."

Most of the time, a TBS-order is combined with an order of mandatory treatment when the safety of persons or the general safety of persons or goods are in danger (Article 37b, Section 1 Sr.). The law requires that *at least* two experts from different disciplines report on the defendant, before the trial court can decide to impose a TBS-order. One of the experts must be a psychiatrist (Article 37a, Section 3 and Article 37, Section 2 Sr.). A TBS-order can be imposed by the court if the following conditions apply (Article 37a Sr.):

1. The defendant must suffer from a mental disorder, which means that his responsibility for the alleged crime is (severely) diminished or absent;[5]

---

[2] In Dutch terminology: *ontslagen van alle rechtsvervolging*.

[3] In the following, the male pronoun is used for referring to either gender.

[4] Thus, Dutch law distinguishes punishability of the acts from punishability of the defendant. Both types of punishability are a precondition for a conviction.

[5] In the following, we will elaborate on the degrees of criminal responsibility in the Dutch legal system.

2. The crime carries a prison sentence of at least four years, or the offense belongs to a category of offenses carrying a lesser sentence specifically mentioned in the law;
3. There is a risk for the safety of other people or for the general safety of persons or goods.

In theory, a TBS-order is of indefinite duration (Article 38e, Section 2 Sr.). Initially imposed for two years (Article 38d, Section 1 Sr.), it may be extended for one or two year periods as the court re-evaluates the patient to determine whether the risk for the safety of other people or for the general safety of persons or goods is still too high (Article 38d, Section 2 Sr.). TBS involves involuntary admission to a specialized maximum-security forensic psychiatric hospital (Article 37d, Section 1 Sr.) aimed at motivating the patient to participate voluntarily in the treatment programs offered by the hospital. The implication for clinical practice is that it is legally permitted to place a patient in a living group with fellow patients and to structure his daily life in such a way that it is almost impossible for him to avoid contact with members of the hospital staff (e.g., sociotherapists). Neither on ethical nor on legal grounds can there be an escape from the obligation to participate in a therapeutic milieu in order to facilitate social contacts aimed at motivating the patient for treatment. However, patients are free to refuse, for example, pharmacotherapy and to avoid participating in specific therapeutic activities such as psychotherapy.[6] Although there are (rather large) differences in the treatment models the nine Dutch forensic psychiatric hospitals adhere to, the treatment provided within the legal framework of the TBS generally strives to effect structural behavioral change that leads to a reduction in violence risk.

In the Dutch criminal law system, which is mainly inquisitorial in nature (as opposed to the adversarial legal systems in most common law systems), forensic reporting on the responsibility of a defendant generally takes place on the initiative of the investigating judge or the court.[7] According to Articles 227–228 Sv., the investigating judge, while conducting a pre-trial investigation, has the competence to appoint behavioral experts, either in his official capacity, or on request of the defense or the public prosecutor. It is this "judicial framework" that serves to guarantee the independence of the expert's contribution, and to avoid a possible

---

[6] Because of the fact that the TBS-order can be extended as long as the TBS-patient poses a risk, refusal of treatment generally implies a prolonged stay in the hospital.

[7] Article 317 CCP recognizes the authority of the trial court to order an investigation into the mental capacities of the defendant. For this purpose, the court may summon that the accused shall be brought to a particular psychiatric hospital or a forensic mental health assessment center.

"mix up" with the interest of the prosecution or the defense. This procedure is in rather extreme contrast to, for example, forensic experts' daily
practice in the United States, where "selection and calling in of the
experts, and their payment, largely belong to the domain [...] of the
defense and the prosecution" (Malsch & Hielkema, 1999, p. 224),[8] which
may compromise the impartiality of the report of the expert; defense
lawyers are known to sometimes "shop" for an expert who will support
their case. On the other hand, professional standards such as the *Daubert*
standard (*Daubert et ux. v. Merrell Dow Pharmaceuticals Inc.*, 1993) on the
admissibility of scientific evidence, provide some safeguards against low
quality reporting and "reading into the test results what one wants to
find."[9] Psychological assessments under *Daubert* have to be based on psychological tests that are reliable and valid and psychological interpretations have to be related to specific test results.

In the Netherlands, the investigating judge or the court generally
requests answers to the following questions:

1. What is the personality of the defendant?
2. Did the defendant, at the time of the alleged crime, suffer from any
   pathological disturbance and/or defective development?
3. If so, what is the relationship between the pathological distur-
   bance/defective development and the committing of the crime?
4. As a result of this relation, to what extent can the defendant be
   held responsible for committing the crime, if proven.
5. To what extent is the defendant likely to recidivate?
6. What is the best treatment for the defendant?

In general, there are two ways in which the forensic assessments of
defendants with suspected mental disorders are conducted: (1) non-residential forensic mental health evaluation and (2) residential observation
and assessment at the Pieter Baan Centrum.[10] The choice for a certain type
of assessment depends on the nature of the suspected mental disorder and
the seriousness of the crime of which the defendant is accused. In general,
residential, multidisciplinary observation in the Pieter Baan Centrum is
requested when a very serious or bizarre crime has been committed that

---

[8] Although behavioral experts are generally appointed by the investigating judge in the
Netherlands, it does occur that the defense lawyer asks for a second opinion by another
expert.

[9] Not everyone would agree on this. See, for example, Hagen (1997), especially pp. 298–299
for a completely different opinion.

[10] For an extensive discussion of the reporting procedure in the Pieter Baan Centrum, see
Mooij, Koenraadt and Lommen-van Alphen (1991).

substantially violated the legal order and non-residential observation is not considered to be an adequate assessment procedure.

The majority of the forensic assessments of the defendant's accountability are conducted on an ambulatory basis. In these cases, in general, both a psychiatrist and a psychologist will answer the forensic questions mentioned above. The Pieter Baan Centrum (PBC) is the Psychiatric Observation Hospital of the Ministry of Justice that conducts multidisciplinary evaluations of defendants as to possible mental defects or disorders and advises on treatment. For about seven weeks, a social worker, a sociotherapist, a psychologist, a legal advisor, and a psychiatrist work together to (1) assess the defendant's accountability for the alleged crime, (2) estimate the risk of recidivism, and (3) formulate recommendations about treatment. The conclusion and recommendation are discussed in a final staff-meeting, which is not only attended by the reporting team, but also by a legal advisor (who does not report but has studied the case), a member of the board of directors and the local probation officer, who is, of course, not responsible for the conclusion and recommendation of the reporting team. The legal advisor has as primary task to ascertain that the final report does not contain any (new) information that is relevant to the legal aspects of the case.

COMPETENCE TO STAND TRIAL

In the United States, but also in some other countries, at the very beginning of a potential court case, before the issue of the insanity defense even arises, the defendant may be examined to determine competency to stand trial. According to Melton, Petrila, Poythress, and Slobogin (1997), competency to stand trial is by far the most frequently adjudicated competency issue in the United States. It generally means that the defendant is capable of assisting in his own defense (*Dusky v. United States*, 1960), that is, the defendant needs to have the capacity to understand the criminal process, including the role of the participants in that process, and he needs to have the ability to function in that process, primarily through consulting with counsel in the preparation of a defense.

Competency focuses on the defendant's *present* ability to consult with counsel and to understand the proceedings. It therefore differs fundamentally from the test of criminal responsibility, which is a retrospective inquiry focusing on the defendant's state of mind at the time of the alleged crime (Melton et al., 1997). If the court finds the defendant incompetent, the trial is suspended. In some cases, in particular if the defendant is charged with a nonserious offense, a case will not be further prosecuted in exchange for the defendant seeking treatment as a civil psychiatric patient. In other cases, in particular if the alleged crime is a more serious one, the accused is often committed to the public mental system for treatment. The stated purpose of treating the person found incompetent to stand trial is to restore competency so that trial may resume (*Jackson v. Indiana*, 1972).

Contrary to legal practice in the United States any defendant can, in principle, be summoned to stand trial in the Netherlands. The question whether someone is "fit for trial" is seldom asked, and therefore not an issue about which forensic mental health experts have to report. Article 16, Section 1 Sv., however, states that the trial court has the authority to adjourn the trial if the accused suffers from such a serious mental disorder that he is not capable of understanding the charges. The defendant's legal counsel serves to defend his interests (Article 331, Section 1 Sv.).

THE DIMINISHED RESPONSIBILITY DOCTRINE

There is a clear distinction between punishment and treatment in the Netherlands. By providing treatment an attempt is made to alter the disturbance in the personality of the offender to such a degree that he will pose less risk and will not commit another serious crime. This so-called dualistic sanctioning system of punishment and coercive measures considers the safeguarding of society to be the main reason for coercive measures; the principle reason for punishment is a certain degree of culpability. The basic principle is that only those who can be held responsible for their behavior will be punished. The choice between punishment and coercive measures is determined by the judge, based on the *degree* of responsibility of the defendant. The basic assumption is that the defendant is fully responsible. In case of a disorder, the court will decide on the basis of reports of behavioral experts *to what extent* this disorder has influenced the behavior of the defendant at the moment of the alleged crime.

Article 37a of the (old) Code of Criminal Law created the possibility of diminished responsibility. On the basis of this, more refined "qualities" of criminal responsibility were introduced in Dutch case law, and eventually a five-point sliding scale (between full responsibility on the one hand, and complete absence of responsibility on the other), emerged, indicating the degree of criminal responsibility: full responsibility, slightly diminished responsibility, diminished responsibility, severely diminished responsibility, and total absence of responsibility. In case of slight or severe diminished responsibility (i.e., the offense is to some extent determined by a mental disorder but cannot be explained in its entirety by this disorder), the judge may sentence a prison term for that part of psychological functioning which the defendant had freedom of choice, i.e., the choice not to commit the offense.

Consequently, offenders considered to have diminished responsibility for the crimes they committed (i.e., those suffering from a serious mental disorder) can (and most of the time will) also be sentenced to imprisonment. On the one hand there is the principle of "no punishment without guilt." On the other hand, however, following decisions of the Dutch Supreme Court, there is *no* such thing as "punishment to the extent of guilt." This is because in determining the sentence the court not only takes into account the degree of guilt of the offender, but also includes among others to what extent society is shocked by the offense, and the deterrent effect of the punishment. This means, for example, that if a person committed a first degree murder under the influence of a mental disorder and the trial court consequently considers this person to have diminished responsibility for the offense, the court can sentence him to a long (e.g., 10 years, which is considered long in the Netherlands) prison sentence in combination with a TBS-order.[11] In theory, and sometimes also in practice, a person found guilty but with diminished capacity can serve the same prison term as a fully-responsible defendant and also faces an additional period of involuntary hospitalization on top of the prison term.

The combination of imprisonment and involuntary admission to a forensic hospital leads to significant ethical questions. As stated before, the TBS is ordered to allow treatment of the psychiatric disorder of the offender and therefore there is an ethical obligation to admit the patient to a hospital as soon as possible. From a medical point of view, one can argue that it is ethically unjust to postpone the treatment the patient needs, i.e., by executing the prison sentence first. On the other hand, it seems also ethically unjust to treat the patient first, and execute the prison sentence after he is successfully treated and no longer considered to be a danger for society.

Contrary to the situation in the Netherlands, American legal practice does not allow much room for degrees of responsibility. In the United States, the diminished or partial responsibility doctrine is considered to be a "mini-insanity" defense, which gives mitigating effect to the presence of a

---

[11] It should be noted that (severely) diminished responsibility does not always result in the recommendation and the imposition of involuntary admission to a forensic hospital under the TBS-order. Only in cases where, in addition to a mental disorder being established, it is judged that the person is at risk to commit another serious (sexually) violent crime in the future again, a involuntary admission to a forensic psychiatric hospital will be imposed. If a person is sentenced to a long penal sanction in conjunction with the measure of TBS (involuntary admission to a forensic hospital), the prison sentence is executed first; after the offender has served his sentence he wil be transferred to a forensic hospital.

mental disorder that causes cognitive or volitional impairment but produces neither insanity nor an inability to form the *mens rea* for the alleged crime.[12] The doctrine of diminished responsibility has rarely enjoyed support in the U.S. courts, if only because it is thought to be very difficult to implement: how does one, for instance, sensibly define partial responsibility and of what crime is the defendant guilty if he is "only" partially responsible?

PSYCHIATRIC DISORDERS IN TBS PATIENTS

A little over 1000 TBS-patients are treated in nine forensic psychiatric hospitals in the Netherlands. They form 7.4% of the total prison population (Dienst Justitiële Inrichtingen, 1999). The Dr. Henri van der Hoeven Kliniek is one of the nine hospitals. Ninety-five percent of patients are male and 28% are nonnative (mostly Antillian, Surinamese, Indonesian, Turkish, and Moroccan). Eighty-three percent have only elementary school or lower vocational training. The offenses for which they are sentenced are, for instance, (attempted) murder or manslaughter, rape, indecent assault, arson, pedosexual offences, robbery and extortion (Van Emmerik, 1997). The mean treatment duration for patients who were released from the Van der Hoeven Kliniek in 1997 and 1998 was 4.2 years.

Research has shown that 25% of TBS-patients suffer from a psychotic disorder (18% schizophrenia, 2% organic psychosis, and 5% other psychotic disorders) and approximately 80% fulfill diagnostic criteria for one or more DSM-III-R or DSM-IV personality disorders (American Psychiatric Association, 1994; Van Emmerik, 1997; Greeven, 1997). Thus, a personality disorder (i.e., independent of Axis I disorders or mental retardation) can be grounds for a TBS sentence, and thus also for a degree of diminished responsibility. This is in contrast to the North American criminal justice systems where personality disorders are considered mental disorders but not a reason for diminished responsibility because for the latter the defendant "must then show that a disease of the mind rendered him incapable either of appreciating the nature and quality of the (criminal) act or of knowing that the act was wrong" (Zinger & Forth, 1999). For instance, psychopathic personality disorder has been found to be "a disease of the mind," but to date the presence of psychopathy alone has

---

[12] Diminished responsibility needs to be distinguished from the diminished capacity doctrine. The latter doctrine, in its broadest sense, permits the defendant to introduce clinical testimony focusing directly on the mens rea for the alleged crime, without having to assert an insanity defense. In contrast to the disposition when insanity is the defense, when the mens rea for a crime is negated by clinical testimony the defendant is acquitted only of that particular charge.

never fulfilled the legislative criterion of not knowing that the act was wrong. Consequently, a diagnosis of psychopathic personality disorder in a defendant in a North American criminal court usually leads to detention in a correctional facility rather than commitment to a psychiatric hospital. In the majority of cases, the diagnosis of psychopathy leads to longer sentences by the court (Zinger & Forth, 1999). In the Netherlands, a diagnosis of psychopathy does not rule out the possibility of a TBS sentence with treatment in a forensic psychiatric hospital. In fact, about 15% of 62 patients committed to one of the Dutch forensic psychiatric hospitals received a diagnosis of psychopathy, based on the Hare Psychopathy Checklist-Revised (PCL-R, see Hare, Vertommen, Verheul, & De Ruiter, 2000; Hildebrand & De Ruiter, 2000).

TREATMENT UNDER THE TBS ORDER

Every forensic psychiatric hospital has a legal obligation to provide security to society, treatment for the offender-patient, and to protect the civil rights of the latter. These three components need to be balanced in the forensic psychiatric setting and each hospital makes its own choices in this regard, in conjunction with its therapeutic ideology and level of security. Although the treatment models of the hospitals vary, they all involve a composite of education, work training, individual and group psychotherapy, creative arts and sports activities. The general treatment aim is a reduction in future violence risk by means of a positive change in those factors that are associated with (sexual) violence for the individual patient. For instance, at the Van der Hoeven Kliniek in cases of schizophrenia treatment is focused on psycho-education about psychosis and its precursors, on medication adherence and daily living skills. Patients with personality disorders participate in various group therapy programs, such as social skills training, aggression and impulsivity management and sex education. There are special programs for substance abusers and sex offenders. Almost all patients receive individual psychotherapy, which focuses on their individual risk factors for reoffending by means of the so-called offense script and relapse prevention (Van Beek, 1999). Education and job training are an important aspect of treatment, because many patients are lacking the skills they need to be successful on the job market (De Ruiter, 2000).

To give the reader an impression of the treatment process and its different stages, the procedures in the Dr. Henri van der Hoeven Kliniek, one of the Dutch forensic psychiatric hospitals, will be described in some detail here. In this way readers will be able to compare "the Dutch approach to treatment of mentally disordered offenders" to the way this group of offenders is dealt with in other jurisdictions. A central concept in the treatment ideology of the Van der Hoeven Kliniek is the stimulation of the patient's awareness that he is responsible for his own life, including his offenses and his progress in treatment. This premise is basic to the way the hospital is organized and to all treatment activities. Only when the patient takes responsibility the road towards freedom can be set in.

OBSERVATION AND ASSESSMENT

Prior to admission to the hospital, the prospective patient is visited twice while he is still in prison: once by a supervising psychologist of the hospital, and once by a group leader and a patient. These visits are meant to provide the new patient with some basic information about the hospital and to get to know him. The first two months of his actual stay at the hospital are used for extensive observation, assessment and preparation for treatment. From the first day on, the patient has a program of daily activities, including work, education, creative arts and sports. Work supervisors and teachers observe patients during their activities and report on their observations. The patient also spends time at his living group (see below), where group leaders make observations during structured and unstructured activities. During this period, psychologists see the patient for personality and educational assessment. When there are doubts about a patient's cognitive functioning, additional intelligence and/or neuropsychological testing is performed. The objective of personality assessment is to obtain insight into the factors that are related to the patient's risk of violence. To this end, semi-structured interviews (for DSM-IV Axis II disorders and the Psychopathy Checklist-Revised interview), self-report personality inventories (e.g., the Minnesota Multiphasic Personality Inventory-2, MMPI-2, Butcher, Dahlstrom, Graham, Tellegen, & Kaemmer, 1989) and anger, impulsivity and interpersonal behavior scales and indirect tests (e.g., the Rorschach Inkblot Method, Exner, 1993) are administered. Also, structured clinical guidelines for the assessment of violence risk (HCR-20, Webster, Douglas, Eaves, & Hart, 1997; Dutch translation: Philipse, De Ruiter, Hildebrand, & Bouman, 2000) and sexual violence risk (SVR-20, Boer, Hart, Kropp, & Webster, 1997; Dutch translation: Hildebrand, De Ruiter, & Van Beek, 2001) have been implemented recently. Personality assessment results are used to help formulate treatment goals and a treatment plan, and to provide standardized information for empirical research. The findings from the educational assessment result in a plan for work and education.

During the first weeks, the patient also meets with one of the psychotherapists and with the social worker who is assigned to his living group. These sessions are scheduled to determine what function the patient's social network and psychotherapy could have in his treatment. The observation and assessment period ends with the so-called "treatment indication meeting," a staff meeting where all hospital staff is invited to discuss the core issues of the patient and his treatment plan. In the meeting room, an inner circle and an outer circle are created. In the inner circle, the patient and a fellow-patient, two group leaders, the patient's work supervisor, his sports teacher, his creative arts teacher, his social worker, one of the psychotherapists and one of the school teachers, and the supervising psychologist take place, as the latter directs the conversation. All other staff members sit in the outer circle. They listen to the conversation among the inner circle members, but do not participate in it. The first half-hour of the meeting is spent discussing the patient's core problems in relation to the offense(s) for which he was sentenced to TBS. During a ten-minute pause, the patients and the group leaders leave the room so that staff members from the inner and outer circles can exchange their views on what has been discussed so far. After the pause, the (provisional) treatment program as it has been determined by the treatment team, is discussed with the patient.

The Central Role of the Living Group

Most patients stay in a living group, where they live with fellow-patients in a kind of "house." Every living group consists of 8 to 10 patients, who are supervised by 5 group leaders. The living groups manage their own household. The money needed for that comes from the hospital's budget and is spent by the groups, because the hospital emphasizes the importance of handling money in a way that is comparable to that in society at large (Wiertsema, Feldbrugge, & Derks, 1995). The hospital provides patients with a hot meal daily, but living groups are allowed to cook for themselves. Daily life in the group provides patients with experiences that have to do with shared responsibility, social skills and spending leisure time. Each patient has his own room.

The treatment team consists of a supervising psychologist, a social worker and the group leaders and is responsible for the planning, progress and evaluation of the patient's treatment. The group leaders have a diversity of tasks: they are present at meals and at group discussions; they supervise the structure of daily life; they write treatment plans and daily logs of their experiences with patients.

The hospital has a special ward for individual treatment, where patients who are unsuitable for placement in a regular living group are admitted. In general, the goal is to place patients in a regular living group after a period of intensive individual treatment, but this objective is not always met. Since the beginning of the 1990s there is a special living group for patients with psychotic disorders. This group is more highly structured and medication adherence and psycho-education are the most important aspects of the treatment here.

Treatment Evaluation

Treatment progress is evaluated every three months, both orally and in writing. The patient's progress is discussed with fellow patients during a meeting with the living group and during a meeting with the persons (teachers, therapists, etc.) who are involved in the patient's treatment. After 18 months of treatment, the patient is retested with a number of the personality tests that were also administered upon admission to the hospital. In this way, objective instruments provide information on the patient's progress. Important phases in the treatment process, such as extended leave, are discussed at evaluations. Subsequently, the patient may be invited to submit a proposal for extension of leave, which needs to include arguments why he thinks he has changed so that extended leave is warranted. Such a proposal is discussed within the patient's living group, in the treatment team and in the so-called Hospital Council, which consists of staff members and patient representatives from all living groups. The Hospital Council meets every day and serves to maintain a safe and viable therapeutic milieu through cooperation between staff members and patients. After the patient's proposal has been discussed in all these organs, the final decision about extension of leave is made in the general staff meeting.

The Resocialization Phase

The staff at the Van der Hoeven Kliniek aims to limit the duration of the inpatient treatment phase for each patient, of course without losing sight of society's safety. When feasible, a patient is placed in a so-called "transmural setting." These patients are supported by a special team of group leaders of the hospital, who supervise them during this resocialization phase. Supervision is sometimes conducted in collaboration with other mental health institutions.

There are several types of transmural settings. *(1) Supervised living in apartments owned by the hospital or in rental apartments.* Characteristic for this type of forensic supervised living is regular contact between the patient and staff members of the hospital, but there is no 24-hour supervision. The patient's daily life mainly takes place outside the walls of the hospital, although in some cases he may visit the hospital almost daily, for example to see his psychotherapist or to go to work training. *(2) Collaboration with a sheltered home organization in the city of Utrecht (SBWU)*. Since 1991, a contract with SBWU allows the hospital to place patients with limited social and cognitive capacities who realize sufficiently that they will need supervision for an extended period of time, in a sheltered home. Most of these patients follow a treatment program in the hospital during the day. After a certain period their activities in the hospital are often replaced by activities in society, such as volunteer work or a paid job in a welfare facility. *(3) Clinical admission in a general psychiatric hospital*. For patients who have insufficient capacities to maintain themselves in a sheltered home, the Van der Hoeven Kliniek has places in a general psychiatric hospital. These patients may suffer from psychoses that cannot be managed adequately with medication or they may be unable to adhere to their medication regimen without intensive external supervision. They need long term, continued clinical treatment to prevent psychotic decompensation.

Treatment Effectiveness Research

Although the TBS order was introduced in the criminal justice system in 1928, research into the effectiveness of the treatments offered in the Dutch forensic psychiatric hospitals is sorely lacking. A number of follow-up studies of different patient cohorts from 1974 through 1993, have documented serious violent recidivism rates between 15 and 20% over follow-up periods of 3 to 8 years for patients for whom the TBS order was terminated (Van Emmerik, 1985, 1989; Leuw, 1995, 1999). Unfortunately, there is currently no research evidence showing that recidivism rates are related to treatment process and outcome. A two-year cross-sectional follow-up study of 59 personality disorder patients, during their inpatient treatment in the Van der Hoeven Kliniek, demonstrated that 25% of these patients changed reliably and to a clinically significant degree on a number of self-report measures of personality and psychopathology (Greeven, 1997). However, the overall personality structure of the patients remained essentially the same, and it remains to be seen how these patients will fare after they have been released into society. These 59 patients were tested last in 1995, and will be traced and tested again in 2001. Recidivism rates can then be examined in relation to objective treatment measures for the first time.

VIOLENCE RISK ASSESSMENT AND MANAGEMENT UNDER THE TBS ORDER

Risk assessment and management are ongoing tasks of the staff of forensic psychiatric hospitals where TBS patients stay. All proposals for extensions of leave have to be announced to the Ministry of Justice, who carries the ultimate responsibility for the execution of the TBS order. The Ministry has the right to raise objections to or question the leave proposals submitted by the hospitals, and withholds permission in some cases. Leave decisions that have to be approved include, for instance, the first time the TBS patient is allowed outside the physical security of the institution, still under staff supervision, travel without staff supervision and leave on probation.

Every one or two years, the patient's case has to be reviewed by the court (Article 38d, Section 1 Sr.), which decides whether the TBS needs to be extended or can be terminated in the individual case. The forensic hospital has to submit a report to the court that gives information on the mental disorder of the patient, treatment progress, the assessment of recidivism risk and advice on the extension or termination of the TBS. Judges do not always follow the hospital's advice; in one in five cases they opt for termination of the TBS against the latter's advice. Several studies have shown that forensic hospital staff are better at predicting recidivism in their patients than judges. In a long-term follow-up (>5 years) of 40 patients who had been treated at the Van der Hoeven Kliniek, recidivism rates of patients who had been released by the judge against the hospital's advice were notably higher than recidivism rates of patients released on the hospital's advice (25% vs. 55% for serious recidivism that resulted in unconditional imprisonment and/or TBS, Niemantsverdriet, 1993). Similar findings are reported by Van Emmerik (1989) and Leuw (1999).

Risk assessments conducted in the forensic psychiatric hospitals are generally based on (behavioral) observations by treatment staff from different roles and professions (nurses, teachers, work supervisors, psychotherapists, etc.). The psychologist or psychiatrist who carries the final treatment responsibility for an individual patient integrates these observations into the report for the court and provides an advice on the patient on the basis of it. Standardized risk assessments, based on psychological testing procedures (e.g., the Psychopathy Checklist-Revised, Hare, 1991) and structured clinical guidelines for conducting risk assessments (e.g., the HCR-20, Webster et al., 1997), conducted by independent assessors, are not yet general practice in Dutch forensic psychiatric hospitals. However, we expect that this will change in the coming years, because Dutch translations of a number of important risk assessment instruments have recently become available (Hare et al., 2000; Hildebrand, De Ruiter, & Van Beek, 2001; Philipse et al., 2000) and the Ministry of Justice has recently appointed a task force that will formulate general guidelines for standardized risk assessment under the TBS order (Ministry of Justice, 2000).

After a patient has been detained under the TBS order for six years, the law (Article 509, Section 4 Sv.) requires two independent behavioral experts, a psychologist and a psychiatrist, to submit a forensic report to inform the court about the mental disorder and the risk of recidivism of the patient. The court then decides about extension or termination of the TBS order on the basis of the reports provided by the hospital where the patient is being treated and those of the two independent experts. This so-called 6-years procedure is to safeguard the patient against the well-known biases that treatment staff are liable to when they have to assess future violence risk in their own patients (Dernevik, 1999).

STRENGTHS AND WEAKNESSES

The Dutch criminal justice system provides a number of procedures that offer possibilities for a unique way of risk assessment, management and treatment of mentally disordered offenders under the TBS order. A number of follow-up studies have documented a 20% violent recidivism rate in former TBS patients (e.g., Leuw, 1995, 1999). Although the TBS population is not completely comparable to a prison population, recidivism rates after long-term prison sentences for similar offenses tend to be higher. The TBS order, with its focus on therapeutic milieu treatment and opportunities for education and work training offers mentally disordered offenders a much valued opportunity towards resocialization and rehabilitation, which is in sharp contrast to the way in which North American criminal justice systems handle this group of offenders.

Still, there are a number of shortcomings in current forensic psychiatric practice in the Netherlands that need to be improved in the coming years. Criticism by politicians and the lay public on the expensive "TBS system" is growing and serves to foster long overdue reconsideration of the current practice. First, there is as yet no official training or certification program for forensic psychologists or psychiatrists in the Netherlands. Psychologists and psychiatrists generally learn their forensic assessment skills more or less "on the job," and in the absence of quality standards and/or a register of certified forensic professionals, the quality of their reports is highly variable (De Ruiter, 2000). Few forensic behavioral experts make use of structured risk assessment instruments, which have been proven to be more reliable and valid than unstructured clinical judgment (Webster et al., 1997). Second, the treatments provided under the TBS order are not "evidence-based." There have not been any studies that examine the relation between treatment outcome and recidivism, which is a prerequisite for determining the effectiveness of the TBS measure. Moreover, there is no information on the differential effectiveness of the treatments provided, i.e., whether the treatment is successful with some types of patients but not with others. Studies that examine changes in violence risk factors during treatment and the predictive validity of different factors with regard to treatment outcome and recidivism are underway in the Van der Hoeven Kliniek.

From the 1950s on, a general optimism about the treatment amenability of mentally disordered offenders has been part of the influential Utrecht school in Dutch penal law (Moedikdo, 1976). The TBS order and the diminished responsibility doctrine provided venues for this optimism. Recently, however, the optimism of the 1950s has been replaced by the realism of the new millennium. A 20% violent recidivism rate looks good on the surface, but looked at more realistically, it means that every one in five ex-TBS patients is arrested for another serious offense that often caused great personal harm and shocked society. We need empirical research to help us to better assess and predict the risk of recidivism and to improve our treatment programs so we may hopefully at some time in the future bring down that "every one in five" figure.

7

The Death Penalty and Adversarial Justice in the United States

SAMUEL R. GROSS

In a volume devoted to comparing adversarial and inquisitorial procedures in Western countries, the subject of the death penalty is an anomaly. Any system of adjudication must address several basic tasks: how to obtain information from parties and witnesses, how to evaluate that information, how to utilize expert knowledge, how to act in the face of uncertainty, how to review and reconsider decisions. By comparing how competing systems deal with these tasks we can hope to learn something about the strengths and weaknesses of alternative approaches to common problems. The death penalty, however, is not an essential function of a system of justice; it is not even a common element. Not a single Western country with an inquisitorial system of justice has retained the death penalty, and neither has any major Western country that uses an adversarial system—except the United States. As a result, it is impossible to compare how modern adversarial and inquisitorial systems handle the difficulties of administering capital punishment. Instead, I will address a different question: How well does the American system of adversarial justice manage the difficulties of capital cases?

The answer (hardly a secret) is that we handle capital cases very badly. Perhaps a discussion of the ways in which American adversarial justice fails in this context will contribute to a comparison between adversarial and inquisitorial systems by identifying weak points in the adversarial method that make it prone to terrible problems when it is subject to the types of stresses that the death penalty creates. But perhaps not. It is by no means clear that Holland or Spain could do much better than Texas if it executed 30 or 40 people a year.

I do not propose to write a comprehensive review of the problems of capital punishment in the United States. There is a voluminous literature on the subject, and it continues to accumulate at a rapid rate. Even a cursory summary would require a book-length treatment. Instead, I will do no more than briefly review three of the major sets of problems that plague the administration of the death penalty in the United States. Moreover, since this volume is a comparison between different legal *procedures*, my review is restricted to practical problems—how the death penalty, as used in America, is discriminatory, arbitrary, and inaccurate. I will not address the arguments that the death penalty, like torture, is inherently immoral and a violation of fundamental human rights.

INADEQUATE RESOURCES FOR LEGAL REPRESENTATION

The American system of adversarial justice is predicated on the assumption that both sides are competently represented and have adequate resources to present their cases. That assumption is often false. In criminal cases, the problems that are caused by inadequate resources are very different depending on the side that is affected. The prosecution in the United States has essentially unlimited discretion to choose which cases to pursue and which to forego. Among those cases that are pursued, the prosecution has equally great discretion to decide when to offer an irresistible plea bargain, and when to insist on trial and severe punishment. An underfunded American prosecutor is likely to respond to limited resources by declining to prosecute cases that seem comparatively unimportant, or those in which convictions may be difficult to obtain because the evidence is weak, and by offering attractive plea bargains to defendants who are prosecuted. The net effect is to exclude or remove cases that are deemed weak or unimportant from the stream of formal criminal adjudication. Only very rarely will inadequate prosecutorial resources result in a full-blown trial at which the prosecution is overwhelmed by a far better prepared defense.

Criminal defense attorneys do not have the power to choose which cases to defend. If they are overworked, underfunded, lazy, or incompetent, they must nonetheless forge ahead and handle the cases that prosecutors bring, however inadequately. In the usual case of bad defense work, that means agreeing to a quick plea bargain without conducting an adequate factual investigation of the case, and without pursuing possible legal and factual defenses. Once in a while an incompetent criminal defense attorney will proceed to trial; usually, they never get that far. Death penalty cases, however, are very different from other criminal prosecutions, even other murder cases. As a result, the consequences of inadequate resources are quite different, on both sides.

On the defense side, the worst problems are well known: defense attorneys who interviewed no witnesses, presented no defense, came to court drunk, fell asleep at trial (Bright, 1994; Jennings, 2000). Despite these outrageous stories, it is no doubt true that overall the resources devoted to the defense are greater in capital cases than in other criminal prosecutions. The problem is in part that these resources are distributed extremely unevenly. In the United States, most criminal justice policy is set by the states and by local governments rather than by the national government (Israel, Kamisr, & LaFave, 2000). In some states, capital defendants benefit from excellent representation by experienced and well-financed criminal lawyers. In others, they suffer from inexcusably incompetent representation by unqualified lawyers who receive nominal compensation and assistance. In addition, capital cases demand far greater defense resources than other criminal proceedings. Obviously, there can be no plea bargain if the prosecution insists on capital punishment. That means that convictions that result in death sentences—unlike the great majority of other criminal convictions—are almost always the result of full-blown jury trials rather than negotiated guilty pleas (Gross, 1998). Inadequate defense attorneys cannot get out of capital cases cheaply and invisibly by engineering plea bargains; they must do their worst at trial.

And these are not just ordinary trials. In addition to all the usual complexities of a murder prosecution, when a defendant is convicted of capital murder in the United States there is an elaborate separate procedure—in effect, a second trial—to decide the punishment, usually before the same jury that convicted him. In this penalty trial the jury is allowed to consider a very wide range of information about the defendant and his crime, and must then make an essentially discretionary decision whether to sentence him to death or to life imprisonment. The outcome is very much up for grabs. The great majority of ordinary criminal trials in America, perhaps 75 or 80%, result in convictions. But among capital penalty trials, only about half or slightly more end in death sentences. In many cases this highly discretionary and variable decision seems to turn on the quality of the defense. On the one hand, clients of the best capital defense attorneys are rarely sentenced to death. On the other hand, there are many cases like that of Horace Dunkins, who was sentenced to death and executed in Alabama in 1989. Before his execution, a juror said publicly that she (and probably other jurors as well) would not have voted for death if she had known that Dunkins was mentally retarded, but his defense attorney never presented that information in court (Applebome, 1989). The result, in Stephen Bright's (1994) words, is that the death penalty, as often as not, is given not for the worst crime but for the worst lawyer.

On the prosecution side, the consequences of limited resources for capital cases are less obvious but just as important. Death penalty prosecutions are very expensive. They are much more complex than other criminal cases at every stage, from initial investigation through trial to review on appeal. And, of course, this costly process cannot be short-circuited by plea bargaining; in order to obtain and execute a death sentence, the state must go through every step at least once—and, as the process typically unfolds, many of them twice or more. As a result, prosecutors are very selective in choosing which cases to prosecute capitally and which not.

In theory, selectivity in capital prosecution is a good thing. Even the strongest advocates of the death penalty agree that it should be used sparingly. But (at least from the point of view of supporters of capital punishment) infrequency is not a virtue in itself. The idea, rather, is that the death penalty should be used sparingly because it should be reserved for the worst cases. Infrequent use because of limited resources constraints is not likely to fit that mold (Liebman, 2000).

Prosecution in the United States is a local function. With few exceptions charging decisions are made by county prosecutors who are elected separately in each of the more than 4,000 counties across the country (Israel et al., 2000). The offices these prosecutors run also pay for the prosecutions. In addition, county governments typically pay the cost of defending capital cases—which (in some states) can be very high. As a result, the effects of the cost of capital prosecutions not only vary enormously from state to state but within states from county to county. Defendants in some areas are far more likely to face the death penalty than those charged with similar crimes in nearby towns. Moreover, in small counties in particular, capital charging decisions may turn on accidents of time and order. A defendant may be subject to capital prosecution if there has been no capital case in the county for a while, or may be spared the ordeal because someone else got there first and already cost the county half a million dollars. This is one aspect of the issue I will address next: patterns in the use of capital punishment in the United States.

ARBITRARINESS AND DISCRIMINATION

Although the United States executes more prisoners than any other democratic nation, the death penalty is still a rare punishment. In 1999, there were 98 executions in the United States (Death Penalty Information Center (DPIC), 2001b), a very large number by modern standards, but they occurred in a country in which there were over 15,000 homicides (Federal Bureau of Investigation (FBI), 2001). Some of those homicides were not legally eligible for capital punishment, either because they were committed in the minority of states that don't use the death penalty or because they clearly did not meet the criteria for capital prosecution. Even so, use of the death penalty in the United States has been restricted to a small fraction of the cases in which it could theoretically be applied, perhaps 1 in 50 or fewer (Gross & Mauro, 1989).

As I have mentioned, infrequency of death sentences and executions would be no problem—indeed, it would be a virtue—if its use were restricted to the worst and most deserving cases. But that is not so. As I have also already mentioned, the fate of a potential capital defendant frequently turns on accidents of geography and timing, or the quality of his legal defense. As often as not, however, there is no apparent reason for the outcome—it is absolutely obscure why some defendants are sentenced to death and others are not. While the most heinous murders are very likely to be subject to the death penalty (serial murders, for example), and the least aggravated ones are very likely to be spared that fate (such as a killing by a jealous spouse), there are exceptions even at those ends of the spectrum, and in between many decisions might as well turn on chance (Baldus, Woodworth, & Pulaski, 1990; Baldus, Woodworth, Zuckerman, Weiner, & Broffitt, 1998).

It would be difficult, perhaps impossible, to devise any evenhanded system for imposing a penalty that is so rare and so severe. In the American system of criminal justice there is no feasible way even to try to do so. At the initial charging stage, decisions are made by numerous locally elected autonomous prosecutors. No state official (let alone any national body) directs their discretion. This means that the criteria that are used will vary greatly from town to town and year to year. Each prosecutor is likely to make only a small number of these difficult decisions—one or two a year, none for years at a time—so it is not feasible to expect most of them to articulate (let alone follow) any sort of systematic policies for choosing capital prosecutions. At the end of the process, the American tradition of jury sentencing in capital cases means that most capital sentencing decisions are made by single-case panels of inexperienced lay decision makers. Jury decision-making is a central aspect of the American context. It is important, among other purposes, as a limitation on the influence of politics on the judicial process (remember, for example, that most state-court judges [as well as prosecutors] are elected, Israel et al., 2000). But it cannot produce consistency in a process of this sort. Juries inevitably reflect local differences in attitudes toward crime and the death penalty in particular, and their decisions frequently turn on accidents of group composition.

If the only problem in the pattern of the use of capital punishment in America were arbitrariness or randomness, that would be bad enough. But the true picture is worse. The use of the death penalty in America is also deeply influenced by systematic illegitimate biases. Some of these are widely suspected but not well proven. For example, it is said that some prosecutors are more likely to ask for the death penalty when they are running for re-election than after they have been recently elected, or that capital prosecutions are more common when the victims are prominent citizens. The most disturbing pattern, however, is well studied and well documented: the death penalty in the United States is infected with racial discrimination (Baldus et al., 1990, 1998; General Accounting Office, 1990; Gross & Mauro, 1989).

Some of the discrimination in the use of the death penalty in the United States is old-fashioned discrimination against black defendants. But the strongest and most pervasive pattern is discrimination by race of victim. Across the country, decade after decade and in state after state, numerous studies have shown that defendants who are charged with killing white victims are several times more likely to be sentenced to death than defendants in similar cases with black victims. This discrimination occurs at both ends of the process, in the initial charging decision of prosecutors, and in the ultimate sentencing decisions of jurors (Baldus et al., 1998; General Accounting Office, 1990).

Discrimination by race of victim seems to be deeply entrenched in the use of the death penalty in America, probably because it has multiple causes. Prosecutors may be more likely to ask for the death penalty in white-victim cases because those homicides attract more attention and concern from the politically powerful white majorities in their districts; they may also respond to the fact that their white constituents favor the death penalty more than the blacks. Jurors may be more likely to sentence a defendant to death if they identify with the victim or see her as a possible friend or relative, because killings that strike closer to home tend to horrify us more than those that seem more remote and abstract. In a largely segregated society in which most jurors are white, this means that defendants who kill white victims will be more likely to be sentenced to death than those who kill blacks. This bias is probably entirely unconscious, but may be quite powerful. And it may also influence prosecutors at charging as well as jurors at sentencing, both because prosecutors may share that emotional response themselves, and because they may anticipate that jurors will be unlikely to return death sentences in black-victim cases, and therefore decide not to ask for the death penalty in the first place.

ERRORS

Finally, the worst problem with the administration of the death penalty in the United States is that it is extraordinarily prone to error. Arbitrariness, which we have already considered, is one type of systemic error. Capital punishment in the United States is supposed to be reserved for the most heinous murders, but many capital cases clearly do not satisfy that criterion (Baldus et al., 1998). In addition many individual cases are plagued by more specific and disturbing errors of law and fact. A recently released study by Liebman (2000) shows that 68% of all capital cases are reversed on review because of legal errors in the determination of guilt or penalty or both. This is a sharp contrast to other criminal cases in the United States, which are rarely reversed (Liebman, 2000).

In part, this astonishingly high rate of legal error is a direct consequence of the procedural nature of capital litigation. In general, American law greatly limits appellate review of convictions based on guilty pleas. In some states, ordinary appeals are not permitted at all following guilty pleas; where they are allowed only a narrow range of issues can be raised since the entry of a guilty plea obviates the need for most of the procedural steps that might be subject to review. Since the vast majority of criminal convictions in America are the result of guilty pleas, usually after plea bargaining, they are only subject to limited appellate review, or none. Death sentences, however, almost always follow full-blown jury trials, which preserve the defendants' rights to appeal on any available issue. These trials are usually much more complicated than other criminal trials, even on the issue of guilt and innocence. In addition, they also include the unique procedure of the capital-sentencing trial, which is subject to its own complex and error-prone legal rules. Finally, American judges are probably more careful and exacting in their review of death sentences than other criminal convictions—at least on the question of penalty, where a finding of error merely requires a reduction or reconsideration of the defendant's death sentence rather than the underlying conviction.

Many of the errors in capital cases in America are peculiar to the legal requirements that govern the use of the death penalty. In some, reviewing courts reverse death sentences on the ground that the defendant was not eligible for treatment as a capital offender. In others, the problems are procedural—typically, that in one manner or another that the defendant was denied the opportunity to argue effectively for a lesser sentence

(*Lockett v. Ohio*, 1978; *Penry v. Lynaugh*, 1989). Other errors are of types that frequently occur in non-capital cases as well—ineffective representation by defense counsel, use of illegally seized evidence or coerced confessions, etc.—but are less likely to lead to reversal because of the prevalence of plea bargaining and the less demanding standard of review. On these issues, the death penalty may simply be a context in which some of the common faults of criminal adjudication in the United States are uncommonly likely to be exposed. Finally, and most important, quite a few capital defendants have been released from prison for the most fundamental and disturbing legal error possible: because they were convicted and sentenced to death for crimes they did not commit.

Since the death penalty was reinstituted in the United States in 1976, 101 prisoners have been released from death row because they were proven to be innocent, or because of serious and unanswerable questions about their guilt (Death Penalty Information Center (DPIC), 2001c). Most spent many years under sentence of death; some decades. New cases of erroneous death sentences continue to come to light regularly, with no end in sight. Some of these defendants may in fact have committed the crimes for which they were condemned, but there is no doubt that the great majority was completely innocent, and that many other innocent defendants remain on death row. Several defendants who were later exonerated came within days, in some cases hours, of executions that were postponed for procedural reasons. Many if not most of these 101 defendants were cleared by a process that depended on blind luck (Gross, 1998). So far, there is no case with incontrovertible evidence that an innocent defendant was put to death, but it is likely that this has already happened and certain that it will happen in the future if we continue to execute at the current rate (Death Penalty Information Center, 2001c).

What accounts for this great concentration of miscarriages of justice among the tiny proportion of criminal cases in which death sentences are pronounced? In part it is due to the great attention that is focused on capital cases, especially on review. Similar errors in other cases—or for that matter in capital cases that do not result in death sentences—are less likely to be detected. In at least one case, for example, a defendant who was prosecuted for a murder he didn't commit and sentenced to life imprisonment was only exonerated after an investigation into the case of a co-defendant who was sentenced to death proved that neither of them was involved in the killing. In addition there is reason to believe that erroneous convictions are more likely in murder cases in general—and in the heinous murder cases that are likely to lead to death sentences in particular—than in other criminal cases. The main underlying process is that the authorities are much more strongly motivated to solve murder cases than lesser crimes, and even more so when the murders are particularly gruesome. This is not a process that is unique to capital case. The same thing may happen in a gruesome rape case, or any notorious case with strong political overtones. But murders are the most common category of criminal cases that command that sort of extraordinary attention from the authorities.

The major effect of this extra attention is that the police and prosecutors use more resources in the investigation and prosecution of homicides, and bring more killers to justice. At the same time, however, the political and emotional pressures to resolve these cases impel the authorities to take cases to trial with weaker evidence than they would for other crimes. As a result, capital juries see a mix of cases that include a disproportionately high number in which the evidence is in serious doubt, and they must make more difficult, close decisions on factual issues than other juries. Inevitably, that leads to a higher proportion of mistakes (Gross, 1998). These same pressures also push prosecutors and police officers to take liberties with the procedural rules that are designed to prevent erroneous convictions. Most of the cases in which innocent defendants have been convicted of capital crimes—and many of the capital cases that have been reversed for other types of error—involve official misconduct. The common, garden-variety type of misconduct is the concealment of evidence favorable to the defendant, but some cases involve more extreme misconduct such as the destruction of physical evidence or the procural of perjury. In part as a result, perjury is the leading cause of erroneous convictions in capital murder cases; in other cases, the dominant cause is eyewitness misidentification (Gross, 1998).

The review process that is supposed to detect these errors has strained the resources of the appellate system in many American states. As a result there is an enormous backlog of cases on death rows across the United States, and long delays in processing those cases. As of January 1, 2001, there were 3,726 prisoners under sentence of death, most of them at the early stages of the complex process of review (Death Penalty Information Center (DPIC), 2001a). The average time between death sentence and execution in the United States is over 10 years and growing, and many prisoners have been under sentence of death for 20 years or more with no execution date in sight. These long delays have produced what has become known as the "death row phenomenon"—the terror of indefinite imprisonment under threat of eventual execution. European courts consider this process a human rights violation in itself (*Pratt v. Attorney General of Jamaica*, 1994; *Soering v. United Kingdom*, 1989). But any attempt to speed up the process of review would come at a cost. Many of the innocent defendants have been released from death row because of information that became available, typically by chance, late in the process of review. If the appellate procedures had been more efficient, they would now be dead.

CONCLUSION

It may be possible to draw comparative procedural lessons from the American experience with capital punishment, but I doubt it. Perhaps the structure of inquisitorial adjudication, with its greater reliance on presumptively impartial official investigation and its reduced dependence on adversarial criminal defense, would do a more even-handed and accurate job of administering this extreme penalty. Maybe the use of professionally trained, non-elected, career prosecutors and judges would improve the process greatly. Perhaps the inquisitorial system of review, with its emphasis on factual accuracy rather than procedural regularity, would do a better job of catching errors. But this is speculation. The central fact remains that there is no Western inquisitorial system that retains the death penalty. Inquisitorial systems are subject to their own pathologies, which I have not explored. If a country that has such a system had retained the death penalty, or were now to restore it, those problems might emerge in full force.

But there is another possible link between the death penalty and adversarial justice that deserves mention. The most striking fact about the death penalty in America is that we continue to use it, and frequently, when every other Western democracy has abandoned the practice. Does our system of adversarial adjudication contribute the retention of the death penalty? The answer, I think, is yes, although the causal connection is indirect.

There are no doubt many reasons for this American exception, but a central one is the politicization of criminal justice in the United States (Gross, 1994). The death penalty is a major context in which this drama is played out—in what other country would the candidates' positions on capital punishment be a major issue in presidential elections?—but not the only one, and probably not the most important. Our drug policies and our astonishingly draconian use of imprisonment are also the products of electoral politics rather than rational policy (Gross & Ellsworth, in press).

Adversarial justice is neither a sufficient condition nor a complete explanation for the political nature of the American practice of punishment. Other countries with adversarial systems do not suffer from intrusion of politics into criminal procedure to the same extent as the United States. But adversarial procedure may contribute to the American way in at least two respects. First, the tradition of citizen participation on juries may foster political interest in criminal justice and perpetuate direct political control over its administration through the local election of prosecutors, judges, and police chiefs. Second, the most powerful position in the system, that of the prosecutor, is assigned to a role that, at least in the context of electoral politics, seems to demand ever-greater punitiveness. Prosecutors run for office on their "toughness" on crime, and then do it again when they run for senator, governor or, president—and their opponents respond in kind (Gross, 1994).

In other words, adversarial justice may be most important to capital punishment in the United States not because it makes the process run better or worse but because it is part of the reason that we continue to use the death penalty at all.

8

Taking Recovered Memories to Court

HARALD MERCKELBACH

From the outset I want to emphasize that as far as psychological issues are concerned, I do not believe in the superiority of inquisitorial legal systems. To the best of my knowledge, there is no empirical evidence that would justify such a belief. A case in point is the popular argument that in inquisitorial systems, triers of fact are professional judges, who therefore reach better decisions than the lay people who serve as jurors in adversarial systems. Although this argument seems to possess some prima facie validity and is often backed up by anecdotal examples of the O.J. Simpson type of trial, it is not based on compelling evidence. In their classic study, Kalven and Zeisel (1966) found that most of the times, professional judges and lay jurors agree in their verdicts, even if cases and the evidence brought forward are quite complex. Or consider risky shift phenomena and other fiascoes that some authors have thought to be typical for group decisions like those made by jurors. Again, there is no convincing support for the idea that group decisions are necessarily more risky than those made by a single individual (e.g., Aldag & Riggs Fuller, 1993). Apart from that it is of course quite misleading to assume that in adversarial systems legal decisions are exclusively reached by jury trials. Thus, although there are many cherished myths about adversarial systems and, especially, their reliance on juries, I agree with Sealy (1998) that there is little reason to believe that these myths are grounded in facts.

Having said this, I now turn to the issue of this chapter, which is how adversarial and inquisitorial systems handle recovered memory cases that go to trial. To preview my argument, I propose that the outcome of recovered memory cases heavily depends on expert testimony. Under the adversarial regime, parties may recruit their own expert witnesses and may challenge those of their opponents (see for details, Shuman, 1997; Spencer, 1998). In contrast, under the inquisitorial regime, expert witnesses are considered to be the court's witnesses and they are explicitly instructed to behave as such (see for details, Spencer, 1998). Whenever experts testify about technical issues and come from scientific disciplines with a high degree of consensus and precision, it probably doesn't matter much whether one of the parties or the court appoints them (but see Williams, 2000). Things are different with recovered memories. The typical recovered memory case rests on many controversial assumptions. In this particular domain, experts may rely on reasonable hypotheses that are not necessarily correct. If in such cases parties are allowed to choose their own experts, they will not experience much difficulty in finding an expert with an impressive curriculum vitae who fits their partisan purpose. Under an inquisitorial regime, such partisan experts are probably more rare and precisely this state of affairs makes the prospects for successful litigation or prosecution in recovered memory cases not very good.

A PROTOTYPICAL CASE

Recovered memories refer to recollections of seemingly forgotten childhood events of a traumatic nature (e.g., physical abuse, sexual abuse, severe neglect). In Schooler's (1999, p. 205) words: "an individual who reports recovering a memory for trauma is really indicating two sentiments: (a) that abuse occurred and (b) that there was a period of time in which the memory was not available." A prototypical case would be that of a woman in her late twenties who suffers from a severe depression, an eating disorder, and/or an anxiety disorder. She decides to consult a psychiatrist or psychologist. This clinician has a strong intuition that the woman's psychopathology originates from repressed or dissociated childhood trauma. That is, the clinician believes that the traumatic memories have no access to consciousness, but do produce psychopathological symptoms. He/she starts using hypnosis or other memory-recovery techniques in order to lift the repression or to circumvent the memory problems caused by dissociation. Eventually, these techniques contribute to the patient's recovery of abuse memories. The patient then decides to bring the recovered memories to court. More specifically, she decides to file a criminal charge and/or a tort damage claim against the perpetrator, who often is a parent.

Case vignettes with this general outline can be found in Loftus and Ketcham (1994), Pendergrast (1995), and Ofshe and Watters (1994), to name but a few authors. It would be a mistake to take these case vignettes as caricatures made up by cynical skeptics. Similar and even more spectacular case reports can be found in the writings of those who have no such a reputation. A fine example is a personal experience recounted by hypnotherapist Dabney Ewin (1994). He tells how one day he came home and asked his wife to fix him a cup of coffee. She refused and Ewin experienced an unbridled rage "that was so out of proportion and so unlike me that I felt I had to analyze it" (p. 175). Ewin used self-hypnosis and regressed to the 12th day of his life. He recovered memories of the day that he was taken off breast-feeding. He adds (p. 175): "The allegory of the woman in my life denying me liquid refreshment is obvious." Apparently, then, the idea that one can apply hypnotic-like techniques to recover memories about the antecedents of behavioral problems is not an invention of skeptics.

The features of our prototypical case also fit well with the basic statistics that have been reported about recovered memory cases (e.g., Gudjonsson, 1997; Van Koppen & Merckelbach, 1999) and with information provided by so called recanters, that is people who declare that their own recovered memories and the accusations based on them are false (e.g., Lief & Fetkewicz, 1995). Most importantly, our prototypical case is consistent with data that come from surveys among certified clinicians. For example, a survey of Andrews et al. (1995) among 180 highly trained practitioners of the British Psychological Society found that a majority of them (i.e., 60%) had seen clients who recovered memories of traumatic incidents. Almost half of the respondents (i.e., 44%) believed that these recovered memories were "usually essentially accurate."

WHAT DOES IT MEAN WHEN YOU SAY THAT RECOVERED MEMORIES ARE ESSENTIALLY ACCURATE?

Although it may be easy for a clinician to tick the "usually" or "always" box in a survey about the accuracy of recovered memories, one should not underestimate the complexity of the issue for an expert witness. When an expert witness testifies that patients' recovered memories are usually correct, he or she really has to believe that the following assumptions refer to facts deserving a place in our psychology textbooks (see for a detailed analysis, Roediger & Bergman, 1998): (1) total amnesia for traumatic childhood events is a common phenomenon; (2) this phenomenon originates from repression or dissociation, which are processes that store aversive childhood memories in a fixed and indelible format and make them temporarily inaccessible for conscious inspection; and (3) when people somehow succeed in retrieving these previously inaccessible memories, they can give a fairly precise report of the content, origins, and temporal characteristics of these memories.

Clearly, each of these assumptions relates to a huge, but also highly controversial corpus of scientific literature (e.g., see for recent reviews, Haber & Haber, 1998; Ornstein, Ceci, & Loftus, 1998; Roediger & Bergman, 1998). Now consider the woman in our prototypical case who seeks criminal prosecution of her biological father or files a civil suit against him on the basis of her recovered memories. Sooner or later, her actions would require expert testimony about the extensive literature on memory and trauma. Her legal prospects would be bad if the expert witness would tell the court that the assumptions listed above lack the status of undisputed facts. Such a conservative position may be expected in a system where the expert is a witness of the court. In contrast, in an adversarial system, the woman's lawyers may shop around for an expert who is willing to adopt a more liberal stance, for example by grounding his or her testimony in what he or she believes to be plausible from a clinical point of view.

A good illustration is provided by the civil trial of *Shahzade v. Gregory* (1996) that took place in the District of Massachusetts. In this trial, a woman brought suit against her male cousin for damages originating from sexual touching that took place several decades earlier. The woman claimed that she only recently regained the memories of these incidents. Referring to the statute of limitations, her cousin objected to the suit. Nevertheless, a U.S. District Judge ruled that the civil suit could go forward. This decision was heavily based on the testimony of a professor of psychiatry who served as an expert witness for the plaintiff. More specifically, the psychiatrist opined that recovery of traumatic memories from amnesia is a robust phenomenon that is widely accepted by clinicians in the field of psychology and psychiatry. The *Boston Globe* (April 10, 1996) quotes the psychiatrist as saying that "there is no scientific basis to believe that Shahzade (i.e., the plaintiff) or other victims could fake such memories and fool psychiatric tests."

According to a large-scale survey among psychologists in the United States, 35 percent of them occasionally appear in court to testify (Dawes, 1994). Although I have no precise estimates, I'm quite sure that this percentage is dramatically smaller in a civil (i.e., inquisitorial) law country like the Netherlands. For example, the number of psychologists who on a regular basis present testimony about criminally insane behavior and its legal consequences (in Dutch *terbeschikkingstelling*) is well below 300 (Malsch, 1998), while the Dutch Psychological Association has more than 10,000 members. The larger the pool of potential expert witnesses, the easier it must be to find an expert willing to testify in a prototypical case that recovered memories are usually essentially accurate. This may be particularly true when the expert is hired by the plaintiff and believes that the plaintiff's health may benefit from his or her testimony.

SOME MORE STATISTICS

In 1996, there were in the United States some 700 lawsuits involving recovered memories at the trial level, while an additional 200 cases reached appellate courts (e.g., Hagen, 1997). For the Netherlands, the best estimate is that in 1996 only 2 or 3 cases involving recovered memories came to the attention of the police, none of them reaching the trial level (Van Koppen & Merckelbach, 1999). Even if you correct for population size, these statistics demonstrate that there is quite a difference between the United States and the Netherlands in terms of the number of recovered memories cases reaching trial level.

One could reason, of course, that this has to do with different prevalence rates of recovered memories in the two countries. Perhaps, there simply are more recovered memories in the United States than in the Netherlands resulting in more criminal or civil proceedings in the former country. However, this explanation can be refuted on the basis of empirical data. Both countries have so called False Memory Syndrome Foundations. Their members claim that they have been falsely accused on the basis of recovered memories, mostly recovered memories of their daughters. These accusations do not necessarily come to the attention of the police or give rise to a tort damage claim. In the United States, a survey among members of the False Memory Syndrome (FMS) Foundation produced a total of 2,300 accusations (FMS Foundation, 1997). A survey among members of the Dutch counterpart of the False Memory Foundation produced a total of 98 accusations (Van Koppen, 1998). Taking population sizes into account, these rates are roughly comparable to each other, which suggest that there is no difference between the United States and the Netherlands in prevalence rates of recovered memories.

Perhaps, then, the higher frequency of recovered memory cases brought to courts in the United States has to do with specific procedural rules of the American legal system. For example, a number of courts ruled that the "delayed discovery doctrine" known from medical malpractice suits may apply to recovered memory cases as well. Accordingly, statutes of limitation were expanded, allowing plaintiffs with recovered memories to pursue their cases in court some time after their abuse memories were revived. The earlier cited *Shazade v. Gregory* (1996) trial illustrates this practice. Experts differ sharply in their opinions about whether such extensions of the statutory period of limitation are justified by psychological data (see for a discussion, Memon & Young, 1997). For example, Dorado (1999, p. 110) argues that it constitutes "some forward progress for incest survivors hoping to sue their perpetrators." On the other hand, Hagen (1997, p. 254) reminds us that "the crucial difference between genuine discovery cases—"My god, he left the sponge in here!"—and recovered memory of trauma cases is that in the former there is no doubt that the sponge is indeed present in the claimant's body because the poor old claimant had to hire another surgeon to remove the disgusting thing…. But with so-called recovered memory cases, there is often no objective or even supporting evidence that the alleged trauma occurred." However that may be, extension of statutes of limitation creates more opportunities for potential lawsuits and one may speculate that this contributes to the relatively high frequency of lawsuits involving recovered memories in the United States. However, the Netherlands has seen a similar liberalization of statutes of limitations, at least for accusations that involve sexual abuse (i.e., Wet Verlenging Verjaringstermijn Zedenzaken, see Van Koppen, 1998). Interestingly, this reform was partly motivated by the belief that victims often react with amnesia to sexual abuse. Thus, regulations surrounding statutes of limitations do not explain why there are more court cases involving recovered memories in the United States than there are in the Netherlands.

What about the admissibility of clinical testimony in recovered memory cases? In the United States, many courts follow some version of the *Daubert* decision (*Daubert v. Merrell Dow Pharmaceuticals Inc.*, 1993) to evaluate the admission of scientific expert testimony. The *Daubert* decision requires a focus on Rule 702 of the Federal Rules of Evidence that emphasizes the helpfulness and relevance of expert testimony to the jury. Some commentators (e.g., Kovera & Borgida, 1998) have argued that *Daubert* has lowered the standards for admissibility of expert evidence. For example, the specialized knowledge of expert witnesses mentioned by Rule 702 may also consist of clinical experience. One could hypothesize that this makes admission of clinical expert testimony more likely, which, in turn, may promote lawsuits based on recovered memories. However, as far as criteria for the admissibility of psychological or psychiatric testimony are concerned, the situation in the Netherlands is roughly comparable to that in the United States. In the words of Van Koppen and Saks (2003) who extensively discuss this issue: "As different as the procedures are in the two systems, as we will see, they often are equally ineffective in screening out poor expert evidence." In sum, then, differences in the legal standards for expert psychologists or psychiatrists do not account for the fact that there are more court cases involving recovered memories in the United States than there are in the Netherlands.

PROFESSIONAL ATTITUDES

Perhaps, then, it is the attitude of psychiatrists and psychologists towards recovered memories that accounts for the difference. In a country where a majority of psychiatrists and psychologists firmly believe that patients' recovered memories of childhood trauma are usually accurate, it is conceivable that many patients feel encouraged to take legal actions on the basis of their recovered memories. There have been a number of surveys addressing professional attitudes towards recovered memories among clinicians in the United States, the United Kingdom, and the Netherlands (e.g., Merckelbach & Wessel, 1998; Poole, Lindsay, Memon, & Bull, 1995; Yapko, 1994). In general, these surveys indicate that there is little reason to believe that skeptics dominate the profession in the Netherlands, whereas believers dominate the profession in the United States or the United Kingdom. For example, one survey (Merckelbach & Wessel, 1998) found that a majority of Dutch psychotherapists believes that repression of memories is a real phenomenon causing psychopathological symptoms. Yapko (1994) obtained similar findings for American psychotherapists.

Why should there be large differences between Dutch and American professionals to begin with, when they all attend the same conferences and read the same literature? Van der Hart, Boon, and Heijtmajer Jansen (1997, pp. 148–149) provide a lively description of how attitudes and insights are transmitted from one country to another. Referring to Dutch professionals' opinions about Dissociative Identity Disorder (DID; formerly Multiple Personality Disorder), a diagnosis often associated with recovered memories, these authors write: "Since the first workshop on DID in the Netherlands in 1984, given by Dr. Bennett Braun of Chicago, a steadily growing number of Dutch clinicians from all over the country have been diagnosing and treating DID patients." Yet, insights in this research domain may change rapidly. The recent survey by Pope, Oliva, Hudson, Bodkin, and Gruber (1999) among board-certified American psychiatrists revealed that only about one-quarter of them feels that the diagnosis of DID is supported by strong scientific evidence. The psychiatric community in the Netherlands lags behind, because in this country about half of the psychiatrists seems to be in favor of the DID diagnosis (Sno & Schalken, 1998). Thus, there is no evidence for the idea that nation-wide differences in professional opinions account for the fact that there are more recovered memory trials in the United States than there are in the Netherlands. Moreover, the fact that a sizable minority or even half of the professionals believes in the existence of DID, dissociation, or repression does not automatically imply that these professionals would also be willing to mount the witness stand and testify about the essentially accurate quality of recovered memories.

MOUNTING THE WITNESS STAND

Suppose you are a psychiatrist who has published numerous articles in psychiatric journals about trauma and dissociation and who has treated many patients with such characteristics. And suppose that one day, a lawyer contacts you. He consults you about a patient who recovered memories of childhood abuse during psychotherapy. The patient now wants to bring a criminal charge against her biological father. The lawyer asks you whether you would be willing to testify as an expert witness on behalf of the patient. More specifically, he wants you to inform the court that recovered memories are usually essentially accurate. You decide to interview the lawyer and his client. You learn that there is no independent corroboration for the recovered memories and, of course, you are not surprised: the absence of such evidence is why they asked you in the first place. It also becomes clear to you that the patient has severe dissociative symptoms and that it would come as a great relief to her if her father were sentenced for his offense.

To be sure, you could testify to the court that memories of the sort recovered by the plaintiff are usually essentially correct. In doing so, you could base your opinion on your extensive clinical experience and on scientific literature. As far as the latter is concerned, you could, and probably should, make explicit to the court that your position rests on the three assumptions mentioned earlier. Thus, you may quote from studies that found that a considerable percentage of victims of childhood abuse fail to report the abuse (e.g., Williams, 1994) and you could present this as evidence for the idea that amnesia for childhood trauma is a common phenomenon. You may then go on summarizing a vast literature indicating that trauma promotes repression and dissociative fragmentarization of memories (e.g., Chu, Frey, Ganzel, & Matthews, 1999). In addition, you may refer to research papers claiming that such traumatic memories, unlike ordinary memories, possess photographic qualities (Van der Kolk, 1994). To make a really impressive case, you could even bring fMRI scans with you. After all, there do exist pictures of the brain that suggest that dissociative patients handle traumatic and neutral memories in qualitatively different ways (e.g., Tsai, Condie, Wu, & Chang, 1999). Finally, you could point out that there are excellent case studies that illustrate that victims can give well-articulated accounts of the circumstances under which their lost memories turned into recovered memories (Terr, 1984).

While testimony along these lines is not unreasonable in a clinical conference room, it might be misleading when it is presented in court. Basically, the misleading potential of this testimony has to do with its selective use of the scientific evidence. For example, the fictional expert witness described above fails to inform the court that several review articles have questioned whether amnesia for traumatic events is a common phenomenon (see for a review, Pope, Hudson, Bodkin, & Oliva, 1998). The expert also ignores studies that have criticized the concept of repression and/or dissociation of traumatic memories (see for reviews, Frankel, 1996; Merckelbach & Muris, 2001). Likewise, the expert's testimony is silent about studies showing that traumatic memories are not immune for distortions which raises doubts about the photographic qualities of such memories (e.g., Bryant & Harvey, 1998; Merckelbach, Muris, Horselenberg, & Rassin, 1998; Roemer, Litz, Orsillo, Ehlich, & Friedman, 1998). If our expert witness would bring fMRI pictures into the court, that maneuver would be difficult to reconcile with the reservations made by authors like Kulynych (1996). Neuroimages have a certain seductive power because they seem to offer a photographic representation of the brain, when, in fact, they are more similar to highly constructed graphs than to photographic pictures.

The expert in our prototypical case also overlooks findings showing that people are not good in judging the temporal characteristics of their memories. Thus, when a patient or client claims that a traumatic childhood event has not been recalled previously (i.e., before therapy), this may be a false impression (e.g., Loftus, Joslyn, & Polage, 1998; Parks, 1999). Finally, and perhaps most importantly, our expert runs the risk that his testimony is biased by a tendency to seek and value supportive evidence at the expense of contrary evidence (e.g., Wedding & Faust, 1989). One potential source of contrary evidence has to do with the fact that the patient recovered memories during psychotherapy. This raises the question whether the memories may have been tainted by treatment. There are a number of studies addressing treatment techniques (e.g., hypnosis, journaling, dream interpretation, imagery) that have the potential to taint memories or to produce complete pseudomemories in patients (e.g., Horselenberg et al., 2000; Hyman, Husband, & Billings, 1995; Rassin, Merckelbach, & Spaan, in press). Thus, it would have behooved the expert to tell the court whether or not these studies bear relevance to the case at hand.

CLINICAL VERSUS JUDICIAL DECISION-MAKING

The problems surrounding expert testimony in recovered memory cases can best be framed in terms of a clash between clinical and judicial decision-making (Appelbaum, 1997; Van Koppen & Saks, 2001; Rassin & Merckelbach, 1999; Shuman, Stuart, Heilbrun, & Foote, 1998). Clinical decision-making is based on clinicians' primary obligation to advance their patients' interest. Therefore, doctors must actively look for symptoms and hidden pathology. Indeed, technology in medicine aims at uncovering hidden pathology and the worst error that a clinician can make is that he or she overlooks such pathology. Thus, a good doctor will act according to the principle that absence of evidence is not evidence of absence (of a disease). The doctor's highest priority is preventing false negative outcomes and this occurs when you overlook latent pathology.

Judicial decision-making is quite different. Central to judicial decision-making is not promoting the well-being of the clientele, but seeking and revealing the truth or—somewhat less ambitious—following fair trial principles. Under judicial decision-making rules, the worst error you can make is contributing to the conviction of an innocent suspect. After all, the presumption of innocence is a corner stone of both inquisitorial and adversarial law systems. Accordingly, preventing false positives (i.e., convicting innocent suspects) has high priority in both legal systems.

There can be little doubt that expert witnesses should adopt judicial decision-making heuristics. That is, the expert witness has an obligation to be equally sensitive to the interests of both plaintiffs and suspects and should therefore refrain from partisan testimony. Under an adversarial regime, expert witnesses may find it sometimes difficult to adopt such a role and this may be particularly true for recovered memory cases because here clinicians are often explicitly hired to serve the interests of one party. Under these circumstances, selective use of what is essentially controversial evidence may lead the expert to endorse hypotheses that are reasonable, but not necessarily correct. Such hypotheses, in turn, may constitute the ingredients of partisan testimony.

Under an inquisitorial regime, the expert witness is court-appointed and, therefore, he or she may find it easier to make the transition from clinical to judicial decision-making. This is not to say that unbalanced and partisan expert testimony on recovered memories is totally absent in an inquisitorial law country such as the Netherlands. In fact, we have previously described such testimony by Dutch expert witnesses in detail (e.g., Van Koppen & Merckelbach, 1998). Interestingly, these civil cases followed an adversarial scenario in that the clinical expert was willing to tell the court that recovered memories are usually essentially correct, thereby showing that he was not able to resist the natural temptation to serve the party that had hired him.

In their thought-provoking review, Lavin and Sales (1998) concluded that it is currently not within the boundaries of a clinician's competence to testify that a plaintiff's recovered memory is veridical, even when such testimony is in principle admissible. Nevertheless, offering expert testimony of this sort is far easier when expert witnesses are adversarially called and this may set a premium on filing lawsuits on the basis of recovered memories. Lavin and Sales (1998, p. 77) also noted that "it is appropriate to testify, for example, that there are many reasons to be skeptical about memory reports of long forgotten events." For an expert called and paid by a plaintiff who brings her recovered memories to court, it will be extremely difficult to offer this type of testimony.

Some may argue that in the adversarial system, unbalanced and selective testimony may be corrected through cross-examination by opposing counsels. However, Kovera and Borgida (1998) summarize evidence showing that once jurors have formed beliefs about the reliability of expert testimony, cross-examination does not sensitize jurors to its potential shortcomings. More importantly, it may be precisely because of the adversarial and hostile style of cross-examination that knowledgeable experts may prefer to avoid the courtroom and retreat to their laboratory instead (e.g., Bruck, 1998).

CONCLUSION

Does this all imply that adversarial legal systems are inferior? No. In the final analysis, the bug in the system is the expert witness, not the adversarial procedure per se. The most obvious solution to the problem of partisan expert testimony is to invite professional organizations to educate their members. Perhaps, such education should start with a demystification of clinical expertise (Dawes, 1994). As the earlier mentioned example of Ewin (1994) illustrates, clinical experience may function as an especially overstated heuristic on which clinical expert witnesses rely. In the words of one skeptic: "Some doctors make the same mistakes for twenty years and call it clinical experience" (Walker, 1996, p. 27).

Good education by professional organizations should also underscore the point that when it comes to traumas and their impact, clinical and judicial domains are not closed circuits. Overstatements in one domain may have their echoes in the other domain. In general terms, it is striking that even recent psychiatric studies in the field of trauma research loosely employ a vocabulary that suggests causality and objective measurement, although they do not reach such standards. Consider the study by Chu et al. (1999). These authors write that "independent corroboration of recovered memories of abuse is often present" (p. 749) when they refer to patients' subjective reports that they (i.e., the patients) had been able to find some kind of verification for the abuse. As another example, Lewis, Yeager, Swica, Pincus, and Lewis (1997) claim that their study establishes "once and for all, the linkage between early severe abuse and dissociative identity disorder" (p. 1703), a claim that suggests a large-scale, longitudinal design, when in fact this study was cross-sectional in nature and relied on a sample of 12 patients. A more technical example is provided by a recent study of Draijer and Langeland (1999). Using a cross-sectional design, these authors gathered retrospective self-reports of trauma and dissociation in a clinical sample. The authors concluded that childhood trauma makes a unique contribution to the severity of patients' dissociative symptoms. While this conclusion more or less reiterates the popular view that trauma causes dissociation, it is misleading in that it is premised on a regression analysis in which trauma self-reports entered as the predictor variable and dissociation served as the criterion, a constellation that one could easily reverse (e.g., Merckelbach, Horselenberg, & Schmidt, in press).

I could go on making a long list of sweeping statements from fairly recent articles that appeared in psychiatric journals, but the message is clear. This type of overstatement may encourage expert witnesses to adopt a partisan attitude. Meanwhile, to educate expert witnesses about the risks of such an attitude is more urgently needed in the United States than in the Netherlands. To the extent that professional organizations do not succeed in disciplining those members who regularly mount the witness stand, the "throw-them-out-of-court" sentiments that were so eloquently articulated by Hagen (1997) become difficult to resist.

9

Adversarial Influences on the Interrogation of Trial Witnesses

ROGER C. PARK

This chapter examines adversarial incentives that affect the interrogation of witnesses by parties harmed by their testimony. It asks whether these incentives help or hamper the discovery of truth.

Putting it another way, this chapter evaluates Wigmore's famous claim that adversarial cross-examination is "beyond any doubt the greatest legal engine ever invented for the discovery of truth" (Wigmore, 1974).[1] In evaluating cross-examination, I have relied, as Wigmore did, on anecdotes, books for lawyers, case law, accounts of trials, and fireside inductions. So far, systematic empirical research has little to contribute in examining the value of cross-examination (see below). I started by reading manuals and books instructing lawyers on how to conduct cross-examination. I then asked whether the recommended techniques were likely to add to the accuracy of verdicts.

Before starting, I will ask readers to note that I am writing about the usefulness of *cross-examination*, not the usefulness of impeachment evidence. They are two different things. Cross-examination refers to the procedure of

---

[1] Wigmore's assertion is frequently cited. The Supreme Court has repeatedly used the great scholar's opinion as authority for the efficacy of cross-examination. See *Lilly v. Virginia*, 527 U.S. 116, 124 (1999); *White v. Illinois*, 502 U.S. 346, 356 (1992); *California v. Green*, 399 U.S. 149, 150 (1970). Others have cited the assertion in a less reverent fashion. See Tillers & Schum (1992) and Wellborn III (1991).

adversarial questioning of a witness called by the opposing party, as opposed to direct examination of one's own witness. Impeachment refers to bringing out evidence that reduces the credibility of a witness who has given unfavorable testimony. Cross-examination is often used to impeach, but it is not always needed for that purpose. Impeachment evidence about motives to falsify, bad character, inconsistent statements, mental illness, or other facts detracting from a witness's credibility could be received through the impeacher's direct examination of other witnesses, including those who sponsor documentary proof. In some instances, it might also come in by stipulation or judicial notice. A cross-examination that is spectacularly successful because it reveals, for example, that the cross-examined witness sent an email urging a fellow witness to lie on the stand is not an example of a *cross-examination* that succeeded. It is an example of a *pretrial investigation* that succeeded because it uncovered the damning facts that were used on cross- examination to impeach. Had cross-examination been unavailable, the impeachment would still been accomplish through other means.

For example, suppose that an eyewitness is unavailable at the time of trial, and the eyewitness's statement identifying the defendant as the perpetrator of the crime is admitted under a hearsay exception. Cross-examination of the eyewitness would be impossible. However, the opposing party could still impeach the eyewitness with evidence, for example, that the eyewitness previously identified another suspect as the perpetrator.[2] Facts that find their way into evidence through alternate routes might not be as dramatic as facts extracted during a confrontation with a lying witness during cross-examination, but the question of the value of cross-examination (from the point of view of the system of justice) lies not in its dramatic value *per se*, but in its value in promoting accuracy of verdicts.

PRECEPTS OF CONTEMPORARY CROSS-EXAMINATION

The principal precept of cross-examination as it is taught in the trial practice courses and in programs for young lawyers[3] is to *take no risks*. These authorities advise preparing extensively before trial, having

---

[2] For example, Fed. R. Evid. 806 provides that when a hearsay statement has been admitted in evidence, "the credibility of the declarant may be attacked, and if attacked may be supported, by any evidence which would be admissible for those purposes if declarant had testified as a witness."

[3] For the precepts I will be stating, I will be relying upon manuals used on law school trial advocacy courses. These include Lubet (1997), Mauet (2000), McElhaney (1994), McElhaney (1974) Jeans Sr. (1993), and on Irving Younger's a famous lecture, still widely used on videotape, entitled *The Ten Commandments of Cross-Examination* (Younger, 1977). The "ten

ammunition ready, and using that ammunition in a way that avoids counter-thrusts and unexpected mishaps.

At the bottom of the "take no risks" attitude is the danger of backfire, a danger that is magnified by the adversarial nature of the proceedings. When the lawyer doing the direct examination presents testimony favorable to that lawyer's client, the jury is always somewhat suspicious; they expect the lawyer to be presenting biased testimony and they take it with a grain of salt. But when the cross-examiner elicits testimony that is favorable to the other side, the backfire is dramatic, humiliating to the lawyer, and harmful to the case.

The corollaries of the "take no risks" precept are never to ask a question without knowing the answer, don't ask the witness to explain, always use leading questions, and never ask one question too many (leave well alone). I will examine the first three precepts more specifically.

Never ask a Question for Which You Don't Know the Answer

Lubet gives the conventional advice "Do not ask questions to which you do not know the answers" (Lubet, 1997, p. 121).[4] Mauet advises "Play it safe. Many witnesses will seize every opportunity to hurt you. This is not a time to fish for interesting information or to satisfy your curiosity" (Mauet, 2000, p. 352). Younger (1977) and others (Iannuzzi, 1998) agree.

The trial practice lore and literature abound with examples of lawyers who are visited with disaster by venturing questions that get surprise answers. A few of these follow.

---

commandments" are: (1) Be brief; (2) Short questions, plain words; (3) Ask only leading questions; (4) Never ask a question to which you do not already know the answer; (5) Listen to the answer; (6) Do not quarrel with the witness; (7) Do not permit the witness to explain; (8) Do not ask the witness to repeat the testimony from direct; (9) Avoid the one question too many; and (10) Save the explanation for summation. For printed versions of the Ten Commandments, see Younger (1987) and (1976). For testimonials about their influence, see Solecki (1982, "The lawyers who have never seen Irving Younger's film, "The Ten Commandments of Cross-Examination," can probably be counted on the fingers of one hand") and Asbill (Asbill, 1994, Younger's Ten Commandments resemble the biblical Ten Commandments in that they are "accepted on faith and followed by nearly all").

[4] Lubet notes that, "A witness, during either direct or cross, may expose an enticing, but incomplete, morsel of information. It is difficult to resist exploring such an opening, just to see if anything is really there" (p. 121). But Lubet, of course, advises against such "fishing". Lubet later qualifies the advice slightly, saying: "Every question on cross-examination should contain a proposition that falls into one of these three categories: (1) you already know the answer; (2) you can otherwise document or prove the answer; (3) any answer will be helpful" (p. 105). He gives as an example of the last: "Were you lying then, or are you lying now?"

Gilbert without Sullivan

Stephen Tumim's (1983) report of W. S. Gilbert's first case has all the elements of a perfect backfire story—a foolish question that brings out devastating evidence; the lawyer hoisted on his own petard; an angry client. Tumim reports that before meeting Arthur Sullivan and becoming part of Gilbert and Sullivan, W. S. Gilbert practiced as a barrister for four years, with an average of five clients a year, earning a total of 75 pounds. His first case was one in which the defendant was accused of being a pickpocket. She denied guilt and said she was just going to tea and prayers with her hymnbook and that the perpetrator must have planted the purse on her. Eager to bring out the fact of the hymnbook, Gilbert asked the arresting officer what the officer found in his client's pocket, and received the answer, "two other purses, a watch with the bow broken, three handkerchiefs, two silver pencil-cases, and a hymn-book." According to the report, the client threw her shoe at her lawyer while she was being taken away to serve her sentence. The shoe missed Gilbert but hit a reporter, a fact that Gilbert later said might explain why the newspapers were so unkind in reporting on his search for a defense.

"Have You Ever Been in Prison?"

Wigmore, who loved cross-examination as a trial procedure, was quite aware that it could backfire. In fact, his treatise included a subsection entitled, "Examples of the inutility of a cross-examination, in bringing out facts which strengthen the witness's credit, or answers which otherwise give him a personal victory" (Wigmore, 1974, pp. 47–54). The subsection includes many backfire reports. In one example (Osborn, 1937, quoted in Wigmore (1974), § 1368 at 52–53), a lawyer asked an unkempt old man, "on bad advice or an unwarranted suspicion," the question whether the witness had ever been in prison. The old man answered "Yes." The lawyer then asked triumphantly, "Where were you in prison?" The witness answered, "In Libby Prison during the Civil War," a blow that made the cross-examiner seem to shrink.

"Did You Ever Hear the Prisoner Threaten the Deceased?"

In another Wigmore (1974, par. 1368) example, the cross-examiner defended a man accused of murdering a barmaid. Confident of getting a favorable answer, the cross-examiner asked the bar owner: "Did you ever hear the prisoner threaten the deceased woman before the date of the alleged murder?" and got the following answer: "Yes, many times, although I never thought the threat serious."

"Isn't that because your recovery has been quicker than expected?"

Lubet hypothesizes a personal injury plaintiff who stated during direct exam that her doctor told her she did not need to go to physical therapy any longer. Hoping this shows her injuries were not severe, the defense lawyer asks, "Isn't that because your recovery has been quicker than expected?" and gets the answer, "No. It is because the therapy was too painful and I wasn't making any progress."[5]

DON'T ASK THE WITNESS TO EXPLAIN

Novice trial lawyers are often advised never to ask the witness to explain, advice sometimes stated as "never ask why or how questions."[6] For example, Professor Lubet cautions: "It is almost impossible to imagine a need to ask a witness to explain something on cross-examination. If you already know the explanation, then use leading questions to tell it to the witness. If you do not already know the explanation, then cross-examination is not the time to learn it. No matter how assiduously you have prepared, no matter how well you think you understand the witness's motives and reasons, a witness can always surprise you by explaining the unexplainable" (pp. 119–120). He gives the example of the witness who explains how he can get from the parking garage to his office in 3–5 minutes by taking a special shuttle bus that has its own lane. "Asking a witness to explain is the equivalent of saying, 'I've grown tired of controlling this cross-examination. Why don't you take over for a while?'" (Lubet, 1997, p. 121). Lubet also cautions the lawyer to avoid "gap" questions. He gives the example of a defendant who testifies to an alibi but leaves several half hour gaps. The prosecutor asks, "Mr. Defendant, you told us where you were at 2:00 p.m., but you didn't say anything about 2:30 p.m., did you?" Lubet advises, "Do not ask that question; you will lose control. It is an unspoken invitation to the witness to fill in the gap. Even if the witness does not take the opportunity to complete his alibi, you can be certain that opposing counsel will do it for him on redirect. The far better tactic is to allow the omission to remain unexplained and then to point it out during final argument." Obviously, from the perspective of a system of justice that aims at discovering the truth, it would be better to fill in the gap.

---

[5] Note that it would be a good idea to find out why the witness did not continue in therapy if the goal is to discover the truth. But if the witness's statement about ending therapy is unexpected, in the context of partisan cross-examination, the fear of backfire may prevent the question from being asked.

[6] As Mauet (2000, p. 253) puts it, "Questions that ask "what," "how," or "why" or elicit explanations of any kind invite disaster."

In short, the lawyer who asks for an explanation is asking for disaster. Here are examples from the literature and lore:

"How come you can testify he bit off the nose when your back was turned?"

Irving Younger's celebrated and influential "Ten Commandments" lecture offers the following example (from Oliphant, 1982; Younger, 1977):[7] A witness testified on direct that the defendant bit off the victim's nose. On cross, he said he was birdwatching at the other end of the field, admitted he had his back turned, and that his attention was first attracted by the victim's scream. The examiner should have stopped there, but he asked further, "How come you can testify he bit off the nose when your back was turned?" The witness answered, "I saw him spit it out."

"Well, explain what you were doing [as you bent over the body]"

Younger's lecture also reports that he once asked the celebrated trial lawyer Edward Bennet Williams for stories about mistakes. Williams reported that as a young lawyer he had been defending a transit company whose vehicle had run over a derelict. The company maintained that the derelict was drunk. No bottle had been found on the derelict's body. The son of the victim, also a derelict, had walked over to the victim and bent over the victim's body after the accident. Williams was convinced that the son had taken the bottle. With proper leading questions, Williams asked "You saw the accident? You knew your father was hurt? You went and bent over him? You took the bottle?" On getting a negative answer to the last question, Williams should have stopped. Instead, he asked, "Well, explain what you *were* doing." The witness answered, "Even though he was an old drunk, he was my father, so I kissed him goodbye."

---

[7] Younger notes during the lecture that the story is probably apocryphal, and offers it merely as a useful fable. The story was probably inspired by the somewhat different example in Wigmore (1974, § 1368 at p. 43, from 13 The Green Bag 423 (1901)), in which a defense witness on direct stated that he was present at the scene and did not see the defendant bite the victim's ear off. In response to an open-ended question on cross-examination asking the witness what he *did* see, the witness conceded that he saw the defendant spit the ear out. Though in the Wigmore example the prosecutor asked an open-ended question, presumably he knew what the answer would be and hence was not violating the precept not to take risks.

"How could you have arrested my client?"

The following fictional example is from Mathew's *Forensic Fables by O* (1961):

MR. WHITEWIG AND THE RASH QUESTION

MR. WHITEWIG was Greatly Gratified when the Judge of Assize invited him to Defend a Prisoner who was Charged with Having Stolen a Pair of Boots, a Mouse-Trap, and Fifteen Packets of Gold Flakes. It was his First Case and he Meant to Make a Good Show. Mr. Whitewig Studied the Depositions Carefully and Came to the Conclusion that a Skillful Cross-Examination of the Witnesses and a Tactful Speech would Secure the Acquittal of the Accused. When the Prisoner (an Ill-Looking Person) was Placed in the Dock, Mr. Whitewig Approached that Receptacle and Informed the Prisoner that he Might, if he Wished, Give Evidence on Oath. From the Prisoner's Reply (in which he Alluded to Grandmothers and Eggs) Mr. Whitewig Gathered that he did not Propose to Avail Himself of this Privilege. The Case Began. At First All Went Well. The Prosecutor Admitted to Mr. Whitewig that he Could not be Sure that the Man he had Seen Lurking in the Neighbourhood of his Emporium was the Prisoner; and the Prosecutor's Assistant Completely Failed to Identify the Boots, the Mouse-Trap, or the Gold Flakes by Pointing to any Distinctive Peculiarities which they Exhibited. By the Time the Police Inspector Entered the witness-Box Mr. Whitewig Felt that the Case was Won. Mr. Whitewig Cunningly Extracted from the Inspector the Fact that the Prisoner had Joined Up in 1914, and that the Prisoner's Wife was Expecting an Addition to her Family. He was about to Sit Down when a Final Question Occurred to him. "Having Regard to this Man's Record," he Stearnly Asked, "How Came You to Arrest him?" The Inspector Drew a Bundle of Blue Documents from the Recesses of his Uniform, and, Moistening his Thumb, Read therefrom. Mr. Whitewig Learned in Silent Horror that the Prisoner's Record Included Nine Previous Convictions. When the Prisoner was Asked whether he had Anything to say why Sentence should not be Passed Upon him, he Said some Very Disagreeable Things about the Mug who had Defended him.

Moral—Leave Well Alone.

USE ONLY LEADING QUESTIONS

The great philosopher and law reformer Jeremy Bentham, in his influential work on judicial evidence, displayed strong belief in the efficacy of interrogation. He even set forth examples of questions that would throw light on a case. Bentham suggested interrogation by asking, "Do you remember nothing more? Did nothing further pass, relative to this or that person or thing (naming them)?" He asserted that "By interrogations thus pointed, such a security for completeness is afforded as can never be afforded by any general engagement [such as oath]" (Bentham, 1827, Book II, Chapter IX, p. 446). These open-ended questions would be anathema to the American lawyer doing trial cross-examination.

As Professor Lubet puts it, "The cardinal rule on cross-examination is to use leading questions. The cardinal sin is to abandon that tool" (Lubet, 1997, p. 117).[8] Roy Black advises to "Think of cross-examination as a series of statements by the lawyer, only occasionally interrupted by a yes from the witness" (Liotti, 1999, p. 81). Younger (1977) and others are in accord.[9]

The following examples illustrate the point.

"And you went in with a pipe and you thought it would be fun, isn't that right?"

Harlan Levy reports an example of effective cross-examination from the Central Park Jogger Trial, a case involving the tragic attacks by a group of teenagers upon random victims, including a young woman who was jogging in Central Park (Levy, 1996, pp. 82–83). Prior to the attack on her, the group, which was "wilding"—attacking people just for fun—had attacked other people, one of whom died. One of the defendants had made a confession to the police and took the stand to deny it:

> Salaam, tall and slender, took the witness stand, and, on direct examination by his own attorney, denied that he told Detective McKenna he had participated in an attack on a female jogger, or in any other attacks. Salaam claimed that he never admitted any involvement in that night's events to McKenna. But he also offered his version of what happened in the park that night, and it was there that he ran into trouble.
>
> According to Salaam, he had entered the park with a group of 50 young men, with no specific purpose in mind. But, Salaam said, he quickly got separated from the group. As he walked through the park, he saw a bum, thought he was dead, and started running because he didn't want to be blamed for killing someone he didn't kill. Then he came upon a group that looked like they were beating somebody up. Again, said Salaam, he started running.

[8] Lubet's exceptions are: (a) when you need a bit of information to continue and it won't hurt you no matter what the answer is. For example, there are two ways the defendant could have driven to his office, and the cross-examiner is prepared to handle either (p. 118), (b) when answer is short, well-documented, and factual, can't hurt you, and would be more impressive coming in witness's own words. For example, Q: "Where did you spend Labor Day weekend?" Answer: "At Eagle River Falls." Cites to other trial practice sources to be added.

[9] Roy Black (1999), from review by Liotti (1999, p. 81): "Don't ask "what happened next." That's like asking the witness to make a speech." For a rare counter-example, see Wellman (1986, p. 186). There, a lawyer asked a paranoid but plausible witness for "the whole truth" on cross-examination, and successfully elicited testimony from the witness about a fantastic conspiracy, thereby discrediting the witness.

Then, something very strange happened during Salaam's questioning by his own attorney. Salaam made the startling admission on his direct examination that he had in fact had a pipe as he entered the park that night. According to Salaam, he didn't do anything with the pipe. It just fell out of his pocket, somewhere in the park. Besides, it wasn't even his pipe. It was his friend Kharey's pipe. Kharey told him to hold it for him, and Salaam forgot that he had it.

As the prosecutor began her cross-examination, she headed straight for the implausibilities and admissions within Salaam's story, and sought to highlight them for the jury.

"You were walking with a group," asked Lederer, "and suddenly everybody was gone?" "We were walking up a hill," said Salaam. "I got real tired, lagged behind them, and suddenly everybody was gone. I don't know where they went."

"Then," said Lederer, "you came upon a person who you thought was dead." "Yes," said Salaam.

"Did you go over to see if he was bleeding?" asked Lederer. "No," said Salaam.

"You just decided to run away from him?" asked Lederer. "If I touched him," said Salaam, "my fingerprints would have been on him."

"You just ran away from him?" asked Lederer. "Yes, I did," answered Salaam.

"You didn't call for help for him?" "No," said Salaam.

"Then," asked Lederer, "you ran further into the park?" "I ran south," answered Salaam. "You stayed in the park?" "Yes."

"You weren't going home at that time?" "I was trying to catch a train," answered Salaam.

"You were running south in Central Park trying to get to a train, is that your testimony?" "Yes," answered Salaam.

"You had a pipe in your pocket?" asked Lederer. "Yes," said Salaam.

"Do you always carry a pipe in your pocket?" asked Lederer. "No," said Salaam, "I don't have a pipe of my own."

"You weren't going into the park for a picnic?" asked Lederer. "No, I wasn't. It was nighttime. I don't have a picnic in the nighttime," said Salaam smugly.

"Good point," said Lederer.

"Did you have any jogging clothes on when you went into the park that night?" asked Lederer. "No, I didn't," said Salaam.

"You didn't take a bicycle to go biking in the park that night, did you?" "I didn't have a bicycle," said Salaam.

"You didn't take any sports equipment; you weren't going to play any sporting games, were you?" "No," said Salaam.

And you went in with a pipe and you thought it would be fun, isn't that right?" "Yes," said Salaam."

This is low-risk cross, a way of dramatizing facts that help the prosecution by putting them to the defendant. Had cross-examination not been permitted, the prosecutor could still have made the same points in summation.

You asked a rapist to find [your friend's] shoes ... in a dark house?

In the celebrated William Kennedy Smith rape trial, Ann Mercer, a friend of the alleged victim, was the first major witness called by the prosecutor. Henry W. Asbill (Asbill, 1994, p. 2):

> Never forget that the examiner is entitled to answers to questions and should politely—but if necessary firmly and rudely—insist on them. A good example of this type of "argument" occurred during Roy Black's cross-examination of Ann Mercer during the Smith trial.
> *Black*: You walked into the house where the rapist is, right? *Mercer*: Yes. *Black*: It was dark in there, right? Mercer: Yes. *Black*: You met with a man who your friend says is a rapist, right? *Mercer*: I was not afraid of him. *Black*: That's not my question. You asked a rapist to find her shoes? *Mercer*: Yes. Black: In a dark house, right? *Mercer*: Yes.
> Black continued this line of questioning: "Onto a dark patio? Down a dark stairway? With a door at the bottom? On a dark beach? With a man who raped your friend?" Then he asked, "Did you tell this man, 'I'm sorry we've met under these circumstances'?" Prosecutor Lasch objected that Black was being too argumentative, but Judge Lupo directed Mercer to respond. "Yes," she answered; and it was then clear to the jury that either Mercer had doubts about her friend's story or she had her own agenda on the evening of the alleged attack."[10]

"You pitched the tent?"

Professor Lubet illustrates the danger of using non-leading questions by hypothesizing a case in which a personal injury plaintiff went on a three-day camping trip, during which she hiked, fished, swam, pitched the tent, carried her backpack, and slept on the ground. Even if she has testified about these acts during her pre-trial deposition, he advises against asking an open-ended question, suggesting that it might lead to the following answer:

> Q.: Ma'am, please tell us all of the things that you were able to do on your recent camping trip.
> A.: I was hardly able to do anything. Everything I tried caused me pain, even sleeping (Lubet, 1997, p. 118).

---

[10] Asbill also reports significant impeachment for bias of Ann Mercer, a major prosecution witness. When defense attorney Roy Black elicited on cross-examination that Mercer had been paid $40,000 for her story by a tabloid television show, the courtroom audience (including the jurors) "erupted." The judge, Mary Lupo, had to "temporarily halt ... the proceedings and threatened to 'clear' the courtroom if there were any more 'audible responses.'" (Smith Case Witness Paid $40,000 by TV, *Washington Post* at A3 (Dec. 4, 1991).)

He suggests that instead the cross-examiner should take refuge in the "greater safety" of leading questions, as follows:

> Q.: Ma'am, you went on a three-day camping trip?
> A.: Yes.
> Q.: You went hiking?
> A.: Yes, but it caused me pain.
> Q.: You went fishing and swimming?
> A.: Yes.
> Q.: You pitched the tent?
> A.: Yes, but that hurt too.
> Q.: You stayed out in the woods for three days?
> A.: Yes (p. 119).

The examples in the literature of eliciting facts to impeach the witness with concessions about known facts are really just a form of dramatized argument, not presentation of new facts. The facts about the witness's camping trip could all have been presented without the witness, through others who had firsthand knowledge, or through the witness's out-of-court statements. If the attorney never asks the question without knowing the answer and takes no risks, these alternative modes of proof *must* be available. Otherwise the attorney would be taking risks. Thus putting the questions to the witness dramatizes them, but does not add facts that could not be shown by other means.[11]

You kept your eye on the knife?

Professor Mauet illustrates the use of leading questions in an example of the defense counsel's cross-examination of a robbery victim (Mauet, 2000, pp. 265–266). The victim identified the defendant as the man who robbed him at knifepoint. To show bad witnessing conditions, including weapon focus, the cross-examination proceeds as follows:

> Q.: Mr. Archer, all this happened around 11:00 at night?
> A.: Yes.
> Q.: It was dark?
> A.: Yes.
> Q.: The robber pushed you from behind into the alley?
> A.: Yes.
> Q.: You never saw the robber until after you were in the alley, right?
> A.: That's right.
> Q.: And there weren't any street lights in the alley, were there?
> A.: No.

---

[11] In addition to the examples presented in text, see Mauet's model cross-examinations on how many letters a secretary has typed and how many police reports an officer has made (Mauet, 1992, pp. 228–230).

Q.: The robber was facing into the alley?
A.: That's right.
Q.: And you were facing toward the street?
A.: Yes.
Q.: Then you noticed he had a knife in his hand?
A.: Yes.
Q.: Describe the knife.
A.: It had a shiny blade, about six inches long, and a wooden handle.
Q.: Mr. Archer, you must have been concerned that he might use the knife against you?
A.: Yes.
Q.: You kept your eye on the knife?
A.: I suppose so.
Q.: He then said "give me your wallet" and you gave it to him?
A.: Yes.
Q.: He then ran down the alley, away from the street?
A.: Yes.
Q.: From the time he said "give me your wallet" to the time he ran past you down the alley, that took about ten seconds?
A.: I'm not sure of the exact time.
Q.: And during that time, he always had the knife where you could see it?
A.: Yes.

Leading questions are a way of pursuing a broader goal, always exercising control over the witness (see Lubet, 1997, p. 104, "The essential goal of cross-examination technique is witness control"). In addition to using leading questions, Lubet suggests that the lawyer try not to read questions from notes (looking away from the witness may cause loss of control, p. 105), to use small, steady steps, creating a "conceptual corral" (p. 106–114) and to avoid long or complicated questions "because they have an almost limitless capacity to deprive a cross examiner of witness control" (p. 122, for example, the witness may ask for clarification.). He adds, "The pitfalls of cross-examination are well known: refusals to answer, unexpected answers, argumentative witnesses, evasive and slippery witnesses. Significantly, virtually all these problems derive from the same basic error on the part of the cross examiner—failure to control the testimony." Lubet urges reasserting control if the witness does not answer the exact question (p. 116), using pointed repetition or subtly scolding the witness for not answering the exact question. Ultimately, one can ask for help from the judge. If the witness asks the lawyer a question, such as "how would you feel," the lawyer should respond that the rules don't allow him to answer questions.

EXCEPTIONS TO THE LOW-RISK PRECEPTS

Most contemporary lawyers and trial advocate teachers recognize and try to follow the precepts of not asking questions unless the answer is known, not asking witnesses to explain, maintaining control, and taking no risks. But it would be misleading to suggest that the precepts are invariably followed. The published literature recognizes exceptions to them. One relatively innocuous one is that one can ask a question without knowing the answer if no answer could hurt (Lubet, 1997, p. 105).[12] A more important one is that when desperate, the lawyer has to take chances (Asbill, 1994; Mauet, 2000; Wellman, 1986). But in the usual contested case, it is probably safe to say that the low-risk strategy is pursued by the vast majority of lawyers.

COMPARISON OF ADVERSARIAL AND INQUISITORIAL INCENTIVES

It seems obvious that the low-risk precepts of adversarial cross-examination have their costs. Tantalizing bits of information go unpursued, even if they might shed some light on the case. Clarifying questions are not asked for fear that they will backfire. Any time that the cross-examiner fails to ask a relevant question because he fears backfire, or the direct examiner does not ask the question for the same reason (or because she knows the answer but doesn't like it) the adversarial climate has obstructed the search for the truth.

My Hastings colleague Gordon Van Kessel has provided me with an example from his trial experience. Prior to becoming a law professor, Van Kessel was the defense counsel in a robbery case. He cross-examined an eyewitness who had identified the defendant as the robber. The witness had observed the defendant from a vantage point across the street. Van Kessel asked the witness, "Do you wear glasses?" On receiving a positive answer, he then asked "Were you wearing them at the time you witnessed the robbery?" The witness answered "no." Following the low-risk precepts, Van Kessel then stopped asking questions. For unknown reasons, the prosecutor had no further questions on re-direct. In other words, the prosecutor did not attempt to clarify how well the witness could see *without* glasses, perhaps fearing to delve into the unknown.[13]

---

[12] His example is the inquiry to a witness who has had to admit to previously having given a false answer, "Were you lying then, or are you lying now." The present author once saw a trial in which the witness answered "neither." The answer went unexplored.

[13] Personal conversation with Gordon Van Kessel, November, 2001. In the case tried by Professor Van Kessel, the judge finally stepped in and tested the witness by having him read a sign in the rear of the courtroom, a task the witness performed with success. Of course, in the adversary system, one cannot often count on a neutral to step in and clarify an ambiguity.

In contrast, the neutral interrogator need not fear embarrassment if the witness gives a surprising answer. Indeed, the question that reveals new information is a successful question that reflects well upon the interrogator's competence, since it has added to or clarified the file.

It is not too early to note, however, that this handicap caused by fear of the unknown is mitigated to some extent by other features of the adversarial system. In major civil cases, it is common to depose major witnesses before trial. Depositions are taken under oath and recorded. They commonly take place in a lawyer's office or other location away from the courtroom, and the lawyers normally conduct them without direct judicial supervision. Lawyers for all parties have the opportunity to ask the witness questions. Where the depositions are conducted merely for discovery, and not as a substitute for trial testimony, the precepts of trial cross-examination do not apply. During a deposition, the party harmed by the witness's testimony will freely elicit concessions, seek unfavorable information, and ask questions without knowing the answer (see, e.g., Haydock, Herr, & Stempel, 2001, pp. 324–325, advising to "ask anything and everything" and "ask who, what, where, when, why and how questions"; Mauet, 1993, pp. 224–225, saying that where purpose of deposition is to get information, lawyer should ask open-ended questions and encourage the witness to volunteer information). The cross-examining attorney will assume that the opponent will put in the unfavorable information at trial, and use the deposition to find out what it is and prepare for it.

Depositions are, however, less common in criminal cases. Criminal discovery in general is less broad, because of fear that criminal defendants will intimidate witnesses or use information learned during discovery to concoct a false story of innocence.[14] Here strict adherence to the precepts of cross-examination undoubtedly results in some loss of information. The same may be said of civil cases in which the amount in controversy is not large enough to justify depositions, where depositions are taken only as a substitute for testimony[15] or where the witness was not deposed for various reasons—for example, the witness was not perceived as important, or the witness's availability was discovered just before trial.

---

[14] Professor Van Kessel suggests an interaction between aggressive cross-examination and other trial features, such as lack of discovery, that favor the prosecution. In his view, the prosecutor has greater control over the presentation and examination of witnesses, and perhaps over keeping facts secret, as a counterbalance of aggressive defense cross-examination (Van Kessel, 1992, pp. 485–486).

[15] Where a videotaped deposition will be shown to the judge or jury at trial, the lawyer has as much reason to fear backfire as in live trial testimony.

WHEN CAN ADVERSARIAL CROSS-EXAMINATION ELICIT NEW FACTS?

If adversarial cross-examination is always, or almost always, simply dramatized argument,[16] then cross-examination doesn't really bring out anything new. It may be effective for advocates, but it doesn't seem to add much to accuracy of fact-finding. It can still serve a useful purpose in cases in which there's no special reason to eliminate it. It can serve as an audit of the cross-examiner's proof. For example, the cross-examiner may have persuasive evidence that the target witness made a prior inconsistent statement, but the evidence may not be conclusive, and if it's presented on cross-examination and the witness admits making the statement, all the better. It can give the witness being impeached a chance to explain the impeaching evidence—perhaps, for example, by saying that the inconsistent statement was made under pressure. And sometimes impeachment by cross-examination and the witness being impeached can simply be more economical than calling extrinsic witnesses.

Of course, in rare situations dramatized cross-examination might do more than elicit nonverbal demeanor or audit probable facts, as in the example of the stubborn uncooperative witness or the insane witness. Or a flukish witness may unexpectedly, on cross-examination as on direct, contradict indisputable facts. But in general, if all that no-risk cross-examination does is to put in facts that can be proven some other way, then it would seem to be a convenience in cases in which it is feasible, but something that can be dispensed with in cases in which there is some harm or cost associated with it.

On the assumption that no-risk cross-examination is the predominant mode of cross, under any reasonable hypothesis does adversarial cross-examination really add anything? This chapter will now examine situations in which cross-examination might yield new information even if the examiner is pursuing a low-risk strategy.

ADDING INFORMATION WITH COMMIT AND CONTRADICT TACTICS

If the lawyer has information that the witness does not know about, or that the witness has forgotten about, then the lawyer can try to get the

---

[16] By dramatized argument, I mean simply putting to the witness facts that can be proven otherwise for the purpose of having a dramatic "face-to-face" presentation. The same thing could be done, less dramatically, through other testimony, supplemented by final argument during which the lawyer states the points that he would have asked the witness to affirm on cross-examination.

witness to make an assertion on cross-examination that can be definitively disproven, thereby showing the witness willing to lie under oath in the very case at bar.

This "commit and contradict" impeachment could occur, for example, in a personal injury case in which the lawyer has a surveillance videotape showing that the allegedly disabled person engaged in some strenuous activity, such as painting his house. The cross-examiner could first try to get the plaintiff to make exaggerated claims of disability, then to specifically deny that he painted the house. Then the irrefutable proof to the contrary would show not only that the plaintiff had less of a physical disability than he claimed, but also that the plaintiff was willing to tell a bald-faced lie under oath about something he was unlikely to be mistaken about.

A similar example occurs where the cross-examiner has evidence of an inconsistent statement that the witness doesn't know about. The cross-examiner can first try to commit the witness to the position that he never would say any such thing, approaching the matter by degrees, and then impeach him with the statement. Again, the cross-examination has a double effect—first, the effect that the inconsistent statement would have if presented by itself; second, the extra mileage given by showing that the witness either forgot it or lied about it.[17]

The following trial anecdotes further illustrate the "commit and contradict" technique.

---

[17] Rule 611(b), abolishing Queen Caroline's Rule, aids this sort of cross-examination by allowing a witness to be asked about a statement before showing it to him. For example, suppose that a witness (Thompson) testified on direct that Mr. Harsh and Mrs. Coles behaved with perfect propriety at the Pudding River picnic. The cross-examiner knows that in an email message, Thomson had written, "You should have seen the way Mr. Harsh and Ms. Coles acted at the Pudding River. It was absolutely disgraceful." Thompson hit the "reply" key and unknown to him, the message went out to the whole Pudding River discussion list instead of just to the friend he meant to write to. The lawyer has a printout of the message in her hand. The following cross-examination would be permissible: Q. Did you ever describe the conduct of Mr. Harsh and Mrs Coles together as disgraceful? A. No. Q. You never said it was disgraceful? A. No. Q. You never wrote it was disgraceful? A. No. Q. Are you as sure of that as you are of the rest of your testimony? A. Yes. Q. Is it possible you called it disgraceful and forgot about it? A. No. Q. You didn't write to your friend Tom Jones and say it was "disgraceful?" A. No. Q. Now would you look at what has been marked as Plaintiff's exhibit 1 for Identification. Is that an email message? A. Yes. Q. Is that your email address in the return address? A. Yes. Q. Did you write that email message to Tom Jones on January 1 of this year? A. Yes. Q. Would you read to the jury the second paragraph of that message you wrote?

*"Won't you be good enough to point out where Ericson
adopts your view of this case?"*

Francis L. Wellman's (1986) celebrated book[18] describes Wellman's cross-examination of Dr. Ranney, a medical expert. Wellman first questioned Dr. Ranney about being a professional witness, getting him to admit that he spent so much time in court that he had comparatively little time to devote to reading and private practice. He then asked if any medical authority agreed with Ranney that the symptoms pointed to this disease only. Ranney, apparently believing he was still being accused of not keeping up in his field, claimed that Ericson on the Spine agreed with him. Asked how he knew, Ranney said he had checked Ericson's book that very morning.

Having done his homework, Wellman knew there was no such statement in all of Ericson. Reaching under the counsel table, Wellman brought out his own copy of Ericson, approached the witness, and asked "Won't you be good enough to point out where Ericson adopts your view of this case?"

The doctor responded, "Oh, I can't do it now, it is a very thick book." Pressed, he said "I have no time to do it now."

Wellman replied, "Time! There's all the time in the world."

The witness and lawyer eyed each other for three minutes in silence. Then the presiding judge asked the witness if he intended to answer the question. The witness said he did not, and he was excused from the stand in breathless silence, completely destroyed (Wellman, 1986, p. 85).

Fuhrman's Use of Racial Epithets

Another example was F. Lee Bailey's cross-examination of the witness Fuhrman in the O.J. Simpson trial. Fuhrman was a police detective who had discovered crucial evidence that Simpson had murdered his wife. The defense already had some evidence of racist statements that Fuhrman had made using the word "nigger" and after cross-examination,

---

[18] This remarkable book, entitled *The Art of Cross-Examination*, was first published in 1903. Working without co-authors, Wellman produced four editions before dying in 1947. Apparently his book has never been out of print. A 1997 paperback reprint of the 1947 edition contains a blurb from a *New York Times* book review calling it an "undisputed classic." The book is full of anecdotes about cross-examination that was devastatingly successful and cross-examination that horribly backfired. Wellman himself was quite a master, and two of the witnesses he cross-examined, one a sitting Congressman and the other a newspaper reporter, left the witness stand in such disgrace that they went into hiding and, in the case of the Congressman, was never heard from again (Wellman, 1986).

tape recordings came to light that conclusively proved Fuhrman's use of the epithet. Bailey got Fuhrman to testify that he had never used the word in the past 10 years and that it would be impossible for him to have used it and forgotten about it. The TV news commentators treated the cross-examination as a victory for Fuhrman, but both Fuhrman and the prosecution were later much harmed when tape recordings of Fuhrman making such statements were presented. Fuhrman was recalled to the stand and refused to answer questions when asked about his lies. He invoked his Fifth Amendment privilege against self-incrimination to protect himself against possible charges of perjury. Then, in order to protect himself from forfeiting his Fifth Amendment rights he also had to refuse to answer the question whether he planted the bloody glove.[19]

"How could you see if you had no candle?"

Another familiar example is the story of Abraham Lincoln and the moon. During his great debate with Douglas, while running for the Senate, Lincoln took time out to try a murder case in which the son of an old friend was accused. The murder took place at eleven o'clock at night. Lincoln elicited facts showing that the nearest light was far away and that the participants did not have a candle. He then induced the witness to claim that he had seen the attack by the light of a nearly full moon. Lincoln showed with an almanac that there was practically no moon at eleven o'clock that night (Wellman, 1986, pp. 76–77).[20]

COMMENTS ON COMMIT AND CONTRADICT

In all of these examples, the cross-examination actually added something that could not have been accomplished by other proof. It could have been shown by other proof that there was not much moonlight or that Fuhrman had made racist statements or that the plaintiff had painted a house, but the willingness to tell a bald-faced lie under oath in that very case is something that is only shown by cross. So the same goal could

[19] The jury was not told that Fuhrman had taken the Fifth Amendment, but it was widely believed the jurors found out about this fact during conjugal visits, since Fuhrman's later appearance, like the rest of the trial, was televised.

[20] It is perhaps worth noting that the form of Lincoln's question ("How could you see"?) seems to violate the maxim about not asking for explanations. Thus, when it is presented in the form presented by Wellman, it seems to implicitly counsel asking for an explanation. But this example may be one of those rare ones where asking for an explanation would be consistent with a low-risk strategy, if the lawyer knows what answer will be given or if any possible answer must favor the cross-examiner.

not have been accomplished by letting in hearsay accompanied by impeachment of the hearsay declarant.

Note in these examples the role of misdirection and the need for careful planning. The lawyer doesn't want the witness to know the goal of cross-examination. So the lawyer pretends to be getting at something else. In Lincoln's case the witness apparently believed that Lincoln was pointing out the absence of light, to argue that the witness could not see well. In the case of Dr. Ranney the witness apparently believed that the cross-examiner was trying to show that the witness had not much time to do research or keep up because he testified so much. In the case of a written inconsistent statement, a lawyer might start out seemingly trying to get concessions that the event affirmed by the statement might have happened, in order to get the witness dug into a hole ("committed") to saying that it absolutely could not have happened, and perhaps also saying that he's sure he never said that it happened.[21]

It seems unlikely that the same sort of impeachment would be attempted if witness examination were conducted by a neutral official. First, setting that sort of tricky trap[22] would take the neutral out of the neutral role, making the neutral seem to be a partisan who was trying to trip up one of parties by concealing information and setting a trap. Secondly, the advocate with high adversarial incentives—the desire to win, compensation and glory dependent upon winning—is more likely to do the groundwork and planning, whereas the neutral, wanting to avoid the appearance of partisanship and perhaps also pursuing what Bentham called "love of ease," is more likely to ask open-ended questions that do not set traps.

ADDING INFORMATION BY SHOWING EVASIVENESS OR SELF-CONTRADICTION

Sometimes the cross-examiner has no ammunition for the commit and contradict strategy and little or none for other purposes, such as eliciting concessions. In such instances, if the witness has done little harm, one option is merely to decline to do any cross-examination (for a discussion, see Mauet, 2000, pp. 247–249). If cross-examination is attempted, the

---

[21] See example in note 16, *supra*.

[22] Wellman (1986, p. 138) spells it out: "One very skillful method of handling a witness, particularly when he is not only intelligent but shifty, is not to disclose your 'trump card'—if you have one—until you have so completely committed the witness to the details of his story as to make it impossible to offer any plausible explanation of the damaging document with which you intend to destroy him."

no-risk strategy would counsel a *pro forma* cross-examination asking about universals that detract from the testimony of virtually all witnesses, e.g., asking about whether the witness has talked to the opposing lawyers about the case.[23] But sometimes lawyers attempt more, especially if the witness is crucial and the benefit is worth the risk. Wellman advises that "When ... you have not the material at hand with which to frighten the witness into correcting his perjured narrative, and yet you have concluded that a cross-examination is necessary then avoid repeating the direct examination, select an area involving attendant circumstances that the witness is least likely to have prepared for."[24]

The anecdotes illustrating this method are not as punchy as other trial anecdotes, because the cross-examination tends to be long and circumstantial, but there are a number of examples of cases in which witnesses just couldn't get their stories straight.[25] The tactic may have worked better in Wellman's day; one wonders whether it would be as good against well-prepared witnesses with basic education, and whether it might not backfire if the witness held up well.

Some witnesses become obviously evasive on cross-examination. They stall, ask that the question be repeated, say "I can't recall," and avoid answering directly. Here the cross-examiner can show something about

---

[23] This is a risk-free question because the witness who answers "no" will not be believed, and the "no" answer will undermine that witness's testimony. See Haydock & Sonsteng (1999, p. 527, discussing "neutral" and "safe" questions which include questioning on whether witness discussed the case with the opposite counsel), Mauet (1996, p. 267, talking about "apparent" cross-examination that attacks witness on collateral issues: i.e. discussion of the case with the opposing counsel) and McElhaney (1987, p. 265, discussing safe areas of questioning, but warning about "getting too greedy").

[24] He adds, "Do not ask your questions in logical order, lest he invent conveniently as he goes along; but dodge him about in his story and pin him down to precise answers on all the accidental circumstances indirectly associated with his main narrative. As he begins to invent his answers, put your questions more rapidly, asking many unimportant ones to one important one, and all in the same voice. If he is not telling the truth, and answering from memory and associated ideas rather than from imagination, he will never be able to invent his answers as quickly as you can frame your questions, and at the same time correctly estimate the bearing his present answer may have upon those that preceded it. If you have the requisite skill to pursue this method of questioning, you will be sure to land him in a maze of self-contradiction from which he will never be able to extricate himself."

[25] For illustrative anecdotes, see Wellman (1948, pp. 413–436, Bellevue case, pp. 55–57, cross-examination by Lincoln in the Grayson case, pp. 124–127, "caveat" case). For recent discussions, similar to Wellman's, on the use of misdirection in cross-examination, see McElhaney (1987, pp. 270–271, discussing the "use of logical relationships" method by taking things out of context to create a wanted inference), Lubet (1993, pp. 60–61, discussing "misdirection" method of cross-examination, a method that conceals the ultimate object of the cross-examination from an intentionally elusive and untruthful witness) and Goldman (Goldman, 1993, p. 159, discussing use of pace to elicit wanted replies while cross-examining).

the witness's lack of candor simply by continuing to ask questions getting as many evasive answers as possible (see Mauet, 2000, p. 299).

Adding Information by Eliciting Honest Concessions

One major function of cross, or of interrogation in any form, is to elicit concessions from a witness aligned with the opposing party.

Where basically honest witnesses have framed their testimony so that it only reveals what helps the party to whom the witness is partial, the function of eliciting honest concessions can be quite important. Gathering information about facts helpful to the cross-examiner's case, and then getting the witness to confirm them, is a valuable adversarial tool.[26]

For example, in a case described by Reed (1885, cited in Wigmore, Evidence, § 1368, at p. 40), the testimony of an honest but not particularly forthcoming witness was offered to prove that a horse was docile. With carefully crafted questions, the direct examiner elicited testimony that the witness, a blacksmith, was able to shoe the horse and that the horse stood

---

[26] See Reed (1912, § 90, cited in Wigmore, Science, § 265, at pp. 581–582): "If you observe the trial of issues of fact, you will note that nearly every witness is made to suppress some important parts of a transaction while replying to the direct examiner; and that often, where he is given free range by being told to make his statement in his own way, he omits some details which would aid the other side should they be proved. To make the witness give a *complete* narrative, if what has been kept back is favorable to your side, may be regarded as the point where cross-examination should generally begin.... (*b*) We now come to what is practically the most effective and most widely useful of all the different sorts of cross-examination. In it you have the opposite witness to prove *independent facts* in your favor.... A person may have been present when a sum of money was borrowed, and he may also have seen the money repaid afterwards to one who is claimed to have been the agent of the lender to receive it. If this witness testifies for the plaintiff on the trial of a suit for the money, his counsel will ask nothing about the repayment. He may not even know it. But you have been told of it by your client, and you therefore will draw it out when you take the witness.... Note the usual cross-examinations by good practitioners, and you will find that in a large proportion they ask hardly any questions except such as are now our special subject. In most cases they see intuitively that there is no very distorted statement to be rectified, and that there are no serious mistakes to be corrected; and they only make the witness reenforce their side as to some detail.... While the kind of cross-examination now in hand is the most important of all, it is also the most easy. It requires no great skill. It will generally be well done if with patience you have had your client and his following to tell you all that the witnesses for the other side know in his favor, and you then question accordingly. As we leave this branch of the subject, we must ask you not to fall into the error of rating its place in practice by the short notice it has received from us. It is too simple to need much explanation. But if you stay at the bar, you will have increasing use for it, and after a while you will, as a general rule, prepare no other sort of cross-examination for the average witness. It is a larger field for your powers than appears at first; ... in short, the details relevant here are as varied and extensive as the entire possibilities of proof."

quietly while being shoed. The cross-examiner did not enquire further about the circumstances of the shoeing, perhaps fearing that he would make things worse by asking questions without knowing the answer. If questioned further about the details, the witness would have conceded that he had to hold the horse with a pair of pincers to make him stand, and that the horse had to be taken to an open lot and cast before he could be shoed.

Honest concessions can frequently be elicited from expert witnesses. For example, an expert physician who has testified on direct examination to a certain conclusion, based on the assumption that a growth was close to the patient's skin, might withdraw that conclusion of asked to assume that the X-ray showed that the growth extended down to the bone (For a description of a case in which this occurred, see Wellman, 1986, p. 119).

Hypothetical questions are frequently used to examine expert witnesses, and concessions can also be elicited by varying the hypothetical on cross-examination. Thus, an expert might be asked whether, if facts a, b, and c are true, consequence d would ensue. If fact c is in controversy, the cross-examiner can ask whether consequence d would still occur if fact c were absent. Hypothetical questions may be carefully tailored by an attorney and the expert prior to trial in order to permit the expert to give answers that appear favorable to the side that called her. Changing the question may elicit an answer with a different cast. Wellman even reports one instance when, on the direct examination of an eminent physician, the opposing lawyer had stated a carefully crafted hypothetical asking the physician whether he could say *"with positiveness"* that a proposition was true. The physician answered in the negative. But when asked by Wellman whether *in his honest opinion* the proposition was true, the physician gave a different answer (Wellman, 1986, p. 121).

HONEST CONCESSIONS: ADVERSARIAL AND INQUISITORIAL COMPARISONS

In comparing adversarial cross-examination with interrogation by a neutral in a non-adversarial setting, then it should be borne in mind that the adversarial setting contributes to the concealment of information. Lawyers prepare the witness for direct examination and rehearse them. This facilitates the slanting of testimony so that it reveals information helpful to the proponent while concealing information helpful to the cross-examiner. If adversarial cross-examination were replaced by a system of neutral investigation and interrogation, under which lawyers did not prepare witnesses for testimony, the concessions might come more freely. In fact, it might be wrong to even call them "concessions," since non-party witnesses would be less likely to become aligned with parties. The system in which witnesses are prepared and called by parties creates subtle incentives for otherwise neutral witnesses to be part of the team.

In assessing the two systems, one must also consider the fact that, though procedures exist for compelling witness testimony, these procedures are not perfect. Witnesses may be able to evade subpoenas or even discourage advocates from issuing them by hinting that they will give hurtful testimony. Hence an inquisitorial system that lacks the fearsome prospect of adversarial cross-examination may be more successful in enlisting the voluntary aid of truly neutral witnesses.

Of course, many witnesses are not neutral. Some are biased from the start, without any aid from the trial process. They have an interest in the lawsuit, either as parties, business associates, friends, or family. Is the adversarial system more successful in eliciting concessions from these witnesses? It might be so, if it leads to more vigorous questioning and if the fear of being exposed inhibits lying. However, the maxim "never ask a question unless you know the answer" means that a cross-examiner using a risk-free strategy will avoid asking for concessions unless the cross-examiner knows that she can prove the conceded fact to be true. When the cross-examiner takes a chance and seeks a concession without knowing it to be true, the results can be disastrous, as the anecdotes set forth in an earlier section illustrate.[27]

ADDING INFORMATION THROUGH USE OF A COURTROOM TEST

Cross-examination can also add information by use of a courtroom test, in which the examiner quizzes the witness about her knowledge of facts, or puts her perception or expertise to a practical test. The use of a courtroom test should be distinguished from questioning about testimonial defects based on information already known. If the cross-examiner knows that an expert has failed a medical board test, then asking about it on cross merely dramatizes the shortcoming. The evidence could be presented by another method. However, if the cross-examiner tests the expert by asking the expert the formula for carbon dioxide, then the answer will reveal new information.

Cross by use of courtroom tests is not limited to experts. A lay witness might be asked to demonstrate a testimonial capacity, such being able to read a sign in the courtroom without glasses or to estimate distances in the courtroom.

Courtroom tests can be dangerous, but they can sometimes work, as the following anecdotes illustrate.

[27] See *supra*.

Successful Courtroom Tests

The trial practice literature contains many examples of successful courtroom tests. Wellman tells the story of the doctor who was asked to put the skeleton of the foot into the ankle joint, and put it into the knee joint instead (Wellman, 1986, p. 104). He also tells an account of the hand-writing expert who was tested by being asked whether three handwriting exemplars were produced by the same person, and who failed by giving an opinion that they were, when in fact they had three different authors (Wellman, 1986, pp. 105–107). He also suggests asking expert witnesses to repeat the substance of complicated hypothetical questions posed by the other side in eliciting the expert's opinion, saying that witnesses are frequently unable to do so, though he warns of backfire in the case of the carefully prepared witness (Wellman, 1986, pp. 120–121). Wigmore even describes a case in which a lawyer brought a hidden skillet of pitch into the courtroom to show that the witness could not, as claimed in his prior testimony, have smelled burning pitch in a police barracks.[28]

The famous rote learning cross-examination in the Triangle Shirtwaist case is a variety of courtroom test (Wellman, 1986, pp. 69–72).[29] There, a witness, apparently one of low intelligence, gave a memorized account of a tragic fire. The cross-examiner asked her, in exactly the same words used earlier by the opposing lawyer, to describe what happened after a certain point. She repeated her narrative in exactly the same words use on direct examination. The cross-examination continued as follows:

Thereupon the subject was once more changed, and nearly a half hour was used in examination upon various matters relating to the fire. At the end of this second half hour the question was for the third time put, and the witness started with the same word and continued to narrate the story in precisely the same words that she had used before, except that she omitted one word. She was asked whether it was not the fact that she had omitted a word, naming the word. Her lips began to move and start the narrative to herself all over again, and when she reached the position where that word belonged she said; "Yes, I made a mistake; I left that word out." Q. "But otherwise your answer was correct?" She again began to move her lips, obviously reciting to herself what she had previously said, and then said, "Yes, otherwise my answer is correct."

---

[28] *The Witness that was able to Smell Pitch* Abbott Parry (1923, p. 923, p. 66), quoted in Wigmore (Wigmore, 1937, § 281 at pp. 634–635).

[29] As one example of a contemporary low-risk author who still has room for courtroom tests in some situations. See Mauet (1996, p. 263). Mauet suggests the Triangle Shirtwaist technique in a paragraph on "memorized or identical stories."

When the question was put to her for the third time the District Attorney vigorously objected, but was overruled. Another period of 20 minutes or more was used in examining her with relation to other matters, and then for the fourth time the question was put to her: "Will you please tell the jury what you saw and what you did after you first observed any sign of the flames?" She started with the same word, and continued her narrative, but again left out one word, this time a different word. Asked whether she had not now omitted a word, naming it, she went through the same lip performance and replied that she had, and upon being asked to place the word where it belonged, she proceeded to do so.

There was no further examination of that witness. There were no more tears in the jury box. The situation had entirely changed. The witness had not hurt, but had very materially helped, the defense; she had succeeded in casting grave suspicion on the testimony of many of the girls who had previously testified; her carefully prepared story had aroused the suspicion of the jury regarding the entire case of the prosecution.

Courtroom Tests that Backfired

The courtroom test can be a high-risk procedure. It can backfire badly if the witness passes the test. Wellman gives the example of a handwriting expert who spectacularly passed the test, revealing in the process that the expert knew the lawyer's handwriting better than the lawyer did himself (Wellman, 1986, pp. 129–130). The following anecdotes also illustrate the danger of backfire:

Trying On the Bloody Glove in the O.J. Simpson Case

A notorious backfire occurred during the O.J. Simpson case, a televised trial in which a sports celebrity was accused of murdering his ex-wife and another person.[30] Chris Darden, a young prosecutor, took a chance, after being egged on by veteran defense lawyer F. Lee Bailey (Toobin, 1996, p. 366), and asked that the defendant try on a bloody glove connected to the crime. The defendant struggled with the gloves, which seemed to be too small (pp. 367–368). This demonstration was a dramatic disaster, one that led to the defense's refrain on closing argument, "If it doesn't fit, you must acquit." If the *defense* had staged the exhibition the jury would have been more suspicious. The prosecution could more

---

[30] Technically, the backfire did not occur during cross-examination, since the defendant did not testify. The prosecution's decision to invite the physical test is, however, illustrative of the dynamics of a cross-examination backfire.

effectively then have done what I did in the real case as damage control: that is get a new pair of gloves of the same size, make and model and have someone else place them on Simpson's hand (p. 369). It could effectively have argued that the defendant had cocked his thumb to prevent the gloves from going on or that the latex gloves he wore underneath (because the bloody gloves were a biohazard) had been put on only partially in a way that impeded the other gloves. It could have argued more effectively that the evidence gloves could have shrunk when left overnight in moisture at the crime scene; and they would have been more effective in pointing out that the defendant was able to take off the gloves in a flash.[31]

"Let the jury see you write" (Wickersham, 1938, quoted in Wigmore, Evidence, § 1368 at pp. 53–54)

> [The pivotal witness against the defendant was an "Eskimo" whose physical appearance was not very impressive to Judge Wickersham.] Everybody in the courtroom felt that his testimony would be utterly destroyed by cross-examination, and especially on the statement he made in support of his certainty of the date because "me lote (wrote) it in me log." Obviously the next inquiry was clear and smashing. "How do you know it was June 7th, maybe it was June 10?" During this direct attack on his principal and apparently helpless old witness, the prosecuting attorney sat silent and unconcerned with the same peaceful look on his face that the cat is said to have on its face after eating the canary. The old chief again repeated *"me lote (wrote) it in my log."* Instantly one of the lawyers for the defense picked up a piece of paper from the clerk's desk, placed it with a pen and an inkstand on a small table before the jury, and said in a sharp and rather boastful tone; "So you can write, can you; well, come over here and let the jury see you write." It was a tense and dramatic moment, for everybody present seemed to know that the old Eskimo could *not* write, and it was a body blow to the prosecution if he failed.
>
> The native seemed to know instantly what was demanded of him when he was offered the pen, and the attorney waved his hand toward the paper on the little table before the jury. He shuffled his ill-smelling clothes for a moment, gave us all a childlike smile, then grasped the pen in his hand, moved over to the table facing the jury—and *wrote his name in a clear and legible script*—in Russian! The old chief looked up at the attorney with his ever-lasting smile. The attorney said, "That will do," and sat down. The cross-examination was over!

Courtroom Tests Using the Low-Risk Strategy

While courtroom tests will trip up the sham expert and perhaps the witness of very low intelligence, there is a great danger of backfire in

---

[31] Darden's biography, addressing the issue, implicitly concedes it was a disaster, and Darden asks himself how he could have done that after telling his trial advocacy students never to ask a question unless they knew the answer. See (Darden, 1996, p. 326). Cf. Vincent Bugliosi (1996, p. 147).

other situations. The lawyer pursuing a low risk strategy will hesitate to use courtroom tests unless their outcome is known or they can do no harm. If their outcome is known, then cross-examination has not contributed anything unique because the underlying knowledge could have been presented instead. In some circumstances, however, courtroom tests that can do little or no harm can sometimes produce useful additional evidence. An example might be asking the witness who has testified to distances to relate the distances to objects in the courtroom. The cross-examination might be seen as merely an attempt to clarify the evidence, not to test the witness's capacity, so the danger of backfire is reduced.

Another low-risk test is the attempt to expose memory lapse or fabrication by asking about surrounding details that are not an essential part of the occurrence in question, but that the witness should remember if the witness remembers the occurrence itself. While there is a danger of reinforcing the direct or of tedium, if the witness answers accurately about such facts the result is not disastrous, while incorrect answers can have strong impeaching effect. For example, the witness who testifies that the defendant was home for the whole month of April might be asked whether the defendant was home on other months (for a successful use of this technique, see Langhorn's Trial (Howell's State Trials, 1679, VII, 452), quoted in Wigmore, 1937, § 248, p. 520). A witness who purports to have recognized an acquaintance's body by the absence of certain teeth might be asked whether specific other acquaintances had missing teeth and, if so, which teeth were missing.[32] Inability to answer would throw doubt upon the claim that he knew about the dead person's missing teeth, but correct answers are not a complete disaster. A witness who claimed to have visited a certain house might be asked to describe the contents of the house.[33] While there is some danger of backfire, the harm would not be great nor would it be accompanied with humiliation for the lawyer.

In short, the degree of danger to the cross-examiner partly depends upon the degree to which the test is presented as a challenge to the witness, and the degree to which it can be slipped in through the back door while seemingly examining about something else. In Wellman's example of the doctor who was unable to put the foot in the ankle joint, the request to do so would not necessarily have backfired even if the witness had

---

[32] For a description of a trial in which a witness failed this test, see *Hillmon v. Insurance Co.* (as summarized by Charles S. Gleed, in the 18th Annual Report of the Kansas State Superintendent of Insurance, 1887, quoted in Wigmore, Science § 248 at pp. 529–530.)

[33] For a vivid description of a trial in which a witness flunked this test, see John H. Surratt's Trial (American *State Trials*, IX, 1, p. 289, quoted in Wigmore, Science, § 48 at pp. 528–529).

been able to do the task successfully. For the cross-examiner could have used the exhibit with the foot in the ankle joint as an illustrative aid in questioning the expert about his client's theory of the nature of the injury. Similarly, asking a witness to spell and define technical terms[34] (or to pronounce them) could be done incidentally while examining the witness about another matter, so that if the witness succeeds then the jury will not know that it was a test. Similarly, a witness might be asked about distances by reference to locations in the courtroom, and only if the witness's estimate was far from a previous estimate expressed in feet would it be necessary for the lawyer to reveal that part of the objective was conducting a test.

It seems likely that adversarial incentives cut both ways in encouraging and discouraging the use of courtroom tests. Tests will be eschewed if they raise dangers of backfire. On the other hand, adversaries will spend more energy and thought on clever ways to trip up the witness. The neutral may be more respectful and, in the case of an expert who is called by the neutral and treated as a colleague, more reluctant to do anything that might embarrass the witness. The neutral-dominated system may be less effective in tripping up incompetent experts while at the same time more effective in enlisting the cooperation of distinguished experts who have an occupation other than testifying in court.[35]

ADDING INFORMATION BY AN ASK AND INVESTIGATE STRATEGY

Sometimes cross-examination will yield leads that can be investigated.[36] The deliberate use of cross for this purpose, however, is less likely in modern civil cases because of the risks involved and the availability of discovery for the same purpose. In criminal cases the risks alone are likely to deter prospecting for leads except in the most desperate cases, and the shortness of the ordinary criminal trial is another limit to its usefulness.

---

[34] Mauet suggests asking experts to spell and define technical terms, warning however of the danger of backfire. See Mauet (1996, p. 267).

[35] For other useful observations on differences in the scrutiny of expertise under the two systems, see the chapter by Van Koppen and Saks in this volume.

[36] See, e.g., Brown excerpt quoted in Wigmore (1974, § 1368 at p. 39, witness testified on cross that he weighed arsenic by shot and found some missing, lawyers gathered samples of shot from local grocers, finding that different parcels of shot varied more in weight than the weight of the allegedly missing arsenic). The cross-examination of Fuhrman in the O.J. Simpson case also helped produce extrinsic evidence. Though the defense had some evidence of racist statements by Fuhrman, the best evidence did not come to light until after the cross-examination. See Rosenberg (1995, pp. 3–4). In televised trials that are lengthy and notorious, it may be reasonable to expect new evidence to come to light as a result of public viewing of the cross-examination.

There is simply not much time to investigate leads except in a few prolonged cases.[37]

Concentrated proceedings are not an inherent feature of an adversarial system, since it is possible to have party control of pleading and proof in segmented proceedings. Concentrated proceedings are, however, associated with the overall institutional context of the adversarial system, where a coordinate ideal of government leads to use of lay decisionmakers, and lay decisionmakers prefer concentrated proceedings.[38] And whatever the reason, in adversarial systems, whether the trial be to judge or jury, concentrated trials are more common than in inquisitorial systems (Damaška, 1997).

In the inquisitorial system, it appears that the process of adjournments allows more follow-up. According to one prominent commentator, this is the reason why the adversarial system's technical rules about hearsay and authentication are absent or muted in an inquisitorial system (Damaška, 1997). There is time to check out the authenticity of documents and the source of hearsay between meetings. Obviously the same principle would apply to leads developed in interrogation in the inquisitorial system. The existence of *de novo* appeals in some systems would add to the amount of time in which new evidence could be developed.

My focus on adversarial versus inquisitorial interrogation at trial encompasses only a small part of the overall truth-finding process. Other trial and pretrial events, such as police interrogation, questioning on direct examination or during depositions and other hearings, formal pretrial discovery, and informal investigation also provide opportunities for discovery of information to provide leads that might be followed. Functionally, the important question is what the overall opportunities for discovery are, not what the opportunity is at a particular phase of the proceeding. Other issues, such as the motivation of the participants and the availability of resources, are also important. These matters are beyond the scope of this chapter.

ADDING INFORMATION WITH OTHER STRATEGIES

The methods listed above do not completely exhaust the ways in which cross-examination might elicit new information, but they probably constitute the principal means. At the least, it may be said that the

---

[37] In the prolonged and highly publicized O.J. Simpson case, evidence of Fuhrman's racism emerged during the course of trial. See *supra*.

[38] See Damaška (1986, p. 62, "An organization composed of part-time laymen prefers to dispose of judicial business in a continuous block of time ... [I]f proceedings were of the installment variety, by the time of the next episode it could be inconvenient or impossible to reconvene ..."). Damaška also states (pp. 51–52) that, in hierarchical systems, a bureaucrat prefers to work in installments in order to have time to reflect and investigate.

instances of successful cross-examination offered by two classic writers and by several modern ones can be categorized in those categories—to the extent that cross-examination actually reveals new information, as opposed to dramatizing what is otherwise known. Many of the other examples are either quirky—as in giving the insane witness enough rope to hang himself[39] or just another form of drama, as in the many instances of repartee reported by Wigmore (1974, p. 50, 52, often repartee in which the lawyer takes the worst of it).[40] Other examples are oil strikes that are the result of the type of wildcatting unlikely to be employed by one using the low-risk strategy, or even by a lawyer who merely obeys the rule that cross-examination questions must have a good faith basis.[41]

PROPHYLACTIC EFFECT OF CROSS-EXAMINATION IN DETERRING DECEPTION

Cross-examination may also add something by deterring deception, just as the polygraph can induce truth-telling because the subject believes it works. Judge Posner speculates that "The significance of cross-examination is often misunderstood, and its social value consequently underappreciated, because of failure to consider the deterrent effect of the right of cross-examination. Because cross-examination *can* destroy a witness's credibility, it rarely does so in practice and is mistakenly denigrated. The witness whose credibility would be destroyed by cross-examination will not be called at all or will try to pull the sting of the cross-examination by acknowledging on direct examination the facts that a cross-examiner could be expected to harp on" (Posner, 1999, p. 1490).

One mechanism that could cause this deterrent effect is the witness's fear of the commit and contradict strategy. For example, in the case of the personal injury plaintiff, the fear that the opponent has evidence that would contradict the claims of disability may cause the witness to agree with the questions on cross about activities of the witness.

Sometimes even the witness who comes prepared to brazen it out will change his mind after a few hard blows, for fear that the examiner

---

[39] Wellman (1986, p. 186) asked for "whole truth," witness describes paranoid fantasy; Wigmore (1937, § 281) witness thought legs made out of red sealing wax.

[40] Wellman (1986, p. 45, on cross, Whistler conceded he painted Nocturne in two days, asked "the labor of two days then is that for which you ask 200 guineas." The witness answered "No. I ask it for the knowledge of a lifetime").

[41] See, e.g., Wellman (1986, pp. 144–145): witness claimed to be ignorant and illiterate. Lawyer took shot in dark and asked, "Were you not a Rabbi in the old country?" to which witness replied, "I don't remember." See also Wigmore's (1937, § 266 at pp. 591–94) description of cross of Fleming.

knows more. For example, in a case defended by Alan Dershowitz in which members of the Jewish Defense League were accused of terrorism, a JDL member who had been cooperating with the police in return for leniency had secretly tape recorded certain conversations he had with a police officer. The crucial statement by the officer was not on the tape, however. The defense decided to keep the existence of the tape secret. The first stage of the defense strategy involved allowing the officer, Parola, to believe that there were no tapes of his conversations with the defendant, Seigel, and that he "could lie with impunity in the expectation that his testimony would be contradicted only by Seigel's own words. We would elicit answers from him that we knew—while he did not—would be exposed as lies by his own words as recorded by the hidden tape machine" (Dershowitz, 1982, pp. 52–54). Then in the second phase the cross-examiners quoted to him verbatim statements that he had made that were on tape, allowing him to infer that he had been tape recorded. Then they asked him about other statements the defendant said he had made but which were not on tape, hoping that he would fear that they were on tape and admit them (pp. 52–54). They put cassette tapes on the table along with boxes of "transcript." When they started quoting exact language to the officer he began to get cautious, saying things like "I don't remember, it sounds familiar." "I possibly would say something like that" (p. 55). The government asked for disclosure of the tapes and the court refused. Then, in a controversial tactic, the defense pretended to read from what seemed to be a transcript of the tape and asked a question about whether he had made a crucial statement to the defendant, getting the answer that it "sounds familiar" (pp. 58–59). The lawyers may have gone too far by indicating by mannerisms and conduct and the apparent verbatim nature of the statements that they read that they had recordings when they did not, but even without that they would probably have been in a position to get additional admissions from the witness once he discovered they had tapes of at least parts of the conversations.

Recognizing the prophylactic effect of cross-examination, Wellman states that "Sometimes … it is advisable to deal the witness a stinging blow with your first few questions … it makes him afraid of you and less hostile in his subsequent answers, not knowing when you will trip him again and give him another fall. This will often enable you to obtain from him truthful answers on subjects about which you are not prepared to contradict him" (Dershowitz, 1982, p. 134). Others advise seeking concessions first, then delivering the blows (Mauet, 2000).

It seems likely that adversarial cross will have more prophylactic effect than either neutral cross or impeachment without cross-examination. But it may also have a discouraging effect on the cooperation of honest witnesses who, despite their good faith efforts to be accurate, fear being embarrassed on cross-examination.

STUDIES COMPARING HEARSAY EVIDENCE TO CROSS-EXAMINED EVIDENCE

There is a growing literature of studies that try to assess the impact and sometimes the probative value of hearsay evidence (Bull Kovera, Park, & Penrod, 1992; Golding, Sanchez, & Sego, 1997; Kandel, 1994; Landsman & Rakos, 1991; Miene, Borgida, & Park, 1993; Miene, Park, & Borgida, 1992; Paglia & Schuller, 1998; Pathak & Thompson, 1999; Rakos & Landsman, 1992; Schuller, 1995; Schuller & Paglia, 1999; Thompson & Pathak, 1999). The question of the value of cross-examination is basically the same as the question of the value of hearsay, since the principal rationale of the hearsay rule is that it protects the right of cross-examination. The alternative to cross-examined testimony is hearsay statements used testimonially.

Unfortunately for the author of this chapter, no one has come close to doing a definitive study, and one could argue that no one has even made a good start. Doing a study of the helpfulness of cross (or the harmfulness of substituting hearsay evidence, which is the same question) is quite a challenge. If used to show something about the value of cross-examination, the hearsay studies are hard to generalize to the courtroom situation.

First, the hearsay studies do not seek to examine a representative sample of the population, except for the population of jurors. In the better studies, realistic courtroom stimuli are videotaped, and then shown to a random sample of juror subjects, who render verdicts and fill out recall measures.[42] There is no attempt, even in these studies, to have representative witnesses and cross-examiners. The cross-examiner is typically one person. The cross-examination she conducts may or may not be typical of cross-examinations; it might be exceptionally adroit or exceptionally poor. The cross-examiner may not be a lawyer at all, or may be a lawyer following a predetermined text set by the experimenters. The same may be said of the witness subjects. They are few in number, not chosen from a random sample, and hence not necessarily representative. They may or may not react to cross-examination in a way typical of witnesses.

Second, the hearsay studies do not attempt to examine situations in which the witness is engaging in deliberate deception. The witnesses are either playing a completely make-believe role, or they are witnesses who

---

[42] Several studies do not go this far, and are basically paper-and-pencil tests where the stimuli are written descriptions of simulated trials, rather than videotapes of simulated trials.

have made an honest mistake on a matter such as the description of a suspect (Miene et al., 1993). Hence the role of cross-examination in revealing deception has not been studied at all by social psychologists. Were it to be studied, the investigators would face the same obstacle faced by those who have sought to study lie detection by demeanor cues or by polygraph: it is difficult to give the experimental subjects the same motives and same emotional stakes as witnesses have in actual courtroom situations.

Third, situational differences make it difficult to generalize about the effectiveness of cross-examination from a small group of experiments. The cross-examination of an expert witness differs from the cross-examination of a criminal defendant or a police officer. The cross-examination of a perjured witness with selfish motives for exaggerating a claim differs from the cross-examination of a neutral witness who has merely identified the perpetrator of a crime. The cross-examination of a child differs from the cross-examination of an adult. The intelligence of the witness, the witness's experience in court, the strength of the witness's knowledge, the witness's emotional makeup, and the witness's stake in the outcome are all relevant factors. Even if studies could be done that surmount other difficulties, they would still be hard to generalize across the variety of cross-examination situations.

CAVEAT: OTHER BENEFITS OF CROSS-EXAMINATION

This chapter's discussion of the merits of cross-examination has focused on the benefits of the procedure in improving the accuracy of verdicts. The discussion that follows will also assume that improving accuracy is the primary goal of the procedure. Nonetheless, it must be acknowledged that cross-examination can have benefits other than improving accuracy. First, it can reduce costs. Impeaching a witness out of the witness's own mouth is cheaper than calling other witnesses to prove the same facts. Second, the right to confront and question may have benefits quite apart from either accuracy or cost, such as showing respect for the dignity of the accused or providing a sense of participation.

THE COSTS AND HARMS OF CROSS-EXAMINATION

One of the principal costs of cross-examination is witness vexation. Lawyers ask witnesses embarrassing questions. Sometimes the questions contain assertions that are not true or that, though true, hurt the witness without much advancing the cause of truth-finding. Abuses are not entirely prevented by the requirement that the cross-examiner have a good faith basis for the question[43] or by protections against inflammatory or prejudicial questions (Federal Rules of Evidence 403 and 408). Some lawyers ignore these rules and get away with it; in any event, a good faith basis is not a requirement that the fact be more probable than not.

As with its benefits, the harms of cross-examination must be compared with the harms of alternatives. A party may be unfairly attacked quite aside from cross-examination—by the testimony of other witnesses, by opening statements and closing arguments, even in the lawyer's press conferences.[44]

It seems likely, nevertheless, that the attack on cross-examination is more harmful to vulnerable witnesses than an attack by other means would be. Moreover, even gentle and appropriate questioning may be harmful to vulnerable witnesses, for example children who have been subjected to sex abuse. And otherwise appropriate techniques may sometimes lead to mistaken verdicts, as where a lawyer defeats a witness in cross-examination while knowing that the witness is truthful (though it appears that the same thing might happen without cross-examination, for example where the impeachment takes the form of evidence about prior convictions of the witness).

Cross-examination, because it is feared, can also cause witnesses to stay away from the courtroom where they can, in one way or another, avoid testifying. Witnesses may succeed in avoiding testimony merely by denying to investigators that they have knowledge, by threatening to testify in a way that harms the party who might subpoena the witness, by leaving the jurisdiction, or, in the case of an expert, by simple refusal to accept an offer to testify. Just as cross-examination deters falsehoods, it can also deter truthful testimony because of a fear of its ordeal.

---

[43] See Lubet (1997, p. 148) noting the requirement of a good faith basis and giving an example of an unfair cross-examination containing details about drinking and running up a $12 bar bill. See also the description of the Marla Hanson case by Debra Baker (1999, p. 42), in which a disfigured rape victim was grilled about not wearing underwear.

[44] Debra Baker (1999, p. 55) contains the following examples: (1) In a case in which the victim was severely injured by insertion of a broomstick into his rectum at a police station house, the lawyer defending one of the officers charged with the crime suggested in opening statement that the injuries came from consensual sex and that another man's DNA had been found in the victim's rectum. After hearing three weeks of testimony, including testimony against the officer-defendant by four other officers, the defendant admitted ramming the broom handle into the victim's rectum and pleaded guilty to all charges, including sexual assault with a weapon. (2) In the "preppie murder" trial of Robert Chambers, the defense attorney, Jack Litman, portrayed the deceased victim (Levin) as a slut and "sought to enter Levin's diary into evidence, alleging it was relevant to show that the victim had a "kinky and aggressive" sex life. After reviewing what turned out to be little more than a date book, the judge said it had no relevance to the case and ruled it inadmissible. By that time, however, Litman's allegations about Levin had been widely publicized. Chambers eventually pleaded guilty to a reduced manslaughter charge."

CAVEAT: TRIAL CROSS-EXAMINATION IN THE CONTEXT OF ASSOCIATED PROCEDURES

This chapter has discussed the value of adversarial cross-examination at trial, not the value of the package of cross-examination plus depositions and/or grand jury appearances. The author has assumed that the cross-examination takes place after the usual trial preparation.

If the entire package is considered together, so that cross-examination includes not only questioning at trial but also on deposition, then the procedure has greater value in uncovering problems of memory and perception and uncovering honest mistake than this text has suggested. During a deposition, the party harmed by the witness's testimony will freely elicit concessions, seek unfavorable information, and ask questions without knowing the answer. The cross-examining attorney will assume that the opponent will put in the unfavorable information at trial, and use the deposition to find out what it is and prepare for it. The precepts of cross-examination at trial do not apply to cross-examination during a deposition. Thus, if the view that cross-examination at trial is not very valuable results in the substitution of depositions for trial testimony, then the *ex ante* effect on depositions will be that the parties will be less willing to take chances there (knowing that questions may backfire when shown to the trier of fact) and hence valuable information may be lost. This danger supports the rule that depositions are admissible only if the witness becomes unavailable or there are special circumstances.[45] However, if depositions were routinely admissible in lieu of trial testimony, the cross-examiner on deposition might assume that the opponent would still offer the live witness at trial for strategic reasons, thinking it would give the favorable testimony more impact. (The belief in greater impact would be stronger if the deposition were not videotaped or otherwise recorded in a fashion that simulates live testimony.) Therefore the opponent might still ask open-ended questions and try to find out information on deposition. Intermediate procedures that attempt to preserve the value of depositions while making their use at trial as substantive evidence more common could be considered. For example, the opponent could be empowered to demand live testimony in lieu of deposition, but only upon paying costs.

In criminal cases, depositions are more rare, and hence there is less danger of loss of the information gained stifling questions at depositions.

---

[45] Variants are worth considering. Depositions are admissible but trial testimony is also admissible, so that opponent would assume that the proponent would normally prefer to have trial testimony from the witness and would still try to find out what it was. Opponent could force testimony by paying costs.

But the substitution of hearsay for cross-examination there raises dangers that government entities might abuse their power by preparing tendentious hearsay in preparation for litigation, in a way hard to penetrate without cross-examination. And if the benefit of confrontation goes beyond giving the defendant a chance to produce facts that support a defense, these benefits will be denied also. Hence it is wise to hesitate before seeking to drastically curtail cross-examination in criminal cases on grounds that it often does not reveal new information but merely dramatizes what could be proved by other means.

CLOSING COMMENT

The question whether cross-examination is the "greatest legal engine ever invented for the discovery of truth" cannot be answered with any assurance. The dominant risk-free strategy limits the amount of new information contributed by trial cross-examination. It seems likely that the greatest legal engine for discovering the truth is discovery and investigation, not trial cross-examination. But trial cross-examination can sometimes commit a witness to a story that can be disproved conclusively, thus contributing new information by showing the witness to be a perjurer.

The adversarial context of cross-examination undoubtedly inhibits the asking of clarifying questions, because fear of backfire prevents advocates from delving into the unknown. Other parts of adversarial procedure may partly take up the slack. For example, lawyers ask clarifying questions at depositions in civil cases, and then present any information that helps them at trial.

In light-discovery civil and criminal cases, perhaps the movement to allow jurors to ask questions will aid in clarification. Perhaps, in high-stake criminal cases, it would be wise to appoint a lawyer to screen the jury's questions and to ask them, along with any necessary follow-up questions.[46]

Adversarial cross-examination probably does inhibit the flow of clarifying information from neutral witnesses. And it has other costs, such as vexation, that have been detailed in this chapter. But if the adversary has sufficient resources, it may be a better protection than neutral questioning against extreme impositions on justice through use of perjured testimony.

---

[46] I leave it to others to devise a name for this functionary, one that does not suggest association with either party or with the judge.

10

Children in Court

INGRID M. CORDON, GAIL S. GOODMAN, AND STACEY J. ANDERSON[1]

In legal proceedings, determination of truth is an essential component of true justice. Determining truth requires the careful examination of evidence. However, when the evidence is eyewitness testimony of a child, complex psycho-legal issues are raised: issues of children's comprehension, competence, accuracy, and emotional resilience, and issues of the legal system's ability to adapt itself to the needs of children so that truth can be ascertained.

The adversarial legal systems of the United States, England, Canada, and other common law countries, have traditionally dealt with these issues in ways that contrast with the procedures used in the inquisitorial legal systems of Continental Europe. Today, a blending of the two traditions is taking place in several countries. Such legal evolution is intriguing, all the more so because of the important role played by scientific research on child witnesses.

In this chapter, we focus on children's experiences in court and children's ability to meet the expectations that the adversarial legal system places on witnesses. At times children's needs, and the various modifications that have been developed to enhance the accuracy and reliability of children's testimony, place children's rights at odds with those of the defendant. We argue that the legal evolution now blending the adversarial and inquisitorial systems may benefit children and justice, and in particular the truth-seeking function of trials. We first discuss many of the

[1] We thank John E. B. Myers and Annika Melinder for their comments on an earlier draft of this chapter.

167

expectations placed on child witnesses when they testify in the adversarial system. In doing so, we review research relevant to children's abilities to meet these expectations. The research derives primarily from studies conducted in reference to criminal courts in the United States and England, and focuses heavily on issues that arise in prosecutions of child sexual abuse. We also review what is known about the emotional effects on children of participating in legal proceedings. We then contrast the expectations placed on children in the adversarial legal system with the expectations placed on children in variants of the inquisitorial legal system. We end with the suggestion that the advantages of both legal traditions should be integrated so as to optimize the efficacy of the fact-finding process and ensure the least emotional burden on the child.

BACKGROUND ON ASSUMPTIONS OF THE ADVERSARIAL SYSTEM

Historically, in the United States, doubts about children's competence and credibility typically prevented many children from participating in legal proceedings (Goodman, 1984). However, in 1975, the Federal Rules of Evidence declared that, "every person is competent to be a witness" (Myers, 1997). The Federal Rules and hundreds of court decisions have paved the way in America for an increasing number of children to participate in legal proceedings as witnesses.

Although many children can provide accurate and reliable testimony, at times child witnesses may appear confused, inconsistent, or contradictory on the witness stand. Saywitz and Snyder (1993) suggest that children's apparent inconsistency and confusion may have more to do with the discrepancy between the expectations for witnesses and the developmental needs of children than with children's ability to provide accurate information. Children's ability to provide optimal testimony is contingent upon not only children's strengths and weaknesses, but also the formal and informal procedures of the legal system and the sensitivity of those involved in the judicial process (Cashmore & Bussey, 1989; Saywitz & Snyder, 1993).

The adversarial legal system holds many implicit expectations of witnesses, including the expectation that witnesses have some knowledge of judicial processes; can understand the language of the courtroom, particularly attorneys' questions; can, if necessary, prove their competence to testify (e.g., possess the skills needed to communicate effectively and understand the difference between truth and falsehood); can, if telling the truth, withstand cross-examination; and can cope emotionally with the stressors inherent in taking the stand. These expectations, reviewed in turn next, can tax children's testimonial capacities, leaving them less capable of providing evidence and more vulnerable to system-related stress (Saywitz & Snyder, 1993). These expectations developed based on adult assumptions, language, and requirements, and not those of children.

CHILDREN'S KNOWLEDGE OF THE COURT

When a witness is called to testify in criminal court, it is expected that the witness understands the general framework of the legal process. However, even adults in the general public have little knowledge about the legal system (Banks, Malloney, & Willock, 1975; Farrington & Hawkins, 1979). Studies conducted with children and adolescents in the United States, Britain, Scotland, Italy, Canada, and France demonstrate age-related differences in children's understanding of the court, its proceedings, and its terminology (Aldridge, Timmins, & Wood, 1997; Berti & Ugolini, 1998; Flin, Stevenson, & Davies, 1989; Freshwater & Aldridge, 1994; Peterson-Badali, Abramovitch, & Duda, 1997; Pierre Puysegur, 1985; Saywitz, 1989; Saywitz, Jaenicke, & Camparo, 1990; Warren Leubecker, Tate, Hinton, & Ozbek, 1989). Although comprehension of court proceedings increases with age, research indicates that children move from a relatively complete lack of knowledge, to incorrect perceptions and assumptions, to relatively accurate comprehension (Saywitz et al., 1990; Warren Leubecker et al., 1989).

Children under 10 years of age understand little about the legal system (Warren Leubecker et al., 1989). Even adolescents who have had experience with the legal system lack an understanding of legal processes (Grisso & Lovinguth, 1982). Saywitz (1989) suggests that experience may actually reduce understanding of legal proceedings because children are presented with complex information in a confusing context. Lack of knowledge about the legal process may create misapprehensions and unnecessary anxiety. Flin et al. (1989), for example, found that most young children believed that courts are for "bad" people, that the child might be put in jail if not believed, and that witnesses were also on trial. Children's knowledge, or lack of knowledge, about the legal system can influence their performance on the witness stand. In a realistic courtroom setting involving direct and cross examination, children with greater legal knowledge provided more correct information to questions than did children with less legal knowledge, even when age was controlled statistically (Goodman et al., 1998).

In regard to children's understanding of the legal system, only a small proportion of young children know what a courtroom is (Warren

Leubecker et al., 1989). Young children typically describe court from the perspective of someone who has done something wrong (Saywitz, 1989). By age 10, the majority of children are familiar with the concept of a courtroom. However, the roles of legal professionals are rarely described correctly, and research indicates that some legal concepts develop sooner than others. For example, understanding of the concept of *judge* develops before the concept of *lawyer* and the concept of *jury* is one of the last concepts children comprehend (Perry & Wrightsman, 1991). The majority of 3-year-olds do not know anything about judges (Warren Leubecker et al., 1989). By age four, an understanding of the concept *judge* begins, although these children's understanding is primarily descriptive, such as that a judge dresses in black. Understanding of a judge's function begins to emerge in the third grade (ages 8–9 years), and by adolescence the concept of *judge* is fairly well established (Saywitz, 1989). As another example, children under seven typically do not understand what a lawyer does. Some children describe a lawyer as someone who loans money or decides who is guilty. By age 10, children begin to understand that an attorney prosecutes or defends the accused, although most 10-year-olds believe that the main function of lawyers is to defend, as opposed to prosecute, criminals (Warren Leubecker et al., 1989). Saywitz (1989) found that most young children lack an understanding of the roles of witnesses, and many young children believe that all witnesses tell the truth and that witnesses are always believed. An understanding of the function of juries does not emerge until the age of 10 to 12. Even at this age, however, children do not understand that, at times, the truth differs from what a judge or jury determines is the truth.

Children's misapprehensions and misunderstandings about the legal system can pose serious difficulties for their ability to provide accurate and consistent evidence in a court of law. If children are anxious because they feel that a courtroom is a place for "bad" people, that witnesses are on trial, and that they may go to jail if they do something wrong, the fact-finding process is jeopardized. In the adversarial system of the United States, most children (child victims and child bystander witnesses) are expected to take the stand, no matter how young or traumatized the child might be, and thus children's misapprehensions and misunderstandings can have serious implications. This is typically not the case in the inquisitorial system.

CHILDREN'S UNDERSTANDING OF LEGAL TERMINOLOGY

Another expectation of the adversarial legal system is that witnesses possess the language skills necessary to understand basic legal terms.

Brennan and Brennan (1988) point out that words "are the currency of the court" (p. 5), and lawyers are masterful language users who build their careers on words. The verbal skills of lawyers, however, can present a barrier to communication with children and adults (Perry & Wrightsman, 1991).

One of the concerns young children have about being in court is not being able to understand questions asked of them and not being able to provide answers (Flin et al., 1989). This anxiety on the part of children is justified because most children under 10 years of age do not clearly understand the terminology used in court. Stevens and Berliner (1980) argue that children in the legal system are regularly subjected to legal jargon that even parents do not comprehend. In addition, lawyers frequently use developmentally inappropriate and often confusing language, requiring children to answer questions that are both semantically and syntactically too complex for them to understand (Brennan & Brennan, 1988; Carter, Bottoms, & Levine, 1996; Perry, McAuliff, Tan, & Claycomb, 1995; Peters & Nunez, 1999; Saywitz et al., 1990; Saywitz & Snyder, 1993; Walker, 1993).

Brennan and Brennan (1988) identified several categories of questions that pose challenges to children, including the use of negatives, double negatives, multipart questions, complex syntax, and difficult vocabulary. Perry et al. (1995) found that multipart questions were the most difficult question form for all interviewees to answer, adults as well as children. When kindergarten (ages 5 to 6 years), 4th grade (ages 9–10 years), 9th grade (ages 13–14 years), and college students were questioned with multipart questions versus simple questions (with sentence length equated), use of the multipart question form reduced correct responses by nearly 100 percent. Full processing of some of the "lawyerese" question forms (e.g., passive voice, complex syntax, multipart questions) is not established until adolescence. Some linguistic forms, such as complex negation, continue to cause processing problems in adulthood (Walker & Warren, 1995).

In daily interactions, children are accustomed to conversations that contain a wide array of different language forms. Courts, however, allow only one of these forms (e.g., questions in which a lawyer asks the questions and witnesses are expected to respond), and this language form is strictly controlled by an established set of procedures. The language devices used in the courtroom involve structures, vocabulary, and language interactions that are seldom found in any other situation, making comprehension difficult for children. Even words that appear simple from an adult perspective, such as *before* and *after*, may pose difficulty for young children (Walker & Warren, 1995).

Children's errors reveal age-related patterns. Young children (under eight) frequently make auditory discrimination errors (e.g., "*jury* is that stuff ladies wear on their fingers and around their neck") and homonym errors (e.g., "a case is something to carry papers," and "parties are places for getting presents", Saywitz et al., 1990). Saywitz et al. (1990) suggest that these errors may reflect children's failure to realize that they have insufficient information to interpret legal terms. Further prompts for other possible definitions of terms such as "jury" failed to elicit any relevant responses from young children. However, when third (ages 8–9 years) and sixth graders (ages 11–12 years) were prompted for other definitions, 31 percent and 46 percent respectively, provided a second solution. Thus, older children recognized that the terms could have another meaning. The strategy chosen by most young children may have been to assume that they had sufficient information to make a correct interpretation of the legal terms, basing their decisions on familiar experiences (Saywitz et al., 1990).

Of particular concern is young children's tendency to answer questions that they clearly misunderstand. Young children have limited ability to monitor their comprehension of questions, and often fail to recognize that they do not understand a question (Dickson, 1981; Flavell, Speer, Green, & August, 1981; Markman, 1979; Saywitz et al., 1990; Saywitz & Snyder, 1993). In complex and unfamiliar settings such as a courtroom, children may have difficulty monitoring their understanding of legal terms and asking for clarification (Cosgrove & Patterson, 1978; Ironsmith & Whitehurst, 1978). Saywitz et al. (1990), for example, found that younger children tended to admit their lack of knowledge of a term but older children attempted to respond even when they did not know the definition. Legal-sounding phrases such as "what if anything," and "who else if anybody," designed to avoid the appearance of leading questions, can also pose difficulty for young children (Walker, 1993).

Adults make many assumptions when they carry on conversations with other adults, and carrying these assumptions over to conversations with children may result in miscommunication. It is not safe in the legal context to take words for granted with young children because they often fail to ask for clarification, repetition, or rephrasing of questions, especially when the speaker is an authority figure (Walker & Warren, 1995). Children also make assumptions about their adult conversationalists. For example, children often assume that adults are always informative, clear, and right (Bonitatibus, Godshall, Kelley, Levering, & Lynch, 1988; Grice, 1975). Teaching young children some basic social conversational rules and changing the ways in which adults elicit information may assist children in providing more accurate information (Cordon, 2000; Perry & Wrightsman, 1991; Walker & Warren, 1995).

Perry and Wrightsman (1991) and Walker and Warren (1995) offer suggestions that may avoid communication errors, suggestions that could be implemented in the adversarial legal system, but that typically are not.

These researchers suggest that legal terms should be defined for children in a way children can understand. Court personnel should use simple words and illustrate these words with concrete examples. Passive voice sentences should be avoided and replaced with more active voice phrases. Double negatives are particularly difficult for children to understand and should be avoided. Attorneys should avoid summarizing the child's testimony and then asking for a general confirmation of accuracy because children tend to categorize multiple statements into "generally" correct or "generally" incorrect and respond accordingly rather than examining each statement for correctness. In addition, questions should contain as few ideas as possible to generate better responses from children. Adult questioners should be alert to words that may have several meanings (e.g., case, charges, court). Walker and Warren (1995) argue that helping children overcome the difficulties they encounter in a forensic setting is the responsibility of the adults.

COMPETENCE EXAMINATIONS

The adversarial legal system also has the expectation that witnesses are competent providers of information, who understand the difference between truths and falsehoods, and understand the obligation to tell the truth. Federal Rule of Evidence 601 states that "every person is competent to be a witness." Thus, although a competency examination of children is not required by law, the issue of competence remains important when the witness is a young child. An attorney can challenge a child's competence, requiring the judge to make a competency determination. *Wheeler v. United States* (1895) outlined some of the elements that need to be considered in determining competency (Myers, 1992; Walker, 1993). Determination of competence includes assessment of the witness's capacity to observe events, adequate memory to recall events, ability to communicate, sufficient intelligence, ability to distinguish fact from fantasy, an understanding of the difference between the truth and a lie, and the appreciation that it is wrong to lie (Myers, 1992, 1997).

In the United States, the trial judge determines whether a child is competent to testify and has broad discretion regarding evaluation of competence (Myers, 1997). On rare occasions, a psychological evaluation may be conducted prior to the competency hearing to assist in the determination of competency (Goodman & Lloyd, 1988; Myers, 1997). Competency decisions are based on a child's answer to questions and overall demeanor. The party challenging a child's competence has the burden of establishing incompetence. When a child's competence is challenged, a competency examination is conducted, usually before the child is sworn in and outside of the presence of the jury. The manner in which the competency examination is conducted is largely at the discretion of the court (Myers, 1992, 1997).

Differentiating between truth and lies, and understanding the obligation to tell the truth in a court of law, are essential components of competency. The child does not need to comprehend the subtleties of truths and falsehoods. What is required is a basic ability to discriminate between truths and lies (Myers, 1997). The child must also demonstrate an understanding that it is wrong to lie, or that the child may be punished if he or she tells a lie in court (Haugaard & Reppucci, 1992). The child may be required to answer questions that indicate concrete knowledge, such as "Has your mother or father ever talked to you about telling the truth or telling a lie," and "Do you think it is a good or bad thing to tell a lie?" (Goodman & Lloyd, 1988).

In general, even young children can distinguish between truth and lies and between lies and mistakes if asked to do so in a concrete manner, using concrete examples (Siegal & Peterson, 1996). Bussey (1992), for example, found that young children appreciate the "naughtiness" of lying, and Haugaard et al. (1991) found that most young children understand that a child who made an inaccurate statement at the request of a parent or friend was telling a lie. However, children seem to find it easier to recognize the difference between truth and lies than to define these terms (Lyon & Saywitz, 1999; Pipe & Wilson, 1994). Asking children what the difference between a truth and a lie is may not allow children to demonstrate their understanding (Huffman, Warren, & Larson, 1999). Requiring children to define truth and lie may understate their competence, especially with maltreated children who tend to lag behind in their linguistic development (Hoffman-Plotkin & Twentyman, 1984; Lyon & Saywitz, 1999). Lyon and Saywitz (1999), for example, found that the majority of the maltreated children studied could identify truthful statements and lies, and understand that lying was wrong. However, maltreated children under seven years of age often could not define "truth" or "lie," nor could they distinguish between the two. Walker (1993) suggests that children should be given truth and lie examples from their everyday lives, such as, "What if your brother ate up all your mom's cookies and said you did it. Is he telling the truth or a lie?" It is also suggested that adult questioners ask children if it is a good or a bad thing to tell a lie and what the consequence of telling a lie is.

To be considered competent, children must posses a sense of the obligation to tell the truth and must understand that untruthful testimony can result in punishment (Myers, 1993). The child does not need to understand or believe in divine punishment for the telling of falsehoods in a court of law. Rather, children must understand that punishment may come from any source such as God, judges, or parents (Myers, 1997). Many children are aware of the importance of telling the truth in court. Flin et al. (1989), for example, found that the common justification for honesty among 6- to 8-year-olds was that lying could lead to being jailed or punished. By age 10, many children understand the importance of telling the truth to determine guilt or innocence.

In addition to competence examinations, several state courts in the United States recently ruled that so-called "taint hearings" can be held if there is some evidence that children have been suggestively interviewed. However, other United States courts have decided that taint hearings are unnecessary additions to competence examinations (Nunez & Krampner, 1999). Competence examinations and taint hearings potentially add to the number of interviews and court appearances child witnesses must endure. It has been argued that such obstacles to children's testimony should be eliminated and that the trier of fact should determine how much weight to place on the child's statements (Lyon, 1995; Wigmore, 1935/1976).

DIRECT-EXAMINATION AND CROSS-EXAMINATION

Another expectation for witnesses within the adversarial legal system is that they submit to direct- and cross-examination. The fact-finding process can be derailed when there is a mismatch between the demands of the courtroom and children's abilities to provide eyewitness evidence during direct- and cross-examination.

To briefly review the typical format of criminal court proceedings in the adversarial system, after the witness is sworn in, testifying begins with direct-examination. During the direct-examination, the witness answers questions from the attorney who asked the witness to testify. The purpose of direct-examination is usually to elicit information favorable to the party on whose behalf the witness testifies and convey this information to the jury. Questions asked in direct-examination are typically open-ended allowing for elaboration or extension (Brennan & Brennan, 1988). Leading questions are usually not allowed during direct-examination, although courts frequently permit leading questions with children who experience difficulty testifying due to fear, confusion, or embarrassment (Myers, 1992). Once the need for leading questions declines, however, use of leading questions should cease. Myers (1997) recommends that during direct-examination, prosecutors ask some of the questions used during competency hearings to dispel any doubts that the jury may have about the child's competency.

Cross-examination follows direct-examination. The cross-examiner controls the witness by requiring short specific answers and seldom asks why or how questions (Brennan & Brennan, 1988; Myers, 1997). Leading questions are permitted and frequently used, and attorneys are given wide latitude in their cross-examination of witnesses (Goodman, Golding, & Haith, 1984). Judges in the adversary system have authority to control cross-examination and to forbid unduly embarrassing questions. Indeed, in the United States, Rule 611(a) of the Federal Rules of Evidence (1975) states that "the court shall exercise reasonable control over the mode and order of interrogating witnesses and presenting evidence so as to [...] protect witnesses from harassment or undue embarrassment." Additionally, several states have laws that give judges the authority to protect witnesses. A New York statue, for example, states that "the judge presiding should be sensitive to the psychological and emotional stress a child witness may undergo when testifying" (N. Y. Executive Law, 1995, § 642-a 4). Judges in the adversarial system, however, are often reluctant to interfere with questioning (Goodman et al., 1992). Attorneys view the use of cross-examination as essential to the search for the truth, and they place great confidence that its use will uncover truth and unmask falsehoods (Myers, 1996). A study by Turtle and Wells (1988), however, found that cross-examination impaired children's ability to report witnessed events accurately.

The role of the cross-examiner is to disprove the case against his or her client. In an adversarial-system jury trial, attorneys' tactics during direct and cross-examination are aimed at influencing jurors' perceptions of child witnesses. Skilled prosecuting and defense attorneys often use jurors' preconceptions of children's characteristics and abilities to influence the jury's perception of the child. For example, the prosecuting attorney may emphasize the child's honesty and accuracy while the defense attorney may highlight the child's inconsistencies and suggestibility (Goodman et al., 1984). Also, attorneys may try to capitalize on children's limited language capacity to call into question the credibility of the child witness (Brennan & Brennan, 1988; Goodman et al., 1984). As mentioned earlier, attorneys may use complex grammatical forms such as double negatives, embedded clauses, or multipart questions to confuse the child.

Myers (1987) describes several of the techniques used by attorneys in the adversarial system to try to discredit child witnesses. One wonders if such techniques serve the ultimate goal of reaching the truth, when a child testifies. One technique, for example, involves asking a series of nonsubstantive questions to which the child will agree and then switching to substantive issues. The child is first asked a series of innocuous questions, the answer to which the attorney displays approval (e.g., "I hear you get good grades, is that right?" "You like music, don't you?"). Once the child is in a mode of agreeing, the attorney subtly moves toward asking more substantive questions designed to elicit favorable information (e.g., "Maybe that's how you thought it happened, but it could have been a little different, couldn't it?"), that is, information that contradicts what the child claimed before or that otherwise helps the attorney's case. The goal is to make the child less cautious in answering questions. Related to this technique is one where the attorney adds a "moderate" level of anxiety, with such questions as "You know you are not supposed to tell a lie, don't you? Do you get into trouble if you tell a lie?", that focus the child's attention on punishment. Attorneys realize that the things that make children anxious change with age and use this knowledge to adjust their intimidation tactics to be age-related. Three-to 5-year olds, for example, are believed to fear getting into trouble; 6- to 11-year-olds are believed to fear social embarrassment; adolescents are believed to fear issues that adversely affect their self-esteem.

Children's tendencies to be suggestible and to fantasize may be capitalized on by attorneys in court. By demonstrating that the child is suggestible or prone to flights of fantasy, the child's credibility in undermined. Questioning might include asking the child about a false event that the jurors know the child never experienced, or an attorney may ask whether cartoon or TV characters are real and can do things like fly.

Another technique tries to induce inconsistencies in children's testimony. The attorney asks leading questions that are designed to introduce changes in the child's account of what happened, asking about the events out of order of their occurrence while keeping two different lines of questioning open. The goal is to keep the child off balance to increase the chances of inconsistencies. Use of such techniques, meant to confuse and discredit child witnesses, have lead many to observe that a child is no match for a defense attorney in a court of law.

Brennan and Brennan (1988) argue that cross-examination is the part of court proceedings in which the rights and interests of the child are most likely ignored and sacrificed. The complexity of the language used, the use of highly restrictive leading questions, and the stress of testifying in an unfamiliar context can lead to an impaired ability to provide evidence, thus discrediting children's testimony before a jury. If the essence of justice is the determination of truth, then social scientists and members of the legal community must find ways of ensuring that both the language and the procedures used in courts of law assist, rather than hinder, children's ability to participate successfully in the fact-finding process.

CHILDREN'S ABILITY TO COPE EMOTIONALLY

Another salient demand of the legal system concerns the expectation that witnesses can cope emotionally with the stress of testifying about a traumatic experience while facing the defendant. These demands tax children's ability to testify and may affect their emotional adjustment and attitudes about the legal system later.

Thinking and talking about the stressful event itself, the event for which the child is called to testify against a defendant, may be disturbing and frightening to a child witness. Testifying against the alleged perpetrator of abuse can be accompanied by feelings of guilt and ambivalence, especially in cases of abuse by a family member or caregiver (Herman, 2000; Katz & Mazur, 1979). In our ongoing study of adults' recollections of their courtroom experiences in childhood, one young adult stated, "I cried and was worried. I wanted to back down." Another stated, "I was just trying not to be nervous. My parents were trying to calm me down and tell me it would be alright." One child tried to commit suicide for fear of testifying. In our earlier research, in which we observed children testifying in criminal court, we saw many children in tears on the stand, clam-up, refuse to testify, and need many recesses. Although further research is required, some children clearly have considerable difficulty coping with the stress of testifying.

Facing the defendant in abuse cases is the main fear expressed by children (Brannon, 1994; Goodman et al., 1992). In our study of children involved in child sexual abuse prosecutions, children who exhibited the most fear of the defendant were less able to answer prosecutors' questions (Goodman et al., 1992). Children who must confront their alleged perpetrators in open court are sometimes less willing to testify than are other witnesses (Goodman et al., 1998) and less able to provide clear, coherent testimonies (Goodman et al., 1992). Although these studies are not free of potential confounds, the accumulated findings of these and other studies provide evidence that facing the defendant hinders children's ability to provide clear and reliable testimony. In practice, Spencer (1989) states, requiring children to give evidence in front of the defendant causes acute distress to child witnesses. Spencer indicates that "time and time again there have been cases where children 'dry up' when called on to give evidence, or break down in tears. A report by the Magistrates' Association describes a case where a little girl tried to dive under the clerk's desk in fright when she first caught sight of the defendant. All this is bad for the child: and it is bad for justice, too, because when the child is unable to utter it means the court is deprived of an important source of evidence" (p. 117). The Dutch legal system addresses this problem by permitting any witness who is threatened, or feels threatened, to testify outside of the defendant's presence.

Finally, the intimidating nature of the courtroom setting (Saywitz & Nathanson, 1993) may affect children's ability to cope with testifying. The antagonism inherent in cross-examination in the adversarial legal system, which takes place in an imposing and authoritarian environment, can induce fear in child witnesses. Even when questioning of children is benign, testimony can be adversely affected by the intimidating atmosphere of the courtroom. Saywitz and Nathanson (1993) found that when children were questioned in a mock courtroom setting, as compared to the familiar surroundings of their own classroom, the children's ability to report from memory was impaired. The children in the mock courtroom setting also rated the experience of being questioned as more stressful than did the children in the classroom setting. Not only is the experience of being in the courtroom stressful in and of itself, which is unfortunate in terms of children's well being, but the impairment in memory accompanying that stress also may lower children's completeness and accuracy, hindering the fact-finding process. Nevertheless, this is what is often required of child victims and child witnesses within the adversarial system.

EMOTIONAL EFFECTS OF CHILDREN'S COURTROOM EXPERIENCES

What are the emotional effects on children of courtroom experiences? Brannon (1994) points to potential benefits to the child of having a forum in which to talk about the abuse episodes and be listened to by adults in authority. For some children under certain circumstances, this is a valid point. However, for other children under different circumstances, court experiences may add to their trauma.

It should be noted that when child victims initially become involved in prosecutions, they may be at a high point of distress (Goodman et al., 1992). It is unclear how much of the stress experienced by such children is a consequence of the victimization itself or of involvement in the legal system. Especially in the first couple of months of a legal proceeding, children's behavioral adjustment is poor relative to the adjustment they can achieve roughly three months or more into the proceedings. If the cause of the stress is indeed the fact of being involved in legal proceedings, the attenuation of children's distress may be due to acclimation to a new and arguably daunting experience imposed on traumatized children.

Most research has concentrated on the relatively short-term (up to three years post-testimony) effects of court experiences within the adversary system. In Australia, Oates and Tong (1987) found that, of 46 children whose sexual abuse cases went to court, most of the children (86%) were rated retrospectively by their parents as being very upset immediately after the hearing. Two and a half years after the prosecution, more than half of the children (57%) were reported as still upset about the legal case and/or to have persisting behavioral problems, compared to only 12 percent of those whose cases did not go to court. Methodological problems with this type of research preclude firm conclusions. Nevertheless, Oates and Tong's early research foreshadowed the results of newer research, which has shown that testimony in criminal court is associated with short-term distress in a sizeable subset of children (Goodman et al., 1992; Whitcomb et al., 1991). Additionally, the newer research has identified several factors associated with short-term distress in children who testified in criminal court. These factors include harsh courtroom treatment (e.g., aggressive or demeaning cross-examination), testifying multiple times, and lack of maternal support (Berliner & Conte, 1995; Goodman et al., 1992; Whitcomb et al., 1991). In contrast, Sas (1993) found that children's psychological adjustment, as rated by clinicians 3 years after criminal case closure, was unrelated to whether or not children testified.

Surprisingly little research exists on the long-term emotional and attitudinal effects of legal involvement, especially testifying in court. In our laboratory, we are currently conducting a prospective, longitudinal study of children who had been involved as victims of child sexual abuse in criminal court prosecutions. Preliminary analyses from this study indicate that, 12–14 years after legal involvement, testifying in the legal case was not significantly associated with mental health problems, at least as assessed by a subset of questions on the Brief Symptom Inventory (Quas, Redlich, Ghetti, & Alexander, 1999). However, children who testified versus those who did not reported significantly more acts of serious delinquency before turning 18 (Redlich et al., 2000). These findings must be qualified by the fact that cases involving incest or male victims were somewhat under-represented in the sample.

In summary, research indicates that court involvement (i.e., testifying in criminal court) in the adversary system is associated in the short-term (at least up to three years) adverse emotional effects in many, but not all, children. In the longer term, we can tentatively say that testifying may not be associated with adverse mental health effects overall, as indexed by items from one standardized measure of mental health, but is associated with greater criminality in adolescence and childhood. Within the next few years, as our study is completed, more will be known about the long-term effects of testifying in the adversarial system's criminal court.

ALTERNATIVE METHODS FOR OBTAINING AND ADMITTING CHILDREN'S EVIDENCE

THE ADVERSARIAL VERSUS THE INQUISITORIAL SYSTEMS

Given that research indicates negative short- and possibly negative long-term effects of legal involvement on some children, what has been suggested and what is being done to make the experience less traumatic? Various modifications and procedural reforms have been suggested. Saywitz and Snyder (1993) distinguish between two types of modifications that can help bridge the gap between the needs of children and the requirements of the legal system: "bottom-up" (child to adult) and "top-down" (adult to child).

Bottom-up modifications involve techniques and programs designed to prepare the child to face the challenges that testifying entails. Thus, the child is prepared to meet the demands of the adult legal system (child to adult). Bottom-up changes include preparing children for the cognitive, communicative, emotional, and social challenges they face as witnesses. A few examples of the bottom-up changes have already been provided in this paper (e.g., teaching the child conversational rules).

Top-down modifications, in contrast, involve changes in legal procedures to accommodate the needs of children and includes additional training for legal professionals. The adult legal system, therefore, is modified to meet the developmental needs of children (adult to child). Myers (1996) lists a number of top-down modifications and techniques that, when used in conjunction, may interact to provide child witnesses with the least distressing courtroom experience possible within the adversarial system. These modifications include admitting children's hearsay statements, allowing support persons to accompany child witnesses, excluding the defendant during a child's testimony, closing the courtroom to the public and press, and allowing closed-circuit television (CCTV) and videotaped testimony. Davies and Seymour (1997) further suggest a reduction in long delays in hearings, providing children with more control over how they give their evidence, debriefing children after the conclusion of the case, and placing greater expectations on judges and attorneys to understand and adapt to the special needs of children. Together, these complementary methods (bottom-up and top-down) can help bridge the gap between the needs of children and the requirements of the legal system.

Thus far, we have been concerned primarily with the adversarial legal system. However, other systems of law, particularly the inquisitorial systems, provide provocative examples of alternative procedures for child witnesses. These examples primarily involve top-down modifications in legal procedures. Therefore, in the next section of our chapter, after first describing a few bottom-up methods that have been attempted in the U.S. and Canada, we then turn to a discussion of some of the top-down procedures that illuminate some of the differences between the adversarial and inquisitorial systems of justice when dealing with child witnesses.

BOTTOM-UP PROCEDURES

Researchers have explored various "bottom-up" methods to elicit accurate and reliable testimony from children in contexts that are linguistically challenging. One important method involves child preparation programs (Peters & Nunez, 1999; Saywitz, Snyder, & Nathanson, 1999). These programs provide children with essential information concerning legal processes, enhance children's communication skills, and reduce anxiety. It should also be noted that the programs described in this section of the chapter do not require substantive preparation or rehearsal of the child's testimony, which may threaten the reliability of the report.

A formal program to prepare children for court was investigated by Sas and her colleagues (Sas, 1993; Sas, Hurley, Austin, & Wolfe, 1991) in Canada, a country that uses the adversary legal model. The program was designed to: (1) demystify the court process through education, and (2) reduce fear and anxiety related to testifying through stress reduction techniques. Although the preparation program was customized for each child, it typically included work with a courtroom model and dolls, role-play, use of booklets, familiarization of the child with court procedures, and a court tour. The child's anxiety was addressed through stress reduction techniques such as breathing exercises, muscle relaxation, and cognitive restructuring. Evaluation of the preparation program revealed that court preparation resulted in less fear, increased knowledge of court, and better performance when the children testified. Saywitz and Snyder (1993) argue that simply providing children with some legal knowledge and a tour of the courtroom, as is the more typical practice by attorneys, is insufficient in reducing stress and improving testimony. Sisterman-Keeney and colleagues (Sisterman-Keeney, Amachev, & Kastankis, 1992) state that traditional procedures used to prepare children for court do not prepare children well enough for the impact of the real experience: "Children who had seen the courtroom and knew the roles and positions of the court personnel still froze when they had to testify at trial" (p. 203, see Spencer & Flin, 1993, for a more complete discussion of court stressors and preparation of children for court). In the United States, it is unclear whether children are sufficiently prepared for testifying in court.

Two recent preparation programs, designed to facilitate children's communication and comprehension monitoring, have explored the use of two types of interventions: task demand training (TDT) and comprehension-monitoring training (CMT). With task demand training, children are instructed to tell the interviewer when they do not understand a question and are helped to understand that this action may cause the adult questioner to rephrase the question in a simpler form. With comprehension-monitoring training, children practice identifying instances of noncomprehension and verbalizing their lack of comprehension. Children also are taught the consequences of responding to questions that are not fully understood. Saywitz et al. (1999) found that 6- and 8-year-olds benefited from these interventions. In their study, children who were provided with TDT and CMT showed marked improvements in performance when compared to a control group. Peters and Nunez (1999) found similar results with preschool and kindergarten children.

In summary, bottom-up modifications such as child preparation programs can provide children with essential information about legal proceedings, thereby easing children's anxiety and fears. Additionally, preparation programs enhance children's communicative skills, helping them deal effectively with instances of noncomprehension, thereby enabling children to accurately convey their experiences in courts of law. Certainly, these modifications assist the fact-finding process by improving children's ability to provide accurate and consistent testimony while reducing the stress that is an inherent part of the adversarial system.

TOP-DOWN PROCEDURES

As mentioned earlier, top-down modifications to accommodate child witnesses involve changes in legal procedures. This is where we see the most important differences between the adversarial and inquisitorial systems.

An examination of various methods of obtaining and admitting children's evidence indicates that in countries that adhere to an inquisitorial system of justice, greater leeway is possible in children's treatment in legal cases. In the adversarial system of justice such as that in the United States, there are constitutional rights given to defendants, such as the right to face-to-face confrontation with their accusers, that must be balanced against the need to protect child witnesses. Constitutional concerns guide and limit procedural reforms.

Spencer (1989) describes several core differences between adversarial systems of justice and other (e.g., inquisitorial) systems, and these differences play important roles in affecting children's legal experiences. We focus on two of the differences here. One difference is a passive versus active role of the judge (in the adversarial system, the parties rather than the judge call the witnesses, and the judge serves as an umpire rather than as an investigator). Another difference concerns what qualifies as evidence and the rules that govern admission of evidence, which affects such matters as the need to establish competence of witnesses, the admission of hearsay, and admission of evidence of defendant's previous misconduct.

Concerning the different roles of the judge in the adversarial versus inquisitorial systems, Davies and Seymour (1997) suggest that greater expectations should be placed on judges in the adversarial system to adapt to the special needs of children. This suggestion points to a fundamental difference between the adversarial and inquisitorial systems of justice. The role of the judge in the adversarial system is in several ways more passive than that of the judge in inquisitorial systems, where in the former the judge acts as an impartial observer and final arbiter, and in the latter the judge acts as a more active seeker of truth and elicitor of information. In the adversarial procedural system, it is the duty of the prosecution and the defense to see that evidence is gathered and presented in court, although neither is obliged to present more than what is helpful to each side, so that the trier of fact can evaluate the evidence and decide the verdict. This process, it is posited, will generate all the information that is relevant to evaluate the case. Judges have the responsibility of ensuring that all the evidence admitted is gathered in a legal and proper manner, following strict rules of evidence (Crombag, 1997).

Although judges have authority to control proceedings and questioning of witnesses, Goodman et al. (1992) found that judges rarely intervened to ensure that developmentally appropriate language was employed or that harsh cross-examination did not take place. One judge in the Goodman et al. (1992) study did take steps to ensure children's comfort, by meeting the child at the courtroom door, and walking the child to and from the stand. This judge's cases, however, were later reversed on appeal precisely because the judge's behavior with the child, which took place in front of the jury, appeared to lack impartiality.

In contrast, Smith (1997) states that judges in Nordic countries (whose systems of justice are strongly influenced by inquisitorial legal processes) are legally obligated to seek the truth. Judges in common law countries are also obligated to ensure the truth-seeking function of the legal process. However, the duty to *actively* seek the truth is a requirement for judges that figures more prominently in inquisitorial proceedings and is set out in a number of codes of criminal procedure such as the *Code de procédure pénale* in France, the *Strafprozeßordnung* in Germany (Spencer, 1998), and the *Straffe prosess loren* in Norway (Melinder, 2000, personal communication). Although in the inquisitorial system questioning of witnesses and defendants is conducted by the prosecution and defense, appointment of and questioning of experts is done by the court using a written format. In Norway, child sexual abuse victims are normally questioned by the judge in the judge's chamber with counsel present. Additionally, the judge may appoint a clinical psychologist to conduct the forensic interview. When this occurs, prosecuting and defense attorneys may pose questions to the child through the clinical psychologist (Melinder, 2000, personal communication).

The legal system in France is also predominantly inquisitorial. In serious criminal cases, the *juge d'instruction* presides over a pretrial phase, or *instruction*, in which the defendant and witnesses are interrogated, their statements are recorded in written form, and a dossier of the case is prepared. The dossier and statements become the basis of the case against the defendant. In addition, the *juge d'instruction* is responsible for calling in expert witnesses when necessary, defining their tasks and supervising their work (Spencer, 1998).

Thus, although judges in both adversarial and inquisitorial legal systems are obligated to seek the truth, inquisitorial systems encourage judges to take a far more active role in the fact-finding process. In Nordic countries, this more active role on the part of judges permits the child witness to participate in the legal process in the less taxing atmosphere of a judge's chamber. In contrast, judges in common law countries are expected to remain impartial and thus take a more passive role. Although in the United States, the Federal Rules of Evidence (611, 1975) authorize judges to take an active role in the protection of child witnesses, judges are hesitant to exercise this authority. A more active role in the fact-finding process on the part of judges, in the adversarial system, would not only lessen the demands placed on children, but also possibly enhance children's ability to give evidence.

Perhaps the most fundamental differences between the adversarial and inquisitorial systems concern what qualifies as evidence and the rules that govern admission of evidence, which as mentioned earlier affects such matters as the need to establish competence of witnesses, the admission of hearsay, and admission of evidence of defendant's previous misconduct. As Spencer (1998) points out "the legal systems of France, Germany, Scandinavia, and Israel all provide for the evidence of children to be taken in advance of trial, stored, and eventually presented to the court at trial in the form of a written transcript or a tape of the earlier examination" (p. 118). In England, where the tradition is adversarial but with newly adopted, inquisitorially inspired procedural reforms for children's testimony, videotaped forensic interviews are now shown at trial in place of children's live testimony, with closed-circuit television (CCTV) used for purposes of cross-examination. However, in the USA, the sixth Amendment of the Constitution dictates that the accused has a right to face-to-face confrontation and cross-examination of the accusing witness, even if the witness is a child. This has traditionally been interpreted as requiring live testimony in court with the witness being subjected to cross-examination. Debate in the USA has centered on the interpretation of face-to-face confrontation; a U.S. Supreme Court decision permits the use of testimony via CCTV for child witnesses under certain prescribed circumstances (*Maryland v. Craig*, 1990).

Research on CCTV largely supports its use. Several authors have highlighted the benefits of non-face-to-face confrontation, such as one-way mirrors, CCTV, or videotaped testimony (Davies & Noon, 1993; Lindsay, Ross, Lea, & Carr, 1995; Whitcomb, 1992), although these procedures are accompanied by their own set of problems. Children often feel more relaxed and less intimidated by non-face-to-face forms of testifying, and this in turn helps them be more accurate in their reports. However, juries tend to find children testifying via CCTV to be less credible, less attract-ive, and less intelligent, and to sympathize with the children less than when children testify in open court (Goodman et al., 1998). Davies (1999) summarizes his view of the diverse findings on the topic as follows:

> Jurors may show a preference for live evidence but the positive attributional effects appear to be short-lived and do not survive the deliberation process. The main function of CCTV appears to be to allow younger and less assertive children to "have their day in court" and allow the jury to hear and weigh evidence in a way that is often not possible in the traditional courtroom setting. (pp. 251–252)

In the United States, balancing the needs of child witnesses with the accused's right to confrontation must be carefully considered when con-templating the use of non-face-to-face forms of testimony. Moreover, to the extent that protective measures may weaken children's credibility, the final outcome of the case may be adversely affected from the child's point of view. Israeli legislators long ago enacted provisions to ensure children were spared the distress of courtroom experiences (Sternberg, Lamb, & Hershkowitz, 1996), but Israel is now in the process of reverting back to children's live courtroom testimony partly out of concern that case out-comes are negatively affected when children do not testify live in court (Hershkowitz, 2000, personal communication).

A related issue concerns the admission of hearsay at trial. Hearsay "is a statement, other than one made by the declarant while testifying at trial or hearing, offered into evidence to prove the truth of the matter asserted" (Federal Rules of Evidence 801(c)). In child abuse cases, this means that a child's words are hearsay when: (1) while not in the courtroom, the child stated that something happened (e.g., that the child was abused); or (2) the child's statements are repeated in court (e.g., by an adult or via a video-taped forensic interview) to prove that what the child said earlier actually happened. In the adversarial system, hearsay is constrained by the rules of evidence, but can be admitted in certain circumstances. For instance, an exception to the rules against hearsay can occur when a child has made statements to a medical professional. In this case, a judge may decide that the hearsay has sufficient "indicia of reliability" because it is assumed that people are more likely to be honest when seeking medical care than they might be at other times. If a child's hearsay does not fit into a traditional exception, the hearsay still may be admitted under a residual or child hearsay exception if the judge decides that the hearsay is sufficiently reliable to be used in court. In contrast, in the inquisitorial system, hearsay is liberally admitted, and indeed may be the primary evidence. Such hearsay could include a forensic interviewer testifying in place of the child, admission of a videotaped forensic interview, or written transcripts of the child's former statements.

Recent research indicates that witnesses providing hearsay may not always be able to recount a child's statements verbatim, although they are more likely to be accurate about the gist of what the child said. Also, witnesses providing hearsay may not always be accurate in their memory of how they questioned a child, for instance, whether leading questioning was used (Bruck, Ceci, & Francoeur, 1999; Warren & Woodall, 1997). Moreover, it is presently unclear how much weight jurors give to the testimony of adult witnesses who repeat children's out-of-court statements (Golding, Sanchez, & Sego, 1997; Goodman et al., 1998; Warren, Nunez, Keeney, Buck, & Smith, 2001). Thus although the introduction of hearsay at trial may help attenuate the short-term negative effects on children of testifying in court, it too, like CCTV, is also not without its own set of problems.

As a consequence of the adversarial system's strict rules governing the admission of evidence, the conduct of the trial can dramatically differ across the adversarial and inquisitorial systems, leading one commentator from an inquisitorial country to state (in assessing the demands placed on children in the adversarial system), "I was appalled" (Smith, 1997). Although as mentioned earlier, hearsay evidence is common in United States criminal prosecutions of child sexual abuse, hearsay in United States prosecutions is typically used in conjunction with children's live testimony in court (Myers, Redlich, Goodman, Prizmich, & Imwinkelried, 1999). In contrast, in continental European countries, such as Belgium, Germany, Netherlands, and France, where civil/inquisitorial law procedures are utilized, the defendant and his or her counsel are never permitted to confront the child victim/witness directly in child sexual abuse cases (Crombag, 1997). Also as mentioned earlier, hearsay evidence plays a crucial role in the criminal proceedings within the inquisitorial legal systems. Generally, in the inquisitorial system most proceedings are decided on the basis of written documents (e.g., statements of witness testimony taken by the police or the investigating judge prior to the trial, written reports by expert witnesses). In Nordic countries, although older children

(12 years and older) may testify in court, younger ones are videotaped during forensic interviews (with defendant's counsel in another room viewing the questioning and able to have the police officer ask additional questions), and the videotape is presented at trial. This may also occur for older children if the crime was particularly distressing (Smith, 1997).

Another potentially important difference between the adversarial and inquisitorial legal systems, in addition to those mentioned by Spencer (1989), concerns the amount of pre-trial interviewing and investigation that occurs. The child's experience during forensic interviews can either help the child adjust positively or further intimidate an already traumatized child; additionally, it can also elicit information from the child that can either increase or decrease the child's credibility when on the witness stand.[2] In Korea, relatively little pre-trial interviewing occurs (Shin, 1974). According to Van Koppen (2000, personal communication), "In the Dutch system, the child is interviewed as soon as possible, by a trained police officer in a special interrogation "studio", and the interview is taped. The child is not interviewed again ... I know of only one exception, in which the court, in closed chambers, reinterviewed a child. That is only done because Dutch judges are well aware that interviewing the child again will not contribute to truth finding." One of the benefits of interviewing and videotaping the child's testimony soon after disclosure is that there is less chance of memory fade and memory contamination (McGough, 1994). These procedures stand in contrast to the extensive investigation and interrogation of children, and long time delays, so common in the American adversarial system.

In summary, consideration of the differences between systems of justice reveals alternative methods of enhancing children's ability to provide accurate and reliable testimony, without jeopardizing the fact-finding process or the demands of justice. Inquisitorial legal systems reduce the demands of testifying on children by permitting them to provide evidence in advance of trial (e.g., videotaped testimony, written transcripts, testimony of a forensic interviewer) and, at least in some countries, minimizing the formal pre-trial evidence gathering. Although these modifications must be carefully considered, adoption of some inquisitorial procedures would reduce the demands placed on child witnesses.

---

[2] Since 1998 the Norwegian legal system has also instituted a new procedure, play observation, as an alternative method of communicating with, and obtaining forensic information from, young children. This controversial approach was not designed to replace the standard forensic interview; rather this method was introduced to supplement standard interviewing techniques. Research, however, will be necessary to determine the effectiveness of this alternative procedure in Norway (Melinder, 2000, personal communication).

CONCLUSIONS

Involvement in the adversary system poses several major challenges to child witnesses. In our chapter, we have focused on children in child sexual abuse cases, because it is in such cases that children are most likely to testify in the United States and about which most research has been conducted (Goodman, Quas, Bulkley, & Shapiro, 1999). We have discussed some of the expectations the adversary system places on children who take the stand and some of the techniques developed to mitigate the adverse effects of testifying on children's accuracy and emotional well-being. Techniques to aid children in court must be carefully considered so as to truly benefit children in the short and long term while not adversely affecting the outcome of the case and while still protecting defendants' rights to a fair trial. Not only is the determination of the truth an essential component of justice, but justice also requires that victims are not further traumatized by involvement in criminal court prosecutions.

As Smith (1997) lamented after observing child sexual abuse trials in the adversarial system:

> To me, it is very disrespectful, not only to the child but also to the court. It makes a mockery out of something much too serious—to the defendant and to the child—to be treated that way. Such a line of questioning would never be allowed in Nordic countries. Certainly not with a child witness but not with any witness for that matter. This again has to do with our principle about trying to find the truth. Intimidating a witness this way is assumed to be counterproductive to that search. (p. 508)

Smith goes on to state that defense attorneys in Denmark are usually gentle with children, primarily because of the Danish tradition of not bullying witnesses.

Our own view is that both the adversarial and inquisitorial systems have their own advantages and disadvantages in the search for truth and in the treatment of child witnesses. However, the adversarial system seems much more inclined than inquisitorial legal systems to expect children to meet adult competencies in terms of knowledge, language, and emotional coping skills. We hope that the best features of the two legal systems can be combined in such a way that children's participation in the legal process will be optimized, defendants' rights will be protected, and the search for truth will lead to true justice.

11

Identification Evidence in Germany and the United States

Common Sense Assumptions, Empirical Evidence, Guidelines, and Judicial Practices[1]

SIEGFRIED L. SPORER AND BRIAN L. CUTLER

Cases of mistaken identification have been documented in the legal literature for more than 200 years in different countries. One of the earliest and most remarkable cases is that of Joseph Lesurques who had been accused of robbing a postal coach, along with four other robbers in 1796 (Sporer, Köhnken, & Malpass, 1996). In the years to follow, a total of approximately 13 persons (the exact number depends on various historical sources, see Sporer, 1984) were identified as robbers, and seven of them were executed—some of them obviously innocent, considering that there were only five robbers. In his 1932 book *Convicting the Innocent*, Yale Law Professor Edwin Borchard identified 65 cases of erroneous conviction in 27 states and in England. Borchard's analysis of the facts of these cases implicated mistaken eyewitness identification as a primary cause. Various researchers in different countries have documented again and again cases of mistaken identification (Clifford & Bull, 1978; Loftus, 1979; Meurer, Sporer, & Rennig, 1990; Shepherd, Ellis, & Davies, 1982; Yarmey, 1979). Most recently, Scheck, Neufeld, and Dwyer (2001), in their book *Actual*

[1] This research was supported by a grant from the Deutsche Forschungsgemeinschaft (Sp 262/3-2) to the first author.

Innocence, reported that, in the year 2000, the Innocence Project had reconstructed 74 cases involving 79 erroneously convicted but subsequently exonerated individuals. Mistaken eyewitnesses were a factor in 82% of these convictions (Scheck et al., 2001). Field experiments on eyewitness identification in which the accuracy of identifications is known for certain likewise produce substantial error rates (Cutler & Penrod, 1995; Ross, Read, & Toglia, 1994; Sporer, Malpass, & Koehnken, 1996) although the delay between observation of a target and the attempted identification is usually quite short in these experiments compared to real life situations.

IDENTIFICATION EVIDENCE IN THE GERMAN LEGAL LITERATURE: FROM PAST TO PRESENT

Within the last two or three decades, there has been a tremendous growth in knowledge about eyewitness identification evidence in the Anglo-American literature on psychology and law (for reviews, see Sporer, Malpass, et al., 1996; Wells et al., 1998). But relatively little is known about identification evidence in non-English speaking countries. Here we examine the treatment of identification evidence in German courts of law.

Lineup procedures have had a long history in German law, and some of the problems and pitfalls of identification evidence that experimental psychologists have recently "discovered" and analyzed in great detail have long been known in German legal and criminological writings. More than 150 years ago, Henke (1838), in his *Handbook of Criminal Law and Criminal Politics*, described in astounding detail the proper administration of an identification procedure.

> Above all, the identification procedure has to be preceded by a comprehensive interrogation of the witness, wherein he is to describe the characteristic features which could facilitate recognition of the persons or objects to which his testimony or statements refer. Thereafter, in the identification procedure itself, he is, whenever possible, to be confronted with several persons or objects resembling the one to be identified. He should be urged to point out, for example, the identified object, without hesitation, and also to give the reasons why he had identified this one as the real one instead of any of the others.
>
> On the one hand, the investigator has to take care, to the best of his ability, to remove any changes that may have occurred in the object to be recognized and that may thus impair recognition: therefore, for example, he must not present the accused in his prison clothes, or with a distorting beard, etc. On the other hand, the investigator must beware of drawing the witness's attention to the

correct object through facial expressions, gestures, or external signs that differ-
entiate the object in question from others. (Henke, 1838, pp. 705–706; transl. in
Sporer, 1982, p. 324)

Henke (1838) thus stressed the importance of a comprehensive interrogation of the witness with regard to potential characteristic features of
the perpetrator prior to the identification, as well as the resemblance of
the persons (or objects) during the identification procedure itself. Henke
also warned against what today we would call "nonverbal cues" from the
investigator in the form of facial expressions, gestures, and external signs
that would draw attention to the "correct" suspect (for further details on
the history of eyewitness testimony, see Sporer, 1982; Wells & Luus, 1990).

However, as sophisticated as this early analysis may seem from a
hindsight perspective, it does not seem to have prevented miscarriages of
justice due to mistaken identification. There has been a plethora of cases
of mistaken identity documented in the German legal literature (e.g.,
Lange, 1980; Nöldeke, 1982; Peters, 1972; Schweling, 1969; Sello, 1911;
Sporer, 1984; Sporer, 1996) that make it clear that these sound warnings
have not always been adhered to. As illuminating as these cases are it is
always difficult to extract, ex post facto, the controlling factors that may or
may not have been at work in a given case to make an identification
attempt likely to have been correct or mistaken (for reviews, see Cutler &
Penrod, 1995; Narby, Cutler, & Penrod, 1996; cf. Wells, 1978, discussion of
estimator vs. system variables).

Nonetheless, the anecdotal evidence that can be gained from these
cases seems to indicate that many of the factors that psychologists have
found to influence identification testimony in their experiments may also
be operative in real criminal cases (e.g., conditions and duration of exposure, interpolated experiences such as mugshot exposure, suggestive lineups, etc.). For example, Peters (1972) and Lange (1980), in their re-analyses
of 1,100 cases under appellate review, found that approximately 40 cases
involved person identifications as an issue, both in a sense that identifications originally believed to have been valid later turned out to have been
mistaken but also vice versa. Of course, cases under appellate review are
only lower-bound estimates of potential miscarriages of justice (see also
Connors, Lundregan, Miller, & McEwan, 1996).

Thus, it appears that in the German legal and criminological literature there has been some concern with identification evidence. But the
accrued knowledge is far from constituting an exhaustive, systematic
treatment. There are numerous gaps and also some unresolved issues and
even contradictions, for example regarding the question of whether there
are specific differences regarding the role of fear, stress, arousal, and emo-
tion in crimes of robbery, rape, and indecent exposure (cf. Peters, 1972).

The explanations offered both for and against the validity of identifications by many legal scholars are based on common sense psychological arguments and have not been linked to any empirical studies in the recent psychological literature (see Meurer et al., 1990, for a detailed analysis; illustrative examples of such arguments are presented in Nöldeke, 1982; Schweling, 1969; Steinke, 1978). Only in recent years have legal scholars in Germany started to pay attention to the psychological literature on person identification (e.g., Eisenberg, 1995; Odenthal, 1999).

Empirical studies on this topic could hardly be expected as the *German psychological* literature on the psychology of testimony has altogether ignored the issue of person identification until about a decade ago. The few cursory remarks in the standard German literature on eyewitness testimony (e.g., Arntzen, 1993; Undeutsch, 1967) do not at all address the intricacies and wealth of empirical studies available in the Anglo-American literature (e.g., Clifford & Bull, 1978; Cutler & Penrod, 1995; Loftus, 1979; Ross et al., 1994; Shepherd et al., 1982; Sporer, Köhnken et al., 1996; Yarmey, 1979). In fact, there have been only very few empirical studies in Germany on issues of person identification at the Universities of Kiel, Marburg, Bremen, and Giessen (Fabian, Stadler, & Wetzels, 1995; Köhnken & Maass, 1985; Maass & Kohnken, 1989; Sporer, 1992, 1993, 1994, 1996, 2001; Sporer, Eickelkamp, & Spitmann-Rex, 1990; Stadler & Fabian, 1995).

PROCEDURAL RULES AND RECOMMENDATIONS FOR LINEUPS IN GERMANY

The German Code of Criminal Procedure (*Strafprozessordnung*, StPO, in § 58 II)[2] provides for the "confrontation of witnesses with other witnesses or the suspect if this appears to be necessary for the further progression of the criminal procedure." Implicit in this provision for a confrontation is, also, the possibility of conducting lineups for the purpose of person identification (Burghard, 1976; Kleinknecht & Meyer-Gossner, 1997a). The "Guidelines for Criminal Procedure and for the Assessment of

---

[2] References to German legal codes and German court decisions are given in the format characteristic for German legal citations. The most commonly used abbreviations are: StPO = *Strafprozessordnung* (Code of Criminal Proceedings); RiStBV = *Richtlinien für das Strafverfahren und Bussgeldverfahren* (Guidelines for Criminal Investigations and Fine Proceedings); BGH = *Bundesgerichtshof in Strafsachen* (German Supreme Court in Criminal Proceedings); AG = *Amtsgericht* (lower court); LG = *Landgericht* (higher court); OLG = *Oberlandesgericht* (appellate court). German legal citations normally refer to individual pages of a decision, not the entire length of a decision, article or commentary.

Fines" (*Richtlinien für das Strafverfahren und das Bussgeldverfahren*, RiStBV: Nr. 18) in the 1977 version that became mandatory for all states of the Federal Republic of Germany as of July 1st, 1982, further specify:

> When a lineup is to be used to clarify whether or not the defendant is the per-petrator the witness is to be confronted not only with the defendant but a row of other persons of the same sex, similar age and similar appearance, and in a manner that does not reveal who the defendant is among the lineup members (choice lineup). Analogous procedures apply to the presentation of photo-graphs. Details are to be recorded. (our translation)

Additionally, the "Rules for Police Service" (Polizeidienstvorschrift 100, cit. in Burghard, 1976, pp. 87–88) also specify that lineups should regu-larly be conducted as a choice lineup (*Wahl-Gegenüberstellung*), that is, a lineup with more than one member whereby the foils should resemble the suspect with respect to sex, appearance, and demeanor. The personal inter-ests of the witness should be considered, and in appropriate cases (especially with children) so-called "covered lineups" (*verdeckte Gegenüberstellungen*), i.e., lineups that do not reveal the identity of the witness to the defendant, should be used (e.g., using one-way mirrors, or more recently, video line-ups). Possibilities of suggestion are to be excluded and procedural details should be documented (Polizeidienstvorschrift 100, cit. in Burghard, 1976, OLG Karlsruhe, NStZ, 1983, pp. 377–378). Several state police depart-ments have developed appropriate forms intended to facilitate proper administration and documentation of procedural details and outcomes of lineups.

Of the various commentaries (e.g., Gross & Geerds, 1978; Kleinknecht & Meyer-Gossner, 1997a) and recommendations (e.g., Kalleichner & Grimm, 1973), we have selected the one by Burghard (1976) for more detailed discussion because (a) it is published by the German police and thus likely to be widely distributed and respected and (b) it contains vari-ous promising suggestions that—to our knowledge—have not all yet been considered in the Anglo-American literature on eyewitness identifi-cation. Some of these suggestions raise interesting empirical questions worthy our attention.

Burghard distinguishes between choice lineups (lineups of between five and eight members) and single confrontations (showups) which may be replaced by photographic displays (mugshot displays of at least 8 three-fold ("Bertillon") photographs in frontal, three-quarter, and profile view). Of more interest is an additional distinction regarding a lineup procedure conducted *at the scene of the crime*. We know both from labora-tory (e.g., Davies, 1988; Davies & Milne, 1982) and field experiments (e.g., Malpass, 1981) that through the reinstatement of context, the likelihood of a positive identification will increase (Cutler & Penrod, 1995; Malpass,

1996). It would be of utmost practical importance to know whether or not this effect also generalizes to the scene of the crime as a recognition cue, and whether or not such a cueing effect may be associated with the cost of increased false alarms.

According to Burghard, recognition may be a function of the suspect's total appearance, his or her voice, gait, and special characteristics. It seems peculiar that Burghard does not stress the specific prominence of facial recognition as is done in most research on eyewitness identification. On the other hand, eyewitness researchers have paid relatively little attention in their research to the total appearance of a person (though see MacLeod, Frowley, & Shepherd, 1994, on whole body recognition; and Cutler, Berman, Penrod, & Fisher, 1993, on comparisons of performance in photographic versus live identification procedures), especially in relationship to movements such as gestures and gait (which lineup members might be asked to perform), or to certain aspects of language, such as dialects (Bull, 1981, on voice recognition), or to distinctive characteristics of a person (cf. Going & Read, 1974; Sporer, 1992; Vokey & Read, 1992). It would be especially important to know whether or not a *combination* of these factors would lead to increased identification performance.

Burghard (1976) also warns against chance encounters between a witness and other witnesses, or between a witness and the suspect before and after the lineup procedure. In the case of Lesurques mentioned in the introduction, two witnesses waiting to be interrogated outside the courtroom encountered Lesurques and "identified" him as one of the robbers of the postal carriage. Lesurques had been at the same tavern as the robbers on the evening of the robbery and murder (Sporer, Köhnken, et al., 1996).

Burghard (1976) acknowledges the inferior probative value of a supplemental corporeal lineup after a successful mugshot identification had already been obtained but does not reject such repeated identifications (see below). With respect to the conduct of the lineup procedure itself, Burghard suggests a rather complicated series of steps, with several officers involved. The provision of special forms both for the reporting officer and for the witness (with a "perpetrator absent" category!) seems especially laudable. But the recommendation that the identification procedure be conducted by the officer in charge of the case appears extremely problematic in light of our knowledge regarding potential (intentional or unintentional) cues from the officer towards the suspect (so called experimenter expectancy effects: Gniech & Stadler, 1981; Wells & Luus, 1990; Wells et al., 1998).

Another interesting empirical issue is raised by the commonly adopted procedure to conduct two (sometimes even three) identification trials with the same witness, after allowing the suspect to determine a new lineup ordering after the first trial. This is supposedly done to increase the reliability of an identification attempt (especially with witnesses of borderline intelligence who might have pointed out the "right" person by chance). To protect the integrity of witnesses and to reduce their fear of retaliation, especially with children and juvenile witnesses, the use of "covered" lineups where the witness is not exposed to the suspect has been variously suggested (e.g., Burghard, 1976; Schweling, 1969). These authors have recommended the use of one-way mirrors which are also frequently used in England and Wales. Dent and Stephenson (1979) have found that the use of one-way mirrors leads to more frequent (and more often correct, with some increase in false alarms) identification attempts (cf. also Cutler & Penrod, 1995; Shepherd, 1982; cf. also below).

Taken together, it appears that lineup procedures in Germany should be quite sophisticated with respect to the avoidance of potential biases or procedural errors that have been amply documented in the Anglo-American literature. Some of these recommendations raise interesting empirical questions awaiting further study. The extent to which these recommendations have been followed in the daily routines of police investigations is another issue, however. In the following section, some recent decisions by the highest German courts are reviewed that have attempted to resolve some of the recurrent issues of identification evidence. They reflect to what extent the high standards developed in procedural rules and recommendations and by court decisions are actually met in everyday practice.

GERMAN SUPREME COURT DECISIONS

A series of decisions by the highest German courts on the proper conduct and the probative value of lineup identifications seem to indicate that there has been growing concern about some of the issues raised above. Most of these decisions have dealt primarily with legal issues and will not be discussed here in any detail (e.g., legal status of lineup identifications as part of the interrogation of a witness and/or of the defendant; the right of the defendant to refuse to cooperate (actively or passively) in a lineup procedure, including the potential application of force by the police; the right of the police to change the appearance of the defendant in the direction of the original witness description (e.g., haircut, beard, glasses—sic!); the right of the defendant for counsel at the lineup (for a detailed discussion of these issues, see Bender & Nack, 1995; Grünwald, 1981; Kleinknecht & Meyer-Gossner, 1997a; Rieder, 1977, with further references).

Other decisions hit right at the heart of psychological issues. We have summarized the various factors and issues contained in appellate court decisions in Table 1. Although some entries in this table resemble, to some extent the well-known, *Biggers* criteria (see Table 2) the United States Supreme Court established in its landmark decision in *Neil v. Biggers* (1972), they differ from the latter insofar as they were not set up in a single decision to be used as guidelines as was the case in the United States Supreme Court decision. Rather, Table 1 was abstracted from a series of decisions over several decades. Space limitations prohibit a detailed discussion of all of the principles outlined in Table 1. We will only highlight a few of the most important issues—these will briefly be discussed in light of empirical research. Similarities and differences to decisions in the United States will be noted.

One of the core issues repeatedly addressed by the German courts is that of "repeated recognition" (*wiederholtes Wiedererkennen*), usually in the form of a first identification from a photograph (e.g., mugshot display),

TABLE 1. CRITERIA USED BY THE GERMAN SUPREME COURT TO ASSESS THE ACCURACY OF EYEWITNESS IDENTIFICATIONS (ADAPTED AND EXTENDED FROM MEURER, SPORER, AND RENNIG, 1990, PP. 3–4)

1. **Factors during the perceptual phase**
   Opportunity to view
   Time for observation (exposure time)
   Special characteristics (distinctiveness) of the perpetrator
2. **Factors during the retention phase**
   Retention interval (longer than 5 years)
   Media publication of photographs of perpetrator
   Repeated identification attempts
3. **Factors during the identification procedure**
   Expectation of presence of perpetrator in lineup
   Showups (one-person "lineups")
   Number of foils in lineup
   Similarity of lineup members
   Live presentation vs. photospread
   Contradictory identifications
   Identification during trial (dock identification)
4. **Factors concerning total statement/witness factors**
   Correspondence between person description and person identification
   Quantity of details in statement regarding the criminal act
   Confidence (subjective certainty) in lineup decision
5. **Witness factors**
   Perceptual deficits and cognitive ability of witness
   Children as identification witnesses
   Police officers as identification witnesses (pressure to succeed)

TABLE 2. CRITERIA USED BY THE UNITED STATES SUPREME COURT
IN *NEIL V. BIGGERS* (1972) TO ASSESS THE ACCURACY OF
EYEWITNESS IDENTIFICATIONS

1. Opportunity to view
2. Degree of attention
3. Accuracy of prior description
4. Amount of time between crime and confrontation (identification)
5. Level of certainty demonstrated at the confrontation

and later a second identification—for "corroboration"—in a lineup or even in the courtroom. Although the lack of probative value of the second recognition was acknowledged in the traditional forensic psychological literature well before the boom of experimental eyewitness research (e.g., Altavilla, 1955; Hellwig, 1951), the German Supreme Court criticized the practice of conducting repeated identification attempts relatively late in a frequently cited 1961 decision (*BGHSt 16, 304*). Other decisions have upheld this decision, and legal commentators have elaborated on the scope of the decision (e.g., Schweling, 1969). It is interesting to note that these intuitive psychological analyses have used concepts very similar to those found in today's experimental literature.

For example, Schweling (1969) has emphasized the "unconscious" nature of these processes, i.e., the later recognition may be due to the fact that the impression at the first test (e.g., a mugshot picture) has superseded, without the awareness of the witness, his/her original memory (cf. also Loftus, 1979; 1993, on "unconscious transference" and "reconstructive memory updating"). Experimental studies by Deffenbacher, Brown and Sturgill (1978), by Davies, Shepherd, and Ellis (1979), and by Gorenstein and Ellsworth (1980) have confirmed these warnings against the contaminating effect of interpolated mugshot exposure (for a review, see Wells et al., 1998). However, an interesting potential exception has been pointed out by Nöldeke (1982), one of the first commentators who cited English-language experimental studies on these issues. Nöldeke has argued that a second lineup, with new suspects, might be used to *disconfirm* a previous misidentification and lead to the incrimination of new suspects if identified. Of course, identifying somebody else after a previous misidentification (cf. the blank lineup procedure investigated by Wells, 1984) would be likely to raise doubts about the reliability of this witness. As we can see, the legal world is by no means less complicated than laboratory psychologists contrive it.

In another interesting decision antedating psychological research on this topic, the German Constitutional Court (*BVerfG, Beschl. v. 27.9.1983*) held that it is not unconstitutional that a lineup procedure be videotaped—both in order to allow the court to assess the probative value of the lineup and to allow for future video rather than live lineups at a lesser cost. Sporer (1992, 1993, 2001) has suggested that videotaping the witness making a decision, not just videotaping the lineup, can later be used for the assessment of confidence, decision-times and other decision-strategies (termed "assessment variables": Sporer, 1993, 1995). The court's progressive decision makes the implicit assumption that live and video lineups can be considered functionally equivalent.

This notion has received experimental support by Shepherd et al. (1982) and by Dent and Stephenson (1979). The latter even achieved higher identification rates (with some increase in false alarms) with video over live lineups. Yuille and Cutshall (1984) reported equivalent correct identification and false alarm rates for live, video, and photo lineups. Cutler, Fisher, and Chicvara (1989) and Cutler and Fisher (1990) similarly found that live and videotaped lineups produced comparable hit-rates and proportions correct and Sporer et al. (1990) found fewer false identifications in sequential photo and in sequential live lineups than in simultaneous live lineups, with no significant differences in correct identifications among these three conditions.

Despite these promising insights displayed by some of these decisions, the common sense psychological arguments characteristic of most legal disputes in the area of person identification demonstrate the basic lack of understanding of the *empirical* nature of these issues. For example, again and again post-hoc justifications for normally inappropriate procedures (e.g., showups instead of lineups, Nöldeke, 1982; first mugshot exposure [with identification] then lineup, OLG Frankfurt/Main, StrVert 1988, 10–11; OLG Düsseldorf, StrVert 1991, 509; BGH, NStZ 1998, 266; see Odenthal, 1999, for further references) are sought that would not hold up if scrutinized from an empirical perspective.

In *live lineups* another relevant issue may arise for which to our knowledge there has been no empirical work. Studies conducted by expert witnesses in Germany who were called upon by the court to evaluate eyewitness identifications in particularly difficult cases have shown that a suspect, irrespective of guilt which obviously is not known to the investigators, may send out subtle nonverbal cues which may draw attention to him- or herself during a lineup parade (Fabian et al., 1995). Fabian et al. (1995) demonstrated that mock witnesses watching a videotape of an authentic live lineup were able to pick out the defendant above chance. The suspect was also rated differently from the other lineup members by mock witnesses along several dimensions (e.g., he appeared more insecure, anxious, apathetic, helpless, introverted, and less self-confident). This potential problem has to be recognized in the evaluation of live or video lineups. To the extent that ethnic groups differ with respect to their habitual nonverbal behavior, some of the cues displayed as part of their "normal" behavior may be interpreted by witnesses of a different (or the same) ethnic group as signs of nervousness, thus drawing attention to particular lineup members (Sporer, 2001).

IDENTIFICATION PROCEDURES IN THE UNITED STATES

Practices in the United States can be examined from at least three different perspectives: (1) actual police practices, (2) recently adopted guidelines for investigative practices, and (3) practices within the courts. We will briefly describe each of these perspectives in turn.

ACTUAL POLICE PRACTICES

Police departments in the United States vary widely with respect to culture, sophistication, and available resources. Characterizing how police departments generally handle eyewitness evidence is extraordinarily difficult. Not only is there considerable diversity in practices, but there is little empirical research on this topic. To our knowledge, there is only one such study.

Wogalter, Burger, and Malpass (1993) surveyed 220 police departments about their identification practices. They found that about 73% of the identifications were from photographic as opposed to live lineups (about 16% were videotaped lineups). In response to a question about how they learned to construct identification tests, 74% of the officers responded that they learned from other officers, 54% from court rulings and case law, 31% from general recommendations or guidelines, and 18% from specific rules or regulations. On average, photographic and live lineups contained between six and seven photographs. Sequential lineups are used only about 10% of the time (the remainder are simultaneous lineups). During live lineups, the suspect has an attorney present in about 61% of the cases. In photographic lineups, an attorney is rarely present. Most officers reported that they instruct witnesses that they may choose to not identify any of the lineup members if they believe the perpetrator is not present, and most officers also assess eyewitness confidence in the lineup decision.

The Wogalter et al. study also reported some data on how foils are chosen for lineups and analyses of differences among jurisdictions. This study is informative about general practices in the United States, but clearly more research is needed on this topic before the practices are well understood.

THE NATIONAL INSTITUTE OF JUSTICE'S GUIDELINES

The fallibility of eyewitness identifications has been made salient in the last decade due to the increasing number of convicted individuals who have been exonerated based on DNA evidence. As noted above, mistaken identification is a common precursor to these erroneous convictions (Scheck et al., 2001). In recognition of this increasingly apparent trend and the fact that no national guidelines exist in the United States for collecting eyewitness evidence, former United States Attorney General Janet Reno took on the task of examining procedures used for handling eyewitness evidence and developing recommendations for reducing the risk of erroneous conviction. Reno accomplished this objective by forming a Technical Working Group for Eyewitness Evidence consisting of police officers, attorneys, and research psychologists. Over the period of a year, this group developed a handbook entitled *Eyewitness Evidence: A Guide for Law Enforcement* (Technical Working Group for Eyewitness Evidence, 1999). In the following, we provide an overview of a few of the NIJ Guidelines and discuss some of their implications for contemporary criminal justice practices.

The Task Force's recommendations were derived from social scientific research, combine research and practical perspectives, and assume good faith on the part of investigators. The goals of the Guidelines were to increase the amount and accuracy of information elicited from eyewitnesses, strengthen the validity or accuracy of eyewitness evidence, and improve the system's ability to evaluate the strength and accuracy of eyewitness evidence. The Guidelines are not meant to be a legal mandate, and reliance on the Guidelines is not intended as a substitute for corroborating evidence.

In total, the group made 19 recommendations, each containing a statement of principle citing what is accomplished by performing the procedure, a statement of policy to the investigator regarding performance of the procedure, the procedure itself, and a summary statement explaining the importance of performing the procedure. The Guidelines are subdivided into five sections. Examples of *policy* recommendations follow:

1. *Initial Report of the Crime/First Responder:* The preliminary investigating officer shall obtain and accurately document and preserve information from the witness(es).

2. *Mugbooks and Composites:* The investigator/mug book preparer shall compose the mug book in such a manner that individual photos are not suggestive. The person conducting the procedure shall preserve

the outcome of the procedure by accurately documenting the type of procedure(s) employed and the results.

3. *Procedures for Interviewing the Witness by the Follow-up Investigator:* Investigators shall conduct themselves in a manner conducive to eliciting the most information from the witness. The investigator shall provide complete and accurate documentation of all information obtained from the witness.

4. *Field Identification Procedure (Showup):* The investigator shall employ procedures that avoid prejudicing the witness. When conducting a showup, the investigator shall preserve the outcome of the procedure by documenting any identification or nonidentification results obtained from the witness.

5. *Procedures for Eyewitness Identification of Suspects:* Prior to presenting a lineup, the investigator shall provide instructions to the witness to ensure the witness understands that the purpose of the identification procedure is to exculpate the innocent as well as to identify the actual perpetrator. The investigator shall conduct the lineup in a manner conducive to obtaining accurate identification or nonidentification decisions.

The NIJ Guidelines adequately reflect beliefs widely held among research psychologists who study human memory. Our perception and memory systems do not behave like video recorders. We do not record into our memories complete and accurate representations of the world around us. When asked to retrieve or recognize information, we do not merely rewind our memories and replay complete and accurate representations of events. In contrast, memory involves an elaborate process whereby we perceive, encode, store, and retrieve information, and each of these four subprocesses may be affected by a host of other factors, such as our biases and expectations, aspects of the to-be-remembered event, interfering information, and the method by which our memories are tested. From the standpoint of investigators, therefore, memory is fragile evidence.

Because eyewitness memory can be influenced by so many factors (for review, see Cutler & Penrod, 1995; Narby et al., 1996), a valid assessment of the accuracy of eyewitness testimony requires a thorough understanding of the conditions under which the event in question occurred and the manner in which the eyewitness's recall or identification was obtained. In recognition of this point, the Task Force, in developing the Guidelines, placed substantial emphasis on the recording and preservation of information, including not only the eyewitness reports but also the interviewing and identification procedures used by the investigator to solicit the eyewitness testimony. Contemporary investigative practices often fall short of the Task Force's recommendations. For example, we know from the research that even subtly suggestive identification test instructions to the eyewitness can have a large impact on the likelihood of false identification (Cutler & Penrod, 1995; Steblay, 1997), yet, in the second author's experience as a consultant and expert witness in cases involving eyewitness identification, reliable records of the instructions used in identification tests have been rare. If the Guidelines are followed, investigators, attorneys, and jurists would be able to make more valid assessments of the accuracy of eyewitness testimony. By comparison, the German guidelines have emphasized the importance of documentation for a long time although enforcement of these guidelines may have been a problem.

The Guidelines are becoming increasingly influential in the United States. They have been widely distributed, and training courses for implementing them have been and continue to be available. The Guidelines are becoming part of Continuing Legal Education (CLE) workshops on eyewitness memory. More directly, the New Jersey Attorney General (State of New Jersey Attorney-General, 2001) issued *Guidelines for Preparing and Conducting Photo and Live Lineup Identification Procedures*. The New Jersey Guidelines incorporated some of the NIJ Guidelines and added these additional recommendations based on the psychological research on eyewitness memory:

> In order to ensure that inadvertent verbal cues or body language [of the investigative officer] do not impact on a witness, whenever practical...the person conducting the photo or live lineup identification procedure should be someone other than the primary investigator assigned to the case...In those cases where the primary investigating officer conducts the photo or live lineup identification procedure, he or she should be careful to avoid inadvertent signaling to the witness of the "correct" response.... When possible, photo or live lineup identification procedures should be conducted sequentially, i.e., showing one photo or one person at a time to the witness, rather than simultaneously.

Regarding the advantage of sequential over simultaneous lineups we should note that a recent meta-analysis by Steblay, Dysart, Fulero, and Lindsay (2001) clearly demonstrated that sequential procedures reduced the number of false identifications when the target was not in the lineup. Across studies there were also fewer correct identifications in sequential compared to simultaneous lineups when the perpetrator was present. However, the advantage of simultaneous lineups when the perpetrator was present was less noticeable when the studies were high in ecological validity (e.g., using a live or filmed incident, using unbiased instructions, or having witnesses give a description of the perpetrator prior to the perpetrator prior to lineup, which is done in most cases). Thus, the advantages of the sequential procedure, in terms of protecting the innocent, appears to far outweigh its disadvantages. Nonetheless, we would like to see more research to further improve sequential (and simultaneous) lineup procedures that have not yet been studied in sufficient detail (e.g., possible effects with different ethnic groups, or the use of videotaped or computerized forms of lineups). This way we hope that current procedures will be refined and newer procedures will be developed which protect the innocent without letting the guilty go free.

PRACTICES IN THE COURTS

Eyewitness identification issues can also be addressed from the perspective of the courts. Eyewitnesses do not convict defendants, judges and juries do. The United States justice system has various safeguards that are designed to protect defendants from erroneous conviction resulting from mistaken identification. These traditional safeguards include: (1) having an attorney present at identification tests, (2) allowing attorneys to submit motions to have identifications suppressed if they were obtained through highly suggestive methods, (3) excusing from service jurors who are unable or unwilling to independently weigh eyewitness evidence, (4) cross-examination of relevant witnesses at trial, and (5) cautionary instructions about eyewitness testimony.

Although these safeguards are helpful, they are of limited effectiveness and do not solve the problem of erroneous conviction resulting from mistaken identification (e.g., Scheck et al., 2001). Considerable research has documented the ineffectiveness of these safeguards. As noted in the Wogalter et al. (1993) survey, most identifications are from photographic lineups, and defense attorneys are rarely present at photographic lineups (the suspect has no legal right to representation at photographic lineups). Likewise, attorneys are frequently not present at live lineups. An absent attorney cannot prevent suggestive procedures or note them for future challenges. The "presence of counsel" safeguard, therefore, is not very helpful. Further, even when attorneys are present, they are limited by their incomplete understanding of how to evaluate lineups (Stinson, Devenport, Cutler, & Kravitz, 1996).

Motions to suppress are likewise of limited effectiveness because judges, who rule on these motions, do not have a complete understanding of the factors that affect the suggestiveness of lineups (Stinson, Devenport, Cutler, & Kravitz, 1997). For cross-examination to be effective, attorneys must know the right questions to ask witnesses, and jurors must have a solid understanding of how to evaluate lineups. Neither group appears to possess the requisite knowledge. Indeed a large volume of research demonstrates the fallibility of lay peoples' assessments of eyewitness testimony (Cutler & Penrod, 1995). Last, judges' instructions are of limited effectiveness, at least in part because the instructions themselves lack useful information (Cutler & Penrod, 1995). The typical instructions do not, for example, explain how to evaluate lineups.

A much less common safeguard but one that is becoming increasingly common is expert testimony on the psychology of eyewitness memory. Such testimony is typically given by cognitive and social psychologists. A recent survey by Kassin, Tubb, Hosch, and Memon (2001) revealed 64 such experts with considerable research expertise and courtroom experience. In total, these experts were asked to testify 3,370 times in the previous 12 years. They agreed to testify in 1,373 (41%) of these cases, and they actually testified in 960 cases (70% of the cases in which they agreed to testify). An opposing expert testified in 76 (8%) of these cases. In 89% of the instances in which an expert was asked to testify, the request came from a criminal defense attorney.

Many experts begin their testimony by describing some general principles about the psychology of eyewitness memory and some background about eyewitness research. In one way or another the experts dispel the myth that the brain works like a camcorder, accurately replaying, on demand, information encoded earlier. They explain that memory is an elaborate cognitive process and that it is susceptible to many influences— when witnessing an event, while details of an event are stored in memory, during the retrieval process (for example, a lineup), and even after the retrieval process.

The main part of the expert testimony involves a discussion of relevant eyewitnessing phenomena. For example, in a case in which the eyewitness is very confident about the accuracy of her or his identification, the expert might discuss the generally weak relation between confidence and accuracy in the large body of eyewitness research and the ease with which confidence levels can be manipulated. The eyewitness expert does not normally give an opinion about the accuracy of an eyewitness, but rather provides a knowledge framework by which the eyewitness can properly evaluate identification accuracy.

Admissibility of this form of expert testimony varies considerably by state and within the federal court system (see Cutler & Penrod, 1995, for a review). Research on the effectiveness of expert testimony as a safeguard reveals that it effectively sensitizes jurors to eyewitnessing conditions and the factors affecting lineup suggestiveness (Cutler & Penrod, 1995; Devenport, Stinson, Cutler, & Kravitz, in press).

CONCLUSIONS

In conclusion, the limited effectiveness of judicial safeguards designed to protect defendants from erroneous conviction resulting from mistaken eyewitness identification highlights the importance of the NIJ Guidelines. If greater care were taken in collecting and preserving eyewitness evidence, the United States would be less reliant on additional safeguards. More effective safeguards would be beneficial as well.

The NIJ Guidelines for collecting and preserving eyewitness evidence represent a significant advance toward creating national standards. The Guidelines are based on good science and were developed for use in contemporary practice. The Guidelines are beginning to influence state policies through formal and less formal channels. States that have not given serious considerations to adopting these guidelines in full or in part should consider doing so. The existence of the Guidelines should put investigators on alert that they have to justify the procedures they use for collecting and preserving eyewitness evidence. The Guidelines further serve as standards against which investigative procedures can be compared. Investigative procedures that follow the Guidelines shall enjoy more accurate and less impeachable eyewitness evidence and should lead to fewer erroneous convictions. Investigative procedures that continue to use careless collection and preservation procedures should be more easily impeached in light of the Guidelines endorsed by the National Institute of Justice.

By comparison, guidelines in Germany as well as court decisions have emphasized the importance of documentation for a long time although enforcement of these guidelines may have been a problem. Interestingly, many of the older German guidelines were developed before the research in the Anglo-American literature on eyewitness identification became available. Apparently, the guidelines have been based on commonsense psychological assumptions of legal practitioners. It is remarkable that some of these guidelines run parallel to the insights gained by scientific empirical analyses which in turn influenced the development of the NIJ Guidelines.

Only recently have practitioners in Germany started to pay attention to psychological research on identification evidence. However, in doing so, they have not examined the original research articles in which the results were presented (with all their limitations and caveats) but have relied on secondary sources that have more or less comprehensively summarized the available empirical evidence, sometimes mixed with the reviewers personal views that are not clearly separated from empirical findings.

The problem with the latter approach is that legal scholars and practitioners (in Germany) when implementing some of their policies have apparently not even been aware that the solutions they propose can be addressed empirically and that many of the underlying psychological assumptions have been investigated by psychological researchers. For example, it has been proposed that live lineup procedures be replaced with video lineups without realizing that the equivalence of live and video lineup procedures is an empirical question for which modest empirical research is available (see Cutler et al., 1993; Sporer et al., 1990).

In summary, today in the United States guidelines are nationally available that have at least been partially based on empirical psychological research. However, it would be desirable that the distribution and implementation of these guidelines in daily practice be monitored empirically and accompanied by systematic evaluation research.

Nonetheless, a comparison of the NIJ Guidelines with some of the issues raised in the court decisions in Germany shows that the former have not addressed some of the issues that have arisen in individual cases in Germany. For example, to our knowledge there is no research other than Fabian et al. (1995) that has addressed nonverbal cues emitted by a suspect in live or video lineups which may detract from the fairness of a lineup (Sporer, 2001). Furthermore, we expect that with the advance and distribution of computerized procedures new issues will arise that should be addressed by empirical research. Looking across the fence of both the legal and the psychological literature and across national borders may turn out to be quite fruitful for justice on either side of the fence.

12

Expert Evidence

The State of the Law in the Netherlands and the United States

PETRA T.C. VAN KAMPEN

July 1999. At a stretch from the Ha'penny Bridge, in one of Europe's unique cities, a curious trial takes place. It is a trial with two defendants facing each other. It is not the state that accuses in this trial; it is the state, or rather the system of law, that is on trial here. And although one could argue that the state is on trial in every case brought to the courtroom, where it needs to ascertain that conviction is the right thing to do in that particular case and based on the (properly obtained) evidence before the court, this trial is different. On trial are the accusatorial and inquisitorial system of law, represented in part by the American criminal justice system on the one hand, and its Dutch counterpart on the other hand. To aid their defense, both counsels have many experts available, ranging from experts on police interviewing and trial procedures in both systems of law, to experts on experts and their role in accusatorial systems on the one hand, and inquisitorial systems on the other. The list of experts is impressive, and so is their standing within their community. The clients—the inquisitorial and adversarial systems—have eloquent representation and advantageous positions. Indeed, as will be shown in this contribution, their positions are much more eloquent and advantageous than most criminal defendants can hope for in either system of law.

In the presence of so many well-versed experts and possibly complex expert testimony, there might be a real question whether the four judges presiding the trial are actually capable of rendering a decision. Yet, these judges will not actually take a vote. Indeed, it could well be argued that they cannot take a vote, for the question they face is which system is "better." In comparative legal research, which is the mandate of this trial, the question of "better" is a somewhat difficult question to answer, as long as one has not defined what "better" means: better in achieving fundamental fairness? In discovering the truth? In efficiency? Also, one must ask what one will gain by deciding that issue. As Damaška has argued, the view that one type of procedure is superior to the other in terms of its fact-finding precision and in terms of its fairness "must be examined with suspicion for it often happens that what is gained on one front is lost on another" (Damaška, 1973, pp. 588–589). In addition, while some systems might perform better in one respect or another, these systems might not be optional for other countries, in view of the intimate link between criminal procedures and culturally-based conceptions about proper governance and the relationship between the state and its citizens, as well as the rights and duties of both in criminal proceedings.

Therefore, the Dublin trial judges will not take a vote. All the judges will do at the end of this trial is sum up the evidence for and against both defendants and venture their own personal opinions; a position quite different from the position of both American and Dutch judges. In many of the American states, as opposed to the United Kingdom, judges are not permitted to sum up and/or comment upon the evidence. To the extent they do have that power, they sparingly use it (Van Kessel, 1992, p. 430). In the Netherlands, where criminal trials are conducted without a jury, there is no need for judges to sum up the evidence, as they are the ones who decide the issues of guilt and sentencing.

The evidence for the United States when it comes to experts and their evidence is impressive; at least in the mind of many Continental lawyers. At face value, the evidence for the Netherlands on the subject of expert evidence is less so. Many believe that a system that uses court-appointed experts, as the Dutch system does, is "of its nature unjust, even totalitarian in its operation" (Howard, 1991). The presence of such experts, some writers believe, smothers debate rather than fostering it, and disproportionally affects the procedure's outcome (Cecil & Willging, 1993, p. 5; Freckelton, 1987, pp. 221–224; Relkin, 1994), notwithstanding the fact that jury simulation experiments appear to show that some of these fears may be unfounded—at least within the American context (e.g. Brekke, Enko, Clavet, & Seelau, 1991, p. 451). The American criminal justice system, these writers believe, is much better suited to the task of "sorting out the truth," whether that "truth" is based on expert evidence or not. It provides elaborate rights for both parties to introduce expert evidence, and no party has a more advantageous position vis-à-vis the trier of fact.

Those, at least, are some the arguments usually advanced in relation to both systems of law with respect to expert evidence. Actual practice, however, belies these arguments. What follows in this contribution is an elaboration on that practice: an analysis and comparison of the legal rules and practices that feature in the American and Dutch criminal justice system as far as expert evidence is concerned, viewed mainly from the perspective of criminal defendants. Five main themes are explored within that context: the ability to secure expert assistance, the right to discover expert evidence, the admissibility and decision rules surrounding expert evidence, the right to confrontation, and the right to compulsory process. I conclude this chapter by drawing some conclusions from the—necessarily limited—comparative analysis offered here.

SECURING EXPERT ASSISTANCE

The American criminal justice system starts from the premise of party-incentive and -autonomy: each party to the criminal suit independently decides whether or not to secure expert assistance and, equally important, if not more, whether or not to present the outcome of that process to the trier of fact in the form of expert testimony. The Dutch criminal justice system, by contrast, starts from the premise that the judge, be it the investigative judge during the preliminary judicial inquiry or the trial judge, decides on the question whether or not experts need to be engaged in the investigative or adjudicative process. In both instances, however, practice significantly diverges from the theory.

In criminal litigation, the central tenet of the American system—party autonomy—is a quite problematical concept. It presumes two equally able and capable parties, both in knowledge and in resources. Usually, however, criminal defendants are no match to the prosecutor in either one of these respects. Most criminal defendants do not have the financial and personal resources to secure expert assistance (Giannelli, 1993b; Harris, 1992; Starrs, 1996). As a consequence, criminal defendants often are unable to secure expert assistance, and thus to offer expert testimony at trial. For the defendant to actually take responsibility for factual investigations, including investigations by experts of various kinds, as the theory presumes, the defendant thus needs serious help from either the legislature or the courts. On a statutory level, most American states have recognized that necessity by providing that the indigent defendant may draw on state funds to secure expert evidence. Most of these statutes are modeled after the Federal Criminal Justice Act 1964 (18 USC § 3006 (e)(1)), providing that the court may authorize expert services "upon a finding, after appropriate inquiry in an ex parte proceeding, that the services are necessary and that the person is financially unable to obtain them." In 1985, the defendant's potential inability to secure expert services was furthermore recognized by the U.S. Supreme Court in the landmark case of *Ake v. Oklahoma* (1985). *Ake* concerned a defendant who was charged with first-degree murder and shooting with intent to kill. Found incompetent to stand trial, he was committed to a state hospital. After he had been found competent to stand trial, the defense requested a psychiatric examination at the state's expense, or alternatively examination by a court-appointed expert. Both motions were denied, and as a consequence the defense was unable to present a defense of insanity at trial, and unable to present mitigating evidence at the following sentencing hearing. Ake was sentenced to death, but the U.S. Supreme Court reversed that decision, holding that the Fourteenth Amendment to the U.S. Constitution, which states that the state is not to deprive any person of life, liberty, or property without "due process of law," requires that the defendant have access "to a competent psychiatrist who will conduct an appropriate examination and assist in evaluation, preparation, and presentation of the defense," when he can make an ex parte threshold showing that his insanity at the time of the defense is likely to be a significant factor at trial (*Id.*, p. 41).

Although *Ake* was certainly a blessing for many criminal defendants, it is not at all clear whether and to what extent criminal defendants benefit from the constitutional right to expert assistance. Various courts have held that *Ake* is limited to capital cases, while others have limited *Ake's* holding to psychiatric assistance. While some courts have held that *Ake* requires partisan experts for the benefit of the defense, other courts have held that the *Ake* requirement is met by providing for the assistance of a court-appointed expert (Van Kampen, 1998, pp. 170–172). And while some courts have held that the required threshold showing is met when it is shown that the expert would be beneficial to the defense, other courts require the defendant to show not only that the expert would assist the defense, but also that the denial of the request would result in an unfair trial (see, e.g., Devlin, 1998, p. 413). Generally speaking, most courts have narrowly interpreted *Ake*, a failure that according to critics casts a dark shadow over its promise (Harris, 1990, p. 780), particularly in light of the growing importance of expert evidence in American criminal trials, as well as the complexities of, and the problems related to such evidence.

Meanwhile, the Dutch criminal justice system has been grappling with similar problems, although the impetus for, as well as the solution to, these problems is different. As has been stated before, the Dutch system is premised on the fact that the expert is summoned to assist by the judge (Van Kampen, 1998, pp. 66–67). That premise, if practiced, has important benefits, one of these being that the expert has no interest in furthering one party's case over the other: the expert assists the court, not one of the parties. That same premise, however, also has a number of drawbacks. One of these drawbacks is that the process is quite time-consuming, a problem which among others arises due to the fact that judges are involved in the criminal process at a relatively late stage of the proceedings. According to the original Code of Criminal Procedure (*Wetboek van Strafvordering*; Sv., 1926), the decision to seek expert assistance was either to be taken by the investigating judge during the so-called preliminary judicial inquiry, or by the trial judge. The prosecutor, according to these same rules, originally did not have the autonomous power to appoint experts outside "pressing matters," for fear of undue influence on the (expert's) investigation as a result of conscious or unconscious biases regarding the defendant's guilt (Van Kampen, 1998, p. 66). In order to avoid these problems, the rules required the prosecutor to *always* involve the (investigating) judge during criminal investigations in matters that required expert assistance. When the expert was so appointed, the defendant had (and has) certain rights at his disposal, including the right to be present during the expert's investigation and comment upon that investigation (Article 231 Sv.), to designate an expert to be present for him (Article 232 CP), as well as the right to designate an expert to review the report from the original expert's investigation (Article 233 Sv.).

The Dutch Supreme Court's case-law, however, in the 1970s turned these rules upside down, by holding that the evidentiary rules incorporated in the Code do not actually prohibit the use of expert evidence as proof of guilt that does not originate from "judge-appointed experts" (HR 21 February 1978, *NJ* 1978, 663). As a consequence, there was no longer a premium on the use of experts appointed by judges, and the time-consuming method of securing expert assistance for the benefit of both parties as well as the judge became the exception to the rule, instead of the principal rule (Van Kampen, 1998, p. 72). Recently, the Code of Criminal Procedure has been amended in order to ensure that the code comports with established practice: it now provides that the prosecutor has the power to appoint experts without judicial involvement (Article 151 Sv.). However, this power is limited to permanent forensic experts: experts who have been sworn in by an appellate court in order to serve the judicial system on a more permanent basis.[1]

---

[1] The fact that the permanent forensic expert is under a permanent oath according to some implies that the expert "is expected to go about his task in a professional way. This means— among other considerations—that he will be working in a certain, somewhat outlined area of expertise, and that he cannot go beyond the generally accepted insights of that field without explicitly motivating why he does so. The administration of the oath thus [...] serves as a guarantee of the expertise of the person concerned." Partiële wijziging Wetboek van Strafvordering, Bijlagen Handelingen Tweede Kamer [1993–1994], 23251, no. 6, 20, my translation.

The Dutch Supreme Court's 1978 decision greatly facilitated the use of expert evidence within the Dutch system. At the same time however, it created some serious problems for criminal defendants. One of these problems is that the defendant's rights provided in Articles 231–233 Sv. (see *supra*), are not triggered unless the investigating judge is involved. And thus, when the prosecutor under the Dutch Supreme Court's case law gained the implicit power to appoint experts (and thereby more or less direct their investigation) the question became how to ensure that the defense is more or less equally able to secure expert assistance. For, although the Dutch criminal justice system is often referred to as an "inquisitorial system of law," it is a well-recognized principle under European law that criminal defendants, ignorant of the "framework" they are tried in, have a right to a fair trial, which—if only by virtue of the rules set forth by the European Convention of Human Rights (1950)—includes the principle of "equality of arms."

There has never been any doubt that defendants tried within the Dutch criminal justice system have a right to secure expert assistance by themselves; no rule ever forbade that practice. There is also little doubt that Dutch defendants as much as their American counterparts cannot actually exercise that right for want of financial (and personal)[2] resources. They too need help. On a statutory level, that help is provided for by a rule that the defendant may request the court that has decided the case to reimburse certain expenses, including the costs related to expert assistance, when these expenses have been made in *"the interest of the investigation"* (Article 591 Sv.). The court may decide to reimburse these costs regardless of the outcome of the case. Thus, even when the defendant has been found guilty as charged and sentenced accordingly, the court may still decide to reimburse the expenses made by the defense. In addition, the defense may request advance payment of these expenses (Article 16 *Wet Tarieven in strafzaken;* Statute on Fees in Criminal Cases). There is only one serious drawback to these rules, and that is that the final decision for reimbursement is only made *after* a decision on guilt (and sentencing) or

---

[2] One of the consequences of a system that is premised upon the theory (and initial practice) that all experts are employed by judges, is that (forensic) expertise has a tendency to become monopolized by state institutions, such as in the Netherlands the Netherlands Forensic Institute (NFI). Because this institute only offers its services to the "system" (i.e. police, prosecutors and judges), Dutch defendants may have a serious problem obtaining a (knowledgeable) expert on a particular subject (Hielkema, 1999, pp. 28–29; Van Kampen, 1998, p. 77). This is particularly true when it comes to forensic science evidence, which is almost exclusively practiced and produced by the NFI. In the United States, a similar problem seems to exist (Giannelli, 1993b, p. 118) although the commercial market for experts and their services is more considerable there (but also much more expensive).

innocence has been made. Should the court at that point in time decide not to reimburse the expenses, the defendant will ultimately end up having to finance the expert's assistance himself. As such, these rules may be quite useless to the defense. Meanwhile, the accompanying *Besluit Tarieven in strafzaken* (Decree on Fees in Criminal Cases), that provides the maximum amounts to be spend on various types of expert assistance, ranging from about $50 per hour for unspecified activities to about $500 in total for extended psychiatric analysis, has been left unchanged for many decades. As a consequence, the amount of compensation that may be provided might be quite unsatisfactory for potential defense experts, further compounding the problem.

A partial solution to the problem how to secure expert assistance in the absence of defense resources came with a decision of the Dutch Supreme Court in 1993, in a case known as the *Peanuts* case (HR 2 February 1993, *NJ* 1993, 476). In that decision, which concerned a violation of the Consumer Good and Health Act (*Warenwet*), the Court recognized that the right to a fair trial, as incorporated in the European Convention, *may* necessitate the granting of a defendant's request to re-analyze samples even in the absence of statutory law that requires judges to do so, when the request is made at a time at which such testing is still possible. In contrast to the U.S. Supreme Court then, which provided the defendant with a right to retain an expert, the Dutch Supreme Court decided upon a right to so-called "retesting": a right that comes to the defendant's avail when the expert's investigation has already taken place, and provides the defendant direct access to *testing*, which does not necessarily mean that the defendant can actually pick his own expert (rather than a particular laboratory). The extent to which defendants under *Peanuts* have a right to secure expertise without testing actually having taken place (thus: the right to *test* rather than *re*test), however, is somewhat uncertain.

Like the decision in *Ake*, the *Peanuts* case in practice may not quite live up to its promise. First of all, the *Peanuts* promise may easily be thwarted when there no longer are samples to (re)test, a problem compounded by the fact that it was originally not quite clear whether there was a general duty to preserve evidence (see *infra*). Secondly, the Dutch Supreme Court in 1997 decided that although the defendant may indeed have a right to retest evidence, that right does not necessarily imply that the costs of such retesting are being paid for by the state. Whether or not the state needs to provide for funds for retesting is decided on the basis of Article 591 Sv., which provides that the court may reimburse expenses made in the interest of the case (HR 13 May 1997, *NJ* 1998, 152). As has been noted, however, that decision is only made after the decision as to guilt or innocence has been made, and thus long after the defendant needs to decide whether or not to make a request to retest the evidence. In that respect, the name of the *Peanuts* case seems well chosen.

Given the potential inability on part of criminal defendants to secure expert assistance, an amendment to the Dutch Code of Criminal Procedure meant to promote the fairness of criminal proceedings came into effect in February 2000 (see, e.g., Dozy, 2000, p. 52). The amendment (Article 36a-e Sv.) provides the defendant with the right to request the investigating judge for investigative action, including investigation by experts, as soon as the defendant has reason to suspect criminal charges will be filed against him. As a result of this so-called "mini-instruction," criminal defendants at a relatively early stage of the proceedings have the ability to search for exculpatory evidence and thus to influence the prose-cutor's decision whether or not to prosecute him, as well as the trial court's decision whether or not to find the defendant guilty as charged (Cleiren & Nijboer, 1999, pp. 94–95; Dozy, 2000, p. 51). According to the Law Reform Commission who proposed the amendment, in order for the investigating judge to grant the request, the defendant must show (a) *which* investigative action he proposes the judge to take; (b) *why* the latter should take such action, and (c) *which experts* should undertake the investigation (Commissie Herijking Wetboek van Strafvordering, 1990, pp. 134–135). Failure to satisfy these requirements will result in a refusal to undertake the requested investigation. Although the amend-ment seems promising for criminal defendants (but see Dozy, 2000), if only because it largely bypasses the question of costs present under *Peanuts* and follow-up decisions, it remains to be seen what becomes of that promise.

Notwithstanding the progress that has been made in this area then, securing expert evidence still seems quite an obstacle for criminal defen-dants in either system of law. The rules in place are theoretically designed to alleviate the problems criminal defendants grapple with. In practice, however, things do not quite work in a manner consistent with their apparent intent, not in the American criminal justice system, and not in its Dutch counterpart.

THE RULES OF DISCOVERY

In the American criminal justice system, the difficulties in securing expert services are somewhat compounded by the fact that the defendant may not be able to fully discover the (expert) evidence against him (Harris, 1990, p. 772). Originally, the rules of discovery were quite limited, particularly in criminal cases, for fear of perjury, witness intimidation and the gaining of an unfair advantage by the defendant. Substantial progress however, has been made in the past forty years (see, e.g., Douglass, 2000, p. 2133ff). In *Brady v. Maryland* (1963), the U.S. Supreme Court held that the concealment by the prosecution of evidence favorable to the defendant upon request of the defendant violates the due process clause where the evidence is material to either guilt or punishment. In *United States v. Agurs* (1976), the U.S. Supreme Court moreover held that a specific defense request is not necessarily to come within the protective scope of *Brady*. As a consequence of these and follow-up decisions, criminal defendants now have a constitutional right to discover *exculpatory* evidence. In addition, most states recognize a—generally more encompassing—right to discovery in their rules of criminal procedure. While most of these statutes at the time that *Brady* was decide where quite limited, the scope of most of these statutes have been substantially expanded since 1963. Federal Rule of Criminal Procedure 16 (a)(1)(C), for example, now provides for a prosecutorial duty to permit, upon request by the defendant, the inspection and copying of any results of scientific tests or experiments which are within the possession, custody or control of the government and which are material to the preparation of the defense or are intended for use by the government as evidence in chief at the trial. In addition, as of December 1993, Rule 16 provides for the disclosure upon request of a written summary of expert testimony the government intends to use during the trial, which summary needs to include the expert witness' opinions, the bases and reasons for those opinions, and the witness' qualifications (subdivision (a)(1)(E)). Each of these obligations on the part of the prosecutor is mirrored by an obligation on the part of the defendant to provide the prosecutor with the same information upon request. In that mirror obligation, the right to discover evidence finds its "natural" boundary within the American criminal justice system. According to the theory, discovery needs to be a "two way street": the parties to the criminal suit need to be subjected to essentially similar obligations. While the defendant cannot be asked to fully disclose his case to the prosecutor given the privilege against self-incrimination, so the prosecutor is under no obligation to fully disclose his case to the defendant (e.g., *State v. Evans*, 1969). Or, as the U.S. Supreme Court put it, "there is no general right to discover evidence in criminal cases, and *Brady* did not create one" (*Weatherford v. Bursey*, 1977, p. 559). While discovery in federal cases is generally much broader than the Federal Rules of Criminal Procedure require (e.g., Douglass, 2000, p. 2140), "there are serious problems with a system that counts on informal, voluntary disclosure to solve most of its discovery problems," if only because that system tends to work best when it matters least (i.e., when the evidence is overwhelming). "In effect, an informal system makes beggars of defense counsel. And, as the old saying goes 'beggars can't be choosers'" (Douglass, 2000, p. 2141).

In the Netherlands, by contrast, such a general defense right to discover evidence does exist. Dutch prosecutors are under a legal obligation to fully disclose the evidence against the defendant, while criminal defendants are under no (formal) obligation to disclose any evidence in return.[3] That is to say: prosecutors in the Netherlands need to disclose the complete contents of the case-file to the defendant upon the latter's request (Article 30.1 Sv.). This case-file, according to the Dutch Supreme Court, needs to include documents that may be *reasonably of interest*, either in the inculpating *or* exculpating sense of the word. Access to these documents may not be withheld from the defendant and his counsel except for temporary restrictions (HR 7 May 1996, *NJ* 1996, 687; *Dev Sol*), that need to be lifted as soon as charges have been filed against the defendant (Article 33 Sv.). If the defendant is temporarily refused access to certain documents, he moreover will need to be informed that the documents he has been given access to are not (yet) complete (Article 30.2 Sv.). In addition, according to the Dutch Supreme Court's decision in *Dev Sol*, counsel for the defense (but not necessary the defendant him- or herself) may need to be provided access to documents not included in the case-file, to the extent that such documents are potentially relevant in assessing the reliability and trustworthiness of the evidence adduced against the defendant.

In the Netherlands, full disclosure of everything that is contained in the case-file thus is the rule. A point at issue, however, is to what extent there is evidence which is not included in the case-file, and thus not necessarily discoverable, yet perhaps should have been. In that respect, the Dutch Supreme Court has maintained that the prosecutor's failure to include evidence in the case-file does not necessarily violate the defendant's right to a fair trial, unless it can be inferred that the omission was deliberate or grossly negligent with respect to the defendant's right to a fair trial (HR 5 December 1995, *NJ* 1996, 422; *Zwolsman*). More often than not, the trial courts have found that not to be the case. This problem was

---

[3] For a variety of reasons, criminal defendants in the Netherlands will usually provide the prosecution with a host of information regarding their defense, for example in order to persuade the prosecutor or investigating judge (under Article 36a Sv.) to seek expert assistance, or by asking the prosecutor to incorporate an expert's report into the case-file, in order for the court to learn the information contained therein prior to the trial. In addition, defendants will sometimes have to disclose to the court (and therefore to the prosecutor, as ex parte proceedings are generally not known in the Netherlands) the specific reasons why they want to summon certain persons, including experts, to the trial hearing in order to testify there.

originally compounded by the fact that it was not quite clear whether or not there existed a duty to preserve evidence. While the Code of Criminal Procedure, as well as related statutes and decrees contain some provisions regarding the duty to preserve evidence (see, e.g., Articles 116–119a Sv.), this duty is generally limited to seized objects. To the extent there is no such unequivocal and general duty, some evidence may ultimately not be discoverable by the defense, which has or may have its consequences for the defendant's ability to exercise his right to retest evidence. In February 1997, the Dutch Supreme Court held that if the defendant requests retesting in a timely manner, and the prosecutor subsequently *knowingly* destroys the samples, the defendant's right to a fair trial may be violated (HR 18 February 1997, *NJ* 1997, 484), an analysis which implies a duty to preserve. In addition, the Dutch Supreme Court in October 1998 decided that the absence of secured samples may be such a serious violation of the unwritten principles of a proper trial (*beginselen van een goede procesorde*) that the prosecutor should be barred from prosecution (*niet-ontvankelijkheid van het Openbaar Ministerie*), and that the prosecution should be halted irrespective of whether sufficient legally obtained evidence is present for convicting the defendant. That sanction, however, will not be imposed upon the prosecutor unless it can be inferred that the omission was deliberate or grossly negligent with respect to the defendant's right to a fair trial (HR 20 October 1998, NJ 1999, 122). In the United States, a duty to preserve evidence is also present, although this duty is limited to evidence that might be expected to play a significant role in the suspect's defense, and a failure to preserve such evidence only constitutes constitutional error if it is done in bad faith (*California v. Trombetta*, 1984). Like deliberate omissions in the Netherlands, however, bad faith is difficult to prove.

In both systems of law, the statutory rules of discovery leave one particular point at issue undecided, and that is the question what actually *is* discoverable as far as expert evidence is concerned. To include certain documents in the case-file is one thing; what these documents contain or should contain is quite another. In the United States, attention has frequently been directed to the fact that the information incorporated in experts' reports is generally rather inadequate for the purpose of preparing a defense (Giannelli, 1991; Moenssens, 1984). Laboratory reports, for example, often only reveal the results of tests performed, but not necessarily the kind of tests conducted, whether a choice has been made for a particular test and what reason caused that decision, nor the qualifications of the person who actually conducted the tests. Since 1993, that omission in the federal American system has been somewhat alleviated by the requirement that government and defense upon request need to disclose a summary of the expert's testimony, including the opinion, bases, reasons and qualifications of the expert witness testifying at trial (Federal Rule of Criminal Procedure 16 (a)(1)(E) and 16 (b)(1)(C)). In the Netherlands, the rules require the expert to provide the reasons that led to his conclusion (Article 299.2 Sv.). Inexplicably, however, the Dutch Supreme Court has never strictly enforced that rule (Van Kampen, 1998). As a consequence, there is no premium on not including one's reasons for "knowing," even though the absence of these reasons may seriously hamper the defense in the preparation for trial.

ADMISSIBILITY AND DECISION RULES ON EXPERT EVIDENCE

One of the defining characteristics of the American criminal justice system is the presence of so-called admissibility rules: rules that determine whether or not evidence that has been proffered by one of the parties may actually be presented at trial, so to be heard (or seen) by the trier of fact. These rules are predicated on the assumption that the evidence will be heard by a jury of laypersons and it is the responsibility of the court to assure that the jury receives evidence the probative value of which outweighs any prejudicial impact the evidence may have on the jury.

The Dutch criminal justice system, by contrast, does not "work" with admissibility rules; that concept is foreign to the system. Instead of screening what may be heard and seen by the trier of fact beforehand, the Dutch system does its screening afterwards, by way of so-called decision and argumentation rules (Nijboer, 2000a, p. 60). These rules determine what the court may use as a basis for its decision, as well as what (generally: adverse) decisions need to be explicitly motivated by the court. While the American Federal Rules of Evidence for example defines what constitutes hearsay evidence and prohibits the jury from receiving hearsay evidence deemed unreliable, the Dutch Code of Criminal Procedure defines what kind of statements and documents the court may use as the evidentiary basis for its decision of guilt (Articles 339–344a Sv.). Additionally, the code provides for some "minimal" evidentiary requirements, for example by stating that a statement of a defendant in and of itself is insufficient basis for a decision of guilt (Article 342.4 Sv.). The idea is that if the decision of guilt is being based upon a means of proof that does not comport with the legal definition, that decision (if an appeal on points of law is lodged with the Dutch Supreme Court) will need to be reversed as not being based on the legally recognized means of evidence only, generally irrespective of the question whether or not sufficient evidence remains for a decision of guilt.

Leaving aside the question whether such a system of output control rather than input control is actually in accordance with the way people make decisions, as well as the question whether it forces judges to disregard particular information—rather than forcing judges present their decision in a particular way (see, e.g., Enschede, 1966, pp. 514–517)—there are certain interesting parallels (as well as differences) between the admissibility rules used in the American criminal justice system related to expert evidence on the one hand, and the decision rules in the Dutch system on that same subject on the other hand.

In the United States, the general rule is that all relevant evidence is admissible (Federal Rule of Evidence 402). For expert evidence to be admissible, however, more specific and diverse rules apply. According to Federal Rule of Evidence (FRE) 702, adopted in 1975, scientific, technical, or other specialized knowledge is admissible when it will assist the trier of fact to understand the evidence or determine a fact in issue. In such a situation, a witness qualified as an expert by knowledge, skill, experience, training or education may testify thereto in the form of an opinion or otherwise. It has long been the subject of debate whether that rule actually incorporated what is known as the *Frye* test, originating from 1923. In *Frye v. United States* (1923), the D.C. district court held that for novel scientific expert evidence to be admissible, "the thing from which the deduction is made must be sufficiently established to have gained general acceptance in the particular field to which it belongs"—the "thing" in *Frye* being a precursor to the modern lie detector. FRE 702 on its face makes no reference to that requirement of "general acceptance," yet many American courts held that scientific expert evidence did in fact needed to comport with that requirement in order to be admissible under FRE 702. In 1993 however, the U.S. Supreme Court for the first time in its history decided the issue of the admissibility of expert evidence, and held otherwise. According to the decision in *Daubert v. Merrell Dow Pharmaceuticals, Inc.* (1993), nothing in the Federal Rules established general acceptance as an absolute prerequisite to admissibility. Instead, the Court held that in order for *scientific* expert evidence to be admissible, it needed not only be relevant, but also reliable. That is to say: it needs to be grounded in the methods and procedures of science, connote more than a subjective belief or unsupported speculation, and assist the trier of fact. In order to make the determination of reliability, the Court admonished the federal trial courts to generally consider certain factors, including (a) the question whether the theory or technique can or has been tested, (b) whether the theory or technique has been subjected to peer review and publication, (c) the known or potential error rate and the existence and maintenance of standards controlling the technique's operation, as well as (d) the question whether the theory has been generally accepted (*Id.*, pp. 2796–2798).

The decision in *Daubert* has been both hailed and severely criticized. One of the questions that loomed large after *Daubert* was whether the admissibility requirements advanced by the U.S. Supreme Court for scientific expert evidence also applied to non-scientific expert evidence and to forensic science evidence. In both situations, the *Daubert* criteria may produce problems. DeVyver for example, has argued that the application of these criteria to non-scientific expert evidence "forces a square peg in a round hole" (DeVyver, 1999, p. 202). As far as forensic science evidence is concerned, problems arise from the facts that many of the assertions underlying forensic science evidence (in the Netherlands also known as *criminalistics*) have not been verified, forensic science generally operates outside the normal peer review system, and little is known about the error rates of the techniques used (Faigman, Kaye, Saks, & Sanders, 1997; Jonakait, 1994). Some American courts subsequently held that forensic science does not pass muster as science under *Daubert*, and may therefore not be introduced as such at trial, which does not necessarily imply that it may not be introduced *at all* under FRE 702, given that this rule also refers to "technical or other specialized knowledge" (see e.g. *United States v. Starzecpyzel*, 1995). In March 1999, the U.S. Supreme Court for the second time in its history confronted the issue of the admissibility of expert evidence in *Kumho Tire Co. v. Carmichael* (1999). In that decision, the Court held that *Daubert*'s general holding (relevance *and* reliability) applies to all expert evidence, whether based on scientific or "technical or otherwise specialized knowledge." In determining the reliability of the latter types of knowledge, the trial court "should consider the specific factors identified in *Daubert*, where they are reasonable measures of the reliability of expert testimony" (*Id.*, at p. 1174).

In the Netherlands, the courts long did without any specific decision and argumentation rules with respect to expert evidence, other than the statutory requirement that an expert's statement needs to be "his opinion, made in the course of the investigation at the trial, as to what his knowledge teaches him about that which was the subject thereof" (Article 343 Sv.). Similarly, Article 344 (1)(4) Sv. states that the expert's report may be used in evidence as well, as long as the report entails his opinion as to what his knowledge teaches him about that which was the subject thereof. The word "knowledge" referred to in these rules thereby is taken to include "all special knowledge one possesses or is assumed to possess, even though such knowledge does not qualify as 'science' in the more limited sense of the word, corresponding to the fact that since long, experts have been heard in criminal cases whose special knowledge did not make them practitioners of science" (HR 24 July 1928, *NJ* 1929, 150). Faced with criticism from defense counsel that the expert evidence used in one particular trial or another was hardly scientific, incomplete, or otherwise defective, the Supreme Court long held that the selection and evaluation of available evidence is for the trial court, and the trial court only, to decide (e.g. HR 21 September 1999, *NJ* 1999, 758). Similarly, the Dutch Supreme Court long maintained that it will not decide the question whether or not the trial court was right either to award or deny a person the status of expert (-witness).[4] That being a factual question, it is not for the Supreme Court to decide. Moreover, the trial court need not justify these decisions. Both holdings, however, have been significantly modified in recent years.

In 1989, the Supreme Court decided a case known as the *Anatomically Correct Dolls*-decision (HR 28 February 1989, *NJ* 1989, 748). This case concerned a defendant who stood accused of sexual abuse. In interviewing the alleged victims, the expert used so-called anatomically correct dolls. On appeal, the defense argued that this method of obtaining testimony from small children was unreliable. In support of that argument, the defense presented its own expert, as well as abstracts from American journals criticizing the method. The appellate court nevertheless convicted the defendant, using the expert's report as proof of guilt (among other evidence). The defense appealed to the Dutch Supreme Court on points of law, whereupon the Supreme Court held that the appellate court, confronted with a detailed attack upon the reliability of the *method* used by the expert, *cannot* rely upon such evidence as a basis of their decision of guilt *without* providing additional explanation why the court deems that method reliable. Nine years later, the Supreme Court tightened its control on experts and their evidence by holding that trial courts, confronted with an attack upon the expert himself (rather than his method), need to ascertain *whether* the expert's knowledge also concerns research on, and analysis of, the matter he testifies to, and if so, *which* method the expert used in investigating the matter, *why* the expert considered that method to be reliable, as well as to what extent the expert was capable of professionally utilizing that method (HR 27 January 1998, *NJ* 1998, 404; *Shoeprint*).

---

[4] The Dutch Code of Criminal Procedure only recognizes two categories of persons who can testify at trial. One is the witness; the other is the expert. The witness, by the legal definition incorporated in the Code of Criminal Procedure (Article 342.1) can only testify to matters he has seen or experienced, while the expert needs to testify what his knowledge teaches him (Article 343 Sv.). As a consequence of these legal definitions, statements made by witnesses that include an opinion or conclusion can formally not be used as evidence, while— and more troubling—statements made by experts and referring to facts or "things" they have witnessed during their expert investigation cannot be used as evidence either. In order to avoid the latter problem, trial courts have since taken up the habit to have the expert sworn in as both an expert and a witness: the expert witness (see Van Kampen 1998, pp. 107–108).

That latter decision closely corresponds with an amendment to FRE 702, which took effect December 1, 2000. According to this amendment, FRE 702 will from that date read as follows: "If scientific, technical, or other specialized knowledge will assist the trier of fact to understand the evidence or to determine a fact in issue, a witness qualified as an expert by knowledge, skill, experience, training, or education, may testify thereto in the form of an opinion or otherwise, *if (1) the testimony is based upon sufficient facts or data, (2) the testimony is the product of reliable principles and methods, and (3) the witness has applied the principles and methods reliably to the facts of the case.*"[5] The amendment, which was introduced prior to *Kumho* yet is consistent with that decision, envisions "a more rigorous and structured approach than some courts are currently employing" (Notes of the Advisory Committee to proposed amendment FRE 701, 2000).

As a consequence of the changes in both systems of law during the last decade, the mainstay of the rules for the admissibility of experts and their evidence (whether *in* evidence or *as* evidence) thus is reliability, a factor that no doubt is quite important for any kind of expert evidence. Yet, reliability may be quite difficult to ascertain by lay people—judges and juries alike. At the same time, it seems quite clear that the American criminal justice system imposes a *higher* threshold upon introducing expert evidence than its Dutch counterpart, at least at the surface. While both *Kumho* and the amendment to FRE 702 bring all expert evidence under reliability scrutiny, the Dutch Supreme Court's *Shoeprint* decision according to some critics only concerns *crucial* expert evidence (Reijntjes in his note to HR 27 January 1998, *NJ* 1998, 404), and it does not ban evidence challenged on reliability grounds as means of proof. Rather, it requires trial courts to respond to reliability arguments from the defense.

The difference in threshold requirements is all the more important given the fact that Dutch trial courts, when deciding whether or not to use expert evidence after a detailed attack upon the expert and/or his method of investigation, have already read the complete case-file and thus are aware of all the evidence incorporated therein, which no doubt influences their decision. In the *Shoeprint* case, for example, the appellate court parried the defense's attack upon the expert by pointing to the fact that his results comported with the results of another expert. The Dutch Supreme

---

[5] The amendments to the Federal Rules of Evidence approved by the U.S. Supreme Court also provide for an amendment to FRE 701, in order to "eliminate the risk that the reliability requirements set forth in FRE 702 will be evaded through the simple expedient of proffering an expert in lay witness clothing," as well as in order to avoid that the disclosure requirements set forth in Federal Rule of Criminal Procedure 16 are evaded (Notes of the Advisory Committee to proposed amendment FRE 701, 2000).

Court however, stated that this is not the way the matter should be solved; the court needs to ascertain the reliability of the expert and his method; not simply point to the similarities between the results of various expert investigation (HR 27 January 1998, *NJ* 1998, 404).

In some respects, however, the Dutch criminal justice system seems to impose higher barriers to the use of expert evidence. Some methods of forensic science investigation, such as the analysis of blood-alcohol levels, are laid down by law. To the extent that these methods are not followed to the letter of the law, the results of that analysis cannot be used as evidence (see, e.g., HR 22 April 1980, *NJ* 1980, 451). The same is true when the particular law at issue provides the defendant with a legal right to retest evidence; to the extent that right was invoked, yet not complied with as a result of a failure on part of the state, the results of the contested analysis cannot be used in evidence (see, e.g., HR 26 May 1987, *NJ* 1988, 176). This is different in the United States, where some courts have held that deficiencies in the testing procedure go to the weight of the evidence, and not to its admissibility (e.g., *United States v. Jakobetz*, 1992; *United States v. Lowe*, 1996). At the same time, the benefit of these strict requirements incorporated in Dutch procedural law is rather limited, as many statutes do not actually require a particular method to be used. In these instances, the strict requirement does not apply (Van Kampen, 1998).

The general absence of threshold standards for expert evidence in the Dutch system, however, is not necessarily any more (or any less) problematic than the use (and application) of such standards in the United States. While admissibility standards are certainly beneficial in some respects, they are quite problematical in others. While a higher threshold may be important to the extent that it makes it more difficult for the prosecutor to introduce such evidence, such a threshold may also make it more difficult for criminal defendants to introduce such testimony—albeit that the compulsory process clause may come to defendants' aid here (see *infra*). In addition, as the developments and discussions in the United States show, such standards are difficult to define, and are always liable to criticism that they are too liberal, too conservative, or simply downright wrong. Secondly, there seems to be a real question as to whether such standards, as well as any alterations in these standards, actually change practices very much. There is for example a real question whether *Daubert* (and *Kumho*) actually set higher barriers for the introduction of expert evidence when compared to the original *Frye* test. While some commentators argue that courts applying *Daubert* exclude "far more experts" from the courtroom then they admit (Note, 1995, p. 135), others argue that the courts admit more scientific evidence than before (Note, 1996, p. 2013). Another segment of writers argue, by contrast, that *Daubert* has changed "almost nothing" (Gross, 1995, p. 169). Meanwhile, even in the absence of such standards, some types of expert evidence frequently (and often severely) criticized in the United States, are not used by the Dutch courts as proof of guilt, simply because they are deemed insufficiently reliable. This applies to bite mark evidence, the results of polygraph tests, hypnosis and the use of truth serum (to name but a few). Interestingly enough, neither the legislature nor the Dutch Supreme Court has ever decided the question whether or not the results of such methods could be used (with the exception of evidence resulting from hypnosis; see *infra*, § 6); the decision not to use these results stems from common opinion (Corstens, 1999, pp. 272–273). From an American perspective, a related and quite interesting aspect is that because Dutch trial courts will not use the results of such methods as proof of guilt, they are almost never used in criminal investigations.[6] Nevertheless, as there is not actually a rule that forbids the use of such methods in criminal investigations, prosecutors may decide to use them as an investigative tool, while courts in turn may decide to use the results of such methods as proof of guilt (as the *Dolls* decision shows). The absence of specific and higher threshold standards for the use of expert evidence in the Dutch system may thus not necessarily be a flaw, yet may certainly be considered a weak link in the whole process. And while the requirements set forth by the Dutch Supreme Court in the *Dolls* decision and the *Shoeprint* case somewhat ameliorate that problem, these decisions do not require such evidence be excluded as proof of guilt, rather than requiring that their use as such be explained to the defendant (and the public at large).

THE RIGHT TO CONFRONTATION

One of the paramount safeguards that exist within the American criminal justice system is the defendant's right to confrontation. This

---

[6] One of the reasons why that fact is not surprising in the Dutch system lies in the structure of the Dutch system. To speak in "Damaškian" terms (Damaška, 1986), the Dutch criminal justice system is a hierarchically structured system, in which the case-file (dossier) functions as the linch-pin. Most of what is in that file may be used as evidence, notwithstanding the original intention of the Dutch legislature, as long as the documents incorporated in the file comport with the evidentiary requirements set forth by the code. "Indeed unless such weight were attributed to it [the case-file], the very foundation of the hierarchical process would begin to tremble" (Damaška, 1986, p. 50). That being the case, the evidentiary rules and common practices related to such rules cast their shadow on everything that precedes the trial in terms of criminal investigations; that which will almost certainly not be used as proof of guilt will not be sought after. "There is a definite tendency to view the entirety of the judicial process from the perspective for a final decision or judgment" (Nijboer, 1992, p. 175).

fundamental right, that has been said to have been incorporated in the Sixth Amendment to the Constitution as a result of Sir Walter Raleigh's conviction for high treason in 1603 (Graham, 1972, pp. 99–100), provides the defendant with the right to confront the witnesses (and expert witnesses) against him. Originally, the Sixth Amendment, like most other amendments to the Constitution, only applied to federal trials. As such, they were of somewhat limited use to most criminal defendants tried in the United States, as most were and are involved in state criminal trials, to which the Bill of Rights—the first 10 amendments to the American Constitution—did not apply. It was only in 1868 that the Fourteenth Amendment was adopted, which specifically addresses the states. That Amendment among others admonishes the states not to deprive any person of life, liberty or property without due process of law—also known as the Due Process Clause. As a result of a decision of 1965, *Pointer v. Texas*, the due process requirement includes the right to confrontation. The primary objective of the right to confrontation is "to prevent dispositions or ex parte affidavits being used against the prisoner in lieu of a personal examination and cross-examination of the witness," by compelling the latter to take the stand (*Mattox v. United States*, 1895). As such, the right is not so much concerned with ensuring reliability, as it is with ensuring fairness (Lilly, 1984, pp. 213–215; Note, 1968, p. 940; Taslitz, 1993, p. 130).

The European Convention of Human Rights (1950)—which by constitutional law takes precedence over Dutch national law should a conflict between the two arise—incorporates a similar right to confront, albeit this right refers to *witnesses* only, and not to experts (Van Kampen, 1998, pp. 284ff). Given that the right to confront is part of the more encompassing right to a fair trial, provided for in Article 6 § 1 of the Convention, however, it is evident that Dutch defendants equally have a right to confront the experts and expert witnesses against them, although the contents as well as the practical meaning of the right to confrontation are somewhat different in both systems of law.

Before delving into the right to confront, however, it is worth mentioning that the right to confront is often "at risk" as far as expert evidence in criminal trials is concerned, while that risk in some ways also seems much more profound in the Dutch criminal justice system than in its American counterpart. The risk to the right to confrontation generally results from two different, yet related situations. The first of these situations arises when the expert testifying in court did not actually perform the analysis, but has merely performed the function of supervisor. In this situation, the defendant is actually confronting the wrong person (Giannelli, 1993a, pp. 56–59). The second of these situations arises when the expert as such does not present life testimony at all; instead, it is his report that is being introduced in evidence. Currently, this still is the prevalent way in which expert evidence is being introduced in criminal trials in the Netherlands. Although the Dutch legislature in the beginning of this century placed paramount importance on what is called the principle of immediacy—a principle necessitating that the primary sources of evidence be produced in court (Garé, 1994, p. 190), an exception was made for expert evidence, given the potentially quite complex nature of such evidence (Van Kampen, 1998, p. 57). As it was felt that some evidence might better be read by the parties and the court rather than orally presented, expert reports are a legal means of evidence under Dutch law, without the expert actually being heard at the trial. Of course, the premise that the expert is being called to assistance by the court significantly fostered the presumption that it is not in all instances necessary to subject the expert to "live" and detailed scrutiny, since he himself has (or should have) no "axe to grind." After all, as Damaška argued, "where greater judicial involvement in fact-finding activities reduces adversary tension, the threat of one-sided distortions of information appears less immediate, and the need to subject means of proof to testing because less compelling" (Damaška, 1997, p. 80). In the United States, by contrast, experts' reports are not commonly used in evidence, since they constitute so-called hearsay evidence: a statement other than the one made by the declarant while testifying at the trial (FRE 801 (c)). Such statements are inadmissible at the trial, because the particular hazards out-of-court statements are subject to (see, e.g., Douglass, 2000, p. 2098, note 2). Only when such reports fall within one of the exceptions to the hearsay rule may they be admitted into evidence, because the hazards generally attributed to out-of-court statements are considered not to be present (or at least less problematical) in these "exceptional" circumstances. Three of such exceptions provided for in the Federal Rules of Evidence are of particular importance to expert evidence: FRE 803 (5) (recorded recollection), FRE 803 (6) (records of a regularly conducted activity), and FRE 803 (8) (public records and reports).

In both situations mentioned above, the defendant is unable to confront the person he means or wants to confront, which may in turn endanger his right to confrontation. Whether the statement bears indicia of reliability, and may therefore constitute sound basis for a decision of guilt, is (or should largely be) irrelevant in that respect; the question under the confrontation clause is not so much reliability, as it is fairness. Until well in the 1960s, the U.S. Supreme Court's decisions on the right to confrontation indeed comported with that idea by holding, in various decisions, that the Confrontation Clause is violated when the defendant is unable to confront the witnesses against him, unless the witness is actually shown to be unavailable for the trial, while the prosecutor needs to have made a good faith effort to obtain the presence of the witness at the trial (*Barber v. Page*, 1968). From the 1970s onwards, however, the U.S. Supreme Court slowly backed away from that strict requirement of showing unavailability, instead focusing on the indicia of reliability incorporated in the out-of-court statement. From the line of cases that has been decided since the 1970s, it can be inferred that a showing of unavailability is not generally required; out-of-court statements are generally admissible without violating the right to confrontation as long as the statement falls within one of the firmly rooted exceptions to the hearsay rule (e.g., *White v. Illinois*, 1992). In these instances, after all, the evidence is sufficiently reliable to be introduced in evidence, as these exceptions are generally made precisely because the presumed reliability of such out-of-court statements. Meanwhile, "the Court has never found a hearsay exception that is not 'firmly rooted'. As a result, ...it seems almost certain that any hearsay admissible today under the Federal Rules of Evidence is likewise admissible under the Confrontation Clause" (Douglass, 2000, p. 2111; but see *Lilly v. Virginia*, 1999). According to the U.S. Supreme Court's case law, if the out-of-court statement does not fall within one of the recognized exceptions to the hearsay rule, it needs to bear particularized indicia of reliability in order to be admissible without running afoul to the confrontation clause (*Ohio v. Roberts*, 1980). Reliability, more crudely put, currently is the main theme of the Confrontation Clause, and one that may actually do away with the element of fairness. Nevertheless, that situation may be more advantageous to criminal defendants than the situation Dutch defendants face as far as confrontation is concerned.

The Dutch criminal justice system recognizes the expert's report as a legal means of evidence (Article 344.1(4) Sv.), and one that can be used ignorant of the question whether or not the expert is available for testimony.[7] While fairness may dictate that the defendant should be able to confront the witness against him, it should be pointed out that the "Dutch" expert is not formally a witness against the defendant (since officially called for assistance by the court). That argument is not necessarily

---

[7] Although this is currently standard practice in the Netherlands, there is in fact evidence that indicates that this practice is contrary to the Dutch legislature's intentions. During the legislative process of the Code of Criminal Procedure, the legislature stated that the use of expert reports as evidence was conditional upon the expert being already under oath when he documented his statements. Alternatively, such documented statements need to be affirmed by the expert at the trial, while under oath (Blok & Besier, 1925, p. 162). None of these requirements has ever been legislated, however, nor enforced by the Dutch Supreme Court.

seriously flawed or any more problematical than the "American" way of thinking on the right to confrontation, yet it does present something of a problem when the expert is not actually called for assistance by a judge, *or* is not fulfilling the premise his activity is being based upon; that of independence and impartiality from the parties to the criminal litigation. At this point, the decisions of the European Court of Human Rights in the cases of *Bönisch* (ECHR 6 May 1985, A-92, *NJ* 1989, 385) and *Brandstetter* (ECHR 28 August 1991, A-211), both directed at the state of Austria, play an ever so important role (e.g., Van Kampen, 2000a). From these decisions, it can be inferred that when there are objectively justified fears about the court-expert's impartiality, thus in effect rendering the expert a witness *against* the defendant, fairness requires that the defendant be presented with the opportunity to secure the attendance of experts on his behalf, while these experts should be treated in the same way as the court treats the experts against the defendant. And although that requirement *may* be met by providing the defendant with the opportunity to present expert testimony at trial, generally—and in light of other subprovisions of Article 6 § 3—it requires the defendant be provided with the right to retest the evidence (Van Kampen, 1998, pp. 123 and 126). Confrontation, in other words, here takes place by way of retesting and presenting the results in documented form, rather than directly facing the "adverse" expert in open court.

One of the interesting parallels between the decisions on the right to confrontation in the American criminal justice system on the one hand, and its Dutch counterpart on the other, is that the focal point of that right lies in the supposed *reliability* of the out-of-court statement of the expert. According to American case law, the right to confrontation is not violated when the expert's out-of-court statement falls within one of the firmly rooted exceptions to the hearsay rule, or otherwise bears particularized indicia of reliability. According to the case law of the European Court on Human Right, fairness is similarly held not generally to be violated when there are no objectively justified fears regarding the expert's impartiality; when, in other words, the expert is indeed performing his duty to the court as he is expected to, thereby ensuring that he has no case to further but the case of the court (and thus, in a way, guaranteeing the reliability of his evidence).

The major and consequential difference that still remains, however, is that Dutch defendants are much more likely to be confronted with expert reports than American defendants, notwithstanding the definite trend in the United States to admit more (and generally quite problematical) hearsay evidence in criminal cases (Douglass, 2000). And given the prevalent trend in Dutch criminal proceedings, such reports are likely to become more and more akin to the dreaded *ex parte* affidavits the (American) Confrontation Clause was meant to protect against. Bias and undue influence, whether conscious or unconscious, simply result from the fact that many experts (and most particularly forensic science experts) within the Dutch system only work on behalf of the state, generally receive their assignments and their information from, and selected by, police officers, while feedback or criticism on part of adverse experts may be totally absent because the defense cannot actually secure either the financial or personal resources to secure expert assistance (Van Kampen, 2000b, pp. 60–70). In that respect, risks loom large. These risks moreover assume greater proportions when it comes to reports from police officers. Such reports routinely qualify as expert reports and can as such be used as proof of guilt. In that instance, there is a forceful argument to be made that such reports are in fact ex parte affidavits. In the United States, reports from police officers are not generally admissible in evidence, as FRE 803 (8) excludes the introduction of public reports setting forth "matters observed by police officers and other law enforcement personnel" (Van Kampen, 1998, pp. 208–211). Perhaps more astonishingly, defense counsel in the Netherlands generally seem oblivious of these risks, and infrequently request retesting even when they have a statutory right to do so (Hielkema, 1996, pp. 270–271; Van Kampen, 1998, p. 82).

THE RIGHT TO COMPULSORY PROCESS

In the American criminal justice system, the right to confrontation has an equally important companion: the so-called right to compulsory process, also incorporated in the Sixth Amendment. Whereas the right to confrontation allows the defendant—at least in theory—to face the witnesses against him in open court, the right to compulsory process allows the defendant to secure the attendance and testimony of the witnesses in his favor. Similarly, the European Convention on Human Rights provides that the defendant has the right to obtain the attendance and examinations of *witnesses* on his behalf (Article 6 § 3(d)). In the United States, the right to compulsory process is considered so fundamental by the U.S. Supreme Court that it may actually transcend legitimate concerns regarding the evidentiary reliability of the evidence presented by the defense. In *Washington v. Texas* (1967), one of the landmark compulsory process cases, the defendant had attempted to put his accomplice on the stand, in order for him to testify that the defendant (Washington) had actually tried to prevent his accomplice from firing the fatal shot. According to the then governing rules in Texas, co-participants were incompetent to testify for one another, and thus the attempt failed. The U.S. Supreme Court, however, reversed the decision, holding that the right to compulsory process is the right to present a defense, and not merely to secure the attendance of witnesses: "The Framers did not intend to commit the futile act of giving a defendant the right to secure the attendance of witnesses whose testimony he has no right to use" (*Id.*, 23).

Similarly, in *Chambers v. Mississippi* (1973), the U.S. Supreme Court held that the hearsay rule, which prevented the defendant in that case from introducing the testimony of three witnesses, may not be applied "mechanistically" where constitutional rights directly affecting the ascertainment of guilt were implicated. And in 1987, in *Rock v. Arkansas*, the U.S. Supreme Court held that while the states have a legitimate interest in protecting the accuracy of the fact-finding process by excluding potentially unreliable evidence, such as the results from hypnosis, the state had failed to show that the evidence resulting from hypnosis—per se excluded by Arkansas law—was always so untrustworthy as to impair the defendant from presenting her version of the events through such testimony in that particular case. As in *Washington* and *Chambers*, the court in *Rock* admonished the trial courts that evidentiary rules pertaining to the reliability of evidence cannot be applied *mechanistically* to critical defense evidence. As is equally clear from these cases, however, the defendant's right to present relevant evidence is not unlimited, but rather subject to "reasonable restrictions" (*Id.*, at 55). Such restrictions are *not* unconstitutional so long as they are not arbitrary or disproportionate to the purpose they are designed to serve (*Id.*, at 56; see also *United States v. Scheffer*, 1998).

Under the European Convention, the content of the right to compulsory process is less clear-cut, if only because the wording of that right refers to witnesses only, while experts and witnesses are not treated alike by the European Court (Van Kampen, 1998, pp. 118ff). Something similar to the U.S. Supreme Court holdings can be inferred, however, from the scant Dutch cases related to the subject. In a 1984 case, the Dutch Supreme Court held that statements made under hypnoses can be introduced on the defendant's behalf in order to show that the defendant is *not* guilty as charged (HR 12 June 1984, *NJ* 1985, 135). Such statements, however, cannot be used in evidence in order to show that the defendant is guilty as charged, given the uncertainty that governs the question as to whether such statements are actually sufficiently reliable (HR 17 March 1998, *NJ* 1998, 798). In a 1993 case, a Dutch Court of Appeal moreover allowed the defendant to present the results of a lie detector test (Recherche Adviescommissie, 1994), whereas such results cannot be used as proof of guilt. Although it is of course a legitimate question to ask whether such cases constitute the rule or the exception to it, there is a general belief that they *are* the rule, given the decisional criterion in criminal cases. In Dutch criminal cases, a powerful legal refrain is *in dubio pro reo* (doubt benefits the defendant).

The defendant merely needs to cast doubt about his guilt; he does not have to prove his innocence (Nijboer, 2000a, p. 28). Thus, he is not strictly held by the evidentiary requirements meant to ensure guilt is being based on sufficiently reliable evidence.

For the Dutch criminal justice system, that may be a relatively simple conclusion to draw, little concerned as it generally is—or at least for the longest time has been—with a case-by-case analysis of the reliability of the evidence presented to the court. The actors within the American criminal justice system, however, are far more concerned with reliability of the evidence, something intrinsically linked with the fact that in that system, the parties present the evidence. In that system of law, the fact that constitutional rights such as the right to compulsory process may actually transcend reliability concerns is far more consequential and important.

Yet, although of paramount importance, the "American" right to compulsory process remains a right that may be far out of reach for most criminal defendants. The right to compulsory process is a trial right, and whether the defendant can actually exercise that right depends largely on the question what evidence he has been able to uncover useful witnesses or evidence, either by exercising his right to discovery or by his right to secure expert assistance. Aside from the fact that the vast majority of cases in the United States are resolved through plea bargaining, even in the tiny minority of cases that go to trial, the requirements and limits on discovery and employment of experts mean that "American" defendants may not actually be able to present anything at trial as far as expert evidence is concerned.

EXPERT EVIDENCE IN THE NETHERLANDS AND THE UNITED STATES: DIFFERENT SHADES OF GRAY

The foregoing analysis leaves many interesting and important subjects related to expert evidence untouched. Can experts in both systems of law testify to (foreign) law? Are experts allowed to testify on the ultimate issue? What kinds of data can the expert base his opinion on? In this contribution, these and related questions have been left unanswered. Instead, this contribution has focused on some of the "overarching" and paramount rights such as the right to expert assistance, to discovery, to confrontation and to compulsory process, and what these rights mean or should be taken to mean in the context of expert evidence. As (almost) always in comparative research, the question is what we can learn from such a comparative analysis. One potential answer to that question is "not much." As is evidenced by the foregoing analysis, there are no clear-cut or definite lessons to be learned from foreign experience on the subject of expert evidence; all one is able to discover are different shades of gray. Some rules and practices seem quite alike in their consequences, others seem to differ more, yet these differences appear closely related to other aspects of the system, and may potentially have quite similar effects. What does seem evident, however, is that these different shades of gray feature against a somewhat bleak background as far as criminal defendants are concerned. For to argue that in essence very similar rights do seem to exist in both systems of law as far as expert evidence is concerned (at least insofar as discussed in this contribution) is not the same as arguing that these rights actually suffice from point of view of defendants. Despite the fact that considerable progress has been made in both systems of law in furthering "the defendant's case," expert evidence remains a potentially difficult type of evidence for criminal defendants to argue against. While such evidence is often depicted as crucial in deciding guilt or innocence, such evidence is as the same time, and as far as defense rights are concerned, quite a weak link in the evidentiary chain that ultimately determines guilt or innocence. And as the Dutch saying goes, "the strength of any chain is determined by its weakest link." Needless to say, that leaves much to be desired for in either system of law under review here.

13

Expert Witnesses in Europe and the United States

MICHAEL J. SAKS

The observations contained in this chapter suggest that, when it comes to coping with scientific and other expert evidence, neither the Anglo-American adversary system nor the Civil Law system is quite up to the task. But they tend to fail in different ways, and that may provide clues to improving both.

PRELIMINARY CONSIDERATIONS

At the outset, perhaps we can agree on some basic beliefs about science and law.

First, science (and other knowledge) can be useful in reducing uncertainty, and therefore can be useful to the courts. For example, one of the earliest common law cases involving scientific expert witnesses confronted the question of whether a young woman found dead had drowned or been thrown into a river after first being murdered. Physicians conducted a series of experiments with dogs to try to learn how to distinguish the lungs of a person who drowned from those of a person who died before going into the water (Howell, 2000).

But expertise of any kind presents a challenge to trial fact finders that may, by definition, be insurmountable: Non-expert judges are given the responsibility to evaluate the asserted expertise of asserted experts. In the adversary system, if the asserted experts pass that gatekeeper's test, then they must be evaluated by non-expert fact finders (judges or jurors).

The problems involved in such an evaluation are manifold. Is the underlying expertise valid (this is the question being confronted increasingly by American federal judges in the wake of the U.S. Supreme Court's decision in *Daubert et ux. v. Merrell Dow Pharmaceuticals, Inc.*, 1993)? If an expertise exists, is the expert offered at trial competent in that expertise? Is the expert sufficiently competent in general or in his or her performance in this particular case? Is a competent expert being honest with the trial fact finder? Or might the expert deliberately be withholding or shading or fabricating testimony? The gatekeeper's or fact finder's own lack of expertness often will result in excessive, mindless, uncritical deference to an expert witness. Or in erroneous dismissal out-of-hand. Neither is a rational appraisal of the information being offered.

How does each of our systems seek to gain the benefits of knowledge and avoid the pitfalls? Which system does a better job in dealing with each of these stages of evaluation? Which system overall screens out bad science better? Which system is better at catching scandalous errors, at spotting poor "science" (Giannelli, 1997; Saks, 1998)? At the end of the day, which system produces fewer erroneous convictions based on faulty expertise or experts (Dwyer, Neufeld, & Scheck, 2000)?

My hunch at present is that the adversarial system, when practiced well, should be better at testing the underlying science. And that the inquisitorial system should be better at the routine application of science that is sound. This state of affairs means that, in both systems, the effective use of good science probably is attributable more to luck than any inherent capacities of the systems to use science to discover truth.

THE ADVERSARIAL SYSTEM: IN THEORY AND IN PRACTICE

The adversary system relies fundamentally on the behavior of organizations that are completely outside of itself. It assumes that knowledge generally will be conscientiously and rigorously developed by its field (this is especially true under the *Frye* test, *Frye v. United States*, 1923). Some fields work vigorously at doing exactly that. In other fields the underlying knowledge development and testing is so weak as to border on the nonexistent (Saks, 1998). If a field falls short of the law's expectations, the system assumes that attorneys motivated to win will draw that failing to the attention of the court. But most lawyers have terribly limited knowledge of most fields, which puts them in a poor position to raise such challenges. To be fair, how can lawyers or judges or anyone be sufficiently knowledgeable about a multitude of fields that they can point out the weaknesses of those fields over the protestations of asserted experts? If there is a practical answer, it is to assume nothing and to seek out experts (or counter-experts) who do have a chance of knowing the flaws. Some books have recently been developed which aim to give lawyers a place to start in this nearly impossible challenge (Faigman, Kaye, Saks, & Sanders, 1997; Federal Judicial Center, 1994). One grows weary reading cases in which lawyers raised typical "legal" challenges to scientific evidence, while completely overlooking challenges to the underlying science (e.g., HIV-testing, forensic science of various types). Thus, one of the weak links in the theory of the adversary process is the capability of the attorneys—both prosecutors and defense counsel—to present and to attack scientific evidence.

The process in court requires the trial judge to decide whether to admit or exclude scientific evidence offered by one of the parties and opposed by the other party. Two alternative legal tests, both with variations, dominate this judicial gate keeping role. Courts in jurisdictions using the *Frye* test are to ask themselves whether the proposed testimony rests on principles that are "generally accepted" within the relevant field. Courts in jurisdictions using the test under the Federal Rules, as interpreted by the United States Supreme Court in *Daubert* and *Kumho Tire* (1999), are to ask themselves whether the underlying principles are sound. It should be obvious that the *Frye* test relies more heavily on the assumption that various fields find a way to produce truth and decide what truth is, and involves more deference to those various fields. But in an adversary system, where judges are dependent upon submissions and challenges by the attorneys, neither test can work particularly well without counsel who know enough to educate the judges.

Moreover, both tests have been known to permit considerable fudging by judges when—for whatever reason—they have a feeling that they want to admit or exclude any particular kind of expert testimony. If one had to name a single principle that drives judges under both systems, it probably would be Conventionalism. Judges want to admit what is thought by the general public to be genuine expertise, or which other judges before them have generally admitted; and to exclude what the general public distrusts, or which other judges before them have generally excluded. If that is the driving force, *Frye* comes close to being the perfect test, and it is easy to apply. But if the underlying validity of an expertise is the goal, as the Supreme Court since *Daubert* has commanded that it be, the strong temptation to remain conventional causes a considerable tension between what judges want to do and what the federal courts are now supposed to do (for examples of cases in which judges reflect the tension described here, see the introductions to various chapters in Faigman et al., 1997).

The American adversary system further assumes that attorneys are deterred from offering unsound testimony by two features. One is the adversary process itself: If unsound scientific evidence manages to get past the gate keeping judge, the attorney on the other side is motivated to cross-examine the expert and reveal to the fact finder the weaknesses of the expert's evidence. In addition, Federal Rule of Evidence 706 empowers the court to appoint its own expert witnesses. This rule has a remarkable theory behind it, namely, that its mere existence will deter attorneys from proffering questionable "expertise"—and therefore it rarely will need to be used (Saks, 1995). One thing we know is that Rule 706 rarely is used (Cecil & Willging, 1993). Whether its purpose is achieved is far more doubtful. The adversarial temptation to approach the borderlines of junk science, and perhaps to put a few toes across that line, do not appear to be dampened by Rule 706—though it is impossible to say what would be offered if Rule 706 did not exist. And the effectiveness of cross-examination of experts is dependent upon the knowledge of counsel doing the cross-examining. As already noted, few attorneys, at least on the criminal side of the courthouse, know much about the sciences being proffered, whether they are doing the proffering or the opposing. Moreover, the witness game may turn at least as much on apparent "credibility" of witnesses as it does on the soundness of the substance. Thus,cross-examining attorneys are more likely to focus on raising concerns about the bias ("you always testify for that side, don't you?") or interest ("isn't it true that you'll testify for either side of these issues, as long as they are paying you?") of the other side's witnesses than on digging down into the content of what they had to say.

In order to make the battle more substantive, the law has mandated more openness. Recent revisions to the federal rules require the disclosure of reports by experts and facilitate discovery of the proposed expert witness's contemplated testimony (see recent amendments to the Federal Rules of Civil Procedure, Rule 26, and the Federal Rules of Criminal Procedure, Rule 16). This seems to work reasonably well in civil (noncriminal) cases, where such mutual disclosure has become familiar to lawyers since the advent of the federal rules of civil procedure in 1938. On the criminal side, there still is a tendency by prosecutors to try to hide their expert evidence, to preserve the tradition of trial by ambus—and with it, the less informative use of expert witnesses.

Although the American adversary system—in contrast to the Dutch (and other) civil law trial systems—generally does not permit expert testimony by witnesses whose job is to assess the credibility of other witnesses, this sort of evidence nevertheless sneaks in. Certain exceptions, often involving psychologists, allow credibility expert testimony to enter through a back door. For example, there might be testimony about psychological syndromes (e.g., Battered Woman Syndrome, Rape Trauma Syndrome) or about examinations of child victims of almost any kind of alleged harm, where the expert's testimony conveys information to the judge and jury about the expert's belief in the truth of the statements given (or not given) by another witness or party (Spencer, 1998).

The difficulties the adversary system has in dealing competently with scientific evidence are in large degree structural. The system assumes a fair fight between two parties who develop their cases before a neutral third party. But criminal defendants usually have far fewer resources than prosecutors. Crime laboratories work for police investigators and with prosecutors. Few defendants have comparable experts of their own to double check, detect errors, and challenge bad science or erroneous applications or interpretations—all of the things the theory of the adversary process expects and intends will happen. But without such resources on both sides, it cannot. Similarly, in civil tort cases, defendants generally have more resources than plaintiffs do.

A second structural problem is that the process itself tends to distort the science. Think of information falling along a more or less normal distribution. In the middle are the facts that are most widely agreed upon. At one tail are the facts and interpretations that one minority subscribes to and at the other extreme are those that their opposite number subscribe to. Different fact-assembling procedures will draw from different parts of that distribution. The adversary system will emphasize the tails of such a distribution to the extent that it is advantageous to the parties to take opposing positions on scientific propositions (Saks & Van Duizend, 1983). This contrasts sharply with systems that seek consensus among those holding diverse views (e.g., medical consensus conferences). Those systems tend to draw from the center of the information distribution posited above.

A final distorting feature I will mention is the test of admission that prevails. One such rule is that scientific expert evidence is admissible only if it enjoys a consensus within its own field, that is, the *Frye* test. That places a considerable amount of the power to decide what is admissible in the field rather than in the court. Fields differ in their rigor and traditions of vigorous testing and debate over their own ideas. Under this rule, the courts will tend to admit evidence more readily from fields with weak scientific traditions and more reluctantly from fields with more vigorous scientific customs. It also creates at least some incentive for a field to maintain a high degree of consensus, and no incentive to improve the quality of their knowledge. This seems to have reached it peak among the forensic sciences: They have no function outside of supplying evidence for possible use in courtrooms (that is, little academic or commercial reason to test and improve their knowledge), they have no competitors, and they have weak scientific traditions (Saks, 1998). Under a rule like *Frye*, such fields are in the enviable position of certifying their own eternal admissibility, yet need not improve the quality or quantity of their knowledge—unless and until they choose to do so. Change the rule to one in which admissibility depends upon the court determining that their knowledge and methods are dependable, and suddenly the likelihood increases that they will fail the new test and be denied admission. And, suddenly, an incentive is created to test and to learn and to advance knowledge and skill. That seems to be exactly what is happening under the test announced by the United States Supreme Court in *Daubert v. Merrell Dow* (see Faigman et al., 1997, Chapter 1).

THE CIVIL LAW SYSTEM: IN THEORY AND IN PRACTICE

Thibaut & Walker's *Theory of Justice* (1978) suggests that when the dispute to be resolved is essentially a cognitive conflict (that is, one in which resolving a factual uncertainty—in contrast to a distributional or attributional uncertainty—resolves the conflict), then the best trial procedure will be the one that has the best ability to provide unambiguous information to the disputants or to a third-party decision-maker. Their empirical work suggests that the search incentives of the adversary trial will transform a skewed distribution of real-world facts and present to the court a more balanced distribution of facts. An inquisitorial system, by contrast, tends to more faithfully reproduce for the court the external distribution of facts.

Additional advantages that have been argued on behalf of the civil law system include the following. One is that it insures the availability of competent experts by having the court pre-screen and enlist such experts. Another is that by having experts identify with the court, and not with a party, experts are more able to be neutral and independent (at least of the partisan positions of the parties) and therefore bias is reduced. Expert witnesses are more able to gain all (not half) of the picture of the evidence in the case, and can give all of the evidence they feel is important to resolving the issues before the court (rather than being limited to answering the questions posed by partisan counsel). Finally, experts in the civil law system are said to be more accountable to their own field, rather than to police or parties or lawyers—especially where their discipline provides to the court a carefully controlled list of representatives of a field who are approved by that field to serve as expert witnesses (Spencer, 1998). Even if this is not as true in practice as it is claimed to be, it should be apparent that the Civilian system can more easily make this feature true. Thus, at least where a dispute turns heavily on factual issues, the civil law system should be advantageous.

On the other hand, we might entertain some concerns. First, the civil law has no built-in skepticism about the question of whether an expertise exists. If there is no expertise, there can be no experts. That is to say, unless and until a body of reliable knowledge and skill can be established, claims to possess such knowledge and skill must be viewed skeptically. Although lawyers and judges in the adversary system do an unimpressive job of evaluating scientific expert offerings, that system nevertheless provides unmistakable opportunities to challenge the expertise—as well as the expert or the application to the particular case. In the adversary system these include legal tests for assessing the admissibility of the asserted expertise and procedural devices for presenting the challenge (pre-trial hearings, motions in limine, voir dire of experts). Once the civil law system comes to accept a field—and by what process that happens it is hard to say, but conventionalism seems a likely explanation—the courts have committed themselves institutionally to belief in the existence of an expertise, to the field that practices it, and to the experts who are authorized by the field to serve as expert witnesses. To challenge the fundamental belief in those fields of asserted expertise comes close to challenging the judicial institution as well. And the process by which the challenge could be posed is difficult to discern. The civil law system implicitly adopts what American jurisdictions call the *Frye* test: if members of the field believe in themselves, then the courts adopt that belief, without any separate test of their validity.

Second, the civil law system frankly permits credibility assessments by supposed experts on such matters. In Germany, indeed, a judge who did not appoint an expert to advise the court on the credibility of a problematic witness could find the verdict appealed because he or she had failed in the duty to take all proper measures to establish the truth (Spencer, 1998, p. 38). These experts include psychiatrists and psychologists offering testimony about the credibility of a child's allegations of sexual abuse, using statement validity analysis (SVA), and so on. My concerns have less to do with notions of invading the province of the fact finder and more to do with the mere fact that the testimony is admitted without first ascertaining whether the techniques are valid in the first place and, if they are, with what limiting conditions. Apparently, it is enough that the experts believe in themselves and their techniques. In order for the courts to reject an expertise once it has been accepted, it would appear to be necessary for the experts to draw the courts' attention to a discovery that the experts cannot, after all, do what they have all along been claiming that they can do. It is hard to imagine many fields of expertise making such confessions.

Expert witnesses in the civil law system are said to be more independent, in that they are not called by either party to a dispute, but by the judge. There is no doubt that experts in the adversary system are too closely allied with one side or another. Though it must be said that this comes about in spite of, not because of, the formal ideology of the system. Over-identification with a party, rather than loyalty to the fact finder, is a byproduct of the structure of the system, which requires the parties to find their own expert witnesses, brief them, prepare them for trial, remunerate them, and present their expert testimony (Saks, 1992; Saks & Van Duizend, 1983). Moreover, these same factors play a part in selecting and shaping, and ultimately distorting, the knowledge "out there" for delivery to a court.

But just how independent are civil system experts? Lack of independence comes from other sources in addition to the attorney representing one side of a case. To the extent that an expert witness is associated with a police agency that took part in the investigation of a case, or pursuant to requests from an investigating magistrate, the witness becomes committed to a viewpoint, not unlike that of adversary witnesses in many contexts. Indeed, this is not unlike the fundamental concern about the neutrality of judges who participate in the investigation (as civilian judges do), and tend to engage in a confirmatory search for evidence that supports hypotheses formed early on the basis of little evidence, in contrast to the position of neutral and passive judges (judges in the adversary system).

Relatedly, do civilian experts become privy to too much other information about a case, and therefore suffer from having too many cues as to the "correct" decisions they "should" be making within their own field of expertise? Ideally, from a methodological viewpoint, experts would be required to offer their opinion on the basis of no more biasing evidence than they truly must have to conduct their own analyses. Indeed, evidence could be presented to experts in much the way lineups are presented to eyewitnesses, and for the same reasons: to obtain evidence about the witness's accuracy as well as about the suspect's culpability. Otherwise, what appears to be multiple independent sources of evidence that all point in the same direction are really an illusion, based on quite a lot of double counting. To give a glaring example: A forensic dentist friend told me that his colleagues had discussed the possibility of adopting a practice whereby they would always withhold their own conclusions until after the results of DNA testing in the same case were in hand. That would prevent them from the embarrassment of being in conflict with the DNA typing results. It also prevents the court from gaining the value of independent evidence.

Finally, judges who call expert witnesses and work with them (which happens rarely in the adversarial system but is typical in the civilian system) tend to place excessive trust in "their" experts. I base this comment on the findings of a study of American federal judges who have employed their own expert witnesses (Cecil & Willging, 1993). These judges come to have an astonishingly high assessment of their own witnesses, and a far lower assessment of the experts called by the parties. I suspect this has more to do with the role relationships and less to do with the actual competence of the experts (Saks, 1995). Judges (like anyone else) be more influenced by the role relationships, and the attributions that engenders, than by the actual competence and value of the experts. Thus, Continental judges may have more faith in their experts and Anglo-American judges less faith, but the actual worth of these experts may not differ.

CONCLUSION

I see no indication that either system has learned to manage expert evidence with any real competence. Neither system does a respectable job of evaluating the claims of expertise of various fields that offer their asserted knowledge to the courts. Though the adversary system has procedures and rules to deal with precisely these issues, few lawyers or judges have sufficient competence to deal with them effectively (Moenssens, Inbau, Starrs, & Henderson, 1995; Snow, 1959). As a result, there is little real judicial scrutiny of expertise. These are daunting problems that neither system has come close to solving. For those fields that truly have sound techniques and apply them with care, the inquisitorial system appears to offer a greater chance of putting that knowledge to use with less distortion.

Perhaps some mixing of adversarial and inquisitorial elements would offer the most advantageous effect: An adversary process for testing admissibility of asserted expertise, and a more civilian approach to bringing the evidence of expert witnesses to the fact finders in particular cases. On the latter point, it may be well worth considering the ideas of Sam Gross, who has proposed that parties nominate the experts they think the court should hear (an adversarial element), the witnesses then are called by and employed by the court (a civilian element), pre-trial meetings with the experts are open to both sides (civilian), but at trial testimony is elicited by the parties (adversarial, Gross, 1991).

Or perhaps the two systems both reflect the desire of lawyers and judges who know little science to remain not having to know much. Perhaps their differences reflect the European faith in experts and authority and the American distrust of government and passion for markets (Reitz, 1990).

14

The Role of the Forensic Expert in an Inquisitorial System

TON BROEDERS

As a forensic expert who is practicing in a country with what is traditionally described as an inquisitorial criminal law system, I have had relatively little professional experience with adversarial type justice systems. My perception of the expert's role in the latter type of system is therefore necessarily largely based on what I have read about it in the scholarly literature as well as, inevitably, by what I have seen in factual and fictional accounts of the adversarial system at work. I am not however entirely destitute of hands-on experience of the role of the expert witness in an adversarial setting, as will appear from the following anecdote.

Some years ago, I received a summons from a British colleague of mine and subsequently found myself being flown at very short notice and no doubt at considerable expense to the beautiful island of Mauritius. I was asked to aid the defense in their challenge of the procedure by which the prosecution had obtained several ear witness identifications of one of two defendants as the woman who had made an extremely incriminating telephone call in association with a fire in which the male defendant's wife had died. This is not the proper place to go into the details of the case or the trial but some aspects of it are clearly relevant to the present discussion. One of the things I remember most vividly was the way I was seated immediately behind the defense lawyers, a position which—during

245

the cross-examination of the prosecution expert—turned out to greatly facilitate the exchange of a steady flow of hastily scribbled messages between the defense lawyers and myself, which procedure enabled the former to put a large number of extremely awkward questions to the prosecution expert with a minimum of delay and sometimes to considerable effect. More generally, what the whole context seemed to promote more than anything was the taking of an undeniably partisan position. By exposing the methodological weaknesses of the procedure used by the prosecution expert, I was in effect helping the defense get the identification evidence ruled inadmissible. Whether in doing so I was making a contribution to the truth-finding process is clearly a different question.

WRITTEN REPORTS

Interestingly enough, my experience as an expert witness in a Dutch court of law is also limited, but for a very different reason. In the vast majority of cases, forensic evidence is supplied by court-appointed experts under permanent oath, many of whom are employed by the Netherlands Forensic Institute, the forensic science laboratory of the Dutch Ministry of Justice. The reputation of this institute in criminal law circles is such that the results of forensic examinations carried out by its experts are rarely challenged by the defense. Like interrogations of suspects and witnesses, which are normally carried out by the police or by an investigating judge and presented to the court in a written format, forensic reports in the Netherlands are typically submitted to the court in written form only, in accordance with the *de auditu* principle, a practice which makes it possible for Dutch court proceedings to rank among the briefest and most efficient in the Western world. It is generally only in the more controversial or recently developed and/or less well-known forensic disciplines as well as in high profile cases that the laboratory's experts are called to testify by the courts, not infrequently at the request of the defense. As I am involved in one such less well-established area, forensic speaker identification and audio analysis, I am called up relatively frequently by Dutch standards. Even then, the defense strategy is not primarily aimed to test the validity of the conclusion that is formulated by the expert but seems almost invariably set to achieve only one thing: to get the expert to say something less specific than the text in the report, not to challenge the expert's methods as such.

EVALUATION OF FORENSIC EVIDENCE

A major difference between the two judicial systems under discussion concerns the role of the judge in determining the admissibility of evidence, including evidence of a forensic nature. In Common Law, adversarial type systems, evidence could be said to be subject to a form of input control. The judge plays an important role as gatekeeper to stop irrelevant or misleading information reaching the jury. On the other hand, Continental Law systems tend to use a form of output control. According to Margot (1998), in the inquisitorial system judges are traditionally led by the three guiding principles of *liberté des preuves, liberté d'appréciation* and *l'intime conviction*. Essentially, the first two of these principles imply that judges are free to accept or reject evidence, and to assess and evaluate it as they see fit, as long as such decisions are duly motivated. As a result, the need to rely on guidelines by means of which the question of the admissibility of evidence can be resolved—of which the *Frye* test, the Federal Rules of Evidence and the *Daubert* ruling are examples in the US context—has clearly traditionally been less strongly felt in the continental European systems. On the other hand, Continental Law systems would seem to be much more concerned with the legal status of the evidence—more specifically with the question whether it may have been obtained in ways which conflict with the law—than with its validity and reliability.

By and large, it seems that judges in Dutch courts tend to admit expert evidence if it comes from what strikes them as a reliable source. A prominent Dutch psychologist who has frequently appeared as an expert witness both in Dutch courts and abroad (Wagenaar, 1988), has often expressed his surprise at being asked to state his age and his academic status only before being allowed to give his expert opinion in a Dutch court, a procedure which contrasts sharply with what is usual in adversarial type courts. A colleague of mine was recently involved as a court appointed firearms expert in a case where the defense had called their own firearms expert. Again, the only question my colleague was asked to prove his status was to give his first name and age while the defense expert had brought and was asked to show all diplomas and certificates deemed even remotely relevant to his expertise before he was allowed to answer a single question. However, there are indications that the tide may be changing (Malsch & Nijboer, 1999). In another recent case, the identification of a suspect of a series of petrol station robberies on the basis of videotapes showing the perpetrator's ear has led to what may be the beginning of an unprecedented discussion of the role of forensic identification methodology in the Dutch criminal context (Van Koppen & Crombag, 2000).

QUALITY ASSURANCE

Clearly, in an inquisitorial system there is the dilemma posed by the two poles of education versus deference: do judges see it as their responsibility to evaluate the quality of the expert evidence presented to them or do they in fact bow to the expert's superior knowledge in his or her field, perhaps even while deluding themselves into thinking that they are able to assess the value of the expert evidence (Allen & Miller, 1993). Partly because they wish to dissociate themselves from this uncomfortable dilemma, forensic science laboratories are increasingly realizing that they have a role to play in ensuring the quality of their forensic casework. In Europe, this work is taken forward within ENFSI, the European Network of Forensic Science Institutes, which was formally established in 1994 and seeks to promote education and training of experts, the introduction and enforcement of quality assurance systems and the harmonization of methods and techniques in the various forensic disciplines. Laboratories like the Forensic Science Service in Britain, SKL in Sweden, NBICL in Finland and NFI, my own laboratory, to mention just a handful, have certified some of their forensic examinations with nationally operating, external and independent laboratory certification boards, such as UKAS in the United Kingdom and the Council for Accreditation in the Netherlands, and are continuing to do so. An increasingly important role in this context is being played by the ENFSI Expert Working Groups which were set up in the last decade. Like their American counterparts, such as the Scientific Working Group for Materials Analysis (SWGMAT) and the Scientific Working Group for Document Examination (SWGDOC) working under the auspices of the FBI, and similar groups in Australia and New Zealand, such as the Scientific Advisory Groups (SAG) operating within the context of SMANZFL (the Senior Managers of Australian and New Zealand Forensic Science Laboratories), many of the ENFSI Expert Working Groups, such as the Drugs, Fibers, Paint, Firearms and DNA Groups are actively involved in drawing up best practice manuals, setting up collaborative tests and education and training programs and working towards increased harmonization and standardization of methods and techniques.

LIMITATIONS OF QUALITY ASSURANCE

While the importance of quality assurance, in the form of certification, proficiency testing or validation is increasingly being recognized and more and more laboratories are implementing quality assurance programs, it should be borne in mind that, in the forensic context in particular, the external validity of quality assurance measures is necessarily limited. Forensic questions often relate to unique situations which cannot usefully be replicated under controlled conditions (Robertson & Vigneaux, 1995). The external validity of the results of controlled laboratory experiments, frequently carried out with university students as subjects, is often questionable and may create an unrealistically gloomy picture. On the other hand, some of the collaborative tests—a euphemism for proficiency tests— that are currently available from organizations like CTS (Collaborative Testing Service) are often felt to be too easy. They may create a false semblance of security in suggesting that forensic standards are up to scratch, while in fact they demonstrate an appalling incompetence on the part of at least some of the—anonymous—participants. As a result, forensic experts are increasingly looking into ways of setting up their own tests within the framework of organizations like ENFSI.

At the same time, the demands imposed on the forensic field by some observers of the scene (e.g., Saks, 1998), are partly based on unrealistic assumptions about scientific progress and procedure. Indeed, if taken to their logical extreme, the views of those critics of the forensic scene who argue that hardly any of the forensic identification disciplines can rightly aspire to the status of a science would lead to the inevitable conclusion that the judicial system itself should be made to grind to an instantaneous halt. After all, in their unique task of converting uncertainty into certainty, judges and juries are no better placed to use scientifically correct procedures than expert witnesses. There is a real danger that valuable expertise can no longer be brought to bear on forensic issues because it fails to meet criteria which, if applied across the board, would affect almost all forensic disciplines. More than a hundred years after its introduction as a crime detection tool, fingerprint identification still lacks a sound scientific basis (Evett & Williams, 1996) and there are regular reports of false identifications (see http://onin.com/fp/problemidents.html for two recent cases). However, presumably not even Saks would advocate throwing the baby out with the bath water, i.e., argue that fingerprint evidence be ruled inadmissible. Yet, it appears that sometimes we are in danger of doing precisely that. Following the *Daubert et ux. v. Merrell Dow Pharmaceuticals, Inc.* (1993), *United States v. Starzecpyzel* (1995) and *Kumho Tire Co. v. Carmichael* (1999) judgments, defense lawyers in the USA would now seem to have powerful precedents to refer to in their efforts to stop potentially damaging evidence reaching the jury. Yet, even in an area of forensic expertise like authorship identification, which, depending on one's point of view, could either be described as obscure or novel, expert testimony may still be judged admissible in part. In a recent case involving the questioned authorship of a number of threatening letters (*United States v. Van Wyk*, 2000), the court did allow the expert, an FBI agent with a degree in criminal justice administration but not in linguistics, to point out linguistic similarities between writings known to have been authored by the defendant and the questioned writings. However, the expert's conclusion regarding the identity of the author of the questioned writings was barred, as the methodology employed was held to be insufficiently reliable under the *Daubert* standard.

INDEPENDENT EXPERTS, PARTISAN EXPERTS, AND HIRED GUNS

While the pursuit of the truth is of course by no means the only objective served by a trial, it is my personal belief that the inquisitorial system is better suited as a way of approximating to the truth in a given case than the adversarial system. Court-appointed experts, whether appointed by an investigating judge or by the court, are more likely to be in a position to make a contribution to the purpose of finding the truth, potentially make forensic expertise equally available to prosecution and defense and avoid the unnecessary duplication which will frequently occur if two experts representing opposing parties examine the same material. The results of the court-appointed expert's work can be made available before the trial rather than during the trial itself, which creates more time for consideration. If conflicting views are expressed by the defense or additional questions need to be answered, the investigating judge can refer these back to the expert or appoint a second expert. However, in order for state employed forensic experts to preserve their independence, it is desirable that state forensic laboratories should be divorced from police organizations, especially from operational police units, and forensic experts in state laboratories should always be aware of the danger of identifying with the prosecution perspective.

There may be another advantage to having independent professional forensic experts. There are indications that experts employed by universities and other research organizations as well as private experts tend to be more willing to act for the defense than as court-appointed experts. I regularly find myself casting around for expertise on a variety of foreign languages which is not available from professional forensic experts. My attempts to secure such expertise on behalf of an investigating judge from the ranks of university faculty or other non-professional experts frequently fail, even though the people I approach are almost invariably appreciative of the importance of expert evidence being available to the court. Nevertheless, they often have powerful reasons not to oblige. Some of the more common reasons for their unwillingness to appear as experts include the fear of reprisals from the suspect and the fear of the unpleasant implications their testimony might have for the suspect. Omenn (1997) discusses some other reasons why people with relevant expertise may be reluctant to act as experts in court, be it as prosecution or defense experts. Court proceedings tend to emphasize differences rather than seek consensus; there is the possible discomfort of having to face another person who is accepted by the court as an expert but who is really only marginally knowledgeable if at all, and there is the danger that in the end the only conclusion the court seems prepared to draw is that "the experts disagree". Further reservations may be due to the reluctance to face potentially hostile examination or to have one's expertise called into question, doubts about the relevance of one's knowledge to the issues being litigated or ambiguities about compensation for one's time. To which may be added: skepticism within scientific communities about getting involved in anything other than "pure" science, and misunderstandings of the role of expert (e.g., a fear that one might "get a guilty person off" rather than understanding that the job is to help decision makers make better decisions).

While state employed professional experts may tend to identify too closely with the prosecution, experts hired by parties will tend to take partisan positions. The involvement of defense experts in particular may tend to prolong the proceedings; they may be hired to confuse the issue, their expert opinions may be cooked, trimmed or entirely suppressed by the defense, who may even resort to expert shopping (Foster & Huber, 1997). During trials presentational skills may (be expressly designed to) divert the court's attention from content to form. By the same token, expert witnesses called by the prosecution may be too willing to cooperate with prosecutors who are eager to secure convictions at any cost, witness many examples of police, prosecutor and expert witness corruption in the USA, involving the use of fabricated evidence and perjured testimony against defendants. Arguably, the problems posed by partisan prosecution experts are potentially more serious than those created on the defense side because defendants, their attorneys, and their evidence tend to be viewed with greater skepticism by judges and juries.

In the civil context, the danger of partisan positions posing as scientific evidence is quite real, even though it may not be quite as common as it sometimes made out to be (Huber, 1991). More recently, Ong and Glantz (2000) exposed what they see as persistent attempts by the tobacco industry to discredit unwelcome results of studies on passive smoking by commissioning several million dollars' worth of new research that might be more favorable to the industry and generally adopting communications strategies aimed to misinform and thus subvert normal decision making processes. On a smaller scale, a Dutch medical consultant participating in a drug testing program was recently convicted for providing a pharmaceutical company with data for scores of patients who either did not exist or had never been prescribed the drug in question.

RECENT DEVELOPMENTS: DNA, THE EUROPEAN COURT OF HUMAN RIGHTS

The increasing prominence of DNA technology as an evidential tool, coupled with the growing interest in the application of Bayesian statistics that has followed in its wake, is making itself increasingly felt in many fields of forensic expertise (Broeders, 1999). Although the degree of quantification of the frequency of relevant characteristics that is possible in most traditional forensic fields does not even begin to compare with that in DNA evidence, there is every reason to believe that, in view of the wide acceptability that DNA evidence has gained, the conceptual framework that is associated with this type of evidence will gradually be expected to apply to other forensic disciplines as well. After all, even in those forensic areas where figures are a rare commodity, the Bayesian or likelihood approach has a lot to commend itself. It clarifies the role of the expert, provides a way of expressing the strength of a particular piece of evidence and stresses the need to formulate rival hypotheses to the prosecutor's hypothesis (Sjerps, 2000).

A second factor which is changing the status of forensic expertise in continental European inquisitorial systems is the increasing influence of Anglo-American adversarial-type procedures, standards and notions like equality of arms and the right to fair trial, as laid down in Article 6 of the European Convention for the Protection of Human Rights and Fundamental Freedoms. *Bönisch v. Austria* (1985), *Brandstetter v. Austria* (1991) and *Mantovanelli v. France* (1997) are some of the recent decisions of the European Court of Human Rights which are gradually beginning to affect the role of the expert in the Dutch criminal justice system. The first two decisions require that the defendant be given the opportunity to enlist the services of an expert of his own if there are objectively justified reasons to fear that the expert consulted by the court is not impartial (see also Van Kampen, this volume); in the third case the Court ruled that plaintiffs should have been afforded the opportunity to comment effectively on the expert's report before the tribunal. In the Netherlands, the most recent example of this trend is the Dutch Supreme Court's "shoemaker-stick-to-thy-last" ruling (HR 27 January 1998, *NJ* p. 404) that the evidence of an orthopedic shoemaker who identified footwear marks found at a scene of crime as originating from the suspect's shoes should not have been admitted by the appellate court because this court had failed to establish whether the shoemaker's expertise as an orthopedic shoemaker also includes the examination and analysis of footwear marks and if so, what method he had used, why he considered this method reliable and to what extent he was capable of applying the method in a competent fashion.

While Continental law systems are increasingly being confronted with adversarial-type procedures and principles when it comes to the role of expert evidence, there are indications that within adversarial type systems, the idea of introducing court appointed experts, a Continental law feature, is slowly gaining ground. Spencer (2000) believes that the Continental law systems are far ahead of common law systems in terms of rules designed to secure neutrality of experts. However, despite the growing awareness that biased expert evidence was a major factor in some of the recent miscarriages of justice in the UK, there is as yet no great enthusiasm for the introduction of court-appointed experts in criminal cases. Interestingly, the new Civil Procedure Rules do involve a clear move towards a single neutral expert, to be appointed jointly by the parties or, failing this, by the court.

CONCLUSION

In recent years, expert evidence has come to be both more commonly used and more closely scrutinized in common law as well as in Continental law systems. While common law systems are showing as yet little or no inclination to move towards the Continental type figure of the court appointed expert, Continental type criminal law systems are increasingly being confronted with the need to adapt to principles stemming from an adversarial type law system, including those affecting the role and position of forensic experts and their expertise. On a more academic level, the growing interest in the Netherlands in recent years in the status of expert evidence in the two legal systems under discussion is reflected in a spate of scholarly publications, of which those by Hielkema (1996), Van Kampen (1998), Malsch and Nijboer (1999), and Nijboer and Sprangers (2000) are likely to be some of the more influential.

15

Psychological Expert Witnesses in Germany and the Netherlands

CLAUDIA KNÖRNSCHILD AND
PETER J. VAN KOPPEN

DIVERSITY WITHIN UNITY

Both the legal system of the Netherlands and that of Germany are inquisitorial systems, at least for criminal cases. One could naively suppose that the differences in legal procedure between the two countries would be negligible compared to differences with accusatorial systems. And, indeed if one spends a day in court in The Netherlands and in Germany the two legal systems seem to share many features. The court—in both countries usually a three judge panel in cases of serious crimes—holds a much stronger position during trial than either the prosecution or the defense. For instance, the judge is the first to question the defendant and the witnesses, only after which the defense and the prosecution are given the opportunity to pose questions. One will look for a jury in vain.

In both countries, the criminal trial is much more envisaged as a quest for the truth, rather than a fair contest between two equal parties. The lack of adversarialness shared by both countries is especially noticeable in the role given to expert witnesses. Both the Dutch and German courts have a preference for expert witnesses appointed by an independent body: the court or the public prosecutor, the latter being a magistrate in both countries. Although the legal systems of the Netherlands and

Germany share such features, however, it would be rash to conclude that all inquisitorial systems are identical.

An investigation of the similarities and differences in treatment of expert witnesses by both countries is the aim of this article. We limited the study to the treatment of psychological experts in criminal cases. For reasons to be discussed below, we further limited the study to expertise in the field of credibility assessment. Within these limitations, however, we approached our task with a broad perspective. So, we compare the type of psychological experts engaged in both countries, the manner in which they are appointed, the reasons they are appointed and the tasks given to them, the instructions they receive, how psychological experts are supposed to conduct their business, the role they have in trial proceedings and, finally, which mechanisms, if any, exist to ensure the quality of their work.

METHOD

We conducted our study in two phases. First we analyzed the relevant articles of codified law (especially the two countries' codes of criminal procedure) and Supreme Court decisions in order to identify the rules that formally apply to psychological expert witnesses. Second we examined how and to what extent these formal regulations are reflected in daily practice and what guidelines have been established additionally. In order to gather further information about daily practice, we interviewed experienced psychological expert witnesses of both countries, as well as judges accustomed to working with psychological expert witnesses.

The available information does not allow for an assessment of the total number of forensic psychologists working as expert witnesses in both countries. For our study we divided psychological expert witnesses into two groups: The first are forensic psychologists whose main profession is that of expert witness. The second group consists of the experts who primarily work as psychotherapists or university researchers and only from time to time serve as expert witnesses. The interviewees were chosen in equal shares from both groups. Another selection criterion was equal spatial distribution of all interviewees within both countries. This made it possible to cover the habits of as many courts as possible in our inquiry. Such an equal distribution was especially necessary in Germany. Due to the country's larger size, experts in Germany work primarily for courts in their own geographical area. Most of the Dutch experts, however, stated that they regularly work for courts all over the country. This may be related to the small number of specialists who are at the court's disposal. Most of the Dutch interviewees work predominantly in the field of credibility assessment. They agreed that less than ten expert witnesses work regularly as credibility assessors at Dutch courts. Finally, we should stress that the interviewees do not form a cross-section of all forensic experts in both countries. For the present study that is no problem, because we were interested in how experts are treated in the criminal justice system rather than their individual behavior. We interviewed one judge and several experts in each country.

FORENSIC PSYCHOLOGICAL ASSESSMENT

In both countries it has long been the task of psychological expert witnesses to assess whether a defendant was *responsible or not* for the crime committed—comparable to the insanity defense in Anglo-American criminal trials. Usually these assessments are done in co-operation between a psychologist and a psychiatrist. In addition, in certain criminal cases there is a demand for a *credibility assessment* from a psychological point of view. In Germany credibility assessment has a longer tradition than it does in the Netherlands (Bullens, 1998; Sporer, 1982; Undeutsch, 1989). In a fewer number of cases the expertise of psychologists is used in both countries, to assess the quality of *identifications* of the suspect by witnesses.[1] In spite of their concentration in specific areas, most of the expert witnesses we interviewed also regularly give opinions on matters outside their specialization. Moreover, experts frequently pointed out that there had been shifts in their specialization over the course of time.

The type of forensic psychological assessments most often conducted in both countries is a *first opinion report*. In such a report, a single expert gives an opinion on a particular case from a psychological point of view. Only very rarely is there a demand for a *second opinion*, for which a second expert is asked to conduct an independent assessment. For a second opinion, the expert sometimes carries out the same work as for a first opinion report. More frequent, however, is a *critique of methodology* used in a psychological assessment. These reports are based on a critical evaluation of the methodological approach and strategies used by the first expert. In the Netherlands there is usually no clear-cut distinction made between a critique of methodology and a second opinion report.

---

[1] Please note that there is great demand for psychological assessments in family law, for example in questions of child custody. Psychologists also work as expert witnesses for juvenile and labor courts, welfare tribunals and administrative courts. The areas are outside the scope of this chapter.

RESTRICTION TO CREDIBILITY ASSESSMENT

If psychological expert witnesses are asked how their clients select and appoint them, certain differences between the two countries' legal systems quickly become apparent. Differences were also identified between parts of one legal system (e.g., between civil and criminal courts) as well as within a single part (e.g., within criminal courts). There are differences in the appointment of expert witnesses as well as in the expert's role during the main hearing at court.[2] In order to produce a clear comparison between the two countries, we restricted our topic to the work done by psychological expert witnesses in Germany and the Netherlands in the field of credibility assessment in criminal cases.[3]

APPOINTMENT OF AN EXPERT WITNESS

Whereas the way of conducting a credibility assessment and the role of the psychological expert during the main hearing differ in several respects between Germany and the Netherlands, the two countries show fewer differences in the appointment of the expert witness.

The criminal codes of both countries stipulate that the public prosecutor is authorized to appoint an expert witness (§ 161a StPO, German Code of Criminal Procedure, *Strafprozessordnung*; Art. 151 Sv., Dutch Code of Criminal Procedure, *Wetboek van Strafvordering*). So is the judge

---

[2] There exist so many differences between an Anglo-Saxon trial and the equivalent in both the Netherlands and Germany, that we will use the term *main hearing*.

[3] That does not mean that there are no differences in the area of the assessment of responsibility of the suspect. In the Netherlands the psychological expert is usually not contacted directly by the court if a report is required on the suspect's soundness of mind. Usually the judge-commissioner appoints the Forensic Psychiatric Service (FPS) as an expert mediator. An FPS psychiatrist then meets the accused for a short examination and gives an initial recommendation, stating what other examinations should be carried out and whether the person is suicidal. If a responsibility assessment is recommended, the case files are handed to the FPS psychologist, who in turn tries to find a suitable psychological expert to do the job. The FPS has a register of psychologists from for this purpose. The psychologists in the register either work as a full time expert witness or as a side occupation, next to their primary occupation in prisons or psychiatric hospitals. The FPS psychologist enters the name of the chosen expert in the criminal judge's blank order and sends this together with the case file to the expert. After writing the assessment, the expert returns the files with the report to the FPS psychologist who then examines the quality of the work and confers with the expert if necessary. Finally the FPS psychologist submits the report to the criminal judge who originally ordered the assessment. Occasionally, Dutch criminal judges also consult the FPS psychologist for a recommendation of an expert for a credibility assessment. In Germany the judge would contact the expert directly.

(§ 73 StPO; Art. 227 Sv.). These are the clients most frequently mentioned by the interviewees. Only one of the Dutch experts reported that he on rare occasions was asked to conduct an assessment directly by the police.

In both countries the defense usually has to be informed whenever an expert witness is appointed. In both countries it is also possible for the defense to ask an expert to conduct an assessment. In this case the defense selects and pays the expert privately. Such a report can be used as evidence at the main hearing. In neither country, however, does the code of criminal procedure provide rules for this situation. The German and Dutch specialists interviewed gave their impression that such private orders constitute a minority of total appointments. Nevertheless, there are experts who report that they receive the majority of their orders from the defense. A number of German experts tend not to accept orders by the defense at all, or only exceptionally. These specialists are afraid, on the one hand, of losing their independence. On the other hand they see their own credibility in the eyes of judges as being at risk if their opinion as an expert witness appears to be purchasable.

In both countries there are ways in which the defense can influence the court's choice of an expert. Criminal procedure stipulates the following:

Germany	The Netherlands
• The prosecutor (or judge) shall provide the defense with the opportunity to express his/her opinion before choosing an expert (Art. 70 RiStBV, *Richtlinien für das Straf-und Bussgeldverfahren*, Guidelines of Penal Proceeding and Fining System)	• The defense has the right to propose the names of one or more experts and has the right to request the appointment of one of these (Art. 227, section 2 Sv).
• The expert who is appointed can be rejected by the defense, by the prosecutor or by the private litigant for any of several reasons (§ 74 StPO), e.g., if it is possible to substantiate to the court that there is convincing doubt about the expert's neutrality.	• The defense has the right to appoint a second specialist to be present while the court-appointed expert is carrying out his/her examination (Art. 232 Sv). Furthermore, the defense has the right to order a second opinion report (Art. 233 Sv).
	• In both cases the second expert is subject to the same regulations as the expert appointed by the court and is paid out of public funds.

While the formal rights of the defendant in Germany are restricted to acceptance by the defense or rejection of an expert, the suspect in the

Netherlands is given broader rights. By law the suspect has the right to request the appointment of a particular expert, although this is dependent on the court's agreement. Additionally, Dutch law allows the defense to entrust an expert with a number of tasks. Moreover, it subjects this expert to the relevant requirements of the Code of Criminal Procedure and guarantees payment out of public funds. In the daily practice of German courts, the defense has a say in the appointment of an expert witness, too. Because of the narrower legal basis, however, it can be assumed that the possibilities of intervention by a defendant in Germany are also narrower, and are more dependent on the judge's (or the prosecutor's) obligingness. Because of this, the defense in Germany may be more inclined to take recourse to privately employing an expert, especially as the court will reimburse the expenses later, depending on the circumstances. A privately employed specialist is not subject to the criminal procedure that applies to expert witnesses appointed by the court. This fact, together with the financial pressure under which freelance experts operate since they depend on their reports for their personal income, may explain the reluctance of some German interviewees to accept appointments by the defense. The lack of integration in criminal procedure and financial dependence on the client may indeed lead some experts to bias, as one German judge interviewed reported. If this assumption is correct, it would facilitate the establishment of the truth if all experts worked under the same rules. In addition, payment of the expert out of public funds, as is the case in the Netherlands, would be advantageous.

ORDERING A CREDIBILITY ASSESSMENT

If the decision is made to bring a psychological expert into the case, the client—judge, prosecution or defense—chooses one. In the Netherlands, as already mentioned, only ten psychologists accept orders of credibility assessments (three of these experts exclusively produce critiques of methodology). In both countries the client is totally free in the choice of an expert. In Germany, where many more experts are working, the client usually consults an expert with whom he or she has previous satisfactory experiences. Recommendations by colleagues are most often used when contacting new experts. Other circumstances that may lead to the employment of a new expert are personal acquaintance, interviews with potential experts, acquaintance with the expert through published work, or the expert already being involved in the case (e.g., as therapist of the alleged victim). The time an expert needs for doing the work is another important consideration in clients' choice of an expert. In

Germany in the interests of economy (traveling time), the expert should be geographically close to the person to be examined.

In both countries the employment of an expert usually starts with a phone call by the client. Topics discussed in this call include a description of the case, date the report is to be submitted, and questions and requests of the expert. Only rarely does the client ask questions about the expert's competence. According to German law (§ 73 StPO) the judge has to make an *arrangement* with the expert, whereas the Dutch judge is authorized to *stipulate* when the expert will begin and end the examination (Art. 229 Sv.). Both countries formally recognize experts' obligation to accept appointment as expert witnesses (if particular conditions are met: § 75 StPO; Art. 227, section 4 Sv.) as well as the right of refusal to act as an expert witness (again, only when particular conditions are met: § 76 StPO; Art. 217 Sv). In daily practice, however, the psychological expert witness may refuse an order, for example because of lack of time or because he/she does not feel competent in the case at hand. Unofficially, interviewees named additional reasons for refusing an order, such as negative experience with a client in the past. Another reason experts gave for refusing an order from a defendant is when the expert has the impression that the defendant is guilty as charged. Once the expert and the client have come to an agreement, the expert always receives a written order. Usually the whole case file or relevant parts of it are enclosed. Infrequently, the client sends the order (including the other documents) directly by mail without phoning first. In both countries the law provides for the deadline for submission of the report to be extended by the client if compelling reasons exist (§ 224, Abs. II ZPO, Zivilprozessordnung, Code of Civil Procedure, cited from Kleinknecht & Meyer-Grossner, 1997b, p. 216, Art. 229 Sv).

At some point in the assessment, the Dutch expert has to swear an oath that he/she will carry out the assigned task to the best of his/her ability. Besides ordinary expert witnesses, there are also specialists in the Netherlands who are permanently under oath. They need not take an oath every time they accept an order. For privately assigned specialists, no swearing in is necessary. When they appear personally at the main hearing, all Dutch experts must take an oath (Art. 296 Sv). German experts are sworn in only if the judge regards this as advisable, or if the prosecution or the defense demand this (§ 79 StPO). The swearing in takes place after the expert has presented the report orally at court. This means that German psychologists become forensic expert witnesses merely by accepting an order; other formal steps are not necessary. It seems unlikely, however, that these difference in procedure between Germany and the Netherlands have any effect on the quality of the reports.

THE INSTRUCTIONS TO PSYCHOLOGICAL EXPERTS

In both countries the written order to the expert usually specifies the questions to be answered. Below, two examples are given of such questions posed to psychological experts for a credibility assessment.

Germany	*The Netherlands*
Can the statement of child X concerning the accused Y be considered credible?	What information, recommendations, and arguments based on observation or behavioral research are you able to put forward concerning the statement of child X? What further remarks do you regard as important to the consideration of the court?

In the Netherlands the experts interviewed agreed on two aspects of questions posed to them: (1) The questions are often formulated inaccurately or are impossible to answer from a psychological point of view. (2) Such questions usually have to be reformulated by the psychologist, i.e., reformulated in a fashion that makes it possible to answer them in the sense of a strictly psychological assessment. German interviewees did not mention similar criticism. This does not necessarily mean that orders in Germany are more suitably formulated. One German expert, who also works as a university professor, pointed out that he views it as sufficient if the term credibility assessment appears in the written order. As the conducting of a credibility assessment in Germany follows strict guidelines—to be discussed below—there is not such a strong need for precision in the formulation of the order (Wagenaar, 1998, proposes adopting such guidelines in the Netherlands).

CONDUCTING A CREDIBILITY ASSESSMENT

TWO DIFFERENT STARTING POINTS: VIDEOTAPE VS. PERSONAL EXAMINATION

The basis for conducting a credibility assessment differs greatly between the two countries in one particular aspect. The German expert meets the witness—usually a child—and examines the witness personally, if necessary several times. The Dutch expert, in contrast, very rarely meets a witness under the age of twelve whose credibility is to be assessed. The reason for this is the Dutch custom to spare a child who has been allegedly sexually abused from having to recount in detail on more than one occasion the abuse they suffered. These children are interviewed in a specially equipped police studio which provides an environment suitable for children as well as enabling the police to record the interview with cameras. The questioning is carried out by specially trained police officers. Some experts interviewed, however, criticized the quality of this police work. In some cases, e.g., for children with a learning disability or a behavioral disorder, a psychologist is also appointed to be present at the interview. According to the psychologists we interviewed, of about 1100 interviews of child-victims per year in the Netherlands, a psychologist is present at about 100 of them. Very young children are interviewed by psychologists. In some cases a psychologist not present at the interview is asked to assess the credibility of the child's statement, based on the video of the interview. For that purpose the expert receives, in addition to the case files, a videotape of the interview and a transcription of it. The Dutch expert therefore does not have the possibility of using psychological diagnosis (such as IQ tests) if the child whose credibility is to be assessed is below the age of 12. If the material provided is insufficient for an assessment, it is possible for the psychologist to receive permission to personally meet the child.

In Germany the expert usually meets the alleged victim whose credibility is to be assessed. The child has previously been questioned by trained police staff. This usually happens at the beginning of the preliminary proceedings. A ruling by the Federal Supreme Court of Germany (BGH, 30.7.99, 1 StR 618/98) specifies that if a sexual offence is suspected, a psychologist should be present when the child is interviewed. This appointed expert is usually a specialist in child psychology. In case a credibility assessment is needed later, however, the ruling does not explicitly state whether the same psychologist or a second psychologist (as in the Netherlands) should be appointed.

The German interviewees explained that, after receiving an assessment order, their first step is to study the case files. Most of the German interviewees explicitly stated that their next step is the formulation of questions relevant to the case and their research method. One of the interviewees emphasized that she always informs the child or the child's guardian that the examination is voluntary, when an appointment is made for the examination. She also pointed out that she makes sure that the judge has informed the child of its right to refuse to be questioned. This consent serves a special purpose: only if a consent has been obtained, is it possible for her as an appointed expert to use the information given by the child during the interview at the main hearing.

This German expert customarily visits the child at the child's home. Her reason for doing so is that the child feels more comfortable in this environment, and at the same time she gets an impression of the family atmosphere. She makes exceptions only if the child shares the house with the accused. During the whole examination only she and the child are present in the room. The dialogue is always recorded on tapes. She spends about five to eight hours a day with the child. In some cases—where there has allegedly been only one instance of abuse—she visits the child only once. Other experts consider a minimum of two shorter visits as necessary.

The information provided by Dutch experts differed markedly on this point from the information given by German experts. In addition to the case files, Dutch experts base their assessments on the content of the videotape and the transcript of the tape only, and do not examine the child directly. German experts, in contrast, personally get to know the child, in its home environment, over a period of several hours. During and outside of this meeting they can collect specific information necessary for the case at hand:

- by observing the child (including the tape and transcription).
- by using psychological diagnostic instruments (to assess the child's IQ, power of imagination, suggestibility, or ability to recall memories, particularly memories of other experiences around the time of the suspected abuse).
- by questioning a third party (e.g., the parents or guardians of the child, the child's teacher, or the person who heard the child's initial statement).

In contrast, German law authorizes the expert to request the judge or prosecutor conduct further investigations, for instance by interrogating the suspect and other witnesses (§ 80 Abs. 1 StPO). The expert is entitled, however, to question both the witnesses and the suspect directly at the main hearing (§ 80 Abs. 2 StPO). The expert is not entitled to carry out an interrogation (*ibid.*). Nevertheless German psychological experts regularly question the child and other witnesses before the main hearing in order to collect information for the credibility assessment. That seems to be a contradiction to German law and the German Supreme Court (BGH, 30.7.99, 1StR618/98) leaves this question explicitly undecided.

In Germany as well as in the Netherlands some of the experts reported that in some cases they consult medical colleagues on particular issues presented in those cases.

IMPACT OF DIFFERENCE OF QUALITY

It seems that the German expert is provided with a wider range of information than the Dutch expert, as the child can be observed in its home environment, other people who have a personal relationship with the child can be interviewed and psychological diagnostic instruments can be used. One might assume that the relatively higher quality and quantity of information contributes to the reliability of the expert's assessment, even though it remains unclear just how much more reliable such an assessment would be. It is not possible to arrive at a clear answer to the question whether the German way inevitably leads to a better assessment. Instead, the question should be whether the gathering of detailed information for non-therapeutic purposes justifies the repeated confrontation of a child with memories of the abuse suffered. In essence there are two conflicting priorities: to gather information which is as reliable as possible, in order to establish the truth versus the need to protect the child's well being.

In the Netherlands the basis of assessment is the videotape of the child's interview in the police studio and the transcript thereof. If the alleged victim is older than twelve years, Dutch experts always meet with them to conduct a psychological examination, e.g., by means of personality, suggestibility and IQ tests. In accordance with Dutch law, the judge, the defense lawyer, and the prosecutor, as well as a second expert appointed by the defense, may attend this examination (Art. 231 and 232 Sv). In German law there is no such provision.

COURT RULINGS ON THE ANALYSIS OF STATEMENTS IN GERMANY

On 30 July 1999 a ruling by the *Bundesgerichtshof* (Federal Supreme Court of Germany; BGH) outlined particular scientific requirements for the psychological assessment of statements (1 StR 618/98). This ruling gives a number of criteria for the content and presentation of credibility assessments ordered by courts. It stipulates that the objective of a credibility report is the critical assessment of whether a statement of particular events can be considered as true. This means that the examination concentrates on discovering whether the subject has really experienced the stated facts or not. The methodological strategy should entail denying credibility until the collected information prove the validity of the statement. In order to test the hypothesis that the statement is not true, at least one other hypothesis must be formulated. If the test leads to the conclusion that the hypothesis is incompatible with the facts, then the hypothesis that the statement is not true is rejected and is replaced by the alternative hypothesis.

This provision by the BGH results in the necessity of a diagnosis led by hypotheses. When searching for such a diagnosis, only appropriate scientific methods are permitted to be used. A detailed description of the methodological approach for an analysis of content—which concentrates on the qualitative assessment of a single statement—and a continuity analysis—which concentrates on the chronological order of several statements—are therefore formulated. The method used for the content analysis usually is Criteria-Based Content Analysis (CBCA, see Horowitz et al., 1997; Lamb & Sternberg, 1997; Ruby & Brigham, 1997; Undeutsch, 1989). The conclusions resulting from both methods then must be compared to the specific experiences and competencies of the subject. There exist three methods of doing this: (1) An analysis of possible sources of errors, which focuses on the emergence of the statement and its development over time (this is to reveal, e.g., suggestive impact on the subject); (2) An analysis of motivation to ascertain whether motives exist that might lead the subject to express a false accusation; (3) An analysis of competence that examines whether the content of the statement may in fact refer to other (though similar) experiences of the subject, or is based on the subject's imagination.

In its decision, the Court discusses the present limits of statement-related psychological methods. The main criteria set by the BGH for the presentation of the assessment report are transparency and comprehensibility. The diagnostic conclusions are to be formulated in a way that can easily be understood by all attending the main hearing. At the same time the methodological strategy must be presented in a fashion that is comprehensible, at least to other experts. Certain binding standards are set that psychological experts writing credibility assessments must meet. At the same time, they are obliged to keep up to date on current scientific developments.

Critics of this BGH decision among the interviewed German experts argue that it occurs rather rarely that credibility assessments are not based on scientific methods of information collection, for instance by interpreting a person's character. Their criticism was mainly aimed at inaccuracy when carrying out the statement-related psychological methods as described above. Mistakes that impact the final results were considered the most serious ones (e.g., a lack of accuracy when testing an alternative hypothesis or a lack of consideration of the circumstances of the witness's initial statement, in other words, the possibility of suggestibility is insufficiently taken into account). In addition, mistakes were named which do not necessarily influence the final results (less serious methodological mistakes in the analysis) as well as mistakes in the form of the report (inaccurate reference to sources, weak distinctions between parts presenting the results and the interpretation, or the absence of a logical connection between the report and its conclusions).

DUTCH METHODS OF STATEMENT ANALYSIS UNDER DISCUSSION

Up until now, the *Hoge Raad der Nederlanden* (Supreme Court of the Netherlands; HR) has not adopted a set of standards to be applied to credibility assessments. In other cases (e.g., the analysis of blood samples for alcohol content) the Dutch court has provided a detailed description of methodological strategies that are to be applied by the medical expert (Corstens, 1993, p. 135). These guidelines are intended to increase the validity of the assessment, and are formulated in co-operation with a forum of experienced experts. Even for areas where quality standards exist, the judge should be open for a methodological critique of an assessment, as changes in methods might have taken place which lead to improvements. Therefore, the Dutch Supreme Court was able to issue guidelines on the methodological approach to be used in credibility assessments as well.

On 30 March 1999 the Supreme Court of the Netherlands ruled on the reliability of a method that had been used by an expert in examining the credibility of a child's statement (HR 30 March 1999, *NJ* 1999, 451). An expert for the defense challenged the reliability of the method in that particular case. The HR ruled that, if a court uses such an assessment as evidence and the defense has argued against the scientific basis of the assessment, the court must argue in its decision why it uses the assessment as evidence nevertheless. In the case in which the HR gave this decision, an expert had assessed a child's statement using CBCA. Two experts proposed by the defense—both were Dutch university professors—had pointed out in a critique of methodology that CBCA used was not reliable enough and that a credibility assessment based on this method was not sufficiently grounded in science.

According to the Dutch interviewees, their credibility assessments usually rely on information obtained with Statement Validity Assessment (SVA) combined with other sources. Usually these are the case files, the videotapes, and also the results of the psychological diagnosis, if the expert has personally examined the subject. The SVA consists of two methodological techniques: CBCA (Criteria-Based Content Analysis) and VCL (Validity Check List). Both have been intensely criticized by Dutch researchers as a method for assessing credibility in court cases. According to Rassin, Merckelbach and Crombag (1997, p. 1929) the CBCA does not have a sound scientific basis. They conclude: "From a scientific perspective, the CBC can be seen as a promising instrument that needs further development" (p. 1929; our translation). Van Koppen and Saks (this volume) describe CBCA as a "fine example of psychologists who overstate their case in court." The Validity Check List (VCL) is, in their view, "neither based on sound empirical research..., nor is it limited to psychological insights." Several Dutch researchers criticize any use of SVA in court if all weaknesses of the method are not revealed to the court. They have carried their criticism of the methodology into the practical field in critiques of methodology of first opinion reports and in published articles in law and psychology journals.

This debate seems to be the reason why Dutch experts who conduct credibility assessments as a main occupation spoke of major changes in their work in recent years. They said that earlier assessment reports contained an explicit statement as to the degree of credibility of the person examined. Nowadays they merely provide the judge with arguments for and against considering the statement to be credible. Alternatively, they explain on what grounds a hypothesis can be considered valid or not valid. Thus the final conclusion is now usually left to the judge.

DIFFERENCES IN INFORMATION AND ANALYTICAL METHODS

One of the judges we interviewed summarized the German situation as follows: the new guidelines recently rendered by the Federal Supreme Court (Bundesgerichtshof; BGH) are clear-cut standards that will safeguard the quality of credibility assessment reports. This judge believes that these guidelines strengthen the judge's authority. It is the judge's task to evaluate the quality of the reports. Now the judge's scope of action has been restored, whereas previously there was a dangerous tendency towards delegation of authority to experts.

In contrast, Dutch interviewees who are not university professors sketch a troublesome situation. They are appointed by the court to write a credibility assessment, which they carry out by using the SVA, a method that, in their opinion, has been developed using a scientific approach. Now, this method has been called scientifically insufficient in methodological critiques by academic researchers. Dutch interviewees felt uncertain how they should make assessments in future.

Given the present situation in Germany, the challenge will be to use the created clarity for safeguarding the quality of court-ordered credibility assessments. However, the regulations should not become inflexibly rigid, or be immune to knowledge resulting from new scientific developments. Although the Bundesgerichtshof has intervened in the work of expert witnesses on a large scale, the decision met with almost unanimous approval (Köhnken, 2000). Various authors (Balloff, 2000; Jansen & Kluck, 2000) pointed out that basically nothing has been changed by this significant, clarifying, establishing and, most important, determining decision of the Bundesgerichtshof. The highest court has not made fundamentally new demands on expert's work, but it established those standards as legally binding which are almost concurring disused and demanded for a long time in relevant text books by leading forensic scientists and experts. Burgsmüller (2000) criticized that a particular method claims general validity in the field of deciding whether or not a testimony is believable. In her point of view on the one hand the method has not sufficiently revealed its own limitation in the face of the court. On the other hand the method offers a way of logic and rationality that can be seductive for people who work in the field of law; the method may have the appearance of clarity, which can deceive. Furthermore Burgsmüller emphasized that there is a risk that the competence of decision-making could be taken from the courts of justice in substantial spheres.

In the Netherlands, the challenge will be to find methods for credibility assessments that appear reliable in terms of scientific standards. At the same time, attention should be paid to the demands of daily work in court. An examination of the model of statement-related psychological assessments as known in Germany might lead to productive results, although a wholesale application of German methods to Dutch court procedure would seem extremely dubious given the differing circumstances. A number of methods and analytic techniques used in German credibility assessments are presumably not applicable, or applicable only in a limited way, in the Netherlands, especially for assessing the credibility of a child below the age of 12:

- In the Netherlands, collecting information to test a hypothesis is normally limited to the material provided (files and videotape). Thus, compared to a German expert, the Dutch expert relies on less diverse information, which is usually gathered by others.
- Dutch experts cannot carry out a continuity analysis, unless multiple statements by the child exist, which is seldom the case.
- When carrying out an analysis of competence, the Dutch expert cannot use psycho-diagnostic tests and results. Instead, the conclusion must be based on indirect means of observation.

In the face of these restrictions, the validity of a credibility report obtained by the German method of statement-related psychological assessment but carried out under Dutch conditions must be considered highly dubious.

THE MAIN HEARING

A main hearing does not take place in every case for which a Dutch or German expert has written a credibility report. Especially if the expert has concluded that the statement is not reliable enough or is even unbelievable, the prosecution will usually drop the case.

If a main hearing is held, reports and testimony of experts are considered as evidence, in accordance with criminal procedure in both countries. In other words, they provide information on which the court bases its final decision. In Germany as well as the Netherlands, the public prosecutor may summon experts to the main hearing (§ 161a StPO; Art. 260 Sv), and they are then obliged to appear (§ 161a StPO; Art. 213 Sv). In both countries there are legal consequences in the case of absence of an expert (§ 77 StPO; Art. 213 Abs. 2 Sv). Experts are treated to a large extent the same way as other witnesses (§72 StPO; Art. 227 Abs. 3 and Art. 296 Sv).

Apart from these common grounds, there are several differences between German and Dutch procedure. These differences result from difference in application of the principle of immediacy. The differences can be summarized as follows:

	The Netherlands	Germany
1. Written report	Always made. A copy of it is handed to (all or to a few) participants at the main hearing before it starts.	
2. Attendance at main hearing	The expert has to be present only in exceptional cases.	The appointed expert always has to be present in court.
3. Summons of expert	Expert is summoned by public prosecutor. Expert is obliged to obey this summons.	
4. Purpose of summons	Answering additional questions about the assessment.	Oral presentation of the assessment on the basis of all facts mentioned during the main hearing (it is the right of the expert to pose questions to the accused as well as to all other witnesses); afterwards, answering questions posed by participating parties at the main hearing.
5. Duration of attendance	As long as the expert's testimony takes.	During the whole main hearing (reading out of the charges, questioning of the accused and other witnesses, and summaries by prosecution and defense).
6. Information about expert	At the beginning of the expert's testimony, personal data (name, age, etc.) are elicited.	

	The Netherlands	*Germany*
7. Swearing in	Always takes place before questioning (both as an expert witness and as a witness).	Prior to reporting on assessment the expert is cautioned (also as witness). If demanded by one of the parties, the expert takes an oath after presenting the assessment report.
8. Qualification of expert	Only rarely are questions concerning the expert's qualifications raised. If so, a short summary of the professional career suffices.	
9. Duration of presentation	Usually 10–15 minutes	Usually 30–45 minutes
10. Discharge of expert	By the court (frequently the experts are not informed of the final verdict in a particular case).	

THE MAIN HEARING IN THE NETHERLANDS

In the Netherlands the main hearing takes only one or two hours. Even in more complicated cases, this time limit is usually not exceeded. As a rule, only formalities are addressed during the hearing. Before the hearing starts, the judges, prosecution and defense have read the files. Apart from the court, the public prosecutor and the defense lawyer, the accused is often the only other person present. Frequently there are no witnesses or experts attending the hearing. The child who is allegedly the victim is never called as a witness. The European Court of Human Rights (ECHR) has reprimanded the Netherlands several times for this, as this is considered a violation of the principle of immediacy (Van Koppen & Saks, this volume). According to some of the interviewees, there are signs of change.

The court often receives the assessment shortly before the main hearing starts, and may therefore have little time to study the report. In the opinion of one of the judges interviewed, this practice also seems to be changing. The reason reports are handed in so late seems to be that the judge, in ordering an assessment, instructs the expert that the report has to be submitted "before the main hearing starts." Most experts seem to take this very literally as "just before."

Normally, Dutch experts submit a written report. They are required to appear in court if they are summoned, but that only happens in exceptional cases, if for instance some important questions remained unanswered, if the assessment lacked formal clarity, or if one of the participating parties demands the presence of the expert at the hearing. The experts interviewed agreed that they appear in court in less than one-third of all cases.

The Role of a Psychological Expert during the Main Hearing in Germany

Before the main hearing, the presiding judge, the public prosecutor, the plaintiff, and the defense receive a copy of the written report. The jurors and the other judges on the panel, however, do not know the content of the assessment. They only receive information that is introduced during the hearing. Thus, in reaching a verdict the only relevant information is the information introduced during the hearing (this meets the requirements of the principle of immediacy).

The German adherence to the immediacy principle has two main consequences for the job of court-appointed psychological experts: (1) They always have to present the results of their assessment orally in court. Delivery of a written report does not suffice. (2) Formally, their oral presentation must be based solely on facts that are introduced during the main hearing. This inevitably leads to the need of the expert's presence during the entire hearing. This also means that the expert can digress from the prepared report in court, either because the person examined is suddenly incapable of recounting details of the offence, or because new information has come up during the hearing. The average duration of an ordinary main hearing in a German criminal court is one to two days, in rare cases a couple of weeks or even longer.

In contrast to Dutch psychological experts, the German expert appointed by the court is authorized to question all witnesses and the suspect during the main hearing. If necessary even the child who is allegedly the victim of an offence is questioned at court, but only under certain conditions. Usually the court expert is the last to take a turn in questioning the witnesses at court. Only rarely and in exceptional cases does the judge allow the expert to be the first to pose questions. Some of the German interviewees stated that they would prefer this more often, as it would make their job more efficient.

At a main hearing in Germany, the psychological expert's task is to answer particular questions on the basis of specific psychological methods. In the course of this, the expert is not allowed to digress into other disciplines such as medicine. The following example clarifies the psychological expert's use of testimony given by other parties at court.

At a main hearing the alleged victim states that she was raped by the accused. When questioned, she reports that she did not bleed even though there was penetration. A medical expert reports that the hymen of the alleged victim is undamaged but very flexible. Because of the hymen's flexibility, it is possible that there was penetration without defloration. The psychological expert can integrate the two statements by statement-related psychological interpretation. It is a common occurrence that penetration leads to defloration of which bleeding is a consequence. If a woman would lie, it is probable that she would do so along these lines. However, in this case the alleged victim states something contrary to that. This statement being contrary to the expected one is compatible with the results of the medical examination, which were unknown to the alleged victim at the time of questioning. The victim is therefore reporting something very unusual, which may indeed apply to her physical condition. From a statement-related psychological point of view, it would be quite an achievement if the witness had lied. The expert can compare this aspect with other results of the psychological examination (e.g., test results) when giving the oral presentation. The German interviewees agreed, however, that in many cases no new facts are uncovered during the main hearing. This means that their presence at the main hearing is not always very productive.

The oral presentation of the expert's assessment follows the examination of all witnesses. At the beginning, the judge tells the expert to be impartial, to tell the truth and that punishment may follow any wrong information given intentionally or unintentionally.

Oral presentations by the German experts we interviewed seem to vary considerably. They range on the one hand from "reading to the audience" to "completely free speeches." Some stick to their written report and there are differences in the extent to which the experts include new information uncovered during the hearing. The oral presentation is followed by the questioning of the expert by other participating parties. According to the German interviewees, it rarely occurs that one of these parties demands the swearing in of the expert. Only very rarely is a German expert summoned to a following session of the court in order to answer further questions on the same case.

If the expert has been appointed by the defense, the assessment is not treated as "evidence given by an expert." Instead, it is introduced by the expert's employer as "present evidence." This means that the treatment of an expert's testimony as described above does not apply to an assessment ordered by the defense.

The Immediacy Principle as a Comparative Criterion

Most of the differences between the main hearings in Germany and the Netherlands stem from the different treatment of the immediacy principle. In both countries, immediacy is one of the fundamental principles of criminal procedure. According to this principle, the court must base its decision exclusively on facts that were obtained from immediate sources (Cleiren & Nijboer, 1997). The principle is mainly understood as implying that the examination of witnesses and experts is carried out in the presence of the court and the parties in the case.

Strict adherence to the immediacy principle would have the following consequences for expert witnesses. An expert who has been appointed to conduct an assessment always has to attend the main hearing. There the expert must present the assessment orally to the court, in the presence of prosecutor and defense. After the presentation, the expert can be questioned by at least the court. In the Netherlands, these procedures are often not followed: the expert is usually not present in court, and if present, usually answers only questions directly related to the report submitted in writing before the main hearing.

The practice in Germany usually exceeds the requirements of the immediacy principle: The psychological expert must be present from the very beginning of the main hearing even though most of the other experts need not be. The psychologist has the right to question the suspect, the witnesses and other experts. The opinion of our interviewees on the necessity and usefulness of this varied widely, an issue that will not be explored further in this article. In addition, the question arises why German courts consider psychological experts' assessments of credibility to be so important and therefore entrust these experts with so many rights. This is another issue that will not be discussed further here.

THE QUALITY OF THE ASSESSMENTS

LEGAL GUIDELINES

In Germany a second assessment is ordered if the judge considers an expert's assessment as qualitatively unsatisfactory (§ 83 StPO). In the Netherlands a second expert may be appointed because of the judge's objections or at the request of other parties involved (Art. 235 Sv). Both codes of criminal procedure give several grounds for ordering an assessment by a second expert. In Germany a second expert can be appointed if (1) the qualifications of the first expert are doubted, (2) the first assessment is based on inappropriate premises, or (3) the first assessment contains contradictions (§ 244 Abs. 4 StPO). In the Netherlands it is even possible that in addition to the court-appointed expert and the expert appointed by the defense, a third expert is appointed. This is done if it is considered necessary (1) because of the methodology used in the assessment, (2) because of factual contradictions between the first two assessments, or (3) because of differences in the conclusions of the first and second experts. Although it is of course the courts responsibility to make a final decision (Corstens, 1993, p. 135; Hellmann, 1998), both German and Dutch interviewees said that the court usually follows their conclusions.

In 1989, the Dutch Supreme Court ruled that a court has to explicitly explain its decision to follow the conclusions of an expert's assessment if that assessment has been seriously criticized by the defense (Van Koppen & Saks, this volume). In 1998 the Dutch Supreme Court extended this decision, ruling that a court must determine (1) whether the expert was indeed a suitable expert for the particular case, (2) which method was used by the expert in arriving at the conclusions, (3) why the expert believes that the method used is sufficiently reliable, and (4) to what extent the expert is capable of competently using the particular method. These guidelines are considered by most of the Dutch interviewees as reasonable safeguards of the quality of assessments. The interviewees of both countries stated, however, that they had only rarely been required to give an account of their qualifications as a psychological expert witness.

The ruling of the German Federal Supreme Court (BGH, 30.7.99, 1 StR 618/98), which issued scientific standards for statement-related psychological assessments, is described above. This ruling also stipulates that the judge is in principle the one who must make sure the stipulated minimum scientific standards have been met. "If one of the parties involved in the case considers that the scientific requirements have not been met, it must request the appointment of a further expert when still at the instance of facts. If the court does not intend to accept this request ... a detailed explanation of the decision to reject it is normally required only if the requesting party has pointed out concrete shortcomings of the prior assessment. After that has happened, and before coming to such a decision, it is recommended that the prior assessor be heard and have the opportunity to give his statement with regard to the shortcomings referred to above" (our translation).

Apart from these legal guidelines, and the two Supreme Court decisions which we already discussed above (BGH, 30.7.99, 1 StR 618/98 and HR 30 March 1999, *NJ* 1999, 451), several quality guidelines can be found in the psychological literature for drawing up a psychological report in general (Berufsverband Deutscher Psychologen e.V., 1988; Kubinger, 1997; Westhoff & Kluck, 1998; Wurzer, 1997) or especially for courts. Van Koppen and Saks (this volume) have developed eight non-binding, self-imposed quality criteria. These criteria are the following:

1. The psychologist should be an expert on the particular subject matter on which he testifies and should explain in his report precisely why he considers himself an expert on the specific issues before the court.

2. The expert witness should show awareness of the limitations of her role. She should remain within her own domain and not intrude on those matters that are properly within the domain of the court.
3. Psychotherapists should never be expert witnesses on the value of evidence.
4. Psychologists who serve as expert witnesses should limit their testimony to subject matter for which psychology is relevant.
5. The psychologist should show that the testimony and the underlying research are relevant for the case in point.
6. The psychologist should show that she is competent to apply the specific method to the specific case.
7. Expert testimony encompasses application of scientific knowledge to a specific case. Thus, the expert should apply sound empirical research, must tell the court which results of research have been applied and why they are relevant to the specific case or its circumstances.
8. In applying sound research, the expert presents the court with sufficient basis for the court to assess its value, which depends upon the extent to which:
   a. It is grounded in the methods and procedures of science;
   b. It is based on empirical research, rather than the expert's subjective belief or unsupported speculation;
   c. The theory or method applied by the expert has been subjected to peer review after as well as before publication;
   d. The methods used are valid enough for the court to base its decision upon;
   e. The expert provides an accurate account of the discussion in the scientific community concerning the concepts or techniques being employed.

FURTHER SAFEGUARDS OF QUALITY

Three further means of safeguarding quality crystallized during our study. The following may be considered particularly effective (1) institutionalized research and publications; (2) education and professional training courses; and (3) changes in law, court, and police practices.

Institutionalized Research and Publications

The degree of institutionalization of forensic psychology is fairly low at German and Dutch universities. Adding academic chairs of forensic psychology would make expanded professional research possible. It would also help improve methods and diagnostic procedures related to credibility assessments. It is not enough, as one of the interviewees put it, to "extend old tracks"; university research should also aim at the development of new methods. This will make it possible to raise the quality of credibility assessments. The publication of new findings should not only be addressed to the international scientific community. Within each country such findings should also be made available to practicing psychologists and legal professionals. At the same time, an increased institutionalization of forensic psychology as a university subject could make an early specialization of psychologists possible, as is customary in other psychology sub disciplines. An academic center of forensic research could even integrate the approaches of different departments. Such an interdisciplinary center could at the same time offer continuing education programs, such as professional training courses for legal professionals and psychologists.

Education and Professional Training

During the education of psychology students, there should be a stronger emphasis on drawing up psychological assessments. Psychologists are often insensitive to the large differences between diagnoses for therapy and assessments in a forensic setting (Rassin & Merckelbach, 1999). Several interviewees doubted that law students should be trained to evaluate the quality of an assessment, as only a small percentage of law students will need this knowledge during their future career. Professional training courses were considered by those interviewed as particularly important: Experts should be able to choose from a large variety of training courses (e.g., on the use of specific diagnostic methods or on the implications of recent scientific research relevant to credibility assessments). Legal professionals should also be offered professional training courses (e.g., on quality control of psychological reports). The more legal professionals are qualified to evaluate the quality of an assessment, the likelier it is that, as a result of competition among experts, the quality of assessments in general will rise. The interviewees also mentioned as a measure for safeguarding quality that it would be useful if there were more courses to teach new judges and public prosecutors the relevant knowledge for dealing with psychological assessments. Postgraduate professional training programs in forensic psychology should enable qualified psychologists to achieve specialized competence while working as professionals. In both countries the founding of such continuing education programs is still in the planning stage. However, how do professionals in the two countries acquire their qualifications now? All experts interviewed in both countries had completed their study of psychology and had chosen different ways of acquiring special skills: (a) through self-study, (b) by pursuing a psychology-related profession that included the writing of assessments (but not credibility assessments), (c) by participating in short training courses, (d) through learning by doing, and (e) through the individual help and supervision of an experienced expert.

Changes within the Law, the Court, and Police

The German experts stated that they consider the recent ruling on credibility assessments by the Supreme Court a measure that sufficiently safeguards the quality of assessments. A Dutch expert and university professor recommended the revision of all relevant passages of the Code of Criminal Procedure. Apart from that, interviewees proposed a number of pragmatic changes in police and court procedure:

- *Changes in the preliminary proceedings*: Only specially trained professionals should carry out the initial interview with the alleged victim. Such an interview should always be videotaped and transcribed.
- *Changes in the appointment of experts*: The period of time between the discovery of an alleged offence and the appointment of an expert to write a credibility report should be reduced. There should be a clear definition of circumstances under which appointment of a psychological expert should be considered. The judge should consider more carefully whether a case in fact requires assessment by a psychological expert witness. In case the judge decides to appoint an expert, the judge should consider thoroughly what exactly needs to be found out, and should formulate a precise question to be answered. The judge should consider more carefully what expert qualifications are appropriate for the particular case. Psychotherapists should normally not be appointed as expert witnesses.
- *Changes in the main hearing*: The expert's report should be handed in well before the main hearing starts. The expert should explain in court what qualifies him or her as an expert on the particular case at hand. German experts would consider it an advantage to be allowed to question the witnesses at an earlier point in the main hearing, instead of being the last to question the witnesses.

The judges and the psychologists we interviewed emphasized the need for better communication between psychologists and legal professionals, both on an individual level, and in representative professional bodies. Clients should give clear feedback. Binding guidelines should be discussed and formulated by representatives of both professional groups. Regular communication could lead to a process of learning from each other.

All of these aspects are intended to raise the quality of psychological assessment reports. Most interviewees agreed that external control and compulsory selection of experts from a register would be disadvantageous. External control (proposed by, for instance, Nijboer, 1997) is usually understood as an external organ to monitor the quality of assessments. Nearly all of the interviewees of both countries suspected this measure would be dangerous, as it would enable a relatively small group of people to evaluate the quality of reports used in court. They pointed out that such a board of examiners could influence content and results. Several interviewees noted that this danger had been experienced in a part of Germany (Nordrhein-Westfalen) in the field of court-appointed culpability report writing.

In some countries (e.g., France) the choice of experts is limited to experts who are registered in a public list. In order to be registered, the expert's qualifications are examined. Interviewees mentioned several reasons for rejecting this form of quality control: (1) A group of people must decide who will be registered and who will not be registered. There is a high probability that the selection will be dominated by non-objective considerations. (2) A register of experts is usually not differentiated by expertise. However, it is crucial for the potential client to know whether a particular expert is qualified to do credibility assessments, or culpability assessments, or whether the expert is competent in identification cases. (3) Free choice by clients, combined with quality control of the resulting report, is enough to drive insufficiently competent experts out of the market or force them to improve their performance (principle of competition)—provided that the supply of experts is large enough.

A further aspect was described as highly delicate by several interviewees, namely the financial pressure under which expert witnesses do their work. This pressure entails several dangers for the highly qualified work of psychological expert witnesses. If financial pressure increases, experts will have less time to dedicate to continuing education or the study of new scientific developments. Furthermore, accepting too many cases will result in lower quality. There is also the danger that the expert will lack the time for extensive investigation needed in unusual cases.

Safeguarding the Quality of the Psychological Expert's Work: A Summary

The legislative bodies of both Germany and the Netherlands have entrusted the court with the evaluation of the quality of the expert's work. The legal guidelines available to the judge are neither numerous nor detailed. Thus a problem of competence versus competence arises: As the court lacks competence in a particular field, it consults an expert in order to use the expert's specific competence. Is it possible under these circumstances that a court can have the competence to evaluate the quality and results of the expert's work? One of the answers to that is that the court has to learn to evaluate the quality of an expert's work, for instance with the help of guidelines fixed by the Supreme Court or by following professional training courses.

The part of the expert's work that can be evaluated is the assessment report. The quality of such reports can be safeguarded in any of several ways: (a) through standards imposed by the experts themselves (e.g., as mentioned in Van Koppen and Saks' list of quality criteria), (b) through professional training courses for experts, and (c) through binding regulations for court-ordered credibility assessments which are established by representatives of all parties involved. Binding regulations for psychologists and legal practitioners for safeguarding and evaluating the quality of the assessment report have already been formulated in Germany. In the Netherlands this has not yet started. At the same time the qualifications of a particular expert should be checked. This means that experts would have to provide the necessary information about their qualifications, and that judges would have to evaluate these carefully in light of the requirements of the particular case. In contrast to Germany, the Netherlands already has a Supreme Court ruling on this matter. However, the ruling has not yet been put into practice.

Besides the judges, there are always other parties involved in a court case who are authorized to evaluate the quality of the report as well as the appointed expert's competence with regard to the case. If these parties express well-founded objections, the court must examine these objections seriously, and if necessary consult a second expert. In Germany as well as in the Netherlands, it seems that requests made by other parties are not always honored.

All of the measures discussed above are intended to raise the competence of all parties to appropriately evaluate the quality of credibility assessments. High quality assessments are a prerequisite for achieving the court's aim of establishing the truth. In this respect, two further means for safeguarding quality appear to be significant: (1) the institutionalized development of scientific knowledge as well as its transfer to practitioners (through publications as well as tertiary education and professional training courses for both psychologists and legal professionals); and (2) assuring high-quality preliminary work, which requires good communication and co-operation among all groups involved in producing credibility assessments (police, psychologists, public prosecutors, judges).

CONCLUSIONS

In this article we described the present situation of psychological expert witnesses who are appointed to conduct psychological assessments for German and Dutch courts. We collected most of our information through interviews with psychologists and judges. In order to provide a clear-cut comparison of both countries, we restricted the study to criminal procedure in general and credibility assessments in particular. The comparison focused on three aspects of accessing credibility, in chronological order: (1) the ordering of an assessment, (2) the production of the assessment, and (3) the role of psychological experts during the main hearing. Similarities and differences were pointed out between the two countries (both are usually considered inquisitorial systems). The reasons for the differences and their consequences were discussed, focusing especially on the impact on the quality of psychological assessments. Several feasible measures that could be implemented to safeguard the quality of psychological assessments in Germany and the Netherlands are described.

In short we found that in the Netherlands all psychological experts conducting an assessment are more closely integrated in criminal procedure and the experts are paid out of public funds. This strengthens the impartiality of the appointed expert and contributes to the establishment of the truth.

When working on an assessment ordered by the court, there is a great difference between the two countries in the material available to the expert: The Dutch expert produces the credibility assessment mainly on the basis of videotapes of a single interview with the alleged victim. The German expert always personally examines the person whose statement is being assessed. The reason for this difference has to do with differing priorities in the two countries. In the Netherlands the well being of the child is considered most important. The particular type of information available to an expert inevitably influences information analysis. Since the Dutch expert does not have the same type of information available, the methods of psychological statement analysis developed in Germany cannot be transferred wholesale to the Netherlands. What, then, is a suitable method of data analysis to use in the Netherlands? The present fierce debate in the Netherlands among researchers and forensic psychologists underscores the unresolved nature of this question.

The degree of integration of psychological experts in the main hearing is another point of difference between the two countries. It results from a different interpretation of the immediacy principle. Dutch court hearings do not conform fully to the immediacy principle. In Germany there is a tendency, to take this principle to an opposite extreme. Whether this is necessary and useful or whether it may have negative effects remains unclear.

In the future the issue of safeguarding the quality of the work of psychological experts continue to be an important topic of discussion in both countries because psychological assessments have a strong impact on the judge's verdict. This chapter suggests a number of quality standards (for both form and content) as well as measures to safeguard the quality of psychological assessments.

16

Preventing Bad Psychological Scientific Evidence in the Netherlands and the United States

PETER J. VAN KOPPEN AND MICHAEL J. SAKS

TWO PROSTITUTES AND THEIR PIMP

In a recent case in the Netherlands, a pimp was accused of molesting two of his prostitutes and also of raping one of them.[1] Although the police knew of the violent character of the pimp, the case confronted them with a problem: the prostitutes had also accused the pimp of forcing them to sell their bodies, but after the pimp was arrested both continued to work in that trade. Were they just making their whole story up or was it typical for women who had been forced into prostitution to continue in the trade even after the force has been removed? To answer these questions, the police called in a psychologist the day before the case was scheduled for trial in the district court.

The prosecution chose this psychologist because she had done some research on prostitutes. She read the police reports of the prostitutes' statements, and spoke to each of them for an hour. The following day she testified in court on the results of her short investigation. First, she told

---

[1] In the Dutch legal system, anonymity of all participants is a highly valued asset. Therefore, we refrain from supplying citations of cases, except from Supreme Court decisions.

that she recognized the pattern of behavior of both girls—they were quite young prostitutes—from her studies of prostitute behavior: "The story they told tallied with the behavior of pimps I encountered before ... I was not surprised by the things I heard and read."[2] Second, she told the court that the girls were speaking the truth: "They did not hesitate and were very consistent during our conversation. Their statements were also synonymous ... I have encountered very few deceitful statements in my research of prostitutes ... I neither had the impression that the things that happened were exaggerated ... From their consistency, I concluded that it is true what the ladies have told."

A statement such as the one by this psychologist is quite common in the Dutch legal system, though generally barred in the American system. Nevertheless, it is deplorable by any standard, legal or psychological. We return to that later.

In the Netherlands psychologists routinely are called upon—either by the investigative judge, the prosecution, the defense, or the court—to testify on a number of subjects. Among the most common subjects are testimony concerning the sanity or insanity of the accused during the course of the crime, a task typically performed by clinical psychologists of whom most are employed by government agencies; and the usefulness of witness statements or, to a lesser extent, statements made by the suspect.

This chapter deals with how Dutch courts use psychologists who testify on the matters noted above, as well as other subject matters, and compares the legal procedures and testimonial content to what is done in the United States after *Daubert* (*Daubert v. Merrell Dow Pharmaceuticals Inc.*, 1993). Our conclusion will be that neither an adversarial nor an inquisitorial system has adequate provisions for excluding bad psychological expert evidence. A partial solution we will propose at the end of this paper is that standards should be set for the content of expert testimony.

EVIDENCE FOR COURTS AND JURIES

Dutch and American courts treat the use—as well as the admissibility—of expert evidence in criminal cases[3] quite differently. In the United States the model of handling evidence is based on a jury trial, in which the jury weighs the evidence admitted by the judge, who serves as gatekeeper. The judge decides whether evidence can be admitted and offered to the

---

[2] These and all following quotes are translated from Dutch.
[3] We leave comparison for civil and administrative cases to others (see, for instance, Van Kampen & Nijboer, 1997).

fact finder for evaluation. This has led to a focus on the issue of admissibility and the development of rules and an extensive case law governing the admissibility of expert evidence.

In the Netherlands the court[4] functions both as gatekeeper and as decision maker (for a comparison, see Van Kampen, 1998). In such a system, there is no reason—indeed, it would be silly—to have the same individuals first decide on the admissibility of evidence and then evaluate the evidence. There is no jury that has to be protected from bad or unsound evidence by a judge; the court itself feels smart enough to evaluate all evidence. This moves decisions on evidence from admissibility rules to rules of decision-making.

Anglo-American judges also believe themselves to be smarter than jurors, and part of the received wisdom of evidence doctrine in North America is that, were there no jurors, there would be few rules of evidence. The question that naturally arises is whether judges really are able to perform cognitive feats that jurors cannot, such as disregarding improper evidence. The few studies that have directly compared judges in the U.S. to jurors on this issue have found judges to make the same mistakes that jurors do (e.g., Landsman & Rakos, 1994). If these few studies accurately reflect the general phenomenon, then dividing the responsibility for admitting evidence from the responsibility for deciding the case would appear to be a wise strategy, whether the distribution of decision-making responsibility is between judge and jury or between two judges.

In the Netherlands there are hardly any rules concerning admissibility of evidence. One would expect that the American admissibility rules would be substituted in the Netherlands with rules on how the court then should use the evidence in its decision-making. These rules, however, are very limited. Simply put, the court can convict a suspect if it is convinced that the suspect is guilty. That resembles the French system, where the judge has to have a *conviction intime* of the guilt of the suspect. In addition, Dutch courts have to base their *conviction* on so-called legal evidence. What is considered legal evidence is enumerated in the Code of Criminal Procedure: (1) Own observation of the judge; (2) Statements made by the suspect; (3) Witness statements; (4) Expert statements; (5) documents (art. 339 ff.). There is one exception: facts that are generally known do not require proof.

That is a meager set of rules indeed. One would expect that through precedents, these simple rules would have been supplemented, but, until

---

[4] The court in more serious and difficult cases consist of three judges at the district court level and of three justices at the appellate court level. At the Supreme Court—a Court of Cassation—cases are decided by a panel of five justices.

recently, that has not happened. That is a consequence of how the Dutch legal system is organized and how the Dutch Supreme Court (Court of Cassation) interprets its task. In the Netherlands most crimes are dealt with by the district courts. After every decision, both the prosecution and the defense have the right to appeal to the appellate court. The appellate court decides the case *de novo* on the basis of the dossier compiled and considered by the trial judge. After the decision of the appellate court, both parties can appeal to the Supreme Court, but that is a cassation court, which decides only on matters of law and the application of law by the lower courts. The Supreme Court tends to leave matters of fact to the inferior courts. Appeals to the Supreme Court on how evidence is handled and what kinds of evidence are accepted by the lower courts are routinely rejected by the Supreme Court.

THE STANDARDS FOR EXPERT WITNESSES

But times are changing. Recently, the Dutch Supreme Court set standards for the testimony of expert witnesses. Under Dutch law that is quite novel, since the decisions about the facts are almost completely left to the inferior—district and appellate—courts (Van Kampen, 1998, Chapter 4; Nijboer, 1992). In 1989, the Supreme Court ruled in a case in which an expert witness used the anatomically correct dolls-test to assess the veracity of a statement made by a minor in a sexual abuse case. The Court decided that if the defense seriously contests the method used by the expert, the court should explain explicitly why it still uses the expert's opinion as evidence (See HR 28 February 1989, *NJ* 1989, 748, *anatomisch correct poppen; anatomically correct dolls*).

In the beginning of 1998, the Dutch Supreme Court expanded this decision by reversing an appellate court decision in a case in which an orthopedic shoemaker had given an expert opinion on identification by means of shoe traces. The Supreme Court ruled that upon a challenge of this evidence by the accused, the appellate court should have investigated (1) whether the expert also was an expert on shoe traces; (2) if so, which methods were used to reach the opinion; (3) why the expert considers this method reliable enough; and (4) to what extend the expert is able to use this method competently (See HR 27 January 1998, *NJ* 1998, 404, *Schoenmaker blijf bij je leest; Shoeprints*). These guidelines may seem meager to the Anglo-Saxon lawyer but they are profoundly new to Dutch criminal procedure.

All of these developments are happening under the influence of the European Court of Human Rights (ECHR) in Strasbourg. ECHR decisions are binding for national courts. Decisions by the ECHR are gradually causing the return of witnesses to the courts. Some 15 years ago, courts decided almost all cases on written documents. Witnesses played a role, but only in the form of their statements as recorded by the police or by the judge-commissioner (*juge d'instruction*). Typically, expert witnesses appeared in court in the form of their written report. Although decisions on written documents are still the rule, in the last few years more and more witnesses and expert witnesses have been summoned to appear at the trial. The example given earlier of the expert in the prostitutes' case is an exception in that the expert wrote no report at all. That is unfortunate, because writing a report might have caused her to think more about her evidence.

Times have been changing for experts in North America as well, in consequence of a series of opinions by the United States Supreme Court, beginning with the case of *Daubert v. Merrell Dow Pharmaceuticals, Inc.* (1993). *Daubert* held that a court might admit scientific expert evidence only if the judge is rationally convinced of its validity. Soon thereafter, in *General Electric Co. v. Joiner* (1997), the Supreme Court held (in addition to a more technical issue concerning the standard of review) that an expert's assertions of belief are not enough; the expert's conclusions must be logically connected to some sound basis: data, research literature, etc. In the third case in this series, *Kumho Tire Co. v. Carmichael* (1999), the Court held that because the line between science and non-science is not well defined, *Daubert* applies to *all* expert testimony, that is, no expert testimony of any kind may be admitted unless the trial judge is persuaded that it is of sufficient soundness.

It is fair to say that, collectively, these cases create a set of rules that are similar in their general outlines to those of the Dutch Supreme Court. Certainly with respect to scientific expert testimony, they establish a focus on the expert's methodology, require trial judges to evaluate the basis for the expert's claim that those methods are valid and reliable, require that a convincing connection be shown between observables and inferences or between a body of research and what the expert is concluding, and that the expert can and has applied these correctly in the case before the court. (For a detailed review of the American cases see Faigman, Kaye, Saks, & Sanders, 1997, Chapter 1; 1999, Chapter 1).

We shall use the guidelines set by the Dutch Supreme Court to assess the testimony of psychologists in court. We will also show how meager the Dutch standards are, but that American practice is not better. We conclude by giving an extended list of standards.

PSYCHOLOGISTS VERSUS FORENSIC PSYCHOLOGISTS

A large part of the work of psychologists consists of drawing inferences about states or traits or behavior that cannot be directly observed, but must be inferred from other indicators, usually other behavior. For instance, psychologists give an estimation of someone's intelligence based on the person's score on a test. Inferences can be about the future (e.g., how dangerous a convict may become in the future) about the present, and about the past. Typical of such inferences is the making of predictions of future behavior, so much so that our discussion will proceed in terms of predictions.

The quality of a prediction mainly depends on the quality of the instrument used to make the prediction. For instance, we know that predictions about someone's intelligence based on a proper intelligence test outperform the clinical judgment of a psychologist (see, for instance, Meehl, 1954).

Predictions in one context differ from predictions in other contexts. Predictions made in a therapeutic context—usually called diagnosis there—are quite different from predictions made in a forensic context. In therapy the diagnosis looks like the diagnosis a general practitioner makes. If you go to your general practitioner with pain in the tummy, the doctor usually cannot make a straightforward diagnosis, because this is a notoriously difficult symptom. The doctor then does two things: tries to exclude the most dangerous possibilities, such as acute appendicitis, and if these are not present, gives you a medicine (or a placebo) and asks you to come back next week. This manner of making a diagnosis is typical for both medical doctors and psychotherapists. It is vital not to miss anything that might be acutely dangerous; for the rest the timing is less essential. If this medicine does not help, the doctor can give another one next week.

The structure of the problems associated with the medical diagnosis looks like Table 1. The most important aim of the diagnosis is not to miss appendicitis, which is not making a *false negative* diagnosis. Avoiding false negatives is considered in the best interest of the patient. Similarly, the diagnosis of a psychologist in the role of therapist is aimed first at detecting and dealing with the most serious problems.

In the Dutch forensic context the role of the prediction is quite different (see Rassin & Merckelbach, 1999). If the psychologist writes a report for the court, the "diagnosis" is final from the perspective of the

TABLE 1. THE STRUCTURE OF THE DIAGNOSIS OF PAIN IN THE TUMMY BY A GENERAL PRACTITIONER

True disease of patient	Medical diagnosis	
	Appendicitis	Something else
Appendicitis	Correct	False negative
Something else	False positive	Correct

psychologist. After submitting the report to the court, it may play a role in the court's decision, without the possibility to adapt the conclusions to new insights in the case. More important, in the Dutch system, the work of the psychologist is unambiguously aimed at aiding the court, not to help the accused or the attorneys or the other witnesses. Consequently, in the Dutch system, it is proper for the psychologist to consider the point of view of the court. That is governed by doctrine and precedents, among which is the proposition that a suspect is to be considered innocent until proven guilty and that a conviction of an innocent suspect is much worse than an acquittal of a guilty one (compare Blackstone, 1769, "The law holds, that it is better than ten guilty persons should escape, than that one innocent suffer"; Fortescue, 1616, "Indeede I would rather wish twentie euill [evil] doers to escape death through pittie, then one man to bee vniustly [unjustly] condempned"; Hale, 1736, "it is better five guilty persons should escape unpunished, than one innocent person should die").

In the Anglo-American system, by contrast, the expert is expected to supply information that will be elicited by lawyers on both sides so as to advance the goals of the prosecution or the defense, respectively. Whether expert witnesses ought to take the, court's viewpoint or the party's viewpoint is, at best, doubtful and debatable. The system sends contradictory messages to expert witnesses (Saks, 1992) and the witnesses tend to conflate the different decision responsibilities (Monahan & Wexler, 1978). Moreover, the use of experts to evaluate the statements of witnesses, while common in the Dutch and other Civil Law systems, is almost unheard of in the Anglo-American system, where such evaluations are considered to be the province of the judge or jury in the role of the trial's fact finder (Spencer, 1998).

In either legal system, however, as Blackstone's famous ratio of erroneous acquittals to erroneous convictions makes clear, the criminal justice process is principally aimed at avoiding *false positives*, rather than false negative judgments (see Table 2). If a psychologist wants to serve the court while evaluating the statement of a witness who accuses the suspect, the psychologist should also try to avoid false positives (see Table 3).

This difference between predictions in the therapeutic context and the forensic context becomes problematic if psychologists serve as expert

TABLE 2. THE STRUCTURE OF THE DECISION BY THE COURT

True state of affairs	Decision of court	
	Suspect is guilty	Suspect is not guilty
Suspect guilty	Correct	False negative
Suspect not guilty	False positive	Correct

TABLE 3. The Structure of the Diagnosis of the Forensic Psychologist

	Judgment of psychologist	
True state of affairs	Witness speaks the truth	Witness does not speak the truth
Witness speaks the truth	Correct	False negative
Witness does not speak the truth	False positive	Correct

witnesses without understanding this crucial difference. Most psychologists are accustomed to the clinical setting where the perception of the client is central to the interaction between psychologist and client, and the truth of the client's statements is of minor importance (see, however, McNulty & Wardle, 1994). A therapist who is too concerned with what really happened to the client may hurt their relationship, which is based on trust, and impair the therapeutic process. For the forensic psychologist the *only* point of interest has to be what really happened (and perhaps secondarily what the defendant believed even if the belief does not comport with reality). Also, the therapist is trained at being empathic for the client. If a therapist is hired by and for the court to evaluate a statement made by a witness, empathy towards the witness is incompatible with the independent role the expert has to play (Greenberg & Shuman, 1997).

In addition, the diagnosis of the forensic expert needs to meet much higher standards than the diagnosis of the therapist. In a therapeutic setting each diagnosis is tentative, so that if during consecutive sessions the diagnosis proves to be wrong, it can be changed without any harm being done. In criminal cases psychologists are usually called in only if there is a problem with the evidence. In most cases that means that there is not much evidence other than the witness statements, which are subjected to the assessment of the expert psychologist. In such cases the expert testimony may make the difference between a conviction and an acquittal. Therefore, the expert opinion generally has to meet higher standards than the diagnosis of the therapist. If, for instance, a psychologist comes to the conclusion that a witness is speaking the truth, the psychologist must be quite sure of that and on the basis of much more than personal intuition (Wagenaar, Van Koppen, & Crombag, 1993).

THE EXPERTISE OF THE PSYCHOLOGIST

Let us return to the decisions of the Supreme Court of the Netherlands in the shoemaker case and compare it to the opinion given by the psychologist in the prostitute case discussed above. The psychologist gave evidence on two questions in that case: first, is the behavior of the prostitutes typical for (that is, diagnostic of) battered prostitutes; and second, do they speak the truth?

The first criterion set by the Supreme Court is that the expert must have expertise in the field in which an opinion is being given. The psychologist has done research on prostitutes and on prostitutes who have been battered. So, she must have expertise on the type of behavior displayed by battered prostitutes in different kinds of situations. But that was not the question asked by the court; rather, the court wanted to know whether displaying certain behavior is diagnostic of the prostitutes being battered. That question is considerably different from the research done by the psychologist. This is a typical error made by psychologists in other cases as well. In turn, the psychologist's error can easily become the court's error. Sexually abused children, for instance, tend to have behavioral problems, start wetting their beds again, and often have nightmares. But how diagnostic of sexual abuse of the child is wetting its bed at a later age.

A somewhat more hidden version of this error also occurs in sexual abuse cases. Consider this example. A 19-year-old girl—let us call her Linda—accuses a much older man of sexually abusing her for some years. The suspect admits their sexual relationship, but claims it has been of a much shorter duration and, more important, that it was a consensual relationship. A clinical psychologist is called in to study the file and talk to the girl. The psychologist concludes that Linda is speaking the truth *because* she is suffering from posttraumatic stress disorder. This diagnosis is derived from the *Diagnostic and Statistical Manual of Mental Disorders* (DSM-IV), a publication of the American Psychiatric Association, which is used worldwide for the classification of psychiatric disorders (American Psychiatric Association, 1994). The DSM-IV also lists a large number of criteria which all have to be met before a patient can be diagnosed as suffering from a posttraumatic stress disorder (American Psychiatric Association, 1994, pp. 427–429).

As is typical in the therapeutic setting, the psychologist diagnoses Linda loosely as suffering from this disorder, without making clear to the court on which DSM-criteria she bases the diagnosis. A much larger problem, however, is that the psychologist argues that *because* Linda is suffering from a posttraumatic stress disorder, it is very likely that she suffered from the sexual trauma inflicted upon her by the suspect.

How does she know? The first criterion in the DSM-IV for posttraumatic stress disorder is that: "The person has been exposed to a traumatic event in which both of the following were present: (1) the person experienced, witnessed, or was confronted with an event or events that involved actual or threatened death or serious injury, or a threat to the physical integrity of self or others; (2) the person's response involved intense fear, helplessness, or horror" (American Psychiatric Association, 1994, p. 427). And how does the psychologist know that Linda suffered a trauma? Because Linda told her. That is an acceptable basis for setting this diagnosis in a therapeutic setting, but if the psychologist then uses the diagnosis to convince the court that Linda indeed was sexually abused, the reasoning has become completely circular. These kinds of expert opinions are particularly dangerous, because psychologists in the Netherlands never tell the court how they reached their diagnosis (and in the United States do not do so unless an explanation is elicited on cross-examination by opposing counsel, who rarely have sufficient knowledge to recognize the problem with the testimony), so the circularity of the testimony remains completely hidden from the court.[5]

The psychologist in the prostitutes' case also gave an opinion on the veracity of the stories told by the two prostitutes. Asked in court what she knew of CBCA,[6] she answered: "This abbreviation means nothing to me." Since CBCA is the method most used for evaluation the veracity of witness statements (see Lamb & Sternberg, 1997; Ruby & Brigham, 1997), the psychologist evidently is no expert on the credibility of witness statements. We know that only because the defense asked her. Dutch courts almost never start questioning the expert with the simple question: "Dear psychologist, just start by telling us why you think you are an expert." But that has changed also since the *Shoeprints* decision of the Dutch Supreme Court (HR 27 January 1998, *NJ* 1998, 404). Nowadays, most courts start by asking why a proffered expert thinks she is an expert. Follow-up questions, however, are still not asked. In American courts, this is the issue of "qualification" of the expert witness. There, the issue is routinely addressed, though often in a perfunctory and superficial way. The opponent of the expert often fails to challenge adequately and with substance, and the proponent wants to use the qualification phase to do nothing more than to emphasize the credentials of the witness so as to boost the witness's credibility in the eyes of the judge or jury. Neither system gains the potential benefit of evaluating the expertise of the proffered expert.

---

[5] Even for the Dutch Supreme Court. See HR 18 November 1995, *NJ* 1996, 666 (Psycholoog ondersteunt getuigenverklaring; Psychologist supports witness statement), in which the court accepted such an expert statement as valid evidence.

[6] That is an abbreviation of Criteria Based Content Analysis, to be discussed below.

METHODS FOR EVALUATING WITNESS STATEMENTS

The second, third, and fourth criteria set by the Dutch Supreme Court in its *Shoeprints* decision are related: all involve the method used by the expert. The method should be explained, should be reliable[7] enough to reach the conclusions given, and the expert must be able to use this method competently. These same criteria for expert testimony have been explicated in the American system most clearly and most recently in the series of cases decided by the U.S. Supreme Court (*Daubert, Joiner,* and *Kumho*). But as mentioned earlier, one of the interesting differences between the Civil and the Common Law rules of evidence is that Common Law courts generally do not allow experts to opine on the veracity of witness statements.

The most common methods for evaluating witness statements are lie detection—which is not used in The Netherlands (van Koppen, Boelhouwer, Merckelbach, & Verbaten, 1996)—and Statement Validity Analysis (SVA) (Raskin & Esplin, 1991). SVA aims at assessing the truthfulness of a witness statement by way of two methods: evaluating an interview with the alleged victim using Criteria Based Content Analysis (CBCA) (Steller & Köhnken, 1989) and evaluating other case information with the Validity Checklist (VCL). Evaluations by psychologists using SVA or CBCA alone are done on a rather large scale in The Netherlands. Let us first discuss the CBCA and later turn to the VCL.

CRITERIA BASED CONTENT ANALYSIS

The CBCA is based on the assumption that a true statement can be distinguished from a false statement because someone who tells about something that really happened tells the story differently than someone who has to tell about something that did not happen. The method was expressly developed for use with children who allegedly were victims in sexual abuse cases, but now is also used for the evaluation of adult alleged victims (see Ruby & Brigham, 1997, p. 729).

In applying CBCA, it is of major importance that others have exerted as little influence as possible on the statement. Also, the interview itself must comply with high standards, especially in the absence of suggestive

---

[7] Both Dutch and American Lawyers use the word "reliable" when they mean an amalgam of reliability and validity (as Justice Blackmun took some pains to do in the *Daubert* opinion). Communication between fields would improve if the lawyers and judges traded in the word "reliability" for "dependability" or if the scientists traded in the word "reliability" for a synonym such as "repeatability."

questioning. Therefore the witness should be interrupted as little as possible and should tell the story as much as possible in free recall. This method of questioning is essential to the CBCA (see, for instance, Undeutsch, 1983). Then the interview must be typed out verbatim and on the written version of the interview the criteria of the CBCA are applied. The most important reason for the latter is that there exists no fixed scoring scheme for the CBCA. To be precise: there exists no scoring scheme for the 19 individual criteria. That is left to the subjective evaluation of the psychologist. There exists a scoring scheme for combining the 19 evaluations into a final judgment by the psychologist (Steller, 1989; Yuille & Cutshall, 1989). That does not help much. The method fully depends on the detailed and argued application of the 19 criteria (see Steller, 1989, p. 137).

Thus far, the research on the CBCA has yielded mixed results (see recent reviews by Horowitz et al., 1997; Lamb & Sternberg, 1998; Ruby & Brigham, 1997). The gist of the argument is that CBCA has some scientific potential but has too low a diagnostic value to be used in a forensic setting. Ruby and Brigham summarize the state of affairs as follows:

> The CBCA may have the potential to enhance the objectivity of the investigation and prosecution of allegations of child sexual abuse. It might also aid in protecting those who are unfortunate enough to be at the receiving end of an unfounded child sexual abuse allegation. But much more empirical validation work is necessary before it can adequately fulfill such a role. (p. 729)

Still, psychologists present results of their CBCA analyses to Dutch courts without any hesitation and without mentioning the controversy over the instrument in the scientific community.

PROTECTING COURTS AGAINST CBCA

CBCA is a fine example of psychologists who overstate their case in court. How would the court know the psychologists do this? They could read the leading law journal in the country, because there Rassin, Merckelbach, and Crombag (1997) fully explained the recognized problems with the CBCA. Otherwise there is no safeguard against unfounded application of the CBCA in the Dutch legal system. The prosecution usually relies on the psychologist's report in which the CBCA is applied. In the reports seen by the first author,[8] psychologists do express their doubts about the case at hand if warranted, but never discuss doubts about the

---

[8] Although these are many, they surely do not form a random sample from all reports. For instance, Van Koppen does not see cases in which the suspect readily confessed.

very method that has been the topic of the scientific discussion. If the suspect is "at the receiving end of an unfounded allegation" it completely depends on the attorney whether another psychologist scrutinizes the psychologist's report. If the defendant lacks an alert attorney, this will not happen. And it does not happen very often, because the part of the Dutch bar that is specialized in sexual abuse cases is very small. There is no "automatic" court check on the quality of expert evidence in the Netherlands. Similarly, in the Anglo-American system, there is no automatic court check. If counsel for the defense does not raise a challenge, then the evidence generally will come in.

VALIDITY CHECK LIST

Evaluations of children's statements in sexual abuse cases have more problems. Some argue that CBCA is valid enough only if it is supplemented with the VCL. Raskin and Esplin propose that a useful statement assessment should be more than just scoring a statement of the 19 criteria on the CBCA (see Raskin & Esplin, 1991). The CBCA should be applied to material drawn from a properly conducted interview in which enough material is gathered to use the criteria upon. In addition, however, information has to be gathered outside the interview. Since children differ in their cognitive abilities and these differences influence the scoring of the criteria, information must be collected on these abilities and other personality characteristics of the interviewee. Also, alternative hypotheses on the genesis of the story as told by the child must be investigated. The story may be in error because of earlier suggestive interviews by parents or others, by deficient memory of the child, or by other pressures on the child. For evaluating the latter elements, the VCL has been developed. The VCL consists of four clusters:

1. Psychological characteristics of the child.
2. Interview characteristics of the child and the examiner.
3. Motivational factors relevant to the child and others involved in the allegations.
4. Investigative questions regarding the consistency and realism of the entire body of data.

Research on the validity and usefulness of the VCL is scarce and does not exceed casuistic illustrations (see Endres, 1997). Thus, it is not clear which role should be assigned to the psychological characteristics or motivational factors of the child in evaluating the veracity of the statements made.

Using the VCL introduces another problem in expert statements, because it is at odds with the role that an expert witness should have in the Dutch court. In American terms: it invades the province of the court (Penrod, Fulero, & Cutler, 1995). The expert's role should be limited to informing the court on subjects which are not part of the common domain of knowledge of members of the judiciary and which can be discussed using knowledge common in the scientific domain. As soon as the psychologist's statement is not based on psychological scientific insights or enters into the domain of the judge, the psychologist should keep quiet. In using the VCL the psychologist oversteps on both points.

The VCL is neither based on sound empirical research (see Horowitz et al., 1997), nor is it limited to psychological insights. Especially Cluster D can pose problems. Assume a case in which the psychologist interviews a child who allegedly is the victim of sexual abuse. After the CBCA analysis, the psychologist considers the story of the child rather trustworthy and then dives into the case file to apply the VCL while answering Cluster D. There the psychologist finds additional clues for the veracity of the child's story and concludes that the child is speaking the truth. In this case, the court can decide that the statement of the child, as it is supported by the expert statement of the psychologist and the clues in the case file, constitute enough evidence for a conviction. In doing so, through the use of the VCL by the psychologist, the court is led to make "double" use of the evidence present in the case file. This danger is particularly present because, since there exists no clear-cut scoring scheme for the CBCA or the VCL, psychologists tend to remain too vague to allow a thorough analysis of their statement, and judges tend to limit their reading to the conclusions of the experts' reports.

In addition, the VCL requires the psychologist to step outside the psychologist's domain and outside the domain of existing knowledge. In one report in a sexual abuse case, for instance, the psychologist argued in answering Cluster A of the VCL that the child's story was supported by the fact that around the time the abuse was supposed to have started, she suffered from hyperventilation. We have been unable to find research supporting a relationship between hyperventilation and sexual abuse in the psychological or medical literature.

METHODS OF OWN DESIGN

Notwithstanding that the VCL and especially the CBCA are the most used methods for evaluation of witness statements by psychologists, some have methods of their own invention and without validation. We have already discussed the psychologist in the prostitutes' case, who believed that telling a story without hesitation, telling it each time in the same manner, plus her own impression was enough support for a conclusion that witnesses are telling the truth.

Another example comes from a case in which a father is accused of, among other crimes, raping his daughter a great many times in a period of four years. A psychologist talks with the daughter, whom we will call Janet. The psychologist concludes "From a behavioral scientific point of view, the following conclusions can be drawn. Based on the results and analyses above, the statement of Janet on the sexual abuse by her father she experienced must be classified as *believable.*"

The analyses of this psychologist can be summarized in the list below. This list is remarkable, because this particular psychologist usually applies CBCA to evaluate children's statements. The cited conclusion was based on the following:

1. Janet shows symptoms that match posttraumatic stress disorder.
2. Janet's mother reports that she observed a change in the development of Janet.
3. Janet suffered from medical problems, i.e. neck trouble.
4. The psychologist believed Janet's story.
5. Janet recounts her story in the form of a script.
6. There is only a short period between discovery of the abuse and the filing of the report to the police.
7. The statements made by Janet about her abuse could hurt the relationship with her boyfriend.
8. Janet ran away from home.
9. Janet accused nobody but her father of sexually abusing her.
10. Janet has made the disclosure of the abuse more implicitly than explicitly.
11. Janet reports that at first she had a "good feeling" when her father touched her (in a false statement the psychologist would expect that an alleged victim would be entirely negative about her father).
12. There is no evident motive to file a false complaint.

Item 1, used by this psychologist, has been discussed earlier. In using Item 2, this psychologist falls prey to an error already discussed. Items 3 falls outside the domain of psychology. Items 7 and 12 have not been studied or systematically theorized about. Item 4, of course, is fully circular: the statement is true because the psychologist thinks it is true. Telling a story in the form of a script, Item 5, seems to be more indicative of an untrue than of a true story (see Memon, Vrij, & Bull, 1998). As for Items 6,

8, 9, and 10: these are more in the domain of the court, since there is no research to support these Items. With Item 11 this psychologist finally uses one, but only one, of the CBCA criteria.

The first author of this paper wrote a report at the request of the defense and pointed out the problems with the bases of this psychologist's conclusions. In a rebuttal the psychologist explained our disagreement by adding that experimental psychology and clinical psychology each have their own philosophy, methods and techniques and thus results from experimental psychology are not valid. In other words, according to that psychologist, clinical psychology does not believe in the need for valid, well tested procedures, and fields that do believe in validity are invalid.

EXPERTS AND COUNTER EXPERTS

Assessing the validity of witness statements by a psychologist is almost the only field in which psychologists in the Netherlands report at the request of the public prosecution.[9] In the United States, such bolstering of witness credibility is generally prohibited, though prosecutors have begun to by-pass this prohibition by offering experts on certain psychological profiles, notably Rape Trauma Syndrome (see generally, Frazier & Borgida, 1997). In most other cases psychologists in both countries are called in by the defense to investigate methods used by the police in interrogations of witnesses and suspects and, most notably, in eyewitness identification of the suspect.[10]

INTERROGATION OF WITNESSES

Most of what can be said about psychology expert testimony on the interrogation of witnesses has been said above. Most expert statements in that vein are made in cases alleging sexual abuse of children. In the last

[9] There are some exceptions. One example, from the first author's experience, is the case in which a man spontaneously went to the police to confess the murder of a young woman and during the interrogation confessed to three more. The judge-commissioner was worried that the confessions might be false, so he called Van Koppen in to at least assess the quality of the interrogation by the police using the videotapes, which turned out to be quite sound.

[10] There is one other terrain that we will leave out of the discussion here, namely expert testimony on the scent line-up performed by tracker dogs. It is an interesting area, since most of the principles that apply to recognition procedures apply to the scent line-up as well (see Van Koppen, 1995).

few years a new category of case has been added: cases in which adult females claim that they have been abused for a long time, but forgot about the abuse for a long time and only recently recovered the memory of the abuse.[11] Both the number of these kinds of cases—allowing for the size of the population—and the type of cases in the Netherlands are the same as in the United States and Great-Britain (compare False Memory Syndrome Foundation, 1997; Gudjonsson, 1997; Van Koppen & Merckelbach, 1999). In the recovered memory cases the same happens as in other sexual abuse cases: psychologists are called in,[12] who then declare the statement of the alleged victim sound and truthful on feeble grounds (for more general discussion of the Dutch situation, see Crombag & Merckelbach, 1996; see, for instance, the case discussed in Van Koppen & Merckelbach, 1998).

These kinds of cases tend to be handled incorrectly by the police and often result in grave problems for the victim, as well as for the suspects and their family (compare Loftus, 1997b). Van Koppen recently wrote a report for the minister of Justice on how to prevent recovered memory cases from getting out of hand (see Van Koppen, 1997, 1998b). At the end of 1999, formal guidelines for the police and the prosecution will be introduced. Part of these binding guidelines is that the prosecution are obliged to consult a team of experts in cases in which the complainant claims the abuse (1) took place before the age of 3, (2) was ritual in nature, and (3) involves recovered memories. Hopefully, problems with recovered memory cases and the expert testimony given in them will be reduced in the future.

INTERROGATION OF SUSPECTS

Until recently, Dutch psychologists were hardly ever involved in evaluating interrogation of suspects by the police. Two developments changed that. First, more and more the police have started to video-tape interrogations in important cases. That makes an analysis of what happened afterwards possible. In other cases, analyses have to be based on the police report of the interrogation. These reports are always a summary in the form of a monologue by the suspect, but written down by and in the words of the interrogating policemen. Only in rare cases do police reports give real insight into what happened in the interrogation room.

Second, the police in Zaanstad, together with somebody who calls himself a communication expert, developed a method to bring virtually

---

[11] This has led to a great controversy, the "Memory Wars," both in the Netherlands and the United States, as well as elsewhere (Loftus, 1997a; Mulhern, 1997; Read & Lindsay, 1997).

[12] Often by the attorney of the alleged victims, since in these cases a criminal procedure is often accompanied by a civil suit for damages.

every suspect to a confession, commonly known as the Zaanse interrogation method (a description is given by Vrij, 1997; Vrij & Lochun, 1997). This
method is based on the one proposed by Inbau, Reed, and Buckley (1986),
and is supplemented with sound and unsound police practices, and covered with a quasi-scientific sauce of neurolinguistic programming (see Vrij
& Lochun, 1997). Quite a bit of uproar in the country was caused by a case
in which the suspect was put under pressure by covering the walls and
ceiling of the interrogation room with photos of the very bloody scene of
the crime along with those of his wife and children (see also European
Committee for the Prevention of Torture and Inhuman and Degrading
Treatment or Punishment (CPT), 1998). Although the minister of Justice
forbade the method,[13] parts of the method are still in use by the police (for
a description of one such case see Van Koppen, 1998a). In these kinds of
cases, psychologists are called in to explain to the court what influence the
interrogation method has had on the confession by the suspect.

Typically, expert testimony in cases like this have fewer problems
than in the cases in which a psychologist is called in to assess the veracity
of statements. The main reason seems to be that in the latter type of cases
the psychologist is hired to solve a problem of the court or the prosecution. They are awaiting the psychologist's conclusion and are less interested in how and why the psychologist reached the conclusion.
Anticipating that, psychologists usually refrain from explaining their
methods and reasoning extensively in their reports. In cases where the
psychologist is asked to comment on police interrogations, usually by
the defense, their reasons for evaluating police methods as faulty or not
are the heart of their testimony, and naturally form a part of it.

The same seems to apply to cases in which psychologists testify on
other kinds of police behavior, as for instance eyewitness identification
procedures. Perhaps explaining methods and reasoning is easier in these
cases, because well established standards exist for eyewitness identifications, and a good deal of research exists to cast light on the effects of various procedures.

EYEWITNESS IDENTIFICATION

Cognitive psychologists most often testify on problems in eyewitness
identification.[14] Much is known of how a proper identification procedure

---

[13] The Dutch Supreme Court is, as usual, more lenient. See HR 22 September 1998, NJ 1999,
104 (Zaanse Verhoormethode; Zaandam Interrogation Method).

[14] This statement is not based on a survey, but on discussions in the rather small community
of psychologists who testify in court.

should be conducted (see recently Cutler & Penrod, 1995; Wells et al., 1998), and in the Netherlands there are clear-cut rules about how the police should conduct such procedures.[15] Still, it frequently is done wrong by the police (Van Koppen & Hessing, 1999). The most common error made is that a one-person show-up is used instead of a proper line-up with a witness who knows the perpetrator just from the crime scene.

A witness confrontation is used to assess whether the appearance of the suspect corresponds to the memory the witness has of the appearance of the perpetrator. A good lineup or photo-spread procedure seeks to accomplish two purposes simultaneously: to try to learn from an eyewitness who perpetrated a crime and, at the same time, to test the accuracy of that eyewitness's identification. This dual objective is achieved by confronting the witness with a line-up of people who all conform to the general description of the perpetrator. One of these is the suspect; the others are innocent foils unknown to the witness. The witness' task is to indicate the one person in the line-up he recognizes, if he recognizes anyone at all.

The result of a properly conducted line-up has a very high diagnostic value (Wagenaar et al., 1993). It is essential, however, that the procedures minimize the likelihood that an identification is the result of judgments of the relative similarity of a member of the lineup to the witness's memory (that is, that the witness chooses the suspect who looks most like the memory for the perpetrator rather than the one who is the perpetrator), or that subtle or not so subtle cues suggest to the witness who is the "right" suspect to choose. For example, the use of foils who are distinguishable from the eyewitnesses' description reduces the effective size of the lineup, as if those foils were not even there. Moreover, it is important that a suspect's confidence in an identification (which may initially be weak) not be artificially bolstered after the lineup by confirmation from the investigators (that the person chosen is the one they thought was the perpetrator) or learning that other witnesses chose the same person (see Wells & Bradfield, 1999).

Accomplishing these things insures that an identification is caused by a witness's memory of the perpetrator and not something else, and calibrates the diagnostic value of the identification. These goals can be accomplished by routinely employing these four procedures: (1) The person or persons who conduct the lineup or photo spread should not be aware of which member of the lineup is the suspect or which photograph is that of

---

[15] The guidelines were set by the Werkgroep Identificatie (1989), and were revised later (Werkgroep Identificatie, 1992). There is also a small booklet which explains everything a policeman might want to know on the subject. (Van Amelsvoort, 1996).

the suspect. (2) Eyewitnesses should be told explicitly that the person being sought might or might not be in the lineup or photo spread and, therefore, that they are not obligated or expected to make an identification. (3) Lineups should be presented sequentially rather than simultaneously (that is, one lineup member at a time rather than all at once, to minimize the tendency of witnesses to look for whichever lineup member comes closest to the description of the perpetrator). (4) A suspect should not stand out in the lineup or photo spread as being different from the other people in the array on the basis of the eyewitness's previous description of the person sought or other irrelevant criteria. (5) At the time of the identification and prior to any feedback from anyone, a clear statement shall be taken from the eyewitness regarding his or her confidence that the identified person actually is the person sought (Wells et al., 1998).

Apart from a proper identity parade, tests of the witness's memory can be conducted in two other manners: (1) mug books, on paper or on a television screen; and (2) a one-person show-up. These serve other purposes. Mug shots are photos of known criminals. If done properly, these are shown only to witnesses in investigations where the police have no idea where or how to find the perpetrator. Therefore, the police show to the witness a selection of photos of known criminals who conform to the description given by the witness. If the witness points one out, that individual always becomes a suspect. This will lead to a suspect driven search (Wagenaar et al., 1993, Chapter 7), which has the potential of generating erroneous identifications, and ultimately a miscarriage of justice. Therefore, the results of examinations by witnesses of mug shots should not be used as evidence by the court.

The one-person show-up should be used in one situation and one situation only: when the witness already knew the perpetrator before the crime took place. The identification then takes place at the scene of the crime and showing the suspect to the witness can only serve to prevent administrative errors ("is this the neighbor you meant?"). If the witness knows the perpetrator by name, this procedure is unnecessary. If used with a witness who saw the perpetrator only at the scene of the crime, the one-person show-up is much more likely to yield false identifications than are properly constructed line-ups (see Dekle, Beale, Elliot, & Huneycutt, 1996; Lindsay, Pozzulo, Craig, Lee, & Corber, 1997; Yarmey, Yarmey, & Yarmey, 1996). The one-person show-up is much too suggestive, because with this procedure the police signal to the witness: "We got him. You just have to confirm it." If, in a proper line-up, the eyewitness has no good recollection of the perpetrator, or the suspect is innocent, it is most likely that he will identify an innocent foil, which can be detected as an error. Such error-detection is impossible with the one-person show-up.

In Dutch police practice most often identifications are attempted using the one-person show-up. This seems to be a structural problem that is caused by two things. First, although the principles of a line-up are simple, organizing one means much work to the police. People must be obtained to serve as foils. They must be present at the same time as the witness, the suspect, the suspect's attorney, the prosecutor, and a number of policemen not involved in the investigation, and then the show must be run by the book (see Van Amelsvoort, 1996). A one-person show-up is much easier. Besides, Dutch courts are very lenient on how identification procedures should be run. Courts routinely accept procedures that violate one or more of the requirements of a proper line-up. So, why should the police bother?

Thus, the police regularly make every conceivable error in conducting identification procedures. A 1998 case provides an example where the flaw is so obvious that one wonders how such errors can happen in the first place. In that case, a witness saw five men in a car. One of them had a gun. Five suspects had been arrested and the policewomen running the investigation showed each of them in a one-person show-up to the witness. Each time, the witness identified the suspect. Now the question remained which of the suspects had held the gun. The police report then reads as follows:

> After Dekkers had been confronted with each of the suspects, he stated that he recognized each of them, but he had not indicated yet which of the suspects had the gun. So I asked him to indicate which suspect had held the gun. Then Dekkers stated that he doubted and hesitated between number 1 and 3. Subsequently, I informed Dekkers that both other witnesses had identified the first suspect as the man with the gun. I said he should not hesitate and point one out with confidence. Then Dekkers stated that he was confident that the suspect number 1 had held the gun.

An example of a more subtle error is where the police officer conducting a lineup tells a witness who is unsure which lineup member the witness recognizes, to "take another look at suspect number 1" or some other inadvertent (or intentional) signal that tells the witness whom to select. In these kinds of cases the defense time and again calls in cognitive psychologists to explain to the court what went wrong.

In the United States, lineups are a more regular part of police investigation practices, but they often are conducted in ways that inadvertently (or intentionally) undermine their potential value as evidence for a fact finder at trial, typically by making it appear that the eyewitness identification is more reliable than it is in fact. Though errors in testing eyewitnesses are common, only occasionally do defendants call psychologists as expert witnesses on eyewitness identification, and only sometimes do courts allow the psychologist to testify. The value of lineups conducted by American police would be greatly improved if they were conducted using the procedures outlined above (see Wells et al., 1998, for a discussion of these procedures and what they achieve).

STANDARDS FOR EXPERT PSYCHOLOGISTS

The above discussion suggests that, although both theory and practice of common law and civil law differ enormously (Damaška, 1973, 1998) the problems encountered in psychological expert testimony in the Netherlands and the United States are not very different. It may be that some solutions to the problems of avoiding bad expert testimony need not be much different.

Those familiar with the civil law system know that it has not worked well to exclude poor expert psychological evidence, but at the same time have no confidence that the adversarial common law system would provide the solution to those shortcomings. Those familiar with the common law system have a mirror image reaction—they know the system has been ineffective in excluding weak psychological expert evidence but have no confidence that the civil law system is the solution.

Some expect that further time and efforts within the respective systems will rectify the problems others and we have discussed. For example, an optimistic view of the American adversarial system's ability to improve on these problems has been offered by Penrod, Fulero, and Cutler (1995). They expect that, before long, experimental psychologists will be called upon often and that even judges will enthusiastically master the psychologist's concepts and tools.[16] The clashing of opposing parties and the procedural principles of a fair trial are expected to eventually

---

[16] To get the full flavor of their optimism: "Experimental psychologists should be able, and increasingly, will be called upon, to talk authoritatively about the role of basic scientific concepts and practices in eyewitness research. We are confident that many of these basic concepts will become part of the basic vocabulary of a good number of trial judges, though we are also confident that judges will rival undergraduate introductory psychology students in their enthusiasm for mastering these important concepts and tools. As a complement to the conceptual armamentaria, we expect that judges will also learn much more about the professional processes that serve as quality controls on what is generated and dispensed as knowledge by research scientists. Thus, a typical proffer of expert testimony might also emphasize elements of peer review mentioned in Daubert, including peer reviews of grant proposals, research reports intended for publication in scientific journals, and even peer review of book chapters and books. Judges may also learn about the sheer quantity of research on eyewitness reliability issues being generated by psychologists" (Penrod et al., 1995, p. 245).

produce, or at least promote, psychological evidence of good quality. Both of the present authors are not so optimistic about the ability of the American system, at least as practiced by real people on a daily basis, to place dependable expert evidence before juries.

Again, both of the present authors are not so optimistic about the ability of the Dutch system, at least as practiced by real people on a daily basis, to place dependable expert evidence before judges.

Let us summarize why the expert testimony in the cases discussed in this paper went wrong. Together, they are quite typical of psychological evidence in the more "difficult" cases in the Netherlands, and, except for the evaluation of witness truth-telling, not very different from what comes before courts in the United States. All of the problems have to do with the knowledge and skills of the participants. Of course, the psychologists who overstate their case, give unwarranted opinions or simply tell nonsense are a problem. A more fundamental problem, however, is that all of the other participants in the procedure—lawyers, judges, defendant, or other witnesses—do not recognize bad expert evidence immediately. It needs an informed and alert prosecutor, defense attorney, or judge to recognize these problems. Since psychology is not their trade, this is not an automatic process. Even the Common Law system, which is structured to produce scrutiny through the clash of competing interests persistently fails to screen out poor expert evidence (see Risinger, 2000; Saks, 1994, 1998; Saks & Koehler, 1991; Stoney, 1997). In both the Dutch as well as the American systems, much bad expert evidence simply goes unquestioned and unchallenged, perhaps because it simply goes unnoticed.

With respect to expert evidence, let us think of both systems as consisting of a series of filters, all of which are intended to screen out bad expert evidence and to allow good expert evidence to pass through and influence the verdict of the court. These "filters" consist of procedural, evidentiary, and ethical rules, prosecutors, defense lawyers, decision-makers (judge sitting with or without a jury), and the experts themselves. If any one filter works successfully, the court will be protected from misleading expert evidence. Only if all fail will the court receive, and perhaps decide on the basis of, expertise that may be incorrect or misleading. To be sure, the nature and configuration of these "filters" differs much between the two systems. But the one that is largely common to both is the experts themselves. A focus on the experts provides a trans-system opportunity to create a "filter" that will help courts in both systems, an opportunity in which educational and professional institutions may contribute in important ways (without relying so heavily in the intervention or control of any court process to police the evidence). Both legal systems may lack adequate filters to protect themselves from weak or misleading expert evidence, but if the experts in both systems are made to be highly competent, both systems can benefit. The solution proposed here is that the experts themselves be bound by strict rules on the content if their testimony.[17]

By way of conclusions, we offer a preliminary list of standards for psychological expert testimony. The list reflects standards suggested by the recent scientific evidence opinions of the Dutch Supreme Court and the United States Supreme Court, by the logic of science and its application, and by the examples given above. In the list that follows, we assume that an expert provides a written report, rather than solely giving oral testimony, which to differing degrees is current practice in both the Dutch and American systems.[18] These are aspirational standards; the closer a psychological expert witness comes to achieving them, the greater will be the psychologist's value to the court.

1. The psychologist should be an expert on the particular subject matter on which he testifies and should explain in his report precisely why he considers himself an expert on the specific issues before the court.

---

[17] Our metaphorical description focuses on the exclusion of bad expert evidence and not the admission of good expert evidence. Not only are courts disadvantaged by admitting misleading evidence, they are, of course also disadvantaged by excluding good and helpful evidence. Erroneous (or unwise) exclusion is perhaps a greater problem in the American courts than in the Dutch courts, because the latter are more inclined to admit expert evidence and allow the judge to assess its value. A good example of this is the courts' response to expert psychological testimony on eyewitness accuracy. This type of evidence had been more readily admitted in Dutch courts, and has faced a more difficult struggle in American courts. But see *United States v. Hines*, 1999 WL 412847 (D. Mass., holding that expert testimony on eyewitness identifications generally is based on a more solid scientific foundation, and at the same time refrains from asserting ultimate conclusions, in contrast to many other kinds of asserted scientific, which has a far shakier basis and yet asserts specific ultimate conclusions).

[18] Clearly it is the Anglo-American system which is more verbal than written. But in recent times the American system increasingly requires experts to provide written reports (Federal Rule of Civil Procedure 26(a)(2)(B)). Complying with these standards is much easier if the expert provides a written report, whether directly to the court or through the parties. Explaining methods and research, for instance, requires reference to and consultation of scientific publications, something that is likely to be accomplished more comprehensively and accurately in writing. Formulating precise conclusions is more easily done in writing. The act of writing helps the expert's thinking and committing one's analysis and conclusions to writing makes it easier to scrutinize what it is the expert has to say. If experts are permitted to evade this discipline by writing reports that hide rather than reveal what they have done and why they conclude what they conclude, then someone does not want the court to have the benefit of sound analysis and meaningful conclusions.

2. The expert witness should show awareness of the limitations of her role. She should remain within her own domain and not intrude on those matters that are properly within the domain of the court.
3. Psychotherapists should never be expert witnesses on the credibility of fact witnesses.
4. Psychologists who serve as expert witnesses should limit their testimony to subject matter for which psychology is relevant.
5. The psychologist should be able to show that the testimony and the underlying research are relevant for the case in point.
6. The psychologist should show that she is competent to apply the specific method to the specific case.
7. Expert testimony encompasses application of scientific knowledge to a specific case. Thus, the expert should apply sound empirical research, must tell the court which results of research have been applied and why they are relevant to the specific case or its circumstances.
8. In applying sound research, the expert presents the court with sufficient basis for the court to assess its value, which depends upon the extent to which:
   a. It is grounded in the methods and procedures of science;
   b. It is based on empirical research, rather than the expert's subjective belief or unsupported speculation;
   c. The theory or method applied by the expert has been subjected to peer review after as well as before publication;
   d. The methods used are valid enough for the court to base its decision upon;
   e. The expert provides an accurate account of the discussion in the scientific community concerning the concepts or techniques being employed.[19]

Psychologists who adhere to such guidelines would almost certainly be doing courts more good and less harm. These, and perhaps other, guidelines are urgently needed in the Netherlands and the United States and probably also in other countries. Perhaps developing such guidelines, and finding ways to promote and enforce them, is a fine task for the flourishing European Association for Psychology and Law in collaboration with the American Psychology-Law Association.

---

[19] The reader will recognize some standards set by the United States Supreme Court in *Daubert*.

17

Styles of Trial Procedure at the International Criminal Tribunal for the Former Yugoslavia

FRANCIS J. PAKES[1]

It is fair to say that international humanitarian law has transformed dramatically in the 1990s. The most tangible developments are the foundation of the International Criminal Tribunal for the former Yugoslavia (ICTY) and its sister court, The International Criminal Tribunal for Rwanda (ICTR). Both have been said to have put "flesh on the bones of international humanitarian law." For the first time, such bodies exist under the umbrella of the United Nations. The International Criminal Tribunal for the former Yugoslavia (ICTY), on which this chapter will focus, was established in 1993 by the UN Security Council. Its specific assignment is to prosecute and sentence persons responsible for the violations since 1991 of international humanitarian law in the former Yugoslavia. The part of its Statute that constitutes the Criminal Code consists of four clusters of crimes. These are grave breaches of the Geneva Conventions of 1949 (Article 2 of the Statute), violations of the laws and customs of war (Article 3), genocide (Article 4), and crimes against humanity (Article 5). Sentencing those responsible would contribute to ensuring that these atrocities are halted, and that

[1] Thanks to Mr. Glyn Morgan, Intelligence Officer, Office of the Prosecutor at ICTY, for helpful comments and advice.

justice would be done. In this fashion, the Tribunal would contribute to the restoration and maintenance of peace.

Apart from its impact on international humanitarian law, the Yugoslav Tribunal can serve as an interesting case study of the differences between adversarial and inquisitorial trial systems. Most legal systems have developed over time, often over centuries. In such systems, the culture and practice of how trials are conducted evolved over time as well. The statute and rules of proceedings at the Tribunal, however, were almost developed from scratch. Its main and almost its only examples are post-World War II Tribunals in Nuremberg and Tokyo. It is interesting to see how trial proceedings develop in a court that had it first contested case only a few years ago and whose rules of procedure have been developed in a matter of months rather than over centuries.

Tochilovski, legal adviser to the Tribunal, argues that the style of trial proceedings is predominantly adversarial. He argues that this choice was not so much informed by assumptions underlying systems of trial, but that it was of a more practical nature. The advisers most forthcoming in the preparatory stage were from an adversarial background, most notably from the United States, so that an adversarial system of trial proceedings emerged as the natural choice (Tochilovski, 1998).

The legislators, a team of international lawyers and diplomats were undoubtedly keen to ensure that they would improve on the Nuremberg (the Nuremberg International Military Tribunal) and Tokyo (the International Military Tribunal for the Far East) Tribunals that followed the end of the Second World War. A few important differences between the Tribunals and the ICTY are worth discussing.

Firstly, in both Nuremberg and Tokyo, all defendants were tried simultaneously, in one "mega-trial." In The Hague, most defendants are tried individually, although joint indictments and trials also do occur.

Secondly, in the Nuremberg and Tokyo trials there were certain restrictions placed on the conduct of the defense. In the Nuremberg trial, the defense was not allowed to discuss potential wrong doings on the part of the Allied forces. Similarly, in the Tokyo trial, the atomic bombs on Hiroshima and Nagasaki were not topic of any debate. The panel of judges of both trials ruled these to be irrelevant to the charges brought. The ICTY, by mouth of the Chief Prosecutor, has stated that the behavior of allied forces during the "Kosovo crisis" does fall under its jurisdiction. ICTY is not aimed to be and clearly does not want to be or seen to be a "victor's tribunal."

Thirdly and relatedly, the judges in Nuremberg and Tokyo primarily came from "victor's countries." This was most notable in Nuremberg, which was conducted by four judges from the United States, the United Kingdom, France, and the Soviet Union, with the inevitable impression left that this trial was primarily about the victors judging the losers of World War II. Defense counsel in Nuremberg were invariably German. In Tokyo, all defendants were also defended by fellow countrymen. However, as it was felt that the trial procedures were largely adversarial, it was later agreed that each defendant was assigned a U.S. defense councilor as well. It was felt that these lawyers would be more equipped to operate effectively in what has been termed a rather adversarial trial system. As Tokyo Judge Röling observed, "the majority of the judges were accustomed to an Anglo-Saxon trial and gradually many Anglo-Saxon features crept into the proceedings by majority decision of the court. Thus it became a kind of trial Japanese lawyers were not accustomed to" (Cassese & Röling, 1993, p. 36). Röling observed a similar tension in Nuremberg where German defense lawyers were operating in a system with which they were not necessarily familiar.

Fourthly, the judges did rely to a relatively large extent on paper work. Documentary evidence such as official documents played a substantial role. This measure to enhance the trials' expedience helped to ensure that the Nuremberg trial (involving 25 defendants) took no more than 11 months (International Military Tribunal, 1947), whereas the Tokyo trial (involving 28 defendants) lasted approximately 2.5 years. Some trials at the ICTY involving a single defendant have lasted almost as long.

CHARACTERISTICS OF THE ICTY

One thing that has remained from the Nuremberg and Tokyo trials is the rather adversarial nature of courtroom procedures (Tochilovski, 1998). The principle of immediacy is strictly adhered to. Until recently judges did not receive a case file beforehand and relied on courtroom witness testimony for acquiring information about the case. Witnesses are examined by the party that called them and subsequently cross-examined by the opposing party. Following this, the party that called the defendant can examine the witness again in a rebuttal, and finally the opposing party has another chance to ask questions in a rejoinder. Judges are also allowed to ask questions themselves.

One consequence of this arrangement is that many vulnerable witnesses are to testify in court whereas they in more inquisitorial trial systems often do not need to make appearances. The Tribunal has the full modern range of technological options available to accommodate the needs of vulnerable witnesses, such as video links, masking devices for appearance as well as for voice distortion, while on occasion a satellite link with a witness in the former Yugoslavia has been used as well.

An obvious departure from the adversarial tradition is the absence of juries anywhere in the proceedings. A panel of three judges decides on guilt as well as on sentencing. A majority finding of two against one is in principle sufficient for a guilty verdict, a state of affairs that has not escaped criticism (Pruitt, 1997).

Judges are appointed after a vote by the UN's General Assembly. States can nominate a maximum of two judges, only one of which can be a national of that country. In order to be nominated, judges have to be eligible for the highest judicial offices in their home countries, and of high moral character, integrity, and impartiality. The UN Security Council processes this list of nominates and produces a "short list" of candidates, "taking due account of the adequate representation of the principal legal systems of the world" (Statute, Article 13.2.c). Judges are appointed for four years with the possibility of re-election. Not more than one judge per state can be appointed to the Tribunal.[2] President of the Tribunal is Judge Claude Jorda from France. Apart from his experience as a judge in France, he was as a prosecutor before his appointment at ICTY. He also has taught at the School of Law at the University of Paris, and has been Secretary-General and Deputy Director of the *Ecole Nationale de la Magistrature* as well as Director of legal services at the French Ministry of Justice.

THE PERFORMANCE OF THE TRIBUNAL

On 10 January 2001 the Tribunal had publicly indicted 97 people. These include Serbs, Bosnians, as well as Croats. Of these, 66 are still outstanding. Partly because of the lack of cooperation of some of the states in the former Yugoslavia, the number of cases that actually have been tried is rather small. One case has been administered following a guilty plea. Erdemovic[3] has been sentenced to five years imprisonment, and is serving his sentence in Norway. Contested trials have resulted in convictions for Tadic,[4] Alexovski,[5] and three of the four defendants who were tried together in the so-called Celebici[6] case. Of these four, only Delalic has been found not guilty on all counts. He regained his freedom after having spent two and a half years in pre-trial detention. Papic is the other defendant

---

[2] In December 2000, a number of 14 Judges were in office. They are from Australia, China, Colombia, Egypt, France, Guyana, Italy, Jamaica, Malaysia, Morocco, Portugal, United Kingdom, United States, and Zambia.

[3] *The Prosecutor v. Erdemovic* (IT-96-22).

[4] *The Prosecutor v. Tadic* (IT-94-01).

[5] *The Prosecutor v. Alexovski* (IT-95-14/1).

[6] *The Prosecutor v. Delalic and others* (IT-96-21) "Celebici".

who was acquitted on all charges. Furthermore, Jelisic[7] pleaded guilty to all counts but one, the one being the sole count of genocide brought against him. He was acquitted on that charge and sentenced for the remaining counts that he did not contest. Alexovski was tried on two counts of Grave Breaches of the Geneva Conventions and found guilty. Also, Furundzija[8] was found guilty of violations of the laws and customs of war and sentenced to 10 years imprisonment. He has lodged an appeal. The case of Tadic is the only case thus far on which the ICTY's appeals court has rendered a verdict. He was found guilty and sentenced to 20 years imprisonment.[9]

Given the fact that the judges are the actual decision makers on guilt or innocence and on sentencing, their role is crucial for how justice is actually administered. The procedural rules give them considerable leeway in deciding how to run a trial. Judges could decide to be largely reactive. They could follow adversarial system practices and choose to let prosecution and defense do the witness examinations and only rule on objections and other issues, such as the admission of items of evidence. On the other hand, judges could decide to adopt a more active position akin to that of traditional inquisitorial systems. They are allowed to ask questions themselves and it is up to them to decide to what extent they wish to exercise that right. In addition, judges can call witnesses themselves. Again, it is a matter of choice or preference to what extent judges regard this as the proper exercise of their role, as they are, in a way, both judge and jury at trial.

Since judges work at the Tribunal for a limited period of time after having been on the bench in their home countries—often for many years—it is not unreasonable to assume that judges might "bring their domestic legal culture with them" when they sit as a judge at the tribunal. Although I have to resort to crude generalizations, I would expect judges accustomed to an adversarial manner of trial proceedings to be more reactive whereas judges from an inquisitorial tradition might be expected to conduct their trials in a more proactive manner.

This chapter examines and evaluates these different styles of courtroom interactions between judges and witnesses in the ICTY's courtrooms.

THE PRESENT STUDY

This research reported in this chapter has used transcripts of trials conducted at the ICTY as the raw data. In two cases, witness examinations,

---

[7] *The Prosecutor v. Jelisic* (IT-95-10).

[8] *The Prosecutor v. Furundzija* (IT-95-17/1-A).

[9] For the latest developments in ongoing cases, see www.un.org/icty.

TABLE 1. CHARACTERISTICS OF THE TRIALS OF TADIC AND BLASKIC

Case	*Prosecutor v. Tadic (IT-94-01)*	*Prosecutor v. Blaskic (IT-95-14-T)*
Defendant	D. Tadic, born 1 October 1955	D. Blaskic, born 2 November 1960
Start date	7 May 1996	24 June 1997
End date	7 November 1996	30 July 1999
Number of witnesses	126	159
Prosecution	86	104
Defense	40	46
Bench	0	9
Exhibits	465	1414
Prosecution	362	787
Defense	103	614
Bench	0	13
Judges	G. Kirk McDonald (presiding), United States	Claude Jorda (presiding), France
	Ninian Stephen, Australia	Mohamed Shahabuddeen, Guyana
	Lal Chand Vohrah, Malaysia	Almiro Rodrigues, Portugal

cross-examinations, rebuttals and rejoinders have been analyzed.[10] The defendants involved were Tadic and Blaskic.[11]

In the case of Blaskic it was alleged that from May 1992 to January 1994 members of the armed forces of the Croatian Defense Council (HVO) committed serious violations of international humanitarian law against Bosnian Muslims in Bosnia and Herzegovina. It is alleged that Blaskic held the rank of Colonel and later of General and Commander in the HVO. The indictment charges the accused with various instances of grave breaches of the 1949 Geneva Conventions, violations of the laws or customs of war, and crimes against humanity. The Trial Chamber is currently considering its judgment.

The indictment involving Tadic alleges that between late May 1992 and 31 December 1992, Dusko Tadic participated in attacks on and the seizure, murder, and maltreatment of Bosnian Muslims and Croats in the Prijedor municipality in Bosnia, both within and outside prison camps. The indictment charged him with several instances of crimes against humanity, grave breaches of the 1949 Geneva Conventions, and violations of the laws or customs of war. Characteristics of both trials are listed in Table 1.

---

[10] Trial transcripts are available on the Tribunal's internet home page: www.un.org/icty.
[11] *The Prosecutor v. Blaskic* (IT-95-14-T).

Both cases were selected because of the composition of the courts. As I assumed that the identity and background of the presiding judge might have a strong impact on how the court would conduct the trial, I decided to examine one case involving a French presiding judge, and one case with an American presiding judge. My rationale was that a judge coming from the French inquisitorial tradition would be more inclined to take an active stance at trial, as is common in France, whereas an American presiding judge would probably more inclined to be more like a passive referee, as is more common in the USA.

In analyzing these witness appearances, I primarily examined the judges' behavior. I examined the nature of interruptions, either prompted by one of the parties, or not; questions asked by one of the judges; the introduction of witnesses; and other interactions with either party or the witness whilst the witness was on the witness stand.

THE ACTIVE POSITION: JUDGE JORDA IN *THE PROSECUTOR V. BLASKIC*

Just by examining the number of questions asked, we can see that Judge Jorda's style of conducting a trial was more active than that of Judge McDonald, who presided over the Tadic trial. The French judge asked more factual questions himself after both parties have finished their questioning, as do both other judges on the panel. Based on a sample of 20 witness examinations, I estimate that judges asked almost twice as many questions directly to the witness in the Blaskic case as compared to the case of Tadic. Witnesses in Tadic were asked 10–12 questions on average whereas witnesses in Blaskic were asked in the order of 25 questions by the judges.

While interruptions by the court during examinations were not particularly frequent in Blaskic's trial, they did occur and show an "active" attitude toward trial proceedings. The French presiding judge sees it as his task to steer the behavior of both parties to a considerable extent. A good example occurred during the examination of witness Ahmic. The presiding judge showed impatience with the prosecution, because of its objection to the defense's summarization of what the witness had said just before. Prosecutor Mr. Kehoe argued that this summarization was inconsistent with what the witness had actually said himself. The presiding judge was clearly not impressed with this objection: "Mr. Prosecutor, this is the last objection, otherwise I am going to ask the questions myself of the witness" (witness Ahmic, 2 October 1997, transcript, p. 7393).

A point of note is that this witness was 18 years of age at the time of the examination. He testified about events in a prison camp that he witnessed when he was only 14 years old. The judge showed great awareness for the distress that the court appearance might have caused for this witness. It is therefore probably fair to say that this is the reason why the judge was rather strict in the manner in which both parties examined this particular witness. The quotation also, obviously, shows that for this presiding judge, examining a witness directly is a distinct possibility, although Judge Jorda did not carry out this threat.

When Judge Jorda felt that a line of questioning was not relevant, or when he was dissatisfied with an answer given by a witness, he regularly interrupted and addressed either the party or the witness directly. When Professor Bilandzic testified about historical aspects of the situation in the former Yugoslavia, the presiding judge was keen to step in when the answers seemed to lose their relevance to the case: "Mr. Professor, it's a legal discussion, this is not a historic conference. I understand you have a great number of things to say, but we need to cut back to the subject at hand" (witness Bilandzic, 9 September 1998, transcript, p. 11383).

When subsequently the prosecutor again asked the witness to cover similar ground another admonition was delivered. These examples illustrate the active manner in which this presiding judge conducted the trial.

Before witnesses actually started their testimony, they were addressed by the presiding judge. Judge Jorda addressed witnesses rather elaborately and in doing so, appeared to be instructing both parties at the same time. Consider the following quotation, which contains the following introduction to the witness, British politician Mr. Paddy Ashdown.

> Mr. Ashdown, you have agreed to testify at the request of the Prosecution as part of the trial before the International Criminal Tribunal for the Former Yugoslavia against General Blaskic, who is in this courtroom. The Prosecutor has given us a summary of the main points of your testimony. You are very well familiar with the type of procedures that are in effect at this Tribunal, which to a large extent come from proceedings which you are familiar with, so you will not be surprised that you will be asked to answer the Prosecutor's questions. However, the Tribunal would very much like this testimony to be as spontaneous as possible, and that of course the Prosecutor can ask you for clarifications about this or that point. (Witness Ashdown, 19 March 1998, trial transcript, p. 7325)

Similarly, the anonymous witness with alias JJ, was introduced to the proceedings as follows:

> You agreed to come to testify in the trial, which is here at the International Tribunal, of General Blaskic who is in this courtroom. Speak without fear. You are being protected by international justice. The Prosecutor told us what the main lines of your statement will be, which will make the proceedings go more smoothly. You will speak freely, and you will be guided by the Prosecutor's questions. (Witness JJ, 19 March 1998, trial transcript, p. 7393)

Both quotations are typical for the fashion in which Judge Jorda introduced witnesses to the courtroom procedure. Notable is the fact that the judge encouraged witnesses to speak freely, saying in one instance that the testimony should be "as spontaneous as possible." In the other instance, the judge emphasized that the prosecutor's questions should be taken as "guidance." The aim of this introduction seems to be to invite the parties to ask broad ranging open questions that the witness can answer without interruption.

A further point of note is the fact that Judge Jorda makes it clear that he regards the proceedings to be Anglo-Saxon in style. He explains to Mr. Paddy Ashdown that he will be familiar with the way the trial is conducted. In Judge Jorda's introduction of British MP Martin Bell he says the following: "I'm sure you know the legal customs of your own country. These are more or less the same that are here" (Witness Martin Bell MP, 15 February 1999, trial transcript, p. 17599).

Additionally, Judge Jorda required both parties to introduce each witness to him before they were called. In this introduction, the identity of the witness was divulged, or their alias if they testified anonymously. It also included an overview of the issues on which the witness will testify, why the testimony will be relevant and what counts of the indictment the testimony will pertain to. These introductions could be quite elaborate. One might speculate whether they served a function similar to reading the case file before trail, which is common practice in many inquisitorial systems whereas it was, until recently, not common practice at the ICTY.

Finally, it must be noted that in the case of Blaskic, nine witnesses were called on initiative of the bench.

THE JUDGE AS REFEREE: JUDGE MACDONALD IN THE PROSECUTOR V. TADIC

Judge MacDonald's style of conducting the trials was rather different from that of Judge Jorda. Whereas Judge Jorda presence is very noticeable in the proceedings, Judge MacDonald tends to assume a rather more passive position. Unprompted interruptions by the bench in the case she presided over were quite rare. Most often, they did not relate to the behavior of the parties, but to either the technical apparatus assisting the court or the translation. Only in a few cases did a judge, usually the presiding judge, intervene during examinations. These were invariably minor interruptions, relating to points of clarification, or a request to one of the parties to repeat a certain question. Witnesses were on average asked less questions by the judges than in Blaskic. Sometimes the presiding judge did not even ask her colleagues on the bench whether they had any questions at all. The behavior of the parties does not seem to be very different in both trials, so that differences in the behavior of the court cannot be attributed to that.

The differences in approach become most apparent when we compare the fashion in which witnesses are introduced to courtroom procedures. In the trial of Tadic, the American judge hardly played a role in this
respect. Apart from having each witness take the oath, she left it to the
parties to get on with their examination. The introductions by the presiding judge for the sake of the witness or the introduction of witnesses to the
bench simply did not occur. The presiding judge usually instructed prosecution or defense counsel to proceed without any form of instruction.
Jorda-style introductions simply did not occur.

Whereas the judges in the case of Blaskic did call a number of witnesses
themselves, this did not occur at all in the case of Tadic. I take this as further
evidence for that fact that the judges in Blaskic are simply more active when
conducting their trial than the bench in Tadic. The judges in the latter case
simply assume a referee-like role and leave it to the parties to elicit the information from witnesses in the fashion they regard as most appropriate.

CONCLUDING REMARKS

In the number and content of the questions they ask, the extent to
which they interrupt proceedings, and in their decision whether or not to
introduce witnesses and have witnesses introduced to them, we can
clearly distinguish two styles of conducting an ICTY trial. One is more
reminiscent of a continental inquisitorial tradition. In this tradition,
judges tend to be important fact finders at trial. This the how the French
Judge Jorda ran his trial. The other style, adopted by Judge MacDonald in
the trial of Tadic, involves a judge as a referee who does very little in
terms of actual fact finding. It more closely resembles the traditional role
of a judge in adversarial proceedings.

So which approach is most appropriate? ICTY "inquisitorial style" or
"adversarial style"? This is arguably a question of comparative criminal justice within one and the same court. Damaška (1986) argues that the difference between adversarial and inquisitorial systems is in its core a difference
between values. The highest value in adversarial systems is assigned to
equality between both parties. Trials are seen as a platform for conflict resolution. If both parties have the opportunity to present their evidence in front of
an impartial decision maker, justice will emerge, provided that both parties
have equal opportunities of putting their views forward. Such an approach
would require for a decision maker to be passive, and to leave it to the parties to produce the goods in terms of evidence.

In inquisitorial systems, *truth* is said to be most important. In order to
find the truth, more responsibilities with regard to information gathering are
put on the shoulders of the actual decision maker. Where finding the truth,

rather than resolution of conflict is the objective, it makes sense to have the decision maker more involved in eliciting information that neither party (for whatever reason) has brought forward. The calling of witnesses on their own initiative would perhaps be the best example of this attitude.

It is safe to say that the ICTY was not just founded as a platform for conflict resolution. The following quotation from their 1998 annual report illustrates this.

> Ensuring that history listens is a most important function of the Tribunal. Through our proceedings we strive to establish as judicial fact the full details of the madness that transpired in the former Yugoslavia. In the years and decades to come, no one will be able to deny the depths to which their brother and sister human beings sank. And by recording the capacity for evil in all of us, it is hoped to recognize warning signs in the future and to act with sufficient speed and determination to prevent such bloodshed. (International Criminal Tribunal for the Former Yugoslavia, 1998, paragraph 294)

Truth finding, as a core objective, fits better with an inquisitorial system involving an active judge who have a certain obligation to ensure that the "whole truth" is laid bare. The bench in Blaskic, who asked more questions themselves, who tend to impose a slightly more inquisitorial style of proceedings and who do call witnesses themselves seem to better meet this obligation. On the other hand, an over-involved judge is traditionally warned against, because it might lead to a loss of impartiality or perceived impartiality of the judge or court. This argument obviously carries weight, not only because of the importance of impartial courts within any formulation of the rule of law, but also because the ICTY's impartiality has been questioned, especially in some of the states in the former Yugoslavia. However, impartiality would hardly be jeopardized by judges adopting a slightly more active stance at trial, and it will prevent acquittals on the basis of what the courts perceives are insufficient witness examinations. It also fits better with ICTY's ambition of leaving a record for future generations relating to what actually happened in the former Yugoslavia. The importance of the latter aim can hardly be overestimated.

One might speculate whether perhaps a slight shift towards a more inquisitorial style of proceeding is currently taking place. The introduction of case files seems to signify this development. The fact that "inquisitorial" Judge Jorda has just been elected to become the new president might be another signal. Thirdly, one main concern of the Tribunal itself is the fact that it suffers from a lack of efficiency. The availability of case files might improve the expediency of witness examinations, since the bench will already be more or less familiar with the content of their testimony. I conclude by saying if such a shift toward a more inquisitorial style of trial proceedings is occurring, there are ideological as well as practical reasons to welcome it.

18

Convergence and Complementarity between Professional Judges and Lay Adjudicators

SHARI SEIDMAN DIAMOND

The American jury is both a popular cultural icon and a favorite scapegoat. Calls for reform are rampant (e.g., Adler, 1994; Wilkinson, Zielinski, & Curtis, 1988). Some proposed reforms are friendly and constructive, such as those advocating that jurors should be permitted to take notes and to submit questions for witnesses during the trial (e.g., Dann, 1993; McLaughlin, 1983). These changes in the jury trial do not assume that juries are failing to perform adequately, but rather are designed to assist them in reaching well-considered judgments, to improve the comfort of the conscripted citizens who serve as jurors, and generally to optimize jury performance and juror satisfaction. Other proposed reforms, however, are aggressively hostile, such as calls for a complexity exception to the right to jury trial in civil cases (Devitt, 1974; Flehner, 1979) and for legislative caps that place a ceiling on jury awards (e.g., *Crookston v. Fire Ins. Exch.*, 1991). Some of the proposed changes in the jury system have been stimulated by particular high profile trials (e.g., the acquittal of white police officers on trial for the beating of African-American Rodney King, St. George, 1993), such as calls for racial quotas to ensure minority representation on the jury (Alschuler, 1995; King & Munsterman, 1996) or the elimination of peremptory challenges (Amar, 1995; Diamond, Ellis, & Schmidt, 1997; Montoya,

321

1996) which can permit criteria such as race and gender to creep into jury selection.

Discourse on the performance of the jury frequently ignores a basic reality of legal systems: in evaluating the jury, the relevant comparison is not with some hypothetical ideal decision maker, whatever qualities such a model decision maker would have. Rather, the appropriate comparison is with the human alternative or set of alternatives that might be used in the jury's stead (Lempert, 1981). Thus, against the background of calls for jury reform in the United States and in light of the expanding interest in lay participation in adjudication internationally (Thaman, 1999), it is worth considering the lay adjudicator in relation to its chief alternative, the professional judge.[1]

I begin with a look at the jury through the eyes of the judge, that daily observer of laypersons in the jury trial. The available evidence indicates that the judicial perspective on the jury is remarkably positive. One potential explanation for this enthusiasm is that judges generally agree with jury verdicts. Next, I compare the verdict preferences of professional judges and lay decision makers, revealing both substantial agreement and some systematic differences. Then, I consider additional ways that judges and legal adjudication benefit from the participation of laypersons in the criminal trial process. I conclude with an assessment of the implications of convergence and complementarity between professional judges and lay adjudicators and its implication for jury reform.

THROUGH THE EYES OF THE JUDGE

Trial court judges who preside over jury trials have a unique opportunity to watch what juries do. Although judges do not sit in the deliberation room and watch the jury deliberate, they have a ringside view of the jury during the trial and are in a position to evaluate the jury's behavior and verdict in light of their own impressions of the same evidence that the jurors have seen and heard. In addition, judges may be asked to answer questions from the jury in the course of the trial and deliberations, they receive the jury's verdict and must deal with post-trial motions in the

---

[1] Some of the benefits of the jury arise from its ability to pool the resources of its various members, raising the question of whether a panel of judges, such as the three-judge panel used in the Netherlands, would offer the same benefits that a 6- or 12-person jury supplies. Although there is no direct empirical evidence on this question, two attributes of the jury would remain: (1) a larger panel of judgments to combine and (2) a more heterogeneous group of perspectives to pool.

wake of that verdict, and they may speak with the jurors before dismissing them at the end of the trial. It is significant, therefore, that judges are among the most enthusiastic supporters of the jury.

The voices of trial court judges are seldom heard when the jury is criticized.[2] In 1987, the National Law Journal surveyed 348 state and federal judges (The View from the Bench, 1987). Asked what they thought was the most frustrating aspect of being a judge, judicial complaints centered on heavy workloads and administrative problems (30%), unprepared and/or unqualified attorneys (16%), and a variety of other non-jury issues (e.g., maintaining neutrality, delays, inadequate pay). Notably absent from the list was frustration with juries. When asked to evaluate jury performance in criminal trials, most of the judges said that they agreed with the jury in the majority of cases. Only 12% of the judges said that juries acquitted when they believed the jury should have convicted more than 10% of the time. In civil cases, 18% of the judges said they disagreed with the jury's verdict more than 10% of the time. Although such aggregate self-reports may be only crude estimates of actual agreement levels, they suggest that judges do not perceive juries as frequently reaching decisions that the judges find unwarranted.

A second survey of 800 state and 200 federal judges who spent at least half their time on civil cases was carried out by Louis Harris and Associates (Harris, 1989). An overwhelming majority of both federal and state judges (99% and 98%) said that jurors usually make a serious effort to apply the law as they are instructed. More than three-quarters of both the federal and state judges viewed the right to trial by jury as an essential safeguard which must be retained in routine civil cases. The judges varied in their interest in considering potential alternatives to the jury in some complex civil cases, but a majority rejected the idea of a limitation on the use of juries for complex civil cases involving highly technical and scientific issues, or for very complicated business cases. Although 66% of federal and 62% of state judges thought juries need more guidance than they usually get, most did not believe that "the feelings of jurors about the parties often cause them to make inappropriate decisions" (80% for federal judges and 69% for state judges).

---

[2] One notable exception to this pattern can be found in the writings of the prominent legal realist, Jerome Frank. Although Frank was critical of judges, he reserved his most aggressive criticism for the jury (see, e.g., Frank, 1950, Chapter VII on juries). Frank was appointed to the Second Circuit from his position as a law professor. He never served as a trial court judge and thus not only lacked the firsthand exposure to trials and juries that trial court judges accumulate, but also saw only the selective sample of jury cases that are appealed.

Similar results were obtained in a 1991 survey of state judges in Georgia (Sentell, 1991).[3] A substantial majority of judges (87%) reported that they agreed with the jury's verdict in negligence cases about 80% of the time. Moreover, they generally did not attribute disagreements to incompetence or bias. Ninety-two percent of the judges rejected the idea that jury miscomprehension was the reason for the disagreement and 79% rejected the notion that bias in favor of a particular party was the explanation for the difference in verdict.

Judges have also expressed their reactions to juries outside of the survey context. One particularly interesting set of judicial reactions to the jury appears in a series of firsthand reports about juries from judges who have served as members of a jury. Although judges were traditionally excluded from jury service in the United States, in recent years most occupational exclusions have been eliminated (see Sarokin & Munsterman, 1993) and judges as well as other attorneys are eligible for jury service. The expectation, however, is that a judge or other attorney is likely to be excused by one side or the other out of concern that the judge or attorney will exert an undue amount of influence on fellow jurors. Nonetheless, judges have served as jurors and a number of them have written about their experiences (see examples collected in Hinchcliff, 1986). It is easy to discount these reports: they may not be representative of the experiences of all juries or even of all judges who have served on juries—these are the judges who have chosen to write publicly about their jury service. Nonetheless, I could find no instance of a judge who expressed disappointment with the jury after serving as a juror. Instead, the common theme in the reports of these professionals was an increased appreciation for the conscientiousness and good sense of their fellow jurors.

The reports from judicial jurors are surprisingly consistent. Judge James Duke Cameron's report is typical, albeit more poetic than most: "One swallow does not a summer make, but I came away with a renewed faith in our jury system .... Many attorneys and judges have become cynical about the jury system. After one chance to participate as a juror, I no longer share any of that cynicism" (Cameron, 1981). Even Justice Shirley Abrahamson, who served as a juror in a trial that ended in a hung jury, reported "The system works. I've seen it" (see also Abrahamson, 1986a, 1986b). The judges were not, however, uncritical of their jury experience and several expressed some frustration, but their frustration was not with their fellow jurors. For example, Judge David Hittner observed: "Many trial judges permit a relatively wide area to be discussed in the redirect examination, resulting in a total rehashing of the witness' direct

---

[3] Sentell (1992) found a similar reaction from federal judges.

testimony. I believe this is a mistake by both a judge and a questioning attorney. I was amazed how attentive the jury was to the evidence. They do not have to hear a witness say the same thing twice" (Hittner, 1984).

Both the judicial surveys and judicial testimonials paint a picture that is inconsistent with the complaints voiced by critics of the jury. A simple explanation for the difference is that the judges are better informed and more objective than are other jury observers, and as a result are better able to appreciate the lay jury. Thus, although the judge may not always agree with the jury's verdict, the process that produces the verdict impresses the judicial observer. Nonetheless, it would be surprising if judges were enthusiastic supporters of the jury merely because they see jurors as conscientious and hard-working decision makers. That is, if juries regularly reached verdicts that judges found unacceptable, we would expect judges to find the jury an unacceptable alternative to the bench trial. A series of studies comparing professional and lay verdict preferences allows us to estimate the frequency of disagreement between judges and juries.

AGREEMENT AND DISAGREEMENT BETWEEN LAYPERSONS AND PROFESSIONAL JUDGES

Studies of judge-jury agreement in both criminal and civil trials reveal substantial, but not uniform agreement levels. In Kalven and Zeisel's classic study of the American jury (Kalven & Zeisel, 1966), judges filled out questionnaires in over 3500 criminal jury trials, indicating how the jury decided the case and how they would have decided it if it had been a bench trial. In 78% of the cases the judge and jury agreed on the verdict. In disagreement cases, the judge would have convicted when the jury acquitted in 19% of the cases and the jury convicted when the judge would have acquitted in 3% of the cases, a net leniency of 16%. These data were collected in the late 1950s, but despite many changes in the make-up of the jury pool and the bench, a very similar pattern was found more recently by Heuer and Penrod (1994). In a sample of 77 criminal trials, they obtained a rate of 74% agreement, with the judge convicting when the jury would have acquitted in 23% of the cases and the jury convicting when the judge would have acquitted in 3%, a net leniency of 20%.

The United States is not alone in this general pattern. Baldwin and McConville (1979) studied reactions to jury verdicts in Birmingham, England and measured the frequency of doubt about the jury's verdict by at least two professionals (judges, attorneys, or police officers). Treating cases in which two professionals had doubts about the verdict as cases of disagreement, the agreement cases constituted 82% of the jury cases, with

12% yielding doubts about an acquittal and 6% yielding doubts about a conviction, producing a net leniency of 6%.

Finally, a study of German lay and professional judges by Casper and Zeisel (1972) produced an initial agreement rate of 90% on the issue of guilt in cases in which there had not been a confession, with professionals favoring conviction and the lay judges favoring acquittal in 7% of the cases and lay judges favoring conviction and the professional acquittal in 3% of the cases, a net leniency of 4%.

What does this pattern indicate? First, it is worth noting that the studies were conducted in very different legal settings. Thus, the highest rate of agreement occurred on the mixed tribunals of Germany where one of the professional judges generally receives the dossier on the case before the trial begins, putting that judge at a distinct advantage in familiarity with the facts and potentially as a source of influence on the other decision makers in the trial. In England, where the agreement rate dropped to 82%, the professional judge has the opportunity to sum up and comment on the evidence, providing clear signals about the judge's impressions of the case to the lay jury. The lowest rate of agreement comes from the studies in the United States, where judges typically do not comment on the evidence and there is significantly less opportunity for the judge to influence the jury's decision, but even here there was agreement in over three-quarters of the cases.

Whether the 74–90% agreement is too high or too low is a judgment call (is the glass half full or half empty?), but two additional pieces of information are relevant. First, Kalven and Zeisel (1966) found that disagreement rates were no higher when the judge characterized the evidence as difficult than when it was characterized as easy, suggesting that the disagreements were not produced by the jury's inability to understand the evidence. Second, they *did* find that disagreement rates rose when the judge characterized the evidence as close rather than clear—suggesting that disagreement cases were, at least in the judge's view, more likely to be those cases that were susceptible to more than one defensible verdict. Finally, the majority of disagreements were characterized by the judge either as one a judge also might come to or as tenable for a jury, though not for a judge. Here again, the evidence suggests that disagreements between the judge and jury do not signal a fundamentally different view—but rather a modest different of opinion that affects a minority of cases.

In all of these studies, we have no measure of the extent to which the independent judgments of multiple professional judges would disagree. We do have evidence from other research that human decision makers, even those drawn from the same population (all judges or all physicians), often differ from one another when they independently make judgments on the same case, whether in judging grant proposals, diagnosing patients, or evaluating job applicants (Diamond, 1983). Some research on the sentencing judgments by federal judges in Chicago and New York reveals an agreement rate of approximately 80% between two judges making independent decisions on whether or not to sentence the defendant to custody (Diamond & Zeisel, 1975). Moreover, the three-judge federal appellate court panels in the United States produce non-unanimous decisions despite the opportunity for the judges to confer and resolve disagreements before the final court decision is issued (George, 1999). Although appealed cases are likely to be more closely contested than the average case decided at trial, and the judges as a result may be less likely to resolve their initial disagreements than they would be in the average case, these non-unanimous verdicts provide additional evidence that judges too show evidence of some inter-judge disparity in their judgments.

Both judges and laypersons are sometimes called upon to make sentencing decisions in criminal cases. The Casper and Zeisel (1972) study of mixed tribunals in Germany reveals a somewhat lower rate of agreement for sentencing than for guilt—80% rather than 90%, preserving a small leniency effect of 3%. Three other sentencing studies used a simulation approach, asking laypersons and criminal court judges to sentence the same defendants. Diamond and Stalans (1989) presented a series of cases that ranged from a drug sale to a burglary to Illinois state court judges and jurors. In each case, the jurors were less likely to favor a prison sentence than were the professional judges. A similar pattern emerged in a study comparing the sentencing preferences of professional and lay magistrates in Great Britain (Diamond, 1990). The average sentence given by the laypersons was consistently lower than that given by the professionals. Moreover, the difference was not attributable to a naive expectation on the part of the laypersons that the offender was unlikely to offend again. Both the lay and the professional magistrates varied their predictions of future offending with the nature of the offense and offender—and the two types of magistrates were nearly identical in their pattern. Finally, Mussweiler and Englich (in press) found that experienced German judges responding to a case of sexual assault gave more severe sentences than did law students presented with the same case.

The pattern across all of these studies is strikingly consistent. In a substantial majority of cases, laypersons and professionals agree in the outcomes they prefer. Where disagreement arises, it generally takes the form of greater leniency on the part of the lay decision makers. When compared to their professional counterparts, laypersons are somewhat more likely both to acquit and to prefer less severe sentences. In retrospect, the high rate of agreement is perhaps not so surprising if we view juries and judges as competent, if imperfect, decision makers. After all, both the judge and the jury or lay tribunal are responding to the same evidence and the same legal structure. Moreover, as human decision makers, both are subject to many of the same weaknesses. The few studies that have examined the impact of extra-legal factors such as inadmissible evidence (Landsman & Rakos, 1994), an irrelevant anchor (Guthrie, Rachlinski, & Wistrich, 2001; Mussweiler & Englich, in press), or the hindsight bias (Anderson, Lowe, & Reckers, 1993; Guthrie, Rachlinski, & Wistrich, 2001) on judges have demonstrated that judges as well as laypersons are influenced by these cognitive biases. Thus, shared reactions to both legal and extra-legal factors may explain high levels of judge-lay agreement. High agreement in turn encourages widespread judicial support, but it is not the only explanation for judicial approval of lay adjudicators. As is suggested below, lay adjudicators provide more than merely an alternative means for resolving disputes.

BEYOND AGREEMENT: OTHER JURY ATTRIBUTES

The jury offers the judge and the legal system a number of potential benefits beyond a high rate of agreement with the judge on the appropriate outcome of the case. The legitimacy of the jury's verdict and its ability to reflect community standards, including its occasional actions as a safety valve that softens the edges of an inflexible legal standard, are attributes that judges may recognize and appreciate. There is, in addition, another value in the jury trial that judges are less likely to recognize. The pretrial activities and rulings that precede a bench trial expose the judge to a range of potentially biasing and legally irrelevant information. Only in a jury trial is the adjudicator protected from exposure to that potentially biasing information.

THE JURY AS A SOURCE OF LEGITIMACY

The jury's role as a safeguard against the tyranny of abusive government and the arbitrary exercise of power is commonly cited as its chief virtue: the jury in a criminal trial can protect the defendant from a corrupt or biased judge or from an overzealous prosecutor. In addition to occupying this role as the "safeguard of liberty" (Hamilton, 1961, p. 499) the jury plays another protective role as well. The jury acts as a lightning rod shielding the judge from responsibility and potential blame.

A lightning rod protects the house that stands beside it by attracting lightning. The jury offers the same support for the judge, absorbing the criticism and the second-guessing that may follow an unpopular verdict. Even or perhaps especially when the judge and jury would agree, the verdict of the jury can carry a legitimacy that the decision of the judge, as an employee of the state may lack. If the jury is viewed as an impartial decision maker representing a fair cross-section of the community, its verdict is likely to be seen as the product of fair consideration. The convictions of popular public officials after a trial by jury have been widely accepted as legitimate and even uncontroversial. Even when the jury is not perceived as a fair cross-section of the community or as an impartial decision maker, it is the jury that will receive the blame for an unpopular verdict rather than the judge. Thus, even if preferences of the judge and jury were identical in all cases, a legal system employing a lay jury of decision makers drawn from the community would offer the benefit of insulating the judge and the state legal system from charges that it unfairly convicted a popular defendant or unfairly acquitted an unpopular defendant charged with a brutal crime. Judges do not write about the jury's ability to protect the judge from scrutiny and potential criticism, but they sometimes express their appreciation for this distinctive role of the jury privately.

The Jury as a Conduit for Community Standards

Although the American jury is charged with merely applying the law as the judge presents it to the facts as the jury determines them, the division between law and facts is not clear-cut. In evaluating a claim of self-defense, for example, the jury must determine what a reasonable person would believe. Unlike a single trial court judge, the jury can pool the experiences of a group of citizens with diverse backgrounds to arrive at its assessment of what this hypothetical reasonable person would believe under the circumstances of the case, infusing the decision making with an estimate of community standards in judging such behavior. The difference in perspective can be a source of disagreement between the judge and jury that reflects an advantage for decision making by a group of laypersons.

In some cases, the verdict that a judge feels compelled to give may not be the verdict that the judge would prefer. Thus, even when the judge would decide a case differently than a jury does, the jury's verdict may satisfy the judge. The first time offender whose trial has been "punishment enough" and the technically guilty defendant whose trial was the result of an overzealous prosecutor may get the judge's sympathy, but an acquittal is likely to result only from a jury that concludes that a conviction is not warranted (for descriptions of some situations in which juries have that exercised their power to acquit, to the satisfaction of a trial court judge who would have convicted, see Diamond & Schklar, 1998). The potential for such jury nullification has been a symbol of the power and virtues of the jury as well as a source of jury criticism (see, e.g., Scheflin & Van Dyke, 1980). Because an acquittal by the jury in a criminal case gives the jury the last word in the United States, some judges and legal scholars have identified jury nullification with lawlessness (the seminal case setting out the opposing views in this controversy is *United States v. Dougherty*, 1972). Yet, although the legal system depends on the high level of consistency between judge and jury decision-making, it also profits from the flexibility of the jury to offer, without setting any precedent, a relief from strict application of the law in a limited number of cases. One poignant example of this behavior occurred in the filming of an actual deliberating jury in the case of *Wisconsin v. Leroy Reed* (Herzberg, 1986). The jurors acquitted the defendant on a weapons charge after a long and difficult deliberation. The jury approved of the gun law, but did not believe it was appropriate to apply the law to a mentally deficient defendant who purchased the gun so he could comply with what a magazine described as what was required for training to be a detective. The jury's ability to acquit in this case left the law intact, but prevented its application the facts of this particular case. To the extent that such a tempering of the law is desirable, the jury is in a far better position than the judge to exercise such discretionary mercy.[4] The judge may sit at the sidelines and privately applaud the jury's actions, but in the role of decision maker would be constrained from adopting the jury's resolution (see cases discussed in Diamond & Schklar, 1998).

The Jury as an Insulated Decision Maker

A third attribute of the jury emphasizes the complementarity of the relationship between the jury and the judge in a jury trial. The jury trial has an important structural feature that may actually decrease the effect of extra-legal influences in the verdict. In an effort to control and channel

---

[4] Peter van Koppen makes the interesting point that it is possible to have a legal system in which judges can "soften the application of general legal rules in a specific case or, if necessary, ignore the rule, without setting a precedent that defeats the general nice rule." His point is more than hypothetical because he provides examples from the Dutch criminal justice system. The American judge is more constrained, however (unlike the American prosecutor or the Dutch judge). The jury provides a safety valve that has the additional virtue of reflecting community values and legitimacy in deviating from the letter of the formal law.

jury decision-making, elaborate rules of evidence blindfold the jury to information that is deemed irrelevant or prejudicial (for a discussion of blindfolding, see Diamond, Casper, and Ostergren, 1989). Although there is evidence that juries can be told much more than they generally are without impairing their performance and in some cases improving it (Diamond & Casper, 1992; Diamond & Vidmar, in press; see also Schwarzer, 1991), insulating the jury from potentially prejudicial information is made possible by the division of responsibility between the judge and the jury in a jury trial. When the trier of fact is the jury, the judge must deal with pretrial motions and rule on the admissibility of evidence, excluding it from the view of the jury. In contrast, the judge in a bench trial is exposed to pretrial as well as trial evidence. The legal system depends on the fiction that the judge (but not the jury) can set such information aside and be uninfluenced by irrelevant or prejudicial knowledge. Yet because judges as well as jurors can be affected by extra-legal factors that are excluded from the jury trial (Landsman & Rakos, 1994), a bench trial may increase the likelihood that legally irrelevant information will influence the decision maker.

CONCLUSION

The benefits of accepting laypersons as adjudicators in criminal trials are not self-evident and it is possible to imagine a competent legal system that excludes ordinary citizens from playing this role. Moreover, there are clearly some costs associated with the jury system, at least as it operates in the United States: an inability to "correct" an unjustifiable acquittal, a potentially greater opportunity for an appellate court to detect and correct an unjustified conviction by a judge who must write an opinion that justifies the verdict,[5] somewhat greater trial costs.[6] Nonetheless, it is striking

[5] It is unclear how often a conviction by a judge would actually be more likely to lead an appellate court to respond than it would if the conviction resulted from a jury verdict. The question is how often the trial court's opinion in such a case would reveal grounds on which the appellate court would reverse or remand for a new trial. Note that the pattern of greater leniency by the jury may offer at least as much protection to the innocent defendant.

[6] It is possible to argue in favor of the efficient continental trial that proceeds swiftly because the judges have read the file before the trial session. The American response is that such apparent efficiency may have non-financial costs that should not be ignored: the loss of procedural justice associated with the opportunity for a full-scale trial in which witnesses must provide the evidence and attorneys must present their arguments, whether to a judge or to a jury. and thus not only lacked the firsthand exposure to trials and juries that trial court judges accumulate, but also saw only the selective sample of jury cases that are appealed.

that professional judges in the United States generally applaud sharing their power and responsibilities with lay jurors in both criminal and civil cases. Adopting the vantage point of the judge reveals a number of explanations for this judicial enthusiasm: a high rate of agreement with jury verdicts, the role that the jury can play in legitimizing decisions and in deflecting potential criticism from the judiciary, and the jury's ability to temper the harshness of the law without introducing a change in precedent. Moreover, the structure of the jury trial introduces an additional rarely acknowledged benefit by insulating the adjudicator from exposure to potentially biasing information.

The recent resurgence of the jury and other forms of lay participation in criminal adjudication around the globe (e.g., Thaman, 1999) reflects a recognition of some of these benefits, accompanied by an appreciation of the traditional merits of the educative value of the jury (De Tocqueville, 1948, 1969) and its political role as an indicator of democratic values (*Id.* at p. 272). Amid the contemporary calls for reform of the American jury, all of these benefits and values are worth acknowledging.

19

The Principle of Open Justice in the Netherlands

RUTH HOEKSTRA AND MARIJKE MALSCH

The principle of open justice (in Dutch *Openbaarheidsbeginsel*) is one of the fundamental pillars on which the Dutch criminal justice system rests. In all democratic Western countries, it is a well-established principle that courts should generally be open to anyone who wishes to attend. This is extremely important in the Dutch inquisitorial system, in which the lay-element has almost totally disappeared. The Netherlands system does not make use of juries, and lay judges are, with a few exceptions, not sitting in criminal cases. Judges are not elected, as is the case in some adversarial systems, but they are appointed by the government. Dutch judges are independent and cannot be discharged because of the sentences they impose. Direct public influence on the appointment of the members of the judiciary is absent. This lack of direct democratic accountability has been complemented by providing the opportunity to the public to be able to review the adjudication of cases by the judiciary, at trial or through the news-media. In order to bridge the gap between the adjudicators and the general public, courts should be open to anyone who wishes to attend.

In contrast to the Netherlands, most adversarial systems, as well as some inquisitorial, provide a direct public influence on the adjudication of cases in the form of lay juries. Moreover, media coverage of trials is in many countries much more extensive than it is in the Netherlands, providing more insight to the general public of what is going on in the courts. The Netherlands system has to do without such opportunities for public control and, therefore, the principle of open justice has to be served in other ways. This chapter examines the scope of the principle of open justice, both in theory and in practice.

The principle of open justice, as it is shaped in Dutch law, refers to the accessibility of the criminal process to both the process participants and the general public (Van de Pol, 1986; Corstens, 1995). Process participants need access to all documents and reports produced in a case to enable a check on the propriety and legal correctness of all actions performed by the police and other investigative officers. This aspect of the principle is generally referred to as the "internal openness" of the trial, or the right of access to the documents. Apart from that, the general public needs access to the public hearing of cases in order to exert democratic control on the adjudication of cases. Criminal processes are not held in secret, as was the case during the Inquisition, but are held in open court. This latter aspect of the principle of open justice is generally referred to as the "external openness" of the trial, or the right to attend court sessions.

This chapter explores the relevance of the principle of open justice for both an inquisitorial and an adversarial system. Attention is paid to the two aspects of the principle: the transparency of cases and the accessibility of public hearings. The role of the public gallery[1] and the news-media in the realization of the latter aspect of the open-justice principle is explored. A side-step is taken into particular characteristics of the Dutch criminal procedure, such as the relatively strong emphasis on the pre-trial investigation, as well as the lack of a thorough judicial examination of all evidence in court. The results of a study on the actual use of the public galleries in Dutch courts are briefly outlined. Where feasible, the influence of the case law of the European Court of Human Rights is discussed. The chapter ends with a number of conclusions that are relevant for both the Dutch criminal justice system and the legal systems of other countries.

SIDE-EFFECTS OF OPEN JUSTICE

The principle of open justice, when realized in legal practice, has a number of side-effects that may enhance the realization of particular goals of punishment. Knowledge of what punishments are imposed for which crimes may have a preventive effect on potential perpetrators. This is known in the Netherlands as the *general preventive effect* of punishment. The prospect of public identification and the chance of being convicted and sent to prison may act as a disincentive to commit crimes, at least that

---

[1] The name of the location where the general public is seated for observation of the trial of cases.

is what utilitarian penologists claim (Walker, 1991). Openness of the courts might enhance this preventive effect of punishment by providing the news media and the public with the opportunity to become acquainted with the adjudication of cases.

A similar effect, but limited to the offender him- or herself, may be exerted by standing trial and being convicted in open court. This is also a proclaimed effect of punishment, in the Netherlands generally known as the *special preventive effect* of punishment. Although this effect is largely attributed to the serving of a prison term, it may also be reinforced by the shaming effects of standing trial and being convicted in front of the "public" and the news media; this may prevent an individual offender from recidivism (Braithwaite, 1989). The principle of open justice might also be expected to have an amplifying role in the operation of this effect.

Other side-effects of the principle of open justice are: public denunciation of criminal conduct and, of course, informing the public about what crimes are committed and how they are punished (Roche, 1999). The whole of all these effects and functions, in combination with the primary aim of democratic accountability of the judiciary, renders the principle of open justice a highly important one.

The principle of open justice is laid down in Article 121 of the Dutch Constitution as well as in international treaties such as the European Convention on the Protection of Human Rights (ECHR, Article 6) and the U.N. Covenant on Civil and Political Rights (Article 14). The Netherlands is a member to both conventions, and the provisions contained in these conventions are binding law in the Netherlands. While Dutch law comprises both the internal and the external effect into one principle, we will make a distinction in this chapter between the aspects of transparency and access to the public hearing of cases.

TRANSPARENCY OF CRIMINAL PROCESS: THE RIGHT OF ACCESS TO THE DOCUMENTS IN A CASE

The first aspect of the open-justice principle discussed here refers to the transparency of the criminal process. It has an internal scope and focuses on the access to the dossier for the process participants in a case. Article 30 of the Dutch Code of Criminal Procedure (*Wetboek van Strafvordering*) states that, during the pre-trial investigation stage, the defendant has the right of access to all documents in the case. There are exceptions to this general rule, however, which refer to situations in which the interests of the investigation require that some documents are kept secret. All restrictions must be lifted, however, as soon as the defendant is summoned to appear at trial.

The question of which documents actually do belong to the "official" case-file, as well as the opportunity to withhold certain pieces from the defense, have been subject to substantial debate in the Netherlands (Myjer, 1997; Peters, 1987; Prakken, 1995). This debate is typical of the Dutch type of criminal process, in which the investigation that takes place in the pre-trial phases of a process is the most important for fact-finding. Investigative acts, performed by the police, the prosecution, and the investigating judge are reported in the case-file, which in turn is the basis for decision-making by the court. Courts, in many cases, confine themselves to using police reports of interrogations of witnesses and experts without interviewing the original declarants at trial (Nijboer, 2000a). Decisions about which evidence is to be presented to the trier of fact do not take place on grounds of admissibility, like in systems where juries operate. In the Netherlands, it is the court that decides which evidence will be used for its decisions. For being able to make such decisions, however, courts are dependent on the materials collected and made available by the police and the prosecution (Nijboer, 2000a).

Over the years, some changes have taken place as a result of the influence of the decisions by the European Court of Human Rights (Swart, 1999), but most investigation of a case is still done prior to trial. Obviously, this type of legal practice renders the aspect of access to case-files for all process participants far more relevant than in a situation where all witnesses and experts appear at trial, since the case-file is the backbone of each case (Nijboer & Sennef, 1999).

The actual legal practice in Dutch criminal cases is strongly related to the origins of the system. Many procedures in Dutch law stem from the Inquisition of the 16th century as well as the French legal influences exerted in the first decades of the 19th century. At the time of the Inquisition, the accused was treated literally as an "object of investigation." There was secrecy in the pre-trial proceedings and a total lack of information for the defendant. The emphasis on the pre-trial stage as the dominant or even decisive stage of the process still remains in today's proceedings, but the lack of information has been replaced by a right to information for both parties, which has to be effectuated before the trial starts. The French occupation brought a trial that largely concentrated on the case-files. The dossier became the central element to which the "internal control" by higher authorities was applied; for the law enforcement officials it was the exclusive source of information about what had happened in a case (Anderson, 1999; Nijboer & Sennef, 1999). This exclusiveness also stresses the importance of the internal aspect of the principle of open justice in the Netherlands system. This right is differently framed in, for example, the US system. There, the defendant's constitutional right to discover evidence is limited to "favorable and material evidence" (Van Kampen, 1999). Under Federal Rule of Criminal Procedure 16, defendants in federal cases have the right to discover both incriminating and exculpatory evidence, as long as the government intends to use such evidence or if such evidence is material to the defense. These two standards may seriously hamper American defendants in becoming knowledgeable of evidence to be introduced against them. In the United Kingdom, the internal openness of cases has recently been substantially reduced by new legislation. According to this act, the Crown Prosecutions Service can decide which documents are relevant for the defense and which are not. The defense's right to inspect documents does not extend to the latter type, thereby substantially reducing the right to transparency of the trial (Swier, 1999).

The debate about the transparency of cases conducted in the Netherlands is concentrated on the question of which documents actually belong to the official dossier and, hence, are covered by the principle of "internal openness." Dutch law provides little guidance on this point and, as a consequence, the contents of the case-files are at the discretion of the police and the prosecution. Unfortunately, these law enforcement professionals do not always include all evidentiary materials (both incriminating *and* exculpatory) in the case-file. Since courts are to a large extent dependent on the police and the prosecution to provide them with the evidence of the alleged crimes, this may obstruct objective judicial weighing of all arguments in favor of *and* against a defendant. A number of decisions, both by Dutch courts and the European Court of Human Rights, have elaborated on the point of the right to inspect case-files (for overviews, see Myjer, 1997; Peters, 1987; Prakken, 1995). Article 6 ECHR does not explicitly mention the defendant's right to access to the documents in the case-file. The decisions by both the European Commission and the European Court of Human Rights, however, have ruled that the requirements of a fair trial demand that the defendant has a right to inspect the case-file, because adequate preparation of the defense of a case would not be possible without such a right. Prosecution authorities must, therefore, disclose to the defense all material evidence for and against the accused.[2]

---

[2] See Edwards v. UK, ECHR 16 december 1992, A 247-B, NJCM (1993) 18-3. The Dutch Court of Cassation has ruled that particular evidentiary material—a book with pictures of persons among whom the defendant might be present—could legally be excluded from inspection by the defendant on grounds that it is not legally part of the official documents of the case-file. Police reports in which this particular piece of evidence was discussed, however, were ruled to belong to the "official" case-file and were, therefore, to be made available to the defendant: HR, 7 mei 1996, *NJ* 1996, 687 (Dev Sol).

A generally accepted and established right to inspect the case-file is one thing. Actually getting hold of the case-file in time to read it before the court session is another. All process participants in the Netherlands are from time to time confronted with the situation of dossiers not being in the right place at the right time, or dossiers that are incomplete or contain documents that greatly overlap. The ongoing process of introducing computer systems into the criminal law system has not yet removed these problems. On the contrary, since a wide variety of computer systems are in use at Dutch police and courts and in many cases are incompatible, communication between law enforcement authorities is still lacking, and the files do not adequately reflect all aspects of the case (Malsch & Jansen, 1998). Because these computer systems will be made compatible in the long run, problems mentioned here will, in all likelihood, largely disappear in the future. At present, however, the incompatibility of systems sometimes hinders the timely availability of complete case-files.

All of these factors contribute to the degree of transparency of the case-files. Ergonomic factors, such as degree of computerization of the file and the points in time in which the documents are available to the process participants, are as important for the realization of this transparency as the official right to inspection of the dossier is.

Transparency also implies that those involved in a case have the right to be present at the investigation of the case at trial. On this point too a number of exceptions applies. We will not discuss these exceptions here (Corstens, 1995). The remainder of this chapter will focus on the external aspect of the principle of open justice.

PUBLIC HEARING

The second aspect of the open-justice principle discussed here is the aspect of opening courts to the general public. This aspect has an external scope. Article 121 of the Dutch Constitution states that, with a few exceptions, trials must take place in open court. Exceptions to this general rule are admitted in view of common decency, public order, the safety of the state, the interests of minors, and the privacy of the defendant, of other process participants, or of persons involved in the case. Court decisions are always pronounced in open court; no exceptions are possible.

Both the public at large and the news-media are given the opportunity to attend court sessions. They may be seated in public galleries or in the courtroom to observe the trial of cases. Public galleries and courtrooms have tables for those members of the press who might wish to write down their observations. The admission of television cameras is dependent on the consent of the president of the panel that is sitting that day. In the Netherlands, it is not a general custom to have television cameras in the courtroom. Although a growing number of cases have been recorded for television, the Dutch judiciary is still hesitant to admit television cameras on a large scale. This reluctance has to do with the presumption of innocence and the privacy of both the defendant and the other trial participants. A defendant must be considered innocent as long as a judge has not yet established his or her guilt. Careless reporting of the case by the news media might invade this right.

During the public hearing of a case, some elements of procedure promote accessibility and comprehensibility of the process for those who attend it. For example, the identity of the defendant is established by the presiding judge, the documents of the case-file are read aloud or summarized, and the prosecutor and the defense counsel express their views orally on the case. All these aspects are designed to provide an opportunity to the general public, as well as the press, to attend court sessions and become acquainted with the adjudication of cases in the Netherlands.

THE PRINCIPLE OF IMMEDIACY

Immediacy refers to the situation where fact-finders have all evidence in its original form before them, such as witnesses, defendants, physical evidence, and experts. The general aim of "immediacy" is to make direct observation and review of evidence possible for both the judge and the other trial participants. This is considered the best method of guaranteeing the correctness of judicial decisions. A side-effect of immediacy is that the public can also make complete and adequate observations of the evaluation of evidence in court. As a consequence, the principle of open justice is served by immediacy.

In the present Code of Criminal Procedure, drafted in 1926, the Dutch criminal trial was originally designed as an "oral" process: all evidence should, in principle, be presented and evaluated at trial. In the same year that this new code came into force, the Dutch Supreme Court (*Hoge Raad der Nederlanden; HR*) ruled that lower courts are, nevertheless, allowed to use reports which describe statements of witnesses (or experts) that were made out of court (HR, 20 December 1926, *NJ* 1927, 85). Moreover, statements in which a person (either witness, expert, or police officer) relates what he or she heard someone else say, were considered acceptable evidence. Both types of statements are known as *de auditu* (hearsay) statements. As a consequence of this decision by the Supreme Court, the Dutch criminal trial became substantially less oral and relied more and more on the written reports of interrogations of witnesses, defendants, and experts made up by the police and by other investigating authorities. It even became custom for courts to almost exclusively use written reports by expert witnesses, and only seldom to summon experts to trial. The dossier became the backbone of each case. It was moved from the police to the prosecution, and from the prosecution to the investigating judge, and then to the trial judges, the clerks and the defense counsel. Each official added reports and other documents to the case-file. All these reports were considered to adequately reflect all investigative actions that had been performed in the case (Nijboer & Sennef, 1999). Since they are the last professionals to be confronted with the extensive case-files, trial judges have the task of forming an opinion about the case after an audit of all these documents at trial.

The somewhat aloof evaluation of evidence at trial, caused by the diminished immediacy, must also have an influence on comprehensiveness for the news-media and the public at large. At trials in the Netherlands, very serious cases are often tried in very little time. The presiding judge summarizes the reports of interrogations of witnesses, defendants, and experts in a few lines and reads aloud only a summary of the extensive reports on the defendant's personality that have been drawn up by various mental health experts. It is highly questionable whether the general public can fully comprehend cases that are compressed to such a minimum. On top of that, the language that is employed by Dutch legal professionals may very well not be understandable for lay people. Legal terms are not always explained in court, and the legal professionals often do not even seem to be aware that their language differs substantially from that of ordinary people.[3] This may undermine the working of the principle of open justice to a great extent.

In the legal systems of most other countries, both of an adversarial and an inquisitorial nature, the presentation and examination of evidence at the actual trial is far more important than it is in the Netherlands, and the trying of each case takes more time. Dutch cases, on the other hand, reach an actual trial more often than criminal cases in other countries do. Cases in the American system are plea-bargained more often; such a common practice does not exist to an equal extent in the Netherlands.[4] This

---

[3] In a number of cases, the District Court of Amsterdam has drafted the allegations in colloquial language, but this was not accepted by the Supreme Court. See HR, 22 juni 1995, *NJ* 1996, 126 and 127.

[4] No exact figures of numbers of cases tried in open court as compared to cases not reaching a trial can be found. The annual report of the Dutch Prosecutions Service suggests that over half of criminal cases do not reach a trial in open court.

also has its ramifications for openness of the legal system, since plea-bargained cases are not open to the public.

THE NEWS MEDIA VERSUS THE PUBLIC GALLERY

The audiovisual press is more often present at Dutch trials now than it was ten years ago. Still, media-coverage is much lower in the Netherlands than in other countries. It is not clear whether increased coverage has influenced individual attendance to the public gallery. Both advantages and disadvantages of trial reporting by the news media and the attendance of the public gallery can be discerned. Both provide an opportunity to inspect and check the legal correctness of criminal processes as well as the fairness of procedures. Television and people's physical presence in court both have the advantage of direct perception of what is going on; newspaper reporting lacks this aspect. There is, however, an old "gentlemen's agreement" in the Netherlands that defendants are not clearly shown on television: they are only presented from the back, or only part of their body is shown. From the public gallery, in contrast, they can be perceived from head to toe.

The press (television, radio, and newspapers) reports only a selection from all materials that are collected during a trial. In doing so they may bias their presentations and give an unbalanced overview of a case. Journalists decide what is important and which cases are interesting enough to report. Attendance at court sessions, on the contrary, provides an opportunity to take in the whole trial from the beginning to the end, which makes more objective evaluation possible.

Television journalists often ask process participants for an explanation of what is going on in the case. Such an explanation may be extremely helpful to the general public in understanding the case, but might also be biased in favor of the party who gives the comment. Visitors to the public gallery generally lack such an explanation and have to understand a case under their own power. This might be too difficult for them, because of the professional language that is employed and the cursory treatment of all documents at the session.

The defendant's privacy may be invaded by both the news media and the attendance of court sessions by the public. News media reach a much wider audience than the public gallery, but those making use of the latter learn a lot more about the defendant because they hear all evidence that is presented, including mental health and probation reports. Moreover, they become acquainted with the names of the defendant, witnesses, and experts (if present). In conformity with the old "gentlemen's agreement" mentioned above, this information is generally not reported by the Dutch news media.

Finally, there is a substantial advantage to television programs: you can sit at home and watch them without having to go out. That may be the reason why many people prefer to stay home and watch television instead of phoning to ask when there is a trial and go to court to attend. The United States has a cable channel entirely devoted to trial reporting. The Netherlands lack such a facility, and it can be doubted whether it will exist in the near future. The reason for this doubt is that Dutch trials are rather boring as compared to trials in some other countries: participants in Dutch cases are often focused on reaching compromises instead of fighting for their standpoints. And, as has been explained above, most investigation in a case has been done before the trial, which gives the session the appearance of an exclusively "formal" check of the dossier. Usually little drama is involved.

As of yet, little is known about who attends criminal trials at the public gallery or how accurate the perceptions from the public gallery actually are. The answer to these questions is required to establish whether the principle of open justice has any relevancy for a democratic check of the adjudication of criminal cases in the Netherlands. Against this background, the authors conducted a study of the operation of the public gallery (Malsch & Hoekstra, 1999).

STUDY ON THE PUBLIC GALLERY

A small-scale observation study was conducted on the role of the public gallery in securing the principle of open justice in the Netherlands. All 19 of the country's district courts were visited twice for the study. The administrators of the courts were contacted by telephone prior to a court session and asked questions about when and which type of criminal cases were to be tried by a three-judge panel. During the court sessions, a checklist was used for scoring those aspects that were related to the openness of justice. In all stages of the study, the investigator presented herself as a person who was interested in visiting a criminal trial. Attention was also paid to the sessions where court decisions were pronounced.[5] In all sessions that were attended, serious criminal cases were tried by a three-judge panel.

---

[5] In the Netherlands, the pronouncing of verdicts and sentences in serious criminal cases is done at a separate court session, which is, in most cases, held 14 days after the case has been tried.

Before the Trial

In the majority of cases, obtaining information by telephone about what type of cases were to be tried within the next week did not appear to cause substantial problems. In general, the court personnel were friendly and helpful. However, on about one third of the occasions in which information was requested, the personnel were less than friendly or even off-hand. In some court districts, the researcher had to wait a long time on the telephone and was switched several times before someone could give her the relevant information. In about half of the cases, the courts could not give exact information about the type of cases that would be tried and the scheduled starting time of each case.

There were substantial differences among the courts in friendliness and helpfulness of the people who gave directions to the researcher. These differences were dependent on which employee was in charge that day. On one occasion, the employee even asserted that trials were not open to the public and, hence, could not be visited.

At the Public Gallery

Three types of public gallery can be found in the Netherlands: the gallery which is located within the courtroom and which shares its entrance with the courtroom; the gallery which is separated from the courtroom and which is accessible through the court-building; and the separate gallery that is located on a sort of balcony, and has its entrance outside the court building. The two types of gallery last-mentioned are separated from the courtroom by glass, and were equipped with microphones for amplifying the spoken language on the other side of the glass. Tidiness of the public gallery was narrowly related to which type of gallery it was. All galleries that had a separate entrance were dirty: there was graffiti on the walls and coffee stains on the chairs. Many of them were regularly populated by vagrants. At one gallery, there were even holes in the glass that strongly resembled bullet-holes. The galleries located in the courtroom were substantially tidier.

There were sufficient seats in all public galleries. Their number varied between 20 and 100, with a mean of 48 seats. The galleries that were located within the courtroom generally had more seats than those with a separate entrance. The mean number of visitors at the gallery was seven. From these seven, one was a reporter for a newspaper and two were friends or family of the defendant. The remaining visitors either were part of a school-class or of a group of law students who visited a trial for educational reasons. A mean of four people per case attended out of general interest in the adjudication of criminal cases (see Roche, 1999, for similar results found in Canberra, Australia, where also few people attend court sessions).

The researcher spent substantial time waiting at each visit to the court: the mean waiting time consisted of about a quarter of all the time spent in court. The reason for this considerable waiting-time was that some cases were cancelled at such a late point in time that the schedule of the trial could not be readjusted anymore. The mean number of cases tried in one day in court by three-judge panels in Dutch District Courts lies somewhere between six and nine. There is a substantial probability that one or more of the cases will fall out, causing a gap in the schedule. For most public galleries that have an entrance outside the court-building, this meant that visitors had to wait outside; it was not always made possible for them to wait inside the court building. Nor were they always warned when the hearing was re-opened.

Visibility and audibility of the process from the public gallery was far from perfect. In two courts that had separate public galleries, the visibility of process participants was very poor: from the back seats, none of the participants could be seen, whereas from seats more in the front, the visitors had to bend over to see all participants. At three other courts, visibility was poor from the seats at the back, and adequate from the front seats. The remaining courts, including those that had a public gallery within the courtroom, provided good visual perspective on the process.

Because of poorly working microphones, the audibility of the process was insufficient in most courts. The clarity of the spoken language differed substantially among the various process participants. Judges, for example, were clearly audible because they faced the gallery and spoke into the microphones. The prosecutor and the defense lawyer were less audible because they did not speak directly into the microphones; both have to stand while talking and the defense lawyer generally stands with his or her back to the audience. Least audible was the defendant, who often did not speak directly into the microphone, or spoke very inarticulately. The microphone of the defendant, moreover, was often not well-adjusted, nor were the microphones of witnesses.

Experts often remain seated in the courtroom and are not asked to come forward while being interrogated. Their voices were, as a consequence, not amplified and not audible at all in the gallery. Interpreters were very audible; to such an extent that they even complicated following the trial. They had to continue talking while other participants spoke because they had to translate what was said to the defendant and vice versa: this reduced audibility of all voices for the visitors in the public gallery.

Some courts and panels did their best to make the trial comprehensible for the audience. They put, for example, signs in front of all participants which indicated their function in the trial. When school classes or groups of students were present at a trial, some judges gave a short explanation of the course of events or told the reasons why a particular case was cancelled. This may substantially enhance the public's insight into what is going on.

THE VERDICT

As has been stated above, sentences are always pronounced in open court. The mean number of visitors attending sessions where sentences are pronounced was five: one reporter, two members of the defendant's family or friends, and two other people. No school classes or groups of students were present at these sessions. These figures are a bit lower than those for the trial. The audibility of the judges who actually pronounced the sentences was adequate, and the waiting-time was acceptable.

CONCLUSIONS

The findings of this study show that the operation of the principle of open justice in public galleries is poor as a result of a number of factors. One issue that has not been investigated within this study is the question whether the visitors who do not possess any legal training actually understand what is said in court. Process participants in Dutch cases often employ language that is to a large extent juridical. In Common Law systems, the necessity to make the process comprehensible for the (lay) members of a jury puts a restraint on the use of too much legal language. In the Dutch system, in which only professional judges act as fact-finders, such an incentive to use simple language is largely absent. The fact that Dutch trials are attended by a rather small number of visitors may partly be caused by the fact that the language that is employed is not comprehensible for them. The issue of comprehensibility as compared to the language used in other legal systems is the subject of current research.[6]

One more reason for the small number of visitors may be that many lay people do not know that trials are open to the public. The authors have met a number of striking examples of lack of such knowledge when

---

[6] In countries that make use of juries, the issue of comprehensibility of jury instructions plays a comparable role. It appears that a substantial proportion of jurors do not understand the judge's instructions (Lieberman & Sales, 1997).

conducting their research, but this has also been reported by researchers from other legal systems (Roche, 1999).

There are some other aspects that are relevant for the realization of the principle of open justice that have not been discussed in this chapter either. Among them are the giving of reasons in the written verdicts and the availability of copies of written verdicts to the public (Crombag, Van Koppen, & Wagenaar, 1994; Wagenaar, Van Koppen, & Crombag, 1993). On both topics, there is a debate taking place in the Netherlands, and new developments occur. They deserve separate attention; however, discussing them here would go beyond the scope of this chapter.[7]

Above, a comparison has been made between the news media and the public gallery with respect to securing the principle of open justice. As explained in the introduction, the Dutch courts admit television cameras during trial substantially less often than many Common Law legal systems do. In the United States, the news media have greater access to cases and there is pretrial publicity on a wider scale, with all the possible negative consequences. Research has demonstrated that this type of publicity may influence the attitude of the fact-finders (Studebaker & Penrod, 1997). Publicity before the court has passed sentence may exert an undesirable influence on the judge.

The dangers of news media bias may be combated by a more systematic and adequate use of the public gallery, both in the Netherlands and in countries where these media play a more radical role. As far as the Dutch criminal justice system is concerned, accessibility of criminal trials can and should be increased. This would render the principle of open justice more effective and make the realization of a democratic check on the adjudication of cases possible.

---

[7] On the Dutch way of justifying court decisions, see Malsch and Nijboer (1999).

20

The John Wayne and Judge Dee Versions of Justice

PETER J. VAN KOPPEN AND
STEVEN D. PENROD

In the previous chapters it has been demonstrated that quite a few differences exist between the adversarial criminal justice system as it is commonly practiced in the United States and the form of inquisitorial system as it is practiced in the Netherlands.[1] It has been argued that these systems are somewhere at opposite extremes of the adversarial–inquisitorial continuum (Nijboer, 2000b; Toornvliet, 2000). In his chapter in the present volume Hans Crombag noted "that the question which of the two models is the better one, is unanswerable, because they do not serve the same (proximate) goals." Although "the ultimate goal of both systems is ... to serve justice," Crombag argued that "in the inquisitorial model truth itself is the proximate goal of the system," while "fair play is the proximate goal of the adversarial model."

Of course, Crombag is right, but in this chapter we attempt to sharpen the contrasts by taking the comparisons a bit further. This chapter is an extension of a series of arguments about the nature and merits of the two systems that the authors have sustained for more than a decade. In preparing this chapter Van Koppen has taken the lead in formulating a series of propositions about the contrasting nature and merits of the two systems and Penrod has responded and offered alternative interpretations and perspectives.

---

[1] Of course, there are other countries with inquisitorial systems that come close to that of the Netherlands, notably France and Belgium. For brevity, we will refrain from discussing these countries. It should be noted that especially the Belgian criminal justice system resembles the Dutch in many ways. It is not clear, however, that all of the other elements of Dutch society hold as strong for Belgium.

DIFFERENT FORMS OF JUSTICE?

In the next several pages we sketch out two contrasting and somewhat idealized visions of Dutch and American legal cultures. These visions underscore the proposition that the two systems have different proximate goals and they do so *because* they serve different forms or ideals of justice. Because the forms of justice served by both systems differ the characteristics of the systems are consequently different in many important aspects. Furthermore, the different forms of justice served by the American and Dutch criminal justice systems are, arguably, deeply rooted in both societies. The form of justice preferred by the Dutch is based on a preference in Dutch society to reach compromises as much as possible. End results of decisions, then, are evaluated by the extent to which they serve justice in a form that conforms as much as possible to this compromising nature of Dutch social relations. The form of justice preferred by Americans in this idealized vision is based on the assertion and vindication of individual rights.

Among the three principles of justice—need, equality, and equity (for a more refined discussion of these concepts, see Berkowitz & Walster, 1976; Cohen, 1987; Walster, Walster, & Berscheid, 1978)—the two former better fit into a compromising point of view than the latter. In the principle of need, decisions are evaluated according to the extent that they serve the needs of the relevant recipients as much as possible. According to the principle of equality, decisions are more just if they reach a division as equal as possible between the recipients. An equitable decision is one in which the "input" of the recipients—often framed in terms of better arguments or stronger positions on some dimension—is reflected best. In short, the Dutch consider an end result right and just if it serves the needs of all people involved as much as possible and at the same time does not diverge too much from an egalitarian division. Thus, the Dutch focus more on principles of justice, need and equality, than on equity. Weighing and balancing of interests and opinions are often much more important than taking firm decisions. This manner of serving justice reflects the compromising nature of Dutch society.[2]

---

[2] It should be noted, however, that especially in Europe today a certain level of osmosis is taking place between the systems (Gutwirth & de Hert, 2001, p. 1051). The European Court of Human Rights in its *Kruslin* decision (ECHR 24 April 1990, Series A, vol. 176-A, par. 29) noted: "but it would be wrong to exaggerate the distinction between common law countries and Continental countries. [...] Statute law is, of course, also of importance in common law countries. Conversely, case law has tradiotionally played a major role in Continental countries, to such an extentthat whole branches of positive law are largely the outcome of decisions by courts." See on this subject also below.

In the idealized vision of American justice the principle of equity seems to be most preferred principle of justice. Decisions often appear to be made in a manner such that one of the recipients prevails rather than arriving at a compromise in which all recipients receive a share. This preference for equity would seem to be rooted in American society in the same manner in which a preference for need and equality is rooted in the Dutch. These differences, to be discussed below, have led to two different types of proceedings. In short, American law is based on an individual conflict type of proceedings, while European continental law is much more based on a policy implementing type of proceedings (Damaška, 1986, pp. 25–27).

The next section focuses on the roots of these differences, and then the discussion turns the consequences of these preferences for the daily practice of the respective criminal justice systems. We start with the Netherlands.

THE COMPROMISING SOCIETY

Especially during the first half of the 20th century, Dutch society was strongly divided in so-called *zuilen* (pillars), parts of society that are divided according to religious and political denominations (Lijphart, 1975). The most important pillars in which Dutch society was divided were Catholics, Protestants, Socialists, and Humanists (an extensive discussion is given by Kossmann, 1978, pp. 567–574). None of the pillars constituted a political majority at any point in time. Although these pillars were in some sense incompatible, still the country needed to be run and thus always political and social coalitions between these pillars were necessary. Thus, to ensure a stable society, the government system was built on negotiation and compromise among the denominations, rather than antagonism between the pillars.

This form of "pacificatory democracy" or pillarization requires, among others, a cabinet to appoint both political allies and allies of the opposition to important offices. If a cabinet did not, it could likewise expect the present opposition to fill every important vacancy with their own allies when the opposition came into power. But, more important, it could be expected that a coalition with the present opposition would be necessary after the next elections. So the opposition cannot be alienated too much at any point in time. In this manner, appointment of allies of the opposition is an essential part of the compromising structure that ensures a stable government, even with incompatible political and religious pillars. As a byproduct, this political situation produces a tendency to "de-politicize" political questions (Andeweg, 2000; Lijphart, 1975).

In the political arena this works as follows. The seats in the lower house of the Dutch Parliament are usually divided among 10 to 15 political parties, none of which either ever had or probably will have the absolute majority. Until recently, cabinets were always based on coalitions between the Christian parties (recently unified into the Christian Democratic party CDA) on the one hand and either the Socialist party (PvdA) or the Conservative party (VVD) on the other. Sometimes other, smaller, parties took part. Until the fall of 1989, a coalition of VVD and CDA was in power; after that a coalition of CDA and PvdA. From 1994, a coalition of PvdA and VVD, together with the smaller liberal party D66 formed a coalition. The coalition structure of Dutch government makes the process of legislating quite tedious, and stimulates compromise, if not ambiguity in most statutes. The need to compromise fragmented political interests also produces complicated and detailed statutes in The Netherlands. In contrast, Atiyah and Summers argue that the sharp political divisions in Britain between the two parties and the prevailing strong party discipline make such compromising legislation unnecessary there, resulting in shorter and clearer statutes (see Atiyah & Summers, 1987).

In fact, the Dutch legislator often refrains from regulating certain issues, and leaves the regulation of these issues to the judiciary. It may be argued that one consequence or aspect of Dutch judicial specialization and differentiation from the legislative branch is that the development of Dutch civil law has almost entirely been left to the Supreme Court. But also in criminal law, the Supreme Court gave rulings on important subjects like abortion, euthanasia, labor strike, and the law of evidence without any legislative intervention.

Especially in the last two decades, the legislature has left more and more subjects to decision by the courts. Indeed statutes often include vague norms that need to be fully defined by judicial decisions (e.g., contract have to be executed in "good faith," behavior of the government has to accord to "principles of decent administration," see Schoordijk, 1988). Partly, these vague concepts are used in statutes because the legislators today realize that it is impossible to make a specific rule for everything; partly these vague concepts are necessary because that is the best political thing that can be attained in a coalition compromise.

It might be noted that judging in the Netherlands is a life-long career—Dutch judges are trained in the law just as are Dutch lawyers but lawyer and judge career paths quickly diverge, with judges receiving special training in their profession. Whether such specialization is a desirable matter (a point we return to below) is subject to debate. During a recent speech concerning the slow pace of federal judicial appointments in the United States, Chief Justice Rehnquist observed "We have never had, and should not want, a judiciary composed only of those persons who are already in the public service .... We must not drastically shrink the number of judicial nominees who have had substantial experience in private practice ....[R]easonable people, not merely here but in Europe [believe European systems of career judges] simply do not command the respect and enjoy the independence of ours" (Greenhouse, 2002). Although we do not tackle the question of independence, survey data presented below cast significant doubt on the respect proposition advanced by the Chief Justice.

THE JUDGE DEE MODEL OF JUSTICE

The compromising nature of Dutch society is not only reflected in the political arena, but is a constituent part of much of Dutch society; also in the subject of the present contribution: the criminal justice system. This compromising nature of the criminal justice system is essential to its operations. We will call this the *Judge Dee version of justice*, after Judge Dee, a Chinese judge who actually lived under T'ang dynasty (618–907 before Christ), but has recently become famous because of the mystery novels written by the Dutch diplomat Robert van Gulik (see for instance van Gulik, 1959, 1961). In the novels, Judge Dee (or in Dutch *rechter Tie*) is the person who is not only a cunning detective, but also a decision maker who achieves quite wise decisions by balancing facts and interests.

THE CONTENDING SOCIETY

It has often been argued that the United States is the most litigious country in the world (Holland, 1988) and this characterization of the American justice system underscores a version of justice that Americans seem to prefer. American society is not a pillarized society of groups with contrasting values but a compromising ethic. In contrast to that vision of Dutch society one can identify a vision of values in the United States where the central moral elements of society are shared by almost all citizens. Huntington describes this phenomenon as follows:

> Ideas of constitutionalism, individualism, liberalism, democracy, and egalitarianism are no monopoly to Americans. In some societies, some people subscribe to many of these ideas and in other societies many people subscribe to some of these ideas. In no other society, however, are all of these ideas so widely adhered to by so many people as they are in the United States. (Huntington, 1981, p. 15)

According to Huntington this has a decisive influence on all of American society. American society has a broadly shared moral passion that distinguishes it from other Western democracies (p. 11) and that has changed remarkably little during the last 200 years since Alexis de Tocqueville (1863) wrote down his observations on America. Bryce (Bryce, 1891, pp. 417–418) summarizes these shared moral values in what he calls the American Creed: (1) the individual has sacred rights; (2) the source of political power is the people; (3) all governments are limited by law and the people; (4) local government is preferred to national government; (5) the majority is wiser than the minority; and (6) the less government, the better. These shared values point to the importance of the rule of law in the United States to govern conflict and social behavior and the limited role for a government. Bryce remarked therefore: "Americans had no theory of the State and felt no need for one…. The nation is nothing but so many individuals. The government is nothing but certain representatives and officials."

This vision of American justice puts—more than in the Netherlands—an emphasis on the individuals and his rights and duties. There is much less need to compromise than in the Netherlands and there is less need for a strong government to pacify incompatible parts of society. In contrast, Americans depend on their individual actions to rectify whatever conflict may arise. This manner in which social relations are managed seems to be related much more to the justice principle of equity (again see Berkowitz & Walster, 1976; Cohen, 1987; Walster et al., 1978). There is no strong government that can equalize the divisions of proceeds—of whatever nature—in society or attend to the needs of individual recipients as in the Netherlands. Rather, individual actions to solve conflict in the United States depend on the "input" individuals can bring to a conflict—be it the rule of law that is on their side or any other input. This will almost automatically lead to a much "tougher" interaction of participants in a conflict. In conflict one does not look for a compromise but try to get one of the parties to prevail. "This is a country in which order exists because basic rules are accepted by the people, or insisted upon by them" (Barone, 1999).

THE JOHN WAYNE MODEL OF JUSTICE

Van Koppen is fond of promoting this idealized American model of justice as a cowboy enterprise and is inclined to see the fictional life and times of John Wayne as a model of this vision. In this vision of American justice John Wayne "said it all" in the movie *The Alamo* (1960): "There's right and there's wrong. You gotta do one or the other. You do the one and you're living. You do the other and you may be walking around, but

you're dead as a beaver hat." Of course, this perception of American values and American justice and a tendency to perceive affairs in black and
white terms are reinforced by American leaders such as Ronald Reagan—
who characterized his Soviet adversary as an "evil empire" and, more
recently, George W. Bush who has described American efforts against terrorism as a "struggle ... between good and evil, and nothing else" and has
most recently characterized the regimes in Iraq, Iran, and North Korea as
an "evil axis." Rhetoric aside, one can, of course, fairly ask whether
American justice is as contentious as these images suggest.

As noted above, the United States certainly has the reputation of
being a highly litigious country. Whether this is really true, of course, may
depend on how one counts. Although the popular image of American litigation is probably the jury trial, it turns out that most cases filed in the
United States never reach trial. For example, when Herbert Kritzer (1986)
analyzed 1649 cases in five federal judicial districts and seven state courts,
he found that only 7% of cases went to full trial and reached a jury verdict
or court decision. Of course, another 15% ended as a result of some other
form of adjudication, such as dismissal or arbitration and a further 9% settled following a judicial ruling on a significant motion. But, in this study
and other studies of civil litigation (e.g., Trubek, Sarat, & Felstiner, 1983) it
is clear that between one-half and two-thirds or cases settle through negotiations between the parties without significant involvement of judges—
in a sense, the system is one in which the vast majority of disputes are
settled through negotiation and the courts are perhaps used mostly to get
the attention of the opposing party. Even on the criminal side, the use of
plea-bargaining assures that the vast majority of cases are resolved
through negotiations; though, of course, there are intense arguments over
the desirability of using plea bargaining to dispose of criminal cases (see
for instance Gorr, 2000; Micelli, 1996; Palermo, White, Wasserman, &
Hanrahan, 1998).

A study by Miller and Sarat (1980–1981) is quite interesting because it
suggests the possibility there is actually too little litigation in the United
States. The study, a survey of 5,000 adults who were queried about a
broad range of tort, consumer, debt, discrimination, government, divorce
and landlord tenant problems (each had to involve stakes of $1000 or
more—in 1980 dollars) revealed that large proportions of some problems
(e.g., 70% of discrimination problems) were unresolved because no complaint was made—probably because those injured had little hope the
problem would be resolved. For most types of problems court filings were
quite uncommon—typically 5–10% or less—with the exception of divorce
problems in which filings occurred in 45% of the "cases." These results
hardly paint a picture of aggressive litigiousness—though, of course, the

possibility remains that the frequency of not following through with complaints is much higher in other countries such as the Netherlands. There is even the possibility that the frequency with which problems arise is lower. This is clearly an arena in which comparative research is needed.

THE CRIMINAL JUSTICE SYSTEMS

In these idealized accounts, the Dutch structure of society has led to a compromising nature in both government and many other parts of society. This compromising nature of society has led to a preference for the use of the principles of justice need and equality. For divisions in society according to need and equality a relatively strong government is necessary. In contrast, American society is much more directed at individual actions that are governed by the justice principle of equity. With a relatively weak ordering of relationships at the governmental level, individuals have to try to prevail in conflict, rather than rely on equitable distributions achieved through governmental action. Individual rights play a much more important role in the United States than in the Netherlands, where often the most "reasonable" solution is sought.

Are the differences discussed above between the Netherlands and the United States reflected in their criminal justice systems? In the Dutch inquisitorial criminal system the government—in the form of the court—plays a much more active role than in the United States adversarial system, where the judge is more an arbiter who has to choose between the position of both antagonist parties. As a consequence, decisions in the Dutch criminal justice system may often reflect the more compromising nature of Dutch society, while decisions in the American criminal justice system more often seem to involve a choice for either one or the other party. In that sense, the Dutch criminal justice system is much "softer" than the American "tough" way of handling cases. Evidence for these differences can be seen in many aspects of the respective criminal justice systems. The following sections highlight differences that surface in previous chapters in this volume.[3]

---

[3] We could also point at elements in civil law. One example: American contracts are much longer than Dutch contracts. This is related to the manner in which courts interpret these contracts if a conflict ensues. In the United States, judges much more than in the Netherlands look at the letter of the contract and provisions in it than Dutch judges do. American judges in that manner evaluate which litigant is right in its interpretation of contractual provisions. Dutch judges take a more compromising stance: they look for what is behind the contractual provisions (what the parties intended to reach with their contract) and judicial decision making in contract law is heavily governed by what is the most resonable in the relation between the parties.

PRETRIAL

Chris Slobogin compared in his chapter, among others, search and seizure in Europe and the United States. He noted that American lawyers often criticize European procedures as "relatively nonchalant." He quotes Justice Jackson, who explained that the Fourth Amendment's protection "consists in requiring that ... inferences [about criminal activity] be drawn by a neutral and detached magistrate instead of being judged by the officer engaged in the often competitive enterprise of ferreting out crime" (*Johnson v. United States*, 1948, p. 14). Doing so without a warrant leads to exclusion of the evidence generated by the then illegal search or seizure. Thus, illegal search and seizure leads to a binary decision by the court.

What Slobogin calls "relatively nonchalant" European rules on search and seizure in fact—at least in the Netherlands—is a compromise between the needs of the police and the needs of the suspect. Indeed, usually a warrant must be issued by a judge before a search can be undertaken, but under certain circumstances searches can be done with the permission of a *officier van justitie* (i.e., a prosecutor, but a different one than the American, see below) and if his or her permission cannot be awaited even without such a permission. In practice, courts are quite lenient to the police on this point and rather than keeping the police strictly to the rules, they tend to weigh the probative results of the search to the violation of the rules.

Of course, one can argue over that question of whether "nonchalant" is an apt characterization of European policies. From a Dutch perspective, search and seizure policies and practices are not a matter of "nonchalance" as Slobogin contends, but rather a search for a reasonable compromise consistent with the compromising nature of Dutch values and politics.[4] From an American perspective—especially from a perspective which exalts the individual and individual privacy over the state—European practices may appear out of balance.

A similar difference between the United States and the Netherlands seems to hold for suspect interrogations. In the United States the interrogation model of Inbau and Read (Inbau, Reed, & Buckley, 1986) may seem predominant (see Vrij in this volume). The essence of their nine-phase

---

[4] Another source of the manner in which Dutch courts handle possibly illegal searches is the general trust courts have in the police (see for a more general discussion of this trust Wagenaar, Van Koppen, & Crombag, 1993, pp. 82 ff.). The central role that the Dutch government plays in the pillarized Dutch society is only possible if government officials are basically trusted. This trust is not only extended to judges, but also to the police. These kinds of decisions in American society are, in contrast, influenced by a basic distruct of government and thus of its officials. For instance, in 2000 a little more that 50% of the district court judges and prosecutors in the Netherlands were female (Bruinsma, 2001).

model of suspect interrogations is that it is assumed that the suspect is guilty. The Inbau-model is aimed at eliciting a confession. In doing so, trickery (as for instance presenting nonexistent evidence to the suspect) is permitted. Slobogin may seem to support this, when he writes: "Based on the work of moral philosopher Sissela Bok, I contended that if the police have probable cause that the suspect is guilty (which is normally the case if custodial interrogation is occurring), they may treat him as an 'enemy,' a situation in which Bok, normally hostile to deceit, would permit it" (Slobogin, 1997).

Deceit and trickery by the police may be common in the United States (Leo, 1996), but it is normally rejected by Dutch courts. Dutch defendants sometimes claim the police lured or tricked them into a confession, but always have great trouble in proving that such really happened. Dutch courts tend to believe the statements by the interrogating officers and it has been suggested that part of the difficulty in demonstrating misconduct by the police arises from the fact that the Dutch do trust their police (Wagenaar et al., 1993).

Of course, the implication of this view is that Americans do not trust their police. One of the difficulties in gauging whether Americans or Europeans have found a better balance with respect to police practices is that such a judgment must be made, at least in part, against the backdrop of public perceptions of the police, the courts and even legislators. Thus, American search and seizure practices might, arguably, arise from an American distrust of the police; although toleration of suspect trickery in some ways suggests that the police are trusted. Ultimately, in any system in which there is some fluidity in the relationships among legal and political actors, we might expect that the systems of checks and balances that prevail among police, courts, legislators and citizenry will reflect general levels of trust and mistrust among those groups. Of course, in democratic countries the perceptions of the citizenry presumably should count more than the perceptions of the institutional actors and there is always a danger that relationships among institutional actors can become "too friendly"—e.g., perhaps Dutch judges, in their role as investigating magistrates, identify too closely with the police and are therefore more inclined than American judges to overlook police misconduct.

In the United States, at least, there has been significant fluidity in perceptions of the police (though less fluidity with respect to courts, judges and politicians). It is true that there is and has been a significant level of distrust of police in the American public—especially in minority communities—but the extent of distrust of police in the United States is easily overstated—particularly in comparison to prior times and in comparison to the levels of distrust of other actors in the political and justice arenas. A 1999 national survey in the United States revealed that less than

43% or respondents had a "great deal" of trust/confidence in local police (Rottman & Tomkins, 1999). This may seem a relatively low number, but police actually fared better than the courts—the corresponding percentage for the U.S. Supreme Court was 32% and for local courts 23%. Though these numbers look low, the police and courts both fared better than state legislatures (18%) and the media (10%).

Similarly, results from a Gallup 2001 survey (Gallup Organization, 2001) which asked respondents to rate the honesty and ethical standards of people in different fields indicate that the percentage saying "very high" or "high" was 68% for police (up from 37% in 1977) which was not as high as the 90% for firefighters or the military (81%), but was on a par with doctors (66%) and clergy (64%) and college teachers (58%) and vastly better than business executives and senators (25% each) and lawyers (18%). In a sense, these numbers do confirm the general view of Americans as distrusting of government, but also indicate that Americans are much less inclined to trust policy makers and the policymaking branches of government (legislatures and courts) than they are to trust the police and military who execute those policies.

Other survey results from Gallup (Gallup Organization, 2001) indicate that other impressions of the police have changed in dramatic ways. In 1965, 9% of the respondents thought there was police brutality in their area. By 1991 the percentage had increased to 39% (38% in 1999). Much more rapid changes occurred with respect to the question: Have you personally ever felt treated unfairly by the police or by a police officer? In 1995, 9% of whites (but 34% of blacks) said "yes." Less than four years later, 24% of whites and 43% of blacks said yes. Clearly, changes in numbers of this magnitude reflect fairly subtly differentiated views of the police: police can be perceived to be honest and doing their essential job well, but perhaps exercising more force than the public is willing to endorse.

Although we are not prepared to undertake comparative analyses of public perceptions of police or other legal actors—nor to explore the more complicated dynamic relationships among public trust of justice actors and the legal relationships among those actors—we do suggest that resolving questions such as what constitutes proper practice in search and seizure and interrogation.

AT TRIAL

PROSECUTORS

The most telling difference between the Dutch Judge Dee and the John Wayne versions of justice may be the roles of the participants at trial.

Typical for the difference under discussion is the role of the prosecution. In the Netherlands the public prosecutor (*officier van justitie*) is a magistrate. He or she leads police investigations, a role that in most investigations is more a formal responsibility. Only in major cases does the public prosecutor really give directives to police officers. Also at the Dutch trial the prosecutor accuses the defendant. But there are two striking differences between the American and the Dutch prosecutors.

First, the Dutch prosecutor is not there to prosecute, but is an independent magistrate. He or she is supposed to form their own opinion on the merits of the cases against the defendant and act accordingly. As a consequence, it sometimes happens in Dutch courts that the prosecutor asks for an acquittal at trial. Why the prosecution did not drop such a case in an earlier stage is generally related to practical matters. After the police complete their investigations and send the case file to the prosecutor's office, it is first handled by a junior employee (*parketsecretaris*) who will prepare the case for trial. Only in the few days before the actual trial does the prosecutor proper prepare the case. At this point in time the prosecutor may decide that the police did not present enough evidence and then ask for an acquittal. More often this happens in appeal (see below) in cases where the prosecutor at the lower court appealed a court decision, but the prosecutor who handles the case at the appellate court considers the evidence too thin for a conviction.

In some ways American prosecutors are, at least in principle, similarly situated. American Bar Association ethical standards governing the function of the prosecutor specify that prosecutors should refrain from prosecuting charges the prosecutor knows are not supported by probable cause, that the prosecutor is an administrator of justice and officer of the court who must exercise sound discretion in the performance of their functions, and that the duty of the prosecutor is to seek justice and not merely to convict. Although the mandates appear to be similar, the extent to which the behavior Dutch and American prosecutors is also similar is a complicated matter. The prevalence of plea bargaining in the United States particularly obscures the extent to which American prosecutors exercise their discretion in dropping charges against defendants for lack of evidence.

A second point in which Dutch cases clearly diverge considerably from U.S. cases is the manner in which witnesses are called at trial. Dutch criminal trials are predominantly conducted using documents; the file of the case. The file is filled with witness statements (as recorded by the police), police reports and all other relevant pieces of information gathered during the investigation. In most cases, the court decides on the file alone, without hearing live testimony from witnesses. If, however, the prosecution, the defense or the court deems it necessary to hear live witnesses, they can be summoned to trial. The prosecution does the summoning. If the defense attorney wants to hear certain witnesses, he or she has to ask the prosecution to do so. The defense has to give reasons for calling witnesses to the prosecutor. The prosecution can refuse to summon all or certain witnesses, and often does so, sometimes with the argument that calling a certain witness is "not in the interest of the defense." Of course this decision can be appealed to the full court—for more serious cases always a three judge panel—and if the court agrees with the defense, the witness in question is summoned for the next session of the court. Because of overloaded court dockets, that session make take place only after three months. In this manner the prosecutor presents the defense with a dilemma: it has to choose between the gamble that its case is sufficiently strong to convince to court without the witness in question and awaiting the next session of the court, including an extra three month of custody for the defendant.

THE ATTORNEYS

The latter nicety of the Dutch system may seem peculiar for foreign lawyers, but it fits into the manner in which criminal cases are handled— or at least used to be handled—in the Netherlands. In the days of old, when the first author's father still was an attorney, a Dutch trial was anything but a battle. It took much more the form of a polite conversation between gentlemen (the vast majority of the professional participants were male in these days) who—although each departing from his own point of view—together were searching for the truth. The conversation was based on mutual trust and each participant expected the others to respect its position. These gentlemen participants also needed each other; they could expect to encounter each other in future and if one of them took a too uncompromising position, it could haphazard future relations (and cases). In this situation, the defendant her- or more often himself really was the object of investigations rather than participant. He could not give directions to his attorney but rather the attorney held the so-called *domus litis*: in the end the defense attorney always decided what procedural strategy should be taken.

In recent years this picture has changed somewhat. Especially in high profile cases (usually major drug cases) both the prosecution and the defense attorneys take a harder stance. This kind of behavior is called, by the way, an American form of trial.

There are a number of causes for this change. First, courts put less trust in the police than they used to. This is the product of a parliamentary investigation on police behavior in the beginning of the 1990s (Van Traa, 1996), which showed that the police conducted investigations in drug cases in an illegal or semi-illegal manner. Second, the prosecution nowadays is much more actively involved in the police investigation in large cases, also as a consequence of the Van Traa-report. Extensive cooperation with the police, however, makes the prosecutor less a magistrate in these cases and more a crime fighter. Third, defense attorneys have changed too. In the last decade a specialized criminal bar has also developed. These specialized attorneys more often than in the past follow their client's strategy, rather than pursuing their own. Fourth, and last, decision making by the European Court on Human Rights in Strasbourg has had an important influence on Dutch criminal procedure. This court—consisting of justices from both inquisitorial and adversarial countries—through its decisions has made the Dutch criminal justice system somewhat more adversarial. One important consequence is that witnesses are to be summoned to trial more often. Their very presence and the interrogation of witnesses leave less room for a polite gentlemen's conversation.

THE WITNESSES

Nonetheless, although there are a few tendencies towards a more American way of criminal procedure, most cases in the Netherlands are conducted in the same manner as decades ago. The manner in which witnesses—both experts and other witnesses—are treated in both systems and how they are supposed to behave at trial is quite different in the United States and the Netherlands. The most striking example is children as witnesses. Cordon, Goodman, and Anderson give a description in this volume of how these witnesses are treated in the United States. The Dutch situation is quite different. In the Netherlands child witnesses—often in sexual abuse cases where they are the alleged victims—are interviewed by a specially trained police officer (Dekens & Van der Sleen, 1997). This is done (with a few exceptions) in a specially designed interview room. The interviews are videotaped from an adjacent room with a view of the interview through a one-way mirror. The colors of the room, the type of furniture and toys are designed to make the child feel as much as possible at ease. In almost all cases the one interview with the child is the only interview that is held; children are never summoned to court to testify. The chapter by Cordon et al. demonstrates that the American practice to hear child witnesses in court brings a host of additional issues. It becomes important to find out how much knowledge these children have of the court, how they react to interrogators who are not very qualified to question children, and, most important, how children are able to cope with testifying in public and in front of the defendant who maybe already victimized them.

THE EXPERTS

The grilling of expert witnesses in the United States (see Loftus & Ketcham, 1991, for some fine examples) is in the same vein. When the first author has served as an expert witness in the Netherlands, he usually delivers a written report and only sometimes is summoned to court to answer some additional questions. If this happens, he is questioned in a cursory manner about his credentials and the discussion quickly centers at the points at issue (see also the description of the differences by Ton Broeders in this volume).

This is strikingly different from the manner in which experts are treated in the United States. For example, when the second author has served as an expert on eyewitness and jury issues in American trials, he has been called by one of the parties, paid by that party and his testimony elicited in a manner that favors that party. The elicitation of testimony favorable to the calling party may sound as though it will produce a biased outcome and/or compromise whatever neutrality the expert possesses. It is true that the expert may be in an awkward position insofar as the calling party is likely to elicit mostly favorable testimony (the attorney, rather than the witness, does after all, set the question/answer agenda). But, the adversarial system is constructed with the clear expectation that cross-examination will reveal any weaknesses in the testimony and elicit contrary evidence from the testifying expert. This does mean that the cross-examiner has to be prepared and know what sorts of useful testimony can be elicited on cross-examination (and in the second author's experience that is the primary weakness of the system, supported in this by the chapter by Roger Park in this volume). With respect to what goes on in the courtroom, it turns out that hearings on the question of whether he will be permitted to testify and on what subject matters (hearings which take place with the jury not present) can commonly take much more court time than the actual testimony in front of the jury.

Of course, it is often the case that an American party has undertaken a significant amount of expert shopping in preparation for trial. Thus, while it may be true that only witnesses who support a position advocated by the party will be called, plenty of witnesses who do not support that position may be contacted by a party. Despite perceptions to the contrary, contact by an attorney does not imply that experts will or are expected to adopt the party's position. They will certainly be called upon to identify what useful testimony they might provide and to further identify weaknesses and contrary evidence that might be elicited on cross-examination—on the basis of such information counsel can determine whether, on balance, the expert is likely to be helpful to the attorney and their client. Of course, expert shopping can certainly present problems that would not arise in a system in which judges look for and recruit an expert whose opinion reflects consideration of a problem from a neutral perspective.

None of this implies that the experts located by the parties in the American system are necessarily biased or are not independent. Even in instances where an expert is known to testify for one side or the other on a regular basis, that fact may simply indicate that the expert reads the evidence—whether that refers to case facts or underlying science in a different, though unbiased, way as compared to an expert who testifies for the opposing side with some regularity—both unreasonable and reasonable people can disagree. Of course, in the Netherlands an expert is always expected to take an independent and neutral position, even if he is called and paid by one of the parties—though this begs the question of how much consistency there might be across experts who are ostensibly evaluating the same evidence and even ostensibly using the same evaluative criteria. Dutch scientific journals are not filled with univocal interpretations of empirical observations and Dutch scientists have not abandoned the process of generating and testing alternative theories and explanations for observed phenomena.

THE FACT-FINDERS

In light of the points discussed above, the reader will probably appreciate the whole atmosphere at the Dutch trial. Foreign colleagues who attend Dutch trials always remark on the rather informal and cordial behavior of all participants. It still is gentlemen-like—although nowadays most professional participants are female[5]—discussion of the problem at hand.

One can easily appreciate that if the Dutch would introduce a jury, a change of atmosphere would result and would make the trial more formal.[6] Among other things, such a change would probably necessitate the formulation of rules of evidence akin to those in the United States—rules which guide the admissibility of evidence in a manner designed to facilitate fair decision-making by laypersons. In that sense, the absence and presence of the jury in the Netherlands and the United States, respectively, seems to make a lot of difference. Whether increased formality would result in increased incivility and contentiousness is a different matter—one need only look at British trials as one indication that the presence of juries does not necessitate increases in contentiousness.

---

[5] In fact the Dutch one knew the jury in criminal cases for a few years in the beginning of the 19th century (see Bossers, 1987).

[6] In the Dutch system there is nothing like a guilty or not guilty plea. Taking such a formal position at trial by the defendant is irrevalant because the court reviews the evidence anyway. The closest Dutch defendants come to a guilty plea is when they confess to the police and maintain their confession until the trial.

In the present volume Shari Diamond makes the case for the jury; though the first author remains unconvinced. She argues that, under some circumstances, jury leniency offers much protection to innocent defendants and that in the majority of cases juries and judges would decide alike. This of course still begs the question of whether juries *and* judges in the United States perform as well as professional, career judges in the Netherlands. Van Koppen has argued, for instance, that he could replace his general practitioner for a week and would probably make the same diagnosis in most cases (most diseases solve themselves anyway). But that would not make him a good GP: what he particularly worries about is the need for an expert doctor who can diagnose the three or four patients each week with minor symptoms but major medical problems.

In the same vein the American jury was summarized by Stern in the following manner: "The first thing that happens when a criminal trial starts is both sides get to inquire of the prospective jurors whether they know the defendant, the victim or any of the witnesses. If so, they are not allowed to serve as a juror. We then eliminate those who have had experience with the particular type of offense involved in this trial. Next, we get rid of those with strong feelings about it. In time, we insure that no one sits on the jury if they know anything about the case, the people involved or the issues involved" (Stern, 2001). Although Stern may overstate his case, it points at a dilemma of the criminal justice system that hold for the United States and the Netherlands alike. On the one hand the Dutch have professional judges and the Americans Stern-like juries because they can judge the case as detached as possible. For the same reason Dutch judges excuse themselves from cases or can be excuses on initiative of one of the parties if they are is some way personally involved in the case. The *voir dire* in the United States and the possibility to excuse judges in the Netherlands may increase detachment, but it also may cause the fact-finders to be too little knowledgeable of the social context in which the crime took place. In this respect the American jury has an advantage if jury selection causes at least some jurors to come from the social circles where crimes usually take place. Dutch judges predominantly come from upper class circles, i.e. 78% of their fathers were senior employees or independent professionals (Bruinsma, 2001, p. 1926, Figure 1). On the other hand jurors are almost always first time decision-makers, while Dutch judges are experienced decision-makers. Whether the social circle arguments outweighs the experience argument or not, remains undecided between the two authors.

The presence of the jury in the United States and the absence in the Netherlands again points at the role of the government in society. It is notable in the historic roots of the jury (see the discussion by Hans & Vidmar, 1986, especially Chapter 2) that the jury originated to protect the parties against arbitrary decisions by the crown. The jury exists, in part, because professional decision makers appointed by authorities whose interests were seen to be adverse to the general population were not trusted. As Diamond describes in her chapter there are still many constraints on the jury—it is not regarded as fully trustworthy as the judge. Indeed, most of the constraints on the jury are really designed to improve the quality of jury decision-making. Rules and procedures are designed with the intent of filtering out "information" that is deemed to be unreliable or biasing. Although this is the sort of information that we might prefer that judges also never hear, the American justice system presumes that such evidence (e.g., hearsay evidence) will not have the same impact on a judge as it will on a jury—that a judge is better situated to ignore information that he or she deems inappropriate for consideration. Some would argue that this is a highly debatable question—subject to empirical investigation.

THE SUSPECT

And where does that leave the suspect and defendant? He faces dilemmas in the American system that are not posed to Dutch defendants, the most important being plea-bargaining (Gorr, 2000; Micelli, 1996; Palermo et al., 1998), which again is a typical instance where Americans resort to individual actions without government interference. Suppose you are an innocent defendant who faces a fair amount of damaging evidence (a fine example is the case of Paul Ingram, see Olio & Cornell, 1998; Wright, 1993a,b)? You are faced with the decision during plea-bargaining to cut your losses or take the chance with an unpredictable jury. Dutch defendants do not face such a dilemma (Gross, 1996). Each case goes to trial and in each case the court reviews the evidence, although there are indications that even in the Netherlands, less attention will be paid to the evidence if the defendants confessed to the police and repeats the confession at trial.[7] This at least gives the innocent defendant a second change to

---

[7,8] Case examples show that miscarriages of justice are prevented by the full appeal in the Netherlands. A recent one is the so-called Fitting Room Murder on November 22, 1984 in Zaandam, the Netherlands, in which a female victim was brutally murdered in a fitting room of a fashion boutique. A bicycle mechanic was prosecuted for this murder. The only direct evidence linking him to the crime was a so-called scent lineup[8] in which the dog identified the smell of the suspect to a handkerchief used to gag the victim. The lineup, however, had been conducted in a flawed manner (see the description by the police officer who conducted the lineup Kaldenbach, 1998, pp. 127–139). The defendant was convicted to 12 years imprisonment by the Haarlem court. With the same evidence, the appellate court acquitted. At the time, this was considered a dubious acquittal by many. In the beginning of 2002, however, a reanalysis of the materials found at the scene of the crime

have the damaging evidence reviewed in court, without being posed which dilemmas in plea-bargaining, and may, at least in some cases, give extra protection to the innocent defendant.

American defendants may also be more harshly treated further along the system. The differences begin right after the verdict of the jury. Appeals to higher courts are much more limited in scope in the United States than in the Netherlands. In the Netherlands, two stages of appeal are possible in a criminal case. After the trial decision in first instance, appeal to the next higher court is possible, and the second decision is subject to appeal in cassation to the Supreme Court. As in the first appeal, leave to appeal in cassation to the Supreme Court is not required. In an appeal in cassation, however, the facts as determined by the lower courts are not reviewable; the Supreme Court can only decide on issues of law. The most important difference to the United States is that the trial at the Appellate Court is a full trial in the sense that the case is treated *de novo*. This gives splendid opportunity to weigh the evidence anew and—if the defendant is convicted again—review the sentence rendered by the lower court.[8] Although American cases are not reviewed *de novo*, cases can actually traverse many layers of appeal—typically, an appeal to an intermediate state court with possible further appeals to state supreme courts, possibly followed by appeals to federal trial and appellate courts and ultimately (though rarely) to the United States Supreme Court.

Whether these differences in procedure produce a material difference in outcomes is difficult to gauge, however. In the United States, the vast majority of cases are disposed of through plea-bargaining and rarely give rise to an appeal (of course, as suggested above, some plea-bargains make reflect pleas to crimes not committed by defendants, though neither author has seen reliable statistics or estimates of the frequency of such events). Appeals from conviction at trial are certainly common and reversals of convictions in criminal cases are not uncommon—one figure circulated is that reversal rates in most types of criminal cases in the United States run about 15% of all appeals—but once plea bargains are factored in, appeals may be taken in only 10% of cases which result in a conviction. On the other hand, the thoroughness of American appellate review might be best indexed by reviews of death penalty cases (which are automatically reviewed in almost all states). A study by Liebman and his colleagues (Liebman, 2000; Liebman, Fagan, & West, 2000) examined reversible error rates in all capital cases from 1973 through 1995. The study covered 4578 capital state appeals and found that 41% of verdicts were reversed on

using newer DNA techniques showed that someone else, the Turkish drug addict Kemal Errol (deceased in 1992)—had been the actual perpetrator.

direct appeal; an additional 10% were reversed at state post-conviction hearings; and of cases that survived state review, 40% were reversed by federal review. Over a 22-year period at least 68% of all capital verdicts were overturned. There are no comparable figures for the Netherlands.

It is much harder to dispute that harsher treatment of American defendants goes on after trial and appeal. In addition to implementing some of the harshest penalties and maintaining incarceration rates that are among the highest in the industrialized world, American judicial discretion in sentencing is much more limited than in the Netherlands. An example is the so-called *three strikes and you are out* guidelines and similar sentencing guidelines that produce a tendency of higher sentences (Dickey & Hollenhorst, 1999; Nsereko, 1999). These guidelines also have racial effects and are more punitive for minorities (Albonetti, 1997; Provine, 1998). In the Netherlands there is a maximum for each kind of crime, but a general minimum for all crimes: 1 day in prison or a 15-guilder fine. The court can even declare someone guilty without imposing a sentence (which is customary, for instance, in euthanasia cases where medical doctors were prosecuted for murder).

Of course, there are strong indications that American prisons are of poorer quality than their European counterparts (Vaughn & Smith, 1999) and there are two further points which characterize the harsher individualized American criminal justice system: treatment of disturbed defendants and the death penalty. The chapter by Corine de Ruiter in this volume is a fine example of how disturbed offenders are treated in the Dutch system. De Ruiter's chapter clearly shows how the Dutch try to compromise the needs of the disturbed offender and the necessity to protect society and do so in a manner that is more respectful of disturbed offenders than is true in the United States.

Of course, the most marked difference in Dutch/European versus American treatment of suspects is the application of the death penalty in the United States. Note that the United States is the only industrialized country that still employs the death penalty (Hood, 2001; Van Koppen, Hessing, & De Poot, 2001). Samuel Gross gives an excellent picture in this volume of all problems surrounding the death penalty. When viewed from Europe, justice in the United States appears much more *punitive* and *retributive* and consequently much tougher than what is practiced on the Continent.

The American system is much tougher on perpetrators, if one considers the three-strikes laws, the use of sentencing guidelines, or the quality of United States prisons. It also involves secondary victimization for victims and other witnesses, where, for example, children testify in open court

(Goodman & Bottoms, 1993). In this respect, the death penalty in the United States mirrors the penal harm version of punishment established there.

CONCLUSIONS

In this chapter we have tried to highlight differences between the United States and the Dutch criminal justice system—many of which may be explained by basic differences in the societies. These differences are generally consistent with the idealized visions of justice that we identified early in this chapter—a Dutch society governed by compromise and a American society that is—at least as reflected in its criminal justice system—governed by an emphases on individual rights. Although we cannot authoritatively say that the differences in legal practices before and during trial lead to decidedly different outcomes, it is fairly obvious that post-trial justice is much tougher in the United States than in the Netherlands.

These analyses do not directly lead to the conclusion that one or the other system is better. The authors have certainly not resolved their differences on this matter—although the first author clearly prefers the Dutch system and the second author is prepared to concede, as a matter of personal conviction, a preference for Dutch post-trial practices, it is not yet clear that one system has an advantage over the other in terms of the quality of pretrial and trial decision-making.

References

Abbott Parry, E. (1923). *What the judge thought.* New York: Knopf.

Abinger, E. (1930). *Forty years at the bar, being the memoirs of Edward Abinger, barrister of the Inner Temple.* London: Hutchinson.

Abrahamson, S.S. (1986a). Justice and juror. *Georgia Law Review, 20,* 257–298.

Abrahamson, S.S. (1986b). A view from the other side of the bench. *Marquette Law Review, 69,* 463–493.

Adler, S. (1994). *The jury: Trial and error in the American courtroom.* New York: Random House.

Ajzen, I. & Madden, T.J. (1986). Prediction of goal-directed behavior: Attitudes, intentions, and perceived behavioral control. *Journal of Experimental Social Psychology, 22,* 453–474.

Akers, R. & Lanza Kaduce, L. (1986). The exclusionary rule: Legal doctrine and social research on constitutional norms. *Sam Houston State University Criminal Justice Center Research Bulletin, 2,* 1–6.

Albonetti, C.A. (1997). Sentencing under the Federal Sentencing Guidelines: Effects of defendant characteristics, guilty pleas, and departures on sentence outcomes for drug offenses, 1991–1992. *Law and Society Review, 31,* 789–822.

Aldag, A. & Riggs Fuller, S. (1993). Beyond fiasco: A reappraisal of the groupthink phenomenon and a new model of group decision processes. *Psychological Bulletin, 113,* 533–552.

Aldridge, M., Timmins, K. & Wood, J. (1997). Children's understanding of legal terminology: Judges get money at pet shows, don't they? *Child Abuse Review, 6,* 141–146.

Allen, R.J. & Miller, J.S. (1993). The common law theory of experts: Deference or education? In J.F. Nijboer, C.R. Callen, & N. Kwak (Eds.), *Forensic expertise and the law of evidence* (pp. 11–19). Amsterdam: North-Holland.

Allen, V.L. & Levine, J.M. (1971). Social support and conformity: The role of independent assessment of reality. *Journal of Experimental Psychology, 7,* 48–58.

Alschuler, A.W. (1995). Racial quota's and the jury. *Duke Law Journal, 44,* 704–743.

Altavilla, E. (1955). *Forensische Psychologie [Forensic psychology]* (2 vols.). Graz: Styria.

Amar, A.R. (1995). Reinventing juries: Ten suggested reforms. *U.C. Davis Law Review, 28,* 1169–1194.

American Bar Association. (1989). *ABA Criminal Justice Mental Health Standards.* Chicago: American Bar Association.

American Bar Association. (1998). *National benchbook on psychiatric and psychological evidence and testimony.* Washington, DC: American Bar Association.

American Psychiatric Association. (1994). *Diagnostic and statistical manual of mental disorders: Fourth edition (DSM-IV).* Washington, DC: American Psychiatric Association.

369

Anderson, J.C. (1999). *Why lawyers derail justice: Probing the roots of legal injustices.* University Park, PA: Pennsylvania State University Press.

Anderson, J.C., Lowe, D.J., & Reckers, P.M.J. (1993). Evaluation of auditor decisions: Hindsight bias effects and the expectation gap. *Journal of Economic Psychology, 14,* 711–737.

Anderson, T.J. (1999). The Netherlands criminal justice system: An audit model of decision-making. In M. Malsch & J.F. Nijboer (Eds.), *Complex cases: Perspectives on the Netherlands criminal justice system* (pp. 47–68). Amsterdam: Thela Thesis.

Andeweg, R.B. (2000). From Dutch disease to Dutch model? Consensus government in practice. *Parliamentary Affairs, 53,* 697–709.

Andrews, B., Morton, J., Bekerian, D.A., Brewin, C.R., Davies, G.M., & Mollon, P. (1995). The recovery of memories in clinical practice: Experiences and beliefs of British Psychological Society practitioners. *The Psychologist, 8,* 209–214.

Appelbaum, P.S. (1997). Ethics in evolution: The incompatibility of clinical and forensic functions. *American Journal of Psychiatry, 154,* 445–446.

Applebome, P. (1989). Two electric jolts in Alabama execution. *New York Times* (July 15), A6.

Ardaiz, J.A. (2000). California's three strikes law: History, expectations, consequences. *McGeorge Law Review, 32,* 1–36.

Arntzen, F. (1993). *Psychologie der Zeugenaussage [Psychology of eyewitness testimony]* (2nd ed.). München: Beck.

Asbill, H.W. (1994). The ten commandments of cross-examination revisited. *Criminal Justice, 8*(4), 2–6, 51–54.

Asch, S.E. (1956). Studies of independence and conformity: A minority of one against a unanimous majority. *Psychological Monographs, 70,* 416.

Atiyah, P. & Summers, R. (1987). *Form and substance in Anglo-American Law.* Oxford: Clarendon.

Baker, D. (1999). Shredding the truth. *American Bar Association Journal, 85,* 40–44.

Baldus, D.C., Woodworth, G., & Pulaski, C.A. (1990). *Equal justice and the death penalty: A legal and empirical analysis.* Boston: Northeastern University Press.

Baldus, D.C., Woodworth, G., Zuckerman, D., Weiner, N.A., & Broffitt, B. (1998). Racial discrimination and the death penalty in the post-Furman era: An empirical and legal overview, with recent findings from Philadelphia. *Cornell Law Review, 83,* 1638–1770.

Baldwin, J. (1992). Legal advice in the police station. *New Law Journal, 142,* 1762–1764.

Baldwin, J. (1993). Police interview techniques: Establishing truth or proof? *British Journal of Criminology, 33,* 325–352.

Baldwin, J. (1994). Police interrogation: What are the rules of the game? In D. Morgan & G.M. Stephenson (Eds.), *Suspicion and silence: The right to silence in criminal investigations* (pp. 66–76). London: Blackstone.

Baldwin, J. & McConville, M. (1979). *Jury trials.* Oxford: Clarendon.

Balloff, R. (2000). Das Urteil des Bundesgerichtshofs vom 30. Juli 1999 zur Frage der wissenschaftlichen Anforderungen an aussagepsychologische Begutachtungen (Glaubhaftigkeitsgutachten) und die Folgen für die Sachverständigentätigkeit. *Praxis der Kinderpsychologie und Kinderpsychiatrie, 49,* 261–274.

Banks, C., Malloney, E., & Willock, H. (1975). Public attitudes to crime and the penal system. *British Journal of Criminology, 15,* 228–240.

Barone, M. (1999). *American politics in the second Tocquevillian age.* Lecture at the Hoover Institution, March 31, 1998.

Bayley, D.H. (1986). Ironies of law enforcement. In D.H. Bayley (Ed.), *Police and law enforcement* (Vol. 2, pp. 45–56). New York: National Affairs.

Bedau, H.A. & Radelet, M.L. (1987). Miscarriages of justice in potential capital cases. *Stanford Law Review, 40,* 21–179.

Beel, J. (1993). The French pre-trial system. In C. Walker & K. Starmer (Eds.), *Justice in error* (pp. 226–244). London: Blackstone.

Belloni, F. & Hodgson, J. (2000). *Criminal injustice: An evaluation of the criminal justice process in Britain.* New York: St. Martin.

Bender, R. & Nack, A. (1995). *Tatsachenfeststellungen vor Gericht [Evaluation of facts in courts of law] (2 vols.).* München: Beck.

Bentham, J. (1827). *Rationale of judicial evidence, specially applied to English practice,* edited by J. S. Mill. London: Hunt & Clarke.

Bentley, I. (1995). *Let him have justice: The true story of Derek Bentley, hanged for a crime he did not commit.* London: Sidwick & Jackson.

Berger, M. (1990). Legislating confession law in Great Britain: A statutory approach to police interrogations. *University Michigan Journal of Law Reform, 24,* 1–64.

Berkowitz, L. & Walster, E. (1976). *Equity theory: Toward a general theory of social interaction.* New York: Academic.

Berliner, L. & Conte, J.R. (1995). The effects of disclosure and intervention on sexually abused children. *Child Abuse and Neglect, 19,* 371–384.

Berti, A.E. & Ugolini, E. (1998). Developing knowledge of the judicial system: A domain-specific approach. *Journal of Genetic Psychology, 159,* 221–236.

Berufsverband Deutscher Psychologen e.V. (1988). *Richtlinien für die Erstellung Psychologischer Gutachten.* Bonn: Deutscher Psychologen Verlag.

Bevan, V. & Lidstone, K. (1985). *A guide to the Police and Criminal Evidence Act 1984.* London: Butterworths.

Bijnoord, A.G. (1989). *De zaak Ina Post.* Baarn: Ambo.

Blaauw, J.A. (1971). 99 tips voor het verhoor. *Algemeen Politieblad van het Koninkrijk der Nederlanden, 120,* 287–295.

Blaauw, J.A. (1996). *Verdacht van moord: Reconstructie van zes dubieuze Nederlandse moor donderzoeken.* Baarn: De Fontein.

Blaauw, J.A. (1998). Dubieuze verhoren, fatale gevolgen. *Justitiële Verkenningen, 24,* 47–60.

Blaauw, J.A. (2000). *De Puttense moordzaak: Reconstructie van een dubieus moordonderzoek.* Baarn: Fontein.

Black, R. (1999). *Black's law: A criminal lawyer reveals his defense strategies in four cliffhanger cases.* New York: Simon & Schuster.

Blackstone, W. (1769). *4 Commentaries on the laws of England 352.* Oxford: Clarendon.

Blok, A.J. & Besier, L.C. (1925). *Het Nederlandse strafproces* (Vol. II). Haarlem: Tjeenk Willink.

Blom-Cooper, L. (1997). *The Birmingham Six and other cases: Victims of circumstance.* London: Duckworth.

Blom-Cooper, L. & Brickell, S.J. (1998). *The un-fixing of the Birmingham bombing cover-up.* Canterbury: Brickell.

Blumenthal, S. & Lavender, T. (2000). *Violence and mental disorder.* Hereford: Zito Trust.

Boer, D.P., Hart, S.D., Kropp, P.R., & Webster, C.D. (1997). *Manual for the Sexual Violence Risk-20: Professional guidelines for assessing risk of sexual violence.* Vancouver: British Columbia Institute against Family Violence.

Bonitatibus, G., Godshall, S., Kelley, M., Levering, T., & Lynch, E. (1988). The role of social cognition in comprehension monitoring. *First Language, 8,* 287–298.

Borchard, E.M. (1932). *Convicting the innocent: Sixty-five actual errors of criminal justice.* Garden City: Doubleday.

Borchard, E.M. (1970). *Convicting the innocent: Errors of criminal justice.* New York: Da Capo.

Borum, R. (1996). Improving the clinical practice of violence risk assessment: Technology, guidelines, and training. *American Psychologist, 51,* 945–948.

Bossers, G. (1987). *Welk eene natie, die de jurij gehad heeft, en ze weder afschaft!* Delft: Eburon.

Boumans, T. & Kayzer, W. (1979). *De zaak Annie E.* Amsterdam: Bert Bakker.

Bradley, C. (1993a). The emerging international consensus as to criminal procedure rules. *Michigan Journal of International Law, 14,* 171–221.

Bradley, C. (1993b). The failure of the criminal procedure revolution. Durham, N.C.: Carolina Academic Press.

Braithwaite, J. (1989). *Crime, shame and reintegration*. Cambridge: Cambridge University Press.

Brandon, R. & Davies, C. (1973). *Wrongful imprisonment: Mistaken convictions and their consequences*. London: Allen and Unwin.

Brannon, L.C. (1994). The trauma of testifying in court for child victims of sexual assault v. the accused's right to confrontation. *Law and Psychology Review, 18*, 439–460.

Brehm, S.S., Kassin, S.M., & Fein, S. (1999). *Social psychology*. Boston: Houghton Mifflin.

Brekke, N.J., Enko, P.J., Clavet, G., & Seelau, E.P. (1991). Of juries and court-appointed experts: The impact of nonadversarial versus adversarial expert testimony. *Law and Human Behavior, 15*, 451–475.

Brennan, M. & Brennan, R.E. (1988). *Strange language: Child victims under cross-examination*. Riverina, Australia: Charles Stuart University.

Bright, S. (1994). Counsel for the poor: The death sentence not for the worst crime but for the worst lawyer. *Yale Law Journal, 103*, 1835–1883.

Broeders, A.P.A. (1999). Some observations on the use of probability scales in forensic identification. *Forensic Linguistics, 6*, 228–241.

Broekhuizen, A. (1991). 12 Jaar voor een natuurlijke dood. *Gay Krant* (29 augustus).

Bruck, M. (1998). The trials and tribulations of a novice expert witness. In S.J. Ceci & H. Hembrooke (Eds.), *Expert witnesses in child abuse cases: What can and should be said in court* (pp. 85–104). Washington, DC: American Psychological Association.

Bruck, M., Ceci, S.J., & Francoeur, E. (1999). The accuracy of mothers' memories of conversations with their preschool children. *Journal of Experimental Psychology: Applied, 5*, 89–106.

Bruinsma, F. (2001). Rechters in Nederland: Een NJB-enquête. *Nederlands Juristenblad, 76*, 1925–1934.

Bryant, R.A. & Harvey, A.G. (1998). Traumatic memories and pseudomemories in posttraumatic stress disorder. *Applied Cognitive Psychology, 12*, 81–88.

Bryce, J. (1891). *The American Commonwealth*. London: Macmillan.

Bugliosi, V. (1996). *Outrage: The five reasons why O.J. Simpson got away with murder*. New York: W.W. Norton.

Bull Kovera, M., Park, R.C., & Penrod, S.D. (1992). Jurors' perceptions of eyewitness and hearsay evidence. *Minnesota Law Review, 76*, 703–722.

Bull, R.H. (1981). Voice identification by man and machine: A review of research. In S. Lloyd-Bostock (Ed.), *Psychology in legal contexts: Applications and limitations* (pp. 28–42). Oxford: Macmillan.

Bull, R.H. (1999). Police investigative interviewing. In A. Memon & R.H. Bull (Eds.), *Handbook of the psychology of interviewing* (pp. 279–292). Chichester: Wiley.

Bullens, R.A.R. (Ed.). (1998). *Getuigedeskundigen in zedenzaken: De positie van de gedragswetenschapper bij strafzaken rondom seksueel misbruik van kinderen*. Leiden: DSWO Press, Rijksuniversiteit Leiden.

Burghard, W. (1976). Gegenüberstellungen in Ermittlungsverfahren [Lineup in criminal investigations]. In Verlaganstalt Deutsche Politzei (Ed.), *Taschenbuch für Kriminalisten* (pp. 87–114, Vol. 26). Hilden: Verlagsanstalt Deutsche Polizei.

Burgsmüller, C. (2000). Das BGH-Urteil zu den Glaubhaftigkeitsgutachten: Eine späte Folge der sog. Wormser Strafverfahren vor dem Landgericht Mainz? *Praxis der Rechtspsychologie, 10*(1), 48–59.

Bussey, K. (1992). Children's lying and truthfulness: Implications for children's testimony. In S.J. Ceci, M.D. Leichtman, & M. Putnick (Eds.), *Cognitive and social factors in early deception* (pp. 89–109). Hillsdale, NJ: Erlbaum.

Butcher, J.N., Dahlstrom, W.G., Graham, J.R., Tellegen, A., & Kaemmer, B. (1989). *Minnesota Multiphasic Personality Inventory-2 (MMPI-2): Manual for administration and scoring*. Minneapolis: University of Minnesota Press.

Callaghan, H. (1994). *Cruel fate: One man's triumph over injustice*. Dublin: Poolbeg.

Cameron, J.D. (1981). A judge in the jury box. *Judicature, 64*, 386 (letter to the editor).

Canon, B.C. (1977). Testing the effectiveness of civil liberties policies at the state and federal level: The case of the exclusionary rule. *American Political Quarterly, 5*, 57–84.

Canter, D.V. & Alison, L. (Eds.). (2001). *Profiling property crimes*. Aldershot: Ashgate.

Carrington, K., Dever, M., Hogg, R., Bargen, J., & Lohrey, A. (Eds.). (1991). *Travesty!: Miscarriages of justice*. Leichhart, NSW: Pluto.

Carter, C.A., Bottoms, B.L., & Levine, M.L. (1996). Linguistic and socioemotional influences on the accuracy of children's reports. *Law and Human Behavior, 20*, 335–358.

Cashmore, J. & Bussey, K. (1989). Children's conceptions of the witness role. In J.R. Spencer, G. Nicholson, R. Flin, & R. Bull (Eds.), *Children's evidence in legal proceedings: An International perspective* (pp. 117–187). Cambridge: Spencer.

Casper, G. & Zeisel, H. (1972). Lay judges in the German criminal courts. *Journal of Legal Studies, 1*, 135–191.

Cassell, P.G. (1996). Miranda's costs: An empirical reassessment. *Northwestern University Law Review, 90*, 387–499.

Cassell, P.G. & Fowles, R. (1998). Handcuffing the cops? A thirty-year perspective on Miranda's harmful effects on law enforcement. *Stanford Law Review, 50*, 1055–1145.

Cassell, P.G. & Hayman, B.S. (1996). Police interrogations in the 1990s: An empirical study of the effects of Miranda. *UCLA Law Review, 43*, 839–931.

Cassese, A. & Röling, B.V.A. (1993). *The Tokyo trial and beyond*. Cambridge: Polity Press.

Cecil, J.S. & Willging, J.E. (1993). *Court-appointed experts: Defining the role of experts appointed under federal rule of evidence 706*. Washington, DC: Federal Judicial Center.

Chamberlain, L. (1990). *Through my eyes: An autobiography*. Port Melbourne, Vic.: Heinemann.

Champion, D. (1994). *Measuring offender risk: A criminal justice sourcebook*. Westport, CT: Greenwood.

Chemineau, J. (1983). *Erreur judiciaire: Affaire Paul Chemineau*. Paris: Pensee universelle.

Cherryman, J. (2000). Police investigative interviewing: Skill analysis and concordance of evaluations. (unpublished PhD thesis, University of Portsmouth).

Chu, J.A., Frey, L.M., Ganzel, B.L., & Matthews, J.A. (1999). Memories of childhood abuse: Dissociation, amnesia, and corroboration. *American Journal of Psychiatry, 156*, 749–755.

Cleiren, C.P.M. & Nijboer, J.F. (Eds.). (1997). *Strafvordering: Tekst en commentaar* (2nd ed.). Deventer: Kluwer.

Cleiren, C.P.M. & Nijboer, J.F. (Eds.). (1999). *Tekst en commentaar strafvordering* (3rd ed.). Deventer: Kluwer.

Clifford, B.R. & Bull, R.H. (1978). *The psychology of person identification*. London: Routledge & Kegan Paul.

Cocozza, J. & Steadman, H. (1976). The failure of psychiatric predictions of dangerousness: Clear and convincing evidence. *Rutgers Law Review, 29*, 1084–1101.

Code de Procédure Pénale. (1988). F.B. Rothman: Littleton, Colo. (English translation by Kock, G.L. & Frase, R.).

Cohen, R.L. (1987). Distributive justice: Theory and research. *Social Justice Research, 1*, 19–41.

Commissie Herijking Wetboek van Strafvordering. (1990). *Herziening van het gerechtelijk vooronderzoek*. Arnhem: Gouda Quint (commissie Moons).

Connors, E., Lundregan, T., Miller, N., & McEwan, T. (1996). *Convicted by juries, exonerated by science: Case studies in the use of DNA evidence to establish innocence after trial*. Alexandria, VA: National Institute for Justice (NIH Research Report, US Department of Justice).

Cordon, I.M. (2000). *Facilitating children's accurate responses: Conversational rules and interview style.* Unpublished master's thesis. California State University, Northridge.

Corstens, G.J.M. (1993). *Het Nederlandse strafprocesrecht.* Arnhem: Gouda Quint.

Corstens, G.J.M. (1995). *Het Nederlandse strafprocesrecht* (2nd ed.). Arnhem: Gouda Quint.

Corstens, G.J.M. (1999). *Het Nederlands strafprocesrecht* (3rd ed.). Arnhem: Gouda Quint.

Cosgrove, J.M. & Patterson, C.J. (1978). Generalization of training for children's listener skills. *Child Development, 49,* 513–516.

Criminal Procedure Code Germany. (1973). (3rd ed.). London: Sweet & Maxwell (English translation by H. Niebler).

Crispin, K. (1987). *Lindy Chamberlain: The full story.* Boise, ID: Pacific.

Crombag, H.F.M. (1992). On the Europeanisation of criminal procedure. In B. de Witte & C. Forder (Eds.), *The common law of Europe and the future of legal education* (pp. 397–414). Deventer: Kluwer.

Crombag, H.F.M. (1997). Evidentiary standards in sexual abuse cases in Continental European legal systems. In J.D. Read & D.S. Lindsay (Eds.), *Recollections of trauma: Scientific evidence and clinical practice* (pp. 501–504). New York: Plenum.

Crombag, H.F.M. & Merckelbach, H.L.G.J. (1996). *Hervonden herinneringen en andere* misverstanden. Amsterdam: Contact.

Crombag, H.F.M., van Koppen, P.J., & Wagenaar, W.A. (1994). *Dubieuze zaken: De psychologie van strafrechtelijk bewijs.* Amsterdam: Contact (2e herziene druk).

Cutler, B.L. & Fisher, R.P. (1990). Live lineups, videotaped lineups, and photoarrays. *Forensic Reports, 3,* 439–448.

Cutler, B.L. & Penrod, S.D. (1995). *Mistaken identification: The eyewitness, psychology, and the law.* Cambridge: Cambridge University Press.

Cutler, B.L., Berman, G.L., Penrod, S.D., & Fisher, R.P. (1993). Conceptual, practical, and empirical issues associated with eyewitness identification. In D.F. Ross, J.D. Read & M.P. Toglia (Eds.), *Adult eyewitness testimony: Current trends and developments* (pp. 163–181). Cambridge: Cambridge University Press.

Cutler, B.L., Fisher, R.P., & Chicvara, C.L. (1989). Eyewitness identification from live versus videotaped lineups. *Forensic Reports, 2,* 93–106.

Damaška, M.R. (1973). Evidentiary barriers to conviction and two models of criminal procedure: A comparative study. *University of Pennsylvania Law Review, 121,* 506–589.

Damaška, M.R. (1986). *The faces of justice and state authority: A comparative approach to the legal process.* New Haven, CT: Yale University Press.

Damaška, M.R. (1997). *Evidence law adrift.* New Haven: Yale University Press.

Damaška, M.R. (1998). Truth in adjudication. *Hastings Law Journal, 49,* 289–308.

Dann, B.M. (1993). 'Learning lessons' and 'speaking rights': Creating educated and democratic juries. *Indiana Law Journal, 68,* 1229–1279.

Darden, C.A. (1996). *In contempt.* Thorndike: Hall.

Davies, E. & Seymour, F.W. (1997). Child witnesses in the criminal courts: Furthering New Zealand's commitment to the United Nations Convention on the Rights of the Child. *Psychiatry, Psychology, and Law, 4,* 13–24.

Davies, G. (1999). The impact of television on the presentation and reception of children's testimony. *International Journal of Law and Psychiatry, 22,* 241–256.

Davies, G. & Noon, E. (1993). Video links: Their impact on child witness trials. *Issues in Criminological and Legal Psychology, 20,* 22–26.

Davies, G.M. (1988). Faces and places: Laboratory research on context and face recognition. In G.M. Davies & D.M. Thomson (Eds.), *Memory in context: context in memory* (pp. 35–53). London: Wiley.

Davies, G.M. & Milne, A. (1982). Recognizing faces in and out of context. *Current Psychological Research, 2,* 235–246.

Davies, G.M., Shepherd, J., & Ellis, H. (1979). Effects of interpolated mugshot exposure on accuracy of eyewitness identification. *Journal of Applied Psychology, 64,* 232–237.

Davies, T.Y. (1974). Critique: On the limitations of empirical evaluations of the exclusionary rule: A critique of the Spiotto research and United States v. Calandra. *Northwestern University Law Review, 69,* 740–798.

Davies, T.Y. (1983). A hard look at what we know (and still need to learn) about the "costs" of the exclusionary rule: The NIJ study and other studies of "lost" arrests. *American Bar Foundation Research Journal, 1983,* 611–698.

Dawes, R.M. (1994). *House of cards: Psychology and psychotherapy built on myth.* New York: Free Press.

de Keijser, J.W. (2000). *Punishment and purpose: From moral theory to punishment in action.* Amsterdam: Thela Thesis.

de Ruiter, C. (2000). Persoonlijkheidsstoornissen en delinquent gedrag, milieutherapie in een forensisch psychiatrisch ziekenhuis. [Personality disorders and delinquent behavior: Milieutherapy in a forensic psychiatric hospital]. In C. Janzing, A. van den Berg, & F. Kruisdijk (Eds.), *Handboek voor mileutherapie: Theorie en praktijk van de klinische psychotherapie. [Handbook for milieutherapy: The theory and practice of clinical psychotherapy]* (pp. 56–71). Assen, the Netherlands: Van Gorcum.

de Ruiter, C. (2000). *Voor verbetering vatbaar.* [*In need of correction*]. Amsterdam, the Netherlands: Vossiuspers AUP. [Inaugural address University of Amsterdam].

de Tocqueville, A. (1948/1969). *Democracy in America.* New York: Harper & Row (Translation J.P. Mayer ed. & G. Lawrence).

de Tocqueville, A.C.H.M.C. (1863). *Democracy in America* (2nd ed.). Cambridge, MA: Sever and Francis.

Death Penalty Information Center (DPIC). (2001a). *Death row USA, winter 2001.* <http://www.deathpenaltyinfo.org/DeathRowUSA1.html> (visited 4/04/01).

Death Penalty Information Center (DPIC). (2001b). *Executions in the U.S. 1999.* <http://www.deathpenaltyinfo.org/dpicexec99.html.> (visited 4/04/01).

Death Penalty Information Center (DPIC). (2001c). *Innocence and the death penalty.* <http://www.deathpenaltyinfo.org/innoc.html.> (visited 4/04/01).

Deffenbacher, K.A., Brown, E.L., & Sturgill, W. (1978). Some predictors of eyewitness memory accuracy. In M.M. Gruneberg, P.E. Morris, & R.N. Sykes (Eds.), *Practical aspects of memory* (pp. 219–226). London: Academic.

Dekens, K.M.K. & van der Sleen, J. (1997). *Het kind als getuige: theorie en praktijk van het verhoor.* 's-Gravenhage: VUGA.

Dekle, D.J., Beale, C.R., Elliot, R., & Huneycutt, D. (1996). Children as witnesses: A comparison of lineup versus showup methods. *Applied Cognitive Psychology, 10,* 1–12.

Dennis, I. (1993). Miscarriages of justice and the law of confessions: Evidentiary issues and solutions. *Public Law, 1993,* 291–313.

Dent, H.R. & Stephenson, G.M. (1979). Identification evidence: Experimental investigations of factors affecting the reliability of juvenile and adult witnesses. In D.P. Farrington, K. Hawkins, & S.M.A. Lloyd-Bostock (Eds.), *Psychology, law and legal processes* (pp. 195–206). London: Macmillan.

Dernevik, M. (1999). *Implementing risk assessment procedures in a forensic psychiatric setting.* Paper presented at the joint conference of the American Psychology-Law Society and the European Association of Psychology and Law. Dublin, Ireland.

Dershowitz, A.M. (1982). *The best defense.* New York: Random House.

Devenport, J.L., Stinson, V., Cutler, B.L., & Kravitz, D.A. (in press). How effective are the expert testimony and cross-examination safeguards? Jurors' perceptions of the suggestiveness and fairness of biased lineup procedures. *Journal of Applied Psychology.*

Devitt, E.J. (1974). Federal civil jury trials should be abolished. *American Bar Association Journal, 60*, 570–574.

Devlin, J. (1998). Genetics and justice: An indigent defendant's right to DNA expert assistance. *The University of Chicago Legal Forum, 1998*, 395–423.

DeVyver, K.I. (1999). Comment: Opening the door but keeping the lights off: *Kumho Tire v. Carmichael* and the applicability of the Daubert Test to nonscientific evidence. *Case Western Reserve Law Review, 50*, 177–202.

Diamond, S.S. (1983). Order in the court: Consistency in criminal court decisions. In C.T. Schreirer & B.L. Hammonds (Eds.), *Psychology and the law* (pp. 123–146). Washington, DC: American Psychological Association (The Master Lecture Series, Vol. II).

Diamond, S.S. (1990). Revising images of public punitiveness: Sentencing by lay and professional English magistrates. *Law and Social Inquiry, 15*, 191–221.

Diamond, S.S. & Casper, J.D. (1992). Blindfolding the jury to verdict consequences: Damages, experts, and the civil jury. *Law and Society Review, 26*, 513–563.

Diamond, S.S. & Schklar, J. (1998). The jury: How does law matter? In B.G. Garth & A. Sarat (Eds.), *How does law matter?* (pp. 191–226). Evanston, IL: Northwestern University Press.

Diamond, S.S. & Stalans, L.J. (1989). The myth of judicial leniency in sentencing. *Behavioral Sciences and the Law, 7*, 73–89.

Diamond, S.S. & Vidmar, N. (2001). Jury room ruminations on forbidden topics. *University of Virginia Law Review, 87*, 1857–1915.

Diamond, S.S. & Zeisel, H. (1975). Sentencing councils: A study of sentence disparity and its reduction. *University of Chicago Law Review, 43*, 109–149.

Diamond, S.S., Casper, J.D., & Ostergren, L. (1989). Blindfolding the jury. *Law and Contemporary Problems, 52*, 247–267.

Diamond, S.S., Ellis, L. & Schmidt, E. (1997). Realistic responses to the limitations of Batson v. Kentucky (106 S. Ct. 1712 (1996)). *Cornell Journal of Law and Public Policy, 7*, 77–95.

Dickey, W.J. & Hollenhorst, P. (1999). Three-strikes laws: Five years later. *Corrections Management Quarterly, 3*, 1–18.

Dickson, B. (1993). The prevention of terrorism acts. In C. Walker & K. Starmer (Eds.), *Justice in error* (pp. 178–194). London: Blackstone.

Dickson, W.P. (1981). *Children's oral communication skills*. New York: Academic Press.

Dienst Justitiële Inrichtingen. (1999). *Facts in figures*. Den Haag.: Lakerveld.

Dillon, W. (1987). *Broken pieces*. Houston: Laser.

Donohue, J.J. (1998). Did Miranda diminish police effectiveness? *Stanford Law Review, 50*, 1147–1181.

Dorado, J.S. (1999). Remembering incest: The complexities of this process and implications for civil statutes of limitations. In L.W. Williams & V.L. Banyard (Eds.), *Trauma and memory* (pp. 93–111). Thousand Oaks, CA: Sage.

Douglas, K.S. & Webster, C.D. (1999). The HCR-20 violence risk assessment scheme: Concurrent validity in a sample of incarcerated offenders. *Criminal Justice and Behavior, 26*, 3–19.

Douglas, K.S., Ogloff, J.R.P., Nicholls, T.L., & Grant, I. (1999). Assessing risk for violence among psychiatric patients: The HCR-20 violence risk assessment scheme and the Psychopathy Checklist: Screening version. *Journal of Consulting and Clinical Psychology, 67*, 917–930.

Douglass, J.G. (2000). Balancing hearsay and criminal discovery. *Fordham Law Review, 68*, 2097–2197.

Dozy, R.A. (2000). Herziening van het gerechtelijk vooronderzoek. *Trema, 2000*, 49–59.

Draijer, N. & Langeland, W. (1999). Childhood trauma and perceived parental dysfunction in the etiology of dissociative symptoms in psychiatric inpatients. *American Journal of Psychiatry, 156*, 379–385.

du Cann, C.G.L. (1960). *Miscarriages of justice*. London: Muller.

Dwyer, J., Neufeld, P., & Scheck, B. (2000). *Actual innocence: Five days to execution and other dispatches from the wrongly convicted*. New York: Doubleday.

Ebermayer, E. (1965). *Sie waren unschuldig: Fehlurteile in Namen der Gerechtigkeit*. Köln: Lübbe.

Eisenberg, U. (1995). Visuelle und auditive Gegenüberstellung im Strafverfahren [Visual and voice lineups in criminal investigations]. *Kriminalistik, 7*, 458–465.

Endres, J. (1997). The suggestibility of the child witness: The role of individual differences and their assessment. *Journal of Credibility Assessment and Witness Psychology, 1*, 44–67.

Engelmayer, S.D. & Wagman, R. (1985). *Lord's justice*. Garden City, NY: Anchor.

Ennis B.J & Litwack T.R. (1974). Psychiatry and the presumption of expertise: Flipping coins in the courtroom. *California Law Review 62*, 693–752.

Enschede, C.J. (1966). Bewijzen in het strafrecht. *Rechtsgeleerd Magazijn Themis*, 488–518.

European Committee for the Prevention of Torture and Inhuman and Degrading Treatment or Punishment (CPT). (1998). *Report to the Netherlands government on the visit to The Netherlands carried out by the European Committee for the Prevention of Torture and Inhuman and Degrading Treatment or Punishment (CPT) from 17 to 27 November 1997*. Strasbourg: Council of Europe.

Evans, R. (1993). *The conduct of police interviews with juveniles*. Royal Commission on Criminal Justice Report. London: Her Majesty's Stationery Office.

Evans, R. (1994). Police interviews with juveniles. In D. Morgan & G.M. Stephenson (Eds.), *Suspicion and silence: The right to silence in criminal investigations* (pp. 77–90). London: Blackstone.

Evett, I.W. & Williams, R.L. (1996). A review of the sixteen points fingerprint standard in England and Wales. *Journal of the Forensic Identification, 46*, 49–73.

Ewin, D.M. (1994). Many memories retrieved with hypnosis are accurate. *American Journal of Clinical Hypnosis, 36*, 174–176.

Exner, J.E. (1993). *The Rorschach: A comprehensive system* (3rd ed., Vol. 1). New York: Wiley.

Fabian, T., Stadler, M., & Wetzels, P. (1995). The "authenticity error" in real lineup procedures. Effects of suspect-status and corresponding psychological dissimilarities between target person and distractors: An experimental study. In G.M. Davies, S.M.A. Lloyd-Bostock, M. McMurran, & C. Wilson (Eds.), *Psychology, law, and criminal justice: International developments in research and practice* (pp. 29–38). Berlin: De Gruyter.

Faigman, D.L., Kaye, D.H., Saks, M.J., & Sanders, J. (Eds.). (1997). *Modern scientific evidence: The law and science of expert testimony* (3rd ed.). St. Paul: West.

Faigman, D.L., Kaye, D.H., Saks, M.J., & Sanders, J. (Eds.). (1999). *Modern scientific evidence: The law and science of expert testimony, Supplement*. St. Paul, MI: West.

False Memory Syndrome Foundation. (1997). Family survey update. *False Memory Syndrome Foundation Newsletter, 6*(4), 3–4.

Farrington, D.P. & Hawkins, K. (1979). Psychological research on behaviour in legal contexts. In D. Farrington, K. Hawkins., & S. Lloyd-Bostock (Eds.), *Psychology, law, and legal processes* (pp. 134–156). London: Macmillan.

Federal Bureau of Investigation (FBI). (2001). *Murder and nonnegligent manslaughter*. <http://www.fbi.gov/ucr/Cius_99/99crime/99c2_03.pdf> (visited 4/04/01).

Federal Judicial Center. (1994). *Reference manual on scientific evidence*. Washington: Federal Judicial Center.

Feeny, F. (2000). Police clearances: A poor way to measure the impact of Miranda on the police. *Rutgers Law Journal, 32*, 1–114.

Feldman, D. (1990). Regulating treatment of suspects in police stations: Judicial interpretation of detention provisions in the police and criminal evidence act 1984. *Criminal Law Review, 1990*, 452–496.

Feldman, D. (1999). England: Rules of criminal procedure. In C. Bradley (Ed.), *Criminal procedure: a worldwide study* (pp. 99–142). Durham, NC: Carolina Academic Press.

Field, S., Alldridge, P. & Jörg, N. (1995). Prosecutors, examining judges, and control of police investigations. In P. Fennell, C. Harding, N. Jörg, B. Swart (Eds.), *Criminal justice in Europe: A comparative study* (pp. 227–250). Oxford: Clarendon.

Fijnaut, C. (1983). *De zaak François: Beschouwingen naar aanleiding van het vonnis.* Antwerpen: Kluwer.

Fijnaut, C. (1988). *De toelating van raadslieden tot het politiële verdachtenverhoor.* Arnhem: Gouda Quint.

Fijnaut, C. (1998). Het politiele verdachtenverhoor: Naar de audio-visuele registratie. *Justitiële Verkenningen, 24,* 118–127.

Flavell, J.H., Speer, J.R., Green, F.L., & August, D.L. (1981). The development of comprehension monitoring and knowledge about communication. *Monographs of the Society for Research in Child Development, 46,* 1–65 (65 Serial No. 192).

Flehner, M. (1979). Note, Jury trials in complex litigation. *St. John's Law Review, 53,* 751-XX.

Flin, R.H., Stevenson, Y. & Davies, G.M. (1989). Children's knowledge of court proceedings. *British Journal of Psychology, 80,* 285–297.

Floroit, R. (1968). *Les erreurs judiciares.* Paris: Flammarion.

FMS Foundation. (1997). Family survey update. *FMS Foundation Newsletter, 6* (March), 3–4.

Folsom, J.R. (1994). *Reversible errors in federal criminal cases: A digest of criminal cases reversed by the* United *States Supreme Court and the Circuit Courts of Appeals.* Fort Worth, TX: Knowles.

Fortescue, J. (1616). *De laudibus legum Angliae 62.* London: Companie of Stationers.

Foster, K.R. & Huber, P.W. (1997). *Judging science: Scientific knowledge and the federal courts.* Cambridge, MA: MIT Press.

Frank, J.N. (1950). *Courts on trial: Myth and reality in American justice* (2nd ed.). Princeton, NJ: Princeton University Press.

Frank, J.N. & Frank, B. (1957). *Not guilty.* New York: Doubleday.

Frankel, F.H. (1996). Dissociation: The clinical realities. *American Journal of Psychiatry, 153,* 64–70 (Festschrift Supplement).

Frasca, J. (1968). *The mulberry tree.* Englewood Cliffs, NJ: Prentice-Hall.

Frase, R.S. (1990). Comparative criminal justice as a guide to American law reform: How do the French do it, how can we find out and why should we care? *California Law Review, 78,* 539–683.

Frase, R.S. (1999). France: Rules of criminal procedure. In C. Bradley (Ed.), *Criminal procedure: a worldwide study* (pp. 143–185). Durham, NC: Carolina Academic Press.

Frase, R.S. & Weigend, T. (1997). German criminal justice as a guide to American law reform: Similar problems, better solutions? *Boston College International and Comparative Law Review, 18,* 317–360.

Frazier, P. & Borgida, E. (1997). Rape trauma syndrome. In D.L. Faigman, D.H. Kaye, M.J. Saks, & J. Sanders (Eds.), *Modern scientific evidence: The law and science of expert testimony* (pp. 402–435). St. Paul, MN: West.

Freckelton, I.R. (1987). *The trial of the expert: A study of expert evidence and forensic experts.* Melbourne: Oxford University Press.

Freshwater, K. & Aldridge, J. (1994). The knowledge and fears about court of child witnesses, school children and adults. *Child Abuse Review, 3,* 183–195.

Fulero, S.M. & Everington, C. (1995). Assessing competency to waive Miranda rights in defendants with mental retardation. *Law and Human Behavior, 19,* 533–543.

Fuller, L.L. (1968). The adversary system. In H.J. Bennan (Ed.), *Talks on American law.* New York: Vintage.

Gallup Organization. (2001). *Survey.* http://www.gallup.com/poll/releases/pr011205.asp and http://www.gallup.com/poll/releases/pr990322.asp.

Gardner, E.S. (1952). *Court of last resort*. New York: Sloane.

Garé, D. (1994). *Het onmiddelijkheidsbeginsel in het Nederlandse strafproces*. Arnhem: Gouda Quint.

Geller, W. (1993). *Police videotaping of suspect interrogations and confessions: A preliminary examination of issues and practices*. Washington, DC: National Institute of Justice.

General Accounting Office, U.S.G. (1990). *Death penalty sentencing: Research indicates pattern of racial disparities*. (Report to Senate and House Committees on the Judiciary [GAO/GGD-90-57]).

George, T.E. (1999). The dynamics and determinants of the decision to grant en banc review. *Washington Law Review, 74*, 213–294.

Gershman, B.L. (1997). *Trial error and misconduct*. Charlottesville, VA: Lexis Law.

Giannelli, P.C. (1991). Criminal discovery, scientific evidence, and DNA. *Vanderbilt Law Review, 44*, 791–825.

Giannelli, P.C. (1993a). Expert testimony and the confrontation clause. *Capital University Law Review, 22*, 45–84.

Giannelli, P.C. (1993b). Junk science: The criminal cases. *Journal of Criminal Law and Criminology, 84*, 105–128.

Giannelli, P.C. (1997). The abuse of scientific evidence in criminal cases: The need for independent crime laboratories. *Virginia Journal of Social Policy and Law, 4*, 439–477.

Gilligan, O. (Ed.). (1990). *The Birmingham Six: An appalling vista*. Dublin: Literéire Publishers.

Gniech, G. & Stadler, M. (1981). Die Wahlgegenüberstellung: Methodische Probleme des kriminalistischen Wiedererkennungsexperiments [The lineup: Methodological problems of person identification procedures]. *Strafverteidiger, 1*, 565–570.

Godwin, G.M. (Ed.). (2000). *Criminal psychology and forensic technology: A collaborative approach to effective profiling*. Boca Raton, FL: CRC Press.

Going, M. & Read, J.D. (1974). Effects of uniqueness, sex of subject and sex of photograph on facial recognition. *Perceptual and Motor Skills, 39*, 109–110.

Golding, J.M., Sanchez, R.P., & Sego, S.A. (1997). The believability of hearsay testimony on a child sexual assault trial. *Law and Human Behavior, 21*, 299–325.

Goldman, R.E. (1993). *The modern art of cross-examination*. Englewood Cliffs, NJ: Prentice-Hall.

Goodman, G.S. (1984). Children's testimony in historical perspective. *Journal of Social Issues, 40*, 9–31.

Goodman, G.S. & Bottoms, B.L. (Eds.). (1993). *Child victims, child witnesses: Understanding and improving testimony*. New York: Guilford.

Goodman, G.S. & Lloyd, D.W. (1988). The child witness: Evaluation and preparation. In D.C. Bross, R.D. Krugman, M.R. Lenherr, D.A. Rosenberg, & B.D. Schmitt (Eds.), *The new child protection handbook* (pp. 414–441). New York: Garland.

Goodman, G.S., Golding, J.M., & Haith, M.M. (1984). Jurors' reactions to child witnesses. *Journal of Social Issues, 40*, 139–156.

Goodman, G.S., Quas, J.A., Bulkley, J., & Shapiro, C. (1999). Innovations for child witnesses: A national survey. *Psychology, Public Policy, and Law, 5*, 255–281.

Goodman, G.S., Taub, E.P., Jones, D.P.H., England, P., Port, L.K., Rudy, L., & Prado, L. (1992). Testifying in criminal court: Emotional effects on child sexual assault victims. *Monographs of the Society for Research in Child Development, 57*, 1–142 (145, Serial No. 229).

Goodman, G.S., Tobey, A.E., Batterman Faunce, J.M., Orcutt, H., Thomas, S., Shapiro, C., & Sachsenmaier, T. (1998). Face-to-face confrontation: Effects of closed-circuit technology on children's eyewitness testimony and jurors' decisions. *Law and Human Behavior, 22*, 165–203.

Gorenstein, G.W. & Ellsworth, P.C. (1980). Effect of choosing an incorrect photograph on a later identification by an eyewitness. *Journal of Applied Psychology, 65*, 616–622.

Gorr, M. (2000). The morality of plea bargaining. *Social Theory and Practice, 26*, 129–151.

Graham, K.J. (1972). The right to confrontation and the hearsay rule: Sir Walter Raleigh loses another one. *Criminal Law Bulletin, 8*, 99.

Greenberg, S.A. & Shuman, D.W. (1997). Irreconcilable conflict between therapeutic and forensic roles. *Professional Psychology: Research and Practice, 28,* 50–57.

Greenhouse, L. (2002). Rehnquist says courts risk losing private-sector nominees. *New York Times,* p. 16.

Greer, S.C. (1994). Miscarriages of criminal justice reconsidered. *The Modern Law Review, 57,* 58–74.

Greeven, P.G.J. (1997). *De intramurale behandeling van forensisch psychiatrische patiënten met een persoonlijkheidsstoornis: een empirisch studie [Treatment outcome in personality disordered forensic patients: An empirical study].* Deventer, the Netherlands: Gouda Quint (diss. University of Utrecht).

Grice, H.P. (1975). Logic and conversation. In P. Cole & J.L. Morgan (Eds.), *Syntax and semantics: Speech acts* (Vol. 3, pp. 41–58). New York: Academic.

Grisso, T. & Lovinguth, T. (1982). Lawyers and child clients: A call for research. In J.S. Henning (Ed.), *The rights of children: Legal and psychological perspectives* (pp. 214–238). Springfield, IL: Thomas.

Gross, H. & Geerds, F. (1978). *Handbuch der Kriminalistik [Handbook of forensic sciences] (2 vols.)* (10th ed.). Berlin: Schweitzer.

Gross, S.R. (1987). Loss of innocence: Eyewitness identification and proof of guilt. *Journal of Legal Studies, 16,* 395–453.

Gross, S.R. (1991). Expert evidence. *Wisconsin Law Review, 1991,* 1113–1232.

Gross, S.R. (1994). The romance of revenge: Capital punishment in America. *Studies in Law, Policy and Society, 13,* 71–104.

Gross, S.R. (1995). Substance and form in scientific evidence: What Daubert didn't do. *Shepard's Expert and Scientific Evidence Quarterly, 3,* 129.

Gross, S.R. (1996). The risks of death: Why erroneous convictions are common in capital cases. *Buffalo Law Review, 44,* 469–500.

Gross, S.R. (1998). Lost lives: Miscarriages of justice in capital cases. *Law and Contemporary Problems, 61,* 125–149.

Gross, S.R. & Ellsworth, P. (in press). Second thoughts: Americans' views on the death penalty at the turn of the century. In S. Garvey (Ed.), *Beyond repair?: America's death penalty.* Durham, NC: Duke University Press.

Gross, S.R. & Mauro, R. (1989). *Death and discrimination: Racial disparities in capital sentencing.* Boston: Northeastern University Press.

Grove, W., Zald, D., Lebow, B., Snitz, B., & Nelson, C. (2000). Clinical versus mechanical prediction: A meta-analysis. *Psychological Assessment, 12,* 19–30.

Gruhl, J. & Spohn, C. (1981). The Supreme Court's post-Miranda rulings: Impact on local prosecutors. *Law and Policy Quarterly, 3,* 29–42.

Grünwald, G. (1981). Probleme der Gegenüberstellung zum Zwecke der Wiedererkennung [Problems of lineups for person identification]. *Juristenzeitung, 36,* 423–429.

Gudjonsson, G.H. (1992). *The psychology of interrogations, confessions, and testimony.* Chichester: Wiley.

Gudjonsson, G.H. (1993). Confession evidence, psychological vulnerability and expert testimony. *Journal of Community and Applied Social Psychology, 3,* 117–129.

Gudjonsson, G.H. (1994a). Investigative interviewing: Recent developments and some fundamental issues. *International Review of Psychiatry, 6,* 237–245.

Gudjonsson, G.H. (1994b). Psychological vulnerability: Suspects at risk. In D. Morgan & G.M. Stephenson (Eds.), *Suspicions and silence: The right to silence in criminal investigations* (pp. 91–106). London: Blackstone.

Gudjonsson, G.H. (1995). The effects of interrogative pressure on strategic coping. *Psychology, Crime, and Law, 1,* 309–318.

Gudjonsson, G.H. (1997). Accusations by adults of childhood sexual abuse: A survey of the members of the British False Memory Society (BFMS). *Applied Cognitive Psychology, 11,* 3–18.

Gudjonsson, G.H. (1999). Police interviewing and disputed confessions. In A. Memon & R.H. Bull (Eds.), *Handbook of the psychology of interviewing* (pp. 327–341). Chichester: Wiley.

Guthrie, C., Rachlinski, J.J., & Wistrich, A.J. (2001). Inside the judicial mind. *Cornell Law Review, 86,* 777–830.

Gutwirth, S. & de Hert, P. (2001). Een theoretische onderbouw voor een legitiem strafproces. *Delikt en Delinkwent, 31,* 1048–1087.

Haber, L. & Haber, R.N. (1998). Criteria for judging the admissibility of eyewitness testimony of long past events. *Psychology, Public Policy, and Law, 4,* 1135–1159.

Hagen, M.A. (1997). *Whores of the court: The fraud of psychiatric testimony and the rape of American justice.* New York: HarperCollins.

Hale, L. (1961). *Hanged in error.* Harmondsworth: Penguin.

Hale, M. (1736). *The history of the pleas of the Crown 289.* In the Savoy: E. & R. Nutt & R. Gosling.

Hamilton, A., Madison, J., & Jay, J. (1961). The Federalist, No. 83. In C. Rossiter (Ed.), *The Federalist papers* (originally published 1788). New York: New American Library.

Hans, V.P. & Vidmar, N.J. (1986). *Judging the jury.* New York: Plenum.

Harding, C., Swart, B., Jörg, N., & Fennell, P. (1995). Europeanization and convergence: The lessons of comparative study. In P. Fennell, C. Harding, N. Jörg, & B. Swart (Eds.), *Criminal justice in Europe: A comparative study.* Oxford: Clarendon.

Hare, R.D. (1991). *Manual for the Hare Psychopathy Checklist-Revised* (3rd ed.). Toronto: Multi-Health Systems.

Hare, R.D., Vertommen, H., Verheul, R., & de Ruiter, C. (2000). *Dutch translation of the PCL-R.* Toronto: Multi Health Systems.

Hargie, O. & Tourish, D. (1999). The psychology of interpersonal skill. In A. Memon & R. Bull (Eds.), *Handbook of the psychology of interviewing* (pp. 71–87). Chichester: Wiley.

Harris, D.A. (1990). Ake (*Ake v. Oklahoma,* 105 S. Ct. 1087) revisited: Expert psychiatric witnesses remain beyond the reach for the indigent. *North Carolina Law Review, 68,* 763–783.

Harris, D.A. (1992). The constitution and truth seeking: A new theory on expert services for indigent defendants. *Journal of Criminal Law and Criminology, 83,* 469–525.

Harris, G.T., Rice, M.E., & Quinsey, V.L. (1993). Violent recidivism of mentally disordered offenders: The development of a statistical prediction instrument. *Criminal Justice and Behavior, 20,* 315–335.

Harris, L. (1989). Judges' opinions on procedural issues: a survey of state and federal trial judges who spend at least half their time on general civil cases. *Boston University Law Review, 69,* 731–763.

Hart, S., Cox, D., & Hare, R. (1995). *The Hare Psychopathy Checklist: Screening Version.* Toronto: Multi-Health Systems.

Hatakka, M., & Klami, H.T. (1990). *Beweismass und Irrtumsrisiko.* Helsinki: Suomalainen Tiedeakatemia.

Haugaard, J.J., & Reppucci, N.D. (1992). Children and the truth. In S.J. Ceci, M.D. Leichtman, & M. Putnick (Eds.), *Cognitive and social factors in early deception* (pp. 29–45). Hillsdale, NJ: Erlbaum.

Haugaard, J.J., Reppucci, N.D., Laird, J., & Nauful, T. (1991). Children's definitions of the truth and their competency as witnesses in legal proceedings. *Law and Human Behavior, 15,* 253–271.

Haydock, R.S. & Sonsteng, J. (1999). *Trial advocacy before judges, jurors and arbitrators* (2nd ed.). St. Paul, MI: West.

Haydock, R.S., Herr, D.F., & Stempel, J.W. (2001). *Fundamentals of pretrial litigation* (5th ed.). St. Paul, MI: West.

Hazelwood, R.R. & Burgess, A.W. (Eds.). (2001). *Practical aspects of rape investigation: A multi-disciplinary approach* (3rd ed.). Boca Raton, FL: CRC Press.

Heffernan, W.C. & Lovely, R.W. (1991). Evaluating the fourth amendment exclusionary rule: The problem of police compliance with the law. *University Michigan Journal of Law Reform, 24,* 311–392.

Hellmann, U. (1998). *Strafprozeßrecht.* Berlin: Springer.

Hellwig, A. (1951). *Psychologie und Vernehmungstechnik bei Tatbestandsermittlungen [Psychology and interrogation technique in criminal investigations].* Stuttgart: Enke.

Henke, E. (1838). *Handbuch des Criminalrechts und der Criminalpolitik, Vierther Teil [Handbook of criminal law and criminal politics, Part 4].* Berlin: Nicolai.

Herman, J.L. (2000). *Father-daughter incest.* Cambridge, MA: Harvard University Press.

Herzberg, S.J. (1986). *Inside the jury room.* Videotape available through the University of Wisconsin-Madison Law Library.

Heuer, L. & Penrod, S.D. (1994). Trial complexity: A field investigation of its meaning and effects. *Law and Human Behavior, 18,* 29–51.

Hielkema, J. (1996). *Deskundigen in Nederlandse strafzaken.* Den Haag: Sdu (diss. Rotterdam).

Hielkema, J. (1999). Expert in Dutch criminal cases. In M. Malsch & J.F. Nijboer (Eds.), *Complex cases: Perspectives on the Netherlands criminal justice system* (pp. 27–46). Amsterdam: Thela Thesis.

Hildebrand, M. & de Ruiter, C. (2000). Terbeschikkingstelling, recidive en risicotaxatie: De rol van psychoathie [Treatment of forensic psychiatric patients, recidivism and risk assessment: The role of psychopathy]. *Delikt en Delinkwent, 30,* 764–774.

Hildebrand, M., de Ruiter, C., & van Beek, D.J. (2001). *SVR-20: Richtlijnen voor het beoordelen van het risico van seksueel gewelddadig gedrag. [Dutch translation of the Sexual Violence Risk-20].* Utrecht: Forum Educatief.

Hill, P., Young, M., & Sergeant, T. (1985). *More rough justice.* Harmondsworth: Penguin.

Hill, P.J. & Hunt, G. (1995). *Forever lost, forever gone.* London: Bloomsbury.

Hinchcliff, C.L. (1986). Portrait of a juror: A selected bibliography. *Marquette Law Review, 69,* 495–514.

Hirschberg, M. (1960). *Das Fehlurteil im Strafprozess: Zur Pathologie der Rechtsprechung.* Stuttgart: Kohlhammer.

Hittner, D. (1984). A judge's view of jury service: A personal perspective. *Texas Bar Journal, 47,* 227–230.

Hoffman-Plotkin, D. & Twentyman, C.T. (1984). A multi-modal assessment of behavioral and cognitive deficits in abused and neglected preschoolers. *Child Development, 55,* 794–802.

Hogg, R. (1991). Identifying and reforming the problems of the justice system. In K. Carrington, M. Dever, R. Hogg, J. Bargen, & A. Lohrey (Eds.), *Travesty!: Miscarriages of justice* (pp. 232–270). Leichhart, NSW: Pluto.

Holland, K.M. (1988). The courts in the United States. In J.L. Waltman & K.M. Holland (Eds.), *The political role of law courts in modern democracies* (pp. 6–30). London: Macmillan.

Hood, R. (2001). Capital punishment: A global perspective. *Punishment and Society, 3,* 331–354.

Horowitz, S.W., Lamb, M.E., Esplin, P.W., Boychuk, T.D., Krispin, O., & Reiter-Lavery, L. (1997). Reliability of criteria-based content analysis of child witness statements. *Legal and Criminal Psychology, 2,* 11–22.

Horselenberg, R., Merckelbach, H., Muris, P., Rassin, E., Sijsenaar, M., & Spaan, V. (2000). Imagining fictitious childhood events: The role of individual differences in imagination inflation. *Clinical Psychology and Psychotherapy, 7,* 128–137.

Howard, M.N. (1991). The neutral expert: A plausible threat to justice. *Criminal Law Review, 1991*, 98–105.

Howell, T.B. (2000). The trial of Spencer Cowper, Ellis Stephens, William Rogers, and John Marson, at Hertford Assizes, for the murder of Mrs. Sarah Stout. In T.B. Howell (Ed.), *A complete collection of state trials and proceedings for high treason and other crimes and misdemeanors* (pp. 1105–1168). Buffalo, NY: Hein.

Huber, P.W. (1991). *Galileo's revenge: Junk science in the courtroom.* New York: Basic Books.

Huff, C.R. & Rattner, A. (1988). Convicted but innocent: False positives and the criminal justice process. In J.E. Scott & T. Hirschi (Eds.), *Controversial issues in crime and justice* (pp. 130–144). Newbury Park, CA: Sage.

Huff, C.R., Rattner, A., & Sagarin, E. (1986). Guilty until proven innocent: Wrongful conviction and public policy. *Crime and Delinquency, 32*, 518–544.

Huff, C.R., Rattner, A., & Sagarin, E. (1996). *Convicted but innocent: Wrongful conviction and public policy.* Thousand Oaks, CA: Sage.

Huffman, M.L., Warren, A.R., & Larson, S.M. (1999). Discussing truth and lies in interviews with children: Whether, why and how? *Applied Developmental Science, 3*, 6–15.

Huntington, S.P. (1981). *American politics: The promise of disharmony.* Cambridge, MA: Belknap.

Hyman, E.M. (1979). In pursuit of a more workable exclusionary rule: A police officer's perspective. *Pacific Law Journal, 10*, 33–68.

Hyman, I.E., Husband, T.H., & Billings, F.J. (1995). False memories of childhood experiences. *Applied Cognitive Psychology, 9*, 181–197.

Iannuzzi, J.N. (1998). *Cross-examination handbook* (2nd ed.). Paramus, NJ: Prentice-Hall.

Inbau, F.E., Reed, J.E., & Buckley, J.P. (1986). *Criminal interrogation and confessions.* Baltimore, MD: Williams & Wilkins.

International Criminal Tribunal for the Former Yugoslavia. (1998). *Fifth annual report of the International Tribunal for the Prosecution of Persons Responsible for Serious Violations of International Humanitarian Law Committed in the Territory of the Former Yugoslavia since 1991.* Den Haag: International Criminal Tribunal for the Former Yugoslavia.

International Military Tribunal. (1947). *Trial of the major war criminals before the International Military Tribunal Blue Series* (Vol. 1). Nuremberg: International Military Tribunal.

Ironsmith, M. & Whitehurst, G.J. (1978). The development of listener abilities in communication: How children deal with ambiguous information. *Child Development, 49*, 348–352.

Israel, J., Kamisr, Y., & LaFave, W. (2000). *Criminal procedure and the Constitution.* Minneapolis: West.

Jansen, G. & Kluck, M.-L. (2000). Unter Kontrolle: Aussagepsychologische Gutachten. *Praxis der Rechtspsychologie, 10*(1), 89–101.

Jeans Sr., J.W. (1993). *Trial advocacy* (2nd ed.). St. Paul, MI: West.

Jennings, D. (2000). Judges say sleeping lawyer may not have harmed case. *Dallas Morning News* (October 28).

Jessel, D. (1994). *Trial and error.* London: Headline.

Jonakait, R.N. (1994). Real science and forensic science. *Shepard's Expert and Scientific Evidence Quarterly, 3*, 435.

Jörg, N., Field, S., & Brants, C. (1995). Are inquisitorial and adversarial systems converging? In P. Fennell, C. Harding, N. Jörg, & B. Swart (Eds.), *Criminal justice in Europe: A comparative study* (pp. 41–56). Oxford: Clarendon.

Judex. (1963). *Irrtümer der Strafjustiz: Eine kriminalistische Untersuchung ihrer Ursachen.* Hamburg.

Kaldenbach, J. (1998). *K9 scent detection: My favorite judge lives in a kennel.* Calgery: Detselig.

Kalleichner, H. & Grimm, K. (1973). Die Gegenüberstellung als kriminaltaktische Massnahme [Identification lineups in criminal proceedings]. In H. Schäfer (Ed.), *Grundlagen der Kriminalistik.* (Vol. 11, pp. 327–345). Hamburg: Steintor.

Kalven, H. & Zeisel, H. (1966). *The American jury.* Boston: Little, Brown.

Kamisar, Y. (1987). 'Comparative reprehensibility' and the fourth amendment exclusionary rule. *Michigan Law Review, 86,* 1–50.

Kamisar, Y. (1990). Remembering the old world of criminal procedure: A reply to professor Grano. *University Michigan Journal of Law Reform, 23,* 537–589.

Kandel, R.F. (1994). Power plays: A sociolinguistic study of inequality in child custody mediation and a hearsay analog solution. *Arizona Law Review, 36,* 879–972.

Kaplan, J. (1974). The limits of the exclusionary rule. *Stanford Law Review, 26,* 1027–1055.

Karp, C. & Rosner, C. (1991). *When justice fails: The David Milgaard story.* Toronto: McClelland & Stewart.

Kassin, S.M. (1997). The psychology of confession evidence. *American Psychologist, 52,* 221–233.

Kassin, S.M. & Fung, C.T. (1999). "I'm innocent!" Effects of training on judgments of truth and deception in the interrogation room. *Law and Human Behavior, 23,* 499–516.

Kassin, S.M. & Wrightsman, L.S. (1985). Confession evidence. In S.M. Kassin & L.S. Wrightsman (Eds.), *The psychology of evidence and trial procedure* (pp. 67–94). Beverly Hills, CA: Sage.

Kassin, S.M., Tubb, V.A., Hosch, H.M., & Memon, A. (2001). On the 'general acceptance' of eyewitness testimony research. *American Psychologist, 56,* 405–416.

Katz, M. (1966). The Supreme Court and the states: An inquiry into Mapp v. Ohio in North Carolina: The study and the implications. *North Carolina Law Review, 45,* 119–162.

Katz, S. & Mazur, M.A. (1979). *Understanding the rape victim: A synthesis of research findings.* New York: Wiley.

Kauper, P.G. (1932). Judicial examination of the accused: A remedy for the third degree. *Michigan Law Review, 30,* 1224–1245.

Kee, R. (1986). *Trial and error: The Maguires, the Guildford pub bombings, and British justice.* London: Hamilton.

Kerr, N.L., Harmon, D.L., & Graves, J.K. (1982). Independence of multiple verdicts by jurors and juries. *Journal of Applied Social Psychology, 12,* 12–29.

King, N.J. & Munsterman, G.T. (1996). Stratified juror selection: Cross-section by design. *Judicature, 79,* 273–278.

Kiwit, W. (1965). *Fehlurteile im Strafrecht.* Köln.

Kleinknecht, T. & Meyer-Gossner, K. (1997a). *Becksche Kurzkommentare: Strafprozessordnung [Beck's short commentaries: Law of criminal procedure]* (43rd ed.). München: Beck.

Kleinknecht, T. & Meyer-Grossner, L. (1997b). *Strafprozeßordnung: Gerichts-verfassungsgesetz, Nebengesetze und ergänzende Bestimmungen.* München: Beck.

Köhnken, G. (1995). Interviewing adults. In R.H. Bull & D. Carson (Eds.), *Handbook of psychology in legal contexts* (pp. 235–246). Chichester: Wiley.

Köhnken, G. (2000). Glaubwürdigkeitsbegutachtung nach Mainz und Montessori: Eine Zwischenbilanz. *Praxis der Rechtspsychologie, 10*(1), 4–8.

Köhnken, G. & Maass, A. (1985). Effects of instructional bias on eyewitness identification in a field setting. In F.L. Denmark & L.S. Sidorowicz (Eds.), *Social/ecological psychology and the psychology of women.* Amsterdam: North-Holland.

Kossmann, E.H. (1978). *The low countries, 1780–1940.* Oxford: Clarendon.

Kovera, M.B. & Borgida, E. (1998). Expert scientific testimony on child witnesses in the age of Daubert. In S.J. Ceci & H. Hembrooke (Eds.), *Expert witnesses in child abuse cases: What can and should be said in court* (pp. 185–215). Washington, DC: American Psychological Association.

Kozol, H., Boucher, R., & Garofalo, R. (1972). The diagnosis and treatment of dangerousness. *Crime and Delinquency, 18,* 371–392.

Krey, V.F. (1999). Characteristic features of German criminal proceedings: An alternative to the criminal procedure law of the United States? *Loyola L.A. International and Comparative Law Journal, 21,* 591–605.

Kritzer, H.M. (1986). Adjudication to settlement: Shading in the gray. *Judicature, 70,* 162–164.

Kubinger, K. (1997). Richtlinien zur Qualitätssicherung von psychologischen Gutachten. *Psychologie in Österreich, 17,* 10–16.

Kulynych, J. (1996). Brain, mind, and criminal behavior: Neuroimages as scientific evidence. *Jurimetrics Journal, 36,* 235–244.

LaFave, W. & Israel, J. (1984). *Criminal procedure* (3rd ed.). St. Paul, MN: West.

Lamb, M.E. & Sternberg, K.J. (1997). Criteria-based content analysis: A field validation study. *Child Abuse and Neglect, 21,* 255–264.

Landsman, S. & Rakos, R.F. (1991). A preliminary empirical enquiry concerning the prohibition of hearsay evidence in American courts. *Law and Psychology Review, 15,* 65–85.

Landsman, S. & Rakos, R.F. (1994). A preliminary inquiry into the effect of potentially biasing information on judges and jurors in civil litigation. *Behavioral Sciences and the Law, 12,* 113–126.

Langbein, J.H. & Weinreb, L.L. (1978). Continental criminal procedure: 'Myth' and reality. *Yale Law Journal, 87,* 1549–1569.

Lange, R. (1980). *Fehlerquellen im Ermittlungsverfahren [Sources of errors in criminal investigations].* Heidelberg: Kriminalistik.

Lassers, W.J. (1973). *Scapegoat justice: Lloyd Miller and the failure of the American legal system.* Bloomington, IN: Indiana University Press.

Lavin, M. & Sales, B.D. (1998). Moral justifications for limits on expert testimony. In S.J. Ceci & H. Hembrooke (Eds.), *Expert witnesses in child abuse cases: What can and should be said in court* (pp. 59–81). Washington, DC: American Psychological Association.

Lempert, R.O. (1981). Civil juries and complex cases: Let's not rush to judgment. *Michigan Law Review, 80,* 68–132.

Lensing, J.A.W. (1988). *Het verhoor van de verdachte in strafzaken.* Arnhem: Gouda Quint.

Lensing, J.A.W. (1998). Controle op het politieverhoor: Meer waarborgen voor de verdachte en de strafrechtspleging. *Justitiële Verkenningen, 24,* 37–46.

Leo, R.A. (1992). From coercion to deception: The changing nature of police interrogation in America. *Crime, Law and Social Change, 18,* 33–59.

Leo, R.A. (1995). The impact of Miranda revisited. *Journal of Criminal Law and Criminology, 86,* 621–692.

Leo, R.A. (1996a). Inside the interrogation room. *Journal of Criminal Law and Criminology, 86,* 266–303.

Leo, R.A. (1996b). Miranda's revenge: Police interrogation as a confidence game. *Law and Society Review, 30,* 259–288.

Leo, R.A. & Ofshe, R.J. (1998). The consequences of false confessions: Deprivations of liberty and miscarriages of justice in the age of psychological interrogation. *Journal of Criminal Law and Criminology, 88,* 429–496.

Leo, R.A. & White, W.S. (1999). Adapting to Miranda: Modern interrogators' strategies for dealing with obstacles posed by Miranda. *Minnesota Law Review, 84,* 397–472.

Leuw, E. (1995). *Recidive na ontslag uit de TBS [Recidivism after forensic-psychiatric treatment].* Arnhem, the Netherlands: Gouda Quint.

Leuw, E. (1999). *Recidive na de TBS: patronen, trends en de inschatting van gevaar. [Recidivism after forensic psychiatric treatment: Patterns, trends, processes and risk assessment].* Deventer, the Netherlands: Gouda Quint.

Levy, H. (1996). *And the blood cried out: A prosecutor's spellbinding account of the power of DNA.* New York: Basic Books.

Lewis, D.O., Yeager, C.A., Swica, Y., Pincus, J.H., & Lewis, M. (1997). Objective documentation of child abuse and dissociation in 12 murderers with dissociative identity disorder. *American Journal of Psychiatry, 154,* 1703–1710.

Lidz, C., Mulvey, E., & Gardner, W. (1993). The accuracy of predictions of violence to others. *Journal of the American Medical Association, 269*, 1007–1011.

Lieberman, J.D. & Sales, B.D. (1997). What social science teaches us about the jury instruction process. *Psychology, Public Policy and Law, 4*, 589–644.

Liebman, J.S. (2000). The overproduction of death. *Columbia Law Review, 100*, 2030–2156.

Liebman, J.S., Fagan, J., & West, V. (2000). *A broken system: Error rates in capital cases, 1973–1995*. <http://justice.policy.net/jpreport/index.html> (visited 4/04/01).

Lief, H.I. & Fetkewicz, J. (1995). Retractors of false memories: The evolution of pseudo-memories. *Journal of Psychiatry and Law, 23*, 421–435.

Lijphart, A. (1975). *The politics of accommodation: Pluralism and democracy in The Netherlands* (2nd ed.). Berkeley, CA: University of California Press.

Lilly, G.C. (1984). Notes on the confrontation clause and *Ohio v. Roberts*. *University of Florida Law Review, 36*, 207–233.

Lind, E.A. & Tyler, T.R. (1988). *The social psychology of procedural justice*. New York: Plenum.

Lindsay, R.C.L., Pozzulo, J.D., Craig, W., Lee, K., & Corber, S. (1997). Simultaneous lineups, sequential lineups, and showups: Eyewitness identification decisions of adults and children. *Law and Human Behavior, 21*, 391–404.

Lindsay, R.C.L., Ross, D.F., Lea, J.A., & Carr, C. (1995). What's fair when a child testifies? *Journal of Applied Social Psychology, 25*, 870–888.

Liotti, T.F. (1999). Black's law: A criminal lawyer reveals his defense strategies in four cliffhanger cases. *The Champion* (November).

Loftus, E.F. (1979). *Eyewitness testimony*. Cambridge, MA: Harvard University Press.

Loftus, E.F. (1993). Psychologists in the eyewitness world. *American Psychologist, 48*, 550–552.

Loftus, E.F. (1997a). Dispatch from the (un)civil memory wars. In J.D. Read & D.S. Lindsay (Eds.), *Recollections of trauma: Scientific evidence and clinical practice* (pp. 171–198). New York: Plenum.

Loftus, E.F. (1997b). Repressed memory accusations: Devastated families and devastated patients. *Applied Cognitive Psychology, 11*, 25–30.

Loftus, E.F. & Ketcham, K. (1991). *Witness for the defense: The accused, the eyewitness, and the expert who puts memory on trial*. New York: St. Martin.

Loftus, E.F. & Ketcham, K. (1994). *The myth of repressed memory: False memories and allegations of sexual abuse*. New York: St. Martin.

Loftus, E.F., Joslyn, S., & Polage, D. (1998). Repression: A mistaken impression. *Development and Psychopathology, 10*, 781–792.

Lubet, S. (1993). *Modern trial advocacy: Analysis and practice*. Notre Dame, IN: National Institute of Trial Advocacy (NITA).

Lubet, S. (1997). *Modern trial advocacy: Analysis and practice* (2nd ed.). Notre Dame, IN: National Institute of Trial Advocacy (NITA).

Luis Carlos, L. (1973). *Erros judiciarios* (Vol. 1). Sao Paulo: Editora Sao Paulo.

Luis Carlos, L. (1975). *Erros judiciarios: O desmemoriado de Collegno e outros erros judiciarios* (Vol. 2). Sao Paulo: Editora Rensenha Universitaria.

Lyon, T.D. (1995). False allegations and false denials in child sexual abuse. *Psychology, Public Policy, and Law, 1*, 429–437.

Lyon, T.D. & Saywitz, K.J. (1999). Young maltreated children's competence to take the oath. *Applied Developmental Science, 3*, 16–27.

Maass, A. & Kohnken, G. (1989). Eyewitness identification: Simulating the 'weapon effect'. *Law and Human Behavior, 13*, 397–408.

MacLeod, M.D., Frowley, J.N., & Shepherd, J.W. (1994). Whole body information: Its relevance to eyewitnesses. In D.F. Ross, J.D. Read, M.P. Toglia (Eds.), *Adult eyewitness testimony: Current trends and developments* (pp. 125–143). New York: Cambridge University Press.

Maclin, T. (1944). When the cure for the fourth amendment is worse than the disease. *Southern California Law Review, 68*, 1–86.

Maguire, M. (1994). The wrong message at the wrong time? The present state of investigative practice. In D. Morgan & G.M. Stephenson (Eds.), *Suspicions and silence: The right to silence in criminal investigations* (pp. 39–49). London: Blackstone.

Malcolm, J. (1999). *The crime of Sheila McGough.* New York: Knopf.

Malpass, R.S. (1981). Effective size and defendant bias in eyewitness identification lineups. *Law and Human Behavior, 5*, 299–309.

Malpass, R.S. (1996). Enhancing eyewitness memory. In S.L. Sporer, R.S. Malpass, & G. Köhnken (Eds.), *Psychological issues in eyewitness identification* (pp. 177–204). Mahwah, NJ: Erlbaum.

Malsch, M. (1998). De rechter en de psycholoog: De praktijk van de forensische gedragskundige rapportage in strafzaken [The judge and the psychologist: the practice of forensic psychological testimony in criminal trials]. *Delikt en Delinkwent, 28*, 644–656.

Malsch, M. & Hielkema, J. (1999). Forensic assessment in Dutch criminal insanity cases: Participants' perspectives. In M. Malsch & J.F. Nijboer (Eds.), *Complex cases: Perspectives on the Netherlands criminal justice system* (pp. 213–228). Amsterdam: Thela Thesis.

Malsch, M. & Hoekstra, R. (1999). De publieke tribune: controlemiddel voor de rechtspraak of opvangruimte voor daklozen? *Delikt en Delinkwent, 29*, 737–754.

Malsch, M. & Jansen, M. (1998). Het dossier: op papier of op het scherm? *Proces*, 11–13.

Malsch, M. & Nijboer, J.F. (Eds.). (1999). *Complex cases: Perspectives on the Netherlands criminal justice system.* Amsterdam: Thela Thesis.

Margot, P. (1998). The role of the forensic scientist in an inquisitorial system of justice. *Science and Justice, 38*, 71–73.

Markman, E.M. (1979). Realizing that you don't understand: Elementary school children's awareness of inconsistencies. *Child Development, 50*, 643–655.

Marvell, T.B. & Moody, C.E. (2001). The lethal effects of three-strikes laws. *Journal of Legal Studies, 30*, 89–106.

Mathew, T. (1961). *Forensic fables by O.* London: Butterworths.

Mauet, T.A. (1992). *Fundamentals of trial techniques.* Boston: Little, Brown.

Mauet, T.A. (1993). *Pretrial* (2nd ed.). Boston: Little, Brown.

Mauet, T.A. (1996). *Trial techniques* (4th ed.). Boston: Little, Brown.

Mauet, T.A. (2000). *Trial techniques* (5th ed.). Gaithersburg: Aspen.

McCann, J.T. (1998). A conceptual framework for identifying various types of confessions. *Behavioral Sciences and the Law, 16*, 441–453.

McConville, M. (1992). Video taping interrogations. *New Law Journal, 142*, 960–962.

McConville, M. & Hodgson, J. (1993). *Custodial legal advice and the right to silence.* London: Her Majesty's Stationery Office (Royal Commission on Criminal Justice Report).

McElhaney, J.W. (1974). *Effective litigation: Trials, problems, and materials.* St. Paul, MI: West.

McElhaney, J.W. (1987). *McElhaney's trial notebook* (2nd ed.). Chicago: Section of Litigation, American Bar Association.

McElhaney, J.W. (1994). *McElhaney's trial notebook* (3rd ed.). Chicago: Section of Litigation, American Bar Association.

McEwan, J. (2000). Decision-making in legal settings. In J. McGuire, T. Mason, & A. O'Kane (Eds.), *Behaviour, crime and legal processes: A guide for forensic practitioners* (pp. 111–134). Chichester: Wiley.

McGough, L.S. (1994). *Child witnesses: Fragile voices in the American legal system.* New Haven, CT: Yale University Press.

McKenzie, I.K. (1994). Regulating custodial interviews: A comparative study. *International Journal of the Sociology of Law, 22*, 239–259.

McLaughlin, M.A. (1983). Questions to witnesses and notetaking by the jury as aids in understanding complex litigation. *New England Law Review, 18*, 687–713.

McNiel, D., Sandberg, D., & Binder, R. (1998). The relationship between confidence and accuracy in clinical assessment of psychiatric patients' potential for violence. *Law and Human Behavior, 22*, 655–669.

McNulty, C. & Wardle, J. (1994). Adult disclosure of sexual abuse: A primary cause of psychological distress? *Child Abuse and Neglect, 18*, 548–555.

Meares, T.L. & Harcourt, B.E. (in press). Foreword: Transparent adjudication and social science research in constitutional criminal procedure. *Journal of Criminal Law and Criminology*.

Meehl, P.E. (1954). *Clinical versus statistical prediction: A theoretical analysis and a review of the evidence*. Minneapolis: University of Minneapolis Press.

Melton, G.B., Petrila, J., Poythress, N.G., & Slobogin, C. (1997). *Psychological evaluations for the courts: A handbook for mental health professionals and lawyers* (2nd ed.). New York: Guilford.

Meltzer, D. (1988). Deterring constitutional violations by law enforcement officials: Plaintiffs and defendants as private attorneys general. *Columbia Law Review, 88*, 247–328.

Memon, A. & Young, M. (1997). Desperately seeking evidence: The recovered memory debate. *Legal and Criminal Psychology, 2*, 131–154.

Memon, A., Vrij, A., & Bull, R.H. (1998). *Psychology and law: Truthfulness accuracy and credibility*. London: McGraw-Hill.

Merckelbach, H. & Muris, P. (2001). The causal link between self-reported trauma and dissociation: A critical review. *Behaviour Research and Therapy, 39*, 245–254.

Merckelbach, H. & Wessel, I. (1998). Assumptions of students and psychotherapists about memory. *Psychological Reports, 82*, 763–770.

Merckelbach, H., Horselenberg, R., & Schmidt, H. (in press). Modeling the connection between self-reported trauma and dissociation in a student sample. *Personality and Individual Differences*.

Merckelbach, H., Muris, P., Horselenberg, R., & Rassin, E. (1998). Traumatic intrusions as worse case scenarios. *Behaviour Research and Therapy, 36*, 245–254.

Meurer, D., Sporer, S.L., & Rennig, C. (1990). Zum Beweiswert von Personenidentifizierungen: Von Alltagspsychologien zu empirisch überprüfbaren Fragestellungen. [The probative value of eyewitness identifications: From common sense psychology to empirically testable hypotheses]. In D. Meurer & S.L. Sporer (Eds.), *Zum Beweiswert von Personenidentifizierungen: Neuere empirische Befunde* (pp. 1–18). Marburg: Elwert.

Micelli, T.J. (1996). Plea bargaining and deterrence: An institutional approach. *European Journal of Law and Economics, 3*, 249–264.

Miene, P., Borgida, E., & Park, R.C. (1993). The evaluation of hearsay evidence: A social psychological approach. In N.J. Castellan Jr. (Ed.), *Individual and group decision-making: Current issues* (pp. 151–166). Hillsdale, NJ: Erlbaum.

Miene, P., Park, R.C., & Borgida, E. (1992). Juror decision making and the evaluation of hearsay evidence. *Minnesota Law Review, 76*, 683–701.

Miller, R.E. & Sarat, A. (1980–1981). Grievances, claims, and disputes: Assessing the adversary culture. *Law and Society Review, 15*, 523–566.

Milne, R. & Bull, R. (1999). *Investigative interviewing: Psychology and practice*. Chichester: Wiley.

Ministry of Justice. (2000). *Toekomst TBS: de weg naar een efficiënte forensische behandeling [The future of TBS: The road to an efficient forensic treatment]*. Zoetermeer, the Netherlands: Ministry of Justice, Department of Corrections.

Moedikdo, P. (1976). De Utrechtse school van Pompe, Baan en Kempe. In C. Kelk, M. Moerings, N. Jörg, & P. Moedikdo (Eds.), *Recht, macht en manipulatie* (2nd ed., pp. 90–154). Utrecht: Spectrum.

Moenssens, A.A. (1984). Admissibility of scientific evidence: An alternative to the Frye (*Frye v. United States*, 293, F. 1013, D.C. Cir. 1923) Rule. *William and Mary Law Review, 25*, 545–575.

Moenssens, A.A., Inbau, F., Starrs, J.E., & Henderson, C.E. (1995). *Scientific evidence in civil and criminal cases* (4th ed.). Mineola, NY: Foundation Press.

Monahan, J. (1981). *The clinical prediction of violent behavior*. Washington, DC: Government Printing Office.

Monahan, J. & Steadman, H. (1994). *Violence and mental disorder: Developments in risk assessment* (2nd ed.). Chicago: University of Chicago Press.

Monahan, J. & Wexler, D.B. (1978). A definite maybe: Proof and probability in civil commitment cases. *Law and Human Behavior, 2*, 37–48.

Monahan, J., Steadman, H.J., Robbins, P.C., Silver, E., Appelbaum, P.S., & Grisso, T. (2000). Developing a clinically useful actuarial tool for assessing violence risk. *British Journal of Psychiatry, 176*, 312–319.

Monahan, J., Steadman, H.J., Silver, E., Appelbaum, A., Robbins, P., Mulvey, E., Roth, L., Grisso, T., & Banks, S. (2001). *Rethinking risk assessment: The MacArthur study of mental disorder and violence* (2nd ed.). New York: Oxford University Press.

Montoya, J. (1996). The future of the post-Batson (Batson v. Kentucky, 106 S. Ct. 1712 (1996)) peremptory challenge: Voir dire by questionnaire and the 'blind' peremptory. *University of Michigan Journal of Law Reform, 29*, 981–1037.

Mooij, A.W.M., Koenraadt, F., & Lommen van Alphen, J.M.J. (1991). *Considering the accused: Forensic examination in a residential setting*. Amsterdam: Swets & Zeitlinger.

Mortimer, A. & Shepherd, E. (1999). Frames of mind: Schemata guiding cognition and conduct in the interviewing of suspected offenders. In A. Memon & R.H. Bull (Eds.), *Handbook of the psychology of interviewing* (pp. 293–315). Chichester: Wiley.

Mossman, D. (1994). Assessing predictions of violence: Being accurate about accuracy. *Journal of Consulting and Clinical Psychology, 62*, 783–792.

Mostar, H. (1956). *Unschuldig verurteilt!: Aus der Chronik der Justizmorde*. Stuttgart: Scherz & Goverts.

Mosteller, R.P. (1997). Moderating investigative lies by disclosure and documentation. *Oregon Law Review, 76*, 833–851.

Moston, S.J. (1996). From denial to admission in police questioning of suspects. In G.M. Davies, S.M.A. Lloyd-Bostock, M. McMurran, & C. Wilson (Eds.), *Psychology, law, and criminal justice: International developments in research and practice* (pp. 91–99). Berlin: De Gruyter.

Moston, S.J. & Engelberg, T. (1993). Police questioning techniques in tape recorded interviews with criminal suspects. *Policing and Society, 3*, 223–237.

Moston, S.J. & Stephenson, G.M. (1992). Predictors of suspect and interviewer behaviour during police questioning. In F. Lösel, D. Bender, & T. Bliesener (Eds.), *Psychology and law: International perspectives* (pp. 212–219). Berlin: De Gruyter.

Moston, S.J. & Stephenson, G.M. (1993). The changing face of police interrogation. *Journal of Community and Applied Social Psychology, 3*, 101–115.

Moston, S.J. & Stephenson, G.M. (1994). Helping the police with the enquiries outside the police station. In D. Morgan & G.M. Stephenson (Eds.), *Suspicion and silence: The right to silence in criminal investigations* (pp. 50–65). London: Blackstone.

Moston, S.J., Stephenson, G.M., & Williamson, T.M. (1993). The incidence, antecedents and consequences of the use of the right to silence during police questioning. *Criminal Behaviour and Mental Health, 3*, 30–47.

Mueller, G.O.W. & Le Poole Griffiths, F. (1969). *Comparative criminal procedure*. New York: New York University Press.

Mulhern, S.A. (1997). Commentary in the logical status of case histories. In J.D. Read & D.S. Lindsay (Eds.), *Recollections of trauma: Scientific evidence and clinical practice* (pp. 126–142). New York: Plenum.

Mullin, C. (1989). *Error of judgment: The truth about the Birmingham bombers.* Dublin: Poolberg.

Mussweiler, T. & Englich, B. (in press). Sentencing under uncertainty: Anchoring effects in the courtroom. *Journal of Applied Social Psychology.*

Myers, J.E.B. (1987). The child witness: Techniques for direct examination, cross examination, and impeachment. *Pacific Law Journal, 18,* 801–942.

Myers, J.E.B. (1992). *Evidence in child abuse and neglect cases* (2nd ed.). New York: Wiley.

Myers, J.E.B. (1993). The competence of young children to testify in legal proceedings. *Behavioral Sciences and the Law, 11,* 121–133.

Myers, J.E.B. (1996). A decade of international reform to accommodate child witnesses. *Criminal Justice and Behavior, 23,* 402–422.

Myers, J.E.B. (1997). *Evidence in child abuse and neglect cases* (3rd ed.). New York: Wiley.

Myers, J.E.B., Redlich, A.D., Goodman, G.S., Prizmich, L.P., & Imwinkelried, E. (1999). Jurors' perceptions of hearsay in child sexual abuse cases. *Psychology, Public Policy, and Law, 5,* 388–419.

Myjer, E. (1997). Over stuk recht en recht op stukken. *Trema,* 179–188.

Nagel, S.S. (1965). Law and society: Testing the effects of excluding illegally seized evidence. *Wisconsin Law Review, 1965,* 283–315.

Narby, D.J., Cutler, B.L., & Penrod, S.D. (1996). The effects of witness, target, and situational factors on eyewitness identifications. In S.L. Sporer, R.S. Malpass, & G. Köhnken (Eds.), *Psychological issues in eyewitness identification* (pp. 23–52). Mahwah, NJ: Erlbaum.

Nardulli, P. (1983). The societal cost of the exclusionary rule: An empirical assessment. *American Bar Foundation Research Journal, 1983,* 585–622.

National Center for State Courts. (1986). Guidelines for involuntary commitment. *Mental and Physical Disability Law Reporter, 10,* 409–514.

Niemantsverdriet, J.R. (1993). *Achteraf bezien: over het evalueren van ter beschikking stellingen [In retrospect: Evaluating committals to a forensic mental hospital].* Utrecht, the Netherlands: Elinkwijk (diss. University of Nijmegen).

Nierop, N. (1998). Het verdachtenverhoor: Een gedragskundig perspectief. *Justitiële Verkenningen, 24,* 101–117.

Nierop, N. & Mooij, A.J.M. (2000). *Het verdachtenverhoor in bijzondere zaken.* Den Haag: Korps Landelijke Politiediensten, Divisie Recherche.

Nijboer, J.F. (1992). Forensic expertise in Dutch criminal procedure. *Cardozo Law Review, 14,* 165–191.

Nijboer, J.F. (1997). *Strafrechtelijk bewijsrecht* (3rd ed.). Nijmegen: Ars Aequi Libri.

Nijboer, J.F. (1999). *De waarde van het bewijs* (2nd ed.). Deventer: Gouda Quint.

Nijboer, J.F. (2000a). *Strafrechtelijk bewijsrecht* (4th ed.). Nijmegen: Ars Aequi.

Nijboer, J.F. (2000b). The significance of comparative legal studies. In J.F. Nijboer & W.J.J.M. Sprangers (Eds.), *Harmonisation in forensic expertise: An inquiry into the desirability of and opportunities for international standards* (pp. 399–410). Amsterdam: Thela Thesis.

Nijboer, J.F. & Sennef, A. (1999). Justification. In M. Malsch & J.F. Nijboer (Eds.), *Complex cases: Perspectives on the Netherlands criminal justice system* (pp. 11–26). Amsterdam: Thela Thesis.

Nijboer, J.F. & Sprangers, W.J.J.M. (Eds.). (2000). *Harmonisation in forensic expertise: An inquiry into the desirability of and opportunities for international standards.* Amsterdam: Thela Thesis.

Nobles, R. & Schiff, D. (1995). Miscarriages of justice: A systems approach. *The Modern Law Review, 58,* 299–320.

Nöldeke, W. (1982). Zum Wiedererkennen des Tatverdächtigen bei Gegenüberstellung und Bildvorlage [The identification of suspects in lineups and photospreads]. *Neue Zeitschrift für Strafrecht, 2,* 193–195.

Note. (1968). Confrontation, cross-examination, and the right to prepare a defense. *Georgetown Law Journal, 56,* 939.

Note. (1995). The limitations of Daubert and its misapplication to quasi-scientific experts, a two-year case review of *Daubert v. Merrell Dow Pharmaceuticals Inc. Washburn Law Journal, 35,* 134–156.

Note. (1996). An autopsy of scientific evidence in a Post-Daubert world. *Georgetown Law Journal, 84,* 1985–2041.

Nsereko, D.D.N. (1999). Minimum sentences and their effect on judicial discretion. *Crime, Law and Social Change, 31,* 363–384.

Nunez, N. & Krampner, M.J. (1999). Tainted testimony and competency of child witnesses. *Newsletter of the Section on Child Maltreatment, Division American Psychological Association, 37,* 7–8.

Oaks, D.H. (1970). Studying the exclusionary rule in search and seizure. *University of Chicago Law Review, 37,* 665–757.

Oates, R. & Tong, L. (1987). Sexual abuse of children: An area with room for professional reforms. *Medical Journal of Australia, 147,* 544–548.

Odenthal, H.-J. (1999). *Die Gegenüberstellung im Strafverfahren [Lineups in criminal investigations]* (3rd ed.). Stuttgart: Richard Boorberg.

Ofshe, R.J. (1989). Coerced confessions: The logic of seemingly irrational action. *Cultic Studies Journal, 6,* 1–15.

Ofshe, R.J. & Leo, R.A. (1997a). The decision to confess falsely: Rational choice and irrational action. *Denver University Law Review, 74,* 979–1122.

Ofshe, R.J. & Leo, R.A. (1997b). The social psychology of police interrogation: The theory and classification of true and false confessions. *Studies in Law, Politics and Society, 16,* 189–251.

Ofshe, R.J. & Watters, E. (1994). *Making monsters: False memories, psychotherapy, and sexual hysteria.* New York: Scribner.

Olio, K.A. & Cornell, W.F. (1998). The facade of scientific documentation: A case of Richard Ofshe's analysis of the Paul Ingram case. *Psychology, Public Policy, and Law, 4,* 1182–1197.

Oliphant, R.E. (1982). *Basic concepts in the law of evidence: An outline of the Younger lectures.*

Omenn, G.S. (1997). Enhancing the role of the scientific expert witness. *International Journal of Forensic Document Examiners, 3,* 218–219.

Ong, E.K. & Glantz, S.A. (2000). Tobacco industry efforts subverting International Agency for Research on Cancer's second-hand smoke study. *The Lancet, 355,* 1253–1259.

Ord, B. & Shaw, G. (1999). *Investigative interviewing explained.* Woking: The New Police Bookshop.

Ornstein, P.A., Ceci, S.J., & Loftus, E.F. (1998). Adult recollections of childhood abuse. *Psychology, Public Policy, and Law, 4,* 1025–1051.

Osborn, A.S. (1937). *The mind of the juror as judge of the facts.* Albany, NY: Boyd.

Otte, M. (1998). Het onderzoek ter terechtzitting: Over de betrekkelijke betekenis van het onmiddellijkheidsbeginsel. *Justitiële Verkenningen, 24,* 26–36.

Otto, A.L., Penrod, S.D., & Dexter, H.R. (1994). The biasing impact of pretrial publicity on juror judgments. *Law and Human Behavior, 18,* 453–469.

Paglia, A. & Schuller, R.A. (1998). Jurors' use of hearsay evidence: The effects of type and timing of instructions. *Law and Human Behavior, 22,* 501–518.

Pakter, W. (1985). Exclusionary rules in France, Germany, and Italy. *Hastings International and Comparative Law Review, 9,* 1–34.

Palermo, G.B., White, M.A., Wasserman, L.A., & Hanrahan, W. (1998). Plea bargaining: Injustice for all? *International Journal of Offender Therapy and Comparative Criminology, 42,* 111–123.

Paris, M.L. (1997). Lying to ourselves. *Oregon Law Review, 76*, 817–832.

Parks, T. (1999). On one aspect of the evidence for recovered memories. *American Journal of Psychology, 112*, 365–370.

Pathak, M.K. & Thompson, W.C. (1999). From child to witness to jury: Effects of suggestion on the transmission and evaluation of hearsay. *Psychology, Public Policy, and Law, 5*, 372–387.

Patton, A.L. (1993). The endless cycle of abuse: Why 42 U.S.C. 1983 is ineffective in deterring police brutality. *Hastings Law Journal, 44*, 753–808.

Pearse, J. (1995). Police interviewing: The identification of vulnerabilities. *Journal of Community and Applied Social Psychology, 5*, 147–159.

Pearse, J. & Gudjonsson, G.H. (1996a). How appropriate are appropriate adults? *Journal of Forensic Psychiatry, 7*, 570–580.

Pearse, J. & Gudjonsson, G.H. (1996b). Police interviewing techniques at two south London police stations. *Psychology, Crime, and Law, 3*, 63–74.

Pearse, J. & Gudjonsson, G.H. (1996c). Understanding the problems of the appropriate adult. *Expert Evidence, 4*, 101–104.

Pearse, J. & Gudjonsson, G.H. (1997a). Police interviewing and legal representation: A field study. *Journal of Forensic Psychiatry, 8*, 200–208.

Pearse, J. & Gudjonsson, G.H. (1997b). Police interviewing and mentally disordered offenders: Changing the role of the legal adviser. *Expert Evidence, 5*, 49–53.

Pearse, J. & Gudjonsson, G.H. (1999). Measuring influential police interviewing tactics: A factor analytic approach. *Legal and Criminological Psychology, 4*, 211–238.

Pearse, J., Gudjonsson, G.H., Clare, I.C.H., & Rutter, S. (1998). Police interviewing and psychological vulnerabilities: Predicting the likelihood of a confession. *Journal of Community and Applied Social Psychology, 8*, 1–21.

Pendergrast, M. (1995). *Victims of memory*. Hinesburg, VT: Upper Access Press.

Penrod, S.D., Fulero, S.M., & Cutler, B.L. (1995). Expert psychological testimony on eyewitness reliability before and after Daubert: The state of the law and the science. *Behavioral Sciences and the Law, 13*, 229–259.

Perrin, T.L. (1999). If it's broken, fix it: Moving beyond the exclusionary rule. *Iowa Law Review, 83*, 669–782.

Perry, N., McAuliff, B., Tan, P., & Claycomb, C. (1995). When lawyers serve children: Is justice served? *Law and Human Behavior, 19*, 609–629.

Perry, N.W. & Wrightsman, L.S. (1991). *The child witness: Legal issues and dilemmas*. Newbury Park, CA: Sage.

Peters, K. (1970). *Fehlerquellen im Strafprozess (1. Band)*. Karlsruhe: Müller.

Peters, K. (1972). *Fehlerquellen im Strafprozess [Sources of errors in trial procedures]* (Vol. 2). Karlsruhe: Müller.

Peters, K. (1987). Artikel 6 EVRM en het recht op inzage van processtukken in het strafrechtelijk vooronderzoek. *NJCM Bulletin: Nederlands Tijdschrift voor de Mensenrechten, 7*, 509–524.

Peters, W.W. & Nunez, N. (1999). Complex language and comprehension monitoring: Teaching child witnesses to recognize linguistic confusion. *Journal of Applied Psychology, 84*, 661–669.

Peterson-Badali, M., Abramovitch, R., & Duda, J. (1997). Young children's legal knowledge and reasoning ability. *Canadian Journal of Criminology, 39*, 145–170.

Philipse, M., de Ruiter, C., Hildebrand, M., & Bouman, Y. (2000). *HCR-20. Beoordelen van het risico van gewelddadig gedrag, Versie 2. [Dutch translation of the HCR-20, Version 2]*. Nijmegen/Utrecht, the Netherlands: Prof.mr. W.P.J. Pompestichting/Dr. Henri van der Hoeven Stichting.

Pierre Puysegur, M. (1985). *The representations of the penal system among children from six to ten years*. Paper presented at the 8th biennial meetings of the International Society for the Study of Behavioral Development, Tours, France.

Pipe, M.E. & Wilson, J.C. (1994). Cues and secrets: Influences on children's event reports. *Developmental Psychology, 30*, 515–525.

Pizzi, W.T. (1999). *Trials without truth: Why our system of criminal trials has become an expensive failure and what we need to do to rebuild it.* New York: New York University Press.

Pizzorusso, A. (1965). *La restituzione degli atti al giudice "A quo" nel processo costituzionale incidentale.* Milano: Giuffre.

Platania, J., Moran, G., & Cutler, B.L. (1994). Prosecution misconduct during the penalty phase of capital trials: Harmless error? *The Champion, (July)*, 19–22.

Poole, D.A., Lindsay, D.S., Memon, A., & Bull, R.H. (1995). Psychotherapy and the recovery of memories in childhood sexual abuse: U.S. and British practitioners' opinions, practices, and experiences. *Journal of Consulting and Clinical Psychology, 63*, 426–437.

Pope, H.G., Hudson, J.I., Bodkin, J.A., & Oliva, P. (1998). Questionable validity of dissociative amnesia in trauma victims. *British Journal of Psychiatry, 172*, 210–215.

Pope, H.G., Oliva, P.S., Hudson, J.I., Bodkin, J.A., & Gruber, A.J. (1999). Attitudes toward DSM-IV dissociative disorders diagnoses among board-certified American psychiatrists. *American Journal of Psychiatry, 156*, 321–323.

Posner, R.A. (1999). An economic approach to the law of evidence. *Stanford Law Review, 51*, 1477–1546.

Prakken, T. (1995). Interne openbaarheid in het strafproces: Een bedreigd goed. *Nederlands Juristenblad, 40*, 1451–1458.

Preute, M. & Preute, G. (1979). *Deutschlands Kriminalfall Nr. 1, Vera Bruhne: Justizirrtum?* München: Goldmann.

Provine, D.M. (1998). Too many black men: The sentencing judge's dilemma. *Law and Social Inquiry, 23*, 823–856.

Pruitt, R.C. (1997). Guilt by majority in the International Criminal Tribunal for the Former Yugoslavia: Does this meet the standard of proof 'beyond reasonable doubt'? *Leiden Journal for International Law, 10*, 557–578.

Quas, J.A., Redlich, A.D., Ghetti, S., & Alexander, K. (1999). *Long-term consequences on child sexual abuse victims of testifying in criminal court: Mental health and revictimization.* Paper presented at the biennial meeting of the Society for Research in Child Development, Albuquerque, New Mexico.

Quinsey, V.L., Harris, G.T., Rice, M.E., & Cormier, C.A. (1998). *Violent offenders: Appraising and managing risk.* Washington, DC: American Psychological Association.

Radelet, M.L., Bedau, H.A., & Putnam, C.E. (1992). *In spite of innocence: Erroneous convictions in capital cases.* Boston: Northeastern University Press.

Radin, E.D. (1964). *The innocents.* New York: Morrow.

Rakos, R.F. & Landsman, S. (1992). Researching the hearsay rule: Emerging findings, general issues, and future directions. *Minnesota Law Review, 76*, 655–682.

Raskin, D.C. & Esplin, P.W. (1991). Assessments of children's statements of sexual abuse. In J. Doris (Ed.), *The suggestibility of children's recollections* (pp. 153–164). Washington, DC: American Psychological Association.

Rassin, E. (1998). Onjuiste verklaringen tijdens het politieverhoor. *Justitiële Verkenningen, 24*, 74–85.

Rassin, E. & Merckelbach, H. (1999). The potential conflict between clinical and judicial decision making heuristics. *Behavioral Sciences and the Law, 17*, 237–248.

Rassin, E., Merckelbach, H., & Crombag, H. (1997). De Criteria Based Content Analysis (CBCA) als instrument om de geloofwaardigheid van getuigenverklaringen te bepalen. *Nederlands Juristenblad, 72*, 1923–1929.

Rassin, E., Merckelbach, H., & Spaan, V. (in press). When dreams become a royal road to confusion: Realistic dreams, dissociation, and fantasy proneness. *Journal of Nervous and Mental Disease.*

Rattner, A. (1988). Convicted but innocent: Wrongful conviction and the criminal justice system. *Law and Human Behavior, 12*, 283–293.

Read, J.D. & Lindsay, D.S. (Eds.). (1997). *Recollections of trauma: Scientific evidence and clinical practice.* New York: Plenum.

Recherche Adviescommissie. (1994). *De leugendetector.* Den Haag, the Netherlands: Ministerie van Justitie.

Redlich, A.D., Alexander, K.W., Goodman, G.S., Quas, J.A., Ghetti, S., & Edelstein, R.S. (2000). *Relations between child sexual abuse and juvenile delinquency: Findings from a prospective study of children and adolescents involved in the legal system.* Poster presented at the American Psychology-Law Society Biennial Conference, New Orleans, LA.

Reed, J.C. (1885). *Conduct of a lawsuit out of and in court.* Boston: Little, Brown.

Reed, J.C. (1912). *Conduct of a lawsuit out of and in court* (2nd ed.). Boston: Little, Brown.

Relkin, E. (1994). Some implications of Daubert and its potential for misuse: Misapplication to environmental tort cases and abuse of FRE 706(a) court-appointed experts. *Cardozo Law Review, 15*, 2255–2269.

Rice, M. & Harris, G. (1995). Violent recidivism: Assessing predictive validity. *Journal of Consulting and Clinical Psychology, 63*, 737–748.

Rieder, H. (1977). Die Gegenüberstellung zur Identifizierung des Beschuldigten [Lineups for the identification of suspects]. *Kriminalistik, 31*, 111–114.

Risinger, D.M. (2000). Preliminary thoughts on a functional taxonomy of expertise for the post-Kumho world. *Seton Hall Law Review 31*, 508–537.

Robertson, B. & Vigneaux, G.A. (1995). *Investigating evidence: Evaluating forensic science in the courtroom.* Chichester: Wiley.

Robertson, G., Pearson, R., & Gibb, R. (1996). Police interviewing and the use of appropriate adults. *Journal of Forensic Psychiatry, 2*, 297–309.

Roche, D. (1999). *Restorative Justice: The need for public accountability the role of open justice.* Paper presented at the Third International Meeting on Restorative Justice for Juveniles, Leuven.

Roediger, H.L. & Bergman, E.T. (1998). The controversy over recovered memories. *Psychology, Public Policy, and Law, 4*, 1091–1109.

Roemer, L., Litz, B.T., Orsillo, S.M., Ehlich, P.J., & Friedman, M.J. (1998). Increases in retrospective accounts of war-zone exposure over time: The role of PTSD symptom severity. *Journal of Traumatic Stress, 11*, 597–604.

Rolph, C.H. (1978). *The Queen's pardon.* London: Cassell.

Rose, D. (1996). *In the name of the law: The collapse of criminal justice.* London: Jonathan Cape.

Rosenberg, C.B. (1995). Detective Fuhrman, the tapes are the ruling: A history, O.J. Simpson case commentaries. *Sept. 5, 1995, WL 519716 at *3—*4*, 3–4.

Ross, D.F., Read, J.D., & Toglia, M.P. (Eds.). (1994). *Adult eyewitness testimony: Current trends and developments.* Cambridge: Cambridge University Press.

Rottman, D.B. & Tomkins, A.J. (1999). Public trust and confidence in the courts: What public opinion surveys mean to judges. *Court Management Review, 36*(Fall), 24–31.

Royal Commission on Criminal Procedure. (1993). *Report.* London: Her Majesty's Printing Office (Cmnd 2263; chaired by Viscount Runciman of Doxford).

Rubinstein, J. (1973). *City police.* New York: Ballintine.

Ruby, C.L. & Brigham, J.C. (1997). The usefulness of the criteria-based-content analysis Technique in distinguishing between truthful and fabricated allegations: A critical review. *Psychology, Public Policy, and Law, 3*, 705–737.

Saks, M.J. (1992). Normative and empirical issues about the role of expert witnesses. In D.K. Kagehiro & W.S. Laufer (Eds.), *Handbook of psychology and law* (pp. 185–203). New York: Springer.

Saks, M.J. (1994). Implications of the Daubert Test for forensic identification science. *Shepard's Expert and Scientific Evidence Quarterly, 1*, 427–434.

Saks, M.J. (1995). Court-appointed experts: Defining the role of experts appointed under federal rule of evidence by Ceci and Willging (Book review). *Jurimetrics Journal*, *35*, 233–242.

Saks, M.J. (1998). Merlin and Solomon: Lessons from the law's formative encounters with forensic identification science. *Hastings Law Journal*, *49*, 1069–1141.

Saks, M.J. & Koehler, J.J. (1991). What DNA 'fingerprinting' can teach the law about the rest of forensic science. *Cardozo Law Review*, *13*, 363–372.

Saks, M.J. & Van Duizend, R. (1983). *The uses of scientific evidence in litigation*. Williamsburg, VA: National Center for State Courts.

Sarokin, H.L. & Munsterman, G.T. (1993). Recent innovations in civil jury trial procedures. In R.E. Litan (Ed.), *Verdict: Assessing the civil jury system* (pp. 378–398). Washington, DC: Brookings Institution.

Sas, L.D. (1993). *Three years after the verdict*. London, Ontario: London Family Court.

Sas, L.D., Hurley, P., Austin, G., & Wolfe, D. (1991). *Reducing the system-induced trauma for child sexual abuse victims through court preparation, assessment, and follow-up*. London, Ontario: London Family Court.

Saywitz, K.J. (1989). Children's conceptions of the legal system: 'Court is a place to play basketball'. In S.J. Ceci, D.F. Ross, & M.P. Toglia (Eds.), *Perspectives on children's testimony* (pp. 131–157). New York: Springer.

Saywitz, K.J. & Nathanson, R. (1993). Children's testimony and their perceptions of stress in and out of the courtroom. *Child Abuse and Neglect*, *17*, 613–622.

Saywitz, K.J. & Snyder, L. (1993). Improving children's testimony with preparation. In G.S. Goodman & B.L. Bottoms (Eds.), *Child victims, child witnesses: Understanding and improving testimony* (pp. 117–146). New York: Guilford.

Saywitz, K.J., Jaenicke, C., & Camparo, L. (1990). Children's knowledge of legal terminology. *Law and Human Behavior*, *14*, 523–535.

Saywitz, K.J., Snyder, L., & Nathanson, R. (1999). Facilitating the communicative competence of the child witness. *Applied Developmental Science*, *3*, 5–68.

Scheck, B., Neufeld, P., & Dwyer, J. (2001). *Actual innocence*. New York: Signet.

Scheflin, A.W. & Van Dyke, J.M. (1980). Jury nullification: The contours of a controversy. *Law and Contemporary Problems*, *43*, 51–115.

Schooler, J.W. (1999). Seeking the core: The issues and evidence surrounding recovered accounts of sexual trauma. In L.M. Williams & V.L. Banyard (Eds.), *Trauma and memory* (pp. 203–216). Thousand Oaks, CA: Sage.

Schoordijk, H.C.F. (1988). Hoe vat(te) de Burgerlijke Kamer van de Hoge Raad zij rechtsvormende taak op?, *De plaats van de Hoge Raad in het huidige staatsbestel: De veranderingen in de rol* (pp. 3–63). Zwolle: Tjeenk Willink.

Schulhofer, S.J. (1996a). Miranda and clearance rates. *Northwestern University Law Review*, *91*, 278–294.

Schulhofer, S.J. (1996b). Miranda's practical effect: Substantial benefits and vanishingly small social costs. *Northwestern University Law Review*, *90*, 500–563.

Schulhofer, S.J. & Nagel, I.H. (1997). Plea negotiations under the Federal Sentencing Guidelines: Guideline circumvention and its dynamics in the post-Mistretta (Mistretta v. United States, 109 S. Ct. 361 (1989)) period. *Northwestern University Law Review*, *91*, 1284–1316.

Schuller, R.A. (1995). Expert evidence and hearsay: The influence of 'secondhand' information on jurors' decisions. *Law and Human Behavior*, *19*, 345–362.

Schuller, R.A. & Paglia, A. (1999). An empirical study: Juror sensitivity to variations in hearsay conveyed via expert evidence. *Law and Psychology Review*, *23*, 131–152.

Schwarzer, W.W. (1991). Reforming jury trials. *Federal Rules Decisions*, *132*, 575–596.

Schweling, D. (1969). Das Wiedererkennen des Täters [The identification of criminals]. *Monatschrift für Deutsches Recht*, *28*, 177–179.

Sealy, A.P. (1998). Decision processes in the jury room. In H. Wegner, F. Lösel, & J. Haisch (Eds.), *Behavior and the justice system: Psychological perspectives* (pp. 163–180). New York: Springer.

Sear, L. & Stephenson, G.M. (1997). Interviewing skills and individual characteristics of police interrogations. In G.M. Stephenson & N.K. Clark (Eds.), *Procedures in criminal justice: Contemporary psychological issues* (pp. 27–34). Leicester: The British Psychological Society.

Sear, L. & Williamson, T. (1999). British and American interrogation strategies. In D. Canter & L. Alison (Eds.), *Interviewing and deception* (pp. 67–81). Darmouth: Ashgate.

Sello, E. (1911). *Die Irrtümer der Strafjustiz und ihre Ursachen [Errors of criminal justice and their causes]* (Vol. 1). Berlin: R. v. Decker's Verlag.

Sentell, R.P., Jr. (1991). The Georgia jury and negligence: The view from the bench. *Georgia Law Review, 26*, 85–178.

Sentell, R.P., Jr. (1992). The Georgia jury and negligence: The view from the (federal) bench. *Georgia Law Review, 27*, 59–120.

Sepejak, D., Menzies, R., Webster, C., & Jensen, F. (1983). Clinical predictions of dangerousness: Two-year follow-up of 408 pre-trial forensic cases. *Bulletin of the American Academy of Psychiatry and the Law, 11*, 171–181.

Sharlitt, J.H. (1989). *Fatal error: The miscarriage of justice that sealed the Rosenberg's fate.* New York: Scribner.

Shepherd, J.W., Ellis, H.E., & Davies, G.M. (1982). *Identification evidence.* Aberdeen: University of Aberdeen Press.

Shin, W.S. (1974). *Comparative analysis of Korean and American judicial systems.* Chicago: American Judicature Society.

Shuman, D.W. (1997). Framing the questions of the admissibility of expert testimony about recollections of trauma in the United States. In J.D. Read & D.S. Lindsay (Eds.), *Recollections of trauma: Scientific evidence and clinical practice* (pp. 495–500). New York: Plenum.

Shuman, D.W., Stuart, G., Heilbrun, K., & Foote, W.E. (1998). An immodest proposal: Should treating mental health professionals be barred from testifying about their patients? *Behavioral Sciences and the Law, 16*, 509–523.

Shuy, R.W. (1998). *The language of confesion, interrogation, and deception.* Thousand Oaks, CA: Sage.

Siegal, M. & Peterson, C.C. (1996). Breaking the mold: A fresh look at children's understanding of questions about lies and mistakes. *Developmental Psychology, 32*, 322–334.

Sisterman-Keeney, K., Amachev, E., & Kastankis, J. (1992). The court prep group: A vital part of the court process. In H. Dent & R. Flin (Eds.), *Child as witnesses* (pp. 201–209). Chichester: Wiley.

Sjerps, M. (2000). Pros and cons of Bayesian reasoning in forensic science. In J.F. Nijboer & W.J.J.M. Sprangers (Eds.), *Harmonisation in forensic expertise: An inquiry into the desirability of and opportunities for international standards* (pp. 557–585). Amsterdam: Thela Thesis.

Skolnick, J.H. & Leo, R.A. (1992). The ethics of deceptive interrogation. In J.W. Bizzack (Ed.), *Issues in policing: New perspectives* (pp. 75–95). Lexiington, KY: Autumn House.

Slobogin, C. (1997). Deceit, pretext, and trickery: Investigative lies by the police. *Oregon Law Review, 76*, 775–816.

Slobogin, C. (1998). *Criminal procedure: Regulation of police investigation: Legal, historical, comparative and empirical materials.* Charlottesville, VA: Lexis.

Slobogin, C. (1999). Why liberals should chuck the exclusionary rule. *Illinois Law Review*, 363–446.

Slobogin, C. & Schumacher, J. (1993). Reasonable expectations of privacy and autonomy in fourth amendment cases: An empirical look at understandings recognized and permitted by society. *Duke Law Journal, 42*, 727–775.

Smith, E. (1997). Evidentiary standards in sexual abuse cases in Nordic legal systems. In J.D. Read & D.S. Lindsay (Eds.), *Recollections of trauma: Scientific evidence and clinical practice* (pp. 505–509). New York: Plenum.

Sno, H.N. & Schalken, H.F.A. (1998). Dissociatieve identiteitsstoornis in Nederland: diagnostiek en behandeling door psychiaters [Dissociative Identity Disorder in the Netherlands: Diagnosis and treatment by psychiatrists]. *Tijdschrift voor Psychiatrie, 40,* 602–614.

Snow, C.P. (1959). *The two cultures and the scientific revolution.* New York: Cambridge University Press.

Solecki, P.K. (1982). (Book review). *Milwaukee Law Review, 98,* 163.

Sotscheck, R. (Ed.). (1990). *The Birmingham Six: An appalling vista.* Dublin: Litereire.

Soukara, S. (2000). Identifying the best strategy to elicit valid information from uncooperative suspects. Paper presented at the departmental seminar programme. University of Portsmouth, Psychology Department.

Spencer, J.R. (1989). Children's evidence in legal proceedings in England. In J.R. Spencer, G. Nicholson, R. Flin, & R. Bull (Eds.), *Children's evidence in legal proceedings: An international perspective* (pp. 113–125). Cambridge.

Spencer, J.R. (1998). The role of experts in the common law and the civil law: A comparison. In S.J. Ceci & H. Hembrooke (Eds.), *Expert witnesses in child abuse cases: What can and should be said in court* (pp. 29–81). Washington, DC: American Psychological Association.

Spencer, J.R. (2000). Evidence and forensic science. In J.F. Nijboer & W.J.J.M. Sprangers (Eds.), *Harmonisation in forensic expertise* (pp. 73–85). Amsterdam: Thela Thesis.

Spencer, J.R. & Flin, R.H. (1993). *The evidence of children: The law and the psychology* (2nd ed.). London: Blackstone.

Sporer, S.L. (1982). A brief history of the psychology of testimony. *Current Psychological Reviews, 2,* 323–340.

Sporer, S.L. (1984). Experimentalpsychologische Grundlagen der Personenidentifizierung und ihre Bedeutung für die Strafrechtspraxis [Experimental psychological foundations of person identifications and their implications for criminal law]. *Monatschrift für Kriminologie und Strafrechtsreform, 67,* 339–348.

Sporer, S.L. (1992). Post-dicting eyewitness accuracy: Confidence, decision-times and person descriptions of choosers and non-choosers. *European Journal of Social Psychology, 22,* 157–180.

Sporer, S.L. (1993). Eyewitness identification accuracy, confidence and decision-times in simultaneous and sequential lineups. *Journal of Applied Psychology, 78,* 22–33.

Sporer, S.L. (1994). Decision-times and eyewitness identification accuracy in simultaneous and sequential lineups. In D.F. Ross, J.D. Read, & M.P. Toglia (Eds.), *Adult eyewitness testimony: Current trends and developments* (pp. 300–327). New York: Cambridge University Press.

Sporer, S.L. (1995). Experimentally induced person mix-ups through media exposure and ways to avoid them. In G.M. Davies, S.M.A. Lloyd-Bostock, M. McMurran, & C. Wilson (Eds.), *Psychology, law, and criminal justice: International developments in research and practice.* Berlin: De Gruyter.

Sporer, S.L. (1996). Psychological aspects of person descriptions. In S.L. Sporer, R.S. Malpass, & G. Köhnken (Eds.), *Psychological issues in eyewitness identification* (pp. 53–86). Mahwah, NJ: Erlbaum.

Sporer, S.L. (2001). The cross-race effect: Beyond recognition of faces in the laboratory. *Psychology, Public Policy, and Law, 7,* 170–200.

Sporer, S.L., Eickelkamp, A., & Spitmann-Rex, D. (1990). Live-Gegenüberstellungen vs. Lichtbildvorlagen: Ein experimenteller Vergleich unterschiedlicher Präsentationsmodi

[Live lineups vs. photospreads: An experimental comparison of different presentation modes]. In D. Meurer & S.L. Sporer (Eds.), *Zum Beweiswert von Personenidentifizierungen: Neuere empirische Befunde* (pp. 48–105). Marburg: N.G. Elwert.

Sporer, S.L., Köhnken, G., & Malpass, R.S. (1996). Introduction: 200 years of mistaken identification. In S.L. Sporer, R.S. Malpass, & G. Köhnken (Eds.), *Psychological issues in eyewitness identification* (pp. 1–6). Mahwah, NJ: Erlbaum.

Sporer, S.L., Malpass, R.S., & Koehnken, G. (Eds.). (1996). *Psychological issues in eyewitness identification*. Mahwah, NJ: Erlbaum.

St. George, D. (1993). Fairness, race, and the jury system. *Philadelphia Inquirer* (April 11), 1.

Stadler, M. & Fabian, T. (1995). Der Erwartungseffekt beim Wiedererkennen von Personen, oder: Über die Tendenz, Wahrnehmungshypothesen zu bestätigen [The expectancy effect in person identification, or: On the tendency to confirm perceptual hypotheses]. *Zeitschrift für experimentelle Psychologie, 57*, 132–151.

Starrs, J.E. (1996). Recent developments in federal and state rules pertaining to medical and scientific testimony. *Duquesne Law Review, 34*, 813.

State of New Jersey Attorney-General. (2001). *Attorney-general guidelines for preparing and conducting photo and live lineup identification procedures.* Trenton, NJ: New Jersey Department of Law and Public Safety, Division of Criminal Justice.

Steadman, H.J. (1977). A new look at recidivism among Patuxent inmates. *Bulletin on the American Academy of Psychiatry and the Law, 5*, 200–209.

Steadman, H.J. & Cocozza, J. (1974). *Careers of the criminally insane.* Lexington, MA: Lexington.

Steblay, N., Dysart, J., Fulero, S.M., & Lindsay, R.C.L. (2001). Eyewitness accuracy rates in sequential and simultaneous lineup presentations: A meta-analytic comparison. *Law and Human Behavior, 25*, 459–473.

Steblay, N.M. (1997). Social influence on eyewitness recall: A meta-analytic review of lineup instruction effects. *Law and Human Behavior, 21*, 283–297.

Steinke, W. (1978). Die Problematik der Wahlgegenüberstellung. *Kriminalistik, 32*, 505–507.

Steller, M. (1989). Recent developments in statement analysis. In J.C. Yuille (Ed.), *Credibility assessment* (pp. 135–154). Dordrecht: Kluwer Academic.

Steller, M. & Köhnken, G. (1989). Criteria-based statement analysis. In D.C. Raskin (Ed.), *Psychological methods for criminal investigation and evidence* (pp. 217–246). New York: Springer.

Stephenson, G.M. & Moston, S.J. (1994). Police interrogation. *Psychology, Crime, and Law, 1*, 151–157.

Stern, P. (2001). *Surviving in the courtroom: Twelve rules of testifying as an expert witness.* Unpublished paper.

Sternberg, K.J., Lamb, M.E., & Hershkowitz, I. (1996). Child sexual abuse investigations in Israel. *Criminal Justice and Behavior, 23*, 322–327.

Stevens, D. & Berliner, L. (1980). Special techniques for child witnesses. In L.G. Schultz (Ed.), *The sexual victimology of youth* (pp. 246–257). Springfield, IL: Thomas.

Stinson, V., Devenport, J.L., Cutler, B.L., & Kravitz, D.A. (1996). How effective is the presence-of-counsel safeguard? Attorney perceptions of suggestiveness, fairness, and correctability of biased lineup procedures. *Journal of Applied Psychology, 81*, 64–75.

Stoney, D.A. (1997). Fingerprint identification: B. Scientific status. In D.L. Faigman, D.H. Kaye, M.J. Saks, & J. Sanders (Eds.), *Modern scientific evidence: The law and science of expert testimony* (Vol. 2, pp. 55–78). St. Paul, MI: West.

Stortino, L. (1976). *L'abuso di potere nel diritto penale.* Milano: Giuffre.

Stricker, G. (1985). Psychological assessment and Miranda rights. *Journal of Personality Assessment, 49*, 656–658.

Studebaker, C.A. & Penrod, S.D. (1997). Pretrial publicity: The media, the law, and common sense. *Psychology, Public Policy, and Law, 3*, 428–460.

Stuntz, W. (1991). Warrants and fourth amendment remedies. *Virginia Law Review, 77,* 881–943.

Stuntz, W. (1997). The uneasy relationship between criminal procedure and criminal justice. *Yale Law Journal, 107,* 1–76.

Subcommittee on Civil and Constitutional Rights of the Committee on the Judiciary. (1994). *Innocence and the death penalty: Assessing the danger of mistaken executions (staff report).* Washington, DC: U.S.G.P.O.

Sutermeister, H.M. (1976). *Summa iniuria: Ein Pitaval der Justiz-irrtümer: Funfhundert Falle menschlichen Versagens im Bereich der Rechtsprechung in kriminal- und sozialpsychologischer Sicht.* Basel: Elfenau.

Swart, B. (1999). The European Convention as an invigorator of domestic law in the Netherlands. *Journal of Law and Society, 26,* 38–53.

Swets, J., Dawes, R., & Monahan, J. (2000). Psychological science can improve diagnostic decisions. *Psychological Science in the Public Interest, 1,* 1–26.

Swier, B. (1999). Nieuwe 'miscarriages of justice' in Engeland door beperking interne openbaarheid? *Delikt and Delinkwent, 29,* 627–644.

Tanford, S. (1985). Decision making processes in joined criminal trials. *Criminal Justice and Behavior, 12,* 367–385.

Tanford, S. & Penrod, S.D. (1982). Biases in trials involving defendants charged with multiple offenses. *Journal of Applied Social Psychology, 12,* 453–480.

Tanford, S. & Penrod, S.D. (1983). Computer modeling of influence in the jury: The role of the consistent juror. *Social Psychology Quarterly, 46,* 200–212.

Tanford, S. & Penrod, S.D. (1984). Social inference processes in juror judgments of multiple-offense trials. *Journal of Personality and Social Psychology, 47,* 749–765.

Tanford, S., Penrod, S.D., & Collins, R. (1985). Decisionmaking in joined criminal trials: The influence of charge similarity, evidence similarity, and limiting instructions. *Law and Human Behavior, 9,* 319–337.

Taslitz, A. (1993). Catharsis, the confrontation clause, and expert testimony. *Capital University Law Review, 22,* 103–144.

Technical Working Group for Eyewitness Evidence. (1999). *Eyewitness evidence: A guide for law enforcement.* Washington, DC: United States Department of Justice, Office of Justice Programs.

Terr, L. (1984). Time and trauma. *Psychoanalytic Study of the Child, 39,* 333–366.

Thaman, S.C. (1999). Europe's new jury systems: The cases of Spain and Russia. *Law and Contemporary Problems, 62,* 233–260.

The View from the Bench (1987). *National Law Journal,* (August 10), S1.

Thibaut, J.W. & Walker, L.J. (1975). *Procedural justice: A psychological analysis.* New York: Wiley.

Thibaut, J.W. & Walker, L.J. (1978). A theory of procedure. *California Law Review, 66,* 541–566.

Thomas, G.C. (1996). Plain talk about the Miranda empirical debate: A "steady-state" theory of confessions. *UCLA Law Review, 43,* 933–959.

Thomas, G.C. (2000). The end of the road for Miranda v. Arizona?: On the history and the future of the rules for police interrogation. *American Criminal Law Review, 37,* 1–48.

Thompson, W.C. (1989). Are juries competent to evaluate statistical evidence? *Law and Contemporary Problems, 52*(4), 9–41.

Thompson, W.C. & Pathak, M.K. (1999). Empirical study of hearsay rules: Bridging the gap between psychology and law. *Psychology, Public Policy, and Law, 5,* 456–472.

Thornberry, T. & Jacoby, J. (1979). *The criminally insane: A community follow-up of mentally ill offenders* (2nd ed.). Chicago: University of Chicago Press.

Thornton, P. (1993). Miscarriages of justice: A lost opportunity. *The Criminal Law Review, 1993,* 926–935.

Tichane, G. (1984). *Coupable a tout prix: L'affaire Luc Tangorre*. Paris: Decouverte.

Tillers, P. & Schum, D. (1992). Hearsay logic. *Minnesota Law Review, 76,* 813–858.

Tochilovski, V. (1998). Trial in international criminal jurisdictions: Battle or scrutiny? *European Journal of Crime, Criminal Law and Criminal Justice, 6,* 55–60.

Toobin, J. (1987). *Viva Miranda*. New Republic (February), 11–12.

Toobin, J. (1996). *The run of his life: The people v. O.J. Simpson*. New York: Random House.

Toornvliet, L.G. (2000). Methodology of the research. In J.F. Nijboer & W.J.J.M. Sprangers (Eds.), *Harmonisation in forensic expertise: An inquiry into the desirability of and opportunities for international standards* (pp. 23–33). Amsterdam: Thela Thesis.

Trubek, D.M., Sarat, A., & Felstiner, W. (1983). The cost of ordinary litigation. *UCLA Law Review, 31,* 72–127.

Tsai, G.E., Condie, D., Wu, M.T., & Chang, I.W. (1999). Functional magnetic resonance imaging of personality switches in a woman with dissociative identity disorder. *Harvard Review of Psychiatry, 7,* 119–122.

Tullock, G. (1994). Court errors. *European Journal of Law and Economics, 1,* 9–21.

Tumim, S. (1983). *Great legal disasters*. London: Barker. Reprinted in J.R. Waltz & R.C. Park (Eds.), (1999), *Evidence: Cases and materials* (9th ed., pp. 472 ff.). New York: Foundation Press).

Turtle, J.W. & Wells, G.L. (1988). Children versus adults as eyewitnesses: Whose testimony holds up under cross-examination? In M.M. Gruneberg, P.E. Morris, & R.N. Sykes (Eds.), *Practical aspects of memory: Current research and issues* (Vol. 1, pp. 27–33). New York: Wiley.

Turvey, B.E. (1999). *Criminal profiling: An introduction to behavioral evidence analysis*. San Diego: Academic Press.

Tyler, T.R. (1990). *Why people obey the law*. New Haven: Yale University Press.

Undeutsch, U. (1967). Beurteilung der Glaubhaftigkeit von Aussagen [Evaluation of the credibility of statements]. In U. Undeutsch (Ed.), *Handbuch der Psychologie: Forensische Psychologie* (pp. 28–181, Vol. 11). Göttingen: Hogrefe.

Undeutsch, U. (1983). Statement reality analysis. In A. Trankell (Ed.), *Reconstructing the past: The role of psychologists in criminal trials* (pp. 27–56). Deventer: Kluwer.

Undeutsch, U. (1989). The development of statement reality analysis. In J.C. Yuille (Ed.), *Credibility assessment* (pp. 101–119). Dordrecht: Kluwer Academic.

Uviller, H.R. (1996). *Virtual justice: The flawed prosecution of crime in America*. New Haven: Yale University Press.

van Amelsvoort, A.G. (1996). *Handleiding confrontatie*. Den Haag: Vuga (2e herziene druk).

van Beek, D.J. (1999). *De delictscenarioprocedure bij seksueel agressieve delinquenten [The offence script procedure with sexually aggressive offenders]*. Deventer, the Netherlands: Gouda Quint (diss. University of Amsterdam).

van Cleave, R.A. (1997). An offer you can't refuse? Punishment without trial in Italy and the United States: The search for truth and an efficient criminal justice system. *Emory International Law Review, 11,* 419–469.

van de Bunt, H.G. (1985). *Officieren van Justitie: Verslag van een participerend observatieonderzoek*. Zwolle: Tjeenk Willink (diss. Utrecht).

van de Pol, U. (1986). *Openbaar terecht. Een onderzoek van het openbaarheidsbeginsel in de strafrechtspleging*. Arnhem: Gouda Quint.

van den Adel, H.M. (1997). *Handleiding verdachtenverhoor: Handhaving, controle en opsporing in de praktijk*. Den Haag: Vuga.

van der Hart, O., Boon, S., & Heijtmajer Jansen, O. (1997). Ritual abuse in European countries: A clinician's perspective. In G.A. Freser (Ed.), *The dilemma of ritual abuse: Cautions and guides for therapists* (pp. 137–163). Washington, DC: American Psychiatric Press.

van der Kolk, B.A. (1994). The body keeps the score: Memory and the evolving psychobiology of posttraumatic stress. *Harvard Review of Psychiatry, 1,* 253–265.

van Duizend, R., Sutton, L.P., & Carter, C.A. (1985). *The search warrant process: Preconceptions, perceptions and practices*. Williamsburg, VA: National Center for State Courts.

van Emmerik, J.L. (1985). *TBS en recidive: Een beschrijving van ter beschikking gestelden van wie de maatregel is beëindigd in de periode 1974–1979. [Recidivism after forensic psychiatric treatment: A description of forensic patients who were released between 1974–1979]*. The Hague, the Netherlands: Staatsuitgeverij.

van Emmerik, J.L. (1989). *TBS en recidive: Een beschrijving van ter beschikking gestelden van wie de maatregel is beëindigd in de periode 1979–1983. [Recidivism after forensic psychiatric treatment: A description of forensic patients who were released between 1973–1983]*. Arnhem: Gouda Quint.

van Emmerik, J.L. (1997). *Prevalence findings TBS 1990–1996*. Utrecht, the Netherlands: Dr. F.S. Meijers Instituut, Department of Monitoring and Research.

van Gulik, R.H. (1959). *The Chinese bell murders: Three cases solved by Judge Dee (A Chinese detective story suggested by three original Chinese plots)*. New York: Harper.

van Gulik, R.H. (1961). *The Chinese nail murders*. London: Joseph.

van Kampen, P.T.C. (1998). *Expert evidence compared: Rules and practices in the Dutch and American criminal justice system*. Antwerpen: Intersentia (diss. Leiden).

van Kampen, P.T.C. (1999). Expert evidence compared. In M. Malsch & J.F. Nijboer (Eds.), *Complex cases: Perspective on the Netherlands criminal justice system*. Amsterdam: Thela Thesis.

van Kampen, P.T.C. (2000a). Confronting expert evidence under the European Convention. In J.F. Nijboer & W.J.J.M. Sprangers (Eds.), *Harmonisation in forensic expertise: An inquiry into the disirability of and opportunities for international standards* (pp. 183–211). Amsterdam: Thela Thesis.

van Kampen, P.T.C. (2000b). De positie van het Gerechtelijk Laboratorium: onafhankelijkheid in meer perspectieven. In K. Boonen, A.C. 't Hart, & T.A. de Roos (Eds.), *Criminalistiek, forensische deskundigen en strafrechtpleging* (pp. 59–73). Deventer: Gouda Quint.

van Kampen, P.T.C. & Nijboer, J.F. (1997). Daubert in the lowlands. *U.C. Davis Law Review, 30*, 951–995.

van Kessel, G. (1986). The suspect as a source of testimonial evidence: A comparison of the English and American approaches. *Hastings Law Journal, 38*, 1–152.

van Kessel, G. (1992). Adversary excesses in the American criminal trial. *Notre Dame Law Review, 67*, 403–551.

van Kessel, G. (1998). European perspectives on the accused as a source of testimonial evidence. *West Virginia Law Review, 100*, 799–845.

van Koppen, P.J. (1995). Sniffing experts: Theory and practise of scent line-ups. *Expert Evidence, 3*, 103–108.

van Koppen, P.J. (1997). *Hervonden misdrijven: Over aangiftes van seksueel misbruik na therapie*. Leiden: Nederlands Studiecentrum Criminaliteit en Rechtshandhaving (NSCR) (Advies aan de Minister van Justitie).

van Koppen, P.J. (1998). *Recovered crimes: Sexual abuse reported to the police after therapy*. Leiden: Netherlands Institute for the Study of Criminality and Law Enforcement (NIS-CALE) (Advice to the Minister of Justice; translation of P.J. van Koppen (1997) Hervonden misdrijven: Over aangiftes van seksueel misbruik na therapie. Leiden: Nederlands Studiecentrum Criminaliteit en Rechtshandhaving (NSCR) (Advies aan de Minister van Justitie).

van Koppen, P.J. (1998a). Bekennen als bewijs: Bedenkingen bij het verhoor van de verdachte. *Justitiële Verkenningen, 24*(4), 61–73.

van Koppen, P.J. (1998b). *Recovered crimes: Sexual abuse reported to the police after therapy*. Leiden: Netherlands Institute for the Study of Criminality and Law Enforcement

(NISCALE) (Advice to the Minister of Justice; translation of P.J. van Koppen (1997) Hervonden misdrijven: Over aangiftes van seksueel misbruik na therapie. Leiden: Nederlands Studiecentrum Criminaliteit en Rechtshandhaving (NSCR) (Advies aan de Minister van Justitie)).

van Koppen, P.J. & Crombag, H.F.M. (2000). Oren, lippen en vingers: De waarde van oud en nieuw identificatiebewijs. *Nederlands Juristenblad, 75*, 6–12.

van Koppen, P.J. & Hessing, D.J. (1999). De confrontatie in de praktijk. *Ars Aequi, 48*, 103–107.

van Koppen, P.J. & Merckelbach, H.L.G.J. (1998). De waarheid in therapie en in rechte: Pseudoherinneringen aan seksueel misbruik [On truth in therapy and in the court: Pseudomemories of sexual abuse]. *Nederlands Juristenblad, 73*, 899–904.

van Koppen, P.J. & Merckelbach, H.L.G.J. (1999). Characteristics of recovered memories: A Dutch replication of Gudjonsson's (1997) British survey. *Applied Cognitive Psychology, 13*, 485–489.

van Koppen, P.J. & Saks, M.J. (2003). Preventing bad psychological scientific evidence in The Netherlands and the United States. In P.J. van Koppen & S.D. Penrod (Eds.), *Adversarial versus inquisitorial justice: Psychological perspectives on criminal justice systems*. New York: Plenum (in press).

van Koppen, P.J., Boelhouwer, A.J.W., Merckelbach, H.L.G.J., & Verbaten, M.N. (1996). *Leugendetectie in actie: Het gebruik van de polygraaf in de praktijk*. Leiden: Nederlands Studiecentrum Criminaliteit en Rechtshandhaving (NSCR) (Rapport aangeboden aan de minister van Justitie).

van Koppen, P.J., Hessing, D.J., & de Poot, C.J. (2001). *Public reasons for abolition and retention of the death penalty* (submitted for publication).

van Langenhove, L. (1989). *Juryrechtspraak en psychologie*. Arnhem: Gouda Quint.

van Straten, H. (1990). *Moordenaarswerk: Nederlandse moordzaken die de experts verbijsterden*. Amsterdam: Arbeiderspers (2e herziene druk).

van Traa, M. (1996). *Inzake opsporing: Enquêtecommissie opsporngsmethoden*. Den Haag: SDU (11 delen).

Vaughn, M.S. & Smith, L.G. (1999). Practicing penal harm medicine in the United States: Prisoners' voices from jail. *Justice Quarterly, 16*, 175–231.

Vidal-Naquet, P. (1984). *De l'erreur judiciaire au crime judiciaire*. Paris: Decouverte.

Vokey, J.R. & Read, J.D. (1992). Familiarity, memorability, and the effect of typicality on the recognition of faces. *Memory and Cognition, 20*, 291–302.

Vosskuhle, A. (1993). *Rechtsschutz gegen den Richter: Zur Integration der Dritten Gewalt in das verfassungsrechtliche Kontrollsystem vor dem Hintergrund des Art. 19 Abs. 4 GG*. München: Beck.

Vrij, A. (1995). Behavioral correlates of deception in a simulated police interview. *Journal of Psychology: Interdisciplinary and Applied, 129*, 15–29.

Vrij, A. (1997). Goede politieverhoren. *Tijdschrift voor de Politie, 59*(12), 27–30.

Vrij, A. (1997). Verhoren van de verdachte en bekentenissen. In P.J. van Koppen, D.J. Hessing, & H.F.M. Crombag (Eds.), *Het hart van de zaak: Psychologie van het recht* (pp. 469–492). Deventer: Gouda Quint.

Vrij, A. (1998a). Interviewing suspects. In A. Memon, A. Vrij, & R.H. Bull (Eds.), *Psychology and law: Truthfulness, accuracy and credibility* (pp. 124–147). London: McGraw Hill.

Vrij, A. (1998b). To lie or not to lie. *Psychologie, 17*, 22–25.

Vrij, A. (2000). *Detecting lies and deceit: The psychology of lying and its implications for professional practice*. Chichester: Wiley.

Vrij, A. (2003). 'We will protect your wife and child, but only if you confess': Police interrogations in England and the Netherlands. In P.J. van Koppen & S.D. Penrod (Eds.), *Adversarial versus inquisitorial justice: Psychological perspectives on criminal justice systems*. New York: Plenum.

Vrij, A. & Lochun, S.K. (1997). Neurolinguïstisch verhoren. In P.J. van Koppen, D.J. Hessing, & H.F.M. Crombag (Eds.), *Het hart van de zaak: Psychologie van het recht* (pp. 493–504). Deventer: Gouda Quint.

Vrij, A. & Mann, S. (2001). Telling and detecting lies in a high-stake situation: The case of a convicted murderer. *Applied Cognitive Psychology, 15*, 187–203.

Vrij, A. & Semin, G.R. (1996). Lie experts' beliefs about nonverbal indicators of deception. *Journal of Nonverbal Behavior, 20*, 65–81.

Vrij, A., Nunkoosing, K., Oosterwegel, A., & Soukara, S. (2000). 'I'm not telling you: It is a secret'. Paper presented at the departmental seminar programme. University of Portsmouth, Psychology Department.

Wadham, J. (1993). Unraveling miscarriages of justice. *New Law Journal, 143*, 1650–1651.

Wagenaar, W.A. (1988). *Identifying Ivan: A case study in legal psychology*. New York: Harvester, Wheatsheaf.

Wagenaar, W.A. (1998). De vraag aan de deskundige. In R.A.R. Bullens (Ed.), *Getuigedeskundigen in zedenzaken: De positie van de gedragswetenschapper bij strafzaken rondom seksueel misbruik van kinderen* (pp. 47–59). Leiden: DSWO Press, Rijksuniversiteit Leiden.

Wagenaar, W.A., van Koppen, P.J., & Crombag, H.F.M. (1993). *Anchored narratives: The psychology of criminal evidence*. London: Harvester Wheatsheaf.

Walker, A.G. (1993). Questioning young children in court: A linguistic case study. *Law and Human Behavior, 17*, 59–81.

Walker, A.G. & Warren, A.R. (1995). The language of the child abuse interview: Asking the questions, understanding the answers. In T. Ney (Ed.), *True and false allegations of child sexual abuse: Assessment and case management* (pp. 153–162). New York: Brunner.

Walker, C. & Starmer, K. (Eds.). (1993). *Justice in error*. London: Blackstone.

Walker, C. & Starmer, K. (Eds.). (1999). *Miscarriages of justice: A review of justice in error*. London: Blackstone.

Walker, N. (1991). *Why punish?* Oxford: Oxford University Press.

Walker, S. (1996). *A dose of sanity: Mind, medicine, and misdiagnosis*. New York: Wiley.

Walkley, J. (1987). *Police interrogation: Handbook for investigators*. London: Police Review Publication.

Wall, J.A. & Rude, D.E. (1985). Judicial mediation: Techniques, strategies and situational effects. *Journal of Social Issues, 41*, 47–63.

Waller, G. (1989). *Miscarriages of justice*. London: Justice.

Walsh, D. (1993). Miscarriages of justice in the Republic of Ireland. In C. Walker & K. Starmer (Eds.), *Justice in error* (pp. 203–222). London: Blackstone.

Walster, G.W., Walster, E., & Berscheid, E. (1978). *Equity: Theory and research*. Boston: Allyn and Bacon.

Warren Leubecker, A., Tate, C., Hinton, I., & Ozbek, N. (1989). What do children know about the legal system and when do they know it? In S.J. Ceci, D.R. Ross, & M.P. Toglia (Eds.), *Perspectives on children's testimony* (pp. 158–183). New York: Springer.

Warren, A. & Woodall, C.E. (1997). The reliability of hearsay testimony: How well do interviewers recall their interviews with children. *Psychology, Public Policy, and Law, 5*, 355–371.

Warren, A.R., Nunez, N., Keeney, J.M., Buck, J.A., & Smith, B. (2001). *Children and hearsay: When less is more* (unpublished manuscript).

Wasby, S.L. (1978). Police training about criminal procedure: Infrequent and inadequate. *Policy Studies Journal, 7*, 461–472.

Webster, C.D., Douglas, K.S., Eaves, D., & Hart, S.D. (1997). *HCR-20: Assessing risk for violence, Version 2*. Burnaby, British Columbia: Simon Fraser University Press.

Wedding, D. & Faust, D. (1989). Clinical judgment and decision making in neuropsychology. *Archives of Clinical Neuropsychology, 4*, 233–265.

Weigend, T. (1999). Germany: rules of criminal procedure. In C. Bradley (Ed.), *Criminal procedure: A worldwide study* (pp. 187–216). Durham, NC: Carolina Academic Press.

Wellborn III, O.G. (1991). Demeanor. *Cornell Law Review, 76*, 1075–1105.

Wellman, F.L. (1948). *The art of cross-examination: With the cross-examinations of important witnesses in some celebrated cases.* Garden City, NY: Garden City Books.

Wellman, F.L. (1986). *The art of cross-examination: With the cross-examinations of important witnesses in some celebrated cases* (4th paperback ed.). New York: Collier.

Wells, G.L. (1978). Applied eyewitness-testimony research: System variables and estimator variables. *Journal of Personality and Social Psychology, 36*, 1546–1557.

Wells, G.L. (1984). The psychology of lineup identifications. *Journal of Applied Social Psychology, 14*, 89–103.

Wells, G.L. & Bradfield, A.L. (1999). Distortions in eyewitnesses' recollections: Can the post-identification feedback effect be moderated? *Psychological Science, 10*, 138–144.

Wells, G.L. & Luus, C.A.E. (1990). Police lineups as experiments: Social methodology as a framework for properly-conducted lineups. *Personality and Social Psychology Bulletin, 16*, 106–117.

Wells, G.L., Small, M., Penrod, S.D., Malpass, R.S., Fulero, S.M., & Brimacombe, C.A.E. (1998). Eyewitness identification procedures: Recommendations for lineups and photospreads. *Law and Human Behavior, 23*, 603–647.

Werkgroep Identificatie. (1989). *Identificatie van personen door ooggetuigen.* Den Haag: Ministerie van Justitie, Recherche Advies Commissie, werkgroep Identificatie (voorzitter P. Bender).

Werkgroep Identificatie. (1992). *Rapport identificatie van personen door ooggetuigen.* Den Haag: Ministerie van Justitie, Recherche Advies Commissie, werkgroep Identificatie (voorzitter P. Bender; 2e herziene druk).

Westervelt, S.D. (Ed.). (2001). *Wrongly convicted: Perspectives on failed justice.* New Brunswick, NJ: Rutgers University Press.

Westhoff, K. & Kluck, M.-L. (1998). *Psychologische Gutachten schreiben und beurteilen.* Berlin: Springer.

Whitcomb, D. (1992). Legal reforms on behalf of child witnesses: Recent developments in American courts. In H. Dent & R. Flin (Eds.), *Children as witnesses* (pp. 151–165). Chichester: Wiley.

Whitcomb, D., Runyan, D.K., DeVos, E., Hunter, W.M., Cross, T.P., Everson, M.D., Peeler, N.A., Porter, C.Q., Toth, P.A., & Cropper, C. (1991). *Child victims as witnesses: Research and development program.* Washington, DC: American Bar Association (Final report to the Office of Juvenile Justice and Delinquency Prevention).

Whitebread, C. & Slobogin, C. (2000). *Criminal procedure: An analysis of cases and concepts.* New York: Foundation Press.

Wickersham, J. (1938). *Old Yukon: Tales—trails—and trials.* Washington, DC: Washington Law Book.

Wiertsema, H., Feldbrugge, J., & Derks, F.C.H. (1995). Money: An important but neglected topic in forensic mental health hospitals. *Therapeutic Communities, 16*, 153–162.

Wigmore, J. (1960). *On evidence* (3rd ed.). Boston: Little, Brown.

Wigmore, J.H. (1935/1976). *Evidence in trials at common law* (Vol. 6). Boston: Little, Brown (revised by J. Chadborn).

Wigmore, J.H. (1937). *The science of judicial proof as given by logic, psychology, and general experience* (3rd ed.). Boston: Little Brown.

Wigmore, J.H. (1974). *Evidence* (4th ed.). Boston: Little Brown (revised by J.H. Chadbourn).

Wilkinson, J.C., Zielinski, F.D., & Curtis, G.M. (1988). A bicentennial transition: Modern alternatives to Seventh Amendment jury trial in complex cases. *Kansas Law Review, 37,* 61–105.

Williams, C. (2000). A controversial expert witness. *Family Law, 30,* 175–180.

Williams, J.L. (1973). *Operant learning: Procedures for changing behavior* (3rd ed.). Monterey, CA: Brooks.

Williams, L.M. (1994). Recall of childhood trauma: A prospective study of women's memories of child sexual abuse. *Journal of Consulting and Clinical Psychology, 62,* 1167–1176.

Williamson, T. (1994). Reflections in current police practice. In D. Morgan & G.M. Stephenson (Eds.), *Suspicion and silence: The right to silence in criminal investigations* (pp. 107–116). London: Blackstone.

Wilson, P. (1991). Miscarriages of justice in serious criminal cases in Australia. In K. Carrington, M. Dever, R. Hogg, J. Bargen, & A. Lohrey (Eds.), *Travesty! Miscarriages of justice* (pp. 1–17). Leichhardt, NSW: Pluto.

Woffinden, B. (1987). *Miscarriages of justice.* London: Hodder & Stoughton.

Wogalter, M.S., Malpass, R.S., & Burger, M.A. (1993). How police officers construct lineups: A national survey, *Proceedings of the Human Factors and Ergonomics Society* (pp. 640–644). Santa Monica, CA: Human Factors and Ergonomics Society.

Wright, L. (1993a). Remembering Satan: Part I. *The New Yorker, (May 17),* 60–81.

Wright, L. (1993b). Remembering Satan: Part II. *The New Yorker, (May 24),* 54–76.

Wurzer, W. (1997). Die Qualitätssicherung in der psychologischen Diagnostik bei der Begutachtung und Befundung. *Psychologie in Österreich, 17,* 16–23.

Yant, M. (1991). *Presumed guilty: When innocent people are wrongly convicted.* Buffalo, NY: Prometheus.

Yapko, M.D. (1994). *Suggestions of abuse: True and false memories of childhood sexual trauma.* New York: Simon & Schuster.

Yarmey, A.D. (1979). *The psychology of eyewitness testimony.* New York: Free Press.

Yarmey, A.D., Yarmey, M.J., & Yarmey, A.L. (1996). Accuracy of eyewitness identifications in show-ups and lineups. *Law and Human Behavior, 20,* 459–477.

Young, M. & Hill, P. (1983). *Rough justice.* London: British Broadcasting Corporation.

Young, N.H. (1989). *Innocence regained: The fight to free Lindy Chamberlain.* Annandale, NSW: Federation Press.

Younger, I. (1976). *The art of cross-examination.* Chicago: American Bar Association, Section of Litigation.

Younger, I. (1977). *The ten commandments of cross-examination.* Videotape (on file at U.C. Hastings College of the Law Instructional Media Services).

Younger, I. (1987). A letter in which Cicero lays down the ten commandments of cross-examination. *Law Institute Journal, 61,* 804–806.

Yuille, J.C. & Cutshall, J. (1989). Analysis of the statements of victims, witnesses and suspects. In J.C. Yuille (Ed.), *Credibility assessment* (pp. 175–191). Dordrecht.

Yuille, J.C. & Cutshall, J.L. (1984). *Live vs. video media in eyewitness research.* Unpublished manuscript, University of British Columbia.

Zander, M. (1995). *The police and Criminal Evidence Act, 1984* (3rd ed.). London: Sweet & Maxwell.

Zimmermann, I. (1964). *Punishment without crime: The true story of a man who spent twenty-four years in prison for a crime he did not commit.* New York: Potter.

Zinger, I. & Forth, A.E. (1999). Psychopathy and Canadian criminal proceedings: The potential for human rights abuses. *Canadian Journal of Criminology, 40,* 237–276.

About the Editors

Peter J. van Koppen is senior researcher at the Netherlands Institute for the Study of Crime and Law Enforcement (NSCR) at Leiden, the Netherlands, and Professor of Law and Psychology at the Department of Law of the University of Antwerp, Belgium. He is a psychologist (Groningen, 1978) and studied law in Groningen, Amsterdam, and Rotterdam (JD, 1984). From 1978 until 1992, he worked at the Faculty of Law at the Erasmus University, Rotterdam, the Netherlands, first in civil law, later in criminal law. He has worked at NSCR since 1992. He was a member of the Haarlem town council (1990–1996), is coeditor of *Psychology, Crime, and Law* (from 1992), and is a fellow of the Netherlands Institute for Advanced Study in the Humanities and Social Sciences (NIAS) at Wassenaar. He has been an expert witness in a large number of court cases, scientific advisor to a interregional police squad, and a member of various ministerial task forces. He has written a large number of articles and books on evidence, psychology, and law, and on police and criminal behavior.

Dr. van Koppen's research encompasses the broad area of social science research in law. He has written widely on negotiation behavior of attorneys in civil cases, recovered memories, geographic profiling of criminal behavior, execution of court decisions, lie detection, judicial decision-making and sentencing, scent lineups with dogs and visual identification by witnesses, the history of appointments to the Dutch Supreme Court, justice decision and police behavior in major cases, police interrogations and false confessions, and phone tapping and the value of forensic evidence.

Steven D. Penrod joined the John Jay College of Criminal Justice faculty as Distinguished Professor of Psychology in 2001. He earned his J.D. from Harvard Law School in 1974 and his Ph.D. in psychology from Harvard

University in 1979. He joined the faculty of the psychology department of the University of Wisconsin-Madison in 1979 and became a professor of law at the University of Minnesota Law School in 1988. In 1995 he joined the faculty at the University of Nebraska-Lincoln, where he was director of the Psychology-Law Program and taught in both the law school and the psychology department. Dr. Penrod received an early-career award in applied psychology from the American Psychological Association in 1986 and has published over 90 scientific articles on eyewitness reliability and jury decision-making. He is coauthor of books on juries, eyewitnesses, and introductory psychology and author of a textbook in social psychology.

Professor Penrod's research and writing have been focused on decision-making in legal contexts. He has written extensively about the jury system, including research on the effects of jury size and decision rules on jury decision-making, death penalty decision-making, jurors' use of probabilistic and hearsay evidence, comprehension of legal instructions, and the impact of extralegal influences such as pretrial publicity, joinder of charges, the effects of cameras in the courtroom, and the effects of juror-questioning of witnesses on jury performance. His research and writing about eyewitness evidence has encompassed factors that reduce eyewitness reliability and interview and lineup procedures that may enhance eyewitness performance, child witnesses, jury assessments of eyewitness evidence, the relationship between eyewitness confidence and eyewitness accuracy, and the effects of eyewitness expert testimony on jury decision-making.

About the Contributors

Stacey J. Anderson is a social psychologist interested in the structure and dynamics of cognitive and affective systems, how they develop, and how they influence and are influenced by social behavior. A central theme in her research concerns individual differences in attitudes and social judgment, with an emphasis on the implications of strict applications of stereotypes for interpersonal and intergroup relations.

A.P.A. (Ton) Broeders received a degree in English from the University of Nijmegen, where he subsequently taught phonetics and linguistics. In 1988 he was asked to set up a forensic phonetics and linguistics facility at the Netherlands Forensic Institute in Rijswijk, where he currently holds the position of chief scientist. His publications deal with a variety of subjects ranging from phonetics and lexicography to forensic speaker identification and forensic science in general. He is chairman of the ENFSI (European Network of Forensic Science Institutes) Expert Working Group for Forensic Speech and Audio Analysis. In addition to acting as court-appointed expert in hundreds of cases in the Netherlands, he has testified for the International Criminal Tribunal for the Former Yugoslavia in The Hague.

Ingrid M. Cordon is a developmental psychologist at the University of California, Davis. Her research interests encompass various facets of cognitive development, including language and memory. Her current work concerns the influence of stereotypes and familiarity on children's memory, the influence of early symbolic representation on memory development, and parental reactions to Child Protective Service investigations.

Hans Crombag (1935) is emeritus professor of law and psychology at the universities of Leyden, Antwerp and Maastricht. E-mail: hans.crombag@metajur.unimaas.nl.

Brian L. Cutler earned his doctorate in social psychology from the University of Wisconsin-Madison in 1987. After serving as a faculty member in the Department of Psychology at Florida International University for 13 years, he formed JuryTactics, LLC, a jury consulting firm located in Chapel Hill, North Carolina. Dr. Cutler has authored (with Steven Penrod) *Mistaken Identification: The Eyewitness, Psychology, and the Law* (1995) and more than 40 other publications on eyewitness memory. His research on eyewitness memory has been funded by the National Science Foundation and has been discussed on National Public Radio, local televised news stations, and in over 35 newspaper articles including several in *The New York Times and The Washington Post*. Dr. Cutler teaches continuing legal education courses on the psychology of eyewitness memory, serves as a consultant to attorneys in cases involving eyewitness identification, and serves as an expert witness in state and federal courts. Dr. Cutler can be reached at (919) 928-9357 or cutler@jurytactics.com.

Shari Seidman Diamond is professor of law and psychology at Northwestern University Law School and a Senior Research Fellow at the American Bar Foundation. She received her Ph.D. in Social Psychology from Northwestern University and her J.D. from the University of Chicago. She has conducted research and published extensively on the jury in law reviews and behavioral science journals, and has testified as an expert on juries, trademarks, and deceptive advertising. She is the author of the chapter on survey evidence for the Federal Judicial Center's *Manual on Scientific and Technical Evidence* (2000). She also practiced law (1985–1987) at Sidley & Austin, served as editor of the *Law & Society Review* (1989–1991), was president of the American-Psychology Law Society (1987–1988), received the 1991 Award for Distinguished Research Contributions in Public Policy from the American Psychological Association, and was a member of the National Academy of Sciences Panel on the Evaluation of Forensic DNA Evidence (1994–1996). She has served on advisory groups for the National Center for State Courts and for the past seven years has been a faculty member in the annual Judging Science Program for judges at Duke University. She is currently completing a book on juries, *Understanding Juries*, with political scientist Jonathan Casper and is in the midst of an unprecedented study of actual jury deliberations in civil cases with psychologist Neil Vidmar.

Gail S. Goodman is professor of psychology at the University of California, Davis. Her work has won numerous awards and has been cited by many courts, including the U. S. Supreme Court. Her expertise encompasses child and adult eyewitness testimony, forensic interviewing, trauma and memory, and emotional reactions to legal involvement.

Samuel R. Gross, professor of law at the University of Michigan, teaches courses on the law of evidence, criminal procedure, and the use of the social sciences in law. His published work focuses on the death penalty, eyewitness identification, the use of expert witnesses in litigation, and the relationship between pretrial bargaining and trial verdicts. He can be reached at srgross@umich.edu.

Martin Hildebrand, studied mental health sciences and law at the University of Maastricht, the Netherlands. He is now working as a researcher at the Dr. Henri van der Hoeven Kliniek, a forensic psychiatric hospital in the Netherlands. His current research topic is "Psychopathy and treatment response in mentally disordered criminal offenders." E-mail: mhildebrand@hoevenstichting.nl.

Ruth Hoekstra is a cognitive psychologist. In 1998 and 1999, she worked at the Netherlands Institute for the Study of Crime and Law Enforcement (NSCR) on a project on the principle of open justice. Since 1999, she has worked at the National Airospace Laboratory on the subject of human error in aircraft maintenance.

Petra T.C. van Kampen was, at the time of writing her contribution, a senior lecturer in the Department of Criminal Law and Procedure, Leiden University, the Netherlands. Most of her publications, including her doctoral dissertation, concern expert evidence in the Netherlands and the United States. Part of her research in relation to expert evidence in the American criminal justice system was done at the University of Michigan Law School (Ann Arbor). She is currently practicing criminal law at Nolst Trenité Advocaten, Rotterdam, the Netherlands.

Claudia Linda Knörnschild currently works at Haina Forensic Psychiatric Hospital in Germany. She studied psychology with an emphasis on forensic psychology start criminology in Bamberg and Erlangen, Germany, Manchester, England, and Leiden, the Netherlands.

Marijke Malsch studied social sciences and law at the Universiteit van Amsterdam. In 1989, she received her doctoral degree on a dissertation entitled *Lawyers' Predictions of Judicial Decisions: A Study on Calibration of Experts*. In 1999, she edited with Hans Nijboer *Complex Cases: Perspectives on the Netherlands Criminal Justice System*. Since 1993, she has been a senior investigator at the Netherlands Institute for the Study of Crime and Law Enforcement (NSCR). Her current research focuses on experts in the criminal justice system, the roles of the victim in the criminal justice system, stalking, and the principle of open justice. Since 1997, she has also worked as an ad hoc judge at the District Court of Haarlem.

Harald Merckelbach is a professor of psychology at the Faculty of Psychology and the Faculty of Law at the University of Maastricht, the Netherlands. His primary research interest is in the psychopathology of memory. His articles address such topics as phobias, obsessive-compulsive disorders, and childhood fears.

John Monahan holds the Doherty Chair in Law at the University of Virginia, where he is also professor of psychology and legal medicine. He has been a Guggenheim Fellow, a Fellow at Harvard Law School, and a Visiting Fellow at All Souls College, Oxford. He won the Manfred Guttmacher Award of the American Psychiatric Association in 1982 for *The Clinical Prediction of Violent Behavior* and again in 2002 for *Rethinking Risk Assessment* (with others).

Francis J. Pakes is a senior lecturer at the Institute for Criminal Justice Studies at the University of Portsmouth, United Kingdom. His Ph.D., completed in 2001, addressed the work of Public Prosecutors in the Netherlands. He writes on Dutch, International, and Comparative Criminal Justice. He is currently writing a book on the latter topic.

Roger C. Park holds the James Edgar Hervey Chair in Litigation at the University of California, Hastings College of Law. He received his J.D and B.A. degrees from Harvard University. Prior to coming to Hastings, he was the Fredrikson & Byron Professor of Law at the University of Minnesota. He has taught as a visitor at Boston University, Stanford University, the University of Michigan, and Wellesley College. E-mail: parkr@uchastings.edu.

Corine de Ruiter is professor of forensic psychology at the University of Amsterdam, the Netherlands. She is author of over 100 publications in the area of psychological assessment, psychopathology, and psychotherapy. She is a licensed clinical psychologist and behavior therapist, and practices psychological assessment for the courts. Her current research interests include psychopathy, violence risk assessment, and quality of care in forensic psychiatry. E-mail: cdruiter@vizzavi.nl.

Michael J. Saks is professor of law at Arizona State University. He earned a Ph.D. from Ohio State University and an M.S.L. from the Yale Law School. Previously, he was the Edward F. Howrey Professor of Law at the University of Iowa; he also taught in the Psychology Department at Boston College and the law schools of the University of Virginia (summer LL.M. program for judges), Boston College, Georgetown University Law Center, and Ohio State University. He was a senior staff member of the National Center for State Courts, has served as editor of *Law & Human Behavior*, and is coeditor of Modern Scientific Evidence. His research has earned a number of awards and has been cited in a number of judicial opinions, including several by the U.S. Supreme Court.

Christopher Slobogin is the Stephen C. O'Connell Professor of Law at the University of Florida Levin College of Law in Gainesville, Florida. He is author of a leading treatise and a casebook on criminal procedure, as well as numerous articles on criminal justice. E-mail: Slobogin@law.ufl.edu.

Siegfried L. Sporer is professor of social psychology at the University of Giessen, Germany. He received his B.A. degree from the University of Colorado at Boulder and his M.A. and Ph.D. degrees from the University of New Hampshire. He has published monographs on judicial sentencing and on facial recognition and has edited several volumes on eyewitness identification evidence (in both English and German). His current research interests are on eyewitness testimony, recognition of faces of different ethnic groups, and the detection of deception.

Aldert Vrij is professor of applied social psychology at the University of Portsmouth, United Kingdom. His main research interests are verbal and nonverbal aspects of deception, interviewing suspects, and police officers' shooting behavior. He has published more than 200 articles and book chapters and several books in these areas. He regularly acts as an expert witness in criminal cases in both the Netherlands and the United Kingdom, and is an associate editor of *Legal and Criminological Psychology*. His research has been sponsored by scientific funding agencies in both the Netherlands and the United Kingdom.

Table of Cases

Author Index

Subject Index